TO DO
- ☐ Review text material for exams.
- ☐ Put together a study plan for midterm.
- ☐ Stop by professor's office for extra help.
- ☐ Pick up supplementary books at the bookstore.

Longman has something to make your *To-Do* list a whole lot shorter.

You have a lot to do to be successful in your history course.

myhistorylab™
Where it's a good time to connect to the past!

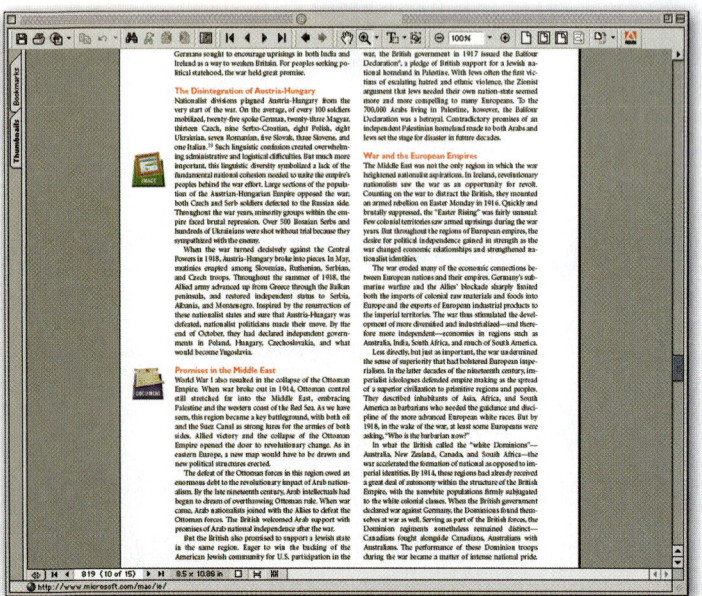

Would your life be easier if you had an electronic version of your textbook?

MyHistoryLab contains the complete text with icons that link to selected sources. You can print sections of the text to read anytime, anywhere.

Are you overwhelmed by the time it takes to find primary source documents, images, maps, and other sources for your research papers?

MyHistoryLab contains hundreds of primary sources, images, and maps— all in one place —to help make writing your research paper easier and more effective, and to help you better understand the course material.

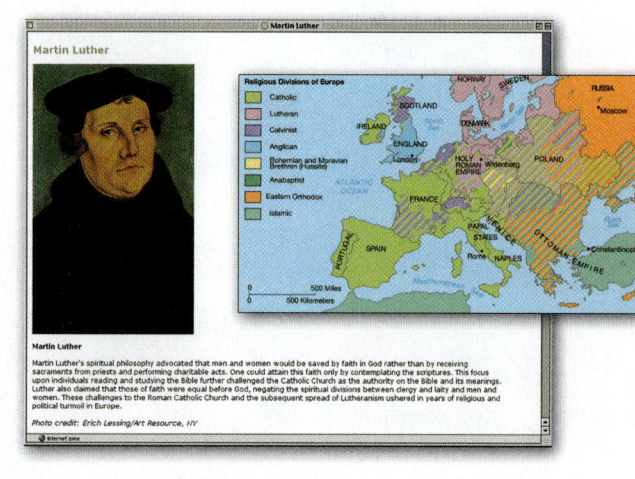

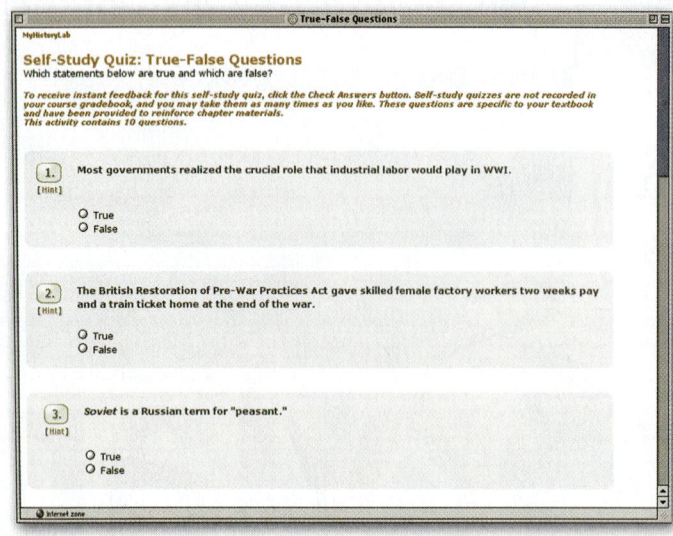

Are you sometimes overwhelmed when you study for exams?

MyHistoryLab gives you a quizzing and testing program that shows what you've mastered, as well as where you need more work. Look for these icons on MyHistoryLab:

Do you sometimes need extra help when your professor isn't in?

Get expert, one-on-one tutoring help with The Tutor Center, available Sunday through Thursday from 5 pm to midnight, Eastern Standard Time – when you're most likely to be completing assignments or preparing for exams, and when your instructor is often unavailable. Tutors can help you use MyHistoryLab to its fullest, or offer advice on writing your research paper.

Did your professor assign other books to read?

MyHistoryLab allows you to read, download, or print over twenty of the most commonly assigned works for this course – all at no additional cost!

Now, flip through *Civilization Past & Present*. You will find the icons shown on the opposite page. Each icon will direct you to a place in MyHistoryLab to help you better understand the material. For example, when reading about classical China or 19th century European politics, you may find an icon that links you to an original source document by **Confucius** or **Karl Marx**.

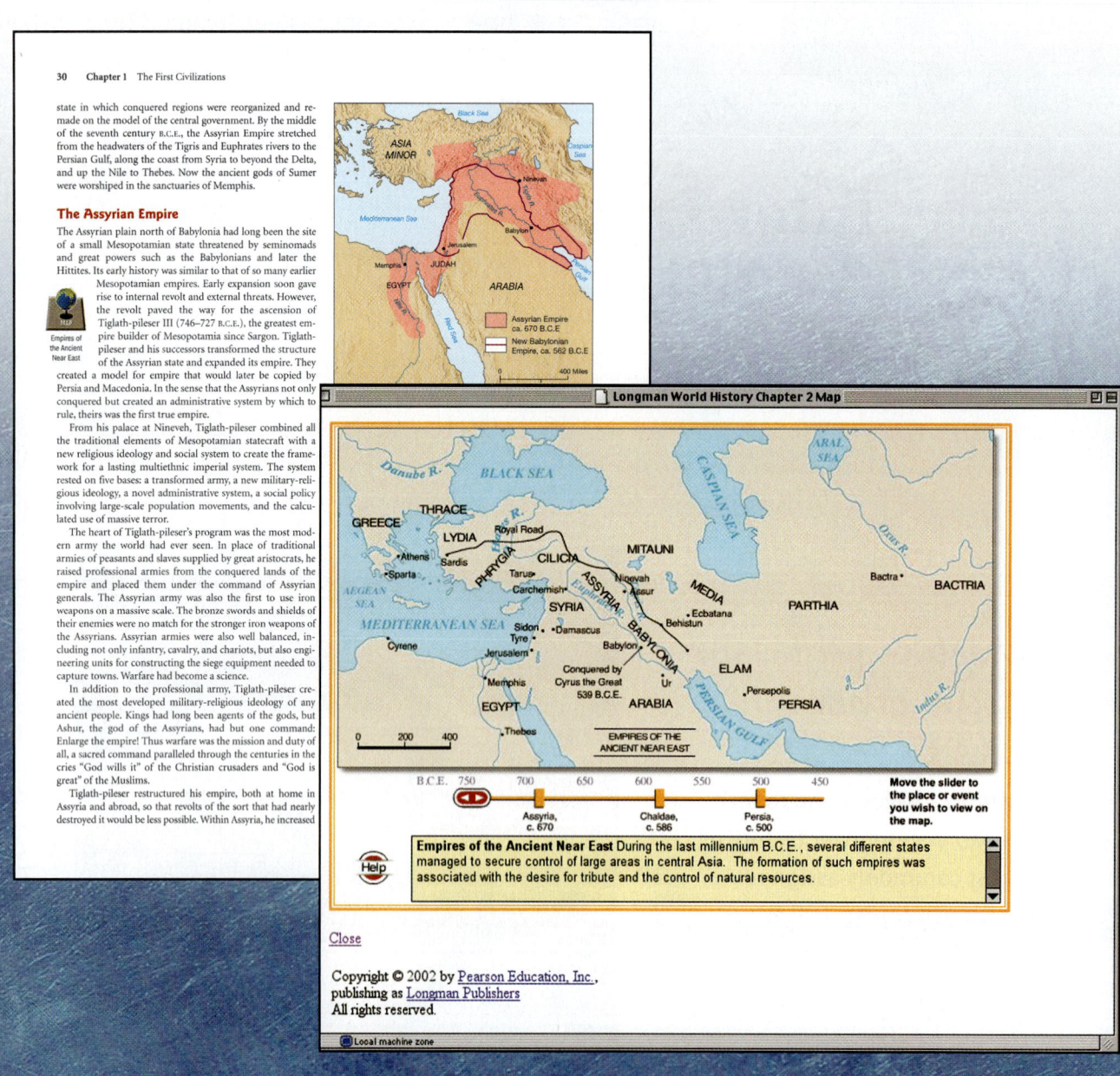

DOCUMENT

This icon will lead you to primary source documents, so you can see the original documents that pertain to the people and events you're studying.

CASE STUDY

Analyze and interpret two or more primary sources on a similar theme or topic. Includes critical thinking questions.

IMAGE

You'll find photos, cartoons, and artwork that relate to the topic you're reading.

MAP

Interactive maps will help you visualize the geography you are exploring in this course. You will also find printable map activities from one of Longman's workbooks.

History Bookshelf Listing

1. *Aesop's Fables*; date unknown
2. *The Iliad,* Homer; 800 BCE
3. *The Upanishads*; 800 BCE
4. *The Analects*, Confucius; circa 500 BCE
5. *The Tao of Teh King*, Lao-Tze;
6. *Histories*, Herodotus; 440 BCE
7. *The Oedipus Trilogy*, Sophocles; circa 400 BCE
8. *The Republic*, Plato; 360 BCE
9. *The Art of War*, Sun Tzu; 100 BCE
10. *The Arabian Nights*; 10 AD
11. Plutarch's *Lives*; 100 AD
12. *The Bhagavad-Gita*; 200 AD
13. *The Holy Koran*; circa 630 AD
14. *Beowulf*; 1100 AD
15. *The Prince*, Machiavelli; 1505 AD
16. *95 Theses*, Martin Luther; 1517 AD
17. *Gulliver's Travels*, Jonathan Swift; 1726 AD
18. *The Communist Manifesto*, Karl Marx; 1848 AD
19. *Origin of Species*, Charles Darwin; 1859 AD
20. *20,000 Leagues Under the Sea*, Jules Verne; 1869 AD
21. *To the Gold Coast for Gold*, Sir Richard Burton; 1883 AD
22. *The Jungle Book*, Rudyard Kipling; 1894 AD
23. *Heart of Darkness*, Joseph Conrad; 1899 AD

myhistorylab™
Where it's a good time to connect to the past!

If your professor has not ordered MyHistoryLab, you can still purchase access to all of these resources.

Go to
www.MyHistoryLab.com
and select the "Register" button. Follow the instructions to purchase online access.

Connecting to the past has never been easier.
MyHistoryLab.com

Civilization
Past & Present
Eleventh Edition

Volume B: From 500–1815

Palmira Brummett
UNIVERSITY OF TENNESSEE

Robert R. Edgar
HOWARD UNIVERSITY

Neil J. Hackett
ST. LOUIS UNIVERSITY

George F. Jewsbury
CENTRE D'ÉTUDES DU MONDE RUSSE
ÉCOLE DES HAUTES ÉTUDES EN SCIENCES SOCIALES

Barbara Molony
SANTA CLARA UNIVERSITY

THIS BOOK HAS BENEFITED FROM THE CONTRIBUTIONS
OVER MANY EDITIONS OF THE FOLLOWING AUTHORS:

T. Walter Wallbank (Late)

Alastair M. Taylor

Nels M. Bailkey

Clyde J. Lewis

New York Boston San Francisco
London Toronto Sydney Tokyo Singapore Madrid
Mexico City Munich Paris Cape Town Hong Kong Montréal

Executive Editor: Michael Boezi
Senior Acquisitions Editor: Janet Lanphier
Senior Development Editor: Dawn Groundwater
Development Editor: Adam Beroud
Executive Marketing Manager: Sue Westmoreland
Media and Supplements Editor: Kristi Olson
Senior Media Editor: Patrick McCarthy
Production Manager: Eric Jorgensen
Project Coordination, Text Design, and Electronic Page Makeup: Electronic Publishing Services Inc., NYC
Photo Research: Photosearch, Inc.
Cover Designer/Manager: Nancy Danahy
Cover Image: Botticelli, Sandro (1444/5–1510). Venus and the Three Graces Offering Gifts to a Young Girl, detail of one of th graces, c. 1483 (fresco) Louvre, Paris, France. © Peter Willi/Bridgeman Art Library.
Manufacturing Buyer: Roy Pickering
Printer and Binder: Courier Corporation
Cover Printer: Coral Graphic Services

For permission to use copyrighted material, grateful acknowledgment is made to the copyright holders on pp. C-1–C-3, which are hereby made part of this copyright page.

Library of Congress Cataloging-in-Publication Data

Civilization past & present / Palmira Brummett ... [et al.].— 11th ed.
  p. cm.
 Includes bibliographical references and index.
 ISBN 0-321-23613-0 — ISBN 0-321-23627-0 — ISBN 0-321-23628-9
 1. Civilization. I. Brummett, Palmira Johnson

CB69.C57 2005
909—dc22   2004029985

Copyright © 2006 by Pearson Education, Inc.

All rights reserved. No part of this publication may be reproduced, stored in a retrieval system, or transmitted, in any form or by any means, electronic, mechanical, photocopying, recording, or otherwise, without the prior written permission of the publisher. Printed in the United States of America.

Visit us at http://www.ablongman.com.

ISBN 0-321-23613-0 (complete volume)
ISBN 0-321-23627-0 (Volume I)
ISBN 0-321-23628-9 (Volume II)
ISBN 0-321-31775-0 (Volume A)
ISBN 0-321-31776-9 (Volume B)
ISBN 0-321-31777-7 (Volume C)

1 2 3 4 5 6 7 8 9 10—CRK—07 06 05 04

Brief Contents

Detailed Contents xi
Documents xiv
Maps xiv
Global Issues xv
Discovery Through Maps xv
Chapter Opening Image Descriptions xv
To the Instructor xvii
To the Student xxviii

CHAPTER 9
The European Middle Ages, 476–1348 C.E. 256

CHAPTER 10
Culture, Power, and Trade in the Era of Asian Hegemony, 220–1350 286

CHAPTER 11
The Americas to 1492 322

CHAPTER 12
The Islamic Gunpowder Empires, 1300–1650 346

CHAPTER 13
East Asian Cultural and Political Systems, 1300–1650 370

CHAPTER 14
European Cultural and Religious Transformations
The Renaissance and the Reformation, 1300–1600 396

CHAPTER 15
The Development of the European State System, 1300–1650 432

CHAPTER 16
Global Encounters
Europe and the New World Economy, 1400–1650 462

CHAPTER 17
Politics in the First Age of Capitalism, 1648–1774
Absolutism and Limited Central Power 490

CHAPTER 18
New Ideas and Their Political Consequences
The Scientific Revolution, the Enlightenment, and the French Revolutions 526

CHAPTER 19
Africa, 1650–1850 560

CHAPTER 20
Asian and Middle Eastern Empires and Nations, 1650–1815 586

Credits C-1

Notes N-1

Index I-1

Detailed Contents

Documents xiv
Maps xiv
Global Issues xv
Discovery Through Maps xv
Chapter Opening Image Descriptions xv
To the Instructor xvii
To the Student xxviii

CHAPTER 9

The European Middle Ages, 476–1348 C.E.   256

    The Church in the Early Middle Ages   258
    The Merovingians and Carolingians   260
    Feudalism and Manorialism   266
    The Revival of Trade and Towns   271
    The Church in the High Middle Ages: 1000–1348   272
    The Crusades   275
    The Development of European States: 1000–1348   278

DOCUMENT
    Charlemagne: A Firsthand Look   263

DOCUMENT
    Muslim and Christian: Two Contemporary Perspectives   277

CHAPTER 10

Culture, Power, and Trade in the Era of Asian Hegemony, 220–1350   286

    India in the Classical and Medieval Eras   288
    China: Cultural and Political Empires   294
    Korea: From Three Kingdoms to One   310
    The Emergence of Japan in East Asia   312

DOCUMENT
    Faxian: A Chinese Buddhist Monk in Gupta India   290

DOCUMENT
    Bo Juyi (772–846): "The Song of Everlasting Sorrow"   300

DISCOVERY THROUGH MAPS
    Gog and Magog in the Ebstorf Mappamundi   309

DOCUMENT
    Sei Shōnagon: The Pillow Book   318

CHAPTER 11

The Americas to 1492   322

    Origins of Americans and Their Cultures   324
    Emerging Civilizations in Mesoamerica   325
    Classical Mayan Civilization   327
    The Postclassical Era   329
    The Amerindians of North America   336

DOCUMENT
    Father Bernabé Cobo, "Pachacuti, the Greatest Inca"   333

GLOBAL ISSUES   LOCATION AND IDENTITY   344

CHAPTER 12

The Islamic Gunpowder Empires, 1300–1650   346

    New Polities in Eurasia   348
    The Ottoman Empire   349
    The Safavid Empire in Persia   357
    The Mughal Empire in South Asia   361
    Networks of Trade and Communication   367

DISCOVERY THROUGH MAPS
    The World Map of Piri Reis   351

DOCUMENT
    Evliya Çelebi, "An Ottoman Official's Wedding Night"   355

DOCUMENT
    The Coming of Ismail Safavi Foretold   358

DOCUMENT
    The Idea of Seclusion and Lady Nurjahan   366

CHAPTER 13

East Asian Cultural and Political Systems, 1300–1650   370

    China: The Ming Dynasty   373

*Each chapter ends with a Conclusion, Suggestions for Web Browsing, Literature and Film, and Suggestions for Reading.

Korea: The Making of a Confucian Society   381
Japan: The Era of Shōguns and Warring States   384
Southeast Asia: States Within a Region   391

DISCOVERY THROUGH MAPS
Map of China's Ancient Heartland, circa 1500 C.E.   375

DOCUMENT
A Censor Accuses a Eunuch   377

DOCUMENT
Sotoba Komachi, a Fourteenth-Century Japanese Nō Play   387

DOCUMENT
A Traveller's Account of Siam   392

CHAPTER 14

European Cultural and Religious Transformations

The Renaissance and the Reformation, 1300–1600   396

Social Upheaval   398
The Italian Renaissance   399
Italian Renaissance Art   404
The Northern Renaissance   408
The Crisis in the Catholic Church: 1300–1517   413
Luther and the German Reformation   416
Henry VIII and the Anglican Reformation   419
Protestantism from Switzerland to Holland: Zwingli and Calvin   421
Reform in the Catholic Church   426

DISCOVERY THROUGH MAPS
The Lagoon of Venice   401

DOCUMENT
Machiavelli, The Prince: On Cruelty and Mercy   403

DOCUMENT
Anne Ayscough (Mrs. Thomas Kyme), English Protestant Martyr   422

CHAPTER 15

The Development of the European State System, 1300–1650   432

Politics in an Age of Crisis: 1300–1500   434
The Religious-Political Fusion   442
Wars of Religions: The Spanish Habsburgs' Quest for European Hegemony, 1556–1598   443
Orthodox Europe: Russian Consolidation and Ottoman Expansion   450
The Austrian Habsburgs' Drive for Superiority and the Thirty Years' War   453

DOCUMENT
The Trial of Joan of Arc   435

DISCOVERY THROUGH MAPS
A Pilgrim's Map of Canterbury   436

DOCUMENT
Simplicissimus on the Horrors of the Thirty Years' War   454

GLOBAL ISSUES   TECHNOLOGICAL EXCHANGE   460

CHAPTER 16

Global Encounters

Europe and the New World Economy, 1400–1650   462

The Iberian Golden Age   464
The Portuguese and Africa   469
The Growth of New Spain   474
Iberian Systems in the New World   477
Beginnings of Northern European Expansion   482

DISCOVERY THROUGH MAPS
Savage Pictures: Sebastian Munster's Map of Africa   471

DOCUMENT
Portuguese Encounters with Africans   473

DOCUMENT
Disease and the Spanish Conquest   480

CHAPTER 17

Politics in the First Age of Capitalism, 1648–1774

Absolutism and Limited Central Power   490

Capitalism and the Forces of Change   492
Social Crises during the Capitalist Revolution   496
Louis XIV, the Sun King: The Model for European Absolutism   502

Detailed Contents xiii

The Gravitational Pull of French Absolutism 507
Holland and England: Limited Central Power 512
Breaking the Bank: Diplomacy and War in the Age of Absolutism: 1650–1774 516
Economic Challenges 520
Louis XV and the Decline of European Absolutism: 1715–1774 522

DOCUMENT
Conditions Among Eighteenth-Century French Peasants 500

DOCUMENT
Louis XIV to His Son 504

DISCOVERY THROUGH MAPS
The Elegant Destruction of Poland 519

CHAPTER 18
New Ideas and Their Political Consequences
The Scientific Revolution, the Enlightenment, and the French Revolutions 526

Revolution in Science: The Laws of Nature 528
The Sciences of Society: The "Age of Reason" 532
The Failure of Monarchical Reform 539
The French Revolution: The Domestic Phase, 1789–1799 541
The French Revolution: The Napoleonic Phase, 1799–1815 552

DISCOVERY THROUGH MAPS
The Heliocentric Cosmos of Copernicus 529
The Widening Scope of Scientific Discovery 530

DOCUMENT
Declaration of the Rights of Man and Citizen 545

DOCUMENT
Olympe de Gouges on the Rights of Women 546

CHAPTER 19
Africa, 1650–1850 560

The Atlantic Slave Trade 562
End of the Slave Trade in West Africa 568
Islamic Africa 569
Africans and European Settlement in Southern Africa 571
African State Formation in Eastern and Northeastern Africa 578

DOCUMENT
A Slave's Memoir 565

DOCUMENT
"Song of the Afflicted" 574

DISCOVERY THROUGH MAPS
The Myth of the Empty Land 577

GLOBAL ISSUES   SLAVERY   584

CHAPTER 20
Asian and Middle Eastern Empires and Nations, 1650–1815 586

The Ottomans in the Early Modern Era 588
Muslim Politics in Persia 593
Early Modern India under the Mughals 594
The Qing Dynasty before the Opium War 598
Korea in the Seventeenth and Eighteenth Centuries 604
Early Modern Japan: The Tokugawa Period 605
Southeast Asia: Political and Cultural Interactions 613
Europeans on New Pacific Frontiers 615

DOCUMENT
Lady Montagu, Florence Nightingale, and the Myths of "Orient" 592

DOCUMENT
Lan Dingyuan, County Magistrate: Depraved Religious Sects Deceive People 603

DOCUMENT
Ihara Saikaku: "The Umbrella Oracle" 612

Credits C-1

Notes N-1

Index I-1

Documents

Charlemagne: A Firsthand Look	263
Muslim and Christian: Two Contemporary Perspectives	277
Faxian: A Chinese Buddhist Monk in Gupta India	290
Bo Juyi (772–846): "The Song of Everlasting Sorrow"	300
Sei Shōnagon: *The Pillow Book*	318
Father Bernabé Cobo, "Pachacuti, the Greatest Inca"	333
Evliya Çelebi, "An Ottoman Official's Wedding Night"	355
The Coming of Ismail Safavi Foretold	358
The Idea of Seclusion and Lady Nurjahan	366
A Censor Accuses a Eunuch	377
Sotoba Komachi, a Fourteenth-Century Japanese Nō Play	387
A Traveller's Account of Siam	392
Machiavelli, *The Prince:* On Cruelty and Mercy	403
Anne Ayscough (Mrs. Thomas Kyme), English Protestant Martyr	422
The Trial of Joan of Arc	435
Simplicissimus on the Horrors of the Thirty Years' War	454
Portuguese Encounters with Africans	473
Disease and the Spanish Conquest	480
Conditions Among Eighteenth-Century French Peasants	500
Louis XIV to His Son	504
Declaration of the Rights of Man and Citizen	545
Olympe de Gouges on the Rights of Women	546
A Slave's Memoir	565
"Song of the Afflicted"	574
Lady Montagu, Florence Nightingale, and the Myths of "Orient"	592
Lan Dingyuan, County Magistrate: Depraved Religious Sects Deceive People	603
Ihara Saikaku: "The Umbrella Oracle"	612

Maps

Charlemagne's Empire	264
Viking, Muslim, and Magyar Invasions, c. 1000	265
Medieval Manor	269
The Crusades	276
England and France, c. 1180	280
Germany, 1000	283
Germany, 1300	283
India, 400–650 C.E.	289
Delhi Sultanate, 1236 C.E.	294
China Under Tang and Song Dynasties	301
The Mongol Empire, c. 1300	306
Civilizations of Central and South America	326
Civilizations of North America	337
The Gunpowder Islamic Empires	348
Ottoman Empire	350
Iran Under the Safavids	357
Mughal Empire	361
Asia, 1300–1650	373
Korea and Japan Before 1500	385
Trade Routes in Southeast Asia, 1300–1650	393
Renaissance Europe	399
Europe After the Reformation	426
Spain, 910	438
Spain, 1491	438
The Hapsburgs in Europe After the Peace of Augsburg, 1555	445
Europe After the Peace of Westphalia, 1648	457
Spanish and Portuguese Explorations, 1400–1600	467
Atlantic Slave Trade	479
European Empires, c. 1660	488
English Common Lands Enclosed by Acts of Parliament, 1700–1850	494
Rise of Prussia, 1440–1795	509
Russia Under Peter the Great	511
Europe After the Treaty of Utrecht, 1714	518
Science and the Enlightenment	538
Revolutionary France	541
Napoleonic Europe	556
Africa, 1500–1800	567
Africa, c. 1830	575
The Great Trek and South Africa in the Nineteenth Century	576
Ottoman Empire, 1699–1791	589
The Maratha Kingdoms	596
Asia and Oceania, 1800	604

Global Issues

Location and Identity	344
Technological Exchange	460
Slavery	584

Discovery Through Maps

Gog and Magog in the Ebstorf Mappamundi	309	Savage Pictures: Sebastian Munster's Map of Africa	471
The World Map of Piri Reis	351	The Elegant Destruction of Poland	519
Map of China's Ancient Heartland, circa 1500 C.E.	375	The Heliocentric Cosmos of Copernicus	529
The Lagoon of Venice	401	The Myth of the Empty Land	577
A Pilgrim's Map of Canterbury	436		

Chapter Opening Image Descriptions

CHAPTER 9

The Gothic-style Benedictine abbey of Mont St. Michel, constructed between the eleventh and sixteenth centuries and built on a rocky inlet amid the sandbanks and tides between Brittany and Normandy, France.

CHAPTER 10

Refined gentlemen of the Tang and Song dynasties, seen in this detail from a scroll by tenth-century artist Gu Hongzhong, displayed their taste and culture in banquets in their own homes. Entertainment by female musicians and courtesans enhanced the opulent foods and rich decorations.

CHAPTER 11

Detail from painted Mayan vase depicting a ceremonially dressed ball player. The ball game served important social, political, and religious functions in Mayan civilization. On a very basic level, it provided the Mayan polity with entertainment. The construction of stone-paved courts, the training of players, and the holding of games also reinforced the prestige of the community. Finally, the game and its players could serve as religious offerings, with losing players sometimes being sacrificed to the gods.

CHAPTER 12

The Ottoman army under Lala Mustafa Pasha parading before the captured fortress of Tiflis. Some janissaries, carrying their gunpowder weapons, are shown in the center of the image.

CHAPTER 13

The Temple of the Golden Pavilion was commissioned by the Japanese shōgun Ashikawa Yoshimitsu in 1397. The building was intimate in scale and designed as part of a garden in which the shōgun could meditate. The building, destroyed by an arsonist in 1950, was rebuilt exactly as the original.

CHAPTER 14

Detail from *The Creation of Adam*, painted by the master Renaissance artist Michelangelo Buonarroti. Ceiling of the Sistine Chapel (1511–1512), in Rome.

CHAPTER 15

The Armada Portrait of Queen Elizabeth I was painted in 1588 to commemorate the English naval victory over the Spanish Armada. Against considerable odds, Elizabeth succeeded in mobilizing her nation to withstand Spanish diplomatic and military pressures. At the same time, she managed to maintain a certain unity in her socially and religiously diverse realm.

CHAPTER 16

This ivory saltcellar, with its carved figure of a Portuguese sailor in crow's nest, makes clear the influence of the West on the artists of Benin.

CHAPTER 17

That the small country of Holland became the richest country in Europe during the seventeenth century is a result of the hard and serious work of a diverse population, including people such as those shown in this detail from Rembrandt's *The Syndics of the Cloth Guild* (1662).

CHAPTER 18

The fury and force of the French Revolution came from people such as these Parisian women advancing on Versailles, October 5, 1789. They were about to bring the King, the Queen, and the entire National Constituent Assembly back to Paris, and the reality of the Revolution.

CHAPTER 19

Europeans usually bought slaves for the trans-Atlantic slave trade at specific locations along the west and central African coast. In *Merchant Slaves of Goree*, the French artists Grasset de St. Sauver and Christian labrousse depicted European and African slave traders negotiating the sale of slaves at Goree, an island off the coast of Senegal.

CHAPTER 20

Large Perspective View of the Theater District in Sakai-cho and Fukiya-cho by Okumura Masanobu (1686–1764). Japan's cities were bustling centers for the arts, culture, and mercantile activities during the Tokugawa period. Artists captured the excitement of urban life in prints depicting what they called the "floating world." This street scene by Masanobu shows theaters, teahouses, restaurants, shops, and a female street vendor selling fish.

To the Instructor

The eleventh edition of *Civilization Past & Present* continues to present a survey of world history, treating the development and growth of civilization as a global phenomenon in which all the world's culture systems have interacted. This new edition, like its predecessors, includes all the elements of history—social, economic, political, military, religious, aesthetic, legal, and technological—to illustrate that global interaction. One of the most significant changes in the eleventh edition is the addition of our new Asian scholar and co-author, Barbara Molony. Barbara is a professor of history at Santa Clara University and is director of Santa Clara's Program for the Study of Women and Gender. Well-versed in modern Asia, she significantly revised the book's Asian chapters.

With the accelerating tempo of developments in business, communication, and technology, every day each part of the world is brought into closer contact with other parts: economic and political events that happen in even the most remote corners of the world affect each of us individually. An appreciation for and an understanding of all the civilizations of the world must be an essential aim of education. Thus, the eleventh edition of *Civilization Past & Present* emphasizes world trends and carefully avoids placing these trends within a Western conceptual basis.

CHANGES TO ORGANIZATION AND CONTENT

The eleventh edition maintains the many strengths that have made *Civilization Past & Present* a highly respected textbook. As the authors revised the text, they relied on the latest historical scholarship and profited from suggestions from adopters of the text and reviewers. Maintained throughout this compelling survey are a fluid writing style and consistent level of presentation seldom found in multi-authored texts.

While the text retains the basic organization of its predecessors, all chapters have been reviewed and revised in light of the globalization of today's changing world. The authors have carefully evaluated, revised, combined, and rewritten chapters to provide balanced coverage of all parts of the world throughout history.

One of the major changes in the eleventh edition is a new chapter, "Latin America: Independence and Dependence, 1825–1945" (Chapter 25). This new chapter provides detailed coverage of Latin America, including the political, social, and economic challenges following independence and into the twentieth century and relations between the Latin American nations and the United States.

Other chapter changes are as follows:

- **Chapter 1:** "Stone Age Societies and the Earliest Civilizations of the Near East" provides coverage of human prehistory, Egyptian civilization, and the development of smaller Near Eastern states.
- **Chapter 2:** "Ancient China—Origins to Empire: From Prehistory to 220 C.E." and **Chapter 3:** "Ancient India: From Origins to 300 C.E." both include expanded coverage of gender and social history.
- **Chapter 6:** "Byzantium and the Orthodox World: Byzantium, Eastern Europe, and Russia, 325–1500" has been revised to stress the independent development of East Rome and includes enhanced information on the development of the Balkan States.
- **Chapter 9:** "The European Middle Ages: 476–1348 C.E." combines the tenth edition's Chapter 9 and Chapter 10, examining the political, religious, and social history of the entire European Middle Ages in one chapter rather than two.
- **Chapter 10:** "Culture, Power, and Trade in the Era of Asian Hegemony, 220–1350" and **Chapter 13:** "East Asian Cultural and Political Systems, 1300–1650" have been thoroughly revised and expanded, with particular attention to gender and social history.
- **Chapter 14:** "European Cultural and Religious Transformations: The Renaissance and the Reformation 1300–1600" combines the tenth edition's Chapter 15 and Chapter 16, exploring the political, religious, and social connections between the European Renaissance and Reformation in one chapter rather than two.
- **Chapter 15:** "The Development of the European State System: 1300–1650" is a new chapter that examines the growth of the European nation-states from the late Middle Ages through the religious wars of the seventeenth century.
- **Chapter 17:** "Politics in the First Age of Capitalism: 1648–1774: Absolutism and Limited Central Power" places more emphasis on the social crises of the first phase of capitalism.
- Reorganized **Chapter 18:** "New Ideas and Their Political Consequences: The Scientific Revolution,

the Enlightenment and the French Revolutions" combines the tenth edition's Chapter 19 and with content from Chapter 22, as the authors believe that intellectual transformations represented by the Enlightenment are directly connected to the political upheavals of French Revolutions and so should be discussed as such in one chapter.
- A recast **Chapter 19:** "Africa, 1650–1850" provides detailed coverage of Africa, including the Atlantic Slave Trade, Islamic Africa, the settlement of South Africa by Africans and Europeans, and state formation in the east and northeast of the continent.
- A recast **Chapter 20:** "Asian and Middle Eastern Empires and Nations, 1650–1815" examines political, social, and cultural developments across Asia, including the Ottoman Empire, Persia, India, China, Korea, Japan, Southeast Asia, and the Pacific.
- **Chapter 21:** "The Americas, 1650–1825: From European Dominance to Independence" offers expanded treatment of the Haitian Revolution.
- Reorganized **Chapter 22:** "Industrialization: Social, Political, and Cultural Transformations," focuses exclusively on the social, ideological, religious, and cultural effects of the Industrial Revolutions in Great Britain, Continental Europe, and the United States.•
- **Chapter 23:** "Africa and the Middle East During the Age of European Imperialism" provides expanded coverage of Islam and Christianity in Africa during the colonial era.
- **Chapter 24:** "Asia, 1815–1914: India, Southeast Asia, China, and Japan" provides expanded coverage of Asian civilizations, with particular emphasis on gender and social history.
- **Chapter 26:** "Politics and Diplomacy in the West: 1815–1914" combines the tenth edition's Chapter 23 and Chapter 27, examining the political changes in Europe between the Congress of Vienna and World War I in one chapter rather than two.
- Expanded **Chapter 28:** "The USSR, Italy, Germany, and Japan: The Failure of Democracy in the Interwar Period" adds coverage of Japan.
- A recast **Chapter 29:** "Forging New Nations in Asia, 1910 to 1950" examines political and social transformations in China, Korea, Southeast Asia, and India.
- A recast **Chapter 30:** "Emerging National Movements in the Middle East and Africa, 1920s to 1950s" explores the rising tide of nationalism in Africa and the Middle East following World War I through the start of the Cold War.
- Expanded **Chapter 31:** "World War II: Origins and Consequences, 1919–1946" adds coverage of the postwar settlements that followed the defeat of the Axis powers in 1945.
- Reorganized **Chapter 32:** "The Bipolar World: Cold War and Decolonization 1945–1991" prefaces its examination of the Cold War by examining the competing economic systems of the United States and the USSR. It also provides a more detailed treatment of decolonization and its relationship to the Cold War.
- Reorganized **Chapter 33:** "The United States and Europe Since 1945: Politics in an Age of Conflict and Change" now stresses the relationship between technology and social change in the United States and Europe and also provides expanded coverage of the Soviet Union and the Russian Republic.
- Reorganized **Chapter 35:** "Asia Since 1945: Political, Economic, and Social Revolutions" integrates coverage of China, Hong Kong, Taiwan, and Singapore.

The eleventh edition of *Civilization Past & Present* is a thorough revision in both its narrative and its pedagogical features. It is intended to provide the reader with an understanding of the legacies of past eras and to illuminate the way in which the study of world history gives insight into the genesis, nature, and direction of global civilization. Given the growing interdependence of the world's nations, the need for this perspective has never been greater.

NEW SPLIT

The split for the two-volume edition has changed for the eleventh edition: Volume I, To 1650, contains Chapters 1–16; Volume II, From 1300, contains Chapters 12–35. The start of Volume II at 1300 accommodates those courses that cover materials beginning earlier than 1650. The eleventh edition also includes a three-volume split edition for schools operating on the quarter system: Volume A, To 1500, contains Chapters 1–11; Volume B, From 500–1815, contains Chapters 9–20; and Volume C, From 1775, contains Chapters 18–35.

FEATURES AND PEDAGOGY

The text has been developed with the dual purpose of helping students acquire a solid knowledge of past events and, equally important, of helping them think more constructively about the significance of those events for the complex times in which we now live. A number of pedagogical features—some well tested in earlier editions and lightly revised here, and a few new ones—will assist students in achieving these goals.

New! *Global Issues* **Essays** These new essays explore seven topics of unique transcultural and transhistorical significance: Migration, Religion and Government, Location and Identity, Technological Exchange, Slavery, Gender, and War and International Law. Each essay employs examples that span both history and the world's many civilizations. As pedagogical tools, the essays are intended to do more than just inform students about global topics; they also reveal challenges that have confronted and still confront civilizations the world over. The essays carefully avoid discussing their topics from a Western conceptual basis and instead strive to examine them using a global framework. Each essay uses art to illustrate its ideas and ends with critical thinking questions. Evenly distributed throughout the book, the essays appear on two-page spreads between chapters.

New! Pronunciation Guide This new feature will help students correctly pronounce key foreign words. Pronunciations appear in parentheses immediately after the first use of a key foreign term in the text.

New! On-page Glossary This new feature provides students with concise definitions of key historical terms. Glossary definitions appear in the footer of the page in which they are discussed.

xx   To the Instructor

Chapter Opening Pages Chapter opening pages again feature an illustration relevant to a major chapter topic, a chapter outline, and a newly designed, easy-to-read chronology of key events—political, social, religious, and cultural—that are discussed in the chapter. Students can easily refer back to the timeline as they read the chapter.

A short text introduction previews the civilizations and themes to be discussed in the chapter. The chronology then sets the major topics within a framework easy for the student to comprehend at a glance. Chapter opening images reflect a wide range of genres, including sculpture, painting, mosaics, tapestries, and illuminated manuscripts. The images have been carefully selected to invoke a particular culture and engage the student visually.

Chronology Tables Throughout each chapter, brief chronology tables once again highlight the major events occurring within a text section. Whether focusing on general trends, as does Religious Reforms and Reactions (Chapter 14), or on a single country, as does China in the Imperialist Era (Chapter 24), the chronology tables give the student an immediate summary view of a topic, at its point of discussion.

Discovery Through Maps This special feature focusing on primary maps in many chapters offers a unique historical view—be it local, city, country, world, or imagined—of the way a particular culture looked at the world at a particular time. Students tend to take the orientation of a map for granted; however, "An Islamic Map of the World" (Chapter 7) makes clear that not all peoples make the same assumptions. The world map of the famous Arab cartographer al-Idrisi is oriented, as was common at the time, with south at the top. Chapter 19's "The Myth of the Empty Land" shows how European settlers of South Africa laid claim to the South African interior by asserting that they were moving into an unpopulated area.

The discussions accompanying these maps have been expanded to emphasize their connection with the text itself; the addition of review questions help students better understand the concepts presented by the maps.

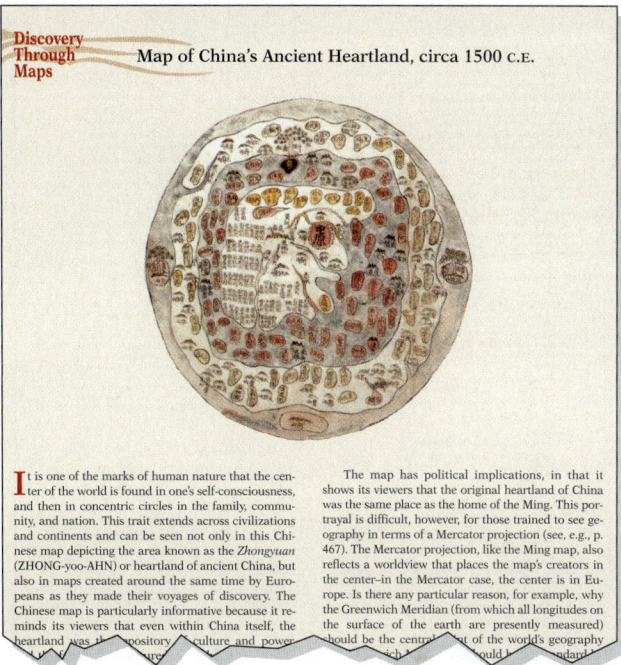

Excerpts from Primary Source Documents Seventeen of the more than 100 primary source documents are new. In "Muslim and Christian: Two Contemporary Perspectives" (Chapter 9), first the Christian knight, then the Muslim physician, write of the bloody fall of Jerusalem with the certainty of religious justification for his cause, and of cultural superiority. Simón Bolívar, in his powerful Proclamation to the People of Venezuela (Chapter 21), addresses his fellow-countrymen to reestablish a republican form of government in the state.

Almost every chapter now includes a document concerning the status of women in general during a particular era or details the accomplishments of a specific woman. In Chapter 35, Benazir Bhutto, Pakistan's first female prime minister, relates the dilemma of being a "foreign" student at Harvard during an era of political turmoil for both Pakistan and the United States.

Headnotes to all have been expanded to better link the documents to the text itself. Several discussion questions now follow each excerpt.

Suggestions for Reading To give the student an additional view of the various cultures and timeframes, a *Literature and Film* section at the end of each chapter offers a listing of novels, poetry, films, and videos. Readings have been updated and carefully trimmed of dated entries. Students can consult these general interpretations, monographs, and collections of traditional source materials to expand their understanding of a particular topic or to prepare reports and papers. *Suggestions for Web Browsing* have also been updated throughout.

Photographs The text's more than 500 photos, most in full color, have been carefully revised to present a diverse range of images from all of the world's civilizations. Special care has again been taken to include images of the lifestyles and contributions of women for all eras and areas.

To the Instructor   xxiii

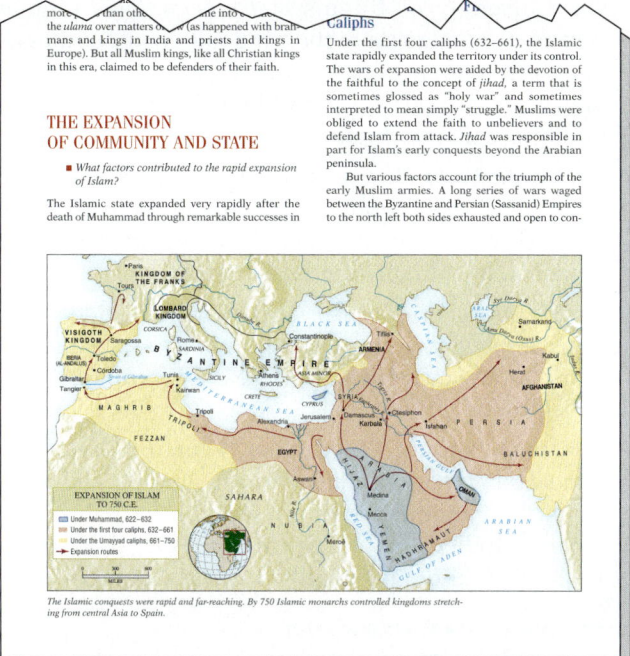

Maps The use of full color allows students more readily to see distinctions on the more than 100 maps in the text. Some maps make clear the nature of a single distinctive event; others illustrate larger trends. For example, Trade and Cultural Interchange, c. 50 B.C.E. (Chapter 2), makes clear that an interconnected world economy existed long before the advent of modern communication and technology. The specific focus of The Persian Gulf Region, c. 1900 (Chapter 23), foretells some of today's complexities in this area of the world. A caption accompanying each map highlights the significance of the map and its relevance to a specific text topic. Many of the maps have been revised, updated, and/or increased in size. Most of the maps also include insets that show where their territory fits within a larger hemisphere or the globe.

FOR QUALIFIED COLLEGE ADOPTERS

Supplements for Instructors

MyHistoryLab With the best of Longman's multimedia solutions for history in one easy-to-use place, MyHistoryLab offers students and instructors a state-of-the-art interactive instructional solution for the World History survey course. Delivered in Course Compass™, Blackboard™, or WebCT™, MyHistoryLab is designed to be used as a supplement to a traditional lecture course, or to administer a completely online course. MyHistoryLab provides helpful tips, review materials, and activities to make the study of history an enjoyable learning experience. Icons in the book lead students to specific assets.

MyHistoryLab includes the following features, all organized according to the text's table of contents:

- **E-Sources:** Each chapter of the book has its own collection of images, individual documents, and case studies.
- **History Bookshelf:** Read, download, or print more than 20 of the most commonly assigned works like Plato's *The Republic,* Machiavelli's *The Prince,* or Confucius' *The Analects.*
- **History Toolkit:** Guided tutorials help students learn to analyze several types of sources.
- **Map Activities:** Each chapter contains a map activity in which students assess a map from the time period covered and take a brief geography quiz for the chapter.
- **Pre-Test and Post-Test Self-Study Quizzes with Targeted Feedback:** Two quizzes per chapter allow students to review their knowledge of the material and concepts. Chapter feedback provides links that take students directly to the relevant section of the textbook online.
- **Chapter Review Materials:** The Study Guide, PowerPoint™ presentations, flashcards, and other features will help students master the contents of the textbook and prepare for exams.
- **The Textbook Online:** Students can read the book online, or print out sections of the book to read anywhere.
- **Chapter Exam:** Each chapter has a chapter exam whose results report to the CourseCompass™, Blackboard™, or WebCT™ online gradebook.
- **Test Bank:** Create your own exams using the Test Bank from your text, and place them right in MyHistoryLab for your students to take as practice quizzes or as graded exams.
- **The Tutor Center:** On-call qualified help is available to answer student questions about MyHistoryLab when an instructor may not be available. The Tutor Center is open Sunday through Thursday from 5 PM to midnight, EST.
- **Unlimited use of Pearson's Research Navigator™:** The EBSCO ContentSelect, Academic Journal & Abstract Database, *The New York Times* Search by Subject Archive, "Best of the Web" Link Library, and *Financial Times* Article Archive and Company Financials offer thousands of credible and reliable articles and websites to get the research process started.
- **A wealth of instructor support material:** Text-specific materials, such as instructor's manuals, test banks, and PowerPoint™ presentations simplify and enrich the teaching experience.

www.LongmanWorldHistory.com This website offers all the best of MyHistoryLab without course management features or the online e-book. As with MyHistoryLab, icons in the book lead students to specific assets on the website.

Instructor's Manual by Rick Whisonant of Winthrop University. This collection of resources includes chapter outlines, definitions, discussion suggestions, critical thinking exercises, term paper and essay topics, and audiovisual suggestions.

Companion Website (www.ablongman.com/brummett). This online course companion provides a wealth of resources for both students and instructors using *Civilization Past & Present,* Eleventh Edition. Students will find chapter summaries, test questions, and links for further research.

SafariX. SafariX Textbooks Online is an exciting new choice for students looking to save money. As an alternative to purchasing the print textbook, students can subscribe to the same content online and save up to 50% off the suggested list price of the print text. With a SafariX WebBook, students can search the text, make notes online, print out reading assignments that incorporate lecture notes, and bookmark important passages for later review. For more information, or to subscribe to the SafariX Web Book, visit www.safarix.com.

Test Bank and Test Generator by Susan Hellert of the University of Wisconsin at Platteville. This easy-to-customize test bank presents a wealth of multiple-choice, true-false, short-answer, and essay questions. Free to qualified college adopters.

Civilization Past & Present PowerPoint™ Presentations. Updated by Pamela Marquez of Metropolitan State College of Denver, these easy-to-customize PowerPoint™ slides outline key points of each chapter of the text and are available for download from the Companion Website (www.ablongman.com/brummett). Free to qualified college adopters.

The History Digital Media Archive CD-ROM. This CD-ROM contains hundreds of images, maps, interactive maps, and audio/video clips ready for classroom presentation, or downloading into PowerPoint™ or any other presentation software. Free to qualified college adopters.

Overhead Transparency Acetates to Accompany Civilization Past & Present. These text-specific acetates are available to all adopters. Every map is represented. Free to qualified college adopters.

Guide to Teaching World History by Palmira Brummett of the University of Tennessee at Knoxville. This guide offers explanations of major issues and themes in world history, sample syllabi and instructions on how to create a manageable syllabus, ideas for cross-cultural and cross-temporal connections, a pronunciation guide, and tips on getting through all the material. Free to qualified college adopters.

Discovering World History Through Maps and Views Overhead Transparency Acetates by Gerald Danzer of the University of Illinois at Chicago. This unique resource contains more than 100 full-color acetates of beautiful reference maps, source maps, urban plans, views, photos, art, and building diagrams. Free to qualified college adopters.

Longman World History Atlas Overhead Transparency Acetates. These acetates are available to instructors who select the *Longman World History Atlas* for their students. Free to qualified college adopters.

Historical Newsreel Video. This 90-minute video contains newsreel excerpts examining U.S. involvement in world affairs over the past 60 years. Free to qualified college adopters.

Longman-Penguin Putnam Inc. Value Bundles. Students and professors alike will love the value and quality of the Penguin books offered at a deep discount when bundled with *Civilization Past & Present,* Eleventh Edition, for qualified college adopters.

Supplements for Students

Companion Website (www.ablongman.com/brummett). This online course companion provides a wealth of resources for both students and instructors using *Civilization Past & Present,* Eleventh Edition. Students will find chapter summaries, test questions, and links for further research.

Student Study Guide in two volumes: Volume 1 (Chapters 1–17) and Volume 2 (Chapters 13–35) revised by Norman Love of El Paso Community College. Each chapter includes chapter overviews, lists of themes and concepts, map exercises, multiple-choice practice tests, and critical thinking and essay questions.

Study Card for World History. Colorful, affordable, and packed with useful information, the *Study Card for World History* makes studying easier, more efficient, and more enjoyable. Course information is distilled down to the basics, helping students quickly master the fundamentals, review a subject for understanding, or prepare for an exam. Because they are laminated for durability, Study Cards can be kept for years to come and be pulled out whenever they are needed for a quick review.

Mapping World History. This workbook was created for use in conjunction with *Discovering World History Through Maps and Views.* Designed to teach students to interpret and analyze cartographic materials as historical documents.

World History Map Workbooks, Second Edition, Volumes I and II. These workbooks, created by Glee Wilson, Kent State University, are designed to explain the correlations between historical events and geography through assignments that involve reading and interpreting maps.

Longman World History Atlas. A comprehensive collection of historical maps that reflects truly global coverage of world history. Each of the atlas's 56 maps are designed to be readable, informative, and accurate as well as beautiful.

Longman Library of World Biography Series. Each interpretive biography in the new Library of World Biography series focuses on a figure whose actions and ideas significantly influenced the course of world history. Pocket-sized and brief, each book relates the life of its subject to the broader themes and developments of the times. Series titles include:

- *Alexander the Great: Legacy of a Conqueror* by Winthrop Lindsay Adams, University of Utah
- *Benito Mussolini: The First Fascist* by Anthony L. Cardoza, Loyola University of Chicago
- *Fukuzawa Yukichi: From Samurai to Capitalist* by Helen M. Hopper, University of Pittsburg
- *Ignatius of Loyola: Founder of the Jesuits* by John Patrick Donnelly, Marquette University
- *Jacques Coeur: Entrepreneur and King's Bursar* by Kathryn L. Reyerson, University of Minnesota
- *Kato Shidzue: A Japanese Feminist* by Helen M. Hopper, University of Pittsburg
- *Simón Bolívar: Liberation and Disappointment* by David Bushnell, University of Florida
- *Vasco da Gama: Renaissance Crusader* by Glenn J. Ames, University of Toledo

Longman World History Series. These books focus on the historical significance of a particular movement, experience, or interaction. Concise and inexpensive, they bring the global connections and consequences of these events to the fore, showing students how events that happened long ago or far away can still affect them. Titles include:

- *Colonial Encounters in the Age of High Imperialism* by Scott B. Cook, Rhode Island School of Design.
- *Environmentalism: A Global History* by Ramachandra Guha
- *Expansion and Global Interaction: 1200–1700* by David Ringrose, University of California at San Diego

ACKNOWLEDGMENTS

A special note of appreciation goes to the following reviewers for providing thorough and expert advice for the *Global Issues* essays. Their suggestions have been of tremendous help in the writing of this new feature:

Milan Andrejevich
Indiana University Northwest

Charles E. Bashaw
College of Charleston

Kevin W. Caldwell
Blue Ridge Community College

Peter Fraunholtz
Northeastern University

James C. Godwin II
University of Delaware

Elizabeth P. Hancock
Gainesville College

Frank Karpiel
College of Charleston

Thomas O. Kay
Wheaton College

Laurence W. Marvin
Berry College

Donald T. McGuire
SUNY Buffalo

Fannie T. Rushing
Benedictine University

Mark B. Tauger
West Virginia University

Rick Whisonant
Winthrop University

We are most grateful to the following reviewers who gave generously of their time and knowledge to provide thoughtful evaluations and many helpful suggestions for the revision of this edition.

Henry Abramson
Florida Atlantic University

Lee Annis
Montgomery College—Rockville

Daniel Ayana
Youngstown State University

James W. Brodman
University of Central Arkansas

Thomas Cary
City University

Edward R. Crowther
Adams State College

Cole P. Dawson
Warner Pacific College

Dr. Michael de Nie
State University of West Georgia

Shannon L. Duffy
Loyola University New Orleans

Charles T. Evans
Northern Virginia Community College

Ronald Fritze
University of Central Arkansas

Richard M. Golden
University of North Texas

Elizabeth P. Hancock
Gainesville College

Eric J. Hanne
Florida Atlantic University

Caroline Hoefferle
Wingate University

Roger L. Jungmeyer
Lincoln University of Missouri

Jeffrrey W. Myers
Avila University

William R. Rogers
Isothermal Community College

Daniel E. Schafer
Belmont University

Acknowledgments

Roger Schlesinger
Washington State University

William Seavey
East Carolina University

Deborah A. Symonds
Drake University

Mark B. Tauger
West Virginia University

Ted Weeks
Southern Illinois University

Rick Whisonant
Winthrop University

We also thank the many conscientious reviewers who reviewed previous editions of this book.

Henry Abramson
Florida Atlantic University

Wayne Ackerson
Salisbury State University

Jay Pascal Anglin
University of Southern Mississippi

Lee Annis
Montgomery County Community College—Maryland

Joseph Appiah
J. Sargeant Reynolds Community College

Michael Auslin
Yale University

Mark C. Bartusis
Northern State University

Charlotte Beahan
Murray State University

Martin Berger
Youngstown State University

Joel Berlatsky
Wilkes College

Jackie R. Booker
Kent State University

Mauricio Borrero
St. John's University

Darwin F. Bostwick
Old Dominion University

Robert F. Brinson Jr.
Santa Fe Community College

Robert H. Buchanan
Adams State College

Nancy Cade
Pikeville College

Michael L. Carrafiello
East Carolina University

James O. Catron Jr.
North Florida Junior College

Mark Chavalas
University of Wisconsin

William H. Cobb
East Carolina University

J. L. Collins
Allan Hancock College

J. R. Crawford
Montreat-Anderson College

Edward R. Crowther
Adams State College

Lawrence J. Daly
Bowling Green State University

Demoral Davis
Jackson State University

Anne Dorazio
Westchester Community College

Dawn Duensing
Maui Community College

Ellen Emerick
Georgetown College

William Edward Ezzell
Georgia Perimeter College

John D. Fair
Auburn University at Montgomery

Nancy Fitch
California State University

Robert B. Florian
Salem-Teikyo University

Nels W. Forde
University of Nebraska

Joseph T. Fuhrmann
Murray State University

Lydia Garner
Southwest Texas State University

Robert J. Gentry
University of Southwestern Louisiana

Paul George
Miami Community College, Dade

David Gleason
Armstrong Atlantic State University

Richard Golden
University of North Texas

Oliver Griffin
Weber State University

Michael Hall
Armstrong Atlantic State University

Paul Halsall
University of North Florida

Jeffrey S. Hamilton
Old Dominion University

Donald E. Harpster
College of St. Joseph

Gordon K. Harrington
Weber State University

J. Drew Harrington
Western Kentucky University

Janine Hartman
University of Cincinnati

Geoff Haywood
Beaver College

Thomas Hegarty
University of Tampa

Madonna Hettinger
McHenry County College

David Hill
McHenry County College

Conrad C. Holcomb, Jr
Surry Community College

Thomas Howell
Louisiana College

Clark Hultquist
University of Montevallo

Scott Jessee
Appalachian State University

Roger L. Jungmeyer
Lincoln University of Missouri

Daniel R. Kazmer
Georgetown University

Bernard Kiernan
Concord College

David Koeller
North Park University

Michael L. Krenn
University of Miami

Teresa Lafer
Pennsylvania State University

Harral E. Landry
Texas Women's University

George Longenecker
Norwich University

Norman Love
El Paso Community College

Marsha K. Marks
Alabama A&M University

Caroline T. Marshall
James Madison University

Eleanor McCluskey
Broward Community College

Robert McCormick
Newman University

Christopher McKay
University of Alberta

David A. Meier
Dickinson State University

Arlin Migliazzo
Whitworth College

William C. Moose
Mitchell Community College

Zachary Morgan
William Patterson University

Wayne Morris
Lees-McRae College

John G. Muncie
East Stroudsburg University

Justin Murphy
Howard Payne University

David Owusu-Ansah
James Madison University

George Pesely
Austin-Peay State

Al Pilant
Cumberland College

Jana Pisani
Texas A&M International University

Sr. Jeannette Plante, CSC
Notre Dame College

Norman Pollock
Old Dominion University

J. Graham Provan
Millikin University

George B. Pruden Jr.
Armstrong State College

John D. Ramsbottom
Northeast Missouri State University

Ruth Richard
College of Lake County

Charles Risher
Montreat College

Hugh I. Rodgers
Columbus College

Ruth Rogaski
Princeton University

William Rogers
Isothermal Community College

Patrick J. Rollins
Old Dominion University

Chad Ronnander
University of Minnesota

R. A. Rotz
Indiana University

Robert Rowland
Loyola University

Barry T. Ryan
Westmont College

Bill Schell
Murray State University

Louis E. Schmier
Valdosta State College

William M. Simpson
Louisiana College

Paul J. Smith
Haverford College

Barbara G. Sniffen
University of Wisconsin—Oshkosh

Lawrence Squeri
East Stroudsburg University

Lawrence Stanley
McHenry County College

Terrence S. Sullivan
University of Nebraska at Omaha

John Swanson
Utica College of Syracuse

Edward Tabri
Columbus State Community College

Gordon L. Teffeteller
Valdosta State College

Malcolm R. Thorp
Brigham Young University

Helen M. Tierney
University of Wisconsin—Platteville

Leslie Tischauser
Prairie State College

Arthur L. Tolson
Southern University

Joseph A. Tomberlin
Valdosta State University

Marcia Vaughan
Murray State University

Thomas Dwight Veve
Dalton College

Chris Warren
Copiah-Lincoln Community College

Mary Watrous
Washington State University

David L. White
Appalachian State University

Thomas Whigham
University of Georgia

John R. Willertz
Saginaw Valley State University

To the Student

We set two goals for ourselves when we wrote *Civilization Past & Present*. The first is to provide you with an understanding of the contributions of past eras in all parts of the globe to the shaping of world history. The second is to illuminate the way in which the study of world history gives us insights into the genesis, nature, and direction of our own civilization.

These are challenging tasks. However, given the globalization of all aspects of our lives, they are essential. When economies in East Asia or Latin America are in a state of crisis, the impact is felt on Wall Street. The culture of the New World—especially music and movies—has spread around the globe. When tragedies occur in the Middle East, we are all affected. Long gone are the days when an occurrence that took place far away could be isolated.

Now you are taking a course in world history to understand the development of the cultures of the world—cultures that are coming together to form a multifaceted world civilization. By understanding how and why other civilizations have chosen differing routes to their future, you can gain an understanding of why your part of civilization has succeeded or failed in attaining its potential. With an understanding of world history, you will be able to respond more knowledgeably to the changes through which you will live and to make informed choices as a world citizen.

History is the study of change over time. A historian is a person who focuses on one aspect of changes in the past, poses questions about why a particular event has taken place, proposes answers—hypotheses—and tests those hypotheses against the evidence—all of the evidence. We do not expect you to be historians at this point in your careers—to form your own hypotheses and write monographs. We have written this book, however, to enable you to study change over the entire course of human history.

We have included a number of tools to help you on your voyage through this text. The new **Global Issues essays** explore seven topics of unique transcultural and trans-historical significance: Migration, Religion and Government, Location and Identity, Technological Exchange, Slavery, Gender, and War and International Law. The essays carefully examine these topics using a global framework, employing examples that span both history and the world's many civilizations. The essays are intended to do more than just inform you about global topics; however; they also reveal challenges that have and still confront civilizations the world over.

As you begin each chapter, take five or ten minutes to look at the **chapter opening pages.** These two pages at the beginning of each chapter reveal what is to come: a photo conceptualizes a main theme of the chapter, and a chapter outline and a timeline allow you to fix beginning and end points in this part of your trip. The chapter introduction sets the stage for the content that follows and indicates the chapter's overall themes—sometimes political or economic, sometimes religious, social, or artistic. Take time to read the introduction and then thumb to the end of the chapter to read the conclusion. Next, go through the chapter reading only the main and secondary headlines. Finally, return to the beginning of the chapter and start to read—knowing in advance where you have come from and which way you are going.

Within each chapter we offer you other tools to gain an understanding of the past. Events take place in a location, and each location has particular features that affect what will happen. Thus the text includes more than 100 full-color **maps,** each with its own explanatory caption. Shaded **insets** on most of the maps help you to locate its territory on its larger hemisphere or the globe. Some maps are designed to make clear the nature of a single distinctive event; others illustrate larger trends.

Each chapter also offers new features to help you better engage with the content. The new **pronunciation guide** will help you correctly pronounce key foreign terms—after each such word within the text a pronunciation appears in parentheses. The new on-page **glossary** provides concise definitions of key historical terms and appears in the footer of the pages in which terms are discussed.

Different civilizations have different visions of themselves and their place in the world. The **Discovery Through Maps** boxes in many of the chapters will give you a notion of the way that various cultures in the world have seen themselves and their relation to the rest of the globe. For example, al-Idrisi's "An Islamic Map of the World" is oriented, as was common in Arab maps of his time, with south at the top; it is centered on the world of his own experience, the sacred city of Mecca in Arabia and the civilized realm of the Mediterranean. A late-nineteenth-century map of southern Africa perpetuated "The Myth of the Empty Land," by which white settlers would claim that they were moving into an unpopulated land and that they had just as much right to it as Africans did.

We also include one or more excerpts from **primary source documents** in each chapter. These excerpts from original sources offer you a window into the way that the people of the time expressed themselves. The documents cover a variety of viewpoints: political, economic, legal, religious, social, artistic, and popular. For example, in "That Was No Brother," two documents—one by an African chief and the other by the English explorer Henry Morton Stanley—give two very different perceptions of the same battle.

The text's 500 **photos,** most in full color, give balanced pictorial coverage of all parts of the world and enhance the reading of each chapter by giving additional context and bringing to life the matters under discussion. For this edition, we have paid special attention in these photos to the lifestyles and contributions of women.

After you have finished each chapter you will find three features to help you prepare a paper or project or simply to learn more. The **Literature and Film** listings offer a listing of novels, poetry, films, and videos. The annotated bibliographies of **Suggestions for Reading** indicate useful general studies, monographs, and source materials. Also included is a list of **Suggestions for Web Browsing** to allow you to hook up to databases, sounds, images, or discussion groups dealing with the topics under consideration.

Robert R. Edgar
Neil J. Hackett
George F. Jewsbury
Barbara Molony

CHAPTER 9

The European Middle Ages, 476–1348 C.E.

CHAPTER CONTENTS

- The Church in the Early Middle Ages
- The Merovingians and Carolingians
  - **DOCUMENT:** *Charlemagne: A Firsthand Look*
- Feudalism and Manorialism
- The Revival of Trade and Towns
- The Church in the High Middle Ages: 1000–1348
- The Crusades
  - **DOCUMENT:** *Muslim and Christian: Two Contemporary Perspectives*
- The Development of European States: 1000–1348

500
590–604 Pontificate of Gregory I, the Great; papacy begins to assert political influence

700
732 Charles Martel defeats Muslims at Tours

c. 790–c. 940 Viking raids and settlements throughout Europe

800
800 Charlemagne crowned emperor by the pope

843 Treaty of Verdun; division of Charlemagne's empire

900
910 Benedictine monastery at Cluny founded

962 Otto the Great crowned emperor by the Pope

987–996 Hugh Capet rules France; beginning of Capetian dynasty

1000
1066 William the Conqueror takes England at the battle of Hastings

1079–1142 Peter Abelard

1095 First Crusade

1100
1152–1190 Reign of Frederick I Barbarossa of Hohenstaufen dynasty in Germany

1154–1189 Reign of Henry II of England, founder of Plantagenet dynasty

1182–1226 St. Francis of Assisi, founder of Franciscan religious order

1198–1226 Pontificate of Innocent III, zenith of papal power

1200
1215 Magna Carta

1212–1250 Reign of Frederick II

1248 Seventh Crusade (last)

The absence of the political unity and military security once provided by the Roman Empire became an obvious fact of life in almost all of western Europe in the fourth and fifth centuries. As the unity and security of the old Roman order collapsed and Germanic chieftains claimed lands and asserted what authority they could, very slowly the civilization of Rome evolved into a culture that was a unique blending of Roman and Germanic institutions. Out of this blending of cultures emerged a distinct pattern of life in western Europe.

One of the institutions that survived the collapse of Roman order was the Christian Church, which, by the beginning of the sixth century, was still in the process of unification under the direction of the bishop of Rome, the Pope. The church increased its efficiency through the centralization of its administration, and unified its efforts to convert all of Europe and eliminate rival religions. Christian efforts to preserve knowledge and learning centered on saving art and literature of the past that was supportive exclusively of the Christian faith; for the most part the art and literature of the non-Christian past was destroyed, suppressed, or ignored—much of the intellectual heritage of the ancient world was lost forever.

The first significant state to emerge out of the fragmentation of old Roman order was that established by the Germanic tribe of the Franks, who gave northern Europe an interim of stability and progress. Military and political security was improved, and Roman Christianity was extended among the barbarian tribes of the north.

But the accomplishments of the Franks were not to be permanent. Their empire did not endure, partly because it lacked the solid economic foundation that had supported the Romans, and because of new and violent invasions. Viking, Magyar, and Muslim incursions had to be addressed through local resistance, since no effective response existed on a national or international level.

Out of the disintegration of the Frankish empire evolved an alternative political order sometimes described as feudalism. Based on formally stated agreements between individuals, this method of government was designed to provide social stability and military security in Europe. And the manorial system, the economic foundation of medieval life, provided stability to the rural economy of Europe. Both institutions attempted to insure security by resisting change and fostering self-sufficiency.

Gradually, the political and military goals of the feudal nobility became aggressive and expansionist. Monarchs once again attempted to increase their authority over the feudal nobility. The growth of trade and commerce slowly provided an economic alternative to the manorial system, and the society of the West changed in the process. In addition, the church increased its power as a political and economic force in European society, in addition to its religious leadership. The church's sponsorship of the Crusading movement of the later Middle Ages was indicative of that power and influence.

The culture of the Later European Middle Ages emerged as greatly distinct from that of the period before 500. The collective and conservative society of the earlier period gave way to a culture becoming more familiar with religious challenge, economic growth, and political centralization. The cultural conservatism and conformity that typified the earlier patterns of medieval life gave way to a society that had to adjust to a more rapid rate of change and challenge in virtually all facets of life. The roots of modern European society are easily found in the civilization of the Late Middle Ages.

THE CHURCH IN THE EARLY MIDDLE AGES

■ *What role did the Church play in stabilizing western European society after the fall of the Roman Empire?*

As Europe formed a unique culture out of the remnants of Roman influence and the injection of Germanic peoples and their traditions, the church played a formative role in shaping this new social fabric. In the Early Middle Ages (500–1000), the administration of the church was centralized through the efforts of the popes and the ever more efficient bureaucracy at Rome. Missionary activity spread Christianity to the borders of the continent and provided a unified cultural and religious foundation for early European society. And, in large part, the church, its missionaries, and its copyists in monasteries should be credited with keeping at least some of the intellectual heritage of the ancient world alive in an age when learning, other than that which supported Christian belief, was considered useless and unnecessary.

The Early Medieval Papacy, 500–1000

Chapter 5 examined the growing authority of the bishops of Rome, the popes, over the Christian Church in western Europe. Not only were the bishops of Rome able to establish control over the church's hierarchy and supervise the spiritual concerns of the believers; often the early popes were looked to for political leadership and guidance in troubled times. During the pontificate of Gregory I, the Great (590–604), the papacy aggressively began to assert its political as well as its spiritual authority. After his election as pope, Gregory assumed the task of protecting Rome and its surrounding territory from the threat of invasion from the Germanic tribe of the Lombards. After successfully negotiating a peace treaty with this tribe, Gregory became the first pope to conduct himself as actual ruler of a part of what later became the Papal States.

Gregory also laid the foundation for the papal machinery of church government. He took the first step in asserting papal control of the church outside Italy by sending a mission of Benedictine monks to convert the non-Christian Anglo-Saxons. The pattern of church government that Gregory established in England—bishops supervised by archbishops, who reported to the pope—became standard.

The task of establishing papal control of the church and extending the pope's **temporal** authority was continued by Gregory's successors. In the eighth century English missionaries transferred to Germany and France the pattern of papal government they had known in England; the Donation of Pepin, a sizable grant of territory in Italy given to the pope by the Merovingian (meh-roh-VIN-gee-ahn) king (see p. 261), greatly increased the pope's temporal power by creating the Papal States.

Missionary Activities of the Church

The early Middle Ages were years of widespread and intense missionary activity. By spreading Christianity,

---

temporal—Having to do with time, or the present life and this world. Worldly or transitory concerns.

The bejeweled front cover of the Lindau Gospels, a work dating from the third quarter of the ninth century, is an example of Carolingian art. The Celtic-Germanic metalwork tradition has been adapted to the religious art produced during the era of Charlemagne. The main clusters of semi-precious stones adorning the gold cover have been raised so that light can penetrate beneath them to make them glow.

missionaries contributed to the confluence of Germanic and Roman cultures. Monasteries, many of which were established in remote territories far from urban centers, served not only as missionary outposts, but also as refuges for those seeking a life of contemplation and prayer, as centers of learning for scholars, and even as progressive farming centers. The dedication and enthusiasm with which many of these monks approached their faith often extended beyond the monastic walls, and resulted ultimately in the virtual elimination of paganism in Europe.

One of the most successful of early Christian missionaries was Ulfilas (OOL-fi-lahs) (c. 311–383), who spent 40 years with the Visigoths and translated most of the Bible into Gothic. Ulfilas and many other early missionaries were followers of Arius, and the heresy of Arianism (see p. 154) was adopted by all the Germanic tribes in the empire, with the exception of the Franks and the Anglo-Saxons.

Missionary activities in Ireland resulted in the founding of numerous monasteries on that island, many of them in remote and isolated locations. In the late sixth and seventh centuries, many of these Irish monks, moved by a passionate devotion to Christianity and dedicated to the elimination of heresy, traveled to Scotland, northern England, the kingdom of the Franks, and even Italy as missionaries to renew the faith and erase the effects of worldly corruption. Irish monks also eagerly pursued scholarship and the preservation of early Christian literary works, and their monasteries became storehouses for priceless manuscripts and exquisite copies of original works.

Early in the seventh century, the papacy, along with the monasteries, took a more aggressive part in directing Christian missionary efforts. Under the direction of the pope, Roman Catholicism was established throughout England, and the Irish church acknowledged the primacy of Rome.

The English church, in turn, played an important role in the expansion of Roman Catholic Christianity on the European mainland. Boniface, the greatest English missionary in the eighth century, spent 35 years among the Germanic tribes and established several important monasteries and bishoprics before he turned to the task of reforming the church in France. There, he revitalized the monasteries, organized a system of local **parishes** to bring Christianity to the countryside, and probably was instrumental in forming the alliance between the papacy and the Carolingian dynasty of kings of the Franks. Roman Catholic missionaries were also sent to work among the Scandinavian peoples and the Slavs.

The Preservation of Knowledge

One of the great contributions of the monasteries was the preservation of the learning of the early church, and some of the literature of the Greek and Roman world that early Christian leaders found compatible with the Christian faith. After the fall of Rome, learning did not entirely die out in western Europe; the knowledge of the classical world was preserved through the efforts of a small number of concerned intellectuals who recognized its lasting value. Seeing that the ability to read Greek was quickly disappearing, the sixth-century Roman scholar Boethius (boh-EE-thee-uhs) (c. 480–525) determined to preserve Greek learning by

---

parish—A local church, with its own priest, and the people under the religious care of that priest.

translating all of Plato and Aristotle into Latin. But only Aristotle's treatises on logic were translated, and these works remained the sole writings of that philosopher available in Europe until the twelfth century. Unjustly accused of treachery by the emperor, Boethius was thrown into prison, where he wrote The Consolation of Philosophy while awaiting execution, which eventually became a medieval textbook on philosophy.

Cassiodorus (cah-si-oh-DOH-ruhs; c. 490–c. 585), a contemporary of Boethius, devoted most of his life to the collection and preservation of classical knowledge. By encouraging the monks to copy valuable manuscripts, he was instrumental in making the monasteries centers of learning. Following his example, many monasteries established *scriptoria*, departments concerned exclusively with copying manuscripts.

During the early Middle Ages, most education took place in the monasteries. In the late sixth and seventh centuries, when political stability was not yet reestablished throughout much of the European continent, Irish monasteries provided a safe haven for learning. There, men studied Greek and Latin, copied and preserved manuscripts, and, in illuminating them, produced masterpieces of art. The *Book of Kells* is a surviving example of their skill. In the early Middle Ages, women were provided no opportunities for such pursuits; the Church limited access to reading and writing to men involved in clerical and business occupations.

DOCUMENT
Rule of St. Benedict

THE MEROVINGIANS AND CAROLINGIANS

■ *How successful were the Merovingian and Carolingian monarchs in preserving Roman institutions and culture?*

In the blending of Roman and Germanic customs and institutions, the Franks played a particularly significant role. Not only was the kingdom of the Franks the most enduring of the early Germanic states, but it became, with the active support of the church, the first European kingdom that attempted to take the place of the Roman Empire in the West.

The Kingdom of the Franks Under Clovis

Before the Germanic invasions of the fourth century, the Franks lived close to the North Sea; late in the fourth century they began to migrate south and west into Roman Gaul. By 481 they occupied the northern part of Gaul as far south as the old Roman city of Paris, and in that same year, Clovis I of the Merovingian dynasty became ruler of one of the small Frankish kingdoms. By the time of his death in 511, Clovis had united the Franks into a single kingdom that stretched south to the Pyrenees.

Clovis was an intelligent manipulator of alliances and a shrewd diplomat who also used religion for political gain. He was converted to Christianity—perhaps through the influence of his Christian wife—and was baptized together with his whole army. He thus became the only Orthodox Christian ruler in the West, since the other Germanic tribes were either still pagan or followers of Arian Christianity (the heresy that maintained that Jesus was not equal to the Father and thereby not completely divine). This conversion of the Franks to Roman Christianity ultimately led to a close alliance of the Franks and the papacy.

Decline of the Merovingians—Rise of the Carolingians

Clovis's sons and grandsons extended Frankish control south to the Mediterranean and east into Germany. But after Clovis's death, the Merovingian dynasty began to decay. The Germanic tradition of treating the kingdom as personal property and dividing it among all the king's sons resulted in constant and bitter civil wars. But most importantly, the Merovingian kings proved themselves incompetent and ineffectual. Soon the Frankish state broke up into three separate kingdoms; in each, power was

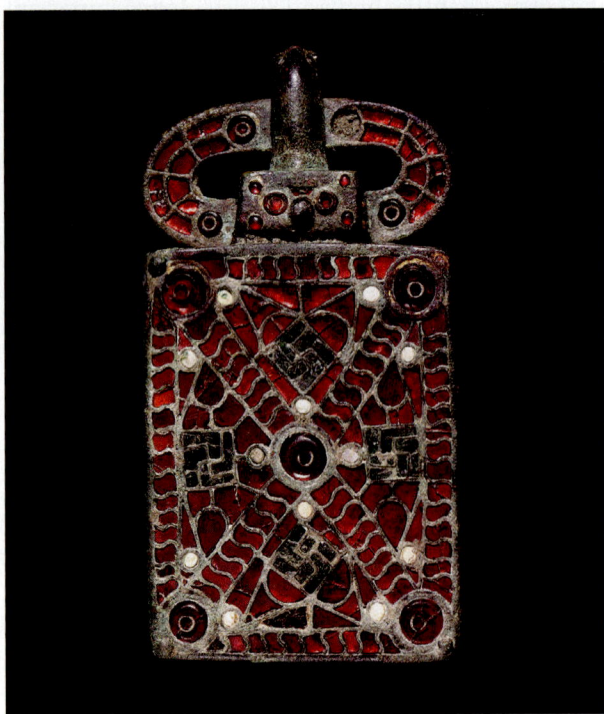
Visigothic belt buckle, circa 525–560. This elaborately crafted buckle is inlaid with finely polished red garnets and was probably worn by a prominent Spanish Visigothic woman. Most Visigothic belt buckles are of the same shape, but the patterns of decoration vary greatly, perhaps to signify the family or clan of the owner.

The Merovingians and the Carolingians

481–511	Clovis unites Franks; beginning of Merovingian dynasty
714–741	Charles Martel mayor of the palace
732	Charles defeats Muslims at Tours
741–768	Pepin the Short mayor of the palace
751	Pepin crowned king of the Franks; beginning of Carolingian dynasty
768–814	Reign of Charlemagne
800	Charlemagne crowned emperor by the pope; beginning of Carolingian Empire
814–840	Reign of Louis the Pious
843	Treaty of Verdun divides Carolingian Empire

concentrated in the hands of the chief official of the royal household—the mayor of the palace, a powerful noble who hoped to keep the king weak and ineffectual. The Merovingian rulers became puppets—"do-nothing kings."

By the middle of the seventh century, the Frankish state had lost most of the essential characteristics of Roman civilization. The Roman system of administration and taxation had collapsed. The dukes and counts who represented the Merovinginan king received no salary and usually acted on their own initiative in commanding the fighting men and presiding over the courts in their districts. International commerce had ceased except for a small-scale trade in luxury items carried on by adventurous Greek, Syrian, and Jewish traders. The old Roman cities served mainly as centers housing the local bishops and their staffs. The virtual absence of a middle class meant that society was composed of the nobility, a union through intermarriage of aristocratic Gallo-Roman and German families who owned and exercised authority over vast estates, and, at the other end of the social scale, the peasants *(coloni)* who worked the land and were considered bound to that estate. These peasants included large numbers of formerly free German farmers. Only about 10 percent of the peasant population of Gaul maintained their status as free individuals.

Coinciding with the Merovingian decay, new waves of invaders threatened every region of Europe. A great movement of Slavic peoples from the area that is now Russia had begun around 500 C.E. From this region the Slavs pushed west, inhabiting the areas left by the Germanic tribes when they advanced into the Roman Empire. By 650 the western Slavs had reached the Elbe River, which they crossed to raid German territory. Another danger threatened western Europe from the south: in the late seventh century the Muslim Moors prepared to invade Spain from North Africa.

The kingdom of the Franks gained strength when Charles Martel became mayor of the palace (or the king's court) in 714. His military skill earned him the surname Martel, "The Hammer." Charles was responsible for introducing a major innovation in European warfare. To counteract the effectiveness of the quick-striking Muslim cavalry, Charles recruited a force of professional mounted soldiers. He rewarded his soldiers with land to enable each of them to support a family, equipment, and war horses. With such a force, Charles Martel won an important victory over the Muslim cavalry at Tours in 732.

Charles's son, Pepin the Short (741–768), legalized the power already being exercised by the mayors of the palace by requesting and receiving from the pope a decision that whoever exercised the actual power in the kingdom should be the legal ruler. In 751 Pepin was elected king by the Franks; the last Merovingian was sent off to a **monastery,** and the Carolingian dynasty came to power. In 754 the pope reaffirmed the election of Pepin by personally anointing him as king of the Franks.

Behind the pope's action was his need for a powerful protector against the Lombards, who had conquered the **Exarchate** of Ravenna (the center of Byzantine government in Italy) and were demanding tribute from the pope. Following Pepin's coronation, the pope secured his promise of armed intervention in Italy and his pledge to give the Exarchate to the papacy, once it was conquered. In 756 a Frankish army forced the Lombard king to withdraw, and Pepin gave Ravenna to the pope. The so-called Donation of Pepin made the pope a temporal ruler over the Papal States, a strip of territory that extended diagonally across northern Italy.

The alliance between the Franks and the papacy affected the course of politics and religion for centuries. It furthered the separation of the Roman from the Greek Christian Church by giving the papacy a dependable Western ally in place of the Byzantines, previously its only protector against the Lombards.

---

monastery—A house or residence of a community of religious men (monks), who live in seclusion from the world and maintain a self-sufficient communal lifestyle.

Exarchate—In the Byzantine empire, the office and/or the area ruled by an official named an exarch—a bishop ranking below the patriarch of the Eastern Orthodox Christian church.

Charlemagne and His Achievements

Under Pepin's son Charlemagne (CHAHR-leh-mayn), or Charles the Great, the Frankish state and the Carolingian dynasty reached the height of its power. Although he was certainly a successful warrior-king, leading his armies on yearly campaigns, Charlemagne, who ruled from 768 to 814, also tried to provide an effective administration for his kingdom. In addition, he had great appreciation for learning; his efforts at furthering the arts produced the revival in learning and letters known as the Carolingian Renaissance.

Charlemagne sought to extend his kingdom southward against the Muslims in Spain. He crossed the Pyrenees and eventually drove the Muslims back to the Ebro River, establishing a frontier area known as the Spanish March, centered near Barcelona. French immigrants moved into the area, later called Catalonia, giving it a character culturally distinct from the rest of Spain.

Charlemagne conquered the Bavarians and the Saxons, the last of the independent Germanic tribes, on his eastern frontier. Even farther to the east, the empire's frontier was continually threatened by the Slavs and the Avars (AY-vahrs), Asiatic nomads related to the Huns. In six campaigns, Charlemagne nearly eliminated the Avars and then set up his own military province in the Danube valley to guard against any future advances by eastern nomads. Called the East March, this territory later became Austria. Like his father Pepin, Charlemagne was deeply involved in Italian politics. The Lombards resented the attempts of the papacy to expand civil control in northern Italy. At the request of the pope, Charlemagne attacked the Lombards in 774, defeated them, and named himself their king.

One of the most important events in Charlemagne's reign took place on Christmas Day, 800. In the previous year the Roman nobility had removed the pope from office, charging him with corruption. But Charlemagne came to Rome and restored the pope to his position. At the Christmas service, Charlemagne knelt before the altar and the pope placed a crown on his head while the congregation shouted: "To Charles Augustus crowned of God, great and pacific Emperor of the Romans, long life and victory!"

This ceremony demonstrated that the memory of the Roman Empire still survived as a meaningful tradition in Europe and that there was a strong desire to reestablish political unity. In fact, Charlemagne had named his capital at Aix-la-Chapelle (AX-lah-shah-PEL), "New Rome," or Aachen (AH-ken), and considered taking the title of emperor in an attempt to revive the idea of the Roman Empire in the West.

The extent of Charlemagne's empire was impressive. His territories included all of the western area of the old Roman Empire except north Africa, Britain, southern Italy, and the majority of Spain. Seven defensive provinces, or *marches*, protected the empire against hostile neighbors.

The Carolingian Empire

The Carolingian territories were divided into some 300 administrative divisions, each under a count (*graf*) or, in the marches along the border, a margrave (*markgraf*). In addition, there were local military officials, the dukes. In an effort to supervise the activities of local officials, Charlemagne issued an ordinance creating the *missi dominici*, the king's envoys. Pairs of these itinerant officials, usually a bishop and a lay noble, traveled throughout the realm to check on the local administration. So that the *missi* were immune to bribes, they were chosen from men of high rank, were frequently transferred from one region to another, and no two of them were teamed for more than one year.

This gold bust of Charlemagne was made in the fourteenth century and is housed now in the treasury of the Palace Chapel of Charlemagne in Aachen, Germany. The reliquary bust contains parts of the emperor's skull.

Charlemagne's Legacy

Charlemagne is considered one of the most significant figures of early European history. He created a state in which law and order were again enforced

Document: Charlemagne: A Firsthand Look

Einhard, born in the kingdom of the Franks in circa 770 C.E., was the emperor Charlemagne's secretary and biographer. The following is an excerpt from Einhard's *Life of Charlemagne*, which he completed some years after the emperor's death. Einhard's biography of the emperor is considered one of the finest works of biography produced in the early Middle Ages. It was modeled after Roman biographies of the later emperors, and intended to give its readers an intimate glimpse of Charlemagne's character, as well as to convince them of the emperor's wisdom and majesty. The following except deals mainly with the emperor's physical appearance and private pleasures:

Charles was large and strong, and of lofty stature, though not disproportionately tall (his height is well known to have been seven times the length of his foot); the upper part of his head was round, his eyes very large and animated, nose a little long, hair fair, and face laughing and merry. Thus his appearance was always stately and dignified, whether he was standing or sitting; although his neck was thick and somewhat short, and his belly rather prominent; but the symmetry of the rest of his body concealed these defects. His gait was firm, his whole carriage manly, and his voice clear, but not so strong as his size led one to expect. His health was excellent, except during the four years preceding his death, when he was subject to frequent fevers; at the last he even limped a little with one foot. Even in those years he consulted rather his own inclinations than the advice of physicians, who were almost hateful to him, because they wanted him to give up roasts, to which he was accustomed, and to eat boiled meat instead. In accordance with the national custom, he took frequent exercise on horseback and in the chase, accomplishments in which scarcely any people in the world can equal the Franks. He enjoyed the exhalations from natural warm springs, and often practiced swimming, in which he was such an adept that none could surpass him; and hence it was that he built his palace at Aix-la-Chapelle, and lived there constantly during his latter years until his death. He used not only to invite his sons to his bath, but his nobles and friends, and now and then a troop of his retinue or bodyguard, so that a hundred or more persons sometimes bathed with him.... Charles was temperate in eating, and particularly so in drinking, for he abominated drunkenness in anybody, much more in himself and those of his household; but he could not easily abstain from food, and often complained that fasts injured his health. He very rarely gave entertainment, only on great feastdays, and then to large numbers of people. His meals ordinarily consisted of four courses, not counting the roast, which his huntsmen used to bring in on the spit; he was more fond of this than of any other dish. While at table, he listened to reading or music....

Charles had the gift of ready and fluent speech, and could express whatever he had to say with the utmost clearness. He was not satisfied with command of his native language merely, but gave attention to the study of foreign ones, and in particular was such a master of Latin that he could speak it as well as his native tongue; but he could understand Greek better than he could speak it. He was so eloquent, indeed, that he might have passed for a teacher of eloquence. He most zealously cultivated the liberal arts, held those who taught them in great esteem, and conferred great honors upon them. He took lessons in grammar of the deacon Peter of Pisa, at that time an aged man. Another deacon, Albin of Britain, surnamed Alcuin, a man of Saxon extraction, who was the greatest scholar of the day, was his teacher in other branches of learning. The King spent much time and labor with him studying rhetoric, dialectics, and especially astronomy; he learned to reckon, and used to investigate the motions of the heavenly bodies most curiously, with an intelligent scrutiny. He also tried to write, and used to keep tablets and blanks in bed under his pillow, that at leisure hours he might accustom his hand to form the letters; however, as he did not begin his efforts in due season, but late in life, they met with ill success.

Questions to Consider

1. What do you suppose is Einhard's real purpose in writing this biography? Do you think it is an impartial account?
2. What could such a biography be used for, especially since it appeared after Charlemagne's death?
3. Do you think there are some exaggerations contained in this except? If so, what might they be, and why do you think they were included?

From Samuel Epes Turner, trans., *Life of Charlemagne by Einhard* (Ann Arbor: University of Michigan Press, 1960), pp. 50–57.

after three centuries of disintegration. His patronage of learning began a cultural revival that later generations would build on, producing a European civilization distinct from the Byzantine to the east and the Muslim to the south.

Charlemagne's empire was not long-lived, however, for its territories were too vast and its nobility too divisive to be held together after the dominating personality of its creator was gone. Charlemagne had no standing army; his foot soldiers were essentially the old Germanic war band summoned to fight by its war leader. The king did not have a bureaucratic administrative machine comparable to that of Roman times. The Frankish economy was agricultural and localized, and there was no system of taxation adequate to maintain an effective and permanent administration. Under Charlemagne's weak successors, the empire collapsed in the confusion of civil wars and devastating new invasions. Progress toward a centralized and effective monarchy in Europe ended with Charlemagne's death.

When he died in 814, Charlemagne was succeeded by his only surviving son, Louis the Pious, a well-meaning but ineffective ruler. Louis, in accordance with Frankish custom, divided the kingdom among his three sons, and bitter rivalry and warfare broke out among the brothers even before Louis died in 840.

In 843 the three brothers met at Verdun, where they agreed to split the Carolingian lands among themselves. Charles the Bald obtained the western part of the empire, and Louis the German the eastern; Lothair, the oldest brother, retained the title of emperor and obtained an elongated middle kingdom, which stretched 1000 miles from the North Sea to central Italy.

The Treaty of Verdun contributed to the shaping of political problems that continued into the twentieth century. Lothair's middle kingdom soon collapsed into three major parts: Lorraine in the north, Burgundy, and Italy in the south. Lorraine included Latin and German cultures, and, although it was divided in 870 between Charles and Louis, the area was disputed for centuries. Lorraine became one of the most frequent battlegrounds of Europe.

Europe Under Attack

During the ninth and tenth centuries, coinciding with the collapse of the Carolingian Empire, western Europe came under attack by Scandinavians from the

Charlemagne was able to rule the largest empire in the West since the collapse of Rome. Although today the emperor is probably remembered most for his administrative and cultural contributions, he conducted campaigns to enlarge his empire during nearly all of his reign.

north and Muslims from the south, while the Magyars, a new band of Asiatic nomads, conducted destructive raids on central Europe and northern Italy. Christian Europe was hard pressed to repel these warlike newcomers who were more threatening to life and property than the Germanic invaders of the fifth century.

From bases in North Africa, Muslim adventurers, in full command of the sea, raided the coasts of Italy and France. In 827 they began the conquest of Byzantine Sicily and southern Italy. From forts erected in southern France they penetrated far inland to attack merchant caravans even in the Alpine passes. What

New invasions in the ninth and tenth centuries threatened the stability of western Europe in much the same way the Germanic invasions had challenged the Roman Empire. Muslim, Viking, and Magyar attacks posed serious threats to Christian European political stability.

trade still existed between Byzantium and western Europe, except for that undertaken by Venice and several other Italian towns, was now almost totally cut off, and the Mediterranean Sea came under almost complete Muslim control.

The most widespread and destructive raids, however, came from Scandinavia. Swedes, Danes, and Norwegians—collectively referred to as Vikings—began to move south. Overpopulation and a surplus of young men are possible reasons for this expansion, but some scholars suggest that these raiders were defeated war bands expelled from their homeland by the emergence of strong royal power. The Vikings had developed seaworthy ships capable of carrying 100 men, powered by long oars or by sail when the wind was favorable. Viking sailors had also developed expert sailing techniques; without benefit of the compass, they were able to navigate by the stars at night and the sun by day.

The range of Viking expansion reached as far as North America to the west, the Caspian Sea to the east, and the Mediterranean to the south. Between 800 and 850, Ireland was raided repeatedly. Many monasteries, the centers of the flourishing Irish Celtic culture, were destroyed. The Icelandic Norsemen ventured on to Greenland and, later, to North America. Other raiders traveled the rivers of Russia as merchants and soldiers of fortune and founded the nucleus of a Russian state. Danes raided Britain and the shores of Germany, France, and Spain. By 840 they had occupied most of Britain north of the Thames. They devastated northwest France, destroying dozens of abbeys and towns. Unable to fend off the Viking attacks, the weak Carolingian king accepted the local Norse chieftain as duke of a Viking state, later called Normandy. Like Viking settlers elsewhere, these Northmen, or Normans, became Christian converts and eventually played an important role in shaping the future of medieval Europe.

FEUDALISM AND MANORIALISM

■ *What influences did feudalism and manorialism have in shaping European society during the Middle Ages and beyond?*

Europe's response to the invasions of the ninth and tenth centuries was not uniform. By 900 the Viking occupation of England had initiated a strong national reaction, which soon led to the creation of a united British kingdom. Germany in 919 repelled the Magyar threat through the efforts of a new and able line of kings who went on to become powerful European monarchs. But Viking attacks on France accelerated a political fragmentation. Since the monarchy could not hold together its vast territory, small independent landowners surrendered both their lands and their personal freedoms to the many counts, dukes, and other local lords in return for protection and security. The decline of trade further strengthened the position of the landed nobility, whose large estates, or manors, sought to become economically self-sufficient. In addition, the nobility became increasingly dependent on military service provided by a professional force of heavily armed mounted knights, many of whom lived in the houses of their noble retainers in return for their military service.

In most parts of western Europe, where an effective centralized government was entirely absent, personal safety and security became the primary concerns of most individuals. Many historians have used the term *feudalism* to apply to the individual and unique political and social patterns resulting from political decentralization and the resulting attempts to ensure personal security.

Feudalism can be described as a system of rights and duties in which political power was exercised locally by private individuals rather than through the bureaucracy of a centralized state. In general, western European feudalism involved three basic elements: (1) a personal element, called *lordship* or *vassalage*, by which one nobleman, the *vassal*, became the follower of a stronger nobleman, the *lord;* (2) a property element, called the ***fief*** or *benefice* (usually land), which the vassal received from his lord to enable him to fulfill the obligations of being a vassal; and (3) a governmental element, the private exercise of governmental functions over vassals and fiefs.

Feudal Society

In theory, feudalism was a vast hierarchy. At the top stood the king; all the land in his kingdom in theory belonged to him. He kept large areas for his personal use (royal or crown lands) and, in return for the military service of a specified number of mounted knights, invested the highest nobles—such as dukes and counts (in Britain, earls)—with the remainder. Those nobles, in turn, in order to obtain the services of the required number of mounted warriors owed to the king, parceled out large portions of their fiefs to lesser nobles. This process, called *subinfeudation*, was continued in theory until the lowest in the scale of vassals

---

fief—A grant made to a vassal by a feudal lord in exchange for services. The grant usually consisted of land and the labor of the peasants who were bound to that estate. The income the land provided supported the vassal. Dignities, offices, and money rents were also given in fief.

was reached—the single knight whose fief was just sufficient to support one mounted warrior.

By maintaining the king at the head of this theoretical feudal hierarchy, the justification for monarchy was preserved, even though some feudal kings were little more than figureheads who were less powerful than their own vassals.

Relation of Lord and Vassal: The Contract

Personal bonds between lord and vassal were sometimes formally recognized. In the ceremony known as **homage,** the vassal knelt before his lord, or **suzerain,** and promised to be his "man." In the *oath of fealty* that followed, the vassal swore on the Bible or some other sacred object that he would remain true to his lord. Next, in the ritual of *investiture,* a lance, a glove, or even a clump of dirt was handed to the vassal to signify his jurisdiction over the fief. As his part of the contract, the lord was usually obliged to give his vassal protection and justice. In return, the vassal's primary duty was military service. But in addition, the vassal could be obliged to assist the lord in rendering justice in the lord's court. At certain times, as when the lord was captured and needed to be ransomed, the lord also had the right to demand special money payments, called *aids.*

The lord also had certain rights, called feudal *incidents,* regarding the administration of the fief. These included *wardship*—the right to administer the fief during the minority of a vassal's heir—and forfeiture of the fief if a vassal failed to honor his feudal obligations.

Feudal Warfare

The final authority in the early Middle Ages was force, and the general atmosphere of the era was one of potential violence. Aggressive vassals frequently made war upon their lords. But warfare was also considered the normal occupation of the nobility, for success offered glory and rich rewards. If successful, warfare might increase a noble's territory; and, if they produced nothing else, wars and raids kept nobles active. To die in battle was an appropriate end for a warrior, much preferred to death in restful circumstances.

Medieval society essentially consisted of three classes: nobles, peasants, and the clergy. Each of these groups had its tasks to perform. The nobles were primarily fighters, belonging to an honored level of society distinct from peasant workers—freemen or serfs. In an age of violence, society obviously accorded prominence to the man with the sword rather than to one with a hoe. The church drew on both the noble and peasant classes for the clergy. Although most higher churchmen were sons of nobles and held land as vassals under the feudal system, the clergy formed a class that was considered separate from the nobility and the peasantry.

The Church and Feudalism

A natural development linked to the decentralization of political power in the early Middle Ages was the involvement of the church in feudalism. The unsettled conditions caused by the Viking and Magyar invasions forced church officials to enter into close relations with the only power able to offer them protection—the feudal nobles in France and Germany. Bishops and abbots often became vassals, receiving fiefs for which they were obligated to provide the usual feudal services. The papacy was also affected; during much of the tenth and early eleventh centuries, the papacy became a political prize sought by Roman nobles.

In spite of its inevitable involvement in politics, the church also sought to influence for the better the behavior of the feudal warrior nobility. In addition to attempting to add Christian virtues to the code of knightly conduct (chivalry), the church sought to impose limitations on feudal warfare. In the eleventh century bishops urged the knights to observe the "Peace of God" and the "Truce of God." The Peace of God banned from the sacraments all those who pillaged sacred places or harmed noncombatants. The Truce of God established "closed seasons" on fighting: from sunset on Wednesday to sunrise on Monday and certain longer periods, such as Lent. These attempts to impose peace, however, were generally unsuccessful.

Chivalry

One of the most interesting legacies of the Middle Ages is its concept of chivalry, a code of conduct that was to govern the behavior of all knights. Early chivalric conduct, emerging during the eleventh century, stressed the warrior virtues that were essential in medieval society: prowess in combat, courage, and loyalty to one's lord and fellow warriors. By the twelfth and thirteenth centuries, many of the rigorous aspects of earlier feudal life had given way to a more peaceful and relaxed lifestyle made possible in a more settled and secure Europe. In a sense, when feudal knights began to occupy themselves with chivalric deeds and

---

homage—A pledge by a vassal to be the lord's "man" (*homo* in Latin means "man"), vowing loyalty and service to his superior. Homage created an unconditional bond between a vassal and his lord.

suzerain—A ruler, or even a state, that exercises political control over a dependent individual or state; a feudal overlord.

gentlemanly pursuits of court life, feudalism itself became a dying institution.

At the height of its development, chivalry was a combination of three elements: warfare, religion, and reverence toward women. It required the knight to fight faithfully for his lord, champion the church, aid the humble, and honor women. Unfortunately, practice often differed from theory. The average knight was more superstitious than religious, and he continued to fight, plunder, and abuse women, especially those of the lower class.

From boyhood, men of the nobility underwent a rigid training for knighthood. At the age of seven, a boy was usually sent to the household of a relative, a friend, or the father's lord. There he became a page, learning the rudiments of manners, hawking, and hunting and undergoing training in the fundamentals of religion. At about 15 or 16, he became a squire and prepared himself seriously for the art of war. He learned to ride a war house with dexterity and to handle a sword, shield, and lance correctly. The squire also waited on his lord and lady at the table and learned music, poetry, and games.

If not already knighted on the battlefield for valor, the squire was usually considered eligible for knighthood at the age of 21. By the twelfth century, the church claimed a role in the ceremony, investing it with impressive symbolism. The future knight took a bath to symbolize purity and washed his weapons before the altar in an all-night vigil, confessing his sins and making a resolution to be a worthy knight. During the solemn Mass that followed, his sword was blessed on the altar by a priest. The climax of the ceremony came when the candidate, kneeling before his lord, received a light blow on the neck or shoulder (the *accolade*). The ceremony was designed to impress upon the knight that he must be virtuous and valiant, loyal to his overlord and his God.

The Lives of the Nobles

Life for the nobles centered around the castle. The earliest of these structures, mere wooden blockhouses, were built in the ninth century. Not until the twelfth and thirteenth centuries were massive castles constructed entirely of stone.

The donjon, or central tower, was the focal point of the castle; it was surrounded by an open space that contained storerooms, workshops, and a chapel. The outside walls of the castle were surrounded by turrets from which arrows, boiling oil, and various missiles might be showered upon attackers. Beyond the wall was the moat, a steep-sided ditch filled with water to deter the enemy. The only entrance to the castle lay across the drawbridge. The portcullis, a heavy iron grating that could be lowered rapidly to protect the gate, was a further barrier against intrusion.

Bodiam Castle, England

Life in the castle was anything but comfortable or ideal. The lord at first dwelt in the donjon, but by the thirteenth century, most had built more spacious quarters. Because the castle was designed for defense, it possessed no large windows, and the rooms were dark and gloomy. The stone walls were bare except for occasional tapestries hung to cut down on drafts and dampness, and a huge fireplace provided the only warmth.

The average noble derived his pleasures primarily from outdoor sports, among which warfare might be included. In peacetime the joust and tournament substituted for actual battle. The joust was a conflict between two armed knights, each equipped with a blunted lance with which one attempted to unseat the other. The tournament was a general melee in which groups of knights attacked each other. Often fierce fighting ensued, with frequent casualties.

The nobles were fond of hunting, and the constant demand for fresh meat afforded a legitimate excuse for galloping over the countryside. Most hunting was done in the nearby forests, but at times an unlucky peasant's crops might be ruined during hunts.

A similar outdoor pastime, which lords, ladies, and even high church dignitaries delighted in, was falconry: hunting with predatory birds. The hawks were reared with great care, and large groups of lords and ladies spent many afternoons eagerly wagering with one another as to whose falcon would bring down the first victim. Nobles often attended Mass with hooded falcons on their wrists.

Indoor amusements included the universally popular diversions of backgammon, dice, and chess. Nights were sometimes enlivened by the entertainment of jesters. At other times, a wandering minstrel entertained his noble hosts in exchange for a bed and a place at the table.

Noble women generally shared the lifestyles of their husbands. Even the nobility had to make the most of life in a crude and often brutal age devoid of many refinements. Like her husband, a medieval woman was expected to devote herself to days of hard work with little time for leisure. Many a noble woman was charged with the administration of the manor and the regulation of its peasants while the lord was otherwise occupied. She may also have presided over the court of the lord's vassals on occasion and generally been charged with the control of the finances for the manor.

The Early Medieval Economy: Manorialism

The economy of the early Middle Ages reflected the localism and self-sufficiency that resulted from the

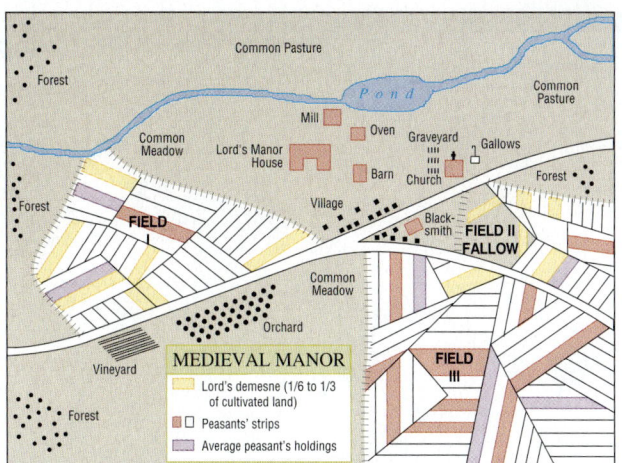

The manor, the self-contained economic unit of early medieval life, operated on a system of reciprocal rights and obligations based on custom. In return for protection, strips of arable land, and the right to use the nonarable common land, the peasant paid dues and worked on the lord's demesne. Under the three-field system, one-third of the land lay fallow so that intensive cultivation did not exhaust the soil.

lack of an effective central government in Europe. The economic and social system based on the manors, the estates held by the nobles, was referred to as *manorialism*.

The manor usually varied in size from one locality to another; a small one might contain only about a dozen households. Since the allotment of land to each family averaged about 30 acres, the smallest manors probably had about 350 acres of land suitable for farming, not counting meadows, woods, wasteland, and the lord's **demesne**—the land reserved for the lord's use alone. A large manor might contain 50 families in a total area of 5000 acres.

The center of the manor was the village, in which the thatched cottages of the peasants were grouped together along one street. Around each cottage was a space large enough for a vegetable patch, chicken yard, haystack, and stable. An important feature of the landscape was the village church, together with the priest's house and the burial ground. The lord's dwelling might be a fortified house or a more modest dwelling.

Distribution of the Land

Every manor contained arable and nonarable land. Part of the arable land was reserved for the lord and was cultivated for him by his serfs; the remainder was held by the villagers. The nonarable land, consisting of meadow, wood, and wasteland, was used in common by the villagers and the lord.

desmesne—Part of the land that is owned by the lord. The demesne is the land upon which the lord built his manor house.

From one-sixth to one-third of the arable land was given over to the lord's demesne. The arable land not held in demesne was allotted among the villagers under the open-field system, in which the fields were subdivided into strips. The strips, each containing about an acre, were separated by narrow paths of uncultivated land. The serf's holding was not all in one plot, for all soil throughout the manor was not equally fertile, and an attempt was made to give each of the villagers land of the same quality. Each tenant was really a shareholder in the village community, not only in the open fields but also in the meadow, pasture, wood, and wastelands.

Wooded land was valuable as an area to graze pigs, the most common animal on the manor. Tenants could also gather dead wood in the forest, but cutting down green wood was prohibited unless authorized by the lord.

Medieval Farming Methods

It is difficult to generalize about agricultural methods, because differences in locality, fertility of soil, crop production, and other factors resulted in a variety of farming approaches. Farming as practiced in northwestern Europe was characterized by some common factors. The implements the peasants used were extremely crude; the plow was a cumbersome instrument with heavy wheels, often requiring as many as eight oxen to pull it. (By the twelfth century the use of plow horses had become common.) Other tools included crude harrows, sickles, beetles for breaking up clods, and flails for threshing.

Inadequate methods of farming soon exhausted the soil. The average yield per acre was only 6 to 8 bushels of wheat, one-fourth the modern yield. In classical times farmers had learned that soil planted continually with one crop rapidly deteriorated. As a counteraction, they employed a two-field system: half of the arable land was planted while the other half lay fallow to recover its fertility. Medieval farmers learned that wheat or rye could be planted in the autumn as well as in the spring. As a result, by the ninth century, they were dividing the land into three fields, with one planted in the fall, another in the spring, and the third left lying fallow. This system not only kept more land in production but also required less plowing in any given year.

Both peasant men and women usually had to endure backbreaking labor. While the men usually attended to the daily manual labor of farming, peasant women cooked, cleaned, made clothing, maintained the animals, milked cows, made butter and cheese, brewed ale and beer, and nurtured the gardens. Women assisted the men during planting and

Both peasant men and women toiled in the fields. Here women reap with sickles, while behind them a man binds the sheaves.

harvesting seasons and with any seasonal or special projects endorsed by the lord. The sexes were treated fairly equally on the lower social levels in the Middle Ages—there was not much difference in the demanding lifestyle all had to endure.

Administration of the Manor

Although the lord might live on one of his manors, each manor was usually administered by such officials as the steward, the bailiff, and the reeve. The steward was the general overseer who supervised the business of all his lord's manors and presided over the manorial court. It was the bailiff's duty to supervise the cultivation of the lord's demesne; collect rents, dues, and fines; and inspect the work done by the free peasants (freemen) and the nonfree peasants (serfs). The reeve was the "foreman" of the villagers, chosen by them and representing their interests.

Freemen often lived on the manor, although they constituted only a small portion of its population. Freemen were not subject to the same demands as the serfs. The freeman did not have to work in the lord's fields himself but could send substitutes. Serfs, however, were bound to the manor and could not leave without the lord's consent. Serfdom was a hereditary status; the children of serfs were attached to the soil, just as their parents were.

The lord of the manor was bound by custom to respect certain rights of his serfs. As long as they paid their dues and services, serfs could not be evicted from their hereditary holdings. Although a serf could not appear in court against his lord or a freeman, he could appeal to the manor court against any of his fellows. To the serfs, the manor was the center of their very existence, but to the lord the manor was essentially a source of income and subsistence.

Life of the Peasants

On the manors of the Middle Ages, the margin between starvation and survival was narrow, and the life of the peasant was not easy. Famines were frequent; warfare was a constant threat; and grasshoppers, locusts, caterpillars, and rats repeatedly destroyed the crops. Men, women, and children alike had to toil long hours in the fields.

Home life offered few comforts. The typical peasant dwelling was a cottage with mud walls, clay floor, and thatched roof. The fire burned on a flat hearthstone in the middle of the floor; unless the peasant was rich enough to afford a chimney, the smoke escaped through a hole in the roof. The window openings had no glass and were stuffed with straw in the winter. Furnishings were meager, usually consisting of a table, a kneading trough for dough, a cupboard, and a bed, often either a heap of straw or a box filled with straw, which served the entire family. Pigs and chickens wandered about the cottage continually; the stable was often under the same roof, next to the family quarters.

The peasants, despite their hard, monotonous life, enjoyed a few pleasures. Wrestling was popular, as were cockfighting, a crude type of football, and fighting with quarterstaves, during which contestants stood an excellent chance of getting their heads bashed in. Dancing, singing, and drinking were popular pastimes, especially on the numerous holy days and festivals promoted by the church.

THE REVIVAL OF TRADE AND TOWNS

- *How did the revival of trade and towns impact the feudal and manorial systems?*

Even though manorialism attempted to secure economic self-sufficiency, an increase in trade and commercial activity in Europe was obvious after the tenth century. The opening of the Mediterranean to European trade was instrumental in increasing trade and commerce. In the eleventh century Normans and Italians broke the Muslim hold on commerce in the eastern Mediterranean, and the First Crusade (see p. 275) revived trade with the Near East. Early in the fourteenth century an all-sea route connected the Mediterranean with northern Europe via the Strait of Gibraltar. The old overland route from northern Italy through the Alpine passes to central Europe was also reopened.

Along the main European trade routes, lords set up fairs, where merchants and goods from Italy and northern Europe met. During the twelfth and thirteenth centuries the fairs of Champagne in France functioned as the major clearinghouse for this international trade.

Factors in the Revival of Towns

The resurgence of trade in Europe was a prime cause of the revival of towns; the towns arose because of trade, but they also stimulated trade by providing greater markets and by producing goods for the merchants to sell. Rivers were important in the development of medieval towns; they were natural highways on which articles of commerce could be easily transported.

Another factor contributing to the rise of towns was population growth. In Britain, for example, the population more than tripled between 1066 and 1350. The reasons for this rapid increase in population are varied. The ending of bloody foreign invasions and, in some areas, the stabilization of feudal society were contributing factors. More significant was an increase in food production brought about by the cultivation of wastelands, clearing of forests, and draining of marshes. Medieval towns were not large by modern standards. Before 1200 a European town of 20,000 was considered very large, in contrast to such cities as Baghdad, Cairo, and Constantinople—all of which were well over 50,000 in population.

Merchant and Craft Guilds

In each town the merchants and artisans organized themselves into **guilds**. There were two kinds of guilds: merchant and craft. The merchant guild, whose members were the more prosperous and influential of the town's commercial leaders, existed to ensure a monopoly of trade for its members within a given locality. All foreign merchants were supervised closely and made to pay tolls. Disputes among merchants were settled at the guild court according to its

---

guilds—An organization of people who practice a similar occupation and come together to protect their own professional standards and social interests.

A guild master judges the work of two craftsmen, a mason and a carpenter.

own legal code. The guilds also tried to ensure that the customers were not cheated: they checked weights and measures and insisted on a standard quality for goods. To allow only a legitimate profit, the guild fixed a "just price," which was fair to both producer and customer.

With the increase of commerce in the towns, artisans and craftspeople in each of the medieval trades—weaving, cobbling, tanning, and so on—began to organize as early as the eleventh century. The result was the craft guild, which differed from the merchant guild in that membership was limited to artisans in one particular craft.

The craft guild also differed from the merchant guild in its recognition of three distinct classes of workers: apprentices, journeymen, and master craftsmen. The apprentice was a youth who lived at the master's house and was taught the trade thoroughly. Although the apprentice received no wages, all his physical needs were supplied. Apprenticeship commonly lasted seven years. When the apprentice's schooling was finished, the youth became a journeyman. He was then eligible to receive wages and to be hired by a master. About age 23, the journeyman sought admission into the guild as a master. To be accepted he had to prove his ability. Some crafts demanded the production of a "master piece," for example, a pair of shoes that the master shoemakers would find acceptable in every way.

Very few women, usually widows of guild members, were allowed admittance into a craft guild. In Paris in 1300, for instance, there were approximately 200 craft guilds, with nearly 80 including members of both sexes. There were, however, about a dozen guilds restricted to female trades, such as the making of garments, silk, and lace.

In spite of restrictions placed on women's full participation in the guild structure, women played a vital role in the functioning of every craft guild. The home remained the center of production in every medieval town, and the wife and daughters of the master craftsman assisted him in every facet of his profession. Not only did they oversee domestic household duties, they also were relied upon to assist in the production of whatever goods the guildsman produced. They would work with the apprentices and the journeymen; if girls were placed as apprentices, they were usually supervised directly by the wife of the guildsman. The wife of the master craftsman was essential to the operation of business; in most cases, she sold merchandise, kept the financial records, and fed and paid the employees. Because of their experience and skills, such women often took over the shop after their husband's death.

The guild's functions stretched beyond business and politics into charitable and social activities. A guild member who fell into poverty received aid from the guild. The guild also provided financial assistance for the burial expense of its members and looked after their dependents. Members attended social meetings in the guildhall and periodically held processions in honor of their patron saints.

The guilds played an important role in local government. Both artisans and merchants were subject to the feudal lord or bishop in whose domain the city stood. Gradually, the citizens of the towns came to resent their overlord's collecting tolls and dues as though they were serfs. The townspeople demanded the privileges of governing themselves—of making their own laws, administering their own justice, levying their own taxes, and issuing their own coinage. The overlord resisted these demands for self-government, but the towns were able to win their independence in various ways.

THE CHURCH IN THE HIGH MIDDLE AGES: 1000–1348

■ *How did the church and its leaders hold such power and influence over European society?*

During the High Middle Ages the church became more extensively involved in the structure of society and, of necessity, more concerned with temporal affairs. Always a spiritual force in Europe, the church grew in political and economic importance through the assertive and able leadership of the papacy and the bureaucracy that served the popes in Rome. By the middle of the fourteenth century, the church had emerged as a dominant political as well as spiritual force in European life.

Monastic Reform

A religious revival, often called the "medieval reformation," began in the tenth century and grew to exercise strong influence in the twelfth and thirteenth centuries. The first manifestation of the revival was the reformed Benedictine order of monks at Cluny (KLOO-nee), in present-day France, founded in 910. The ultimate goal of these Cluniac reformers was to free the church from secular control and subject it to papal authority.

CASE STUDY
Monks and Warriors

The most aggressive advocate of church reform in the High Middle Ages was Pope Gregory VII (1073–1085), who claimed unprecedented power for the papacy. In 1075 Gregory VII formally prohibited lay investiture (bestowal of the symbols of the churchman's office by a secular official such as a king) and

	Monastic Reform and the Investiture Controversy
910	Benedictine monastery at Cluny founded
1059	College of Cardinals founded
1073–1085	Pontificate of Gregory VII; struggle over lay investiture
1077	Emperor Henry IV begs forgiveness at Canossa
1091–1153	St. Bernard of Clairvaux, founder of the Cisterian religious order

threatened to excommunicate (expel from the Roman Catholic Church) any layman who performed it. The climax to the struggle occurred in Gregory's clash with the German emperor Henry IV (see p. 282).

Late in the eleventh century a second wave of monastic reform produced several new orders of monks, among which were the Cistercians. The Cistercian movement received its greatest inspiration from the efforts of St. Bernard of Clairvaux (klahr-VOH; 1091–1153). This order's abbeys were intentionally located in solitary places, and their strict discipline emphasized fasts and vigils, manual labor, and a vegetarian diet. Their churches contained neither stained glass nor statues, and Bernard denounced the beautification of churches in general as unnecessary distraction from spiritual dedication.

The Papacy's Zenith: Innocent III

Under Innocent III (1198–1216) a new type of administrator-pope emerged, and papal power reached an unprecedented height. Unlike Gregory VII and other earlier reform popes, who were monks, Innocent and other great popes of the late twelfth and thirteenth centuries were lawyers trained in the newly revived and enlarged church, or canon, law.

The unity and power of the church rested not only on a systematized, uniform religious creed but also on the most highly organized and efficient administrative system in western Europe. The church was far ahead of secular states in developing a system of courts and a body of law. Canon law was based on the Scriptures, the writings of the church fathers, and the decrees of church councils and popes. But the papacy's chief weapons to support its authority were spiritual penalties. The most powerful of these was excommunication. A person who was excommunicated was deprived of the sacraments of the church and in effect condemned to hell should a person die while excommunicated.

Interdict was also a powerful instrument of punishment and control. While excommunication was directed against individuals, interdiction suspended all public worship and withheld most sacraments in the realm of a disobedient subject. Pope Innocent III successfully applied or threatened the interdict 85 times against disobedient kings and princes.

Heresy

Heresy, the belief in doctrines officially condemned by the church, once again became a great concern in the High Middle Ages. Numerous spiritual ideas found new audiences particularly in the newly revived towns, where changing social and spiritual needs went largely ignored by churchmen more traditional in outlook.

For ten years Innocent III tried to combat the growth and popularity of new heretical groups. Unsuccessful, he instigated a crusade against the prosperous and cultured French region of Toulouse, where

Giotto, Pope Innocent III (1198–1216) Approves the Franciscan Rule. *In this predella (part of a series of paintings on the base of an altar) by the Florentine painter Giotto (1266–1337), Innocent III, accompanied by high-ranking churchmen, is shown approving the Franciscan order of monks by giving the approving document to St. Francis (center) and his humble followers. Legend says that the pope had a dream in which he was instructed by God to give approval to the Franciscans.*

the heretics were attacked in 1208 with the approval of the pope. Soon, the original religious motive was lost in a selfish rush to seize the wealth of the accused.

In 1233 a special papal court, the Inquisition, was established to cope with the rising tide of heresy and to bring about religious conformity. Those accused were tried in secret without the aid of legal counsel. Those who confessed and renounced heresy were "reconciled" with the church on performance of penance. Those who did not voluntarily confess could be tortured. If torture failed, the prisoners could be declared heretics and turned over to the secular authorities, usually to be burned at the stake.

Franciscans and Dominicans

As a more positive response to the spread of heresy and the conditions that caused it, Innocent III approved the founding of the Franciscan and Dominican orders of *friars* ("brothers"). Instead of living in remote monasteries, the friars of these orders moved among the people—especially in the quickly growing towns—ministering to their needs, preaching the Gospel, and teaching in the schools.

The Franciscans were founded by St. Francis of Assisi (c. 1182–1226), who rejected riches and emphasized a spiritual message of poverty and Christian simplicity. Love of one's fellow human beings and all God's creatures, even "brother worm," was basic in the Rule of St. Francis.

The second order of friars was founded by St. Dominic (1170–1221), a well-educated Spaniard who had fought the heretics in southern France. There, he decided that to combat the strength and zeal of its opponents, the church should have champions who could preach the Gospel with the dedication of the apostles. The friar-preachers of Dominic's order dedicated themselves to preaching as a means of maintaining the doctrines of the church and of converting heretics.

The enthusiasm and sincerity of the friars in their early years made a profound impact on an age that had grown increasingly critical of the worldliness of the church. But after they took charge of the Inquisition, became professors in the universities, and served in the papal bureaucracy in a variety of capacities, the original simplicity of the spiritual message became lost. Yet their message and zeal had done much to provide the church with moral and intellectual leadership at a time when such leadership was badly needed.

Education and the Origins of Universities

Before the twelfth century, almost all education was under the control and direction of the church. When schools run by monasteries began limiting their admissions to men preparing for church careers, students interested in educations for careers outside the church began to pressure for admittance to schools administered by cathedrals. Although the cathedral schools were still run by churchmen and taught a curriculum centered on religion, these schools steadily expanded their subject offerings to attract students who were pursuing secular careers. Cathedral schools were also more accepting of the new knowledge made available to western Europe by Byzantine and Moslem scholars. Translations of classical works of philosophy (most importantly the works of Aristotle on logic), medicine, and Roman law, accompanied by analyses and commentaries by Islamic scholars, were reintroduced to western Europe. Much of this revived interest can be attributed to an increasing interest in Islamic culture, brought about partially through contacts established during the crusades, and through the revival of international trade. The result was an intellectual revival that invigorated the interest of scholars and students in the cathedral schools.

The development of professional studies in law, medicine, and theology led to the development of universities, which soon eclipsed or expanded the cathedral schools as centers of learning. The word *university* meant a group of persons pursuing a common purpose—a guild of learners, both teachers and students, similar to a craft guild with their masters and apprentices. In the thirteenth century universities had no campuses and little or no money, and the masters taught in rented rooms or religious buildings. If the university was dissatisfied with its treatment by townspeople or the administration, it could move elsewhere. The earliest universities—at Bologna, Paris, and Oxford—were not officially founded, but in time popes or kings granted them and other universities charters of self-government.

Scholasticism

Most medieval scholars did not think of truth as something to be discovered by themselves: They saw it as already existing in the authoritative Christian and a select few non-Christian texts of antiquity. By employing reason (through the use of logic or **dialectic**), scholars of the twelfth and thirteenth centuries attempted to understand and express truth through this process of explanation. Since this task was carried out almost exclusively in the schools, these scholars are known as Scholastics, and the intellectual method they designed is called *Scholasticism*.

Scholasticism reached its highest development in the works of Thomas Aquinas (ah-KWAI-nahs;

---

dialectic—Logical discussion or logical argumentation.

c. 1225–1274). In his *Summa Theologica* ("summation of theology") this brilliant Dominican philosopher and theologian attempted to reconcile the works of Aristotle with church **dogma**—in other words, the truths obvious through natural reason with the truths held through faith. There can be no real contradiction between the two, he argued, since all truth comes ultimately from God. In case of an unresolved contradiction, however, faith won out because of the possibility of human error in reasoning.

Women and Learning

In the early Middle Ages, and especially after the eighth century, the convents of Europe served as centers of learned activity for a very select group of aristocratic and middle-class women who pursued an intellectual life as well as one devoted to faith. But outside the convents, a life devoted to scholarship was almost impossible for a medieval woman; the church taught that a woman should be either a housewife or a virgin in service to her God. Rarely was it possible for a woman to write, compose, or create works of scholarship or literature in such a society.

But intellectual achievement by some exceptional medieval women was possible. One such remarkable example was Hildegard of Bingen (1098–1179), the leader of a community of Benedictine nuns in Germany. Hildegard wrote a mystical work describing her visions, which she began to receive at the age of 42. She was also a skilled composer and the author of a morality play and several scientific works, which cataloged nearly 500 plants, animals, and stones, assessing their medicinal values.

THE CRUSADES

- What was the influence of the Crusades on European and world history?

An Arab-Syrian Discusses the Franks

The Crusades, a series of campaigns that began toward the end of the eleventh century, were a remarkable expression of European self-confidence and expansion in the High Middle Ages. The church was instrumental in beginning these efforts to recapture the Holy Land from Muslim control. But by the conclusion of the crusading era, the church, and the papacy in particular, had suffered a serious loss of prestige, largely because of its actions related to the crusading movement.

---

dogma—A set of beliefs that are accepted as true by a church. A doctrine put forward with authority. From a Greek word meaning "to seem (good)."

For hundreds of years peaceful pilgrims had been traveling from Europe to worship at the sites held to be significant to events described in the New Testament. But during the eleventh century, Christian pilgrims to the Holy Land became especially concerned when the Seljuk Turks, recent and fervent converts to Islam, took over Jerusalem from the more lenient Abbasid Muslims.

In 1095 Pope Urban II proclaimed the First Crusade to establish Christian control of the Holy Land. Preaching at the Council of Clermont in that year, he called on Christians to take up the cross and strive for a cause that promised not merely spiritual rewards but material gain as well. Following Urban's appeal, there was a spontaneous outpouring of religious enthusiasm. The word *crusade* itself is derived from "taking the cross," after the example of Christ.

The Crusading Expeditions

From the end of the eleventh through the thirteenth century, seven major crusades, as well as numerous small expeditions, warred against the Muslims, whom the crusaders called *Saracens*. The First Crusade, composed of feudal nobles from France, parts of Germany, and Norman Italy, marched overland through eastern Europe to Constantinople. Expecting the help of skilled European mercenaries against the Seljuk Turks, the Byzantine emperor Alexius Comnenus was shocked when confronted by a disorderly mob of crusaders and quickly ushered them out of Constantinople to fight the Turks. This First Crusade was the most successful of the seven;  Crusaders Besieging a Medieval Castle

with not more than 5000 knights and infantry, it overcame the resistance of the Turks, who were at the time no longer united. It captured Jerusalem and a narrow strip of land stretching from there to Antioch, which became known as the Latin Kingdom of Jerusalem, and over which crusaders and Islamic armies continued to battle until the region was finally retaken by the Muslims in 1291.

The fall of Jerusalem to the Muslims, reinvigorated under the leadership of Salah-al-Din (SAH-lah-ahl-DEEN) or Saladin, the sultan of Egypt and Syria, inspired the Third Crusade in 1189. Its leaders were three of the most famous medieval kings—Frederick Barbarossa of Germany, Richard the Lion-Hearted of England, and Philip Augustus of France. Frederick drowned in Asia Minor, and, after many quarrels with Richard, Philip returned home. Saladin and Richard remained to fight but finally agreed to a three-year truce and free access to Jerusalem for Christian pilgrims.

The Fourth Crusade (1202–1204) was a disaster from both a religious and economic perspective. No kings answered the call of Pope Innocent III for the crusade, and the knights who did participate were unable to pay the Venetians  The Crusades

the agreed-on transport charges. The Venetians persuaded the crusaders to pay off their debts by capturing the Christian town of Zara on the Adriatic coast, which had long proved a successful rival to Venetian trading interests. Then, in order to eliminate Byzantine commercial competition, the Venetians pressured the crusaders to attack Constantinople itself. After conquering and sacking the great city, the crusaders set up the Latin Empire of Constantinople and forgot about their intentions of recovering the Holy Land.

The thirteenth century produced other crusading failures. The boys and girls participating in the Children's Crusade of 1212 fully expected the waters of the Mediterranean to part and make a path from southern France to the Holy Land, which they would take without fighting; instead, thousands of them were sold into slavery by the merchants of Marseilles. The Seventh Crusade was the last major attempt to regain Jerusalem; the crusading movement ended in 1291 when Acre, the last stronghold of the Christians in the Holy Land, fell to the Muslims.

The Crusader States

Four crusader states, with the kingdom of Jerusalem dominant, were established along the eastern Mediterranean coast as a result of the crusading movement. By the time Jerusalem fell to Saladin in 1187, however, only isolated pockets of Christians remained, surrounded by Muslims. The crusader states were able to cling to survival only through frequent delivery of supplies and manpower from Europe.

The crusader states were defended primarily by three semimonastic military orders: the Templars, or Knights of the Temple, so called because their first headquarters was on the site of the old Temple of Jerusalem; the Hospitalers, or Knights of St. John of Jerusalem, who were founded originally to care for the sick and wounded; and the Teutonic Knights, exclusively a German order. Combining monasticism and militarism, these orders served to protect all pilgrims and to wage perpetual war against the Muslims.

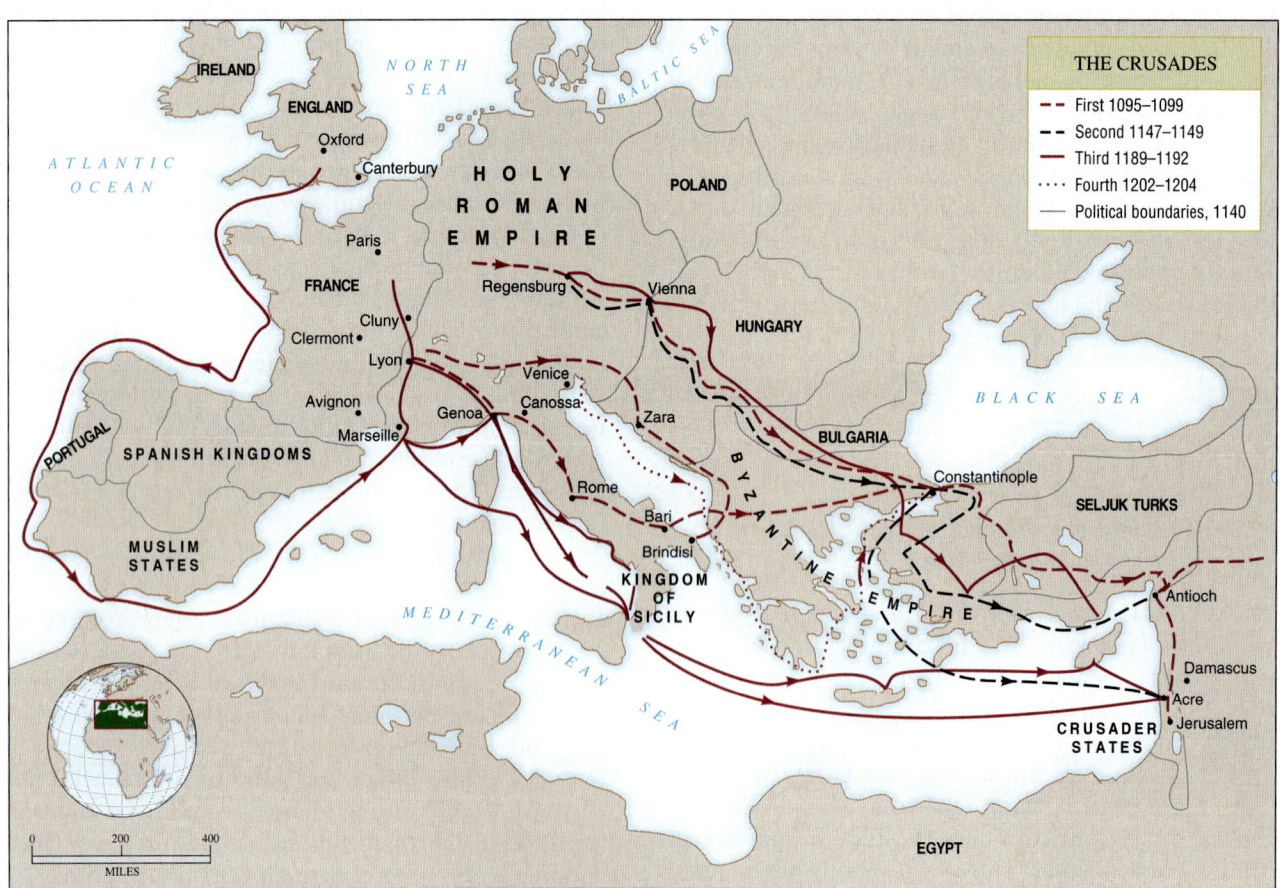

From the eleventh to the thirteenth century, seven major crusades were launched from western Europe for the purpose of taking possession of the Holy Land—portions of the eastern Mediterranean significant to Christians because of their association with the life of Jesus. Although the Crusades eventually failed to annex large amounts of territory for western states, they brought about a broadening perspective and appreciation for Byzantine and Muslim culture on the part of many western Europeans.

Document: Muslim and Christian: Two Contemporary Perspectives

This first selection describes the bloody fall of Jerusalem to the Christians during the First Crusade in 1099, as witnessed by the author, a Frankish knight. He writes with the certainty of religious justification for his cause, and cultural superiority to the Muslim enemy.

In comparison to the Frankish evaluations of their Islamic rivals, the second account, from the Muslim perspective, appears in the writings of a Muslim physician who encountered the crusaders and obviously found their culture not as impressive as his own.

During this siege, we suffered so badly from thirst that we sewed up the skins of oxen and buffaloes, and we used to carry water in them for the distance of nearly six miles. We drank the water from these vessels, although it stank, and what with foul water and barley bread we suffered great distress and affliction every day, for the Saracens used to lie in wait for our men by every spring and pool, where they killed them and cut them to pieces; moreover they used to carry off the beasts into their caves and secret places in the rocks.

At last, when the pagans were defeated, our men took many prisoners, both men and women, in the Temple. They killed whom they chose, and whom they chose they saved alive. After this our men rushed round the whole city, seizing the gold and silver, horses and mules, and houses full of all sorts of goods, and they all came rejoicing and weeping from excess of gladness to worship at the Sepulchre of our Savior Jesus, and there they fulfilled their vows to him. Next morning they went cautiously up on to the Temple roof and attacked the Saracens, both men and women, cutting off their heads with drawn swords. No-one has ever seen or heard of such a slaughter of pagans, for they were burned on pyres like pyramids, and no-one save God alone knows how many there were.

From Rosalind Hill, ed., *Gesta Francorum* (London: Nelson, 1962). Reprinted by permission of Oxford University Press, Oxford.

Glory be to Allah, the creator and author of all things! Anyone who is acquainted with what concerns the Franks can only glorify and sanctify Allah the All-Powerful; for he has seen in them animals who are superior in courage and in zeal for fighting but in nothing else, just as beasts are superior in strength and aggressiveness.

I will report some Frankish characteristics and my . . . surprise as to their intelligence. . . .

Among the curiosities of medicine among the Franks, I will tell how the governor of Al-Mounaitira wrote to my uncle to ask him to send him a doctor who would look after some urgent cases. My uncle chose a Christian doctor named Thabit (?). . . . Thabit replied: "They brought before me a knight with an abscess which had formed in his leg and a woman who was wasting away with a consumptive fever. I applied a little plaster to the knight; his abscess opened and took a turn for the better; the woman I forbade certain food and improved her condition." It was at this point that a Frankish doctor came up and said: "This man is incapable of curing them." Then, turning to the knight, he asked, "Which do you prefer, to live with one leg or die with two?" "I would rather live with one leg," the knight answered. "Bring a stalwart knight," said the Frankish doctor, "and a sharp hatchet." Knight and hatchet soon appeared. I was present at the scene. The doctor stretched the patient's leg on a block of wood and then said to the knight, "Strike off his leg with the hatchet; take it off at one blow." Under my eyes the knight aimed a violent blow at it without cutting through the leg. He aimed another blow at the unfortunate man, as a result of which his marrow came from his leg and the knight died instantly. As for the woman, the doctor examined her and said, "She is a woman in whose head there is a devil who has taken possession of her. Shave off her hair!" His prescription was carried out, and like her fellows, she began once again to eat garlic and mustard. Her consumption became worse. The doctor then said, "It is because the devil has entered her head." Taking a razor, the doctor cut open her head in the shape of a cross and scraped away the skin in the centre so deeply that her very bones were showing. He then rubbed the head with salt. In her turn, the woman died instantly. After having asked them whether my services were still required and obtained an answer in the negative, I came back, having learnt to know what I had formerly been ignorant of about their medicine.

—*Usamah Ibn-Munqidh*

From G. R. Potter, trans., *The Autobiography of Ousama (1095–1188)* (London: George Routledge and Sons, 1929), pp. 172–175, 181–182, in Perry M. Rogers, *Aspects of Western Civilization*, Vol. I, 4th ed. (Prentice Hall, 2000), pp. 311–312.

Questions to Consider

1. What seem to be the most significant obstacles to cultural understanding and tolerance in these two accounts of contact between Christian and Muslim cultures?
2. How might we, as modern analysts of this medieval clash of cultures, misinterpret the sentiments expressed in these two documents? What insights might be gained from a comparison of these two viewpoints?

Significance of the Crusades

Even though the Crusades failed to achieve their permanent objective, they were much more than mere military adventures. Much of the crusading fervor spilled over into the Christian attacks against the Muslims in Spain and the Slavs in eastern Europe. The Crusades crucially weakened the Byzantine Empire and accelerated its fall. Although the early Crusades strengthened the moral leadership of the papacy in Europe, the misadventures of the later Crusades, together with the church's preaching of Crusades against Christian heretics and political opponents, weakened both the crusading ideal and respect for the papacy.

But contact with the East through the crusading movement widened the scope of many Europeans, ended their isolation, and exposed them to a civilization with much within it to be admired. The Crusades did influence the reopening of the eastern Mediterranean to Western commerce, a factor that in itself had an effect on the revival of cities and the emergence of a money economy in the West.

THE DEVELOPMENT OF EUROPEAN STATES: 1000–1348

■ *How successful were European monarchs in establishing authority over their territories?*

The first three centuries of the Later Middle Ages in Europe are often described as the High Middle Ages, since many experts see in this period the full development of the earlier culture of post-Roman Europe. In this era, European monarchies struggled to emerge from the decentralized feudal organization of an earlier time. The church rose to great heights of power and authority. The revival of trade and the rebirth of towns altered the economy of Europe and offered an alternative to manorialism. And this period gave birth to developments in art, architecture, and literature that stand as some of the most significant achievements in European civilization.

The High Middle Ages witnessed the efforts of kings to assert themselves once again as forceful rulers of their lands. As we have seen, feudalism was a system founded on the decentralization of authority; the king was often no more than a figurehead in the feudal order. Now, the monarchs of most European states gradually increased their powers at the expense of their feudal nobility. Through such efforts, several of which took centuries to bear results, national monarchies began to take form on the European continent.

The Capetians and the Beginnings of France

In France, by the beginning of the tenth century, more than 30 great feudal princes were vassals of the king, but they gave him little or no support. When the last Carolingian monarch died in 987, the nobles elected one of their number, Hugh Capet (kah-PAY), count of Paris, as successor. The territory that Hugh Capet (987–996) actually controlled was a small feudal county, the Île-de-France (EEL-duh-FRAHNS), extending from Paris to Orléans. These royal lands were surrounded by many large duchies and counties, such as Flanders, Normandy, Anjou, and Champagne, which were fiercely independent.

The major accomplishment of the first four Capetian (kah-PEE-shi-ahn) kings was their success at keeping the French crown within their own family and at slowly expanding their influence, largely through marriage alliances and the efficiency of the royal courts. With the support of the church, the Capetians cleverly arranged for the election and coronation of their heirs. For 300 years the House of Capet never lacked a male heir.

Philip II Augustus

The first great expansion of the royal domain was the work of Philip II Augustus (1180–1223). Philip's great ambition was to seize from the English kings the vast territory they held in France. Philip took Normandy, Maine, Anjou, and Touraine from the English, and by doing so, he tripled the size of the monarchy's land holdings.

After the brief reign of Philip II's son Louis VIII, France came under the rule of Louis IX (1226–1270), better known as St. Louis. Louis's ideal was to rule justly, and in so doing, he became one of the most beloved kings of France. The king believed himself responsible only to God, who had put him on the throne to lead his people out of a life of sin. Just, sympathetic, and peace-loving, Louis IX convinced his subjects that the monarchy was the most important agency for ensuring their happiness and well-being.

Nation-Building in France	
987–996	Reign of Hugh Capet
1108–1137	Reign of Louis VI
1180–1223	Reign of Philip II Augustus
1226–1270	Reign of Louis IX
1285–1314	Reign of Philip IV, the Fair

Height of Capetian Rule Under Philip IV

The reign of Philip IV, known as Philip the Fair (1285–1314), culminated three centuries of Capetian rule. The opposite of his saintly grandfather, Philip was a man of violence and cunning, tireless in his effort to make the monarchy supreme in France. Aware that anti-Semitism was growing in Europe in the wake of the Crusades, he expelled the Jews from France and confiscated their possessions.

Philip's need for money also brought him into conflict with the last great medieval pope. Boniface VIII refused to allow Philip to tax the French clergy and made sweeping claims to supremacy over secular powers. But Philip IV would not tolerate papal interference, and the result was the humiliation of Boniface (see Chapter 14), a blow from which the influence of the medieval papacy never recovered. In domestic affairs, the real importance of Philip's reign lay in the king's ability to increase the power and improve the organization of the royal government. Philip's astute civil servants, recruited mainly from the middle class, sought to make the power of the monarch absolute.

DOCUMENT
Summa de legibus

Philip enlarged his feudal council to include representatives of the third "estate" or class, the townspeople. This Estates-General of nobles, clergy, and burghers was used to obtain popular support for Philip's policies, including the announcement of new taxes. Philip did not ask the Estates-General's consent for his tax measures; thus, this body did not acquire a role in decisions affecting taxation. By the middle of the fourteenth century, France was well organized, unified in support of a strong monarch, and ready to assert itself as a power on the continent.

England to 1348

Most of England in 1000 was ruled by an Anglo-Saxon monarchy threatened by conquest from the Danish king Canute (ka-NOOT). In 1016 Canute conquered the island and ruled it until his death in 1035, when England returned to an Anglo-Saxon monarchy that was challenged both by the Danes and by William, the duke of Normandy, who claimed the throne on a questionable hereditary right.

William and his army of 5000 men crossed the English Channel to enforce his claim to the throne. In 1066 the duke's mounted knights defeated the English infantry at Hastings, and William became king of England (1066–1087), where he began to introduce the Norman, feudal style of administration. The new king retained some land as his royal domain and granted the remainder as fiefs to royal vassals called *tenants-in-chief*. In return for their fiefs, the tenants-in-chief provided William with a number of knights to serve in his royal army. From all the landholders in England, regardless of whether they were his immediate vassals, William exacted an oath that they would "be faithful to him against all

The Bayeux tapestry, a woolen embroidery on linen, dates from the eleventh century. Over 230 feet long, it depicts the events in the Norman conquest of England in 1066, accompanied by a commentary in Latin and surrounded by a decorative border portraying scenes from fables and everyday life.

other men." Both tenants-in-chief and lesser vassals owed their first allegiance to William.

Henry II

William was succeeded by a number of average or ineffectual rulers, but the monarchy was strengthened by Henry II (1154–1189), the founder of the Plantagenet (plahn-TAH-jehn-et), or Angevin, dynasty. As a result of his inheritance (Normandy and Anjou) and his marriage to Eleanor of Aquitaine (AH-kwi-tayn), the richest heiress in France, Henry's possessions extended from Scotland to the Pyrenees. Henry's great military skill and restless energy were important assets to his reign. He quickly began rebuilding the power of the monarchy in England.

Henry's chief contribution to the development of the English monarchy was to increase the jurisdiction of the royal courts at the expense of the feudal courts. Henry's courts also used the jury system to settle private lawsuits; circuit judges handed down quick decisions based on evidence sworn to by a jury of men selected because they were acquainted with the facts of the case. His judicial reforms stimulated the growth of the common law, one of the most important factors in unifying the English people; the decisions of the royal justices became the basis for future decisions made in the king's courts and became the law common to all English people.

Thomas à Becket

Although Henry strengthened the royal courts, he was not as successful in regulating the church courts. When he appointed his trusted friend Thomas à Becket archbishop of Canterbury, the king assumed that Becket could easily be persuaded to cooperate, but the new archbishop proved stubbornly independent in upholding the authority of the church courts over the king's. After a number of disagreements in which Becket defended the independence of the English church from royal authority, Henry was reputed to have remarked that he would be relieved if someone would rid England of the troublesome Becket. Responding to this angry remark, four knights went to Canterbury and murdered Becket before the high altar of the cathedral. Popular outrage over this murder destroyed Henry's chances of reducing the power of the church courts.

The Successors of Henry II

Henry's many accomplishments were marred by the mistakes of his successors. Richard the Lion-Hearted (1189–1199) spent only five months of his ten-year reign in Britain, which he regarded as a source of money for his overseas adventures. Richard's successor, his brother John (1199–1216), was an inept and cruel ruler whose unscrupulousness cost him the support of his barons, at the time he needed them most, in his struggles with the two ablest men of the age, Philip II of France and Pope Innocent III. As feudal overlord of John's possessions in France, Philip declared John an unfaithful vassal and his claims to lands in France unwarranted. He also became involved in a struggle with Innocent III that ended in John's complete surrender.

In the meantime, the king alienated the British barons, who rebelled and in 1215 forced him to agree to the Magna Carta, a document that bound the king to observe all feudal rights and privileges. Although in later centuries people looked back on the Magna Carta as one of the most important documents in the history of political freedom, to the English nobility of John's time, the Magna Carta did not appear to break any new constitutional ground. It was essentially a feudal agreement between the barons and the king, the aristocracy and the monarchy. However, two great principles were contained in the charter: The law is above the king, and the king can be compelled by force to obey the law of the land.

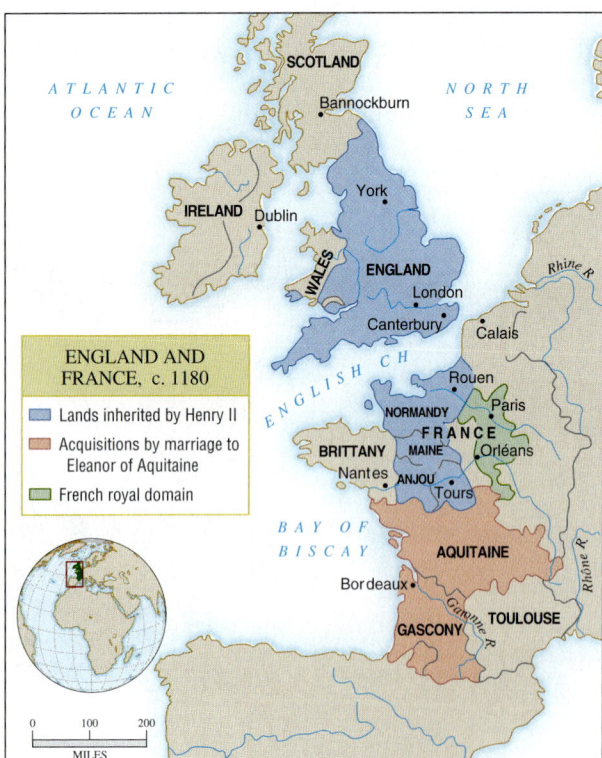

Henry II's claims to lands in France threatened to absorb the kingdom of France. Note the sizable territory claimed by the English king through his marriage to Eleanor of Aquitaine, once wife of the French king. Though it took hundreds of years, the French eventually gained control of all of the French territories claimed by England.

A detail of the Carrow Psalter depicts the murder of Thomas à Becket by the knights of Henry II in Canterbury Cathedral. One knight has broken his sword over the archbishop's head.

The Origins of Parliament

The French-speaking Normans commonly used the word *parlement* (from *parler*, "to speak") for the great council. Anglicized as *parliament*, the term was used interchangeably with *great council* and *Curia Regis*.

Nation-Building in England

871–899	Reign of Alfred the Great of Wessex
1016–1035	Reign of Canute
1066	Battle of Hastings
1066–1087	Reign of William the Conqueror
1154–1189	Henry II begins Plantagenet dynasty
1189–1199	Reign of Richard I, the Lion-Hearted
1199–1216	Reign of John I
1215	Magna Carta
1272–1307	Reign of Edward I

Modern historians, however, generally apply the term to the great council only after 1265, when its membership was radically enlarged. Parliament first became truly influential during the reign of Edward I (1272–1307), one of England's most outstanding monarchs. Beginning with the so-called Model Parliament of 1295, Edward followed the pattern of summoning representatives of shires and towns to meetings of the great council. In calling parliaments, Edward had no intention of making any concession to popular government; rather, he hoped to build popular consensus to support his own policies.

Early in the fourteenth century the representatives of the knights and the townsmen, called the Commons, adopted the practice of meeting separately from the lords. This resulted in the division of Parliament into what came to be called the House of Commons and the House of Lords. Parliament, particularly the Commons, soon discovered its power as a major source of revenue for the king. It gradually became the custom for Parliament to exercise this power by withholding its financial grants until the king had redressed grievances, made known by petitions. Parliament also presented petitions to the king with the request that they be recognized as statutes (laws drawn up by the king and his council and confirmed in Parliament). Gradually, Parliament assumed the right to initiate legislation through petition.

Edward I was the first English king with the goal of being master of the whole island of Great Britain—Wales, Scotland, and England. In 1284, after a five-year struggle, English law and administration were imposed on Wales, and numerous attempts were made to conquer the Scots, who continued to offer Edward serious resistance up to the time of his death. By the time of Edward's death in 1307, England was efficiently organized under a strong monarchy and ready to assert itself in the quest for power on the continent.

Spain to 1348

Unification in Spain took a different course from that in either France or England. Customary rivalry between the Christian feudal nobles and royal authority was complicated by another element: religious fervor. Unification of Christian Spain was not thought possible without the expulsion of the Muslims, with their non-Christian religion and culture.

During the long struggle to drive the Muslims from Spain, patriotism blended with fierce religious devotion. This movement became known as the *Reconquista* (ree-kon-KEE-stah)—the reconquest of Spain from Muslim control. As early as the ninth century, northern Spain became committed to a religious effort to drive all Muslims out of territory Christian Spaniards considered theirs. In the early thirteenth century they captured first Cordova and Seville. The conquest of Seville effectively doubled the territory of the Spanish kingdom. From the end of the thirteenth century, when the Reconquista slowed, until the latter part of the fifteenth century, Muslim political control was confined to Granada. Until the fifteenth century, the Christian victors usually allowed their new Muslim subjects to practice their own religion and traditions. Muslim traders and artisans were protected because of their economic value, and Muslim culture—art in particular—influenced Christian designs and preferences.

Disunity in Germany and Italy

When the last Carolingian ruler of the kingdom of the East Franks died in 911, the great German dukes elected the weakest of their number to hold the title of king. But an exceptionally strong ruler inherited the throne in 936—Otto the Great (936–973), duke of Saxony and founder of the Saxon dynasty of kings. Otto attempted to control the great dukes by appointing his own relatives and favorites as their rulers. Through alliance with the church, he constructed a stronger German monarchy. Otto himself appointed German bishops and abbots, a practice known as lay investiture; since their offices were not hereditary, he expected that their first obedience was to the king.

Otto the Great wanted to establish a German empire, modeled after Roman and Carolingian examples. The conquest and incorporation of the Italian peninsula into that empire were Otto's primary objectives. He proclaimed himself king of Italy, and in 962 he was crowned emperor by the pope. His empire later became known as the Holy Roman Empire.

The Saxon rulers were the most powerful in Europe. They had permanently halted Magyar advances and, by utilizing the German church as an ally, reduced feudal fragmentation in their homeland. They also fostered economic progress. German eastward expansion had begun, and the Alpine passes had been freed from Muslim control and made safe for Italian merchants.

The Salian Emperors

The Saxon kings were succeeded by the Salian dynasty (1024–1125), whose members also tried to establish a centralized monarchy. Under the emperor Henry IV (1056–1106) the monarchy reached the height of its power, but it also experienced a major reverse. The revival of a powerful papacy led to a bitter conflict with Henry, centering on the king's right to appoint church officials who were also his most loyal supporters (lay investiture). This disagreement between state and church culminated in Henry's begging the pope's forgiveness at Canossa in 1077. This conflict, the Investiture Controversy, resulted in the loss of the monarchy's major sources of strength: the loyalty of the German church, now transferred to the papacy; and the support of the great nobles, now openly rebellious and insistent on their "inborn rights."

The second emperor of the new Hohenstaufen (HOH-hen-stahw-fen) dynasty, Frederick I Barbarossa ("Redbeard"), who ruled from 1152 to 1190, also sought to force the great nobles to acknowledge his overlordship. To maintain his hold over Germany, Frederick needed the resources of Italy. But encouraged by the papacy, the cities of northern Italy had joined together in the Lombard League to resist him. Frederick spent about 25 years fighting intermittently in Italy, but the final result was failure: opposition from the popes and the Lombard League was too strong. Frederick did, however, succeed in marrying his son to the heiress of the throne of the kingdom of Naples and Sicily.

Ivory plaque of Christ and the Emperor Otto I (962–968). This ivory carving shows Christ on a throne and in the process of blessing a model of a church presented to him by the German emperor Otto I (left) and a number of saints (right), including St. Peter, who holds his symbolic keys to the kingdom of heaven. The artist was probably influenced by both Carolingian and Byzantine artistic traditions.

The Holy Roman Empire

962	Otto the Great crowned emperor by the pope
1056–1106	Reign of Henry IV
1152–1190	Frederick I Barbarossa begins Hohenstaufen dynasty
1212–1250	Reign of Frederick II

Barbarossa's grandson, Frederick II (1212–1250), was a remarkable individual. Orphaned at an early age, Frederick was brought up as the ward of Innocent III, the most powerful medieval pope. With the pope's support, Frederick was elected emperor in 1215, one year before Innocent's death. Frederick sacrificed Germany in his efforts to unite Italy under his rule. He transferred crown lands and royal rights to the German princes in order to win their support for his Italian wars. Born in Sicily, he remained devoted to the southern part of his empire. He shaped his kingdom there into a vibrant state. Administered by paid officials who were trained at the University of Naples, which he founded for that purpose, his kingdom was the most centralized and efficiently administered in Europe.

After Frederick's death in 1250, the Holy Roman Empire never again achieved the brilliance it had once enjoyed. Later emperors usually did not try to interfere in Italian affairs, and they ceased going to Rome to receive the imperial crown from the pope. In German affairs the emperors no longer even attempted to assert their authority over the increasingly powerful nobles. By the middle of the fourteenth century Germany was hopelessly divided into more than two hundred political units, each striving for separation from the control of the other.

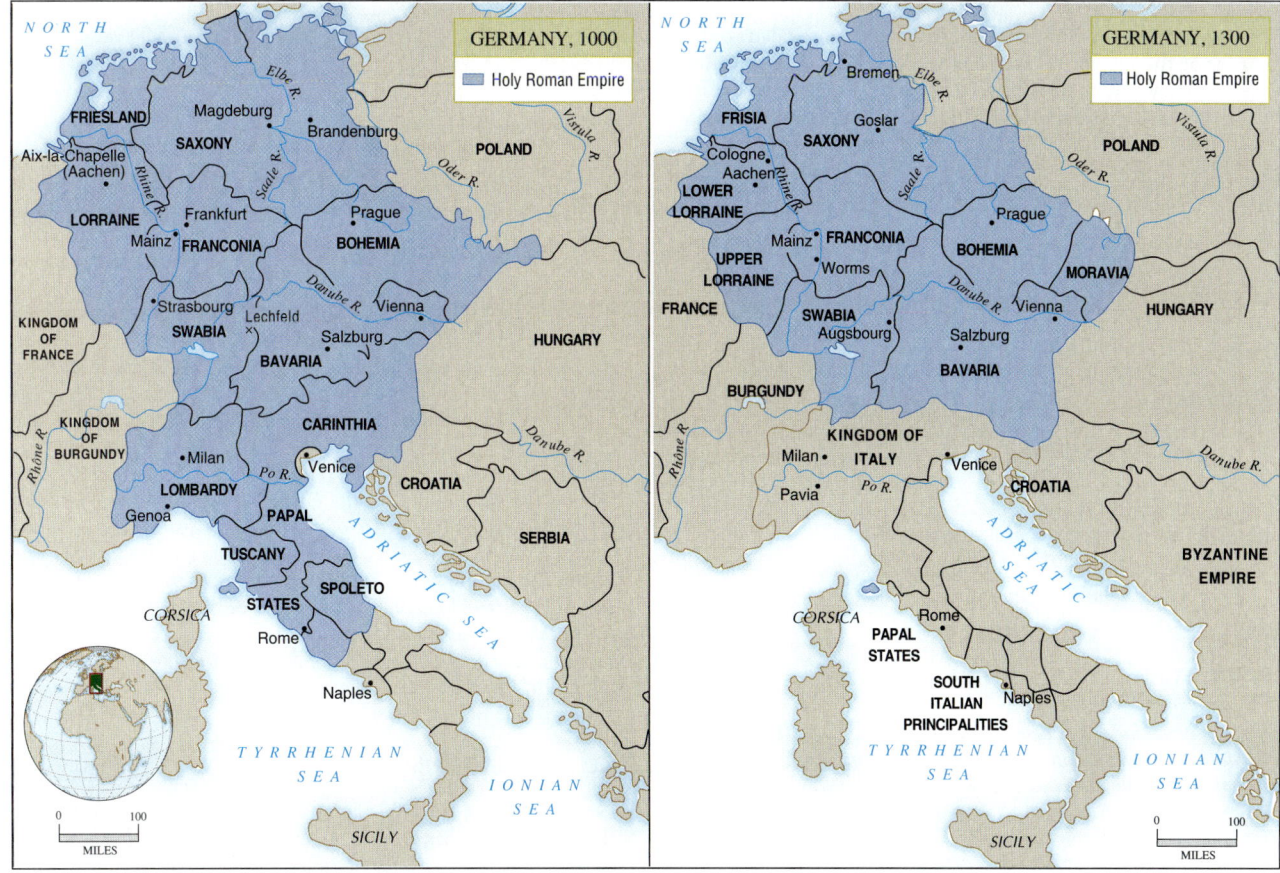

In 962, Otto the Great was crowned as Holy Roman Emperor by the pope. The dreams of recreating a Christian empire to rival the achievements of ancient Rome were never to be realized. Resistance from powerful German nobles and forceful opposition from the northern Italian communes continually frustrated the ambitions of Otto and his successors, so that the Holy Roman Empire was never able to achieve political centralization.

CONCLUSION

This chapter discusses almost one thousand years of European history: from the collapse of Roman political and economic organization, the migrations of new peoples into the old empire, and the growth in influence of a new religion and culture, to the emergence of strong European states under the leadership of ambitious monarchs. Most of the centuries that we call the European Middle Ages were times typified by conservatism and preservation. Political and economic disunity gave rise to institutions that sought to provide protection and security to all segments of society. That quest for security and stability was also evident in early European Christianity, which rejected the cultural heritage of the ancient world in return for a uniform orthodoxy of belief which sought to provide stability in troubled times. But by the eleventh century European self-imposed isolation and the quest for changelessness was challenged on several fronts. Monarchs disrupted the feudal order by setting in motion the drive toward creation of the modern nation-state. The growth of towns and revival of trade brought about new economic and social priorities. The church, once the partner of the state and the unchallenged authority in matters of spirituality and culture, came under increasing examination and challenge. The unique circumstances brought about in Europe by the collapse of Rome, the rise of Christianity, and the Germanic migrations had produced a society unlike any other in world history—one that would emerge by the fourteenth century as vibrant, creative, aggressive, and about to take a more active part in events on a world stage.

Suggestions for Web Browsing

You can obtain more information about topics included in this chapter at the websites listed below. See also the companion website that accompanies this text, **http://www.ablongman.com/brummett**, which contains an online study guide and additional resources.

Medieval Studies
http://labyrinth.georgetown.edu/

The Labyrinth project at Georgetown University offers numerous links categorized by national cultures and by artistic genre.

Women in the Middle Ages
http://info-center.ccit.arizona.edu/~ws/ws200/fall97/grp7/grp7.htm

An excellent site for examining the many activities and responsibilities of medieval women, from peasants to nobility.

Internet Medieval Sourcebook
http://www.fordham.edu/halsall/sbook.html

Extremely helpful site containing original course materials from medieval authors and secondary sources dealing with a large variety of medieval subjects.

Middle Ages
http://www.learner.org/exhibits/middleages/

This site, under the direction of the Annenberg/CBS Project, features information and exhibits illustrating what daily life was really like during the Middle Ages.

Medieval Women
http://labyrinth.georgetown.edu/display.cfm?Action=View&Category=Women

Site details the individual lives and works of medieval women, including Hildegard of Bingen; women rulers and creators; and the impact of the Crusades on women, in addition to numerous general resources.

Women Writers of the Middle Ages
http://lib.rochester.edu/camelot/womenbib.htm

Site offers bibliographies of primary and secondary sources by and about medieval women writers.

World of the Vikings
http://www.worldofthevikings.com/

This well-indexed site provides links to almost everything there is to know about these medieval seafarers—their everyday life, their travels, their influence.

Literature and Film

An excellent new edition of the Beowulf epic is Seamus Heaney, ed., *Beowulf: A New Verse Translation* (W. W. Norton, 2001). Outstanding video presentations on the Middle Ages are *Charlemagne* (2000; 5 tapes, Acorn Media); *Landmarks of Western Art: The Medieval World*, Vol. I (Kultur Video, 1999); *The Vikings* (Nova, 2000); *Just the Facts—The Middle Ages* (Goldhil Home Media, 2001); *Music of the Middle Ages* (Timeless Multimedia, 1994); *Sienna: Chronicle of a Medieval Commune* (Home Vision Entertainment, 2000); *Living in the Past: Life in Medieval Times* (Kultur Video, 2000); and *Medieval Warfare* (2000; 3 tapes, Kultur Video). An award-winning feature film set in France during this period is *The Return of Martin Guerre* (Nelson Entertainment, 1982).

Suggestions for Reading

Three excellent surveys of the early Middle Ages are Robert Bartlett, *The Making of Europe: Conquest, Colonization, and Cultural Change, 950–1350* (Princeton University Press, 1993); Rosamond McKitterick, ed., *The Early Middle Ages: Europe 400–1000* (Oxford University Press, 2001); and Richard W. Southern, *The Making of the Middle Ages* (Yale University Press, 1992). For economic and social history, see Werner Roesener, *Peasants in the Middle Ages* (Polity Press, 1996) and Frances Gies and Joseph Gies, *Women in the Middle Ages* (Perennial, 1991), *Life in a Medieval Village* (HarperPerennial, 1991), and *Marriage and Family in the Middle Ages* (HarperPerennial, 1989). For the history of the church, see Peter Brown et al., *The Rise of Western Christendom*, 2nd ed. (Blackwell, 2003), and Jaroslav Pelikan, *The Growth of Medieval Theology*, Vol. 3: The Christian Tradition (University of Chicago Press, 1978), and Michael Haren, *Medieval Thought* (Dublin University Press, 1992). On the Crusades, see Jonathan Riley-Smith, ed., *The Oxford History of the Crusades* (Oxford University Press, 1997), and Malcolm Billings, *The Cross and the Crescent* (Sterling, 1987). John Burrow, *The Ages of Man: A Study in Medieval Writing and Thought* (Oxford University Press, 1989) is an outstanding review of medieval literature.

CHAPTER 10

Culture, Power, and Trade in the Era of Asian Hegemony, 220–1350

CHAPTER CONTENTS

- **India in the Classical and Medieval Eras**
  DOCUMENT: *Faxian: A Chinese Buddhist Monk in Gupta India*
- **China: Cultural and Political Empires**
  DOCUMENT: *Bo Juyi (772–846): "The Song of Everlasting Sorrow"*
- **DISCOVERY THROUGH MAPS:** *Gog and Magog in the Ebstorf Mappamundi*
- **Korea: From Three Kingdoms to One**
- **The Emergence of Japan in East Asia**
  DOCUMENT: *Sei Shōnagon: The Pillow Book*

300
c. 300 Yamato clan emerges in central Japan
320–515 Gupta dynasty in India
380s Buddhism adopted in Korea

400
439–534 Northern Wei dynasty in China

500
515 Huna seize northwestern India

600
606–647 Reign of Harsha in north India
618–907 Tang dynasty in China
676 Tang driven out of Korea; Silla unifies Korea

700
710–784 Nara period in Japan
755–763 An Lushan Rebellion in China
788–820 Hindu philosopher Shankara
794–1181 Heian period in Japan

900
960–1279 Song dynasty in China
c. 978–1016 Murasaki Shikibu, writer of *The Tale of Genji*

1100
1130–1200 Zhu Xi, Neo-Confucian scholar in China
1185 Minamoto clan establishes Kamakura Shogunate in Japan

1200
1206 Beginning of Delhi Sultanate in India; Chinggis Khan launches invasions that create Mongol Empire
1279–1368 Yuan dynasty in China

Asia served as an incubator and transmitter of cultures and religions with global reach from 220 to 1350. As empires consolidated and expanded their boundaries, trade and commerce accompanied cultural diffusion. Human cultures had long migrated globally, but during this long millennium, the pace of international contacts accelerated. Religions, philosophies, and arts deepened their roots in areas that had spawned them, and at the same time, new ideas spread throughout the region.

The first half millennium was, in some ways, Asia's Buddhist Age. In South Asia, Hinduism, and in East Asia, Daoism and Confucianism as well as indigenous religions continued to play important roles. But a Buddhist traveler from East Asia would find co-religionists in lands with remarkably distinct cultures. Buddhism was spread by both missionary activity and commercial activity along the Silk Roads. The second half of the millennium was likewise influenced by a global religion—Islam. South and Southeast Asian rulers either adopted Islam or resisted it, and power and trade networks were influenced by Islamic missionary and commercial activities. China and Northeast Asia felt the impact of nomadic cultures throughout the millennium, and in the twelfth and thirteenth centuries much of East and Central Asia was integrated into a trade and power network controlled by originally nomadic Mongols. Disease—bubonic plague—took advantage of these networks to spread the hand of death throughout Eurasia in the mid-fourteenth century, and ironically, fatally weakened the Mongols, whose dominance in China created fourteenth-century globalism. While Asian power and culture were in many ways hegemonic until that time and Asia would continue to grow and dominate world trade until the eighteenth century, the door was open to the rise of new sites of power, particularly in Europe, during the next few hundred years.

Each Asian civilization produced significant contributions to the world's common culture. India made remarkable advances in mathematics, medicine, chemistry, textile production, and literature, and Buddhism continued its dramatic spread to East and Southeast Asia. China excelled in political organization, scholarship, and the arts, and at the same time produced such revolutionary technical inventions as printing,

287

gunpowder, and the mariner's compass. Maritime trade flourished as Arab, Jewish, and Indian traders crisscrossed the Indian Ocean to the west of the subcontinent, while Indian and Southeast Asian traders plied the waters to the east as far as China and Japan.

Growth in the old Asian centers led naturally toward outward cultural diffusion and a varied exchange of goods, philosophies, literatures, and fashions with bordering civilizations. In Southeast Asia these arose from increasing contacts with India and China through trade, missionary efforts, colonizing, and conquest. First Korea, and then Japan, imported cultural bases from China. Similarly, nomads of Central Asia—Turks, Uighurs (WEE-ghers), Mongols, and numerous other steppe peoples—engaged in a vigorous exchange with China and India (often assimilating the cultural patterns of those civilizations) as merchants, subjects, or conquerors. The conquest of China by the Mongols during the thirteenth and fourteenth centuries facilitated the passing of those influences to the peoples of the Middle East and Europe. Nor was the diffusion of cultural influences and material culture a one-way process. The great cultural centers of Persia, India, and China adapted dress styles, military tactics, literature, and the hardy Mongol horse from the Central Asians.

INDIA IN THE CLASSICAL AND MEDIEVAL ERAS

■ *What factors contributed to a diversity of religions and cultures in classical and medieval India?*

The Classical Age

The political fragmentation of India during the 500 years from 184 B.C.E. to 320 C.E. permitted the spread of new Indian religions and the introduction of ideas and technologies from east and west of India. But it was not until the reunification of India's north under the Guptas that the classical age of Hindu culture emerged. India's cultural renaissance took root in the Gupta dynasty (320–500) and attempted to recapture the territorial and cultural grandeur of the Mauryas (MOW-ree-yahs). Its monarchs gained control over northern India while fostering traditional religions, Sanskrit literature, and indigenous art. Hindu and Buddhist culture also spread widely throughout Southeast Asia in this period.

The Gupta state began its rise in 320 with the accession to power of Chandra Gupta I (not related to his earlier Mauryan namesake). His son Samudra Gupta (r. 335–375) and grandson Chandra Gupta II (r. 375–415) were successful conquerors, extending the boundaries of an original petty state in Maghada (mah-GAH-dah) until it included most of northern India, from the Himalayas to the Narmada River and east to west from sea to sea. Within this domain the Gupta monarchs developed a political structure along ancient Mauryan lines, with provincial governors, district officials, state-controlled industries, and an imperial secret service. This centralized system, however, was effective only on royal lands, which were much less extensive than in Mauryan times. With a smaller bureaucracy, the Gupta rulers depended on local authorities and communal institutions. Peasants were obligated to pay as taxes to the state one-fourth of their harvest, one-fiftieth of their cattle and gold, one-sixth of their wealth in meat, fruit, honey and trees, and a day of labor per month for road repair or irrigation maintenance. Despite such high taxes, Indian farmers appeared in reports by foreign visitors to successfully produce an abundance of food. Artisans were organized in guilds which negotiated relationships with state and religious institutions. Military forces were raised by feudal levy.

Gupta India

320	Accession of Chandra Gupta I
c. 335–375	Reign of Samudra Gupta
c. 376–414	Reign of Chandra Gupta II
515	Huna (Huns) seize northwest India; Gupta Empire collapses

Marriage alliances aided the Guptas' rise to power. Chandra Gupta I married a princess from the powerful Licchavi (leek-CHAH-vee) clan; his coins show the king and his queen, Kumaradevi (koo-MAH-rah-DEH-vee), on one side and a lion with his queen's clan name on the other. Chandra Gupta II gave his daughter, Prabhavati (prah-bah-VAH-tee) Gupta, in marriage to Rudrasena II (roo-DRAH-seh-nah), king of the powerful Vakataka dynasty in central India. Rudrasena died after a short reign, and his wife then took control of his kingdom for about 20 years as regent for her minor sons. The two kingdoms maintained close ties even after her death.

Peace and stable government under the later Guptas increased agricultural productivity and foreign trade. Commerce with Rome brought a great influx of gold and silver as well as Arabian horses into the Gupta Empire in exchange for Indian textiles, jewels, spices, perfumes, and wood. In fact, Rome's net deficit in gold exports led to the weakening of its economy. Indian traders were also active in Southeast Asia, particularly in Burma, Vietnam, and Cambodia, where they brought not only new products but also Buddhist culture. India's resulting prosperity was reflected in great public and religious buildings and in the luxuries of the elite, particularly at the Gupta court.

Although the Gupta rulers generally favored Hinduism, they practiced religious pluralism, patronizing and building temples for Hindus, Buddhists, and Jains. The Brahmans provided the Guptas with religious legitimacy, and the Guptas rewarded them with significant grants of land. Hinduism dominated the subcontinent. The Hindu revival of this period brought a great upsurge of devotion to Vishnu, Shiva, and Durga. This religious fervor was reflected in a series of religious books, the *Puranas,* which emphasized the compassion of the personal gods. The *Puranas* are a collection of myths, philosophical dialogues, ritual prescriptions, and dynastic genealogies gathered in the third and fourth centuries. The tales of the gods were popular. Among their legends, for example, is a recounting of the deeds of the goddess Durga and her fight against the buffalo demon. By promoting the devotional Hinduism reflected in these tales, the Gupta monarchs gained great favor among all classes of their subjects.

The *Bhagavad-Gita* (BAH-gah-vahd-GHEE-tah; *Song of the Blessed One*), written during this time, assured Hindus that salvation was possible, regardless of one's station in life. **Bhakti** (BAHK-tee; "devotion") was introduced as a path to salvation. Revealing himself as the Divine Savior Vishnu, the *Gita*'s protagonist Krishna explained: "Those who revere me with devotion (bhakti), they are in me and I too am in them. . . . Even those who may be of base origin, women, men of the artisan caste, and serfs, too."[1] Though inequality remained embedded in the status system that differentiated one's religious duties by caste, Hindu salvation was, in the *Bhagavad-Gita,* made accessible to all.

Much of our knowledge of Gupta society comes from the journal of a Chinese Buddhist monk, Faxian (fah-SHEN), who traveled in India for 14 years at the opening of the fifth century. Despite the Guptas' preference for Hinduism, thousands of Buddhist monks and nuns practiced their religion. Buddhist stupas (funerary mounds) dotted the landscape. In the fourth century, only Sri Lanka was more Buddhist than India. Buddhism was an important bridge linking China and India and stimulating commerce in both East and Southeast Asia.

Faxian was primarily interested in Buddhism in India, but he also commented on social customs. He reported the people to be happy, relatively free of government oppression, and inclined toward courtesy and charity. He mentions the caste system and its associations with purity and impurity, including "untouchability," the social isolation of a lowest class that is doomed to menial labor. Of course, travelers' accounts never tell the entire story and must be read with some caution. Each traveler sees bits and pieces of the society he or she is visiting and looks at the society in ways that may be very different from those of other travelers of different

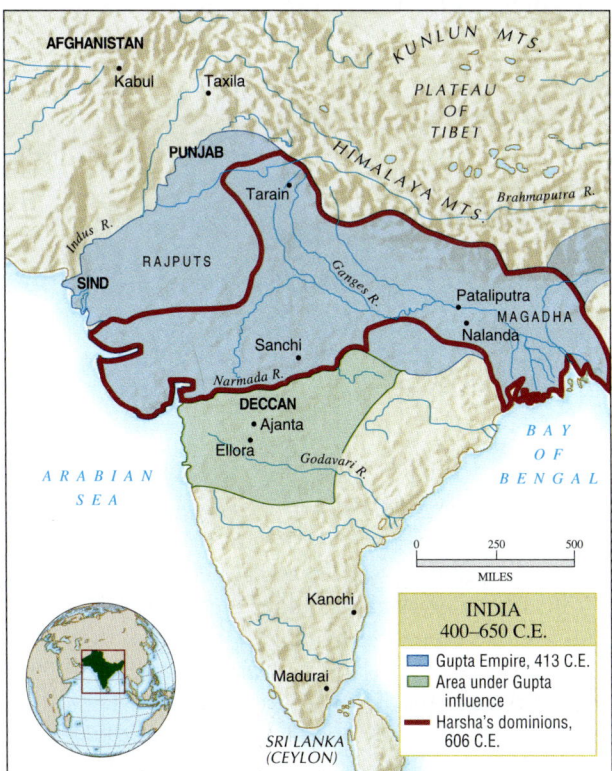

The Guptas extended their rule over northern and central India but never managed to control the southern peninsula.

---

bhakti—Hindu devotion.

Document: Faxian: A Chinese Buddhist Monk in Gupta India

Faxian is an important source on India around 400 C.E. A Buddhist monk, he left China as a pilgrim to India in search of spiritual knowledge and Buddhist texts; he was away from home for 14 years. Faxian reached northern India on foot, via the grueling route over the mountains from China. When he returned home, he translated various Indian works and wrote the account of his travels. Faxian's story and long arduous journey illustrate both the effects of the spread of Buddhism and the draw that the Indian heartland had on Buddhists abroad. Here he describes Pataliputra (modern Patna), where Ashoka once reigned. The festival illustrates the amalgamation of Buddhist and Hindu ritual and suggests the joyous nature of some popular urban religious celebrations. Faxian's account of hospitals gives us some insight into the quality of medical care available free to the poor.

By the side of the tower of King Ashoka is built a monastery belonging to the Great Vehicle [Mahayana Buddhism], very imposing and elegant. There is also a temple belonging to the Little Vehicle [Theravada Buddhism]. Together they contain about 600 or 700 priests; their behavior is decorous and orderly.... Of all the kingdoms in Mid-India, the towns of this country are especially large. The people are rich and prosperous; they practice virtue and justice. Every year on the eighth day of the second month, there is a procession of images. On this occasion, they construct a four-wheeled cart, and erect upon it a tower of five stages, composed of bamboos lashed together, the whole being supported by a center post resembling a large spear with three points, in height twenty-two feet or more. So it looks like a pagoda. They then cover it with fine white linen, which they afterward paint with gaudy colors. Having made figures of the *devas* [gods], and decorated them with gold, silver, and glass, they place them under canopies of embroidered silk. Then at the four corners [of the vehicle] they construct niches in which they place figures of Buddha in a sitting posture, with a Bodhisattva [a Buddha in the making] standing in attendance. There are perhaps twenty cars thus prepared and differently decorated. During the day of the procession both priests and laymen assemble in great numbers. There are games and music, whilst they offer flowers and incense.... Then all night long they burn lamps, indulge in games and music, and make religious offerings. Such is the custom of all those who assemble on this occasion from the different countries round about. The nobles and householders of this country have founded hospitals within the city, to which the poor of all countries, the destitute, cripples, and the diseased may repair. They receive every kind of requisite help gratuitously. Physicians inspect their diseases, and according to their cases order them food and drink, medicine or decoctions, everything in fact that may contribute to their ease. When cured they depart at their convenience.

Questions to Consider

1. What does this story suggest about the institutionalization of Buddhism and its integration into city life in India?
2. Why might the people in Patna place figures of the Hindu gods and of the Buddha on the same float or cart used in a festival procession?

From Samuel Beal, ed., *Buddhist Records of the Western World*, translated from the Chinese of Hiuen Tsiang (629) (Delhi: Oriental Books, 1969), pp. lvi–lvii.

---

class, gender, upbringing, or motive for travel. Nonetheless, travelers like Faxian, who wrote down their observations in some detail, often provide us with the clearest glimpse we can obtain of past societies.

Gupta Art and Literature

Indian art of the Gupta period depicts a golden age of classical brilliance, combining stability and serenity with an exuberant love of life. The Gupta artistic spirit is well expressed in the 28 monasteries and temples at Ajanta, hewn out of a solid rock cliff and portraying in their wall frescoes not only the life of Buddha but also life in general: lovers embracing, beds of colorful flowers, musicians, and dancers. These sculptures reveal the beauty of the human form and provide us with a sense of Indian culture beyond that found in theological texts. The various incarnations of Vishnu and the deeds of the goddess Durga were also common subjects of Gupta sculpture. Hundreds of workers and artisans were employed in this work of building and

IMAGE
Classical Indian Sculpture

The Gupta era is justly renowned for its sculpture. This fifth-century terra-cotta piece shows the young Lord Krishna fighting the horse demon. According to Hindu religious tradition, Krishna, even as a baby, was formidably powerful; he battled a whole assortment of demons before reaching adolescence.

decorating temples that might, as Faxian points out, house hundreds of monks.

The Gupta era was also a golden age for literature, written in Sanskrit, the ancient language of the Brahmans. Authors supported by royal patronage poured forth a wealth of sacred, philosophical, and dramatic works in prose and poetry, including fables, fairy tales, and adventure stories featuring a wide range of characters—thieves, courtesans, hypocritical monks, and strange beasts. The *Panchatantra* is a manual of political wisdom employing animal tales to advise the king on proper rule.

The most renowned literary figure of the Gupta era was India's greatest poet and dramatist, Kalidasa, who wrote at the court of Chandra Gupta II. His best-known work in the West is *Shakuntala*, a great drama of lovers separated by adversity for many years and then by chance reunited. This universal theme of separated lovers is found in the epic stories of many Eurasian peoples in this era—the Arabian story of *Layla and Majnun*, for example.

DOCUMENT
Tales of Ten Princes

Gupta Scholarship and Science

The Gupta era brought a great stimulus to learning. Brahman traditions were revitalized, and Buddhist centers, which had spread after the Mauryan period, were given new support. The foremost Indian university, founded in the fifth century, was the Buddhist university at Nalanda in northeastern India. Accomplishments in science were no less remarkable than those in art, literature, scholarship, and philosophy. The university had a diverse population, with students from China and Southeast Asia also attending classes. The most famous Gupta scientist was the astronomer-mathematician Aryabhatta (AH-ree-ah-BAHT-tah), who lived in the fifth century. He elaborated (in verse) on quadratic equations, solstices, and equinoxes, along with the spherical shape of the earth and its rotation. Other Hindu mathematicians of this period popularized the use of a special sign for zero, passing it on later to the Arabs. Mathematical achievements were matched by those in medicine. Hindu physicians sterilized wounds, prepared for surgery by fumigation, performed cesarean operations, set bones, and were skilled in plastic surgery. They used drugs then unknown in the West, such as chaulmoogra oil for leprosy, a treatment still used during the first half of the twentieth century. With these accomplishments in pure science came many effective practical applications by Gupta craftsmen, who made soap, cement, superior dyes, and the finest tempered steel in the world.

India is famous for its rock carved temples. Kings or affluent families often financed such temples (both Hindu and Buddhist) with spectacular carvings as acts of devotion. This is the Kailasanatha Temple at Ellora, dedicated to the Hindu god Shiva and dating to approximately 765 C.E.

New Political and Religious Orders

Gupta hegemony began to collapse in the second half of the fifth century with attempted invasions by the Huna (called Xiongnu (SHONG-noo) in China and Huns in Europe) from the north. Although the Guptas held out for several decades, they ruled only in parts of northern India after 497. In 515 the Huna—who had already menaced the Roman Empire and successfully invaded Persia—seized first northwestern India and then the Ganges plain. Huna rule did not endure, but it led to several smaller kingdoms breaking free of the Gupta and prompted the migration of more Central Asian tribesmen into India. This resulted in a period in which India was generally divided into regional kingdoms rather than more expansive empires like that of the Guptas. The Central Asian tribesmen also intermarried with local populations to produce a class of fighting aristocrats known as *Rajputs* (RAHJ-poots). These fierce warriors carved out kingdoms among the Hindu states of northern India. Extensive intermarriage was common in frontier areas, blurring the boundaries between ethnolinguistic groups and even creating new identities.

In the seventh century the unity of northern India was revived for a short while by Harsha (r. 606–647), a strong leader. In 6 years he reconquered much of what had been the Gupta Empire, restoring order and partially reviving learning. However, Harsha failed in his bid to conquer the Deccan, and no ruler would do so until 1206. A tolerant leader, he was a strong supporter of Buddhism; during his reign Hinduism also grew in popularity. Harsha's support for Buddhism made possible several successful visits by Chinese ambassadors. In 643 the large delegation sent by the Tang court was received by Harsha who held a Buddhist ceremony in their honor. This diplomatic mission visited Buddhist sites and brought along an artisan to copy Buddhist architecture and sculpture. In addition to making spiritual overtures, the Chinese mission had a key commercial success—acquiring sugar-making technology from the South Asians.

When Harsha died in 647, regional kingdoms again prevailed. The period of the regional kingdoms was not a sterile one. In this era the great Hindu philosopher Shankara (c. 788–820) brilliantly argued a mystical philosophy based on the *Upanishads;* literature, especially in Tamil in the south, flourished; and Brahmans and

Buddhist monks continued to carry their religious and cultural ideas to Southeast Asia and China. Their crucial role in the "Indianization" of Southeast Asia is reflected in the great temples there. It is also reflected in Chinese sources that note 162 visits of Buddhist monks from the fifth to the eighth centuries.[2]

The Chola kingdom on India's southeastern coast played a significant role in the commercial and cultural exchange with Southeast Asia as well. The Chola had long lived in the Tamil south but were apparently a tributary lineage to the more powerful Pallavar dynasty. They began to challenge the Pallavars in the late ninth century and emerged as a ruling force in their own right within a century. Chola rulers in the eleventh century exchanged embassies with China, Sumatra, Malaya, and Cambodia; Chola fleets took Sri Lanka (Ceylon) and challenged the power of the Southeast Asian kingdom of Srivijaya (SHREE-vee-JAH-yah). When a Chola king conquered Bengal, he ordered the defeated princes to carry the holy water of the Ganges River to his new capital to celebrate his victory. Through this ceremony, he not only forced his enemies to perform a ritual act of submission but enhanced his legitimacy in Hindu terms by linking his own lands to those watered by the sacred Ganges.

Muslims in India

The prophet Muhammad founded an Arab Muslim state in Arabia in the seventh century (see Chapter 7); soon the Arab conquerors had defeated the Sassanids in Persia, and Muslim armies arrived at the boundaries of the Indian subcontinent. In 712 an Arab force seized Sind, a coastal outpost in northwestern India. During the next 300 years, Arabic-speaking Muslims established trading posts throughout the Indian Ocean region. Although the existence of the Muslim kingdom at Sind did not serve as a springboard for Arab Muslim penetration of India, Muslim traders did facilitate the integration of India into an Islamic world system. This system was a trading network that did not require participants to be Muslim but did take advantage of Muslim political expansion. The significant expansion of Muslim political control in India 300 years later, beginning in 997, had Turkish, Persian, and Afghan rather than Arabian roots.

Armies of Central Asian and Turkish slaves, originally purchased to support Muslim rulers at Baghdad, began to form independent kingdoms in Afghanistan and Persia. One of them, a kingdom ruled by Mahmud of Ghazni (MAH-mood, GAHZ-nee), launched a series of campaigns into northwestern India. He gained a reputation as a destroyer for his 17 campaigns over the course of 25 years that devastated northern India. One notable episode during these campaigns was Mahmud's destruction of Shiva's large temple complex in Gujarat and the slaughter of its defenders who, according to legend, numbered 50,000 men. These campaigns of pillage rather than conquest made Mahmud a name that to the present day evokes powerful emotions among Hindus.

DOCUMENT
Al-Biruni on India's Hindus

Mahmud is also known for the famous scholars at his court, among them Firdawsi (feer-DOW-see; 940–1020), who wrote the great epic Persian poem the *Shahnamah* (SHAH-NAH-mah), and al-Biruni (b. 973), author of a major history of India. Al-Biruni wrote that it was the caste system that prevented Muslims and Hindus from ever reaching any understanding because the Muslims considered "all men as equal, except in piety."[3] Of course, al-Biruni was minimizing the hierarchies that existed in Muslim society. But the caste system did indeed serve as a significant barrier between Hindus and Muslims (although, over time, Hindus and Muslims intermarried and some Muslim groups adapted castelike social divisions).

Firdawsi's career is an illustration of the vagaries of life at court. He spent many years writing the 60,000 verses of the *Shahnamah* but was then disappointed when the king did not reward him properly. So he penned a savage satire of Mahmud and fled to his home region of Khurasan in Persia. Legend has it that Mahmud later realized the value of Firdawsi's work and sent a large reward after him, but by the time it arrived, the poet was already dead.

The date 1206 stands out as the next significant marker of Muslim conquest in India. In the same year that the Mongol Chinggis (Genghis) Khan mobilized his campaigns of conquest and expansion in Central Asia, the general Qutb ud-Din Aibak (KOOT-buh ood-DIN ai-BAHK) seized power as sultan at Delhi. Qutb ud-Din had been a commander in the army of the Afghan ruler Muhammad of Ghur, who seized Delhi in 1193 from the Rajputs, Hindus who mounted a staunch defense in the northwest. Qutb ud-Din founded a new dynasty in 1206 that lasted for 320 years. He was followed on the throne by his son-in-law, Iltutmish (il-TOOT-mish; r. 1211–1236), and by the latter's daughter, Raziyya (ra-ZEE-yah; r. 1236–1240). According to the Muslim chronicler Minhaju-s Siraj, Sultana Raziyya was "wise, just and generous.... She was endowed with all the qualities befitting a king, but she was not born of the right sex, so in the estimation of men all these virtues were worthless."[4] Raziyya's father Iltutmish had himself been formally consecrated in 1229 as sultan of Delhi by a representative of the Abbasid sultan in Baghdad. Even though the Abbasid sultan wielded little power at this time, he was still a source of Islamic legitimacy for South Asian Muslim rulers. Less than 30 years later, the Abbasid caliphate would fall prey to the Mongol descendants of Chinggis Khan.

At the peak of its power in the thirteenth century, the Delhi Sultanate held not only the north but also part of the Deccan Plateau in the south. When Sultan

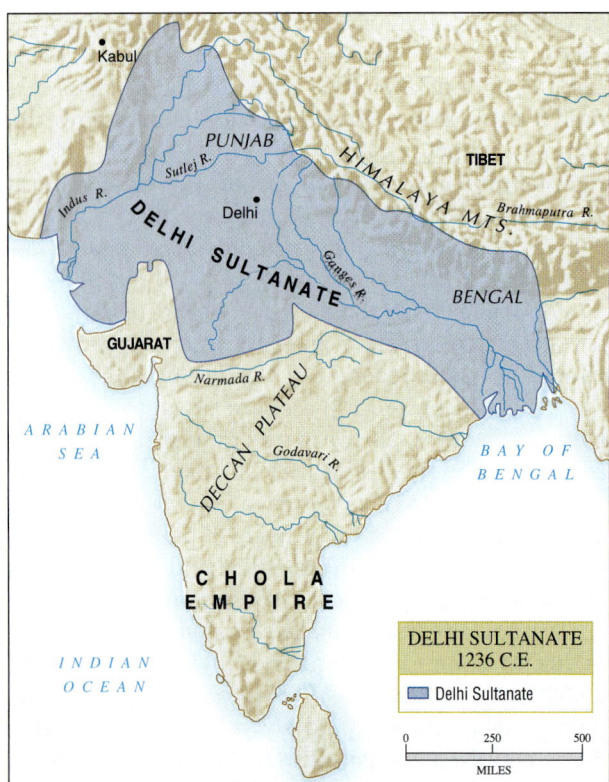

Muslim rulers established a sultanate in northern India, and Delhi flourished as its imperial capital.

Ala ud-Din (r. 1296–1316) invaded the Deccan, he called himself the "Second Alexander," a title that was emblazoned on his coins. The Delhi Sultanate also managed to ward off the Mongol invaders who seized the Punjab (poon-JAHB), thus avoiding the fate of Persia and Iraq. Delhi, under the sultanate, emerged as a great imperial capital. The Delhi sultans were patrons of the arts, builders of splendid monuments, and proponents of philosophy. The Tughluks (TOOG-looks), a Muslim dynasty who ruled Delhi for most of the fourteenth century, held an uneasy rule over the majority Hindu populace as well as over rival Muslim rulers. Ibn Battuta (IH-buhn bah-TOO-tah), the famed Muslim world traveler from north Africa, served the Tughluk court as its chief judge, observing it closely and leaving a detailed historical record. By the middle of the fourteenth century, the Tughluks had lost control of the south (upon the rise of the Hindu Vijayangar (vee-JAH-yahn-gahr) Empire in 1336) and the northeast (Sufi Muslim leaders there declared their independence of Delhi in 1338). Although experiencing brief periods of revival, the regime continued to decline internally before it was terminally fragmented by the brutal destruction of Delhi at the hands of the Turco-Mongol Timur (Tamerlane) in 1398. Timur's army wrought such destruction in Delhi that in his autobiography he denied

DOCUMENT
The Ideal Muslim King

DOCUMENT
A World Traveler in India

responsibility and blamed the slaughter on his soldiers. Numerous rulers, espousing a variety of religious faiths, emerged throughout India as Delhi declined, until a century later, when Timur's great-grandson Babur would return to establish the Mughal dynasty.

Pre-Mughal Muslim rule in India brought some cultural integration as local lords and warriors were incorporated into the new Muslim court. Some Hindus found emotional appeal in the Muslim faith, which had no caste system, or sought to lighten their taxes and qualify for public service by converting to Islam. Others formed new religious groups synthesizing aspects of Hinduism and Islam—for example, **Sikhism**. Another typical example of cultural integration was the spread of Urdu, a spoken Indian language incorporating Persian, Arabic, and Turkish words. The Sikh religion and the Urdu language illustrate how difficult it is to maintain strict boundaries (whether ethnic, linguistic, or spiritual) between peoples who regularly interact with each other, especially in frontier areas.

DOCUMENT
Indian Poetry

Cultural synthesis, however, could not eliminate Hindu-Muslim contention over polytheism, religious images, and closed castes. Many aristocratic Hindu leaders continued to resist Islam. The Muslim centuries should not be seen as a takeover of Indian society and culture by foreigners. Scholars today stress that though the rulers were Islamic, their governments ruled in ways similar to non-Islamic Indian rulers. Religion and caste remained significant barriers to assimilation, and mass conversions did not occur. The Delhi Sultanate remained a Muslim military-administrative class that ruled over a predominantly Hindu population. The impact on Buddhism was, however, far greater. The university at Nalanda and other major Buddhist centers were destroyed in 1202, driving thousands of monks and scholars to Nepal and Tibet. Buddhism was, then, effectively erased from India.

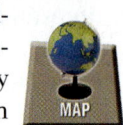
MAP
The Delhi Sultanate and Mughal India

CHINA: CULTURAL AND POLITICAL EMPIRES

■ *How did cross-cultural interaction with indigenous culture and ideology define China as a nation?*

The fall of the Han in 220 was followed by three and a half centuries of political disunity. Unity was regained under the Sui dynasty (589–618), consolidated under the Tang (618–907), maintained precariously under the Song (960–1279), and reasserted

---

Sikhism—Indian religion blending elements of Hinduism and Islam.

under the Yuan (1279–1368). Despite periods of internal disruption, this political system, recreated from Han precedents, survived repeated invasions and civil wars. For the 90-year Yuan dynasty, China was ruled by Central Asian invaders, the Mongols, but despite foreign control at the top, Chinese culture survived and reclaimed the emperorship in 1368. Throughout the millennium, stability resulted from a common written language, a strong family structure, an enduring Confucian tradition, an elite of scholar bureaucrats who shared power while contending for dominance, and the strength of China's economy and material culture. In the first half millennium, including the centuries of political disunity, China was part of the expanding Buddhist world. In the second half, the efforts of China's Confucian scholars promoted a flowering of Chinese culture during the expansionist Tang period, when China was the largest state in the world; during the ensuing economic prosperity of the Song; and in the Yuan period, in which China's economy dominated Eurasian trade.

Period of Division

No single dynasty was able to unite North and South China and establish a long-lasting dynasty from the fall of the Han to the rise of the Sui more than 360 years later. Yet this was a vibrant age of artistic creation, intellectual growth, and profound religious development. The divisions between north and south created dynamic differences in the two regions over time, and the reuniting of the two in the late sixth century led to a fertile synthesis of ideas and practices. Following the fall of the Han Empire various nomadic peoples, mainly Xiongnu and Yuezhi (yoo-EH-juh; "Turks"), interacted with Chinese in the border areas. At the same time, Chinese claimants to power—the ideal of a unified country persisted throughout the age of division—struggled with other Chinese as well as with sinified non-Chinese for dominance. (*Sinification* or *sinicization* meant adopting varying degrees of Chinese civilization, culture, governance, philosophy, and economic organization.) During the third century, three kingdoms vied for supremacy, and one, Jin, seemed to be on the verge of reuniting China in 280. Soon, however, succession disputes pitted Jin factions, joined by Chinese and non-Chinese allies, against one another. Unity was not to be at that time.

Xiongnu and other northern people had been invited inside the Han dynasty's borders in the second century as a way of gaining their support and decreasing the possibility of barbarian conquest. Many were used as soldiers by Chinese generals. By 304, some Xiongnu, sensing an opportunity during the fratricidal wars of the Jin, rose up, declared themselves the new kings of Han, and sacked Luoyang and Chang'an.

For the next century (304–439), China was involved in constant warfare during the period known as the Sixteen Kingdoms. Many aristocrats fled southward, populating the south and bringing Chinese culture with them. This was a demographically significant move, extending the reach of Chinese civilization and developing the south's fertile agricultural economy. When, centuries later, the Grand Canal was built, food could be transported from this "rice basket" to the north, where China's defensive armies had long been dependent on either growing their own food or striking bargains with their barbarian neighbors.

In the North, a clan originally from Manchuria but sinified by the fifth century established the Northern Wei dynasty (439–534). Like other successful outsiders, the Northern Wei had adopted Chinese methods, creating an effective administration by blending their indigenous ways with Chinese ways. Throughout history, China was challenged by the question of maintaining Chinese culture and institutions—especially rule by scholars according to Confucian principles—while learning from the outsider (or barbarians, as they were ungenerously called) to create a hybrid culture, economy, and military. The question of how to maximize borrowing without compromising Chinese culture was most evident in times of strong central government. But religious, cultural, and economic blending occurred at all times. The Northern Wei instituted an **equal-field system** of land tenure that resembled the ancient "well-field" system to overcome the rise of powerful land owners whose control of land and serfs cut the tax roles. They also adopted Chinese language and dress. Their capital at Luoyang was a grand Chinese city, with palaces, 500,000 inhabitants, and 1000 Buddhist temples.

While the Northern Wei controlled the North, other rulers controlled the South. Northern aristocratic families contributed to state building through their interest in Confucianism, while leading southern families were more focused on religion and the arts. Southerners seemed somewhat effete to northerners, but when the two regions reunited in 589, the blend of both styles led to a stronger and more cultured civilization. Each region was differently influenced by foreign cultures as well, stimulating intellectual inquiry and encouraging trade.

The hallmark of the period of political disunity was its cultural growth. At the beginning of the period, the incessant military struggles led many intellectuals to abandon public service. Why bother being a serious Confucian scholar in such times, many concluded, giving themselves up to hedonism and artistic performance, often simultaneously expressing itself in

---

equal-field system—Division of land to peasants, who tilled it, rather than to wealthy landholders; adopted in China, spread to Korea and Japan.

Huge Buddhist rock carvings (these are around 50 feet tall) were commissioned by the Northern Wei at the end of the fifth century. These large figures are part of a collection of thousands of carvings at Yungang in North China. They may have been inspired by earlier Buddhist carvings, recently destroyed by the Taliban in Afghanistan.

poetry or unconventional behavior. The Seven Sages of the Bamboo Grove were the most famous of many talented poets and although one was executed for scandalous behavior, they continue to be celebrated to this day.

Buddhism and Daoism emerged as more spiritual alternatives to Confucian government service. While Daoism had indigenous roots, Buddhism came to China as part of a great expansion of a universal religion. From its origins in India, Buddhism traveled along trade routes to China, bringing international (Greek, Afghan, and Indian) arts and ideas. Missionaries aided the transmission of Buddhism as did Chinese travelers like Faxian.

Buddhism provided comfort in times of crisis. Its promise of salvation (to all, including common people), special appeal to the supposed natural compassion of women and men, offer of monastic security to men in troubled times, and long incubation within Chinese culture all ensured its popularity. China's dominant form of Buddhism, Mahayana, focused on **bodhisattvas** (BOH-dee-SAHT-vahs), individuals who had achieved salvation but chose to postpone their release from the cycle of birth and rebirth in order to save others. Bodhisattvas were technically sexless beings (though identified in popular forms of religion as female) and transcended class and culture as well as gender. The notion of salvation through faith was developed in the **Pure Land** sect of Buddhism in the fourth century; this made Buddhism increasingly appealing to those not able to enter monastic life. Developments in the Tang dynasty would broaden Buddhism's appeal further.

Daoism was encouraged to enhance its dogma and organization by the rise of Buddhism. Like Buddhists, Daoists formed monastic communities and wrote scriptures, although many of these scriptures were kept hidden from non-Daoists, unlike the widely circulated Buddhist texts. Daoists were particularly important in the study of alchemy as a route to immortality; alchemy, in turn, led to scientific discoveries. Although challenged by native Daoism, scorned by some Confucian intellectuals, and periodically persecuted by rulers jealous of its strength, Buddhism ultimately won adherents throughout China. The monarchs of the North patronized Buddhism by building splendid temples and generously endowing monasteries. From the fourth to the ninth centuries, Buddhism interacted with Chinese religious and philosophical traditions to create a complex new synthesis of ideas and art.

The Sui dynasty (589–618), descended from the Northern Wei, presented themselves as Chinese defenders of Buddhism. Emperor Wendi (r. 581–604), the first Sui ruler, and his son Yangdi (r. 604–618) established an imperial military force and a land-based militia, centralized the administration, and revived the civil service system. Between 605 and 609, Yangdi built a great waterway, the Grand Canal, to link the rice-growing Yangzi basin with northern China; this helped to overcome regional differences. This canal eventually stretched 1200 miles and permitted some later governments to locate their seats of power in the less productive but strategically important North. Building this canal, in addition to a massive conscription of soldiers (over one million) to fight in Korea, took huge amounts of labor. Disgust with this exploitation led to numerous rebellions, and in 618 Yangdi's cousin overthrew the Sui. The new Tang dynasty, like the Sui, was a hybrid of North and South, Chinese and foreign.

---

bodhisattvas—In Mahayana Buddhism, an enlightened being who chooses to postpone salvation to aid others in reaching enlightenment.

Pure Land—A place for those saved by faith in the Amida Buddha.

Political Developments Under the Early Tang Dynasty, 618–756

During the first half of the Tang period, China attained a new pinnacle of glory. The first three emperors, Gaozu (GOW-dzuh; r. 618–626), Taizong (TAI-dzong; r. 626–649), and Gaozong (GOW-dzong; r. 650–683), subjugated Turkish Central Asia and conquered Annam (northern Vietnam). Tang cultural influence extended north to Manchuria, east to Korea and Japan, and south to parts of Southeast Asia. It controlled Central Asia all the way to Afghanistan during the seventh century and maintained extensive trade routes. Along with territorial expansion came a deepening of state power.

The legal code of 653 combined northern and southern legal traditions, and the reemphasized **examination system** recruited officials from all regions and, in theory, all classes. This system was based on Confucian texts that were, in principle, accessible to all men (women were not allowed to take the examinations), but in reality were more likely studied in families financially able to educate their sons. This bought the elite's loyalty and focused the ideology of those who wished to be rulers, who were selected by their answers on exams based on the Confucian classics, on a unified body of scholarship. Thus, although the expansion of the empire depended on the promotion of *wu* (military), its maintenance was even more dependent on its promotion of *wen* (civil arts). Though strong supporters of Buddhism, early Tang rulers elevated the principles of Confucianism to rule the state and to define its Chinese nature.

The era of growth and grandeur was marked by the extraordinary reign of the able Empress Wu (r. 690–705), a concubine of the second and third emperors, who controlled the government for 20 years after the latter's death, eliminating her political opponents and firmly establishing the Tang dynasty. She greatly weakened the old aristocracy by favoring Buddhism and strengthening the examination system for recruiting civil servants. Moreover, she decisively defeated the Koreans, making Korea a loyal vassal state. As a woman and a widow, she was considered a usurper and was later criticized by Chinese historians and politicians who emphasized her vices, particularly her many favorites and lovers. She was overthrown in 705. Her grandson, Emperor Xuanzong (SHWAHN-dzong; r. 712–756), was also known for his long reign filled with cultural growth.

Tang rulers perfected a highly centralized government, using a complex bureaucracy organized in specialized councils, boards, and ministries, all directly responsible to the emperor. Local government functioned under 15 provincial governors, aided by subordinates down to the district level. Military commanders supervised tribute collections in semiautonomous conquered territories. Officeholders throughout the empire were, by the eighth century, usually degree-holders from government schools and universities who had qualified by passing the regularly scheduled examinations. These scholar-bureaucrats were steeped in Confucian conservatism but were more efficient than the remaining minority of aristocratic hereditary officials. The Tang retained the nationalized land register under the equal-field system, designed to check the growth of large estates, guarantee land to peasants, and relate their land tenure to both their taxes and their militia service. Until well into the eighth century, when abuses began to appear, the system worked to merge the interests of state and people.

Tang Economic and Social Changes

The early Tang economy was extremely prosperous, supported by thriving cities and the always busy trade routes through Central Asia, along the southeastern coast, and up and down the Grand Canal. Economic productivity, both agricultural and industrial, rose steadily during the early Tang period. The introduction of tea and wet rice from Annam turned the Yangzi area into a vast irrigated food bank and the economic base for Tang power. Tea became a staple throughout China during the Tang. More food and rising population brought increasing manufactures. Population growth was most impressive in the south, where it increased form one-quarter of the realm's population in the early seventh century to half by 742. Chinese techniques in the newly discovered craft of papermaking, along with iron casting, porcelain production, and silk processing, improved tremendously and spread west to the Middle East.

Foreign trade and influence increased significantly under the Tang emperors in a development that would continue through the Song era (960–1279). Chinese control in Central Asia facilitated trade along the old overland silk route; but as porcelain became the most profitable export and could not be easily transported by caravan, it swelled the volume of sea trade through Southeast Asia. Most of this trade left from southern ports, particularly from Guangzhou (gwahng-JOH; Canton), where more than 100,000 non-Chinese Indians, Persians, Arabs, and Malays handled the goods. Foreign merchants were equally visible at Chang'an, the Tang capital and eastern terminus of the silk route. Chang'an, a planned city of 30 square miles, not counting the imperial palace, was the largest planned city in the world, and the most populous. The imperial palace at the north of the city was flanked on either side by a market. The "West Market" dealt in foreign goods, food, and wine and exhibited foreign entertainers and magi-

---

examination system—The selection of scholar-officials through examination in Confucian texts.

cians; the "East Market" was for domestic items. The city was vibrant, but it was also controlled, for Chang'an was planned on a grid, and every resident lived in a rectangular ward, surrounded by walls. The gate to the ward was locked at night.

Although largely state-controlled and aristocratic, Tang society was particularly responsive to new foreign stimuli, which it swiftly absorbed. A strongly pervasive Buddhism, a rising population, and steady urbanization fostered this cross-cultural exchange. Many city populations exceeded 100,000, and four cities had more than a million people. Their cosmopolitan residents enjoyed products from foreign lands, including luxury goods, musical instruments, and textiles. The foreign practice of sitting on chairs replaced sitting on floor mats. Hairstyles and games were adopted from abroad. Foreign religions, including Islam, Nestorian Christianity, Judaism, Zoroastrianism, and Manichaeism (MAN-ih-KEE-ism), were practiced freely by the thousands of international residents in Chang'an and Luoyang, though few Chinese converted to these religions as they had earlier to Buddhism. Merchants clearly benefited, but despite their wealth, they were still considered socially inferior. They often used their wealth to educate their sons for the civil service examination, thus promoting a rising class of scholar-bureaucrats. The latter, as they acquired land, gained status and power at the expense of the old aristocratic families. Conditions among artisans and the expanding mass of peasants improved somewhat, but life for them remained hard and precarious.

By the eighth century, Tang legal codes had imposed severe punishments for wifely disobedience or infidelity to husbands. New laws also limited women's rights to divorce, inheritance of property, and remarriage as widows. Women were, however, still active in the arts and literature. Although some wielded influence and power at royal courts, many were confined to harems. This subordinate position was partly balanced by the continued high status and authority of older women within families.

Class and education played an important role in women's status. Women poets were sought after by men of distinction, and one father of a poet, himself a writer of note, was promoted to a prestigious government position on the strength of his daughter's writing. Empress Wu wrote powerful poetry, some of it recalling her mother, some longing for her late husband, some expressing political ideas. Other women wrote of love and longing, military events, affairs at court, and a wide variety of topics. Not all Tang women poets were genteel. In a poem entitled "Getting It Off My Chest," Xu Yueying (SHOO yoo-eh-YING), a late Tang poet wrote: "I've broken the rules—obedience to father, husband, son. That's why I cry so much. This body? What way, what use to stick to what proper people do?"[5]

Fashions in female beauty change from place to place and over time. Figurines like this one of a mounted woman, possibly playing polo, show that physical activity and a plump physique were esteemed. This style also influenced standards of beauty in Korea and Japan at that time.

Tang Religion and Culture

Buddhism and Daoism blossomed alongside Confucian scholarship and government service. Poets, artists, architects, and painters were all inspired by religious as well as secular themes. Buddhism was particularly dynamic in the early Tang dynasty. Buddhist monasteries and temples educated children in their schools, rural temples gave lodging to travelers, and monasteries ran large-scale farms. Buddhist themes permeated folk tales. Most important, faith-based Buddhist sects, especially Pure Land, spread throughout China, offering peasants a route to salvation. Pure Land Buddhism was a vastly different form of devotion from the earlier sects that required years of good living and often many rebirths on earth before attaining salvation. **Chan** (Zen in Japanese) Buddhism developed in the Tang as well. Chan appealed more to the elite and focused on sudden enlightenment rather than scripture.

Chan—A form of Buddhism that seeks sudden enlightenment through techniques and rituals intended to quiet the mind. Known as Zen in Japan.

A fresh flowering of literature occurred during the early Tang period. It followed naturally from a dynamic society, but it was also furthered by the development of papermaking and the invention, in about 600, of block printing, which soon spread to Korea and Japan. Movable type, which would later revolutionize Europe, was little used in China during this period because it was less efficient in printing Chinese characters. Printing helped meet a growing demand for the religious and educational materials generated by Buddhism and the examination system.

Tang scholarship is best remembered for historical writing. Chinese of this period firmly believed that lessons from the past could be guides for the future. As an early Tang emperor noted, "By using a mirror of brass, you may . . . adjust your cap; by using antiquity as a mirror you may . . . foresee the rise and fall of empires."[6] In addition to universal works, the period produced many studies of particular subjects. History itself came under investigation, as illustrated by *The Understanding of History*, a work that stressed the need for analysis and evaluation in the narration of events. Writers produced works of all types, but poetry was the accepted medium, composed and repeated by emperors, scholars, singing courtesans, and common people in the marketplaces. Tang poetry was marked by ironic humor, deep sensitivity to human feeling, concern for social justice, and a near-worshipful love of nature. Two of the most famous among some 3000 recognized poets of the era were Li Bo (701–763; also known as Li Bai) and Du Fu (712–770). The former was an admitted lover of pleasure, especially of wine. A famous story about him is that during a drinking party on a lake, he leaned over the side of the boat in order to scoop out the moon and drowned. But he also had his philosophical side as seen in the following poem inspired by Daoism:

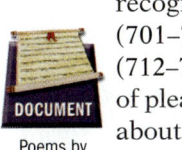
DOCUMENT
Poems by Li Bai (also known as Li Bo) and Du Fu

Zhuangzi in a dream
became a butterfly,
And the butterfly became
Zhuangzi at waking.
Which was the real, the
butterfly or the man?[7]

Du Fu, one of the great landscape poets, also wrote of suffering, especially suffering brought about by rebellions toward the end of his life.

The war-chariots rattle,
The war-horses whinny.
Each man of you has a bow and quiver at his
  belt. . . .
At the border where the blood of men spills like
  the sea—
And still the heart of Emperor Wu is beating for
  war. . . .
In thousands of villages, nothing grows but
  weeds,
And though strong women have bent to the
  ploughing,
East and west the furrows are all broken down
  . . .
It is very much better to have a daughter
Who can marry and live in the house of a
  neighbor,
While under the sod we bury our boys. . . .[8]

The Tang literary revival was paralleled by movements in painting and sculpture. The plastic arts, dealing with both religious and secular subjects, became a major medium for the first time in China. Small tomb statues depicted both Chinese and foreign life with realism, verve, and diversity. These figures—warriors, servants, and traders—were buried with the dead and believed to serve them in the afterlife. Religious statuary, even in Buddhist shrines, showed strong humanistic emphases, often juxtaposed with the naive sublimity of Buddhas carved in the Gandaran (Greek Hellenistic) style of northwestern India. Similar themes were developed in Tang painting, but the traditional preoccupation with nature prevailed in both the northern and southern landscape schools. The most famous Tang painter was Wu Daozi (WOO DOW-zuh), whose landscapes and religious scenes were produced at the court of the emperor Xuanzong in the early eighth century.

Tang Decline and the Transition to Premodern China

The cultural flowering of Xuanzong's reign was matched, in its early years, by vigorous and effective leadership. He fixed problems in the tax system, curbed the power of imperial relatives, and strengthened defenses against the Turks, Uighurs, and Tibetans. His method of strengthening border defenses by giving authority to commanders of military provinces backfired, however. One of these commanders, a protégé of the emperor's favorite concubine, Yang Guifei (YAHNG gwei-FAY), was doted on by the emperor to please his concubine. The commander, An Lushan, built up an army of 160,000 troops along the border, but then turned and marched on Chang'an and Luoyang in 755.

The aged emperor Xuanzong, while fleeing for his life from the capital, was forced by his troops to approve the execution of Yang Guifei, who was seen as having dominated him and his court. According to legend, he died of sorrow less than a month later. Yang

Document: Bo Juyi (772–846): "The Song of Everlasting Sorrow"

This poem by one of the late Tang dynasty's most respected poets recounts the love of Emperor Xuanzong and his beloved concubine, Yang Guifei, who was blamed by her contemporaries for the An Lushan Rebellion. Bo Juyi's poem was esteemed not only in China but also in Japan. Lady Murasaki cited it repeatedly in *The Tale of Genji*.

China's Emperor, craving beauty that might shake an empire,
Was on the throne for many years, searching, never finding,
Till a little child of the Yang clan, hardly even grown,
Bred in an inner chamber, with no one knowing her,
But with graces granted by heaven and not to be concealed,
At last one day was chosen for the imperial household.
If she but turned her head and smiled, there were cast a hundred spells,
And the powder and paint of the Six Palaces faded into nothing.
. . . There were other ladies in his court, three thousand of rare beauty,
But his favours to three thousand were concentered in one body.
. . . Her sisters and her brothers all were given titles;
And, because she so illumined and glorified her clan,
She brought to every father, every mother through the empire,
Happiness when a girl was born rather than a boy.
. . . The Emperor's eyes could never gaze on her enough—
Till war-drums, booming from Yuyang, shocked the whole earth
And broke the tunes of The Rainbow Skirt and the Feathered Coat.
The Forbidden City, the nine-tiered palace, loomed in the dust
From thousands of horses and chariots headed southwest.
The imperial flag opened the way, now moving and now pausing—
But thirty miles from the capital, beyond the western gate,
The men of the army stopped, not one of them would stir
Till under their horses' hoofs they might trample those moth-eyebrows.
Flowery hairpins fell to the ground, no one picked them up,
And a green and white jade hair-tassel and a yellow gold hair-bird.
The Emperor could not save her, he could only cover his face.
And later when he turned to look, the place of blood and tears
Was hidden in a yellow dust blown by a cold wind.
. . . And people were so moved by the Emperor's constant brooding
That they besought the Daoist priest to see if he could find her.
. . . He searched the Green Void, below, the Yellow Spring;
But he failed, in either place, to find the one he looked for.
And then he heard accounts of an enchanted isle at sea,
. . . And the lady, at news of an envoy from the Emperor of China,
Was startled out of dreams in her nine-flowered canopy.
. . . She took out, with emotion, the pledges he had given
And, through his envoy, sent him back a shell box and gold hairpin,
But kept one branch of the hairpin and one side of the box,
Breaking the gold of the hairpin, breaking the shell of the box;
Our souls belong together," she said, "like this gold and this shell—
Somewhere, sometime, on earth or in heaven, we shall surely meet."
. . . Earth endures, heaven endures; some time both shall end,
While this unending sorrow goes on and on for ever.

Questions to Consider

1. Why did the Emperor's soldiers execute Yang Guifei, and why was the Emperor unable to protect her?
2. What does this poem suggest about the role of women in the Emperor's court in the Tang?
3. Why was this poem loved not only in China but also throughout East Asia?

Excerpted from Bo Juyi (Po Chi-yi), "A Song of Unending Sorrow," in Cyril Birch, ed., *Anthology of Chinese Literature: From Early Times to the Fourteenth Century* (New York: Grove Press, 1965), pp. 266–269.

Guifei became a model of female perfidy, fueling misogynistic notions of women's control over men.

It took 8 years to put down An Lushan's rebellion, but the ensuing disruption was so extensive that the late Tang emperors never recovered their former power. In several key areas, military governors acted as independent rulers, paying no taxes to Chang'an. In the rest of China, the equal-field system was replaced with twice yearly taxation on the value of the land. This **two tax system** persisted for the next 700 years in China. Regions were allowed to fill their tax responsibilities as they wished with little government supervision. In addition, the government instituted salt, wine, and tea monopolies to raise revenues. Government receipts to merchants came to be used as a kind of currency, becoming the antecedent for paper money that was developed during the Song dynasty. Though private trade was stimulated by the government's declining economic role, government revenues declined, and taxes on peasants were raised. Falling revenues brought deterioration of the state education establishment and a corresponding drop in administrative efficiency. The government further alienated some groups by seizing Buddhist property and persecuting all "foreign" religions. Buddhism was suppressed in 841. Tens of thousands of monasteries and temples were destroyed and 250,000 monks and nuns were returned to lay life. Except for the popular sects of Pure Land and Chan, most other sects of Buddhism soon declined.

In response to the threat posed by autonomous regional commanders, the court created armies led by eunuchs, originally personal servants to the emperor or to his women's quarters. In time, these eunuchs gained their own power, manipulating and even murdering emperors and scholar-officials. Bandits and other gangs ravaged the country after 860. Chang'an was captured in 881, and the brutal warlord who took the city killed all the foreign residents. Chang'an would never again be capital of China. In 907, the pretense of Tang rule was ended.

Political Developments During the Song Era, 960–1279

For a half-century after the fall of the Tang dynasty, China experienced political division, at times approaching anarchy. During this period of five dynasties in the north and ten kingdoms in the south, attacks by "barbarian" raiders alternated with internal con-

two tax system—Twice yearly tax payment based on value of land rather than on output as under the earlier equal field system.

China expanded to the south, west, and north during the Tang dynasty. Northern Vietnam (Annam) and Turkish Central Asia came under Chinese control.

flicts among contending warlords. One military leader in the north—who reigned as Song Taizu (r. 960–76)—was finally able to unify all of China, founding the Song dynasty in 960. Taizu and his successors were never able to regain all the territories, however. Militarily powerful non-Chinese states bordered the Song, and the new rulers had to devise ways to keep them in check. Several were hybrid states, using Chinese methods of governance to rule over populations that included many Chinese immigrants. The Song responded by building a large military—their army had 1.25 million men by 1040—and producing large quantities of armaments. Military technology advanced as well; after using gunpowder to launch grenades, the Song invented the cannon. At the same time, scholar-officials were used to strengthen the centralizing power of the state. While this did help consolidate Song authority, in time excessive bureaucratization crept in, and rules and regulations began to impede creative governing.

Another consequence of the Song's strong focus on rule by scholar-officials was the rise of factionalism. As the state experienced mounting budgetary deficits and confronted peasant unrest, the emperor Shenzong (SHEN-dzhong; r. 1067–1085) called on an eminent statesman, Wang Anshi (WAHNG ahn-SHUH), to resolve these difficulties. Wang sponsored a thoroughgoing—and therefore threatening—reform program that granted interest-bearing agricultural loans to peasants, fixed commodity prices, provided unemployment benefits, established old-age pensions, converted labor service to monetary taxes, mobilized local militias, increased the number of schools, and reformed the examination system by stressing practical rather than literary knowledge. Although these measures brought some improvements, they evoked fanatical opposition from scholars, bureaucrats, and moneylenders. The internal debate resembled that of more than 1000 years earlier (the Salt and Iron Debates of the Han dynasty) over the propriety of the government's involvement in the economy. In the next generation most of Wang Anshi's reforms were rescinded.

Song ministers faced continuous threats along their northern and western frontiers. To placate their neighbors, the Liao (around Beijing) and the Xia (in the northwest), the Song paid them annual tribute payments in silk and silver. These payments indicated Song subordination or at least a desire for peace. In 1115, the Jurchen, a nomadic people from Manchuria, challenged the Liao. Believing the Jurchen would be good allies against their old rivals in Liao, the Song made a pact with them to divide Liao. Soon the alliance broke apart, and the Jurchen took the Song capital at Kaifeng (kai-FUHNG) in 1126. Ruling northern China, the Jurchen became increasingly sinified, ruling according to Chinese ways and intermarrying with Chinese. The Song court fled in panic to Nanjing and later set up a new capital at Hangzhou (hahng-JOH), thus bringing to an end the Song effort to govern a realm united from north to south. The period from 960 to 1127 is often called the Northern Song, and that from 1127 to 1279 the Southern Song.

After a decade of indecisive war, a treaty in 1142 stipulated that the Song had to pay tribute of silk and silver to the Jurchen whose new dynasty was called Jin (1115–1234). It also prescribed that the Jin monarch be addressed as "lord" and the Song emperor as "servant" in all official communications. The subordination of the Song was thus formalized in language and in tribute payments.

Despite these disasters, the Song rulers enjoyed somewhat better economic conditions. The country experienced unprecedented economic and cultural advances, particularly after its territory was reduced to only southern China, and it turned increasingly toward using the many canals and streams throughout the South to move products. In addition, trade with the Jin state continued as before. One and a half centuries later, a new band of Central Asian nomads, the Mongols, conquered the Jin and went on to take

Tang, Song, and Yuan China

618–907	Tang dynasty
c. 690–705	Reign of Empress Wu
701–763	Poet Li Bo
712–756	Cultural flowering under Emperor Xuanzong
712–770	Poet Du Fu
755–763	An Lushan Rebellion
960–1279	Song dynasty
1005, 1042	Song sign treaties of subordination with Liao and Xia
1019–1086	Sima Guang, historian
1067–1085	Emperor Shenzong and Wang Anshi Reforms
1126–1134	Jin dynasty established in north
1162–1227	Chinggis becomes Mongol Khan (Supreme King)
1260–1294	Khubilai becomes Khan
1279–1368	Yuan dynasty

all of the Southern Song. From 1279 to 1368, China was ruled by Mongols who established a dynasty they called Yuan.

Song Economic and Social Conditions

Economic growth was rapid. Agricultural growth sustained a population that doubled between 750 and 1100. Farmers used their surpluses to buy charcoal, tea, and wine. Many raised and sold silk, sugar, vegetables, cotton, fruit, and wood products. The government maintained some monopolies, taxed trade moderately, built great water-control projects, and aided intensive agriculture, but otherwise loosened control over individual enterprise. Rice production doubled within a century after 1050, and industry grew rapidly, pouring out, for home and foreign markets, fine silk, lacquer wares, porcelain, and paper for writing, books, money and wrapping gifts. Heavy industry, especially iron, grew rapidly, and was used for tools, suspension bridges, and nails for construction. Song economic advances were furthered by such technical innovations as water clocks, explosives for mining, hydraulic machinery, paddleboats, seagoing junks, the stern post rudder, and the mariner's compass. These commercial developments were paralleled by the development of an oceangoing navy. The resulting commercial expansion prompted banks to depend on paper currency and specialized commercial instruments. Trade with the outside world, formerly dominated by Indians and Southeast Asians, was taken over by the Chinese, who established trading colonies throughout East Asia.

The Song economic revolution exerted tremendous foreign influence abroad. Paper money, dating from the eleventh century in the south, was soon copied in the Liao state and issued by the Jin government in 1153; its use then spread steadily in all directions. Other Song economic innovations appeared quickly in coastal areas from Japan and Korea to the East Indies, where Chinese merchants were immigrant culture carriers. Song technology also spread to India, the Middle East, and even Europe. From China, Europe acquired metal horseshoes, the padded horse collar, and the wheelbarrow. Chinese mapping skills, along with the compass and the stern post ship rudder, helped prepare the way for Europe's age of expansion. Later, gunpowder and movable type, both pioneered in Song China, arrived in Europe via Asian intermediaries.

Profound and rapid change brought many tensions to Song society. Some arose from urban expansion in a population that swelled from 60 to 115 million, a growth rate of more than twice the world average. A rise in population unaccompanied by a rise in the number of officials meant that passing the exams to enter officialdom became increasingly, and frustratingly, difficult. On the other hand, life was dynamic and cosmopolitan. Cities offered residents and travelers alike access to international culture, restaurants, plays, artwork, and civic organizations. Rural life was far less exciting, but farmers could go to regularly scheduled rural markets and read printed books published on a variety of topics, including agriculture, rituals, and childbirth. The spread of books and literacy created a national culture that transcended the localism of most rural societies. Unlike Europe, cities were not islands of merchant liberation in a rural sea of aristocratic domination; rather, scholar-officials ruled everywhere. Merchants did not have power, although they could take the exams to enter the scholarly class.

Women's lives were varied though lacking in power. While lively physical activity had been encouraged in the Tang—as evidenced in art work showing women playing vigorous sports like polo—a more demure and modest demeanor was expected of women in the Song. To be sure, the extant records of the Song show women who ran inns, delivered babies as midwives, worked as entertainers, sold their sewing and weaving, wrote poetry, and served as shamans (religious mediums). As wives and mothers, women had a voice in childrearing and spouse selection for their children, despite Confucian ideas that called for women to take a back seat to men in the family. Court records in inheritance cases indicate that judges made sure that daughters received money for dowries by which they could make more successful marriages. The availability of a great number of printed materials opened doors to literature for women of educated families.

At the same time, however, the resurgence of Confucian thinking reinforced a view that demure and even physically weak women were attractive. Women were told to be modest, which limited their public role, and footbinding carried this injunction to an extreme. Begun by dancers in the tenth century, the tight binding of a little girl's feet till they were broken, bent, and ideally just three inches long came to be a symbol both of beauty and of a girl's modesty and refinement. Bound feet attracted better marriage prospects but did little to expand girls' horizons. Though it began in the Song, footbinding was still uncommon at that time and was never mentioned by the Song's greatest woman poet, Li Qingzhao (LEE ching-JOW; 1094–1152). Female infanticide, restriction on remarriage of widows, and harsh legal penalties, including death, for violating the accepted code of prescribed wifely conduct were also Song social phenomena. Women were told to put their families first, but so, too, were men. All family members were under the rule of the patriarchal (male) family head,

Song Philosophy, Literature, and Art

The rapidly changing Song society was reflected in its philosophy, literature, and art. Poets wrote of people's inner lives, joys, and misfortunes. Song aesthetic expression encouraged versatility; as during the later European Renaissance, the universal man, public servant, scholar, poet, or painter was the ideal. Song's most famous woman poet, Li Qingzhao, whose work was enthusiastically promoted by her scholar husband, wrote personalized verse describing the early years of her marriage in which she and her husband engaged in lively intellectual discussions. Su Shi (1037–1101) was a northern Song poet who excelled in painting and calligraphy as well as writing. Writing his poems on his paintings, he combined the three arts of the Confucian gentleman-scholar in a single work. In another genre, Sima Guang (SUH-muh GWAHNG; 1019–1086) was an outstanding Confucian historian. Known for his bitter attacks on his contemporary Wang Anshi, he also was an astute observer of the past, looking to it for moral guidance, and a critic of those who misread historical sources. Artists depicted the beauty of nature in widely varied styles, all involving great attention to detail. Landscapes embraced all of nature in a single work, removing humans from the central position they had had in earlier works. Darker tones and sharper lines replaced the decorative lightness of Tang works. The greatest Song landscape painter was Fan Kuan (FAHN KWAHN; active 990–1020).

Buddhism lost its appeal to Song's rulers as it was associated with their Liao, Xia, and Jin rivals, all of whom were ardent Buddhists. Confucianism, as a result, had a revival. The brothers Cheng Hao (1032–1085) and Cheng Yi (1033–1108) developed metaphysical approaches to Confucianism. They asserted that *li* (principle or pattern) was inherent in all things. *Qi* (CHEE; material force or energy) gives substance to things for which *li* is the blueprint. Mencius's contention that humans are fundamentally good (see Chapter 2) was always hard to explain in light of people's bad behavior. The Song **"Neo-Confucians"** could now claim that humankind's blueprint *(li)* was good but *qi* was sometimes impure and in need of cleaning. The Cheng brothers' most important follower was Zhu Xi (JOO SHEE; 1130–1200). His White Deer Grotto Academy was one of many that trained students in new approaches to Confucianism. He differed from the Chengs by ascribing greater importance to *li* over *qi* and by positing the existence of a Supreme Ultimate to which all *li* was connected. Zhu Xi contended that self-cultivation required the extension of knowledge, best achieved by the "investigation of things." In time, Neo-Confucianism was identified with Zhu Xi's philosophy, though it had many varieties and proponents.

The Song renaissance in scholarship was accompanied by significant advances in the experimental and applied sciences. Chinese doctors introduced inoculation against smallpox, and their education and hospital facilities surpassed anything in the West. In addition, there were notable achievements in astronomy, chemistry, zoology, botany, cartography, and algebra.

The Yuan Dynasty (1279–1368)

The Mongol conquest of the Song followed three-quarters of a century of Mongol growth and expansion in Central and Western Asia. The Mongol Khubilai's (1215–1294) takeover of the southern Song in 1279 furthered China's position as the center of Eurasia. Thus, although the Mongol era was a short dynasty despised by many Chinese and having a relatively minor impact on Chinese culture, it played a very significant role in world history. More than during the

This Song landscape painting, Snow Mountain and Forest, *was painted by the artist Fan Kuan.*

Neo-Confucianism—Metaphysical form of Confucianism developed by the Cheng brothers and Zhu Xi; later became the dominant form of Confucianism throughout East Asia.

Song dynasty, with its lively international trade, and the early Ming, with its unprecedented maritime explorations, during the Yuan the five main areas of Eurasia—China, Southeast Asia, South Asia, Central Asia, and Europe—were part of a single world trading system. Europe was able to acquire Asian goods at low cost during this period; thus, when the Ming drove the Mongols out of China in 1368 and the Turks came to dominate western Asian trade routes, Europeans were inspired to seek maritime access to Asia. This, in turn, led to Europe's encounter with the Americas. Therefore, the brief Mongol period has an importance that belies both its brevity and its very limited demographic extent (the total Mongol population of about 1.5 million ruled over 100 times as many non-Mongols). Some background on earlier Central Asian tribes is helpful to understand the rise of the Mongols.

An earlier precedent for invasions out of Central Asia came from the Turkic peoples, who had figured in Eurasian history for a thousand years before the emergence of the Mongols. Between the sixth and eighth centuries, Turkic and Chinese regimes competed for control of the steppes. With Chinese support, the first Turkish Empire emerged in 552 and extended its dominion over much of Central Asia before it was conquered by the early Tang emperors. (An Lushan was of Turkish background.) During and after their imperial expansion, the Turks absorbed and transmitted much of the culture from their more advanced neighbors. Trade, religion, and warfare facilitated the process. Eastern Turks borrowed early from China, adopting Buddhism and converting their western kinsmen in far distant Ferghana. After the eighth century, when the Abbasid caliphate brought Islam to the steppes, Turkic invaders launched conquests in the Middle East and India. Through the fifteenth century, there were waves of migration and conquest out of Central Asia and into the settled territories of Eurasia. Such incursions usually brought short-term disaster to occupied regions, but effected a great synthesis of peoples and cultures and ultimately led to the establishment of Turkic regimes from India to the Middle East.

For more than five centuries before the Mongol conquests, this process had been growing in intensity. Westward and to the north of the Chinese frontiers, a series of large states, partially settled but still containing nomadic or seminomadic populations, rose and fell. Among them were the Uighur Empire of the ninth century and the Tangut state. Both of these regimes prospered by providing goods, protection, and transport for the overland trade with China, which continued to grow. For many peoples of Central Asia—Turks, Uighurs, Tanguts, Tibetans, Mongols, and a host of others—trade, especially the silk trade, was one of many stimuli that turned their attention toward the outside world in the thirteenth century.

Debate continues over what sparked Mongol expansion: climatic changes that ruined Mongol pasture lands, military capability, or the inspiration of an ambitious warlord. The Mongols, horse- and sheep-raising nomads and formidable mounted warriors, began conquering cities and trade routes in the early

Two views of Mongols as seen by their contemporaries. Left is a Persian miniature showing Mongols preparing food at their tents. Right is a Chinese painting of a mounted Mongol archer. Tents and horses were critical elements of Mongol life and status. The Mongol khans gave tents and horses as gifts to honor their subordinates and Central Asian horses were in great demand in China and Japan. In Central Asian culture a warrior was, by definition, a horseman.

thirteenth century on the way to establishing an empire that controlled most of Eurasia a century later. Beginning with Temujin, known in the West as Chinggis (1162–1227), who was selected Great Khan (Supreme King) in 1206, they claimed that they were destined by "heaven" to subdue all peoples. Chinggis was likely motivated to begin his quest for power to avenge his father's death. The Mongols were remarkably successful in launching large-scale military operations throughout Eurasia. They seized Persia, toppled the Islamic Abbasid caliphate in Baghdad, established their rule in Russia, and sacked Delhi, though they made no further inroads into India before moving on to China. From North China, they invaded Korea (1231 and 1258) and attempted unsuccessfully to invade Japan (1274 and 1281) and Java (1281 and 1292).

The Mongols have often been represented as destroyers par excellence, sacking cities, disrupting trade, and building towers of the heads of their conquered foes. The Mongols often used terror to control conquered peoples, particularly during the early conquests. Mongol commanders regularly imposed mass murder, torture, and resettlement on resisting populations. One million residents of the Chinese city of Chengdu (chuhng-DOO) were slaughtered in 1236 although that city had already been taken with little fighting. But Mongol presence also facilitated trade and diplomatic activity by providing security and postal service on Eurasian trade routes.

The Mongols Before the Conquest of the Song

Prior to their expansion in the early thirteenth century, Mongols had ranged widely in Central Asia, pitching their black felt tents, pasturing their animals, and fighting the elements much like other peoples who had raided and traded with settled Eurasian populations since the fourth century B.C.E. Mongol chiefs contended to be the "first among equals," decisions were made by councils of warriors, and women enjoyed a high degree of respect and influence. Polygamy was practiced among the warriors, but not all marriages were polygamous, and marital fidelity was enforced equally for men and women. Wives sometimes rode and fought beside their husbands; in a harsh environment where raiding and warfare were common, women as well as men had sometimes to defend the hearth and livestock.

At the opening of the thirteenth century, the Mongols began their campaign of conquests and empire building. Within less than a century, they had subdued most populations from the Pacific to the Caspian Sea,

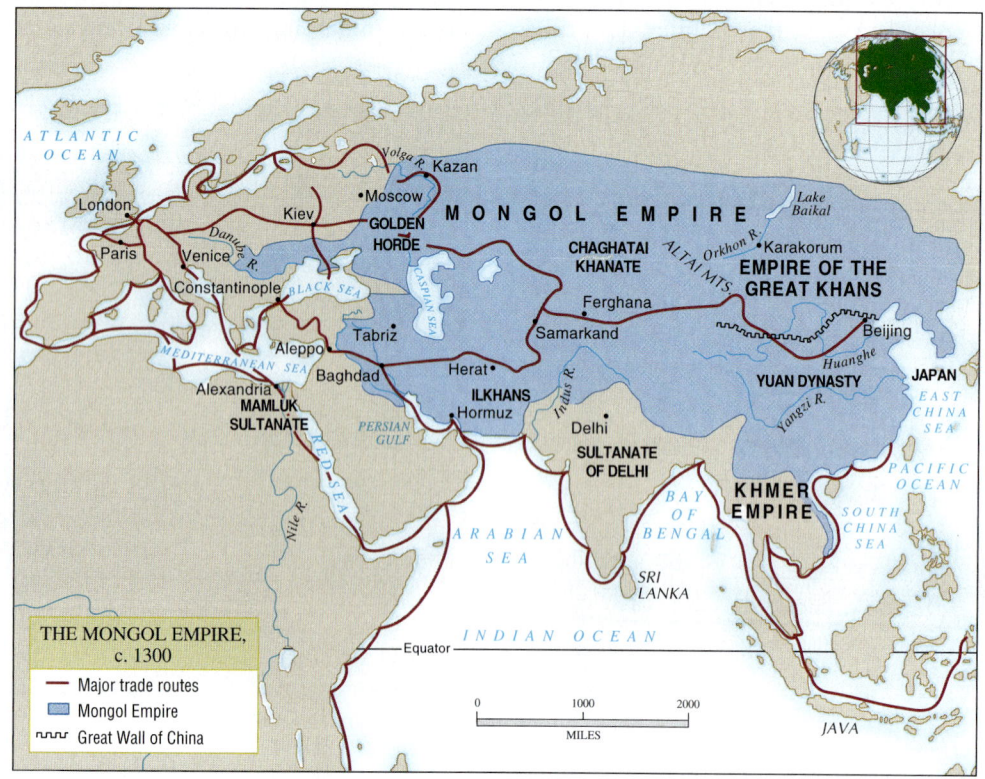

The Mongols extended their hegemony over a major part of Eurasia from the Danube to the Pacific from the mid-thirteenth to the mid-fourteenth centuries.

terrorized the rest, and gained luxuries beyond their imaginings. Trade and travel across Eurasia were facilitated. In most cases, however, they left a light cultural footprint. While the population of China did, indeed, decline from 120 million in 1207 to 60 million in 1290 (after the Mongol conquest), the cultural effects were less drastic. Chinese religion, painting, poetry, and social structure were not touched by the Mongols. Tolerance for foreign religions was promoted, but few Chinese changed their religious beliefs because of the presence of new sects.

During the first stage of their empire building, to 1241, the Mongols concentrated on the Central Asian steppe and its less developed border areas. Chinggis subordinated the Uighurs and Tanguts, seized Turkestan and Afghanistan, and invaded Persia. After his death in 1227, the campaigns halted and the Mongol forces reassembled in Mongolia to elect Chinggis's designated successor, his son Ögödei (EU-guh-dai; 1229–1241). Ögödei was granted Mongolia, from which he took the Jin Empire in northern China in 1234.

Between 1251 and 1259, during the reign of Ögödei's son, Möngke (MUHNG-kuh), Mongol armies conquered eastern Tibet (1252) and Korea (1259) while Möngke's brother, Hülegü (hoo-LEH-goo), toppled the Abbasid caliphate, absorbing every subsidiary state in Persia, Palestine, and Syria. Hülegü's campaign reflected the cosmopolitan nature of the Mongol army, with its Chinese catapult operators, and its court, with its Chinese physicians. The Mongols integrated the commanders, bureaucrats, artisans, and professionals of the conquered peoples into their armies and courts, thereby enhancing their ability to conquer and govern through borrowing the best practices of the conquered people.

Khubilai Khan (r. 1260–1294) emerged as dominant following a struggle from power among Mongol kings in 1260. After 1264 the empire broke up into four parts with only nominal central administration: Mongolia and China under Khubilai; and three other khanates in western Turkestan, Russia, and Persia and Iraq.

Mongol rulers of the mid-thirteenth century were forced to learn quickly how to organize and operate the largest imperial state that had ever existed. Although the ultimate base of authority in the sprawling Mongol territories was military power whose nucleus was a cavalry force of potentially 130,000 Mongols, civil administration and taxation were necessary. They developed a complex courier system linking the empire and created a written form of their language by using the script of the conquered Uighur people to transmit messages and records. The nomadic methods of the steppes were obviously no longer effective and had to be integrated with those of more experienced conquered bureaucrats.

Khubilai Khan hunting with his wife or a consort in a scroll painted in the late thirteenth century. Mongol women and men were expected to be vigorous and talented equestrians.

Before the conquest of the Song dynasty, Möngke revised the law code of Chinggis Khan to accommodate native cultural differences and meet practical needs. He minted coins, issued paper currency, collected taxes in money, and perfected a census system as a basis for taxes and military service. To support military operations, his state industries mined ores and produced arms. Other measures regularized trade tolls, improved roads, and provided for the safety of travelers, especially merchants. These reforms encouraged support from subject peoples, many of whom were now employed in the khan's service. Other areas were under lighter Mongol control. In these, local rulers proclaimed their submission publicly, left hostages with the khans, paid annual tribute, and provided troops for military campaigns. Such tributary rulers who served the khans loyally were guaranteed political security, honored publicly, and rewarded with lavish gifts (e.g., horses, daggers, furs, or silk garments).

China Under the Yuan Dynasty

Khubilai, who reigned as Great Khan from 1260 to 1294, turned his sights to the conquest of the Southern Song. After moving his capital to Beijing in 1264, he adopted a Chinese name for his dynasty in 1271. Like other Central Asian rulers who sought power in the east, Khubilai relied heavily on the advice of his Chinese and non-Chinese sinified advisors. One Song general offered advice on the construction of boats capable of navigating the many rivers and canals of South China. Khubilai, who had relied on cavalry and massive armies for his earlier conquests, thus became the first Central Asian conqueror of South China. Making use of a multiethnic force of Jurchen, Mongols, Persians, Uighurs, Koreans, and Chinese, Khubilai's forces laid siege to the Song. When the Yuan conquered all of China in 1279, Khubilai had gained the richest empire on earth. But even as he gained the wealth of China, the Mongol Empire had already ceased to be a unified Asian empire. Each of the four major khanates had developed its own state, and these were often at odds with one another. Though it is inaccurate to consider the Mongol realm a single political entity, the Mongol bonds of the khanates facilitated trade across the numerous Central Asian routes. Moreover, Turks and other West-Central Asians who had tried to take advantage of the commercial caravans themselves were suppressed during this period, making transport cheaper and easier.

Life under the Mongols was hard for most Chinese. While the Mongols did not prevent Chinese cultural expression, they did treat ethnic Chinese as distinctly inferior. A hierarchy dominated by foreigners was established: Mongols at the top, other peoples of Central Asia on the next rung, northern Chinese in lower positions, and southern Chinese almost completely excluded from office or public life. Taxation of Chinese was high. Many southern Chinese were subjected to serfdom or slavery. Though Khubilai retained the traditional ministries and local governmental structure, he staffed them with those in higher hierarchical positions. Generally, Mongol law prevailed, but the conquerors were often influenced by Chinese legal precedents, as in the acceptance of brutal punishments for loose or unfaithful women. Most religions were tolerated unless they violated Mongol laws.

According to Marco Polo, a Venetian traveler who arrived at Khubilai's court around 1275 and served the Khan for 17 years, the ethnic Chinese deeply resented unequal treatment. On the other hand, Polo also noted that the state insured against famine, kept order, and provided care for the sick, the aged, and the orphaned. To the awed Venetian, the Yuan state appeared fabulously wealthy, as indicated by the khan's 12,000 personal retainers, bedecked in silks, furs, fine leathers, and sparkling jewels.⁹ Polo's fabulous story, dictated to a fellow prisoner of war in Genoa, reported the wondrous world of Cathay (China)—its canals, granaries, social services, technology, and such customs (strange to much of Europe) as regular bathing. Polo's account, like many travelogues of the period, is an interesting mix of fact and fantasy based on impressionistic observations and probably prompted by the desire to entertain as well as inform a specific audience. Polo was not the only observer of China, but his work at the court gave him an unusual vantage point.

DOCUMENT
Marco Polo on Chinese Society

The Yuan court's social practices, in addition to the discriminatory ethnic hierarchy, included the requirement that individuals register by occupation in order to pay labor services. In the realm of culture, the Yuan borrowed some Chinese traditions. At first, Daoism and Confucianism were subordinated to Buddhism, but both were revived during Khubilai's reign. The examination system was sporadically revived after 1315 but was weighted in favor of Mongols, so ethnic Chinese grew disillusioned. Chinese drama remained popular, influenced somewhat by the dance of Central Asia. Interest in drama encouraged the development of classical Chinese opera, a combination of singing, dancing, and acting, which reached maturity in the Yuan period. Some of the most influential Chinese painters were also producing at this time, and the novel emerged as a reflection of Chinese concerns. An example is *Romance of the Three Kingdoms*, a long and rambling tale set in late Han times but written in the fourteenth century.

During the Yuan dynasty, hosts of missionaries, traders, and adventurers continued to journey to and from Asia, Africa, and Europe. These travelers describe the opulence of China and the Mongol court. Even before the Polos, Christian missionaries had proceeded eastward, encouraged by hopes of converting the Mongols and, more important, gaining allies against the Muslims. John of Plano Carpini (PLAH-noh car-PEE-nee), dispatched by Pope Innocent IV, visited the Great Khan in 1246 but failed to convert the ruler or enlist him as a papal vassal. In fact, the khan sent him home with a letter demanding that Europe's monarchs submit to him and that the pope attend the khan's court to pay homage. Later, a Flemish Franciscan, William of Rubruck, visited Möngke's court in 1254 and 1255 and met with similar results; but another Franciscan, John of Monte Corvino, attracted thousands of converts to Christianity between his arrival in Beijing in 1289 and his death in 1322. Meanwhile, Mongol religious toleration had drawn Christians into Central Asia and Buddhists into the Middle East.

In addition to the missionaries, swarms of other people visited China and Mongolia. One was Guillaume Boucier, a Parisian architect, who trekked to Karakorum, where he constructed a palace fountain capable of dispensing four different alcoholic beverages. Other adventurers, equally distinct, moved continuously on the travel routes. Between 1325 and 1354, Ibn Battuta, the famous Muslim globetrotter from Morocco, visited Constantinople, every Middle Eastern Islamic state, India, Sri Lanka, Indonesia, and China. In Hangzhou he encountered a man from

Discovery Through Maps

Gog and Magog in the Ebstorf Mappamundi

Maps depict more than geographical observations; they tell us the beliefs and imaginings of the people who produce them and reflect the point of view of the mapmaker. Historically, when people lacked a clear picture of far-off lands, they employed fantastic stories to describe what lay beyond their own known world. Like myths and folktales, maps from different eras illustrate some of the ways that societies have imagined apparently "strange" or "foreign" lands. We have seen that there was considerable commercial and intellectual exchange among Europe, India, China, and Central Asia in the years 220–1350 C.E. Nonetheless, the "Orient" remained a mysterious place in the imagination of many Westerners, a sometimes frightening place inhabited by strange creatures.

The thirteenth-century Ebstorf Mappamundi (map of the world), discovered in a Benedictine monastery in Germany, presents a geographical vision that combines Christian historiography, geographical observation, biblical mythology, the legends of Alexander the Great, and ancient tales of beastlike races inhabiting the "ends of the earth." It incorporates the idea of Gog and Magog, the homelands of apocalyptic destroyers, drawn from the New Testament (Revelation 20:7–8), into the description of the territory of northeastern Asia, the Mongol territory to the north of the Caucasus Mountains. On medieval Christian maps Gog and Magog were equated with barbarian races, with the Ten Lost Tribes of Israel, and with the armies of the Anti-Christ. According to legend, these ferocious peoples had been trapped by Alexander the Great, who built a great wall to contain them; they would break out at the end of time and overwhelm civilized societies. On the Ebsdorf map the people of Gog and Magog are tribes of savages who are shown eating human body parts and drinking blood. They are walled off in the far northeast of the world. Their identification with the Tartars suggests the fear of Turco-Mongol invaders that pervaded the mapmaker's society in the thirteenth century. Given the striking success of the Mongols' conquests in this era, it is no wonder that they came to be associated with Gog and Magog. Gog and Magog also appear on the twelfth-century Islamic world map of al-Idrīsī (see Chapter 7).

Questions to Consider

1. Why might medieval Europeans have imagined that a "hero" like Alexander the Great put a wall around such fearsome peoples?
2. Do you think the mapmakers took the idea of Gog and Magog literally? Why or why not?
3. What other examples do you know reflecting ideas about frightful peoples that live in far-off lands or about terrible events occurring at the "end of time?"

Morocco whom he had met before in Delhi. Some travelers went the opposite way. Rabban Sauma, a monk from Central Asia, traveled to Paris; and a Chinese Christian monk from Beijing, while in Europe as an envoy from the Persian khan to the pope, had audiences with the English and French kings.

Eurasian traders—Persians, Arabs, Greeks, and western Europeans—were numerous and worldly wise travelers. They were enticed by Mongol policies that lowered tolls in the commercial cities and provided special protection for merchants' goods. Land trade between Europe and China, particularly in silk and spices, increased rapidly in the fourteenth century. The main western terminals were Nizhni Novgorod, east of Moscow, where the China caravans made contact with merchants of the Hanseatic League, a coalition of German merchant companies; Tabriz, in northeastern Persia, which served as the eastern terminal for Constantinople; and the Syrian coastal cities, where the caravans met Mediterranean ships, mostly from Venice.

Expanding land trade along the old silk route did not diminish the growing volume of sea commerce. Indeed, the Mongol devastation of Middle Eastern cities provided a quick stimulus, particularly to the spice trade, which was partly redirected through the Red Sea and Egypt to Europe. Within a few decades, however, the Mamluk monopoly in Egypt drove prices up sharply, and the European demand for cheaper spices helped revive overland trade. By now, however, the southern sea route was thriving for other reasons. The Mongol conquest of China had immediately opened opportunities to Japanese and Malayan sea merchants, causing a modest commercial revolution. Later, after the government in China stabilized and became involved in the exchange, the volume of ocean trade between northeastern Asia and the Middle East surpassed that of Song times.

Although their conquests were accompanied by horrifying slaughter and wrought considerable havoc, Mongol control also spread knowledge of explosives, printing, medicine, shipbuilding, and navigation from China to the West. In the Middle East they furthered art, architecture, and historical writing. To China they brought Persian astronomy and ceramics, in addition to sorghum, a new food from India.

In the end, the Yuan dynasty was short-lived. Khubilai was its last effective leader. A powerful chancellor attempted to build a new canal to transport southern grain after the Yellow River burst its dikes in the 1340s, but his conscription of 150,000 laborers strained China's resources. In response, a messianic religion, the **White Lotus Society,** claimed numerous adherents anxious for Maitreya, the messiah Buddha, to bring about an end to suffering and injustice. Devastating epidemics hit cities already weakened by Mongol subjection; in 1232, Kaifeng lost one million people to the plague in three months. By mid-century, plague ravaged China and spread via the trade routes to the rest of Eurasia. A great rebellion, beginning in southern China and led by Zhu Yuanzhang (JOO yoo-ahn-JAHNG; 1328–1398)—known to history as Taizu, the first emperor of the Ming dynasty—ultimately ended the weakened Yuan. After the Chinese reconquered most of Mongolia and Manchuria, many northern Mongols reverted to nomadism. Others, on the western steppes, were absorbed into Turkic states.

KOREA: FROM THREE KINGDOMS TO ONE

■ *How did Buddhism and Confucianism contribute to Korean culture and politics?*

In the third century C.E. the land inhabited by modern Koreans was divided in three kingdoms—one in the north and two in the south. Despite the common stereotype of Korea as an isolated "hermit kingdom," these three kingdoms were very much part of East Asian international culture. They adopted religion, arts, philosophy, and means of governance from China, transmitted culture and material goods to Japan, and fought battles against and in alliance with Chinese and Japanese rulers at various times. The fate of Koreans was closely integrated with the rise and fall of empires on the continent. By the fourteenth century, domestic and international influences led to the merger of the Korean kingdoms into one kingdom.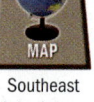

Southeast Asia, Japan, and Korea

According to legend, Ko Chosŏn (KOH CHO-son), the earliest kingdom of Korea, was established in the third millennium B.C.E., but bronze age remnants date it from about 1500 B.C.E. Archaeological remains show that Koreans grew millet, soybeans, red beans, and rice; used ploughs and knives; developed metallurgy; and had an animistic form of religion in which all natural objects had spirits. Labor became specialized into peasant and artisan categories. In 109 B.C.E., this productive territory attracted the attention of the Han dynasty in China. Emperor Wudi conquered Ko Chosŏn and established four Chinese provincial commanderies in the north, permitting the introduction of Chinese culture. The decline of the Han allowed the newly arising Korean states to push the Chinese out and compete for dominance.

Koguryŏ (KOH-goo-ree-oh) was founded in 37 B.C.E. and by the first century C.E. had adopted a Chi-

---

White Lotus Society—Messianic religion that blended Manichaeism, Maitreya Buddhism, Daoism, and Confucianism. Appealed to people in times of crisis.

Korea

57 B.C.E.	Silla established
37 B.C.E.	Koguryŏ established
200s C.E.	Paekche established
383	Buddhism adopted in Korea
668	Silla defeats Paekche and Koguryŏ, unites Korea
936–1392	Koryŏ dynasty
1238	Mongol Invasion

nese style of kingship. Free peasants, living in villages under headmen, formed the bulk of society. Legal codes punished murder, theft, and bodily injury as well as female (though not male) adultery and jealousy—underscoring the importance of life and property in addition to the centrality of the polygamous, patriarchal family. The rise of the southern state of Paekche (PAIK-cheh) in the third century led Koguryŏ to strengthen its institutions: Koguryŏ's King Sosurim (r. 371–384) adopted Buddhism, set up a National Confucian Academy, and developed an administrative law code, all of which made Koguryŏ a centralized aristocratic state. In 433 Paekche formed an alliance with Silla (SHIL-lah; founded 57 B.C.E.), the other southern state. Koguryŏ fought against its Korean neighbors, sometimes in alliance with Chinese or Japanese forces. Koguryŏ was a powerful kingdom, later launching attacks on the Sui in China. (Its victories against the Sui army are part of the Korean annals of resistance.)

All three kingdoms were culturally Buddhist; Paekche adopted Buddhism in 384 and Silla in 528. Their poetry and arts followed Buddhist themes. Because most buildings were made of wood, none remain, but paintings and sculpture from this period, many with religious themes, are plentiful. A major **pagoda** (the East Asian form of the stupa) was built in Silla in 645, and lasted till it was destroyed by the Mongols in the thirteenth century.

Silla began to assert its power in the fifth century. Silla had an aristocratic society in which officials' positions were determined by "bone-rank" (that is, one's bloodline or status). Officials met in the Council of Nobles, and young men were placed in the Flower of Youth Corps, a powerful military organization. Silla allied with the Tang to defeat Koguryŏ and Paekche in the 660s, but, worried about Tang expansionism, Silla decided to push the Tang out of the Korean peninsula in 676. Lively trade between Silla and the Tang ensued, taking the place of conquest. Koreans were drawn into the international system promoted by the Tang; a Silla general in service to the Tang conquered Tashkent and Silla monks traveled to India. The eighth century, in which Pure Land Buddhism and Zen were introduced to Korea and the agricultural output was plentiful and varied, was the high point of Silla rule. By the ninth and tenth centuries, powerful landowners emerged, breaking apart the equal-field system applied in Silla.

In 936, one of many rebels succeeded in unifying the peninsula under a new dynasty he called the Koryŏ (KOH-ree-oh). This leader, King Taejo, and his immediate successors emancipated slaves (while retaining some forms of labor taxes), instituted an examination system (though preserving some aristocratic privilege), collected all arms held by private individuals, built a major university, supported Buddhism, and attempted to model the kingdom on Song Confucianism. Throughout its early years, Koryŏ faced threats from the Liao. The Jurchen's defeat of Liao and then of the northern Song left Koryŏ temporarily at peace with its neighbors. Domestically, however, the civilian leadership of Koryŏ was removed by a bloody coup by military officials in 1170, and peasant uprisings

This crown made of gold and jade is from the Kingdom of Silla and was made in the fifth or sixth century. Its opulence is a symbol for the national unification of Korea under a monarch.

---

pagoda—A Buddhist reliquary/monument, the East Asian equivalent of the Indian stupa.

around the same time weakened, but did not destroy, the state.

The Mongols invaded the weakened Koryŏ state in 1238. In the 1270s and 1280s, Koryŏ joined the Mongols in two unsuccessful invasions of Japan. Destructive Mongol rule led to uprisings throughout Korea in the 1340s, and soon King Kongmin (r. 1351–1374) restored Koryŏ rule. But he was doomed to failure. His bold initiatives at land reform were resisted by officials, tensions between Buddhists and Neo-Confucians of the Zhu Xi school erupted, and Japanese pirates plagued coastal trade. When he was assassinated in 1374, uprisings broke out all over Korea. The newly risen Ming dynasty in China took advantage of Koryŏ's instability, and was poised to invade in 1392. The Koryŏ general facing the Ming saw the writing on the wall, negotiated a treaty that made Korea a Ming tributary state, and marched back to the court to take over as the founder of the Yi or Chosŏn dynasty (1392–1910).

Even in times of trouble, however, Korean culture blossomed. When the great royal library was burnt in 1126, a new collection of Buddhist works was commissioned. Movable type to print this great collection was cast and used three centuries before Gutenberg first used movable type in Europe. Buddhist works of literature, painting, and sculpture as well as a beautiful stone pagoda were also produced during the Mongol era.

of aristocratic society that developed in the classical age that followed the tomb period. How did Japan develop before the tomb period?

Classical Asian culture—religions, philosophies, arts, and means of governance developed on the continent—flowed into Japan first from Korea and later from China. During the Ice Age, land bridges had connected Japan with the continent. Tools dating from 30,000 B.C.E. and pottery dating from 10,000 B.C.E. (the world's oldest examples of pottery) have been found by archaeologists. Whether these were developed in Japan itself or transmitted from elsewhere is uncertain. An increasingly sophisticated Neolithic culture, called Jōmon (JOH-mon) by scholars, developed distinctive pottery and, between 5000 and 3500 B.C.E., the ancient Japanese language. But it was around 300 B.C.E. that a large migration of Koreans to Japan's westernmost large island, Kyūshū, brought about a revolution in agricultural technology (paddy-field rice) as well as bronze and iron technology. By the time the Chinese observers commented on life in Japan in the late third century, the civilization that blended the new continental ideas with indigenous culture had been established for over 600 years. The period from about 300 B.C.E. to 300 C.E. is called the Yayoi (yah-YOI) period for the district in Tokyo in which the period's pottery was first unearthed.

THE EMERGENCE OF JAPAN IN EAST ASIA

■ *Did Japan's distance from the continent allow it to retain more of its indigenous culture than the other countries of Asia in the classical and medieval eras?*

Separated from the Asian mainland by more than 100 miles of open sea since the end of the last Ice Age (around 12,000 B.C.E.), Japan was something of a curiosity to Chinese observers in the late third century C.E. These Chinese chroniclers found the Japanese law-abiding, adept at farming, fond of alcohol, expert at weaving and fishing, interested in divination, and perhaps most surprising, governed by both male and female shamanistic rulers. They described one of these rulers, Queen Himiko (also known as Pimiko), as a powerful priestess/monarch who, after her death, was interred in a remarkably large funeral mound. These tombs, some of which were twice the volume of the Great Pyramid in Egypt, tell historians that Japan was likely a hierarchical society able to mobilize labor during the tomb period, c. 300–645 C.E. The existence of religious leadership, especially female religious leadership, helps to explain the type

Clay figures like this happy dancing peasant couple were placed in the huge tombs built for Japanese uji *leaders in the third, fourth, and fifth centuries.*

The following era, the tomb period, gave birth to what might be called Japan's first organized governments, ruled by those whose remains are in the great tombs. At first, the extent of a leader's control was likely no more than a clan located in one village, but in time, successful leaders brought more and more villages under their control until they had something like a province. Political authority was intimately connected to religious authority. The original clans, called *uji*, were led by a head priest or priestess believed to be descended from the clan's own deity or *kami*. In ancient Japanese religion—later called **Shintō** ("Way of the Gods") when the introduction of Buddhism made it obvious that Japan's intrinsic belief system deserved a religious name—*kami* were believed to be everywhere in nature. The world of the living was seen as connected to the world of the gods, and governance was a part of religious ritual. Thus, women were not barred from what we would consider administrative leadership, and the Chinese observers found that fact sufficiently interesting to comment on it.

The *uji* in the Yamato region, near the area in which the cities of Nara and Kyoto were later built, possessed the most fertile agricultural land in ancient Japan. It is small wonder that the Yamato leaders, able to build on their productive wealth to support military strength, emerged as the most powerful *uji* by the fifth century. The Japanese language did not yet have its own written form, so historians rely on Chinese observers' reports from the fifth century, rich archaeological remains in tombs, and Japanese histories (*Kojiki*—Records of Ancient Matters—and *Nihongi*—Records of Japan), written in the early eighth century and based on orally transmitted tales, for evidence about people's lives at that time. Tomb artifacts throughout the period included jewels, mirrors, and, most interestingly, clay statues of human figures like warriors, musicians, courtiers, and dancing peasants, all showing expressions of joy, as well as of horses, boats and model houses. From the fifth century on, these tombs increasingly held military objects brought in by a new wave of people from the Korean peninsula. Outside the tombs, archaeological remains of peasant villages suggest farmers lived in pit dwellings.

The power of the Yamato *uji* vis-à-vis the other *uji* throughout Japan was bolstered by its alliance with Paekche. Korean artisans and scribes brought a wealth of Korean and Chinese culture with them to Japan, strengthening the prestige, authority, and administrative competence of the Yamato state. Imported weapons allowed the Yamato warriors to hold sway over their neighbors. As in Korea, Chinese characters were used to transcribe Japanese. Confucian scholarship was introduced around 513, and Buddhism made

Shintō—Indigenous Japanese religion focused on innumerable gods in nature; animistic belief system tied to government in antiquity.

Japan

c. 300 B.C.E.–300 C.E.	Yayoi period
late 200s	Queen Himiko of Yamato
c. 300	Yamato clan dominates central Japan
c. 538	Buddhism introduced to Japan
645	Taika Reform
710–784	Nara period
760s	Compilation of *Man'yōshū*
794–1181	Heian period
c. 800	Introduction of Tendai and Shingon Buddhism
995–1027	Regency of Fujiwara Michinaga
c. 1000	Lady Murasaki, *The Tale of Genji*
1185–1333	Kamakura Shogunate
1274, 1281	Mongol Invasions

a grand entrance, possibly in 538, when the king of Paekche sent Yamato a statue of the Buddha and copies of Buddhist scriptures. Though the ties with Paekche soon ended, the coming of continental culture in general and Buddhism in particular set in motion a cultural and intellectual revolution in Japan. After Silla's unification of the Korean peninsula in the 670s, the Yamato leaders turned to the Tang dynasty for cultural models, diplomatic ties, and trade. At the same time, the Japanese retained significant indigenous customs. These included marriage practices that emphasized the central role of the bride and her family, practices that would later play an important political role. They also included the old religions of Japan. The Yamato family, while welcoming Buddhism following a sixth-century struggle between Shintō ritualists and proponents of Buddhism that was won by the latter, nevertheless retained the worship of the Shintō gods. At some earlier time, as the Yamato were rising to power, a myth of Japan's creation that blended several *uji*'s founding myths and placed the Yamato's ancestral deity Amaterasu (AH-mah-teh-RAH-soo), the sun goddess, at the top of the hierarchy, developed. The Yamato would use this to legitimize their political dominance for many centuries to come.

The victorious proponents of Buddhism, the Soga family, greatly influenced the Yamato family. During his aunt's reign as the Yamato ruler, Prince Shōtoku (SHOH-toh-koo), head of the Soga, apparently undertook so many reforms that Japan was forever changed. He is credited with scholarly commentary (in flawless Chinese) on Buddhist scriptures; with building many temples, including, in 607, Hōryūji (hoh-ree-OO-jee), which contains the world's oldest extant wooden buildings; with opening diplomatic relations with the Sui and later Tang; with adopting the Chinese calendar; with reorganizing the Yamato governing structure on the model of the Confucian state to make it the central monarchy of Japan; and with writing, in 604, the "Seventeen-Article Constitution." These accomplishments were detailed in one of the eighth-century histories of Japan and undoubtedly exaggerated the Prince's personal contributions, but most of them did take place either during his service as regent to the throne or in the decades after his death. Shōtoku's death in 622 led to a struggle for power, ending with the victory of one courtly faction led by the head of the Nakatomi family (renamed Fujiwara in 645). The Yamato family retained the throne, as they do to this day, but the Fujiwara family replaced the Soga as their main advisors. In 645, the Fujiwara carried out the Taika (Great change) Reforms, which centralized economic control under the equal-field system imported from China and Korea. Two rulers, Emperor Temmu (r. 672–686) and Empress Jito (r. 686–697), implemented additional changes; they and their successors were simultaneously continental-style rulers empowered by the prestige of Confucian authority and Shintō rulers legitimized by descent from Amaterasu.

Government in the Classical Era— Nara and Heian

An important step toward Chinese-style centralization was the building of a permanent capital. In 710, the Yamato, by then considered the imperial family, built the city of Nara on the model of Chang'an. Although today's Nara is located in a different site, the eighth-century capital's grid of streets and ancient Buddhist temples are still evident in the Japanese countryside. The rise of powerful Buddhist monasteries and temples may have challenged the power of the court sufficiently to force it to abandon Nara in 784 and build a new capital, Heian (now called Kyoto), in 794. Like Nara, Heian was originally laid out on a grid pattern preserved in modern Kyoto's downtown boulevards and streets. Historians designate the years 710–784 as the Nara Period and 794–1181 (or 1185) as the Heian Period.

To make the capital the sole seat of power, the court enticed all *uji* leaders, who might be potential rivals for power, to live there by granting them titles of nobility and making the court too glamorous to avoid. Many of these *uji* families' provincial lands were con-

A fine example of architecture during the mid-Heian period in Japan is Phoenix Hall, near the modern city of Kyoto. Used by Fujiwara Michinaga as a villa, it later became a temple honoring Amida.

fiscated and redistributed under the equal-field system in the seventh and eighth centuries, but the *uji* were allowed to retain some lands, as were religious institutions and individual farmers who opened new fields to cultivation. Such private estates, unlike the lands farmed by average peasants, were exempt from taxation by the court. Though these estates, called **shōen**, were but a small percentage of Japan's cultivated fields in the eighth century, during the next several centuries peasants wishing to escape taxation commended their lands to private estate owners. This led to the gradual reduction in taxable lands, as farmers paid rents to large owners rather than the often higher taxes to the court. The replacement of tax revenues by rents did not at first appear problematic, however. The great families not only lived at or near the court but also, as we shall see, were often tied by blood to the imperial family. By the eleventh century, however, the gradual erosion of the tax base undermined the central authority of the court. In addition, the absence of a government-run military—a conscript army was one of the Chinese institutions not implemented by the Japanese court because Japan appeared not to face external enemies as did the Chinese—induced estate owners to hire guards to protect their provincial economic interests. These guards eventually became the samurai or warrior class. When they served as guards, they presented no threat to the throne, but when they banded together, as they did in the tenth century and then, most disastrously for the court, in 1181, they could become an alternate political authority to the throne.

Even during the height of the throne's power, its authority was dependent on a balance with one great family, the northern branch of the Fujiwara family. The Fujiwara had earned a special role as advisors at the time of the Taika Reform, but they preserved their dominant position through Japan's traditional marriage practices. Japanese couples married extremely young by today's standards—often as young as 12 or 13. Though girls of the elite spent most of their time indoors and spoke with men not of their immediate families from behind a screen to maintain their propriety, they were very well educated and could communicate easily by letters. Literature describes the lives of women and girls at the court as much more open, and these courtly women communicated more freely with men and with one another. In either case, women and girls played an important role in selection of their sexual and marital partners.

Women in the Imperial Courts of China and Japan

A young man interested in a woman at court might find few barriers to a liaison with her. If the young woman lived at home with her parents, courtship was a bit more complicated. The suitor would call on a potential lover by slipping, under cover of night, through the windows of her room, taking care not to wake her parents. She would speak to him, exchanging poetry and observing his character and attractiveness, from behind her screen. If his clothes, language, scholarly ability, scent, musical talent, and sensitive heart were sufficiently appealing, it was proper for her to invite him behind her screen. If not, she sent him packing, and her propriety was not compromised. If he spent the night, he would have to sneak out at the first rays of morning light. Repeated visits would trigger the parents' investigation of the young man and his career prospects, and if they approved, they would indicate the couple's marriage by leaving ritual food and drink outside their daughter's bedroom door. Thereafter, the young man could come and go during the day, as he was now part of the family as the daughter's husband. The young man would be known as the husband of his bride's house, her parents would make sure he was beautifully outfitted to present himself well at court, and in some cases, once the bride was mature enough to run her own household, the parents and other children might move to another house and leave the teenage bride in charge of her own home. Most likely, she would already have one or two children, raised in their early years by their maternal grandparents, as women usually had their first child in their teens. Grandparents thus had a particularly strong bond with their grandchildren. Property was inherited by daughters, children were their mothers' and maternal grandparents' responsibility, and respectable men and women—though not *married* women—could have more than one sexual partner. Once married, a woman should be unavailable to other men, but serial monogamy was practiced.

Fujiwara influence over the throne depended on marriage customs and family relations. When an 8-year-old boy ascended the throne as emperor in 858, his maternal grandfather, a Fujiwara who was already Grand Minister to the court, assumed even greater control as regent for his grandson. This pattern of Fujiwara patriarchs' control of child emperors, and even some adult emperors who were their grandsons or other relatives, continued for the next 200 years. The pinnacle of Fujiwara dominance was in the early eleventh century. Fujiwara Michinaga (MEE-chee-NAH-gah), who held dominion over the court from 995 to 1027, was the brother of two empresses and the father of four, the uncle of two emperors, the grandfather of two more, and the great-grandfather of another. Some non-Fujiwara protested, but until an emperor whose mother had not been a Fujiwara ascended the throne in the late eleventh century, the Fujiwara controlled the throne. Through this control, the Fujiwara were able to have the tax-free ownership status of their shōen estates confirmed, as only an official could grant that status. For the next century, retired emperors took the place of the Fujiwara as

---

shōen—A tax-free estate in Heian Japan.

regents for their youthful sons whom they placed on the throne. In the late twelfth century, disputes over succession to the throne led to the development of factions at court, and with each faction backed by a powerful samurai family, civil war raged throughout the country from 1181 to 1186. When it was over, the imperial institution survived, but it no longer had the authority to rule Japan. That power fell to the victorious samurai leader, Minamoto Yoritomo (MEE-nah-MOH-toh YOH-ree-TOH-moh; 1147–1199), his wife, Hōjō Masako (HOH-joh MAH-sah-ko; 1157–1225), and her family, who exercised their power from the medieval town of Kamakura in eastern Japan.

Classical Arts and Literature

Japanese emperors sent numerous embassies to the Tang court and brought back a continuing stream of up-to-date culture and material goods. New developments in Chinese poetry were reflected in Japanese verse; new schools of Buddhism influenced Japanese religion; and plump Tang beauties set the standard for female pulchritude at the Japanese court. Yet Japan preserved many of its own practices, including an emphasis on aristocracy, a rejection of eunuchs at court, and unique marriage customs. In 839, as the Tang dynasty was clearly declining, the court ceased to send embassies to China.

Courtly society from the Nara through the Heian periods was extraordinarily refined. The record left from those centuries includes great volumes of poetry, diaries, the world's first novel—the massive *Tale of Genji* by Lady Murasaki—as well as paintings, sculpture, temples, monasteries, and other buildings. Art works from distant lands in Eurasia, brought to Japan by travelers to China, show Japan's integration with the international culture of the Buddhist Age in the Nara and early Heian eras. And music preserved in Japan's court until the present day is the only extant record of Tang musical styles borrowed in the classical era. Impressive though this body of culture is, it was the creation of just a tiny group of people; aristocrats were no more than one tenth of one percent of the population, with urban residents influenced by those aristocrats perhaps an additional several percent.

Unlike aristocrats, farmers were not literate. Tax rates appear high, as evidenced by peasants' attempts to escape the tax roles. Pestilence devastated farmers and city-folk alike. Men, women, and children worked hard. Despite these difficulties, folk tales and written stories abound with examples of farm women's high status relative to their husbands. Women likely selected their own spouses, and many made important economic contributions to their households. Wives' infidelity was treated as a joke rather than as a capital crime in folk tales.

The poetry of the literate elite reflected the importance of sentiment. The *Man'yōshū* (mahn-YOH-shoo; *The Collection of Ten Thousand Leaves*), compiled in the 760s, contains over 4000 poems, many of which date to the fifth century, composed by emperors, empresses, courtesans, frontier guards, and commoners. These brief and direct compositions covered such themes as parting of lovers, loyalty to one's lord, love of nature, grief over the death of a child, and the Buddhist theme of the fleeting nature of human life, give us a rich sense of early Japanese society and culture. Two *Man'yōshū* poems, the first a love poem by a woman, the second a poem of grief for his wife by a man, give a sense of this collection:[10]

Court ladies and their maids in The Tale of Genji. *Heian court women were ideally plump, had hair longer than their bodies, and wore many layers of robes. The* Genji *scrolls integrated text and images.*

*Oh, how steadily I love you—
You who awe me
Like the thunderous waves
That lash the seacoast of Ise!*

　　　　　　　　　　Lady Kasa

*In our chamber, where our two pillows lie,
Where we two used to sleep together,
Days I spend alone, broken-hearted:
Nights I pass, sighing till dawn.*

　　　　　　　　　Kakinomoto Hitomaro

The imperial treasury at Nara, built in the eighth century, contains works of art by both Japanese and continental artists, indicating Japan's increasing international contacts in the Nara period. This small silver jar depicts a hunting scene that includes a deer, still one of the symbols of Nara.

Because the Japanese language did not have a written form, it was represented with Chinese characters. Aristocratic men and some women were able to read and write in Chinese and thus sought to use characters to record Japanese. The two languages are not related linguistically, so the characters were used in several different ways. One was to represent meaning—the Chinese character for "tree," for example, would be applied to the Japanese word for "tree." The other was to represent sounds without any consideration for the meaning of the character. This led to a virtually indecipherable script, so *kana*, a syllabic script, was devised in the early ninth century. Soon poetry, diaries, essays, and novels were written in this script. Aristocratic authors, especially but not exclusively women, produced an outpouring of creative works. Women's dominance in the literary arts at that time was due, in part, to the fact that men spent a lot of their time writing government documents in Chinese. But the fact that creativity, including calligraphic, artistic, and sensory abilities, was not gendered at that time, as well as the leisure time their aristocratic privilege gave them, may have had more to do with offering women opportunities to produce fine works.

The most important work of the Heian period—and some might say of the entire body of Japanese literary arts—was *The Tale of Genji*, written over the course of perhaps two decades by Lady Murasaki, who was sometimes praised, sometimes ridiculed for her exceptional knowledge of both Japanese and Chinese scholarship.[11] *The Tale of Genji* describes the life, loves, escapades, and sorrows of the sensitive and talented Prince Genji, a paragon of male virtue; his son Kaoru; Genji's steadfast male friends; and his beloved wife Murasaki. The novel is an intriguing look into courtly life around the year 1000. An excellent parallel to *Genji* is *The Pillow Book* by Sei Shōnagon (SAY SHOH-nah-gon), a contemporary and professional rival of Lady Murasaki at another empress's court. *The Pillow Book* contains often racy, amusing and satirical essays that give good insight into the life of the court.

DOCUMENT
Excerpt from Lady Murasaki Shikibu's Diary

From the sixth century through the first half of the Heian period, religious themes predominated in the arts. Statues and paintings of various manifestations of the Buddha, indicating changes in artistic style and notions of physical beauty over the centuries, were common. But decorated items for aristocratic pleasure, such as musical instruments, boxes, and tables are also among the treasury of early Japanese art. By the tenth century, paintings of highly secular themes emerged. Fans with themes from literature were made and used by court ladies, and the *Genji* scrolls of the eleventh century were a multimedia production interspersing gorgeous paintings with Murasaki's text. Comic scrolls appeared by the late Heian period. The architecture of the court and of private mansions was elegant, with raised floors of polished wood, sliding screen doors, wooden buildings connected to one another by covered corridors, windows with hinged shutters (through which suitors could climb), all surrounded by carefully landscaped gardens with streams and ponds.

Japanese Buddhism in the Classical and Early Medieval Eras

Mahayana Buddhism reached entered Japan in the sixth century and was well established among the aristocracy by the eighth. To further the secular reach of the Nara state, the court established branch temples throughout the country, staffed by monks trained in the capital. Most commoners, especially those in the countryside, continued to carry out Shintō rituals. Except for the struggles in the sixth century, there was little conflict between Buddhism and either indigenous Shintō and the imported philosophy of Confucianism as there had been in China, and Buddhism was eventually

Document: Sei Shōnagon: *The Pillow Book*

Sei Shōnagon was a contemporary and literary rival of Lady Murasaki. The two served different empresses of the reigning emperor; Sei Shōnagon's court was considered more fashionable and Lady Murasaki's more erudite. Sei Shōnagon was a witty and talented writer. In her diary, Murasaki describes Sei Shōnagon as "a very proud person. She values herself highly and scatters her Chinese writings all about.... How can such a vain and reckless person end her days happily!"[11] Below is an excerpt from Sei Shōnagon's *Pillow Book* in which she describes distressing things.

One has been expecting someone, and rather late at night there is a stealthy tapping at the door. One sends a maid to see who it is, and lies waiting, with some flutter of the breast. But the name one hears when she returns is that of someone completely different, who does not concern one at all. Of all depressing experiences, this is by far the worst.

It is very tiresome when a lover who is leaving at dawn says that he must look for a fan or a pocketbook that he left somewhere about the room last night.... Instead of experiencing the feelings of regret proper to such an occasion, one merely feels irritated at his clumsiness.... It is important that a lover should know how to make his departure. To begin with, he ought not to be too ready to get up, but should require a little coaxing.... He should not pull on his trousers the moment he is up, but should first of all come close to one's ear and in a whisper finish off whatever was left half-said in the course of the night.... If he springs to his feet with a jerk and at once begins fussing around, one begins to hate him.

I like to think of a bachelor ... returning at dawn from some amorous excursion.... As soon as he is home ... he begins to write his next-morning letter.... When he has washed and got into his court cloak ... he takes the sixth chapter of the Lotus Sutra and reads it silently. Precisely at the most solemn moment of his reading, the messenger returns.... With an amusing if blasphemous rapidity the lover transfers his attention from the book he is reading to the business of framing an answer.

Questions to Consider

1. How important was romantic love to Heian aristocrats?
2. The ideal bachelor Sei Shōnagon describes reads Buddhist scriptures before heading off to work at the court. What other tasks take priority over his religious practice?
3. Did women have a choice in the selection of their suitors?

From "The Pillow Book of Sei Shōnagon," in Donald Keene, *Anthology of Japanese Literature* (New York: Grove Press, 1955), pp. 137–139.

---

indigenized as the dominant religion of Japan following new theological directions in the Heian period.

Two new sects of Buddhism were brought to Japan by student monks who had journeyed to China in 804. Tendai, introduced by Saichō in 805, and Shingon, brought back by Kūkai in 806, both made it possible to develop mass participation in Buddhist worship. Tendai doctrine stated that those who led a life of purity and contemplation could realize enlightenment and their "Buddha nature." Saichō established an important monastery at Mt. Hiei (HEE-ay), which several centuries later became a source of trouble for the court as it supported not only devotion and learning but also a large army of warrior-monks who demanded land rights and privileges. Shingon was an esoteric faith, with secret and seemingly magical rites. It was extremely popular in the Heian period, as it encouraged art, medicinal use of herbs, incantations, and pageantry. It also appealed to Shintō adherents, as its central deity was Dainichi (DAI-nee-chee), the "Great Sun" Buddha, who was identified with the Sun Goddess in the popular mind.

Buddhist Monks

In the mid-tenth century, itinerant monks spread a simplified version of the Tendai doctrine of enlightenment, stating that salvation was possible only for those who called on the name of Amida, the Buddha of the Pure Land. But it was not until the end of the Heian period, with its natural disasters, earthquakes, fires, and fearsome warfare that a proponent of Pure Land Buddhism succeeded in establishing a new type of Buddhism. The monk Hōnen (1133–1212) preached that faith in Amida alone, without relying on good works, was the only route to salvation. He endured persecution for his propagation of Pure Land ideas. His follower Shinran (1173–1262) took these ideas even further. He said that perfect faith was shown by uttering the name of Amida just once, and that an evil man of perfect faith was able to enter the Pure Land. Shinran broke with Buddhist tradition—eating meat,

The pagodas of Yakushi-ji at Nara. Built in the eighth century, Yakushi-ji is one of Japan's earliest wooden temple compounds. Buddhist temples of that era challenged the secular power of the government, so the emperor's court moved to Heian in 794.

marrying a nun, and advocating the equality of all occupations if performed with a pure heart. His True Pure Land sect eventually became the largest in Japan. The other important faith sect was Nichiren (NEE-chee-ren) Buddhism, founded by the monk Nichiren (1222–1282), who stated that one should place faith in the Lotus Sutra, a key Buddhist scripture, rather than Amida. Known for his Japanese nationalism, he predicted the Mongol invasions. By the twelfth century, Buddhism had spread to all classes of society.

Two major **Zen** sects were also brought back to Japan by Japanese student monks. Eisai (1141–1215) introduced the Rinzai sect and Dōgen (1200–1253) the Sōtō sect. Rinzai stressed complicated riddles to achieve enlightenment, while Sōtō emphasized long hours of meditation. Both methods were increasingly popular with samurai who were attracted to the sudden enlightenment they promised.

Early Medieval Government and Culture

Minamoto Yoritomo's victory over the other major warrior band, the Taira, in 1185 ushered in the era of warrior dominance. He never claimed the throne, as victorious generals elsewhere in Asia had, but rather had the emperor confer on him a new position, *shōgun* (great general), a title which would remain in use for most of the next 700 years. The shōgun theoretically served at the pleasure of the emperor, but (until 1868) when emperors attempted to assert their rights, the struggle was always won by the shōgun, who, of course, claimed to be serving the emperor. (An attempted imperial uprising in 1221 was suppressed.) The shōgun set up his seat of power in Kamakura, away from the capital, and the era of Kamakura dominance is called the Kamakura Period (1185–1333).

Minamoto Yoritomo's legitimacy as a ruler was based on his own institutions in addition to his symbolic subordination to the emperor. First, he made use of the loyalty of his samurai. Like feudal lords in Europe, he used a bond of loyalty to motivate his samurai warriors, whom he called "honorable house men" or vassals. These vassals were appointed constables of provinces, with the duty to raise up armies if necessary, and stewards or overseers on the shōen estates owned by the rich old Heian families. To show his authority over the estates, he allowed the stewards to collect a small amount of revenue—so small that owners did not bother to contest it as they had contested the imperial court's ability to collect taxes on private lands. By paying the small fees, however, owners acknowledged the legitimacy of Kamakura's right to collect it. During the next century, the stewards would use these locally collected resources to establish their own landed power base in the countryside, and they would eventually turn on their supposed overlords in Kamakura. Second, Minamoto Yoritomo and his successors made use of much of the provincial governing structure of the old imperial system for most of the next century. The vassal samurai were too few in number to rule on their own, so the previous system was retained in many places. Third, Minamoto established three new offices: the samurai board, which controlled the vassals; the judicial board, which settled suits over land holdings as well as criminal issues; and the administrative board, to carry out his policies. The judicial board was particularly important in gaining the support of the people, as it was known for its impartiality in settling disputes. The administrative board was headed by his Hōjō in-laws, and was used by them to increase their power after Yoritomo's death in 1199. Indeed, power passed into Hōjō hands, where it remained until the Kamakura shogunate (government by shōgun) was overthrown.

Zen—The Japanese form of Chan Buddhism. Popular with the samurai.

By the end of the thirteenth century, samurai ties to Kamakura had become attenuated. Allegiance to the dominant Hōjō was not as certain as allegiance to the Minamoto had been earlier. Far from Kamakura, samurai stewards out in the provinces developed local ties, both political and economic. When the Mongols attacked in 1274 and again in 1281, the samurai, especially those of the western island of Kyūshū, where the attack came, fought bravely, but none was rewarded, because there were no spoils of war to divide. The invasion in 1274 threw 30,000 attackers against Japan; the second invasion was mounted by 140,000. Commoners built a sea wall whose remnants are still visible today to keep the Mongols out; it helped the Japanese warriors hold the Mongols out until typhoon winds, called *kamikaze* (divine winds), blew many of the Mongol vessels out to sea, forcing them to withdraw. Japan was saved, but the invasions had some very significant outcomes. Disgruntled warriors who had fought, commoners whose labor had built the fortifications, and religious people who claimed their prayers brought about the divine winds eventually moved against Kamakura when succession disputes at court gave them an excuse to join one side or the other in the 1330s. Also, the practice of daughter inheritance and multiple inheritance gave way to unigeniture or inheritance by one son in order to keep samurai lands intact to support a mounted warrior now deemed necessary for national defense. Single inheritance weakened family ties, as younger sons sought new patrons to protect them. This strengthened the lord-vassal bond at the heart of feudalism, which became increasingly important in the next three centuries.

Kamakura was home to numerous beautiful temples, built in harmony with the verdant hills, a new style of construction. A huge outdoor Great Buddha statue that still attracts thousands of tourists every day was cast in the early Kamakura period. But much of Japan's culture in this era emanated from Heian (now increasingly called Kyoto). The court commissioned great collections of poetry as they had in earlier centuries, and court ladies wrote, for an aristocratic readership, tales of great emotional depth. Periodic markets began to bring rural people into a larger national culture, but the arts were still fairly elite. This would change in the next century, as a national culture, enhanced by new infusions of Asian styles, entered Japan.

CONCLUSION

During the centuries following the collapse of the Mauryan dynasty in India (184 B.C.E.) and, much later, the Han dynasty in China (220 C.E.), significant cultural revivals occurred in Asia. First India and then China experienced golden ages when political unity was restored and social systems were revitalized. In India, the Gupta era encouraged the development of Hindu thought, along with notable advances in painting, architecture, literature, drama, medicine, and the physical sciences. At the same time, India continued to be part of an emerging international Buddhist culture, helping to link it to other Buddhist countries along the East-West trade routes. Later, international Islam tied rising Indian dynasties, some of them Islamic, to other centers of power and trade. China experimented with blending "barbarian" and indigenous means of government in the millennium from the fall of the Han to the fall of the Mongols. Cosmopolitan blending of culture made China the East Asian center of both cultural consumption and production. Scholarship and art blossomed even in the period of disunity and flourished in the lively international Tang dynasty and the technologically sophisticated early modern Song dynasty. Korea and Japan, while retaining much of their own culture, adopted a number of aspects of Chinese governance, art, philosophy, religion, and means of communication. Rivalries at times impeded trade, but diffusion of material and other forms of culture made Eurasia a single system, often dominated by its eastern side, during much of the millennium. Over the centuries, cultural diffusion gained increasing momentum throughout Eurasia. Goods and cultural patterns spread through migrations, invasions, missionary activities, and trade to China, India, Southeast Asia, Japan, Korea, the Asian steppes, and Europe.

Suggestions for Web Browsing

You can obtain more information about topics included in this chapter at the websites listed below. See also the companion website that accompanies this text, **http://www.ablongman.com/brummett,** which contains an online study guide and additional resources.

Ancient and Medieval India
http://www.fordham.edu/halsall/india/indiasbook.html
Extensive collection of materials on ancient and medieval India; most entries include subsites with text and images.

Gupta Period
http://www.wsu.edu:8080/~dee/ANCINDIA/GUPTA.HTM
Indian history in the Gupta era.

Medieval India
http://www.goindiago.com/history/medieval.htm
Site discussing the history, sites and monuments, and classical texts of medieval India, 600 B.C.E.–1526 C.E.

Chinese Empire
http://www.wsu.edu/~dee/CHEMPIRE/CHEMPIRE.HTM
Chinese history from 256 B.C.E. to 1300 C.E., with details about philosophy and culture.

The Heian Era
http://www.wsu.edu:8080/~dee/ANCJAPAN/HEIAN.HTM
This site gives a valuable context to the Heian era.

Ancient Japan
http://www.wsu.edu:8080/~dee/ANCJAPAN/ANCJAPAN.HTM

> Website on ancient Japan includes political, religious, and cultural history, details about women and women's communities, and a portfolio of art from the era.

Samurai Archives
http://www.samurai-archives.com/

> Extensive collection of information about individuals and events in the samurai millennium.

Empires Beyond the Great Wall: The Heritage of Chinggis Khan
http://web.archive.org/web/20000815214514/http://vvv.com/khan/

> A rich site (now archived) offering a biography of Chinggis Khan and information about the history and culture of the Mongol Empire.

Literature and Film

The following works give the flavor of this long millennium in India: *The Panchatantra*, trans. Arthur W. Ryder (University of Chicago, 1967); Prince Ilangô Adigal, *Shilappadikaram (The Ankle Bracelet)*, trans. Alain Daniélou (New Directions, 1965); Somadeva, *Tales from the Kathāsaritsāgara*, trans. Arshia Sattar (Penguin, 1994); Cornelia Dimmitt, ed., *Classical Hindu Mythology: A Reader in Sanskrit Puranas*, trans. J. A. Van Buitenen (Temple University, 1994).

For a fictional treatment about Empress Wu that offers a picture of Tang court opulence and intrigue see Evelyn McCune, *Empress* (Fawcett Columbine, 1994). For Japan, Lady Murasaki's *Tale of Genji* is available in several excellent translations. The newest is by Royall Tyler (Penguin Publishers, 2002). A 1991 animated film (subtitled) is a good introduction to the first third of the book.

Suggestions for Reading

Informative surveys of India's medieval history include Hermann A. Kulke, *A History of India*, 3rd ed. (Routledge, 1998); and Tej Ram Sharma, *The Political History of the Imperial Guptas* (Concept, 1989). On the Delhi Sultanate, see Peter Jackson, *The Delhi Sultanate: A Political and Military History* (Cambridge University Press, 2003). On women, see Tracy Pintchman, *The Rise of the Goddess in the Hindu Tradition* (State University of New York Press, 1994); and Leslie Orr, *Donors, Devotees, and Daughters of God: Temple Women in Medieval Tamilnadu* (Oxford University Press, 2000).

Two of many fine general histories of China in the post-Han, Tang, Song, and Yuan periods are Patricia Buckley Ebrey, *Cambridge Illustrated History of China* (Cambridge University Press, 1996); and Charles O. Hucker, *China's Imperial Past* (Stanford University Press, 1975). A comprehensive work on Chinese painting is *Three Thousand Years of Chinese Painting*, eds. Richard M. Barnhart, Nie Chongzheng, Lang Shaojun, James Cahill, and Wu Hung (Yale University Press, 1998). Dorothy Ko, Jahyun Kim Haboush, and Joan R. Piggott's *Women and Confucian Cultures in Premodern China, Korea, and Japan* (University of California Press, 2003) is an excellent overview of the role of women in each of the three countries. For a classic though still excellent introduction to the Song, see Jacques Gernet, *Daily Life in China on the Eve of the Mongol Invasion, 1250–76* (Stanford University Press, 1962). Valerie Hansen, *The Open Empire: A History of China to 1600* (W. W. Norton, 2000) explicates Tang and Song foreign relations and the domestic repercussions of economic expansion. On women and family relationships see Patricia Buckley Ebrey, *The Inner Quarters: Marriage and the Lives of Chinese Women in the Sung Period* (University of California Press, 1993). Katherine Bernhardt's *Women and Property in China, 960–1949* (Stanford University Press, 1999) gives us a legal history of family law in Song China with its social repercussions. On the Yuan dynasty see Elizabeth Endicott West, *Mongolian Rule in China* (Harvard University Press, 1989).

An excellent study of networks of trade and communication in the Mongol era is Janet Abu-Lughod, *Before European Hegemony: The World System, A.D. 1250–1350* (Oxford University Press, 1989). A recent work that treats Asia as an interacting unit is Warren I. Cohen, *East Asia at the Center: Four Thousand Years of Engagement with the World* (Columbia University Press, 2000).

A solid survey of Korean history is Carter J. Eckert, et al., *Korea Old and New: A History* (Harvard University Press, 1990). Surveys of Japanese history in the classical and medieval eras include *The Cambridge History of Japan: Ancient Japan*, eds. Delmer M. Brown, John Whitney Hall, Marius B. Jansen, Madoka Kanai, and Denis Twitchett (Cambridge University Press, 1993); John W. Hall, *Government and Local Power in Japan, 500–1700* (University of Michigan Press, 1999); and Wayne Farris, *Heavenly Warriors: The Evolution of Japan's Military, 500–1300* (Harvard University Press, 1996). Karen Brazell's translation of *The Confessions of Lady Nijo* (Stanford University Press, 1976) offers a fascinating account by an itinerant woman, once a court lady, now a nun, in the early thirteenth century, and is a wonderful addition to the larger body of work on women writers in the Heian period.

The Americas to 1492

CHAPTER 11

CHAPTER CONTENTS

- Origins of Americans and Their Cultures
- Emerging Civilizations in Mesoamerica
- Classical Mayan Civilization
- The Postclassical Era
  DOCUMENT: *Father Bernabé Cobo, "Pachacuti, the Greatest Inca"*
- The Amerindians of North America

Early civilizations in the Americas followed a social sequence similar to that found in Africa and Eurasia. As agriculture became more diversified, food supplies increased and some cultures became more and more able to support cities, highly skilled crafts, expanding commerce, complex social structures, and the emergence of powerful states. The most noteworthy were the civilizations of the Mayas in Yucatán and Guatemala, the Aztecs in central Mexico, and the Incas in Peru. The Mayas are particularly recognized for their mathematics, solar calendar, and writing system—70 percent of which has only recently been deciphered. The Aztecs and Incas conquered large populations and governed extensive states. Each civilization produced distinctive customs, values, art, and religion, many of which have become part of the Latin American heritage. Spanish adventurers who invaded these civilizations were shocked by the religious sacrifices of human beings but astonished by the wealth, grandeur, technical efficiency, urban populations, and institutional complexity they saw in Central America and Peru. For example, Tenochtitlán (te-nohch-teet-LAHN), the Aztec capital with its 150,000 inhabitants, was larger and probably better administered than any European city of its time.

To the north of Mesoamerica, hundreds of Amerindian tribes developed diverse social patterns, languages, and economic pursuits as they adapted to the differing environments they faced. Around 4000 B.C.E. Amerindians in the southwestern part of present-day Florida founded villages along the coast in which they enjoyed a rich diet of fish, shellfish, grains, and berries and lived in accord with a sophisticated religious system that included the burial of the dead in funeral mounds. Recent archaeological finds indicate that still earlier in the present-day state of Washington, Amerindians founded villages with their own unique cultures and economic activities. The Amerindians to the north never attained the centralized power or wealth of the Mayas, Aztecs, and Incas. However, they left behind a variety of archaeological sites that attest to their sophistication and creativity.

40,000

c. 40,000–10,000 B.C.E. Movement back and forth across the Bering Strait land bridge

10,000

10,000 B.C.E. Nomadic migrations from Asia reach tip of South America

c. 5000 B.C.E. Development of maize agriculture

2000

c. 2000 B.C.E. Divergence of Inuits and Aleuts

c. 1200 B.C.E.–150 C.E. Formative period of Mesoamerica culture (Olmec)

c. 800 B.C.E.–600 C.E. Adena and Hopewell cultures

1 C.E.

c. 150–900 Classical period in Mesoamerica culture (Maya)

c. 300 Beginning of Anasazi culture

500

c. 500–600 Beginning of Mississippian culture

c. 900–1500 Postclassical period of Mesoamerican culture (Toltec, Aztec)

1000

c. 1100–1500 Development of Inca empire

c. 1300 Height of Cahokia culture

1500

c. 1500s Inca Empire in South America reaches maturity

323

ORIGINS OF AMERICANS AND THEIR CULTURES

■ *Does the development of Amerindian cultures support or negate the theory of parallel development?*

Many of the American cultures can be traced back to nomadic migrations from Asia to Alaska, across the Bering Strait land bridge. During the Pleistocene epoch, coinciding with the last great ice age, humans established themselves in Siberia where they built underground shelters and hunted large mammals such as mammoths. The most recent ice advance, beginning some 65,000 years ago, locked up immense amounts of global water and lowered sea levels, creating a land bridge that enabled Paleolithic people to follow the animals they hunted into North America. Later, as increasing global temperatures melted the ice and raised water levels, the bridge slowly disappeared around 10,000 years ago, after an estimated 30,000 years of sporadic human migrations. Recent discoveries indicate that there also may have been other routes of entry into the Americas, including those by sea from Iceland and Greenland and across the Pacific into Chile and Peru.

Archaeological work throughout the twentieth century continually pushed back the estimates of the time of the first permanent residents. Artifacts known as Clovis spear points, the oldest of which are about 11,200 years old, were found from Mexico to Nova Scotia. Continued discoveries across North America revised the estimates of when human beings settled in the Americas to around 20,000 years ago. Some archaeologists think humans could have lived in North America even earlier. However, the most widely accepted estimates of the first human settlement in the Americas are 14,000 years ago, with humans reaching southern Chile by circa 12,500 years ago. Recent discoveries in Peru indicate that the first city in the Americas was that at Caral, founded around 2600 B.C.E. Archaeologists believe that the pyramids built there were constructed a century before the Great Pyramid at Giza in Egypt.

Over this protracted period the Amerindians split into eight major ethnolinguistic groups and hundreds of subgroups and adapted to numerous physical environments. New research has shown the Americas to be far more densely populated in the fifteenth century than the European invaders believed—perhaps by as many as 75 million people before the massive population decline caused by climatic changes and foreign diseases such as small pox in the fifteenth and sixteenth centuries.

The development of agriculture in the Mexican highlands, along the Peruvian coastal plain, and in what is now the southwestern United States caused major changes in indigenous American culture after 7000 B.C.E. This development occurred considerably later than in the Near East, and the plants that the Amerindians domesticated were different from those in other parts of the world. They also domesticated animals such as alpacas and llamas in the Andes—there were no cattle, sheep, or horses until the Europeans arrived in 1492. The major agricultural contribution came with the cultivation of maize (corn), shortly before 5000 B.C.E., in the Tehuacán (ti-wah-CAN) valley of Mexico. From this center, maize culture spread widely. After 1000 B.C.E. it became the staple food for hundreds of societies, from the Mississippi River valley to the Argentine pampas. The Aztec Confederacy and Inca Empire, which so awed the Spanish *conquistadores* after 1500, were dependent on the raising of maize.

Beyond these mature civilizations, cultural levels varied widely among the Amerindians by the end of the fifteenth century. Some powerful cultures, like that of the Mound Builders of the Mississippi valley, borrowed heavily from Mexico. Cahokia, a major capital and trade center near contemporary St. Louis, Missouri, housed approximately 25,000 people during the thirteenth century. Other sophisticated cultures north of the Rio Grande ranged from the Pueblo of the southwest to the large Iroquois Confederacy of the eastern woodlands. In South America, complex cultures lived along the north coast and near the mouth of the Amazon. Other societies developed on Caribbean islands, in the South American pampas, and in Chile. Other Amerindians—probably a majority of them—were still hunters and gatherers. These included the Eskimo peoples of Alaska and the Inuit peoples of Arctic Canada; jungle groups such as the Jivaro (he-VAR-oh) of the upper Amazon; and the peoples of Tierra del Fuego, at the southern tip of South America.

Despite differing timeframes, Amerindian cultures differed little from cultures in Africa and Eurasia in their progression from Paleolithic hunting and food gathering to Mesolithic semifixed communities to Neolithic food production and settled communal life and then to urban centers and the emergence of political states. They also displayed common traits with other civilizations in their theocratic systems, sun cults, and human sacrifices. Like the African cultures, they were in transition from matriarchal to patriarchal institutions, although further along in the process. Finally, a common belief in monarchy among Aztecs and Incas was also typical of many other peoples in the ancient river civilizations of Eurasia.

EMERGING CIVILIZATIONS IN MESOAMERICA

■ *What geographical and climatic factors permitted the rise of Mesoamerican civilization?*

A variety of related cultures flourished in **Mesoamerica,** a zone ranging from roughly 100 miles north of Mexico City to Costa Rica. The region varies greatly in landforms, climate, and vegetation. Two mountain ranges run through northern Mexico to join a central highland block in the region of the Valley of Mexico. The Pacific coastal region is relatively narrow while that on the Atlantic side is wide. The north and west have dry lands with sparse vegetation; the south and east are marked by tropical rain forests and savannas.

Central and South American Civilizations

Despite these physical differences, the early cultures were unified by their economic interdependence, because no one region was self-sufficient. They shared a complex calendar, hieroglyphic writing, bark paper, deerskin books, team games played with balls of solid rubber, chocolate bean money, widespread upper-class polygamy, large markets, and common legends. A popular one featured a god-man symbolized by a feathered serpent. We may conveniently divide Mesoamerican history into three main periods: formative (to 150 C.E.), classical (150–900), and postclassical (900–1492).

The Formative Period

For a millennium after 1500 B.C.E., villages in the regions of Mexico and Central America grew steadily to become cities. Scattered throughout this region at the beginning of this period were some 350,000 people, living in relatively sparsely populated ceremonial trading centers and villages. Labor and stone for the massive construction projects, jade for carving, luxury goods, raw materials for the crafts, and food were brought to the centers often from distant places—without the use of horses, mules, or oxen. These goods were probably not the spoils of conquest; Olmec society left little evidence of war or violence, although some security would have been present to protect trading missions.

In these settlements artisans worked at pottery making, weaving, feather design, and masonry. Merchants ranked second only to the priesthood in social status, as they conducted trade among the temple cities. As population increased and society became

Mesoamerica—A cultural zone in Central America ranging from roughly 100 miles north of Mexico City to Costa Rica.

Mesoamerican and South American Civilizations

2500s B.C.E.–400s C.E.	Olmec
300s–900s C.E.	Mayas
900s–1200s C.E.	Toltecs
1100s–1500s C.E.	Incas
1300s–1500s C.E.	Aztecs

more complex, priests came to dominate governments. They governed by enjoying respect and exploiting fear rather than relying on force. The general theocratic orientation is reflected most clearly in the great temple mounds; in the huge stone conical pyramid at La Venta, rising some 100 feet; and in the characteristic carved statuary that represented the dominance of the Olmec cults.

In time the common culture, known as the Olmec, centered in five geographical areas. One was in the Oaxaca (wah-HAHK-ah) region of western Mexico; another was in the inland Valley of Mexico; a third straddled the present Mexican-Guatemalan border; and a fourth (the later Mayan) arose in the southern highlands and lowlands of Yucatán, Honduras, and Guatemala. The fifth, and at the time most significant, area spread over some 125 miles of the eastern Mexican coast and its hinterlands, near present-day Veracruz.

Archaeological research in Olmec sites reveals exceptional wealth, technical efficiency, and artistic sensitivity. In many Olmec sites, the oldest at San Lorenzo, there were great stone buildings and pyramids dating from 1200 B.C.E. The culture is perhaps best known for its colossal heads and its fine jade carving, featuring jaguars. This cultural maturity was not matched by military advancements: San Lorenzo was destroyed by invaders about 900 B.C.E.; another ceremonial center at La Venta, in Tabasco, assumed leadership until it, too, fell, six centuries later.

Olmec influence permeated most of present-day Mexico and Central America. A few independent Olmec centers may have been established farther to the north, but it was probably more common for a number of Olmec priests and traders to live among native populations, conducting religious rites and arranging for the transport of goods to the homeland. Such enclaves were typical of regions as distant as the Pacific coast of Central America. In other places, such as the Oaxaca valley to the west, the southwestern

Ranging from the lowland and jungles of Central America to the arctic cold of the Andes, the civilizations of Central and South America exhibited a rich and sophisticated diversity.

Mexican highlands, or the southern Mayan regions, Olmec influence was more indirect, possibly resulting from trade or Olmec marriage into local elites. By such varied means, Olmec foundations were laid for the religion, art, architecture, and characteristic ball games—and possibly for the calendars, mathematics, and writing systems—of later civilizations, including the Mayan and the Aztec.

The Classical Period

After the fall of La Venta, Olmec prestige waned, but by the second century C.E., cultural developments progressed to a point known as the classical period, which would last until the tenth century. This was a golden age when, across the region, written communication, complex time reckoning, a pantheon of gods, interregional trade, and a 40-fold population increase over the Olmec period occurred. Hundreds of communities raised great buildings, decorated them with beautiful frescoes, produced pottery, figurines, and sculptures in large quantities. Although classical Mayan culture of the Yucatán lowlands is perhaps best known, Teotihuacán (te-oh-tee-wah-KAHN), in the northeastern valley, also generated an impressive culture.

At its peak about 500 C.E., Teotihuacán was the sixth largest city in the world, with a population of 125,000 to 200,000. Three and a half miles long and nearly two miles wide, it was laid out in a grid of sorts

The colossal Pyramid of the Sun rose above the metropolis of Teotihuacán. Measuring 650 feet at its base and 213 feet high, the structure is more than four times larger than the Great Pyramid of Khufu (Cheops) in Egypt.

and paved with a plaster floor on which clusters of imposing edifices were erected. This ceremonial center is dominated by the temple-pyramids dedicated to the moon and the sun. The first pyramid was cut off at the top to provide for a temple with a broad step ascending from a wide rectangular court. Running south is a long ceremonial axis, and adjacent to it the Pyramid of the Sun. Also truncated, it measures 650 feet at the base and rises in four terraces to 213 feet above the valley floor. The interior contains more than a million cubic yards of sun-dried bricks, and the exterior was once faced entirely with stone. As with other pyramids throughout Mesoamerica, these structures, with their ceremonial staircases, led to temples at the summit where rites and sacrifices were offered to the gods.

Teotihuacán was noted for its specialized craftspeople who came from all over Mexico and occupied designated quarters of the city. Its streets were studded with bustling markets, where all types of goods were available from foreign as well as local sources. This wealth permitted a governing elite of priests, civil officials, military leaders, and merchants to enjoy great luxury. Teotihuacán exerted a powerful influence over other states, including some among the lowland Mayas, because of its cultural reputation, social connections, and commercial advantages. When necessary, it used its formidable military power to enforce trade and tribute agreements. Above all, Teotihuacán marks the high point of priestly power over the rest of society. Thereafter, especially with the Toltecs, the cultures came to be far more military in character.

Another impressive classical center in Mexico was located at Monte Alban in the Oaxaca valley. In 200 B.C.E. it already had a population of 15,000, and its fortifications dominated the valley. In Teotihuacán's era, this concentration of temples, pyramids, and shrines was a theocratic state, still drawing tribute from adjacent hill settlements and a valley population of over 75,000 people. Although developed on a smaller scale than Teotihuacán, Monte Alban produced a similar pattern of foreign trade, class distinctions, elaborate religious architecture, artistic creativity, writing, and time reckoning. It derived most of its art styles from Teotihuacán and some from the Mayas but synthesized both in its own traditions. Politically, it remained independent through the classical era, although its elite sought the luxury goods and favor of Teotihuacán.

CLASSICAL MAYAN CIVILIZATION

■ *What were the economic, political, cultural, and religious characteristics of Mayan civilization?*

While Teotihuacán and Monte Alban flourished, Mayan peoples farther south in Yucatán and Guatemala brought artistic and intellectual activity to new heights in more than 100 Mayan centers, each boasting temples, palaces, observatories, and ball courts. Although it borrowed from Teotihuacán before the latter's decay in the eighth century C.E., Mayan civilization subsequently cast a brilliant light over the whole of Mexico and Central America.

A Mayan Town

The earliest Mayas are thought to have migrated from the northwest coast of California to the Guatemalan highlands during the third millennium B.C.E. From that homeland, Yucatec- and Cholian-speaking peoples settled the northern and central lowlands, respectively, between 1500 B.C.E. and 100 C.E. Mayan villages developed steadily, many becoming ceremonial centers by the start of the Common Era. In the highlands, Kaminaljuyu (kah-MEEN-ah-leu-yeu) had by then developed architecture and primitive writing under the influence of Oaxaca and Teotihuacán. But in the early classical period, before 550 C.E., Tikal, in the central lowlands, assumed Mayan leadership as it traded with Teotihuacán and allied itself with Kaminaljuyu. The fall of Teotihuacán brought temporary confusion, soon followed by the glorious renaissance of the late classical era at Tikal, Palenque, Yaxchilán (yahks-chee-LAHN), Uxmal, and other Mayan centers.

A number of distinguished scholars such as Linda Schele and David Friedel, Jeremy Sobloff, and Michael D. Coe have given us a detailed view of the Mayas. Their communities had productive economies based not only on agriculture but also on handicrafts and long-distance trade. In often barren soil, except in some parts of the highlands, Mayan farmers used intensive agriculture, clearing, irrigating, and terracing to raise squash, chili peppers, and many other crops, including maize—which supplied 80 percent of their food. Mayan metalwork, cotton cloth, and chipped stone implements were traded widely, carried in large dugout canoes along the rivers and the Atlantic coast. Exchange was facilitated by the use of common goods as media of exchange, including cocoa beans, polished beads, salt, and lengths of cotton cloth.

Mayan society in this period was a rich mixture of old and new. An ancient kinship system prevailed among all classes, with lands assigned and controlled by the clans. Matriarchal values persisted, as indicated by some queens who retained power and influence. Women were generally respected, held some legal rights, and did some of the most important work, such as weaving. The shift toward patriarchy, however, was definite and unmistakable, as was seen in priorities accorded men in most social situations, such as being served first by women at meals. A more fundamental change involved the rise of social classes. Hereditary male nobles and priests were in most positions of authority and power, but craftspeople and merchants enjoyed privileges and status. Slaves, captured in military campaigns or kidnapped, did most of the hard work, particularly in the continuous heavy construction of ceremonial buildings. They were also subject to being used in religious sacrifice, although this was far less common than among the later Aztecs.

A hereditary priest-king, usually considered to be a descendant of a god, governed each Mayan center. He was assisted by a council of priests and nobles. His government levied taxes, supervised local government in outlying villages, and administered justice. It also was responsible for conducting foreign relations and making war. The Mayas were not very successful in large-scale military operations because their armies were drawn mainly from the nobility and were therefore limited in size. Nevertheless, armed with their obsidian-bladed weapons, they were equal to their neighbors in making war. Indeed, as time passed and cities vied for supremacy, wars became increasingly common. In the process, some centers remained independent, but most joined loosely organized leagues, based on common religious traditions, dynastic marriages, or diplomatic alignments.

Religion permeated all phases of Mayan life. Like the later Aztecs, the Mayas saw life as a burden and time as its measure, and they deified many natural phenomena, particularly the planets and stars, as powers to be appeased by human pain and suffering. Public blood-letting was part of normal ritualistic worship. Human sacrifice, usually accomplished by decapitation, was common, and wars to obtain prisoners for sacrifice were sometimes waged. The dominance of religion over everyday life is further illustrated by the general interpretation of law as religious principle and taxation as religious offerings. Economic value derived as much from the religious sanctity of a thing as from its material utility or scarcity. Moreover, education was aimed primarily at training priests; reading and writing were considered necessary religious skills, and mathematics and astronomy were valued mainly because they were required in scheduling ceremonies honoring the gods.

The two most significant achievements of the Mayas were their calendar and their writing system. Neither of these was original, but both were more efficient than those of earlier peoples. The Mayan astronomers, using only naked-eye observation, surpassed their European contemporaries. Their constant scanning of the heavens allowed them to perfect a solar calendar with 18 months of 20 days each and a five-day period for religious festivals. Using an ingenious cyclical system of notation known as the "long count," they dated events of the distant past for accurate record keeping and the scheduling of astronomical observations. Their notational mathematics, based on 20 rather than 10 as in the decimal system, employed combinations of dots and bars in vertical sequences, to indicate numbers above 20. For nonnumerical records, they combined **pictographs** and **glyphs,** which have recently been deciphered sufficiently to reveal specific historic events and their human dimensions.

DOCUMENT

Anonymous: Victory over the Underworld

These remarkable accomplishments in mathematics, astronomy, and writing were more than matched by the magnificent Mayan art and architecture. The plaza of each Mayan community was marked by at least one pyramid, topped by a temple. The one at Tikal towered to 229 feet, 16 feet higher than the Pyramid of the Sun at Teotihuacán. With their terraced sides and horizontal lines, Mayan pyramids showed a skilled sense of proportion. The highly stylized sculpture dec-

---

pictographs—Picture symbols.

glyphs—Symbolic characters in writing.

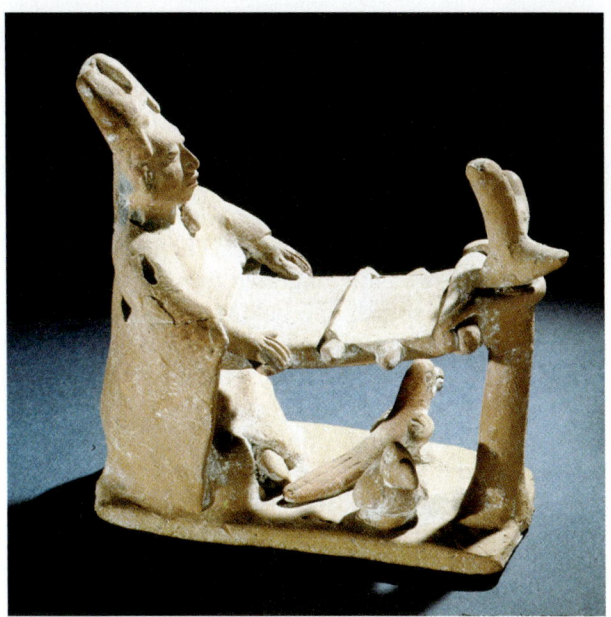

The Mesoamerican societies were at the same time sophisticated, complex, and powerful—and bloody in their human sacrifices to the gods. This seated figure, surrounded by winged messengers, seems to be looking off in the distance to anticipate what the divine powers might next demand from him.

orating their terraces is regarded by some authorities as the world's finest, even though the Mayan sculptors accomplished their intricate carving with only stone tools—there were no bronze or iron implements in the Americas at that time. The Mayas also developed mural painting to a high level of expression. Even their crafts, such as weaving, ceramics, and jewelry making, reveal a great aesthetic sense, subtlety of design, and manipulative skill.

THE POSTCLASSICAL ERA

- Which civilizations rose to prominence after the end of the classical era of Mesoamerican civilization?

The region's classical artistic development ended during the eighth and ninth centuries. The causes, not yet fully uncovered, have been generally attributed to factors ranging from overpopulation and internal struggles to soil exhaustion and Chichimec invasions from the north. Amid the accompanying upheavals, urban populations dwindled, and most of Teotihuacán's residents scattered in all directions, even into the Mayan lands. But there was no complete collapse; trade continued on a large scale, and the expanded use of writing indicated more social complexity and interstate competition, which contributed to intensified politi-

cal conflict. Consequently, the age produced a new cultural mode, with heavier emphases on militarism, war, and gods thirsting for human blood. Among many smaller but thriving city-states, in addition to the dying Teotihuacán, were the Mayan polities of Tikal, Chichén Itzá (cheech-EN eet-SAH), and Mayapán. Farther north, the Oaxacan centers were still flourishing after the tenth century, as were Atzcapotzalco (ahts-kah-poh-TSAL-koh), Xochicalco (hoh-chee-KAL-koh), and Cholula, with its colossal pyramid.

The Toltecs

Most prominent of all these centers was Tollan, the Toltec capital. Toltec history is unclear before 980, when Topiltzin (to-PIL-tzin), a legendary king, founded the city and created a new power located in the central Valley of Mexico. His subjects were a mixture of Chichimecs and former urbanites of the area, who may have served for a while as peacekeepers in the north. Over the next two centuries, the city became a great urban complex of 120,000 people, a hub of trade, and the center of an evolving Toltec confederacy that assumed the leading role formerly played by Teotihuacán. Meanwhile, Tollan's future was shaped by a struggle for power between Topiltzin and his enemies. The king had early adopted the Teotihuacán god **Quetzalcoatl** (kets-al-koh-AHT-el), who opposed human sacrifice; but followers of the traditional Toltec war god, **Tezcatlipoca** (tez-kat-le-POH-ka), ultimately rebelled and forced Topiltzin into exile. The victorious war cult took over, steadily expanding its hegemony, by conquest and trade, into an empire stretching from the Gulf of Mexico to the Pacific, including some Mayan cities of the south.

The tumultuous political conditions of the early postclassical period finally brought disaster to the Toltecs. Failing crops and internal dissension caused great outward migrations from Tollan and abandonment of the capital at the end of the twelfth century. Shortly after, the city was burned by Chichimecs. For two centuries thereafter, the area was a land of warring states and constantly forming and dissolving federations. Some cultural continuity, however, was maintained by peoples in the Oaxaca valley, notably the Zapotecs, whose culture was as old as the Olmec. Although they struggled constantly with neighboring peoples for supremacy and survival, the Zapotecs maintained towns, temples, ball courts, and art that helped preserve Mesoamerican traditions for later times.

Quetzalcoatl—The Toltec god of the civilization, goodness, and light; literally "plumed serpent."

Tezcatlipoca—The god of the night sky and sorcery; literally "smoking mirror"; initially Toltec in origin but also adopted by subsequent peoples, including the Aztecs.

This Aztec mask is a figure within a figure, and the person wearing the mask would hope to project animal strength and unearthly terror.

Toltec militarism spread from central to southern Mexico. It left the less developed Mayan highlands relatively undisturbed but brought decline and reorientation to the old lowland centers, such as Tikal. Severe droughts also drove migrants into northern Yucatán, where a developing cistern technology provided more water. At Chichén Itzá in the tenth century, a cosmopolitan Mexican-Mayan military elite established their dominance and maintained a trading network, by land and sea, throughout the southern region. From the early thirteenth into the fifteenth century, Mayapán was a fortified center, defended by mercenaries and maintaining leverage over subkingdoms by holding hostages from dependent royal families. Trade continued to grow, along with population, among the postclassical Mayas; but art, cultural pursuits, and even architecture deteriorated. The Spaniards were later to describe the Mayan people as fiercely independent, bloodthirsty, and, like the Aztecs, inclined to sacrifice war captives' hearts on their gods' altars.

The Aztecs

Arising in the confusion of the late postclassical era, the Aztec Confederacy came to conquer and dominate central Mexico from coast to coast in less than two centuries. The Aztecs, like the Toltecs before them, retained many of their old traditions while freely borrowing from the culture, religion, and technology of their neighbors and victims. The most significant example of this borrowing was their hydraulic agriculture. It was the major factor by which they increased population in the central Mexico to more than a million people living in some 50 city-states.

The Aztecs' story really begins with the founding of the capital at Tenochtitlán; their earlier history is quite obscure. They evidently migrated from the north into central Mexico some time before 1200. For a while they were dominated by other peoples, including the Toltecs. About 1325 they settled on an island in Lake Texcoco (the site of present-day Mexico City), later connecting their new town to the mainland by causeways. In its later days Tenochtitlán was an architectural wonder. The Aztecs built a dam to control the lake level, completed a freshwater aqueduct, and created floating artificial islands where irrigated fields supplied food for the capital. Within the imperial metropolis, beautiful avenues, canals, temples, and monuments symbolized increasing Aztec power, particularly after the early fifteenth century.

IMAGE
Aztec Warriors

The Aztecs completed the formation of their confederacy at the same time. During the early decades at Tenochtitlán, the Aztecs had fought as tributaries of Atzcapotzalco, the dominant city-state in the valley. In 1370 they accepted a king of assumed Toltec lineage. For decades they won victories and prospered in concert with their overlords, but in 1427 they rebelled, forming a "triple alliance" with nearby Texcoco and Tlacopán, which defeated Atzcapotzalco and became the major power in the region. For the Aztecs, these events brought great change. Internally, they shifted power from the old clan leaders to a rising military aristocracy. Externally, they started a series of conquests and trading agreements. A new imperial order developed, shared at first by the other two allies but increasingly dominated by Tenochitlán, whose ruler imposed his will as head of the army, leader of the state, and chief priest. The reigns of the Aztec kings Itzcoatl (1427–1440) and his nephew Montezuma I (1440–1468), ushered in this new era of rising centralism, efficiency, and expansion. It was still in progress under the ninth monarch, Montezuma II (1502–1520), at the time of the Spanish invasion.

DOCUMENT
Xicohtencatl, the Elder: "I Say This"

As the empire expanded, so did the state-controlled economy. Its base was agricultural land, particularly floating plots installed on the lake after the 1430s. Most were built by the government. Some were allotted to the ***calpulli*** (clans)—made up of the remnants of diverse ethnic groups that came together on the island of Tenochtitlán—for distribution to families. Others were developed as estates for the monarch

---

calpulli—Aztec social units based on family clans.

and the nobility; the latter were worked by tenants under government supervision. Rising agricultural production supported not only the engineering, dredging, stonework, and carpentry required for heavy construction but also artisans turning out weapons, cloth, ceramics, feather work, jewelry, and hundreds of other goods. Porters from distant places backpacked over mountains to the markets of the valley. A later Spanish observer reported that the great market at Tlatelolco (tlah-tel-LOHL-koh), serving Tenochtitlán, attracted 25,000 people daily.

Conquest and the increasing wealth that accompanied it modified the ancient social structure. The old *calpulli* developed into city wards, identified largely by occupational specialties. By 1500 most *calpulli* families were headed by men. Women could inherit property and divorce their husbands but were confined mostly to household tasks, except for midwives, healers, and prostitutes. Kinship still promoted social cohesion, but class status provided major incentives. The appointed nobility *(pipiltin)*, along with the priests, held both power and social status, but they were burdened with heavy responsibilities. Moreover, they held appointed rather than hereditary posts, although they could inherit property. Commoners could be made nobles by performing superior service, particularly in war. Craftspeople and merchants paid taxes but were exempt from military service; some long-distance merchants *(pochteca)* served the government as diplomats or spies in foreign states. Peasants worked their plots and served in the army; nonmembers of *calpulli* were tenants. Their lot was hardly better than that of the numerous slaves, except for the latter's potential role as ceremonial sacrifice victims.

Official documents of the period and other written accounts focus mainly on Mesoamerican social and political elites and conditions in the imperial capitals. However, recent archaeological studies throw fresh light on the lives of the Aztec common people and conditions in the provinces. Surveys of settlement patterns show that Aztec society experienced one of the most significant population explosions of premodern times. In the Valley of Mexico, the heartland of the Aztec Empire, population increased from 175,000 in the early Aztec period (1150–1350) to almost one million in the late period (1350–1519). This pattern of growth was duplicated elsewhere in the empire. To cope with this population explosion, the environment was altered: Farmers built dams and canals to irrigate cropland, constructed terraced stone walls on hillsides to form new fields, and drained swamps outside Tenochtitlán to create **chinampas** or floating gardens. With these changes emerged new villages and towns.

Excavations of rural sites near modern Cuernavaca (kwehr-nah-VAH-kah) disclose that provincial society was much more complex than previously thought. Commoners created a thriving marketing system whereby craft goods produced in their homes were exchanged for a variety of foreign goods. Houses at these sites were small, built of adobe brick walls supported on stone foundations. These houses were furnished with mats and baskets and had a shrine with two or three figurines and an incense burner on one of the walls. In this region the household production of cotton textiles was the major craft. All Aztec women spun and wove cloth, which provided garments, constituted the most common item of tribute demanded by the state, and served as currency in the marketplaces for obtaining other goods and services. In addition to textiles, some residents made paper out of the bark of the wild fig tree, used to produce books of pictographs and to burn in ritual offerings. According to written sources, Aztec commoners were subject to the nobles, who possessed most of the land and monopolized power in the polity. But new archaeological excavations show that the commoners were relatively prosperous people whose market system operated largely beyond state control.

The Aztec polity included subordinated allies and 38 provinces. The latter were taxed directly; most of the former paid tribute in some form; and all were denied free foreign relations. This polyglot empire was headed by a member of the royal family proclaimed to be the incarnation of the sun-god. His household was more lavish than many in Europe and swarmed with servants. A head wife supervised the concubines and scheduled their assignments, but Aztec queens rarely engaged in court intrigues or offered advice to the emperor, for he usually ruled without concern for other opinions. He was assisted in his official duties by a chief minister and subordinate bureaucracies for war, religion, justice, treasury, storehouses, and personnel. The capital and each province were administered directly by governors, most of whom were descended from former kings. They collected taxes, held court, arranged religious ceremonies, regulated economic affairs, and directed police activities. In addition, urban guilds, villages, and tribes had their own local officials. Vassal states were governed under their own laws but observed by resident Aztec emissaries. This whole system was defended by a large military organization, comprising allied forces, local militias, and an imperial guard of elite troops.

Aztec religion developed from the worship of animistic spirits, symbolizing natural forces seeking balance while in constant conflict. A pessimistic obsession with human futility also dominated the Aztec world-

"Song of Tlaltecatzin"

Chinampas—The floating gardens the Aztecs of Tenochtitlán built and tended on Lake Texcoco.

Admonishing Those Who Seek No Honor in War

view, perpetuating the common belief that the gods required human blood to sustain life. Thus, as they assembled their empire, the Aztecs came to envision their sun deity, **Huitzilopochtli** (wheet-tsee-loh-POHCHT-lee), as a bloodthirsty war god with an appetite for warriors captured in battle. In every city, the Aztecs built pyramids, topped by their two temples to the sun deity and Tlatelolco, god of rain. Here they honored Huitzilopochtli in great public ceremonies such as one in 1487 when bloodstained priests at the high altars tore out the living hearts of thousands of victims and held them up, quivering, to the sun. The need for sacrificial victims forced continuing conquests and later weakened the state as it faced the Spanish threat.

Comparing the Aztecs and Mayas with the Romans and Greeks can be an interesting theoretical exercise. The Aztec calendar, mathematics, and writing were derived mainly from Mayan sources, somewhat the way that Roman philosophy and science were based on Greek models. Although Aztec culture spawned skilled sculptors, painters, and craftspeople who produced in great numbers, they lacked the imagination of the Mayas, whom they indirectly copied, just as Roman artists largely imitated their Greek predecessors. Similarly, both Roman and Aztec cultures were characterized by respect for discipline, practicality, directness, and force. Each was highly skilled in engineering, as attested, for example, by their aqueducts and other feats for furnishing copious amounts of water to their respective capitals. They also shared a militaristic ethos and powerful standing armies.

The Inca

The great Inca Empire in the Andean highlands of South America reached its height in the early 1500s.

Inca Expansion

It extended 3500 miles between Ecuador and Chile, including almost impassable mountain ranges that separate the upper Amazon forests from the Pacific. The empire contained at least ten million people in 200 ethnolinguistic groups. It was six times the size of Texas. The capital, Cuzco, which had an estimated 200,000 inhabitants, was governed in a more centralized way than any city in Europe at the time. The Incas produced fine art and architecture and were superb engineers, but their major achievement was imperial organization. In this respect they compared favorably with the Romans and the Chinese.

A long tradition of scholarship, exemplified by researchers such as Ian Cameron, Richard W. Keating,

---

Huitzilopochtli—The patron deity of the Aztecs, god of the sun and of war.

and J. Alden Mason, gives us a detailed idea of Inca society. Although it rose very rapidly just before the Spanish conquest, Inca civilization evolved from ancient cultural foundations. Ceremonial and commercial centers had existed on the Peruvian plateau well before the Common Era. About 600 C.E. cities began rising in the highlands of the interior. During the next two centuries, tributary kingdoms drew together formerly isolated ceremonial centers of the Peruvian highlands. Some of the resulting states exercised control over the plain, along with territories in what are now Bolivia and Chile. Two kingdoms had capitals at Huari (WHA-ree) and Tiahuanaco (tee-ah-wah-NAH-koh) in south central Peru. When these states collapsed in the tenth century, they were succeeded by independent agrarian villages, which were nearly consumed by continuous warfare. A completely different situation developed along the northern coast, where the kingdom of Chimu developed a civilization, marked by extensive irrigation, rising population, centralized government, public works, high craft production, widespread trade, and an expanding tributary domain. This polity was conquered and its culture absorbed by the Incas in 1476.

The Incas created their empire while waging ruthless struggles in the highlands. According to their own legends, these "children of the sun" settled the valley of Cuzco, in the heartland of the Andes, about 1200 C.E., having migrated from the south, possibly from the region of Tiahuanaco. During the next hundred years they were a simple peasant people, organized by kinship in clans *(ayllu)*, living in villages, fulfilling mutual labor obligations, and worshipping their local demigods *(chuacas)*. To strengthen their unity and better protect themselves in constant wars for survival, they formed a monarchy, developed their military, and began taking over territory near Cuzco. In this competition they were only moderately successful during the reigns of the first seven kings, to the early fifteenth century.

Like the Aztec state at almost the same time, the Inca polity began a climactic period of rapid development with a memorable series of rulers. Viracocha (veh-rah-CO-cha) (d. 1438), the eighth emperor, turned his ragtag army into a formidable fighting machine, conquered adjoining territories, and instituted a divine monarchy, with his lineage accepted as descendants of the sun-god. His son, Pachacuti (pahch-ah-KEU-tee) (1438–1471), was a reformer, religious leader, and builder who stands among the most powerful people ever to rule in the New World, and received the admiration of the Spanish occupiers. He began arduous campaigns to the north and south, notably against Chimu. Topa Yupanqui (yeu-PAHN-kee) (1471–1493), Pachacuti's son and successor who commanded the Inca armies after 1463, completed the

Document: Father Bernabé Cobo, "Pachacuti, the Greatest Inca"

Bernabé Cobo (1582–1657) spent 61 of his 75 years in the Americas, from his first arrival in the Antilles to his death in Lima. During that time the Jesuit priest combined his duties with his qualities as a scientist and observer to write at great length about the flora and fauna of Latin and southern America. He entered into close relations with the Indians, as he spread the faith, and came to have a deep understanding of respect for them.

This selection is from Chapter 12 of his *History of the Inca Empire*. Cobo relied on Indian legends and contemporary Indian testimony, as well as earlier Spanish writings as he dealt with the civilization his countrymen had attacked. Far from viewing the Incans as barbaric and "uncivilized" as later, nineteenth-century missionaries would do, Cobo showed the capacity to understand and even admire them.

Viracocha Inca left four sons by his principal wife; they were called Pachacuti Inca Yupanqui, Inca Roca, Tupa Yupanqui, and Capac Yupanqui. The first one succeeded him in the kingdom, and concerning the rest, although they were lords and grandees, nothing is said. Pachacuti married a lady named Mama Anahuarque, native to the town of Choco, near Cuzco, and he founded a family that they call Iñaca Panaca. This king was the most valiant and warlike, wise and statesmanlike of all the Incas, because he organized the republic with the harmony, laws, and statutes that it maintained from that time until the arrival of the Spaniards. He injected order and reason into everything; eliminated and added rites and ceremonies; made the religious cult more extensive; established the sacrifices and the solemnity with which the gods were to be venerated, enlarged and embellished the temples with magnificent structures, income, and a great number of priests and ministers; reformed the calendar; divided the year into twelve months, giving each one its name; and designated the solemn fiestas and sacrifices to be held each month. He composed many elegant prayers with which the gods were to be invoked, and he ordered that these prayers be recited at the same time that the sacrifices were offered. He was no less careful and diligent in matters pertaining to the temporal welfare of the republic; he gave his vassals a method of working the fields and taking advantage of the lands that were so rough and uneven as to be useless and unfruitful; he ordered that rough hillsides be terraced and that ditches be made from the rivers to irrigate them. In short, nothing was overlooked by him in which he did not impose all good order and harmony; for this reason he was given the name of Pachacuti, which means "change of time or of the world"; this is because as a result of his excellent government things improved to such an extent that times seemed to have changed and the world seemed to have turned around; thus, his memory was very celebrated among the Indians, and he was given more honor in their songs and poems than any of the other kings that either preceded him or came after him.

After having shown himself to be so devoted to the sun and having taken the care just mentioned that all worship him in the same way that his ancestors had done, one day Pachacuti began to wonder how it was possible that a thing could be God if it was so subject to movement as the Sun, that it never stops or rests for a moment since it turns around the world every day; and he inferred from this meditation that the Sun must not be more than a messenger sent by the Creator to visit the universe; besides, if he were God, it would not be possible for a few clouds to get in front of him and obscure his splendor and rays so that he could not shine; and if he were the universal Creator and lord of all things, sometimes he would rest and from his place of rest he would illuminate all the world and command whatever he wished; and thus, there had to be another more powerful lord who ruled and governed the Sun; and no doubt this was Pachayachachic. He communicated this thought to the members of his council, and in agreement with them, he decided that Pachayachachic was to be preferred to the Sun, and within the city of Cuzco, he built the Creator his own temple which he called Quishuarcancha, and in it he put the image of the Creator of the world, Viracocha Pachayachachic.

Questions to Consider

1. What was there in Pachacuti's quest to understand the universe that would appeal to Bernabé Cobo?
2. Discuss Pachacuti's accomplishments as enumerated by Cobo. Do you think that the Spaniard's admiration came because the Incan chief possessed "European" qualities, or because he chose local solutions to local problems?
3. Would you like to be a citizen in a state led by Pachacuti? Why? Why not?

From *History of the Inca Empire*, trans. and ed. Roland Hamilton from the holograph manuscript in the *Biblioteca Capitular y Colombina de Sevilla*, © 1979. Reprinted by permission of the University of Texas Press.

Machu Picchu, a natural fortress on a narrow ridge between two mountains, was built by the Incas probably after 1440. When the last Inca ruler died, the fortress was abandoned and lost until its rediscovery in 1911.

annexation of Chimu and extended the empire south into central Chile. The next emperor, Huayna Capac (WHAY-nah KAH-pahk) (1493–1527), completed the subjugation of Ecuador, put down rebellions, and attempted to impose order, although the empire was seething with internal discontent when the Spaniards arrived in 1532.

Despite internal problems, intensified by the steep slopes and harsh weather of the Andes, the Incas demonstrated rare technical skills in fashioning their civilization in difficult and often dangerous circumstances. They were master engineers, carrying water long distances by canals and aqueducts, using techniques borrowed from the Chimu Empire, building cities high in the Andes, and constructing networks of roads along the coast and through the mountains, along with suspension bridges and interconnecting valley roadways. All were designed to knit together a vast region that in the Inca Empire covered some 380,000 square miles.

Archaeologists have long known that the Incas gained a knowledge of canals and irrigation systems from the Chimu: Recent excavation have revealed new evidence about their sophisticated use of that technology. Canals are difficult to construct: If the slope is too narrow, the canal silts up; if it is too steep, its sides erode. Inca engineers devised different canal shapes to control the water's speed and prevent its velocity from ruining the canal. One "intervalley" canal carried water to a city from 60 miles away; it was only one of many networks, involving thousands of feeder canals, that stretched for hundreds of miles. These hydraulic techniques have been described as deserving to stand with Egypt's pyramids and China's Great Wall as among the world's greatest engineering feats. With irrigation canals constructed far removed from the water's source, the Incas farmed 40 percent more land than is achieved today. But if skills fail, land can quickly return to desert conditions. We have yet to learn what caused the destruction or abandonment of these canal systems—was it human or environmental forces, or both?

Hydraulic feats were matched by sophisticated organizational skills. To link the empire together, Inca leaders established a communication service, using state-built roads, runner-messengers, rest houses, and smoke signals. Governing by means of a divide-and-rule technique, they appealed wherever possible to traditional prejudices among conquered peoples, perpetuating feuds, courting native leaders, settling colonies of subjects among their enemies, and generally provoking disunity among potentially rebellious areas. They also relied on a common official language and the cult of divine monarchy to unify their own people, particularly the elite. Every part of their system was fitted together in a highly disciplined and integrated whole. Before the Incas, few other states had succeeded so effectively in regimenting millions of people over such great distances and against such formidable obstacles.

Like all civilized peoples, the Incas faced the problem of population expansion and a limited food supply. They solved it well enough to support large military, bureaucratic, and priestly establishments by developing what economists call a *command economy*. They used no money, no credit, and very little trade beyond local barter. The state planned all economic operations and kept all accounts. Government assigned to families the land to be worked; local family heads, under government supervision, directed workers who produced the crops and saw that harvests were brought to state warehouses. Labor taxes provided work done on public projects, the nobles' estates, and royal lands. A similar approach was used in manufacturing, with craftspeople producing in local guilds, noble households, and palace workshops. From its storehouses, the government distributed goods to individuals, to the military, and to government projects. In the process, it built roads, operated hospitals, and maintained schools. All property, even the nobles' land, was state-owned and assigned, except for distinctly personal possessions, including some luxury goods owned by the privileged classes.

This state-controlled economy functioned by way of a precisely defined class structure, built on the lingering kinship tradition. Commoners were kept loyal and disciplined by identifying the state with their ancient *ayllus*. Inca nobles maintained respect because they were all related directly or indirectly to the royal lineage and therefore shared the divine mandate to rule. They held the highest positions in government, the army, and the priesthood. A notch lower were lesser aristocrats and nobles among conquered peoples, who held local offices, up to subgovernors in the provinces. The two upper classes made up a privileged elite. Trained in special schools, they were rewarded with luxuries in food, dress, and housing. They were also exempted from taxes and cruel punishments. At the third level were common workers. They were generally confined to their villages; their work was prescribed; their dress and food were restricted; and government checked even the cleanliness of their houses. Commoners were thus little better off than the lowest class of slaves, who were often taken as prisoners of war and assigned to serve the upper classes.

The shift from kinship toward class division was accompanied by a decline of matriarchal values. Upper-class women shared some social status with their husbands, and all women could inherit property when they were widowed; but they were generally subordinated and exploited. Indeed, a fifteenth-century royal decree prohibited women from testifying in court because they were by nature "deceitful, mendacious, and fainthearted."[1] Female commoners worked in the fields, while women of all classes were expected to keep house, mind the children, and serve the needs of men. Many were concubines or surplus wives, the number depending on the husbands' wealth and status. The most beautiful and intelligent young girls were drafted as "chosen women." Some would become "virgins of the sun," serving as nuns and weavers in the temple workshops; others would become concubines of the emperor or nobles; a few would be sacrificed. All were honored as servants of the state.

All authority in the Inca state originated with the hereditary divine emperor, who exercised the power of life and death over all his subjects. He was usually aloof, even with his own immediate family, although he might, if he chose, delegate authority to the queen (his full sister after 1438) or take advice from his mother. With its thousands of servants and concubines, his court was a magnificent display of wealth and power. It was also the locus of a central government that included agencies for rituals (religion), war, treasury, accounts, and public works. The chief ministers were advisers to the Imperial Council, consisting of the emperor and four viceroys, who governed the four provinces. Each province, about the size of New York State, was divided into approximately 40 districts, under subgovernors and their assistants. Authority in the districts was further subdivided, ultimately into units of ten families. Officials at each level reported regularly to superiors and were subject to frequent inspections. This system regulated every aspect of life, including labor, justice, marriage, and even morals.

The power of the ruler depended largely on an excellent military system, which featured compulsory service. Instructors in the villages trained peasant boys for the army; the most promising were marked for advancement when they were called to active service in their twenties. They served for two years before retiring to the labor reserve and militia. The army was organized in units of 10, 50, 100, 1000, and 10,000, under officers who held complete authority over subordinates. A combat force of 200,000, with support units, was always under arms. It was supplied from military storehouses throughout the country and garrisoned in mighty stone fortresses, each with independent water sources. Troops from these centers ruthlessly suppressed any resistance to the regime.

A second base for Inca authority was religion. As the empire grew, its priests appropriated the gods of conquered peoples and included them in a vast pantheon, headed by the Inca sun-god. For example, the virgins of the sun, with their ceremonies and temples, evolved from an earlier moon goddess cult among **matrilineal** societies. War victims would on occasion be sacrificed to the sun, as would some children of "chosen women." In later times the servants of an emperor, as well as his favorite concubines, were sent with him, at his death, to serve him in the hereafter. To emphasize the emperors' divinity and symbolize the state's continuity, dead emperors were mummified, seated on thrones in their sacred palaces, and attended by living servants, wives, and priests. On public occasions these figures were paraded before the people, who bowed before them in reverence. Such ceremonies were conducted by a clerical establishment of 4000 priests in the capital and many scores of thousands more throughout the country.

CASE STUDY
Death in War and Childbirth in the Americas

There was a remarkable exception to this religious mind-set in the person of the emperor Pachacuti. A highly successful military leader who largely laid the empire's foundation by consolidating the area around Cuzco and annexing the rich Titicaca basin, this multitalented innovator established **Quechua** (KECH-wah) as the administrative language, reformed the calendar, introduced methods of terracing the hillsides and extending irrigation, and created an efficient public service. Although regarded as a direct descendant of the sun-god, Pachacuti asked himself how the sun could be the supreme deity since it never rested but

---

matrilineal—Tracing hereditary descent through the mother, not the father.

Quechua—A language of the Central Andes, spoken by the Incas and today the most widely spoken indigenous tongue of the Americas.

revolved endlessly around the earth. He concluded that the sun was itself a messenger sent by a more powerful being who from his place of rest could illuminate and command the world. This must be the universal Creator, Viracocha ("Lord"), who governed the sun and had brought into being all other deities. And in his honor the emperor constructed a temple in Cuzco. But, as in the case of Akhenaton, his conceptual forerunner in Egypt, Pachacuti's nascent monotheism did not prevail; later rulers continued to sacrifice victims to the sun-god—though not to the extent practiced by the Aztecs.

Order and security were dominant values in Inca cultural expression, and neither aesthetic concerns nor philosophical speculation received much attention. As we have seen, religious innovation was given short shrift, and any theorizing was subordinated to the practicalities of a state cult and the morality of power—treason and cowardice were considered the worst sins. The Incas had no written records and seem to have lacked even the pictographs of Mesoamerica. Instead they relied on oral traditions, supplemented by mnemonic devices such as the system of knotted strings called **quipus** (KE-peuz). These oral traditions were dealt a lethal blow by the Spanish conquest.

The Inca lunar calendar was inaccurate and provided no starting point for the identification of historical events. Although the Incas were excellent craftspeople, capable of producing fine pottery and metalwork in copper and gold, their most striking technical and cultural accomplishments were in engineering and massive architecture. Without using mortar, they fitted immense slabs of stone into temple and fortress walls. This efficiency is still exhibited in existing roads, bridges, terraced fields, and stone fortresses, such as Machu Picchu.

THE AMERINDIANS OF NORTH AMERICA

- *Why was there no unification of the North American Amerindians, such as there was in Mesoamerica?*

In the past century Hollywood and the popular media reinforced the fallacy that all Native Americans in North America constituted a single culture with a common lifestyle. The mounted, war-bonneted warrior of the plains has too often been considered the archetype of the "Red Man," presented in the "Wild West Shows" of the last century. Some Plains Indians were indeed fine mounted warriors, but they were only a fraction of the complex family of North American Indians.

European settlers found the Native Americans more diverse in their languages and appearances than the Europeans themselves. Two hundred distinct North American languages have been classified. Amerindian societies presented a wide spectrum of variation: from small bands of hunter-gatherers and farmers to well-organized states. A similar diversity was found in their arts and crafts; various regions excelled in basketry, weaving, sculpture, totem-carving, and boat making.

There is a serious debate among scholars as to the number of Native Americans at the time of the European invasions. Estimates range from as low as 2 million to as many as 18 million people in the area north of Mexico—most estimates fall between these extremes. In any case, much of North America was well populated at the end of the fifteenth century. Amerindians north of the Rio Grande did not produce the massive technological and governmental achievements found in Mesoamerica and South America. As with Paleolithic and Neolithic societies in Asia, Africa, and Europe before the Common Era, their populations were smaller, and consequently, they did not create large cities, with their complex division of labor and urban way of life. More often, they typically survived by hunting and fishing until knowledge of food raising spread north from Mesoamerica.

For North American Indians before 1492, agriculture where it could be practiced had the same effect as elsewhere in the world. A more dependable food supply made possible stable settlements in which men cleared the fields and women tended the crops. Marked population growth, with accompanying large village or town centers, and political and military power occurred in the Rio Grande, Ohio, Mississippi, and St.

North American Civilizations

c. 3000–2500 B.C.E.	Watson Brake settlements
c. 800 B.C.E.–600 C.E.	Adena and Hopewell cultures
c. 900–1300	Cahokia flourishes
c. 300 B.C.E.–1350 C.E.	Mogollon culture
c. 1100	Establishment of Navajo culture
c. 1300	Arrival of Mandans in Great Plains

---

quipus—A mnemonic system based on knotted strings used by the Inca to keep records and send messages.

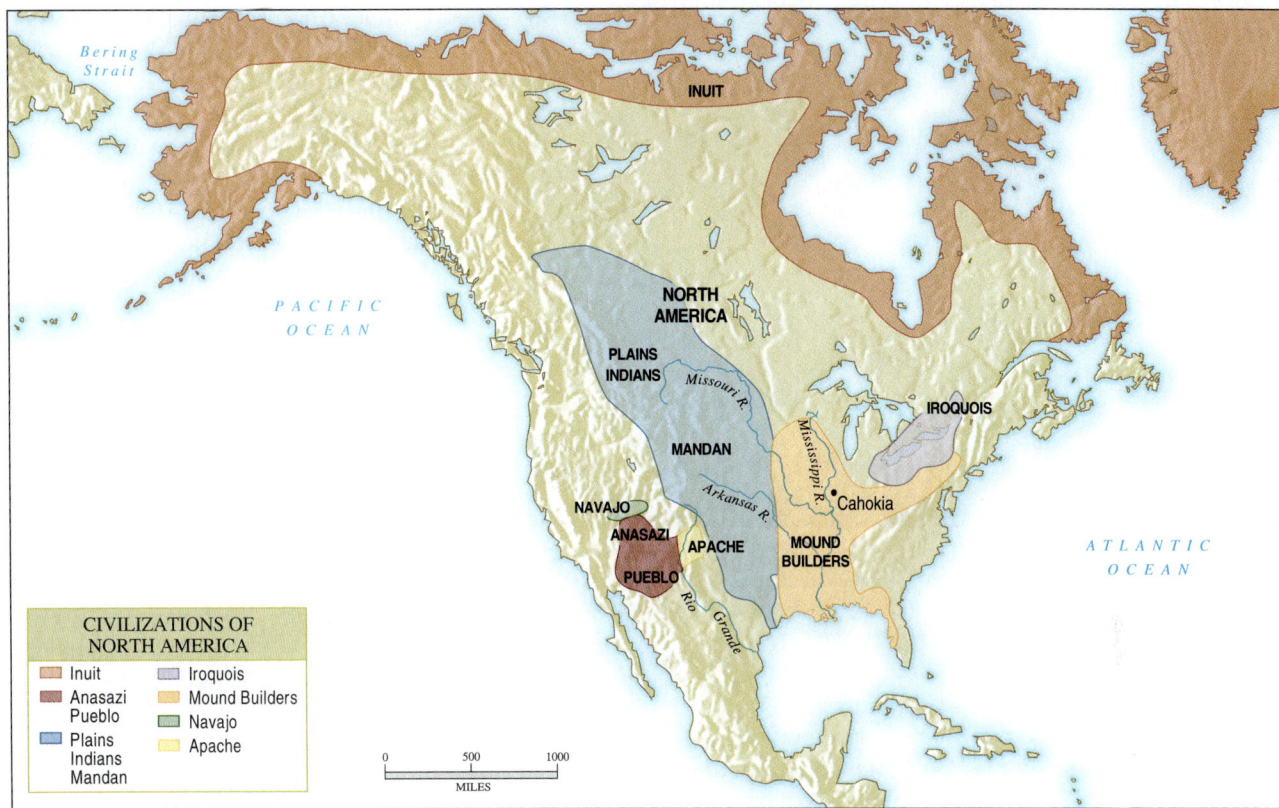

In the vastness of the North American continent, the varied environmental challenges led to the development of hundreds of different Indian tribes—more than 250 alone in the present-day state of California.

Lawrence valleys. In these places, overpopulation exhausted the soil and occasionally created environmental problems that led to the decline of the urban centers. Climate changes and European-borne pandemics in the fifteenth and sixteenth centuries devastated the Native American population, both those settled in the cities and the nomadic peoples.

The Iroquois of the Northeast Woodlands

Europeans arriving in what is now upper New York State found various groups speaking dialects of a common Iroquoian language. They had created a distinctive culture by 1000 C.E. and subsequently formed the League of the Five Nations. They used the metaphor of the longhouse, their traditional communal dwelling, to describe their political alliance: the Mohawk along the Hudson were the "keepers of the eastern door," adjoined in sequence by the Oneida, Onondaga, and Cayuga, with the Seneca, "keepers of the western door." When the Tuscarora joined in the early eighteenth century, the confederacy became known as the Six Nations. The Iroquois eventually extended their control from the Great Lakes toward the Atlantic by subjugating the nomadic, food-gathering Algonquin people.

The Iroquois had the advantage of being agriculturists with permanent villages. Some of these had several hundred residents and extensive fields where maize, beans, squash, and tobacco were grown. Fish traps were built across streams, and smokehouses preserved joints of game. Related families lived in the longhouses, long rectangular buildings protected by high wooden palisades. Women played a notable part: They owned the homes and gardens, and, since descent was matrilineal, chose the leaders. If the men chosen did not give good leadership, they could be replaced.

The Adena and Hopewell of the Ohio Valley

In the area of present-day Kentucky and Ohio, important Amerindian settlements took root between 800 B.C.E. and 600 C.E. Known generally as the Adena and Hopewell cultures, these Amerindians developed complex societies from the Missouri River to the Appalachians and from the Great Lakes to the Gulf of Mexico. Their settlements were based on the work of Indian women who, over two to three millennia,

The Great Serpent Mound in Ohio is a rich repository of the North American Indian life centered in the Adena culture. Active between 500 B.C.E. and 100 C.E. the Indians of the Adena culture had a well-developed village life and traded with other peoples from Canada to the Gulf of Mexico.

mastered the cultivation of seed plants such as sunflowers and squash and maize that arrived in the area in the fourth century B.C.E. As in Mesoamerica and South America, by 1000, maize cultivation sustained the peoples of the Ohio and Mississippi valley regions. Archaeologists think that the Hopewell and Adena cultures survived on a diet of fish, game, nuts, and other plant life.

The Adena and Hopewell cultures developed differing ways to construct their homes: the Adena chose to live in circular houses made out of poles and covered with mats and thatched roofs, while the Hopewell built round or oval houses with more protective roofs made of skins, bark from trees, and a combination of thatch and clay. They had a sophisticated view of the afterlife, as can be seen in the effort they took to bury their dead. The Native Americans near Watson Brake in northeast Louisiana (3000–2500 B.C.E.) and the peoples of the Adena culture at the beginning of the Common Era built thousands of earthen mounds for their dead. The Adena interred their deceased in vast cone-shaped mounds of earth, sometimes 500 feet around. Sometimes the dead were cremated, and the ashes were placed in the mounds along with all sorts of relics such as carved stone tablets, pipes smoked during religious ceremonies, and jewelry. The Hopewell did the same on an even larger scale for the more distinguished members of their families. Archaeologists have found evidence in these mounds of stone and clay items from both coasts, imported copper from the Great Lakes, and flaked stone items from the Tennessee valley.

Along with the impressive burial mounds, archaeologists have found indications of other projects indicating the combined efforts of hundreds of people in addition to a substantial investment of wealth. At Newark, Ohio, for example, the ceremonial site covers 4 square miles. Such enterprises indicate a long period of relative peace, generations remaining in the same place, and a substantial level of wealth. Archaeologists have also found indications of contacts with tribes across North America. Whether through trading or tribute, the Ohio valley societies had access to metals and goods found only in the Rocky Mountain area and shells from the Gulf coast. They had mastered the manufacture of tools, pottery, and copper jewelry.

The Mississippian Culture

At the end of the sixth century C.E. another major Amerindian culture made its appearance in the area just east of present-day St. Louis. Archaeologists are still investigating the origins and extent of this culture from the various burial sites, the most important of which is that at Cahokia, Illinois. Unlike the Adena and Hopewell cultures, the Mississippian culture lived in houses made out of thin pieces of wood (laths) covered with clay—so-called wattle-and-daub houses. These took various shapes in the large villages of the area. So influential was this culture that it came to dominate most of the region west of the Mississippi to the Plains, as can be seen in the Spiro Mounds in eastern Oklahoma.

The Mississippian peoples benefited from mastering the raising of maize, beans, and squash, and they tied their religion to the planting and harvesting cycles. Their burial mounds took the form of flat-topped pyramids, arranged around a central square. In the most developed regions, fortresslike palisades surrounded the site. The Cahokia complex was constructed over a period of nearly three centuries (c. 900–c. 1150). The centerpiece of the Cahokia site is a pyramid with a base of more than 18 acres, reaching a height of almost 100 feet. This is only one of more than 80 such mounds to be found at Cahokia, a city more than 6 miles long. There was no set burial practice for the Mississippian culture—remains have also been found in cemeteries, in urns, and under the floors of houses.

After the twelfth century the peoples in the Mississippian culture passed a highly complex religion along from generation to generation—an indication of their stability, continuity, and sophistication. The extent of their wealth enabled them to construct temples filled with ceremonial objects such as large stone scepters and copper plates. Their religion used symbols such as the cross, the sun, arrows surrounded by

An artist's creation of what Cahokia might have been like at its height.

semicircles, a sunburst, and—most intriguing—an outstretched hand with an eye in the palm. The art that derived from the religion featured portrayals of gods based on animals, rattlesnakes with feathers and wings, and people portrayed as birds. Vessels found at the sites indicate the presence of human sacrifice: jars with human faces painted on them and portrayals of the heads of sacrificed victims. These are indications that not only adults but also infants were given up to the higher deity the Mississippi culture believed controlled their lives.

Excavations of the Cahokia mounds give evidence of an hierarchical society that maintained order and productivity through brutality. Even though it was far distant from the Aztec and Incan Empires, there were several similarities between the political and religious systems and social repression of Cahokia and the systems in Mesoamerica and South America. For a while at the beginning of the thirteenth century, Cahokia was probably the largest city in North America, with a population larger than that of medieval London. At the end of the fourteenth century Cahokia began to decline. Archaeologists point to climate change, soil exhaustion, and the unification of those peoples Cahokia had repressed as an effective enemy force as likely causes for the end of Cahokia as a major power.

The Mogollon, the Hohokam, the Anasazi, and the Fremont Culture

The southwestern Amerindian cultures lived in the most environmentally challenging part of the continental United States, the dry and rocky regions of present-day Utah, Arizona, New Mexico, and Colorado. In response to their surroundings, they produced the most advanced levels of technology and agriculture around 300 B.C.E. The Mogollon, Hohokam, and Anasazi grew maize, beans, and squash, each group evolving its own techniques. The homes of each group were built out of adobe brick or other techniques of masonry, sometimes on extremely challenging sites.

Each group also produced pottery that could rank in beauty with any in the world.

The Mogollon culture of southwestern New Mexico lasted almost 1600 years, from around 300 B.C.E. to 1350 C.E. Its people built their homes low to the ground along the tops of ridges. Villages were built around large underground buildings used for religious ceremonies and as pit houses until the eleventh century; thereafter, they built these structures at ground level. Because of the constant threat of drought, they developed a diversified economy based on hunting, gathering, and farming. Relatively isolated, they saw little need to change over the centuries.

The Hohokam culture grew along the valleys of the Salt and Gila Rivers. Its architecture was similar to that of the early Mogollon, although the Hohokam built not just ceremonial structures but also their homes inside underground pits. Perhaps learning from the Mesoamerican cultures, the Hohokam constructed an impressive network of canals, some more than 30 miles long, 6 to 10 feet deep, and 15 to 30 feet wide. The extent of these canals proves the existence not only of wealth but also of substantial social organization. The Hohokam also borrowed their religion, their burial practices, and even some of their games from the Mesoamericans.

Deriving from these two cultures was the Anasazi, which appeared around 300 C.E. Of the three cultures, the Anasazi had the most sophisticated and most impressive architecture and the largest area of influence—from the Idaho-Utah border to the Gulf of California. Early on, they built their homes in the shape of beehive-shaped domes made out of logs held together by a mudlike mortar. They grew maize and made pottery, like the Mississippian culture, and stored both in warehouse-like structures. Around 700 C.E. they took their economic development one step further by beginning the manufacture of cotton cloth. Their technological genius is apparent from their use of two forms of irrigation: runoff by building dikes and terracing hills and subsoil by constructing sand dunes at the base of hills to hold the runoff of the

The Cliff Palace of the Anasazi, Mesa Verde National Park, Colorado, is among the important Anasazi ruins to be found in the southwestern United States.

sometimes torrential rains. Their lives revolved around their religion, with ceremonies to placate the gods to hold off storms and to ensure fertility.

The Anasazi are best known today for their architectural accomplishments. Around the eleventh century they began to construct cities, with houses built in the shapes of squares and semicircles. They used all of the available materials to build these settlements; with wood, mud, and stone, they erected cliff dwellings and the equivalent of terraced apartment houses. One such structure, with some 500 living units, was the largest residential building in the North America until the completion of an apartment house in New York in 1882. At their height, these master architects constructed around a dozen towns and nearly 200 villages. The disappearance of the Anasazi around 1300 remains a mystery. It is believed that a combination of a long drought, internecine conflicts, and the arrivals of the Navajo and the Apache led to their demise.

To the north of the Anasazi there were a number of different societies spread across the Colorado Plateau and into Idaho. They were a diverse group: Some depended on farming while others were hunters and they spoke different languages. Anthropologists have labeled this group the Fremont culture. They shared traits with the Navajo in that they raised corn, used the same kinds of tools, and lived in pit houses. The culture flourished between the sixth and the fourteenth centuries. Recently one of the best-preserved settlements of the Fremont culture was revealed to have been found near Horse Canyon, Utah in the Range Creek site.

The Navajo, the Apache, and the Mandan

Three other Amerindian civilizations established their presence before the arrival of Europeans. The Navajo, the largest Native American group in the United States, came down from the north to the Southwest sometime in the eleventh century. There they borrowed extensively from the indigenous cultures.

A century or so later, the Apache, who speak a language close to that of the Navajo, arrived in the southwest and by the end of the 1500s lived in parts of the present states of Arizona, Colorado, and New Mexico. They, too, were heavily influenced by the cultures present there.

Finally, the Mandan, who based their economy on fur trading and hunting, came to the vast valley of the Missouri River from east of the Mississippi in the late 1300s. There had been Amerindians in this region since 12,000–8,000 B.C.E. who hunted on foot on the Great Plains for mammoths, mastodons, and bison using spears tipped with Clovis points. Archaeological sites in Canada indicate that Indians hunted and slaughtered buffalo for more than 7000 years. By 1000 C.E. the use of bows and arrows was common throughout the plains. When the Mandan moved west, they became yet another in a long series of Amerindians who harvested the animal wealth of the mid-continent.

The Far North: Inuit and Aleut

The appearance of the Inuit, also known as the Eskimos, is shrouded in controversy. Some observers assert that they descended from ancient seagoing peoples; others believe that they developed their culture in Alaska after the last ice age. They speak much the same language as the Aleut, whose origins are similarly unclear. It is accepted that the two groups split apart more than 4000 years ago and that they are tied more closely to Asians than the Amerindians are.

The Aleut stayed largely in the area that is now known as the Alaskan peninsula, the Aleutian Islands, and the far eastern portion of Russia. The Inuit spread along the area south of the Arctic Circle from the Bering Strait across the top of Canada to Greenland. Both peoples lived by hunting and fishing. The Aleut hunted sea lions, otters, and seals from kayaks—small boats made of a wood frame over which skins were stretched. The Inuit showed more flexibility, hunting both sea and land animals, fishing in fresh and salt water. Their diet was based primarily on the caribou, musk-ox, walruses, and whales. They used the kayak too, but supplemented it with canoes and dogsleds.

The Navajos constructed houses called hogans *to shelter themselves from the often harsh climate of the high desert in the American Southwest.*

Their greatest accomplishment in seafaring, whaling vessels was the umiak, a larger boat with a wood frame covered with caribou hide, in which several people could row.

By about 100 C.E. the Inuit had established large villages; one of the biggest, with around 400 homes, was near present-day Nome, Alaska. To counter the arctic cold, they dug as much as 20 inches into the permafrost to erect their homes, which they then covered with poles and sod. In settlements such as that near present-day Nome, archaeologists have found large structures for the performance of religious rites, led by shamans who claimed to be able to heal diseases and wounds.

CONCLUSION

Before the European invasions and colonization, the Americas produced a rich variety of highly sophisticated and complex civilizations in response to the varied environmental challenges and opportunities of the Western Hemisphere. Some of these groups made the transition from food hunting to food raising, and some did not.

In Central and South America advanced agriculture supplied the foundation to support growing populations. This in turn led to the establishment of villages, and then cities, and, finally, far-flung states. More food and more wealth made possible leisure and priestly classes who had the time and resources to consolidate their power through control of religion as well as producing an advanced art, architecture, and discoveries in mathematics and astronomy.

In North America, environmental conditions were harsher and did not permit a similar accumulation of wealth as in Central and South America. Some Indian tribes remained hunter-gatherers. Others established settled villages and complex civilizations, but without the power and sophistication of the peoples to the south.

Tragically, a combination of climate changes, pandemics—both indigenous and foreign—and European invasions diminished the population by an estimated 80 percent by 1650. Those who survived were subjugated or later forced from their lands. Although they fought bravely against overwhelming odds, the Amerindians would have to struggle to maintain their identities in the centuries to come.

Suggestions for Web Browsing

You can obtain more information about topics included in this chapter at the websites listed below. See also the companion website that accompanies this text, **http://www.ablongman.com/brummett,** which contains an online study guide and additional resources.

Mesoweb, including Illustrated Encyclopedia of Mesoamerica
http://www.mesoweb.com/

Mesoweb is devoted to ancient Mesoamerica and its cultures: the Olmec, Mayas, Aztecs, Toltecs, Mixtecs, Zapotecs, and others.

University of Pennsylvania Museum of Archaeology and Art: Mesoamerica
http://www.museum.upenn.edu/new/exhibits/galleries/mesoamericaframedoc1.html

A history of Mesoamerican culture as reflected by the many artifacts in the university's museum.

National Museum of the American Indian
http://www.nmai.si.edu/

Website of the Smithsonian Institution's National Museum of the American Indian offers a look at one of the finest and most complete collections of items from the indigenous peoples of the Western Hemisphere.

Arctic Studies Center
http://www.mnh.si.edu/arctic/

Smithsonian Institution site dedicated to the study of Arctic peoples, culture, and environments includes numerous images, as well as audio and video segments of dance and discussion.

Literature and Film

For a sensitive and moving portrayal of the Indian life before Columbus in North America see Ruth B. Hill's *Hanta Yo: An American Saga* (Doubleday, 1979). Kathleen King's *Cricket Sings: A Novel of Pre-Columbian Cahokia* (Ohio University Press, 1983) gives an imaginative presentation of life in that Mississippian metropolis. An amusing concoction is A. Tanner Smith's *Anasazi and the Viking* (Sunstock, 1992), a not-totally-inconceivable meeting of Europeans and Amerindians. Insights into the Iroquois world can be gained from Joseph Bruchac, *The Boy Who Lived with the Bears and Other Iroquois Stories* (HarperCollins, 1995). A penetrating novel first published in 1826 has been recently translated by Guillermo I. Castillo-Feliis Félix Varela, *Xicoténcatl: An anonymous historical novel about the events leading up to the conquest of the Aztec Empire* (University of Texas, 1999). Another viewpoint on the Spanish conquest from the viewpoint of Atahualpa is given in Suzanne Alles Blom, *Inca, the Scarlet Fringe* (Forge, 2000). David Drew provides a window into the rich Mayan culture in his *The Lost Chronicles of the Maya Kings* (University of California, 1999).

PBS offers presentations on the Incas and the Mayas in their *Odyssey* series. See also the PBS series: *Seeking the First Americans, Surviving Columbus, Myths and Moundbuilders,* and the *Chaco Legacy*.

Suggestions for Reading

For a useful summary of the theories of migration into the Americas, see Sasha Nemecek, "Who were the First Americans," in *Scientific American,* September 2000, pp. 80–87. A sound, in-depth introduction to indigenous cultures in the New World is Alvin M. Josephy, ed., *America in 1492* (Knopf, 1992). See also Robert Wauchope's *Indian Background of Latin American History* (Knopf, 1970).

Among the most informative works on pre-Columbian Mesoamerica are Ross Hassig, *War and Society in Ancient Mesoamerica* (University of California Press, 1992); Richard A. Dieh and Janet C. Berlo, eds., *Mesoamerica After the Decline of Teotihuacán* (Dumbarton Oaks, 1989); and Robert R. Miller, *Mexico: A History* (University of Oklahoma Press, 1989). Special insights into the Mayan experience are provided in Jeremy A. Sobloff, *A New Archeology and the Ancient Maya* (Scientific American Library, 1990). A recent study of the darker side of Aztec society is David L. Carrasco and Micah Kleist, eds., *City of Sacrifice: The Aztec Empire and the Role of Violence in Civilization* (Beacon, 1998). Michael A. Malpass presents *Daily Life in the Inca Empire* (Greenwood Press, 1996).

E. James Dixon's *Bones, Boats, and Bison* (University of New Mexico Press, 1999) guides the reader through complex archaeological questions surround the question of the first colonization in western North America. Colin G. Galloway's documentary survey of American Indian History, *First Peoples* (Bedford/St. Martin's, 1999), is the best introduction to the general discussion of Native Americans in North America.

GLOBAL ISSUES

LOCATION AND IDENTITY

Why do people use location to identify themselves?

Two foreigners on horseback with Mount Fuji and telegraph wires in the background, woodblock print, Hiroshige Utagawa, 1873.

"*East is East, and West is West, and never the twain shall meet.*"
Ballad of East and West, Rudyard Kipling, 1889

Though Kipling's long ballad goes on to reject that assertion, most Europeans and Americans ("West") and perhaps most Asians ("East") of his day would have accepted it. Of course, it is purely arbitrary to designate one area as "West" and one as "East" on a spherical earth rotating on a north-south axis, but historians, politicians, philosophers, generals, and clerics have all done so for millennia. People have long found ways to distinguish themselves from people in other places or even from people in their own backyard, and location has been one of the ways they have done so.

When the line-drawing seems to fail—for example, Morocco, often considered part of the Middle East, is actually west of London, and Japanese maps in the nineteenth century designated the United States as the East because it lies to Japan's east—the East then gets designated as a cultural place rather than one defined by location. But whose culture? Some would say that the culture of the rulers determines the country's identity. But this can be misleading. For instance, largely Hindu (and therefore Eastern) India did not become Middle Eastern under the Muslim Mughals or Western under British rule. Maps in the twentieth century can be equally confusing. They often painted colonies in the hues of their imperialist rulers, which seems to suggest countries could be culturally relocated by a change in rulers. Is Australia Western because its settlers mostly came from Europe, even as its leaders are currently trying to join the lucrative Asian/Eastern economic zone? Are the mostly Christian Philippines Eastern or Western?

For many centuries Europeans associated continents with the cardinal directions. Asia was East, Europe was West, and Africa was South. Later, America was sometimes considered a "new" world and therefore off the directional map, and sometimes part of the West. At first glance, continents seem to be a helpful way to divide the world into areas with some internal similarities. But the continental framework also has some inconsistencies. The Panama Canal now divides North and South America and the Suez Canal divides Africa from Eurasia. Both of those canals were dug through solid ground that had been traversed by people for millennia. And what about Eurasia? If continents have been viewed, since the eighteenth century, as "large space[s] of dry land comprehending many countries all joined together, without any separation by water,"[1] Europe and Asia are no more independent continents than the world's only "subcontinent" of India.

During the Cold War, East and West took on different meanings. The Communist anthem claimed, "The East [was] Red." A line so rigid it was called "an iron curtain" supposedly divided East from West. Many countries did not fit into those categories, however, calling themselves part of the "non-aligned movement." In time, the wealthy capitalist countries, many but not all allied with the United States, came to be called the First World; the Communist countries aligned with the Soviet Union, the Second World; and all others, including Communist China, the Third World. The Second World ended with the break-up of the Soviet Union, and the First and Third Worlds are more commonly referred to as Developed Countries and Developing Countries or by the cardinal directions North and South, with most of the old Second World countries assigned to the North. But many are uncomfortable with these terms, too.

The cardinal directions do not represent the only way that location has been used to identify people and cultures. Until the late nineteenth century, for example, Chinese rulers viewed the world as centered in China, which is reflected in the name for the Chinese realm, Central Kingdom. Chinese maps paralleled this politically inspired world view. (Religiously inspired worldviews differed in China; India was placed at the center of maps by Chinese

Buddhists.) The Chinese view explained what was essentially a power relationship in terms of the ethical virtue of the emperor. Unlike Europeans, the Chinese, who divided the world into cultured and barbarian spheres, did not ascribe these qualities to the cardinal directions East and West. Instead, distance in any direction would lessen the ethical influence of the Chinese center, which was located in the emperor's court.[2] Early modern Indian geographers centered their maps on India. One Indian geographer designated Europe, at his map's margin, as "England, France, and other hat-wearing islands."[3] Medieval Islamic mapmakers centered their world on Dar al-Islam (abode of Islam). Crossing this huge stretch of territory from southern Spain to China, starting in 1325, North African adventurer Ibn Battuta found recognizable Islamic culture throughout the region.[4]

Europeans, however, were more likely to use cardinal directions to define the world's areas. These directions were conflated with cultural characteristics, most of which have been shown by historians to be inaccurate. Thus, geography became destiny—if you're in the West, you must have certain characteristics, and if you're in the East, you have a different set of cultural behaviors. This was constantly inverted as well. When those doing the defining—the "West"—decided a country had cultural characteristics that were undesirable, it could be excluded from the West or Europe by being redefined as Eastern. Even the historical insistence on calling Europe a "continent" when it met none of the usual requirements for that label was a way of setting it aside as a place with a supposedly homogenous culture, distinct from those elsewhere in Africa or the rest of Eurasia. That culture was "Western."

The ancient Greeks had divided the world they knew into three parts, which loosely corresponded to what we call Europe, Asia, and North Africa. They disagreed, however, on the boundaries between those parts. Before 500 B.C.E., the Greeks used the term "Europe" to refer to Greece and the term "Asia" for all foreign lands other than Europe. They soon expanded Europe to include the land north and west of Greece and separated "Africa" from "Asia." Later, that three-part division was given a religious underpinning when Christians asserted that God had divided the world in three parts, giving one to each son of Noah.[5] From the eleventh-century split in Christendom between a Rome-based Catholic Church and a Constantinople-based Orthodox Church, the terms *West* and *East* were increasingly used for Europe and Asia, respectively. While the East was originally a small area in the eastern Mediterranean, it grew in the popular imagination as the Europeans learned more about India and later East Asia. Seeking wealth and riches, spices and textiles, Europeans looked eastward. The East was seen as different, but not necessarily inferior.

Looking for access to the East took Columbus to a "new" world, neither Western nor Eastern but a hybrid—a "West Indies" inhabited by "Indians." In the next several centuries, European countries established relationships of imperialism over many Asians, Africans, Americans, and Australians. But it was concerning Asians that Europeans of the nineteenth century articulated theories of Western superiority. The others were viewed as barbarians, and European dominance did not seem to need explanation. Later, as categories like "Third World" and "South" replaced "East," so-called Eastern characteristics were easily transferred to Africa or South America.

The East came to be seen as the opposite of the West.[6] This was expressed in a series of stereotyped comparisons. For example, where the East contained countries whose people valued irrationality, the West esteemed rationality. Where the West promoted democracy, the East was run by autocratic rulers whose role derived from what was called, as late as the mid-twentieth century, an "Asiatic Mode of Production."[7] While the West was dynamic and thus had a history, Asia was stagnant and unchanging; and even if it had had a history in the murky past, scholars like Karl Marx and G. W. F. Hegel contended that it no longer did. While Europe enjoyed a temperate climate, permitting it to embark on industrialization, the East did not. Many outside of Europe or the United States also absorbed these stereotypes. In the late nineteenth century, Fukuzawa Yukichi, an advocate of modernizing Japan, accepted these supposed characteristics as natural and called on the Japanese to "leave Asia" and join the West. Though scholars have debunked all these notions as having no grounding in historical fact, they continue to influence the meanings of East and West.

A few additional categories were developed in the twentieth century. The Middle East (East of what? The Middle of what?) came into being as a category for military planning during World War II. Its boundaries are as shifting and political as those of Europe and Asia. Africa is also subjected to a number of different slicings—is North Africa separate from sub-Saharan Africa?

Locational designations, groupings by political allegiance, classification by assumed cultural characteristics, and organization by stages of economic development all influence each other. Assumed cultural characteristics today lead to the redrawing of geographic lines in places like the Balkans, where the break-up of Yugoslavia in the 1990s produced warfare over ethnically defined borders. But location may also lead to our ascribing cultural characteristics or history to a country that never even had that history. North-South and East-West are always relative categories and reflect power relations in addition to designations of cultural identity.

Questions

1. Why do people define their world geographically?
2. How are the ways in which people define locations related to politics or power?
3. Do nations' identities change when their rulers, ideology, or dominant religions change?

CHAPTER 12

The Islamic Gunpowder Empires, 1300–1650

CHAPTER CONTENTS

- New Polities in Eurasia
- The Ottoman Empire

  DISCOVERY THROUGH MAPS: *The World Map of Piri Reis*

  DOCUMENT: *Evliya Çelebi, "An Ottoman Official's Wedding Night"*

- The Safavid Empire in Persia

  DOCUMENT: *The Coming of Ismail Safavi Foretold*

- The Mughal Empire in South Asia

  DOCUMENT: *The Idea of Seclusion and Lady Nurjahan*

- Networks of Trade and Communication

1300
1324 End of the reign of Osman, first Ottoman ruler

1398–1402 Timur invades India and Anatolia

1400
1453 Mehmed II conquers Constantinople

1500
1501 Ismail Safavi launches Safavid dynasty

1517 Ottomans conquer Cairo and gain control of Mecca

1517 Piri Reis world map

1520–1566 Reign of Ottoman Suleiman the Magnificent

1525 Babur, first Mughal emperor, invades India

1538–1588 Sinan Pasha, Ottoman royal architect

1556–1605 Reign of Akbar over the Mughal domains

1588–1629 Reign of Shah Abbas in Persia

1597 Shah Abbas begins building imperial Isfahan

1600
1634–1654 Taj Mahal built

1658–1707 Reign of Mughal emperor Aurangzeb in India

By the fourteenth century the waves of migration and conquest out of Central Asia that had established the Mongol Empire and altered the political configurations of the Islamic world had mostly ceased. Late in that century a new Turco-Mongol conqueror called Timur began a campaign that ravaged northern India, Persia, Iraq, and Anatolia, but his empire was not enduring. In the fifteenth and sixteenth centuries, however, three great Turkic empires gained preeminence in the old Mongol and Byzantine domains. The Ottoman, Safavid, and Mughal empires flourished on the bases of preexisting civilizations, Turco-Mongol military organization, and enhanced firepower; in the process they also crafted a new cultural synthesis. These empires are sometimes called the gunpowder empires because, like their European counterparts, they incorporated gunpowder weaponry into their traditional military systems. All three formed parts of a vast trading network reaching from the Pacific to the Atlantic Ocean. At the same time that the Ming Chinese were launching voyages that reached the East African coast, the Ottoman Turks were building an empire in the eastern Mediterranean that, in the sixteenth century, would dominate the region and challenge the Portuguese in the Indian Ocean.

Europeans were active in Asia during this period but exerted relatively little influence. Awed by the wealth and power of Muslim empires, they were generally held in disdain by Asian elites, who considered their own cultures superior. Akbar, the great Mughal emperor, referred to the "savage Portuguese" at his court,[1] Ottoman sultans regarded European envoys as supplicants, and the Safavid shah kept English merchants waiting for weeks while he attended to more important matters.

347

NEW POLITIES IN EURASIA

■ *How did political conditions in Central Asia influence the rise of the Ottoman, Safavid, and Mughal empires?*

For the kingdoms of Europe, the Ottoman conquest of Constantinople in 1453 signaled a catastrophe: the end of the Eastern Roman Empire and a disruption in established commercial patterns. Preachers and writers in Europe depicted the Ottoman victories as a type of divine punishment for the sins of Christendom. Even more significant, the Ottomans symbolized a new Muslim world emerging between the eastern Mediterranean and Southeast Asia. In that expansive territory, the three new Turkic empires would hold sway for centuries. Geographically, this world was centered in Persia, under its Shi'ite Safavid (sah-FAH-weed) dynasty. Culturally, it was influenced by Persian, Arab, and Byzantine courtly traditions. To the east, the magnificent Mughal (moo-GUL) Empire emerged at a crucial crossroads of the east-west and north-south trade. Militarily, this Muslim world was dominated by the forces of the Ottoman Empire, which were far more formidable than those of any country in Europe at the time. War often raged among these contending states. Nevertheless, they shared the Islamic faith, common steppe antecedents, and Persian artistic and literary traditions.

Background: The Steppe Frontier

After the mid-fourteenth century, tumultuous conditions in Central Asia helped generate the Muslim empires to the south. The fragmented Mongol Empire left the steppe politically divided into states that dissolved and re-formed in new combinations. While the old **khanates** survived for a while, war was almost continuous along the southern steppe frontier, from the Crimea to China.

The continuing steppe influence was well illustrated by the quick rise and collapse of the Timurid (ti-MOR-id) Empire at the close of the fourteenth century. Timur the Lame, the "Tamerlane" celebrated in Western literature, who claimed descent from Ching-

---

khanate—A Turkic state ruled by a khan.

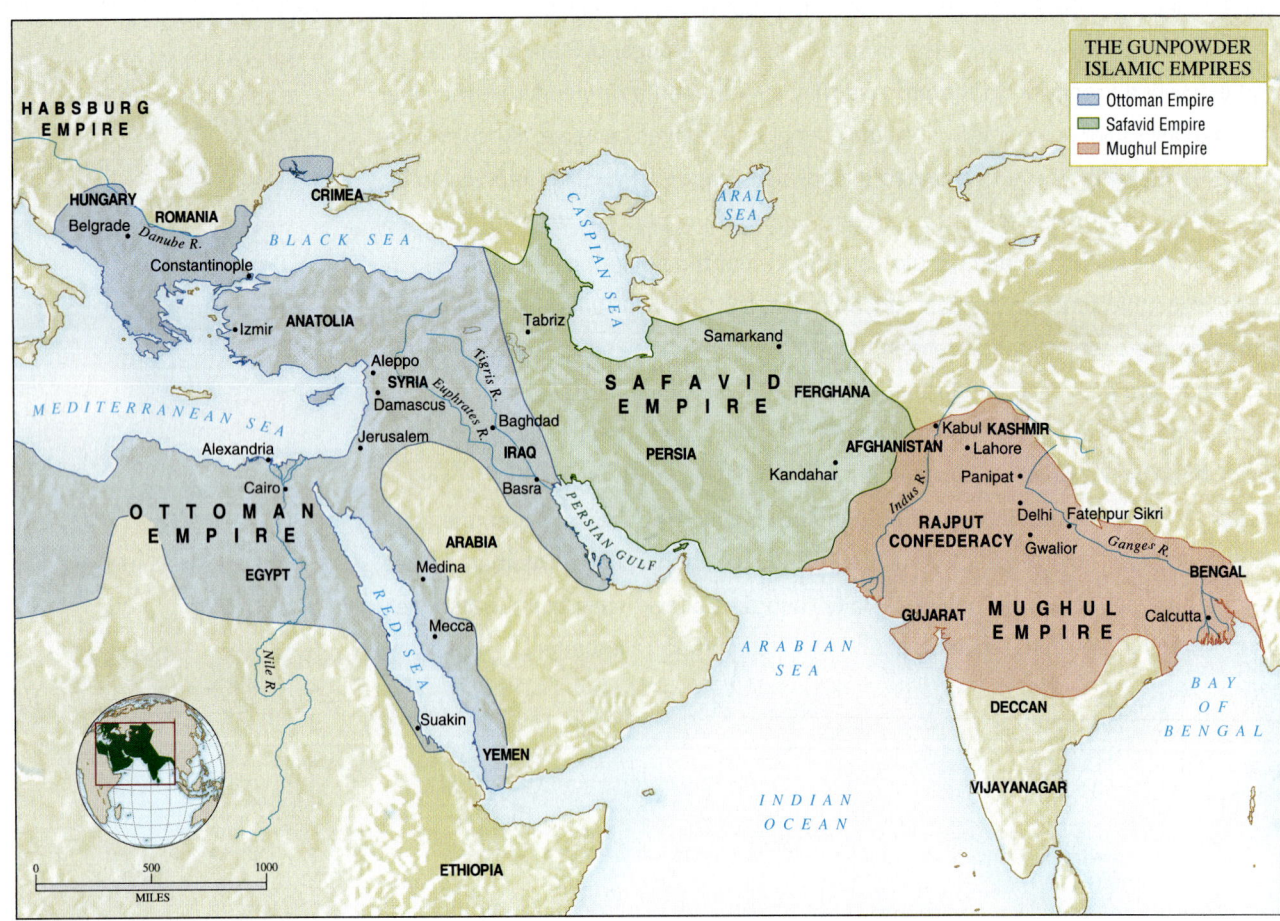

The gunpowder empires dominated south and west Asia, North Africa, and southeastern Europe in the sixteenth century.

gis (Genghis) Khan, rose to power during the 1370s as an *emir* ("commander") in the Chaghatai (chahg-HAH-tai) khanate of Central Asia. In his quest to restore the original Mongol Empire, Timur led whirlwind campaigns through the western steppe, the Crimea, Persia, and Anatolia. He crushed Ottoman resistance and carted the defeated Ottoman sultan, Bayezid I, off across Anatolia in a cage, subjecting him to ridicule. Timur terrorized northern India and was planning to invade Ming China when he died in 1405. But once Timur's army withdrew, the leaders who had submitted to him were less likely to comply with his demands. A conqueror's real domains were those from which he could effectively collect taxes and levy troops.

For more than a century after Timur had resurrected the spirit of Chinggis Khan, a dream of universal empire—real or imagined—lingered in the minds of his descendants, among the many Turco-Mongol rulers in northern Persia and Transoxiana (trahnz-OX-ee-ahn-ah) to its east. The Ottoman sultans, who had established their hegemony in Anatolia before Timur's time and only barely survived his onslaught, were not direct heirs of his traditions, but they too aspired to the conquests and prestige of Chinggis Khan and Alexander the Great. Russia and particularly northern India, where Muslim regimes took hold after Timur's armies devastated Delhi in 1398, were also sites of a renewed struggle for power.

Drastic change marked the steppe frontier after the late fifteenth century, as populations settled around cities and firearms moderated the advantages of tribal cavalry. Indeed, the Uzbeks, who seized most of Transoxiana in this era, were among the last steppe conquerors. Like their predecessors, they were integrated into the courtly cultures of the lands they conquered. But long after the Uzbek conquest, old nomadic traditions continued to shape the rituals and military ethos of Turco-Mongol dynasties.

THE OTTOMAN EMPIRE

■ *How did the Ottoman Turks create and sustain their empire?*

The most powerful of the new Muslim empires was that of the Ottoman Turks. Centered in Anatolia, its military might cast long shadows over southeastern Europe, western Asia, and North Africa. By the middle of the sixteenth century the Ottoman patrimony stretched from Hungary to Ethiopia and from the borders of Morocco to Arabia and Iraq.

CASE STUDY
The Ottoman Empire in the Late Sixteenth Century

The origin myth of the Ottomans suggests the unique role that both the Central Asian warrior traditions and sufi Islam played in the legitimation of kingship. The founder of the Ottoman line was called Osman. According to legend, he was a valiant young warrior, fighting as a Seljuk subordinate on the frontiers of the Byzantine Empire in the late thirteenth century. Osman had, as a warrior must, a good horse, a strong arm, and a loyal companion. He fell in love with the daughter of a revered sufi **shaykh** and asked for her hand in marriage. Her father refused; but that night the *shaykh* dreamed that he saw the moon descending on his sleeping daughter, merging into her

This miniature painting depicts the envoy of Timur at the court of the Ottoman sultan Bayezid I. The sultan is surrounded by his courtiers, with pages to his right and janissaries and officials in the foreground. Bayezid looks imposing, but he was defeated and killed by Timur. Note the fine carpets around the sultan's throne and the soldiers armed with gunpowder weapons in the foreground.

shaykh—An Arabic term for a tribal chief or religious master.

The Ottomans

c. 1281	Osman establishes the Ottoman dynasty
1453	Ottomans capture Constantinople
1517	Sultan Selim conquers Cairo, becomes Protector of the Holy Cities
1520–1566	Reign of Suleiman the Magnificent, Ottoman Golden Age

breast. From this union grew a huge and imposing tree that spread its branches over many lands and many flowing streams. When he awoke, the *shaykh* decided to approve the marriage.

Dreams play an important role in Middle Eastern literatures, and many kings took the interpretation of dreams seriously. The legend of the *shaykh*'s dream linked the warrior tradition to the mystical religious authority of the sufis, thus legitimizing Osman's rule. His dynasty, like the tree, did endure and expand to control many and prosperous territories. As the dynasty grew more powerful, the Ottomans also falsified a genealogy linking them to the prophet Muhammad. This Ottoman claim, like Timur's claim to be a descendent of Chinggis Khan, also lent an aura of legitimacy to their rule. The Ottomans were not the first or the last family to imagine for themselves illustrious ancestors. Osman's line was spectacularly successful; it ruled for over six centuries, from the late thirteenth century until World War I.

Osman's successors won independence from their Seljuk Turk overlords and gradually conquered the surrounding principalities. They had gained control over most of Asia Minor when Timur's army invaded Anatolia, defeated the Ottomans, and forced a half-century of internal restoration. Then two remarkable sultans resumed the Ottoman conquests. The first, Mehmed II (second reign 1451–1481), took Constantinople, Romania, and the Crimea. The second, Selim I (1512–1520), annexed Kurdistan, northern Iraq, Syria,

DOCUMENT Mehmed II

By the mid-sixteenth century the Ottoman Empire encompassed much of the Mediterranean. It included the core territories (excluding Persia) of the Middle East and extended across North Africa and into Europe.

Discovery Through Maps

The World Map of Piri Reis

Western historiography has highlighted Europeans' "discovery" of the New World. But the Age of Discovery produced many visions of the world, only some of which were preoccupied with the Americas. Ottoman cartographers were interested in the Americas, although Ottoman ambitions for conquest were directed primarily eastward to Asia. Mapping in this era was intimately associated with the objectives of merchants and sailors, and the most famous of Ottoman cartographers was a skilled sea captain named Piri Reis. Like other members of the Ottoman military-administrative class, Piri Reis was a man of diverse talents. In 1517, when his sovereign, Sultan Selim, conquered Cairo, Piri Reis presented him with a parchment map of the world, only part of which survives. The segment reproduced here shows the Atlantic Ocean, the western shores of Africa and Europe, and the eastern shores of South and Central America. Piri Reis's map incorporates elaborate illustrations of ships, kings, wildlife, and mythical creatures. It depicts strange tales (like the sailors who landed on a whale's back, mistaking it for an island, at top left) and gives nautical distances. The cartographer provided a list of 20 Western and Islamic sources he consulted, including a map of Christopher Columbus. Piri Reis's map suggests the currents of shared knowledge that linked the scholars, merchants, and sailors of Asia, Africa, and Europe at this time. The boundaries of scholarship were fluid, and learned men eagerly sought out new information. Cartographers like Piri Reis benefited from and contributed to the knowledge assembled by peoples of many nations and religions.

For the sailor or merchant, any map that was more accurate, regardless of its provenance (Portuguese, Ottoman, Christian, Muslim), was a tool for ensuring a more successful and safer journey.

Questions to Consider

1. In the sixteenth century, why would a sea captain be a good mapmaker?
2. Think about the different kinds of maps you have seen in this text and elsewhere. How does the way a map is constructed and illustrated tell us something about the beliefs and objectives of the mapmaker and the people for whom he makes the map?
3. Why do you think there are figures of people and animals on this map?

and Egypt. Mehmed's conquests terrorized European Christendom and brought the Ottoman state considerable wealth and prestige. The sultan repopulated Constantinople, renamed Istanbul in the nineteenth century, using a combination of tax breaks and forced population transfers. The declining but intrepid old warrior was planning new campaigns when he died.

Mehmet II

Mehmed's son, Bayezid II, acquired further territories and built up a powerful fleet. Then, Selim's conquest of Egypt and Arabia brought added prestige: control of another great imperial capital, Cairo, and claim to the title Protector of the Holy Cities (Mecca and Medina), coveted by all Muslim monarchs. It also gave him control over the wealth and grain of Egypt and all the Mediterranean outlets of the eastern trade in spices, textiles, and jewels. Under Selim, the Ottoman navy dominated the eastern Mediterranean.

Ottoman power increased under Selim's only son, Suleiman (SOO-lay-mahn; 1520–1566). This determined campaigner soon became the most feared ruler among a generation of monarchs that included Henry VIII of England, Francis I of France, and Charles V of Spain. Suleiman's estimation of his own supremacy is illustrated in a letter to the French monarch in which Suleiman claimed glorious and elaborate titles but addressed Francis simply as "King."

Suleiman extended all his borders, particularly those touching Habsburg lands in Europe. After taking Belgrade in 1521 and the island of Rhodes from the Knights of St. John in 1522, he invaded Hungary in 1526 with 100,000 men and 300 artillery pieces. At Mohacs the Turks won an overwhelming victory. Hungary was then integrated into the Ottoman Empire. Although many Hungarian nobles were slaughtered in the war, Suleiman continued the Ottoman practice of integrating nobles and military men from his defeated foe into his own administration. If a governor submitted, he was often allowed to retain his post; this pragmatic administrative flexibility helped ensure the success of Ottoman conquests.

Suleiman aspired to the conquest of even further territory, aiming particularly at the rich agricultural lands, timber sources, and mines of eastern Europe; he also proposed to control the rich commerce of the Mediterranean. Meanwhile, his forces took Iraq from the Safavids, thus acquiring access to the Persian Gulf. This monarch, who built the great wall around Jerusalem that is still standing today, claimed to be "Lord of the two lands and two seas." His conquests provoked conflicts with the Portuguese in the Red Sea and Indian Ocean. The Portuguese imagined taking Mecca to chastise the "heathen" Ottomans, but no such attack ever materialized.

The Islamic World: The Ottoman Empire

Suleiman responded harshly to challenges to his authority. He executed his own favorite son and a grandson who rebelled against him. His palace life was marked by pomp and splendor exceeding that of Louis XIV's France. An army of servants attended him, and those men who worked in his palace inner service gained prestige and status because of their proximity to the sultan. The sultan's banquets were served on elaborate tableware of gold, silver, and an expanding collection of fine Chinese porcelain. In the hours between waking and sleeping, Suleiman met with advisers and petitioners, read, or listened to music. For amusement he watched wrestling matches and listened to court poets and jesters. He was trained in the fine art of goldsmithing, also wrote poetry, and had a keen interest in maps. Foreign ambassadors, such as those from the French king or Habsburg emperor, were forced to prostrate themselves before the sultan,

An illuminated tughra *of Sultan Suleiman. The* tughra *was the sultan's signature, used to validate imperial documents and mark coinage. It included the sultan's name and his father's name and designated the sultan as "eternally victorious." The palace employed hundreds of artists, including the designers who fashioned and illuminated such beautiful* tughras.

an indication of the perceived balance of power. European observers commented on the intimidating nature of a visit to Suleiman's court, where thousands of massed troops would stand for hours in absolute silence. In Europe he was known as Suleiman the Magnificent; in the Ottoman Empire he was called Suleiman the Lawgiver.

The sultan's rule was based on an ideal of Persian origin called the "circle of justice." This ideal stated that in order for the kingdom to be prosperous and secure, the sultan required a strong army. To provide for this army, the state needed tax revenues from its citizens, and in order for the citizens to pay their taxes they had to receive in return security and justice from the sultan. Although there were many abuses at various levels of government, the Ottoman sultans did adhere to this ideal. Any of the sultan's subjects could submit a petition to the palace asking redress of wrongs—sometimes the sultan rode out into the streets while his attendants gathered petitions from the crowd. Ottoman court records show many instances in which peasants complained to the local judge *(kadi)* that officials were extracting extra taxes or labor from them. These complaints were then forwarded to the central government, which punished or replaced the offenders.

The Empire Under Suleiman

Suleiman governed the mightiest state of his day. Extending from Poland to Yemen and from Persia to Tripoli, it included 21 provinces and many linguistic and ethnic groups, such as Magyars, Armenians, Bosnians, Albanians, Greeks, Tartars, Kurds, Arabs, Copts, and Jews. "Multiculturalism," often thought of as a twentieth-century concept, was in fact typical of many large agrarian empires of this age.

DOCUMENT
An Ambassador's Report on the Ottoman Empire

Economically, Suleiman's empire was nearly self-sufficient, with expanding production and flourishing trade. The Ottoman dominions produced annual revenues greater than those available to any contemporary European monarch and grain surpluses that gave the Ottomans considerable leverage in the Mediterranean region, where grain shortages were endemic. Merchants smuggled grain out despite government attempts to control them, and Ottoman rivals like Venice often purchased grain supplies from the sultan's **pashas.** Indeed, food has been, and still is, one of the most powerful motivating forces in history.

Power in such a far-flung empire could never be absolute. The sultan delegated authority to local governors and to pashas. Rule in distant provinces, like Egypt, was more flexible and less direct. Conquered lands closer to the capital were given to Ottoman *sipahis* (se-PAH-hee) or "fief" holders, who were expected to bring cavalry contingents for military campaigns. At other times *sipahis* lived on their lands *(timars)*, administering local affairs, collecting taxes, and keeping order. Unlike European feudal lords, they were not usually local residents and were often away in distant wars. Provincial governors *(pashas* or *beys)* were drawn from the higher-ranking Ottoman commanders. All members of this governing class were thus heavily dependent on the sultan, who might suddenly change their assignments or revoke their land holdings. By Suleiman's reign, the political power of the *sipahis* over their *timars* had been partly usurped by the sultan's central bureaucracy. It functioned under a **vizir,** or chief minister, with a host of subordinate officials. The top officials met regularly as the sultan's **divan** or council to advise the ruler, but his word was law (although top officials and religious authorities—the **ulama**—might use their authority to challenge or moderate his decrees).

The Ottomans developed a unique "slave" *(kul)* system that was a major factor in their success. The system was based on the *devshirme* (dev-SHEHR-me), a levy of boys from the non-Muslim subjects of the empire, which functioned as a special type of "human tax" on the Balkan provinces. These boys were brought to the capital, converted to Islam, and taught Turkish. Most of them went to the **janissaries** (JAN-i-sehr-ees), the famed elite Ottoman infantry corps that was armed with gunpowder weapons. They formed the backbone of the formidable Ottoman armies. The smartest and most talented of the boys, however, were sent to the palace to be educated in literature, science, the arts, religion, and military skills. These boys, when they reached maturity, were given the highest military and administrative posts in the state. Ideally, the *kul* system provided the state with a group of expert administrators who, because they had been separated from their families and homes, would remain loyal to the sultan, to whom they owed everything. These "slaves," rather than occupying the lowest level of the social order, controlled much of the wealth and power in Ottoman society. Many of the buildings they endowed are still standing today. The more common type of domestic or agricultural slave did, of course, also exist in Ottoman society. Slavery and slave markets were scattered

---

pasha—Top military-administrative official (governor) in the Ottoman Empire.

vizir—A chief minister or comparable high-ranking government official in the Muslim world, but most particularly in the Ottoman Empire.

divan—A council or place of administrative assembly within the Ottoman Empire.

ulama—Islamic religious authorities; men versed in Islamic sciences and law.

janissaries—An elite Ottoman infantry corps armed with gunpowder weapons and composed mostly of converted Balkan slaves.

European writers and their audiences were fascinated by the Ottoman harem and often depicted it in exaggerated erotic terms. This engraving from a seventeenth-century French history of the Ottoman palace imagines the sultan taking his bath attended by naked harem women. In fact, this image is pure fantasy; both sexuality and reproduction in the harem were tightly controlled, and the sultan's attendants were male, not female.

throughout the Afro-Eurasian world, although Islam prohibited the enslaving of fellow Muslims.

Western literature has produced an exotic, erotic image of the Ottoman sultan's **harem** (the sacred area of the palace, or of any home, forbidden to outsiders). But much of this image is a myth produced by the overactive imaginations or hostile sentiments of European men inspired by the prospect of several hundred women in one household. In fact, sexuality in the palace was tightly controlled. Like women in other traditional patriarchal societies, most Ottoman women had to work in the fields and towns. Only the women of the elite classes could be fully veiled and secluded. In the palace, the harem women were arranged in a rigid hierarchy much like that of the men; each was paid according to her rank. Most of the women were not destined for the sultan's bed; instead they were married to the sultan's officers to create further ties of loyalty to the palace. A select few were chosen to bear the sultan's heirs.

The harem women wielded power because of their wealth, their connections, and their proximity to the sultan. The most powerful among them was the sultan's mother (the **valide sultan**), not his wife. The *valide sultans* participated actively (although behind the scenes) in court politics. Petitioners, including pashas, applied to these high-ranking women to intercede on their behalf with the sultan. Some *valide sultans* even served a diplomatic function, corresponding with European rulers like the Venetian doge, Catherine de' Medici in France, and Queen Elizabeth in England.

In the Ottoman system, proximity to the sultan was the primary avenue to power, and membership in the royal household or military class brought with it the highest status in society. But pashas, palace women, religious officials, and members of the palace staff jockeyed for positions of power and formed alliances to advance their own interests. Harem politics, illustrated in Suleiman's reign by the contending influences of his mother and his wife, have often been blamed for weakening the Ottoman state. In fact, however, the factors that compromised Ottoman power were much more complex. Continued conquests produced serious communication and transportation problems, and long wars and failure to pay the troops on time caused rebellions in the ranks. Religious contention, provoked by the rise of the Shi'ite Safavids in Persia, also threatened the empire.

Another important factor in Ottoman politics was the fact that the eldest son had no automatic claim to the throne. The sultan's sons thus contended to succeed him, sometimes producing extended periods of interregnum. That was the case with Bayezid II, whose sons got tired of waiting for him to die and launched a civil war to determine who would sit on the throne in his stead. Once a prince established himself as sultan, he would often have his brothers exe-

---

harem—In Arabic, literally "forbidden." A sacred area of palace or home forbidden to outsiders, often but not always used to protect and sequester women.

valide sultan—The mother of the Ottoman sultan; generally the most powerful and influential woman in the empire.

Document: Evliya Çelebi, "An Ottoman Official's Wedding Night"

Marriages in the Ottoman administrative system were often arranged to link powerful families, consolidate wealth, and secure loyalty. Love matches were also made, but sometimes officials were forced into marriages at the sultan's command. That was the fate of Melek Ahmed Pasha, who, after the death of his beloved first wife, was forced to marry the elderly and intransigent Fatma Sultan, daughter of Sultan Ahmed I. This passage, in which Melek Ahmed tells his tale of woe to the chronicler Evliya Çelebi, suggests that marriage to a princess, however prestigious, could be burdensome. It also illustrates the consumption of goods by royal households and the power and status of royal women, who could supersede the wishes of influential men. Note that Melek Pasha addressed his new wife as "Sultan." That title was used for royal princesses.

As soon as I entered the harem, having uttered a *besmele* [invocation of God's name], I saw her. Now I am supposed to be her husband, and this is our first night—she ought to show me just a little respect. She just sat there stock still, not moving an inch. I went up and kissed her hand.

"Pasha," she says, "welcome."

"God be praised that I have seen my sultan's smiling beauty," say I, and I shower her with all sorts of self-deprecating flatteries. Not once does she invite me to sit down. And she puts on all kinds of virginal airs, as though she weren't an ancient crone who has gone through twelve husbands!

The first pearl from her lips is this: "My dear pasha, if you want to get along with me, whether you are present at court or absent in some government post, my expenses are 15 purses each and every month. Also I owe my steward, Kermetçi Mustafa Agha, 100 purses: pay my debt in the morning. And every year I get six Marmara boatloads of firewood. And my retainers Selman Beg and Ömer Beg and Mukbil Agha and my steward get as a daily stipend 100 bushels of barley each, 10 okkas of coffee, 10 okkas of fine sugar, and nightly 10 okkas of camphor beeswax"—and on and on with suchlike nonsense, spouting these expenses like a talking inventory. Several times she pinched my cheeks. . . .

Now her stewardess and treasuress and ladies in waiting and, in short, 300 or more women came to kiss my hand and stand there in rows. "Well, my dear pasha, these are my servants of the interior. I also have as many or more manumitted [legally freed] slave girls on the exterior. Together with children and dependents, they total 700 souls. You will provide all of them with their annual stipend of silk and gauze and brocade and broadcloth. And you will pay the annual stipend of my halberdiers and cooks and gardeners and coachmen and eunuchs and *begs*, as well as those serving them, numbering 500 people. And if you don't—well, you know the consequence!"

Melek Ahmed replied: "I swear by God, my sultan," say I, "that I have just returned from the Transylvania campaign. I am a vizir who fights the holy war. In that campaign I had 7,000 men to feed. I spent 170,000 goldpieces and 600 purses. I even had to sell quite a lot of equipment and arms and armor and helmets and to borrow money from the janissary corps. . . . I am unable to bear such expenses."

After this "wedding night" Melek prayed for death and complained that he had been asked to "feed the state elephant." He vowed never to see Fatma Sultan again.

Questions to Consider

1. What does this story suggest about the lives and expenses of both males and females in the Ottoman elite class?
2. Does gender or status take precedence in the dealings of Melek and Fatma?
3. When such a story is incorporated into a history such as Evliya's, should we assume that the dialog is reported word-for-word as it occurred? What factors might affect the accuracy of this account? (Remember that Melek was Evliya's patron.)

From Robert Dankoff, trans., *The Intimate Life of an Ottoman Statesman, Melek Ahmed Pasha (1588–1662), as Portrayed in Evliya Çelebi's Book of Travels* (Albany: State University of New York Press 1991), pp. 259–261.

---

cuted, a grim task designed to ensure the stability of the state and avoid further struggles. A wise prince would try to gain the favor of the janissary corps, for their support might make or break him.

Religion was an integral part of government and society. But as in other Muslim lands, the religious authorities *(ulama)* did not run the government; they were subordinated to the state and the sultan. The grand **mufti,** as head of the Islamic establishment, was also the chief religious and legal adviser to the sul-

---

mufti—A high-ranking Islamic religious and legal adviser.

tan. The sultan approved religious appointments and might dismiss any religious officer, including the grand mufti. A corps of learned religious scholars represented the sultan as judges *(kadis)*, dispensers of charities, and teachers. Non-Muslim subjects or **dhimmis** were regarded as inferior but were granted a significant degree of legal and religious toleration through government arrangements with their religious leaders (rabbis and priests, for example), who were responsible for their civil obedience. Non-Muslim subjects lived under their own laws and customs, pursuing their private interests within limits imposed by Islamic law and Ottoman economic needs. As in other Islamic lands, they had to pay the *jizya,* an additional head tax.

Ottoman society, like other societies, can be divided along different types of lines based on gender, occupation, class, religion, or race. For tax purposes, Ottoman society was divided roughly between taxpaying subjects (*reaya,* or flock) and the military-administrative class *(askeri).* This division between *askeri* and *reaya* was the primary determinant of status, crossing lines of gender, race, and sometimes religion. A woman of the *askeri* class could command authority over a man of lesser status. People of various races could be members of the *askeri* class; the chief black eunuch, for example, was one of the most powerful men in the state. Although merchants and members of the *ulama* might achieve considerable wealth and authority, they did not have access to the same type of power and status as the military administrative class.

Artistic Production

Ottoman success resulted in a vigorous cultural renaissance, most evident in monumental architecture and decorative tile work. Mehmed II rebuilt his decaying capital, from sewers to palaces. His monumental Fatih Mosque and splendid Topkapi Palace, with its fortress walls, fountains, and courtyards, were models of the new Ottoman style, which was influenced by the Byzantine artistic tradition. The palace was divided into three courts that reflected Ottoman concepts of power and space. The outer court was for public affairs, as well as stable and kitchen facilities. The second court provided a dividing line between the public and private life of the sultan. There the sultan met with diplomats and built his library. The inner court was reserved for the sultan and his intimates, a place for relaxation and privacy. Suleiman surpassed Topkapi's splendor with the beautiful and elegant Suleimaniye, his own mosque and mausoleum. These were but three architectural wonders among thousands scattered throughout the empire, many of which remain today.

In addition, the period was marked by wondrous productions in the realms of decorative arts. Calligraphy could take the form of birds or boats in official documents. Elaborate calligraphy and stunning painted tiles decorated Ottoman mosques and buildings. For example, Suleiman added luminous tiles to the Dome of the Rock in Jerusalem. Ottoman high culture also produced a great outpouring of scholarship and literature, mostly following Persian traditions but also reflecting a unique Ottoman synthesis. Poets, artists,

Portrait of a Sufi, c. 1535, was attributed to the painter Shaykh-Zadeh who studied in Herat and then painted and instructed disciples at the Safavid Court in Tabriz. Talented painters were in great demand in the courts of the gunpowder empires. Sufi shaykhs often served as influential advisors to the sultans and shahs.

---

dhimmis—Non-Muslim subjects of a Muslim state.

jizya—An additional head tax imposed on non-Muslims living under Muslim rule.

and historians vied for the attentions—and rewards (silver, sable furs, robes of honor, even houses)—of the sultan. Some achieved remarkable rank and success; others left the palace disheartened and poor. The great majority of artisans, however, held relatively low status. They lived and worked in the palace or in the cities, grouped often according to their occupations on "the street of the gold-thread makers" or "the street of the coppersmiths."

The Suleymaniye Mosque

Challenges to Ottoman Supremacy

Beginning in Suleiman's reign, cheap silver from the Americas and a population increase led to rising inflation, rebellions, and military mutinies, all of which weakened the government. None of the eight sultans who followed Suleiman before 1648 could duplicate his successes. Selim II was known as "the drunkard"; another sultan gained notoriety by having 19 of his brothers killed on his accession. Increasingly, the sultans did not themselves lead their troops into battle. Other problems plaguing Suleiman's successors were the rising power of the Russians and Habsburgs in Europe, stalemated wars with Persia, and the end of Ottoman naval supremacy in the Red Sea. Nonetheless, the period between 1566 and 1650 should be viewed as one of reorganization and retrenchment rather than decline. The Ottoman Empire was adjusting to newly emerging global configurations of power and commerce, and Ottoman armies still managed to gain important victories in this era, notably the reconquest of Iraq by Murad IV (1623–1640) in 1638.

With Suleiman's death the Ottoman Empire passed its zenith, but it remained a significant contender for power in the Afro-Eurasian sphere well into the eighteenth century. It continued to dominate the overland trade with Asia. Moreover, the sultans moderated Portuguese domination of the Indian Ocean, ultimately aiding the Dutch and English seaborne empires in the East while humbling their Habsburg rivals in Europe.

The Decline of the Ottomans

THE SAFAVID EMPIRE IN PERSIA

■ *What role did Shi'ism play in the Safavid Empire?*

In the beginning of the sixteenth century a new Turkic dynasty came to power in Iran, led by a charismatic, red-headed, adolescent, sufi *shaykh*. This dynasty, emerging out of the Safavid sufi religious order, would unite Iran, challenge the Ottoman empire, and shift Iran's predominantly Sunni population to Shi'ism. The Safavid dynasty had its origins in an Islamic mystical order founded by Safi al-Din (c. 1252–1334). One of his descendants, Ismail (ruled 1501–1524), gathered an army of devoted followers and began a series of lightning campaigns that united Persia, conquered Iraq, and posed a formidable challenge to the Ottomans on their eastern frontiers. Ismail was only 14 when he seized his first territories. Although such precocity may seem unusual today, it was common enough in this era for the sons of powerful men to be trained to fight and rule while still boys.

Ismail was not only a successful military commander; he was also the head of a Shi'ite Muslim sect.

The Safavid Empire was based on the broad, semiarid Iranian plateau. The Safavids and Ottomans contended for control of Iraq and Azerbaijan.

Document: The Coming of Ismail Safavi Foretold

Histories and legends of famous leaders and religious figures often recount the ways in which the coming of these men was predicted or foretold. In this selection, from an anonymous Persian manuscript, the story is told of a sufi mystic named Dede Mohammad. This sufi, or *darwish*, while returning from a pilgrimage to Mecca, becomes separated from his caravan in the desert. Dying of thirst, he is rescued by a mysterious youth who takes him to a magnificent encampment in a flowering plain. There he sees a veiled prince, whom he does not realize is the Twelfth *Imam*, a descendant of the Prophet revered by the Shi'ite Muslims who is believed to be in occultation (that is, he has disappeared but is not dead). In this vision, the Twelfth *Imam* girds and sends forth the young Ismail Safavi, thus legitimizing his reign to the Shi'ites.

After his rescue, Dede Mohammad ... walked by the young man's side, until they came to a palace, whose cupola outrivaled the sun and moon.... Golden thrones were arranged side by side, and on one of the thrones a person was seated whose face was covered by a veil. Dede Mohammad, placing his hand on his breast, made a salutation, whereupon an answer to his salutation came from the veiled one, who having bidden him be seated, ordered food to be brought for him. The like of this food he had never seen in his life before.... As soon as he had finished his repast, he saw that a party of men had entered, bringing a boy of about fourteen years of age, with red hair, a white face, and dark grey eyes; on his head was a scarlet cap.... The veiled youth then said to him, "Oh! Ismail, the hour of your 'coming' has now arrived." The other replied: "It is for your Holiness to command." ... His Holiness, taking his belt three times lifted it up and placed it on the ground again. He then, with his own blessed hands, fastened on the girdle and taking [Ismail's] cap from his head, raised it and then replaced it.... His Holiness then told his servants to bring his own sword which, when brought, he fastened with his own hands on the girdle of the child. Then he said, "You may now depart." [The Arab youth then guided Dede Mohammad back to his caravan, and the sufi asked his guide to reveal the identity of the veiled prince.] He replied, "Did you not know that the prince you saw was no other than the Lord of the Age?" When Dede Mohammad heard this name he stood up and said: "Oh! youth, for the love of God take me back again that I may once more kiss the feet of His Holiness [the Twelfth *Imam*], and ask a blessing of him, perchance I might be allowed to wait on him." But the youth replied: "It is impossible. You should have made your request at first. You cannot return. But you can make your request where you will, for His Holiness is everywhere present and will hear your prayers."

Questions to Consider

1. This manuscript apparently dates from the seventeenth century. Why was it important for the Safavids to relate in this way such stories of the predicted coming of Ismail?
2. The Twelfth *Imam* tied a belt or sash around Ismail's waist, placed his cap on his head, and gave him his own sword. What is the significance of this ceremony? Can you think of similar rituals that take place today?
3. What is the significance of the flowering plain in the middle of a desert and of the miraculous food?

From E. Dennison Ross, "The Early Years of Shah Ismail," *Journal of the Royal Asiatic Society* (1896), pp. 328–331.

Contemporary accounts portray him as a charismatic leader whose army thought him invincible. They followed him into battle crying *"Shaykh, Shaykh!"* The Safavid troops wore red headgear with 12 folds to commemorate the 12 Shi'ite *imams* (descendants of the prophet Muhammad); because of this headgear, they were called "redheads."

Ismail angered the Ottoman sultan by sending missionaries and agitators to stir up the sultan's subjects on the Ottoman eastern frontiers. He also launched a sometimes violent campaign to convert the Sunni Muslims of his domain to Shi'ism. Because Persia had been predominantly Sunni, he had to import Shi'ite scholars and jurists from the Arab lands, such as Syria and Iraq. Under the Safavid shahs (kings), Persia became overwhelmingly Shi'ite, as it is today.

Power is acquired not only on the field of battle but also in the arenas of reputation and diplomacy. Legends grew up around the youthful leader Ismail because of his many and rapid conquests. He was also supposed to have received the secret knowledge of the Safavi mystical order, passed down from his brother as he lay dying. Hence he had a powerful aura of both political and religious legitimacy. European rulers, including the Portuguese king and the pope, were inspired by the accounts of Ismail's victories and the rumors of his quasi-divine prowess. Hoping that the Safavids would help them defeat the Ottomans, who were Sunni Muslims, these rulers sent envoys to the young shah. Ismail had some interest in exploring possibilities with European powers, but he was apparently more interested in acquiring European artillery and defeating the Ottomans than in a Christian-Shi'ite alliance.

Because transport and communication technology was so primitive in the sixteenth century, rulers often knew little about their rivals. Diplomatic missions were thus crucially important as a means by which a ruler might establish his reputation and gain information about foreign powers. The Portuguese, for example, thought of the Safavids as barbarians, but they were interested in securing an ally against the Ottomans. Their envoy to Ismail was instructed to brag to the Safavids about the fine quality of Portuguese horses, table service, and women (all considered prize possessions). Envoys were also used to send messages of intimidation. When, in 1510, Ismail defeated Shaibani Khan, the Uzbek ruler in Central Asia, he had the Khan's skull gilded and made into a drinking cup. He sent an envoy with the grisly trophy, along with a taunting message, to the Ottoman sultan, Bayezid II. Of course, being an envoy in this era was dangerous, especially for the bearers of rude messages. The Ottoman sultans often imprisoned Safavid envoys, and messengers to the Safavid court were sometimes detained or abused. When Ismail sent another arrogant message to the Mamluk sultan in Egypt, the latter was so enraged that he sponsored a poetry contest to see which of his poets could write the most insulting reply in verse. But he did not harm Ismail's messenger because he was afraid of a Safavid invasion.

The Ottomans were intimidated by Ismail's early successes. In 1514, however, they soundly defeated Ismail's forces on the frontier between Anatolia and Persia. This victory is often attributed to the fact that the Ottomans had more and better gunpowder weaponry. Demoralized, Ismail withdrew to his palace, having lost his reputation for invincibility. After his death, the Safavids fought a series of long wars against the Ottomans to the west and the Uzbeks to the east.

None of his successors wielded the same charismatic religious power as Ismail. They were kings, not *shaykhs* (holy men), even though Ismail's son Tahmasp still claimed the headship of the Safavid sufi order.

Islam shares the story of Adam and Eve with Christianity and Judaism, with certain variations. In this Persian manuscript Adam rides a dragonlike serpent and Eve rides a peacock; these two beasts facilitated the entrance of Iblis [Satan] *into the Garden of Eden.*

Still, the next hundred years of Safavid rule were characterized by a consolidation of state power, lavish patronage of the arts, and an exploration of diplomatic and commercial relations with Europe. European merchants visited the shah's court, trying to gain access to the coveted Iranian silk trade, but they met with little success. Tahmasp ruled for half a century (1524–1576), despite having to contend with foreign invasions, religious factionalism, and power struggles among the tribal leaders. The Safavids, with the aid of European renegades, developed their gunpowder weaponry but never to the same extent as the Ottomans. Nor did they imitate the elaborate "slave"-based hierarchy and infantry corps (janissaries) that became the basis for Ottoman success. In Persia, the tribal leaders and their cavalry-based militaries retained their position of power.

The Reign of Abbas the Great

The reign of Shah Abbas (1588–1629) is considered a "golden age" of Safavid power, comparable to that of Suleiman in the Ottoman Empire. Ascending the throne at the age of 17, Abbas ultimately became a pragmatic politician, a wise statesman, a brilliant strategist, and a generous patron of the arts. During his reign, Persia acquired security, stability, and a reputation for cultural creativity, symbolized by the shah's splendid new capital at Isfahan.

Abbas directed much of his attention to the threat posed by an Ottoman-Uzbek alliance, which had almost destroyed his country. He held his holy men in political check but labored to project an image of Shi'ite piety. He reorganized his government and army, creating a personal force of "slaves" of the royal household. This force acted as a counterweight to the ambitious and often unruly tribal chiefs. Within the army, Abbas increased his artillery and musket forces, relying less on traditional cavalry. During the 1590s, he slowly recovered territory lost by his less adept predecessors.

Persia prospered under Abbas, and Isfahan was a great center of trade, production, and consumption. The government employed thousands of workers, and the shah, his family, and retainers consumed great quantities of luxury textiles, jade vessels, jeweled weapons, and exotic food items. Government monopolies, particularly in silk, promoted various crafts such as weaving and dying. Hundreds of new roads, bridges, hostels, and irrigation projects promoted agriculture, encouraged trade, and swelled urban populations. These projects also enhanced the prestige of the ruler. Contemporaries noted that a person could travel from one end of the empire to another in safety, without fear of bandits. That was a significant claim in an age when bandits roamed the countryside and merchants traveled at their own risk, often with large retinues of armed guards.

The silk trade was so lucrative that merchants on both sides conspired to get the shipments through, even when the Safavids and the Ottomans were at war. Persia was an important center in the networks of East-West trade. Its silk was in such demand in Europe that Venetian, French, and other traders would wait in the Syrian entrepots for the caravans of Persian silk to come in. They negotiated with local agents, trying to outbid each other for the rights to purchase each incoming load. One Venetian observer stated that a merchant would willingly pluck out his own eye to triumph over a competitor. The British tried for years to gain concessions from the Safavids on Persian silk. Ultimately, the shah signed a commercial agreement with the British, and the Portuguese were forcibly ejected from Hormuz in the Persian Gulf, moves allowing direct shipment of Persian silk to Europe by sea, and thus the avoidance of Ottoman tolls on the overland routes.

Persia at this time was one of the primary cultural centers of the world. It was a conduit to the West not only for the goods but also for the spiritual and literary influences of India. Meanwhile, sufi Muslim missionaries traveled to South and Southeast Asia, transmitting their own ideas and bringing a synthesis of

Nominally, this image illustrates a story about an elderly dervish who is in love with a handsome young man. But miniatures often depicted scenes of everyday life like this sixteenth-century Safavid scene of a bath house. On the roof, servants shake out towels. In the dressing room men are shown changing their clothes and an attendant brings a man who appears to be the bath keeper some food. A father carries his son into the bath while outside a servant takes care of a horse with rich saddle cloths. Inside the bath (hammam), assisted by bath-attendants, men of various ages wash, get their hair trimmed, or enjoy a massage. The bath was a place for socializing, relaxing, and conducting business. Bathing was a same-sex activity. Women, who either attended separate baths or attended on different days, might bring their children or use the bath as an opportunity to evaluate potential brides for their sons.

mystical ideas and practices back to the Islamic heartlands. Persia's fine arts—ceramics, tapestries, and carpets—were eagerly sought from Alexandria to Calcutta. Persian literary forms, particularly the exquisite imagery of Persian poetry, were imitated at both the Ottoman and Mughal courts, even by the rulers themselves. Persian painters explored realist styles and erotic themes. They were recruited from abroad, as were two émigrés, Khwaja Abdus Samad and Mir Sayyid Ali, who founded the famous Mughal school of painting in India.

Major Middle Eastern courts housed large workshops of artists, sometimes numbering in the hundreds. The Safavid shahs paid their painters to produce lavish manuscripts. Ismail commissioned a wondrous illustrated version of the *Epic of Kings (Shahnamah)*, a long rhyming poem by Firdawsi, that was not finished in the shah's lifetime. Five court calligraphers spent nine years transcribing a single edition of the poet Jami's *Seven Thrones*, for Prince Ibrahim Mirza; it was then turned over to a group of painters who produced its lavish illustrations. When the Ottomans conquered the Persian capital of Tabriz, they carried back many of the Safavid artists and their works as a valuable part of the booty.

Persian architecture, with its jewel-like colors, intricate geometric and floral patterns, luxurious gardens, and artificial streams, exerted considerable influence on the architecture of the Islamic world. Abbas made the capital at Isfahan a showcase for these artistic and architectural talents. One of the largest cities of its time, Isfahan had a million inhabitants. Its public life centered around a broad square (used for assemblies and polo matches), the palace compound, a huge bazaar, and the main mosque. Five hundred years later the beauty of Abbas's surviving monuments still inspires awe in visitors. As one Persian writer put it in his boyhood memoirs, "Isfahan is half the world."

THE MUGHAL EMPIRE IN SOUTH ASIA

■ *How did the Turco-Islamic Mughals modify their rule to accommodate a Hindu majority population?*

The Safavid and Ottoman states were contemporaries of the mighty Mughal Empire in India. It too was ruled by a Turkic dynasty. But unlike the Ottoman sultans and Safavid shahs, the Mughals ruled a population that was predominantly Hindu rather than Muslim. That fact marked the Mughal Empire indelibly and helped craft its distinctive character.

The Mughals

1525	Babur invades India
1556–1605	Reign of Akbar, Mughal Golden Age
1632	Shah Jahan commissions the Taj Mahal
1658–1707	Reign of Aurangzeb, reasserts Islamic orthodoxy

Origins

The Ottoman Empire emerged out of a warrior principality in what is now Turkey, and the Safavid Empire was established by a sufi boy-king who commanded both political and religious authority in Persia. The origin of the Mughal Empire was different from each of these; one might say it was founded by a determined prince in search of a kingdom.

The establishment of the Mughal Empire was not the first instance of Muslim contact with the diverse, but predominantly Hindu, population of India. Mus-

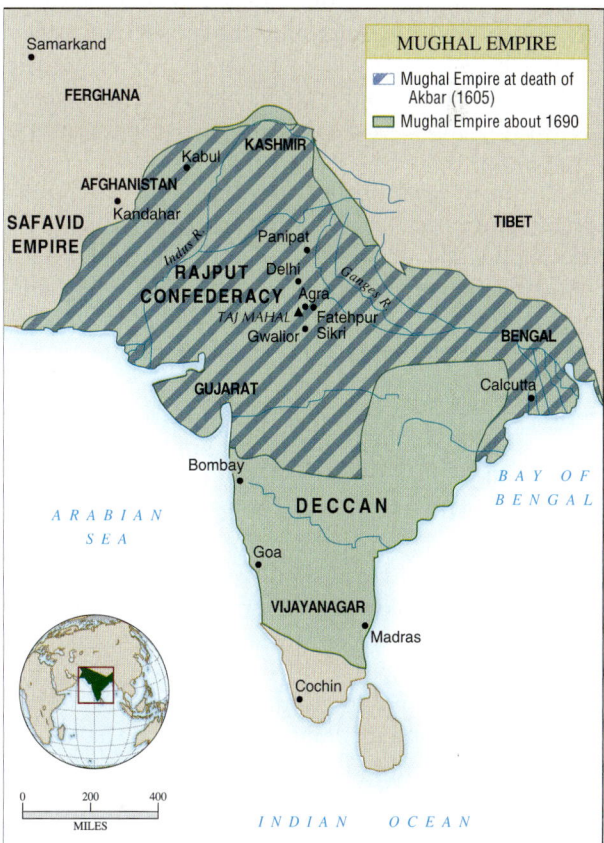

At its height the Mughal Empire comprised most of the Indian subcontinent.

lim merchants and sufi mystics had traveled to India from the Islamic heartlands for many centuries. From the seventh century onward Muslim rulers extended the frontiers of Islam eastward to the borders of South Asia. Then a Turkic warrior, Mahmud of Ghazna (c. 971–1030), gained control of Khurasan province in eastern Persia and Afghanistan and seized control of northern India. Muslim sultanates were also established on the west coast of India, and the Muslim Delhi Sultanate ruled in the thirteenth and fourteenth centuries until Timur's invasion. Thus, by the sixteenth century, much of South Asian society had had some contact with Islamic culture and political power

India is a land of many peoples, many languages, and diverse terrain. At the beginning of the sixteenth century it was politically fragmented. The Delhi Sultanate, having spawned a number of independent contending Muslim states, had been partially resurrected under the Lodi Afghan dynasty. The Rajput Confederacy held sway in the northwest, the Vijayangar Empire controlled much of southern India, and a string of commercial city-states held sway along the southwestern coast. Although many rulers had aspired to unite the entire subcontinent, that goal remained daunting.

Early in the sixteenth century, a new conqueror cast his eye on India. The adventurous Turco-Mongol ruler of Kabul, Babur ("the Tiger"; 1483–1530), was a descendant of both Timur and Chinggis Khan. Babur did not begin his career in India. He inherited the Afghan principality of Ferghana and twice conquered the Timurid capital at Samarkand before losing everything to the Uzbeks. He and his troops finally seized the throne of Kabul in 1504. Babur is a striking historical figure because, unlike many rulers of his time, he compiled his memoirs. They are a tale of triumphs and losses that reveal Babur as a straightforward narrator who built gardens wherever he went, paid careful attention to geography, was solicitous of his mother, and seemed to enjoy good wine and a good fight. He also loved to compose and recite poetry. Babur's memoirs tell of rhinoceros hunts and military relations. He notes, rather ruefully, that he had sworn to give up drink when he reached the age of 40 but now felt compelled to drink out of anxiety because he was already 39. Armed with Turkish artillery, this intrepid warrior mobilized an invasion in 1525, winning decisive battles against the Afghan Sultanate at Delhi and the Rajput Confederacy. Babur was not impressed with Indian culture. He criticized native dress, religion, and the failure of Indians to have running water in their gardens.

> *Hindustan [India] is a place of little charm. There is no beauty in its people, no graceful social intercourse, no poetic talent or understanding, no etiquette, nobility or manliness.... There are no good horses, meat, grapes, melons, or other fruit. There is no ice, cold water, good food or bread in the markets.*[2]

Like many travelers, Babur tended to find his own culture superior to those of other peoples. He did, however, admire the Indian systems of numbers, weights, and measures and the country's vast array of craftsmen. Speaking as a prospective ruler, he could not help but remark that "the one nice aspect of Hindustan is that it is a large country with lots of gold and money."[3] When Babur died, soon after the conquest, the hard-living and thoughtful ruler had laid the foun-

Babur, conqueror of northern India, surveying the spectacular rock-cut Hindu sculptures at Urwa fortress in Gwalior, from an illustrated manuscript of Babur's memoirs. Babur ordered these sculptures defaced, probably to fulfill the perceived Islamic prohibition against depicting the human form. Muslim rulers defaced many such Hindu and Buddhist statues, although some Muslim courts also patronized the production of images of the human form.

dations for a Mughal empire that would dominate most of the subcontinent and endure into the eighteenth century.

Babur was succeeded by his able but erratic son, Humayun (hu-MAH-yoon). After ten years of rule during which he expanded Mughal domains, Humayun was overthrown by his vassal Sher Khan. He then fled to the Safavid court of Tahmasp in Persia. The Safavid shah welcomed Humayun. It was always useful for monarchs of the time to shelter in their courts the sons or rivals of neighboring kings, as such refugees gave rulers leverage against their enemies. Rulers also demanded that vassals send their sons to reside at court; it was a practical way to ensure the loyalty of subordinates.

In 1555 Shah Tahmasp helped Humayun regain his kingdom, no doubt presuming that Humayun would prove a significant ally on the Safavids' eastern frontiers. But Humayun died shortly thereafter in a fall down his library steps—perhaps a fitting end for a learned man, but a rather ignominious one for a warrior.

The Reign of Akbar

Humayun's son Akbar (1556–1605) was 14 years old when he succeeded his father, about the same age as Shah Ismail when he commenced his reign. During a half century of rule, Akbar united northern India, advanced against the sultanates in the south of the subcontinent, and presided over a glorious courtly culture. Akbar ruled an empire more populous than those of the Ottoman sultan and the Persian shah; Mughal subjects numbered between 100 and 150 million.

Unlike Ismail, Akbar did not immediately consolidate his power. Initially, he was controlled by a regent. As often happens when a prince comes to power at an early age, powerful men in the court used the prince's youth to advance their own influence and objectives. By the age of 20, however, Akbar took charge and began a determined campaign of conquest that would continue into his old age.

This Mughal potentate was the counterpart of Suleiman in the Ottoman Empire and Shah Abbas in Safavid Persia. His reign is associated with military might, prosperity, and patronage of the arts at a spectacular level. At 13, Akbar led troops in battle; in his thirties, he challenged an enemy commander to personal combat; in late middle age, he still hunted wild animals with sword and lance. Akbar's concern for morality and social justice was indicated by his advice to a son: "Avoid religious persecution; be strong but magnanimous; accept apologies, sincerely given."[4]

A significant aspect of Akbar's reign is that he adapted the Islamic state to the conditions of ruling a non-Muslim population. In so doing, he promoted cultural synthesis, incorporated Hindus and others into the inner workings of government, and showed himself to be a pragmatic monarch. He married a number of Rajput princesses and made alliances with Hindu families, taking the men into his service. The mother of his heir, Jahangir, was a Hindu. He also abolished the *jizya*, the head tax on non-Muslims. This decision may seem like a simple matter, but the *jizya* was a standard of Islamic rule and had been institutionalized in the Sharia Islamic law. By abolishing it, Akbar gave notice to his Hindu subjects that they were granted a more equitable position vis-á-vis the Muslims, who constituted the ruling class.

Akbar also stopped taxing Hindu pilgrims, financed the construction of Hindu temples, and forbade Muslims to kill or eat the cow, which was sacred to Hindus. These measures alienated the *ulama* and the diverse Muslim elite of Turks, Afghans, Mongols, and Persians but won new support among the majority. Akbar, however, also initiated certain measures designed to force Hindu practice into compliance with Islamic law; he issued decrees outlawing Hindu child marriages and **sati** (the self-burning of widows), two reforms that violated Hindu traditions.

Akbar's tolerance in public administration was matched by his pursuit of knowledge and personal explorations of various religious faiths. He was devoted to certain sufi *shaykhs* and launched at his court a "house of worship," a forum for religious discussion to which he invited Muslims, Christians, Jews, Jains, Hindus, and Zoroastrians. In 1582 Akbar proclaimed a new cult, the *Din-i-Ilahi* (deen-i-eel-AH-hee), or "Divine Faith," which centered on Akbar himself and was highly influenced by **Zoroastrianism.** The new creed gained few adherents, but it further antagonized the *ulama* and demonstrated Akbar's religious eclecticism.

Akbar and the Jesuits

St. Francis Xavier, Jesuit in India

The Mughal State and Its Culture

One of the great accomplishments of the Mughal Empire was its establishment of a highly organized and intrusive central administration. In many ways like that of the Ottomans, it was designed to produce a consistent supply of taxes and troops for the government and to manage distant provinces. Akbar's military administrators, about two-thirds of whom were

---

sati—The practice by Hindu widows of self-immolation on their husbands' funeral pyres.

Zoroastrianism—A religion founded by the Persian prophet and mystic Zoroaster in the fifth century; initially monotheistic, it evolved into a dualistic faith in which the gods of light and good, led by Ahura-Mazda, opposed the gods of darkness and evil, led by Ahriman; influenced the development of Judaism and Christianity; Zoroastrians who migrated to India are known as Parsees.

foreign-born Muslims, were organized in military ranks and paid salaries according to the number of soldiers they commanded. Promotion for these military administrators, who were called **mansabdars** (mahn-SAHB-dahrs), was, ideally, based on merit. Their ranks were open to Hindus, and their positions were not hereditary, like those of European nobles. Like the Ottoman *kul* system, the *mansabdar* system was designed to produce loyalty to the state. Officials, in turn, were now made more dependent on the emperor. Like the Ottomans and Safavids, Akbar drew conquered foes into his service as long as they offered their submission. In this way, he took advantage of the military expertise of defeated commanders.

In the early seventeenth century the Mughal Empire was one of the wealthiest states in the world, with revenues ten times greater than those of France. Cities were numerous and large by European standards. Akbar's capital at Agra, for example, housed 200,000 people—twice the population of contemporary London. In the towns and villages, many industries flourished, particularly cotton textiles, which were exported to most of Asia and Africa. The majority of subjects were Hindu peasants. One-third to one-half of their produce, paid in land taxes, supported the army and kept the administrative elite in considerable luxury.

The early Mughal period saw a new Hindu-Muslim cultural synthesis, well illustrated in literature. Beginning with Babur, each emperor considered himself a poet, a scholar, and a collector of books. Akbar himself could not read, but he founded a great library housing over 20,000 illustrated manuscripts. The Mughals used their wealth to patronize the arts. Their literature was cosmopolitan, reflected a fresh originality, and was expressed in a variety of languages, including Turkish, Persian, Hindi, Arabic, and Urdu (an Indo-Persian fusion).

Despite the Muslim prohibition of representational figures, human or animal, painting developed rapidly as an art in the early Mughal period. Akbar had studied art as a child under Abdus Samad and Mir Sayyid Ali, two Safavid court painters whom Humayan brought to Kabul and later took to India. Akbar's royal studio employed over a hundred artists, mostly Hindus, who created works of great variety including miniatures of courtly life and large murals for Akbar's palaces.

mansabdars—Mughal military-administrative official.

In 1632 the Mughal emperor, Shah Jahan, commissioned the building of the resplendent Taj Mahal as a memorial to his late wife. Tall minarets surround a central dome, and a reflecting pool perfectly mirrors the white marble building, one of the glories of Mughal architecture. The Taj Mahal is one of the more spectacular examples of the ways in which various peoples commemorate their dead.

The royal studio produced beautifully illustrated manuscripts requiring many painters and many years to complete. Foremost among these is the spectacular *Hamzanamah* (hahm-ZAHN-ah-mah), which includes 1400 illustrations on cloth. Akbar also sponsored illustrated versions of Babur's memoirs and of the great Sanskrit epics the *Mahabharata* (MAH-he-BAH-re-te) and the *Ramayana* (rah-MAI-yah-nah). The Mughal school of painters under Jahangir, Akbar's son, produced wonderful animal and bird imagery, developed new strains of sensual and realist representation, and expertly incorporated motifs of European painting into Mughal art.

The most imposing symbols of Mughal glory are to be seen in architecture. Fusing Persian and Indic styles, it featured the lavish use of mosaics, bulbous domes, cupolas, slender spires, lofty vaulted gateways, and formal gardens, all carefully harmonized. Akbar's major building project was his palace complex at Fatehpur Sikri (fe-te-POOR SIK-ree). Akbar wanted to build his new palace on a site dedicated to a famous sufi holy man, *Shaykh* Salim Chishti. But Fatehpur Sikri became a monument to man's vanity and lack of planning. Akbar's court abandoned the complex (which took 15 years to build) after only 14 years because the water supply was inadequate. But visitors still marvel at the red sandstone blocks of the monumental fortress, which were hewn so precisely that they needed no fasteners or mortar.

Akbar's son Jahangir and his grandson Shah Jahan continued the tradition of monumental building. The latter replaced Akbar's sandstone buildings at Delhi with new ones of marble. At Agra, Shah Jahan erected the famous Taj Mahal, a tomb for his favorite wife, Mumtaz Mahal, who died while giving birth to her fifteenth child. This elaborate tomb, set in beautiful gardens, took over 20 years to build. Its luminous white marble, beautiful tracery of semiprecious stones, and elegant lines make the Taj Mahal one of the best-known buildings in the world today.

Akbar's Successors: Contesting the Hindu-Muslim Synthesis

Like most empires, the Mughal polity fared best when its administration was relatively tolerant, its treasury full, and its military successful. Jahangir (1605–1627) and Shah Jahan (1628–1658) continued Akbar's policies of relative tolerance. Jahangir was learned and artistically sensitive (as demonstrated in his memoirs), but he was also a drunkard and a drug addict, often lacking the strength to act decisively and conduct policy. He lost Kandahar to the Persians. Shah Jahan launched three costly and unsuccessful campaigns to retake Kandahar, a disastrous thrust into Central Asia, four costly invasions of the Deccan, and an extravagant expedition to oust a Portuguese enclave on the Indian coast. To compensate for these military expeditions, he had to raise land taxes, thus oppressing the peasantry.

The tension between Mughal tolerance and Muslim rule culminated in the seventeenth century with Akbar's great-grandsons, Dara Shikoh and Aurangzeb (1658–1707). Dara Shikoh took Akbar's tolerance one step further. He was a devoted sufi and wrote his own mystical works; he also studied Hindu mysticism. In the end this prince's attempt to find a middle ground between Islam and Hinduism provoked a violent response from the empire's Muslims and from his brother, Aurangzeb (OR-ang-zeb). Dara Shikoh was his father's favorite, but in the battle to succeed Shah Jahan, Aurangzeb was victorious. Charging his brother with apostasy, Aurangzeb marched him through the streets of Delhi in humiliation and had him executed.

Both sufi orders and the *ulama* opposed the ecumenicalism of Akbar and Dara Shikoh. With their support, Aurangzeb, having gained the throne, was determined to restore Sunni orthodoxy to the Mughal

Miniatures were not painted solely for artistic expression; they also suggested relationships. In this Mughal painting of Shah Jahangir and the Safavid Shah Abbas, Jahangir's artist portrayed his master as big and powerful, dominating his rather puny-looking Safavid rival. The monarchs stand on the globe, but Jahangir's lion is much more imposing than Abbas' lamb. The angels supporting the rulers' halo show the influence of European art motifs on Mughal imagery. According to the inscription on this miniature, Jahangir commissioned the painting after having a dream about Shah Abbas.

dominions. He reimposed the *jizya* and enforced the Sharia more stringently. Many Hindu temples were destroyed during his reign, and his intolerance and rigid orthodoxy weakened the Mughal hold on its diverse Hindu populations.

The Mughal Social Order

As already noted, Mughal society comprised a series of hierarchies based on a Hindu majority and a predominantly Muslim ruling class. The vast majority of

---

Document — The Idea of Seclusion and Lady Nurjahan

The idea of seclusion (being hidden away from view) is often associated with women in Muslim societies. But historically, we find that women in all Muslim households were clearly not secluded and that "seclusion" itself is a notion that varies over time, place, class, status, and culture. Even when women were considered to be "secluded," they might have been engaged in a variety of activities that we don't ordinarily associate with seclusion. So, one question for historians, of any time, place, and group of women is: "What were those women doing?" Some examples of what elite, secluded women were doing are found in the memoirs of the Mughal emperor Jahangir. Like those of his forefather, Babur, Jahangir's memoirs are full of minute and interesting details, including discussion of the affairs of his principal wife Nurjahan (1577–1645). Nurjahan was the daughter of a Mughal vizir, and, at the end of Jahangir's reign, she, along with her brother, took over effective control of the empire. In her husband's account, we find Nurjahan portrayed as an avid hunter, an owner of estates, and a mover-and-shaker in political affairs. She engaged in all these activities while "secluded." These selections from Jahangir's memoirs (and an appendix by his historian Muhammad-Hadi) give some idea of Nurjahan's activities.

On April 16 [1617] ... the scouts had cornered four lions. I [Jahangir] set out with the ladies of the harem to hunt them. When the lions came into view, Nurjahan Begam said, "If so commanded, I will shoot the lions." I said, "Let it be so." She hit two of them with one shot each and the other two with two shots, and in the twinkling of an eye the four lions were deprived of life with six shots. Until now such marksmanship has not been seen—from atop an elephant and from inside a howdah [covered seat] she had fired six shots, none of which missed.... As a reward for such marksmanship I scattered a thousand ashrafis [coins] over her head and gave her a pair of pearls and a diamond worth a lac [100,000] of rupees.

When Jahangir was suffering from chest pain and shortness of breath, his physicians could not ease his discomfort, so he committed himself to his wife's care:

Nurjahan Begam's remedies and experience were greater than any of the physicians', especially since she treated me with affection and sympathy. She made me drink less and applied remedies that were suitable and efficacious. Although the treatments the physicians had prescribed before were done with her approval, I now relied on her affection, gradually reduced my intake of wine, and avoided unsuitable things and disagreeable food. It is hoped that the True Physician will grant me a complete recovery from the other world.

When Nurjahan's father died, Jahangir awarded his estate to her:

I awarded I'timaduddawla's jagir [a type of fief, revenue from land], household, and paraphernalia of chieftainship and amirship to Nurjahan Begam, and I ordered that her drums should be sounded after the imperial ones.

When Mahabat Khan mounted a rebellion against Jahangir, Nurjahan escaped and mobilized for the emperor's defense:

[She] convened the grandees of the empire and addressed them in rebuke, saying, "It was through your negligence that things have gone so far and the unimaginable has happened. You have been disgraced before God and the people by your own actions. Now it must be made up for. Tell each other what the best thing to do is."

Questions to Consider

1. Nurjahan was a royal woman. What do these stories suggest about class and gender as determinants of women's activities?
2. What do these excerpts suggest about the relationship between Jahangir and his wife?
3. If royal women routinely went on hunting expeditions with the emperor, how could they still be secluded?

From Wheeler Thackston, ed. and trans., *The Jahangirnama: Memoirs of Jahangir, Emperor of India* (New York: Oxford University Press, 1999), pp. xx–xxi, 219, 368, 376, 441.

the populace, as in China, the Middle East, and Europe, consisted of illiterate peasants who provided the bulk of the empire's revenue through agricultural taxes. Wealth was an important factor in determining status, but it was not the primary factor. A merchant could be very wealthy but could not achieve the same status as a member of the elite military-administrative class. Among Hindus, status was intimately linked to caste.

Mughal society, like most societies, was also patriarchal; it allocated family, religious, and political dominance to men. This system of male dominance is often attributed to Islam, but patriarchy predated Islam in India, as it did in the Middle East. In general, it would be more accurate to say that Islam both reinforced pre-existing patriarchal structures and improved the position of women by forbidding female infanticide and granting women inheritance rights. In India under Islamic rule, the position of women derived from a synthesis of Hindu custom and Islamic law. Despite Akbar's reform-minded decrees, *sati* and child marriages continued. Formal education of females, as in most societies, was practically nonexistent, except in a few affluent or learned families.

These practices must, of course, be understood in their temporal and social contexts. In Hindu society, as in Muslim society, in which marriage is considered a preferred state (especially for women), early marriage age acted to prevent the girl's sexual purity from being compromised or questioned. By social convention, women were deemed to need male protectors, and when a woman married, she left the protection of her father or brother and became part of her husband's household. By immolating herself on her husband's funeral pyre, a widow prevented herself from becoming a social burden on her husband's family or the family she was born into.

As for female education, we should remember that the overwhelming majority of people, in all the world civilizations of this era, were illiterate. Only certain of the elites could read, and even many people of rank, like Akbar, were illiterate. Men's and women's roles were considered complementary, not equal. Because men were expected to perform the political, religious, and administrative tasks that required literacy, formal education tended to be reserved for them.

NETWORKS OF TRADE AND COMMUNICATION

■ *What role do trade and communication play in the maintenance of the Ottoman, Safavid, and Mughal empires?*

The gunpowder empires emerged in a set of interconnected regions that were in turn imbedded in even more extensive networks of trade and communication. The primitive nature of transport and communications technology limited the flow of goods, knowledge, and information. But all three circulated in ways that might seem surprising, given that the only ways to get from one place to another were on foot, on animalback, or aboard oared and sailing vessels. Despite these limitations, scholars traveled from one court to another, enjoying the patronage of Ottoman, Safavid, or Mughal emperors and sharing literary, artistic, and legal traditions. The royal courts consumed prodigiously and supported the exchange of goods and culture on a grand scale. Mehmed II had his portrait painted by the famous Italian painter Bellini. Babur brought Persian artists into India, and the Safavid court imported Arab jurists. Rulers in all three empires drank from Chinese porcelain cups.

The Ottoman, Safavid, and Mughal Empires derived most of their income from agriculture. But trade was their second source of wealth. None of these empires invented the trading routes. Rather, these routes emerged and expanded across a set of well-established commercial networks linking urban centers.

The birth of a prince in the Mughal harem. This unusual scene shows the numerous female attendants of the princely court and suggests the ceremonial significance of such an event. Note the varying dress styles of the women and the rich textiles surrounding the princess.

They inherited these networks from their predecessors and competed with rival kingdoms to monopolize goods and collect commercial taxes. To understand how these empires worked, we must abandon the notion of modern boundaries that are marked, fixed, and defended. Rulers could not control frontiers absolutely; instead they defended and taxed key routes, fortresses, and cities. The porous nature of borders encouraged tax evaders. If officials demanded high taxes along one route, merchants might shift to another route. If taxes were collected by the camel-load, merchants stopped their beasts outside of town and repacked in order to have fewer loads.

In this context of flexible boundaries, trading communities developed that facilitated the flow of goods from one place to another. Although the Ottomans fought long wars with both Christian states in Europe and Muslim competitors in Persia and Egypt, trade among these regions was seldom squelched for long. The furs of Muscovy flowed south into the empire and the gold of Africa came north. Armenian merchants played a prominent role in the Persian silk trade, which drew European silver in large quantities into the Safavid Empire. Jewish merchants traded copper to Arab merchants, who sold it to South Asian traders in return for cotton, jewels, and spices.

Many great trading centers were scattered throughout the territories of the gunpowder empires. Babur described the emporium of Kabul, located between Persia and India, as receiving merchant caravans of 15,000 or 20,000 pack animals carrying slaves, textiles, sugar, and spices. Kabul channeled the trade of China and India westward in exchange for goods coming eastward from the Ottoman and Safavid realms.

The merchants in turn served an information function. Because communication technologies were so limited, rulers used travelers of all sorts to gain knowledge about the rest of the world. Scholars, sufis, traders, envoys, and spies all served this purpose. Monarchs used envoys as spies, and their rivals tried to control information by keeping visiting envoys sequestered and by intimidating them with military displays. Response to another ruler's challenge could never be swift because it was often months or years before a monarch received a reply or news about his envoy's fate.

Outside these channels of communication, relations between the gunpowder empires and European or East Asian states were still quite limited. Only the Ottomans had resident consuls from some of the European states in their capital. In this era, the balance of trade was tipped very much in favor of the East, with eastern goods flowing into Europe and cash flowing back. European imports, with the exception of certain kinds of textiles, were negligible by comparison.

DOCUMENT
The English in South Asia

CONCLUSION

In the three and a half centuries before 1650, Europe still lagged behind Asia in many respects. No European state, not even the polyglot empire of Charles V, could compare in manpower and resources with the realms of Suleiman or Akbar. Europeans were impressed by the resources and taxation capabilities of the Ottoman governing system. Opportunities for minorities and toleration for dissenting religions were greater in the Muslim countries than in Europe. Asian cities were usually better planned, more tastefully adorned with works of art, and even better supplied with water and with sewage disposal.

Europe's advantages, which began to be more apparent after the beginning of the seventeenth century, were most evident in the realm of technology, specifically in the production of field artillery and oceangoing ships. These technical assets helped certain of the European states gain leverage in a new age, when powerful states would depend on strategic control of sea lanes and world markets. But in the period from 1300 to 1650 it was the gunpowder empires that tended to dominate, using their resources and militaries to become the great imperial powers of that age.

Suggestions for Web Browsing

You can obtain more information about topics included in this chapter at the websites listed below. See also the companion website that accompanies this text, http://www.ablongman.com/brummett, which contains an online study guide and additional resources.

Islam and Islamic History in Arabia and the Middle East
http://www.islamic.org/Mosque/ihame/Sec11.htm
http://www.islamic.org/Mosque/ihame/Sec12.htm
http://www.islamic.org/Mosque/ihame/Sec13.htm

Related sites detailing the enormous legacy of the early Islamic civilization, a history of Mongol destruction and Mamluk victory, and the rise of the Ottoman Empire.

Ottoman Page
http://ottoman.home.mindspring.com/

Site dedicated to classical Ottoman history, 1300–1600, offering numerous links to other sites.

Topkapi Palace
http://www.ee.bilkent.edu.tr/~history/topkapi.html

A guide to Topkapi Palace, with numerous images of the palace rooms and grounds and its phenomenal artifacts, including portraits of the sultans, manuscripts, clothing, porcelains, and armaments.

Internet Islamic History Sourcebook: The Persians
http://www.fordham.edu/halsall/islam/islamsbook.html

Links to a variety of documents detailing the rise and spread of the Safavid Empire.

Internet Indian History Sourcebook
http://www.fordham.edu/halsall/india/indiasbook.html

Extensive indexed site of primary sources for medieval India.

Mughal Monarchs
http://rubens.anu.edu.au/student.projects/tajmahal/mughal.html

A detailed introduction to the Mughal dynasty and the city of Agra, whose images emphasize the superb architecture of the time.

Literature and Film

A short primary source on Jahangir, available in paperback, is Mutribi al-Asamm, *Conversations with Emperor Jahangir*, trans. Richard Foltz (Mazda, 1998). *The Intimate Life of an Ottoman Statesman: Melek Ahmed Pasha (1588–1662)*, trans. Robert Dankoff (SUNY Press, 1991) is a wonderful portrayal of the realities of Ottoman administration. An excellent selection of Ottoman poetry can be found in *Ottoman Lyric Poetry: An Anthology*, eds. Walter Andrews, Najaat Black, Mehmet Kalpakli (University of Texas Press, 1997).

The University of North Carolina library (Chapel Hill) has a large collection of films on the Islamic world which are cataloged by topic. These include films on the Ottoman Empire and the Modern Middle East. See listings on their website at http://www.lib.unc.edu/house/nonprint.

Suleiman the Magnificent depicts the life, accomplishments and regional significance of this Ottoman sultan.

Isfahan: A City Known as "Half the World" is a great video, in Farsi and English, about Isfahan and its historic sites. For additional information, see http://www.iranianmovies.com/reviews/isfahan.html.

Suggestions for Reading

On Inner Asia and Turkic groups, see Peter Golden, *An Introduction to the History of the Turkic Peoples* (Harassowitz, 1992). Luc Kwanten, *Imperial Nomads, a History of Central Asia, 500–1500* (University of Pennsylvania Press, 1979), is an illuminating study of a subject long neglected in standard texts.

The Ottoman Golden Age is ably depicted in Halil Inalcik, *Phoenix: The Ottoman Empire, the Classical Age 1300–1600* (Phoenix Press, 2001); Norman Itzkowitz, *The Ottoman Empire and the Islamic Tradition* (University of Oklahoma Press, 1980); and Stanford Shaw, *A History of the Ottoman Empire and Modern Turkey*, 2 vols. (Cambridge University Press, 1976–1977). On Sultan Suleiman, see Metin Kunt and Christine Woodhead, eds., *Süleyman the Magnificent and His Age* (Longman, 1995). The harem is covered in Leslie P. Peirce, *The Imperial Harem* (Oxford University Press, 1993).

On medieval Persia, see Ann Lambton, *Continuity and Change in Medieval Persia* (Persian Heritage Foundation, 1988), and David Morgan, *Medieval Persia, 1040–1797* (Longman, 1988). See also Roger Savory, *Iran Under the Safavids* (Cambridge University Press, 1980). Coverage in English of the Safavid period is still limited; an old standard is Percy M. Sykes, *A History of Persia*, (Routledge/Curzon, 2003), first published in 1938 and now in its third edition. On Safavid trade, see Rudolph Matthee, *The Politics of Trade in Safavid Iran: Silk for Silver, 1600–1730* (Cambridge University Press, 1999).

The Mughal system is ably described in John F. Richards, Gordon Johnson, and C. A. Bayly, eds., *The Mughul Empire* (Cambridge University Press, 1996); Douglas E. Streusand, *The Formation of the Mughal Empire* (Oxford University Press, 1990); and Neelam Chaudhary, *Socio-Economic History of Mughal India* (Discovery, 1987). For studies of individual emperors, see Gul Badan Begam, *The History of Humayun*, trans. A. S. Beveridge (B. R. Publishers, 1989); Bamber Gascoigne, *The Great Moghuls* (Harper & Row, 1971); and J. M. Shelat, *Akbar* (Bharatiya Bidya Bhavan, 1964).

CHAPTER 13
East Asian Cultural and Political Systems, 1300–1650

CHAPTER CONTENTS

- China: The Ming Dynasty

  DISCOVERY THROUGH MAPS: Map of China's Ancient Heartland, circa 1500 C.E.

  DOCUMENT: A Censor Accuses a Eunuch

- Korea: The Making of a Confucian Society

- Japan: The Era of Shōguns and Warring States

  DOCUMENT: Sotoba Komachi, a Fourteenth-Century Japanese Nō Play

- Southeast Asia: States Within a Region

  DOCUMENT: A Traveller's Account of Siam

1300

1283–1317 Rama Khamheng, Thai king who established independent Thai state, created Thai alphabet

1338 Ashikaga Shogunate succeeds Kamakura Shogunate in Japan

1368–1644 Ming dynasty rules China

1392–1910 Chosŏn dynasty rules Korea

1400

15th century Islam spreads in Indonesia

15th century Nō plays flourish in Japan

15th century Vietnam and Thailand control mainland Southeast Asia

1402 Malacca founded

1403–1424 Reign of Yongle, emperor of China; Forbidden City built

1405–1433 Chinese maritime expeditions by Zheng He

1418–1450 Reign of King Sejong of Chosŏn dynasty, creator of han'gul alphabet

1467–1600 Warring States Period in Japan

1500

16th century Era of Chinese popular novels such as *The Water Margin, Journey to the West*

1557 Ming grants Portuguese traders limited operations in Macao

1592–1598 Korea repulses invasions by Japan

1600

1603 Tokugawa Shogunate in Japan begins

1627, 1636 Korea invaded by Manchus

1639 Japanese restriction of trade to Chinese, Koreans, and Dutch

---

This chapter discusses the development and mutual influences of China, Korea, Japan, and the countries of Southeast Asia from the fourteenth into the seventeenth centuries. During this time, ideologies, religions, and cultural traditions continued to be shared. Trade was maintained, though greatly modified in the middle of the period by the introduction of new players and products from Europe and the Americas and by the severe restriction of Japanese international commerce in the early seventeenth century. China was still the dominant actor in East Asia, but while its power and influence may have seemed paramount, individual nations were forming their own political and cultural traditions and identities.

Throughout its history, Chinese civilization has synthesized outside influences and its own indigenous culture. Culture rather than ethnicity generally defined what it was to be Chinese. Indeed, before the end of the seventeenth century, China was generally seen as a civilization rather than a place inhabited by a dominant ethnic group. Outsiders who adopted Chinese ways could rise to high stations, even rule China. Those who had not sufficiently assimilated Chinese culture were often not viewed as fully Chinese.

China's view of itself as a civilization was just as important as its view of itself as a political entity. Frequently called the "Central Flower," its culture and civilization were seen as having broad universal appeal. As the "Central Kingdom," a term that emphasized *political* unity, China could also justify its international relations based on the tribute system. The tribute system encompassed China's relationships with East Asian nations. It was an unequal system that required peripheral countries to indicate their loyal subordination by donating tribute to China and receiving gifts in return according to a planned schedule of visits—a form of strictly regulated trade. China acted as a protective "parent" toward neighbors who were not entirely independent of China in terms of their foreign relations. The early Ming's place in the larger Eurasian continent was perhaps even more important. It launched the world's largest maritime explorations, dominated world trade, and was deeply connected to the world's silver-based economy.

In Korea, the Koryŏ dynasty, struggling with slave-owning landholders, many of whom had been allied with the Mongols who had themselves just been forced out of China, was overturned by a reformist faction in 1392. The founder of the new Chosŏn dynasty, King T'aejo (1335–1408), sent tribute missions to the Ming, cut all ties to the Mongols, and strengthened Chinese institutions in Korea. The Chosŏn dynasty was known for such cultural advances as the development of an indigenous alphabet, a lively publishing trade, an active scholarly world of competing schools of thought, and refined arts of painting and pottery that blended Korean and Chinese models. Korea retained much of its indigenous aristocratic structure during the long Chosŏn dynasty (1392–1910), but its culture was deeply imbued with neo-Confucianism, originally Chinese but now assimilated into Korean culture.

Japan was also connected with Korea and China in this era. In the first half of the three-century period, refined art collectors revered continental arts. As samurai settled in Kyoto (formerly called *Heian*) in the late fourteenth century, they outdid one another in displaying Chinese, Korean, and Japanese works readily available to wealthy collectors. Although the Ming, in theory, controlled the volume of trade within its tribute system, freebooting Japanese, Chinese, and Korean pirates imported a far greater volume of products through nongovernmental channels. Japanese ships transported products throughout northeast and Southeast Asia, purchased with various currencies, exchange of other goods, and Japanese and New World silver. In the sixteenth century, Japanese silver far surpassed New World silver as the fuel that drove the East Asian trade at the heart of the world economy.

While Confucianism was not yet established in Japan, Buddhism continued to prosper there until the end of the sixteenth century. The breakdown of peace at the end of the fifteenth century and the coming of Iberian missionaries in the sixteenth century, who brought guns along with religion, radically altered Japan's history. In 1600, Japan was once again unified, and by 1640, it would severely restrict its trade to just three partners—China, Korea, and Holland.

The lands and islands southeast of China, today called Southeast Asia, were long influenced by Indian culture and religions. Chinese culture deeply influenced Vietnam. Buddhism, Hinduism, and local religions were celebrated in the kingdoms of Southeast Asia. In Vietnam, a millennium of Chinese rule made the Chinese both despised as overlords and worthy of emulation as bearers of advanced means of governance. With the exception of a period of Mongol attack and, later, a brief occupation by Ming forces, Vietnam was politically independent of China after 939. But Vietnam's government was in many ways an ideal Confucian state, and Vietnam and China were closely bound through the tribute system.

Maritime Southeast Asia—today's Philippines, Malaysia, and Indonesia—was dependent on trade. Important maritime empires, including a succession of rulers on the island of Java, occupied most of modern Malaysia and Indonesia. In the thirteenth century, one of Java's great powers, Majapahit, held off the Mongols' attempted invasion and unified many of the islands of the Indonesian archipelago. In the fourteenth and fifteenth centuries, Islam spread to maritime Southeast Asia as merchants recognized the benefit of Muslim ties in expediting trade in the Indian Ocean. Chinese and Indian traders continued to operate throughout Southeast Asia. The coming of first Portuguese and Spanish and later British and Dutch merchants and missionaries influenced Southeast Asian life by the beginning of the seventeenth century.

CHINA: THE MING DYNASTY

■ *In what ways can Ming China be considered an early modern state?*

Before the modern period, Chinese historians wrote the history of their country as a series of consecutive dynastic waves—as one dynasty declined after a period of growth, another would rise and receive Heaven's mandate (see Chapter 2). The struggle to overthrow the Yuan in the fourteenth century was brutal, but it contained many of the elements of dynastic change identified by contemporaries in China. That is, natural disasters and disease accompanied by religious uprisings suggested Heaven was shifting its support from the Yuan emperor to new rulers. The traditional dynastic cycle model downplays change over time. The Yuan dynasty's brevity gave it little opportunity to change China in lasting ways, and this seemed to confirm the dynastic cycle's validity. Yet, as we have seen in Chapter 10, the Yuan was at the center of a cosmopolitan Eurasian commercial world which influenced culture far beyond China's borders.

The Yuan dynasty declined after Khubilai's death in 1294. The north of China began to decline economically, and southerners suffered discriminatory treatment. Everywhere, the pre-Yuan power structure had been challenged, as the Mongols had altered civil service recruitment policies. Many peasants were brought to the brink of despair in the face of natural

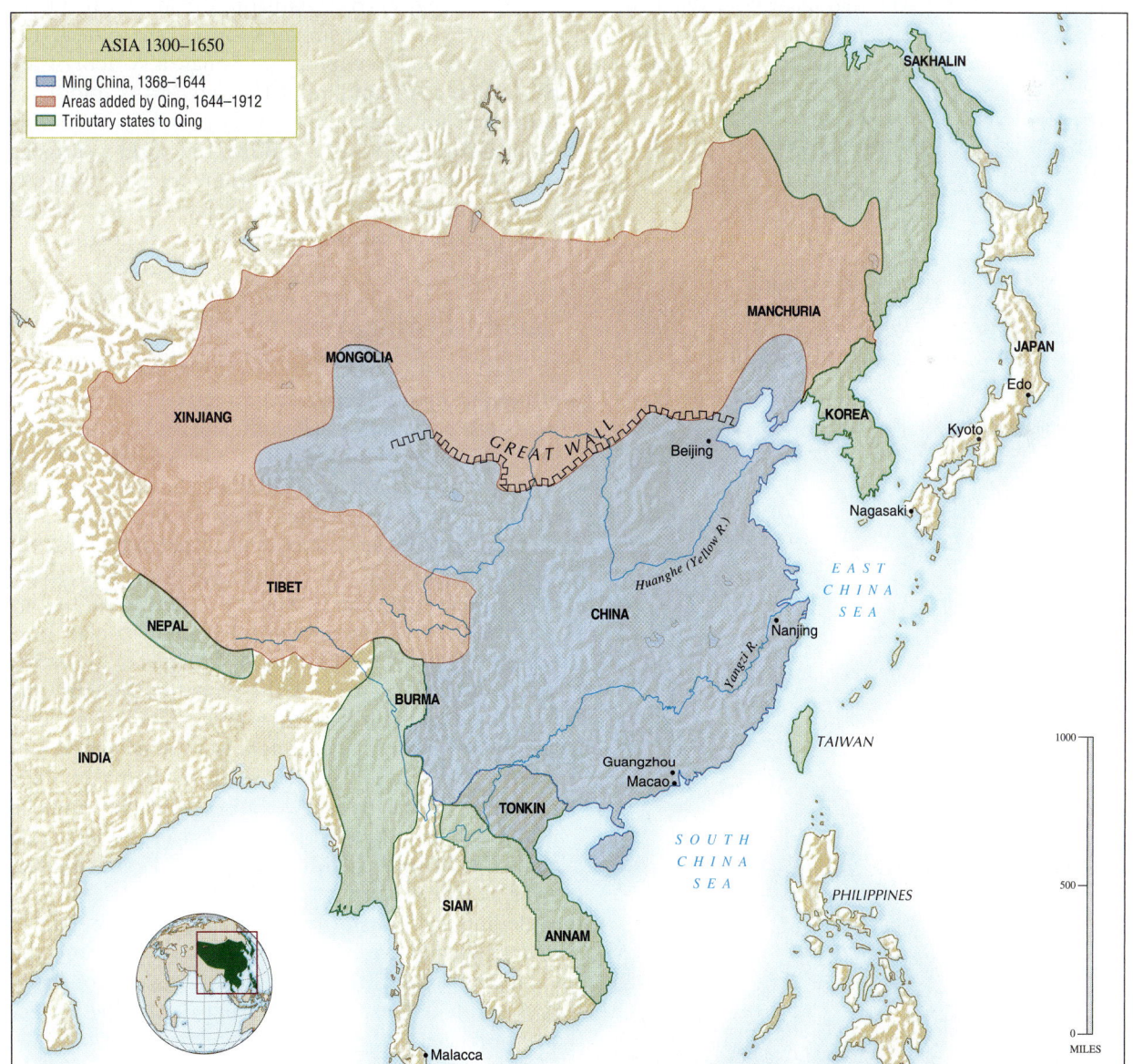

After the first two Ming emperors consolidated and expanded their rule, the rest of the dynasty remained content with the extent of their realm. The Chinese realm was greatly expanded under the Qing, who took power in the second half of the seventeenth century.

disasters in the fourteenth century, especially the Huanghe River's change in course and outbreaks of the plague. Further, the traditionally nomadic Mongol soldiers, now serving in permanent posts, lost some of their toughness and discipline. In the 39 years after Khubilai's death and the installation of the last Mongol sovereign in 1333, disorder also prevailed at the highest level of government. The Mongol royal clan had no orderly method for determining succession, and eight of the nine emperors were either overthrown or killed. Bureaucratic breakdown weakened the base of Yuan power at a time when the Mongols were severely challenged. Religious rebellions sparked by peasant discontent spread throughout southern China in the 1350s.

In 1356, a former Buddhist monk, Zhu Yuanzhang (JOO yoo-ahn-JAHNG), who had taken over the leadership of a religious-based rebel group, the **Red Turbans,** captured Nanjing. Using that city as his capital, Zhu—better known by his reign name, Ming Hongwu (hong-WOO)—conquered other warlords until he was able to march on the Yuan capital at Beijing. The Mongol emperor fled with his court to Mongolia. Hongwu thus founded a new dynasty, the Ming, without actually conquering the old. Hongwu (r. 1368–1398) attempted to assert strong imperial control, even killing thousands of scholars he believed were scheming against or ridiculing him. Neither he nor his successors were model rulers, and the last decades of Ming rule were marked by administrative failure and corruption. The strength of the Ming era lay less in its monarchs and more in the contributions of its artisans, scholars, and philosophers to a Chinese society increasingly claimed by people of all walks of life as their own.

After a period of expansion, the Ming ruled over China until factionalism, corruption, and natural disasters again led to popular uprisings, a symbol of the passage of the Mandate of Heaven, in the middle of the seventeenth century. Although modern historians often judge the Ming a failure, the three centuries were, in fact, an era of population growth, commercial expansion, and a broadening of average Chinese people's participation in the culture of the country.

Red Turbans—A branch of White Lotus Society, a millenarian Buddhist group that used Confucian and Daoist ideas as well. One of several anti-Yuan religious groups.

The Early Ming Era

Hongwu was a rather brutal and paranoid emperor, although he tried to govern effectively. He believed that people should be self-sufficient and motivated to serve their community without having to be paid. He sought to lighten the tax burden of the poor and gave the families of China's 2 million soldiers plots to farm themselves to be self-supporting. More successful villagers were to look out for their less fortunate neighbors, collect village taxes, and serve their communities essentially as administrators but without formal government appointment or pay. At the level of the court, Hongwu tried to cut back the power of the **eunuchs** by forbidding them a role in politics. All these policies failed, however. Village leaders were overworked and undercompensated for their work, soldiers who were unable to support themselves absconded, and eunuchs became more powerful than ever over the next two centuries. The third Ming emperor, Hongwu's son Yongle (YAWNG-luh; r. 1403–1424), moved the capital to Beijing and transformed it into a grand city. He also undertook massive engineering projects, especially the enlarging of the Grand Canal including the construction of fifteen locks, and the expansion of the protective northern wall into the Great Wall of China we know today.

Portrait of Hongwu, the first emperor of the Ming dynasty.

eunuchs—Castrated males who served as palace attendants and administrators for the emperor.

Discovery Through Maps

Map of China's Ancient Heartland, circa 1500 C.E.

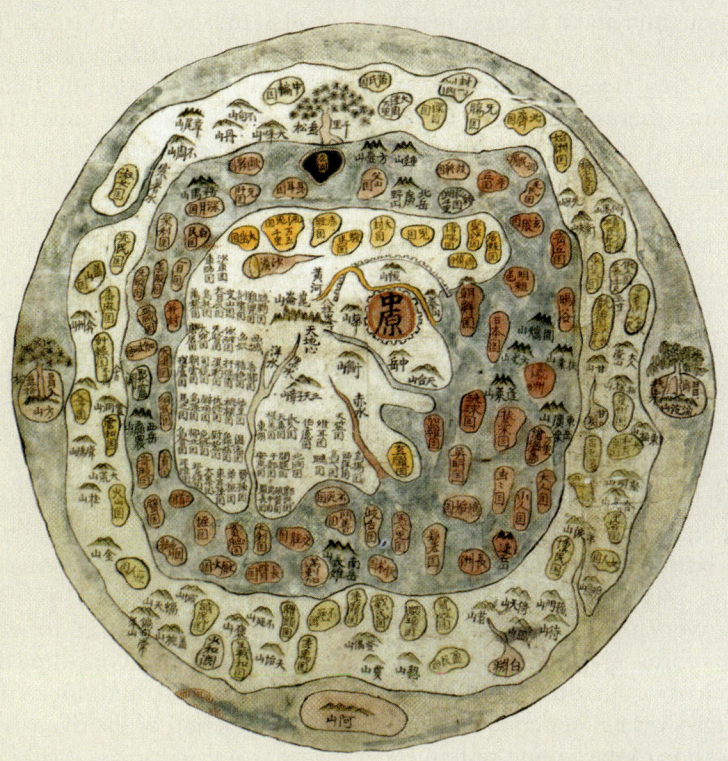

It is one of the marks of human nature that the center of the world is found in one's self-consciousness, and then in concentric circles in the family, community, and nation. This trait extends across civilizations and continents and can be seen not only in this Chinese map depicting the area known as the *Zhongyuan* (ZHONG-yoo-AHN) or heartland of ancient China, but also in maps created around the same time by Europeans as they made their voyages of discovery. The Chinese map is particularly informative because it reminds its viewers that even within China itself, the heartland was the repository of culture and power, and the farther one ventured from the center of that circle, the less likely one was to be influenced by the virtue embodied in the Son of Heaven.

By 1500, the Ming had moved their capital to Beijing, which lay in the northern region in which Chinese civilization was born; thus, the radiance of the Ming emperor was fortuitously in the same region as the birthplace of the culture he represented. In concentric circles around the Central Plain were other areas of China or countries involved in tributary relations with China. The term *central* may also be seen in a common name for China, *Zhongguo* (JONG-gwaw), meaning "Central Kingdom." The Chinese worldview placed it at the center of the world, and it was very much part of the world in terms of cultural and commercial interactions.

The map has political implications, in that it shows its viewers that the original heartland of China was the same place as the home of the Ming. This portrayal is difficult, however, for those trained to see geography in terms of a Mercator projection (see, e.g., p. 467). The Mercator projection, like the Ming map, also reflects a worldview that places the map's creators in the center–in the Mercator case, the center is in Europe. Is there any particular reason, for example, why the Greenwich Meridian (from which all longitudes on the surface of the earth are presently measured) should be the central point of the world's geography and Greenwich Mean Time should be the standard by which most clocks of the world are presently set? English dominance in the eighteenth and nineteenth centuries proved to be only a temporary moment in history, but enough to establish at least a cartographic and chronological centrality.

Questions to Consider

1. Compare and contrast this map with the view of the world on page 467. How are the maps the same? How are they different?
2. Given the particular approach of the China map, draw a simple circular map of the United States. Would Washington, D.C., or some other city be appropriately located at the center of your map? Is the Mercator Projection that is generally used today (see, for example, p. 467) necessarily better in portraying sense and relationship?

Policy in the first century of the Ming reflected a definite interest in border areas and beyond. Non-Chinese tribes, especially the Miao (mee-OW) and the Yao (YOW) in the southwest, were brought under Ming control, engendering a discussion about Chinese identity and cultural blending.

The expansive early Ming invaded Vietnam in 1407, but popular resistance there soon forced them out. The early Ming government, unlike its sixteenth-century successors, encouraged foreign trade with Japan, Southeast Asia, and India. Private trade surpassed the official trade permitted under the tribute system. Yongle regularly sent diplomatic and commercial missions to neighboring states and encouraged Chinese migration south into the Malay Archipelago and north into Mongolia. In 1405 Yongle sponsored a series of naval expeditions to potential tributary states. The greatest were led by Zheng He (JUHNG HUH), a trusted eunuch (see p. 374). The Chinese flotilla of 62 large and 225 small ships (with some ships exceeding 500 tons and carrying crews of 700) visited Sumatra, India, the Persian Gulf, Aden, and East Africa. There they exchanged porcelain for ivory, ostrich feathers, and exotic animals such as zebras and giraffes. These fancy goods were a source of fascination, but the primary purpose of the voyages was neither conquest nor trade but rather the expansion of the tribute system at the heart of Ming foreign relations. China had already penetrated the Indian Ocean while Portuguese captains were just beginning to explore the Atlantic coast of Morocco.

A Ming Naval Expedition

Voyages of Zheng He

The voyages ended in 1433. They were considered too expensive compared to the potential gains of enrolling additional countries in the tribute system. China maintained a powerful, dominant position in that system with its closest neighbors. These neighbors received Chinese support and reciprocal gifts but were also subjected to Chinese domination—at times even invasion—and to the requirement that they humbly present gifts to the Son of Heaven, the Chinese emperor, as a sign of subordination in an almost parent-child relationship. People in distant lands were far less likely to comprehend that particular Confucian proprieties were at the heart of Chinese identity, and enrolling distant people in a tribute relationship was much less useful than demanding the subordination of a neighbor. In time, maritime exploration came to be seen as an unwise investment when costly defense against land-based border tribes was more crucial. Chinese emperors never again sponsored such path-breaking journeys.

Administration of the realm was seen as central to Ming power throughout the period. While foreign adventures could be curtailed, good government demanded that emperors lead by example and that the examination system bring in loyal and honest bureaucrats.

Yet despite their attempts at eliminating past problems, the Ming emperors perpetuated many of the corrupt and weak practices they wanted to reform. The excesses of court eunuchs—male children sold by their parents to be castrated for court service—continued. At the beginning of the Ming dynasty only 100 eunuchs were employed, and not in direct government posts, but by the end of the dynasty 300 years later, 100,000 were working for the throne. Eunuchs had served as court advisers and servants since the Zhou dynasty; under the Ming, they included men from Annam and Korea, some brought as tribute, and some captured in war. Under the Ming, 28 Korean-born eunuchs served as leaders of missions to Seoul. Although eunuchs served as generals, admirals, explorers, diplomats, architects, secret police, and hydraulic engineers, the majority of them were servants of low and even slave status. The increased number of eunuchs was due not only to the expansion of the imperial family under the Ming but also to the influx of men, many self-castrated, who poured into Beijing, hoping to find a secure livelihood after escaping from poverty or famine in the countryside.

The growth in the number and influence of eunuchs was paralleled by an expansion of Confucian scholarship and scholars. Preparing for a career as a bureaucrat became increasingly attractive despite the danger of repression by paranoid emperors like Hongwu. The Ming decreed that the examinations for entering the civil service be written in a strict, formal style, but at the same time they opened opportunities for students from less advanced regions of the country to pass the exams. A new lower level category was created, permitting locally successful exam candidates to become local leaders even if they were not eligible for a better government post. In time, wealthy families perpetu-

Ming China

1368–1398	Reign of Hongwu
1403–1424	Reign of Yongle, sponsor of encyclopedia
1405–1433	Naval expeditions led by Zheng He
1472–1529	Wang Yangming, philosopher
1583–1610	Matteo Ricci at Ming court
1644	Founding of Qing dynasty

Document: A Censor Accuses a Eunuch

This memorial was submitted to the emperor in 1624 by the official Yang Lien, accusing the eunuch, Wei Zhongxian (WAY jong-shee-AHN). It illustrates how the power of the eunuchs was resented by scholar-bureaucrats while giving a sense of palace politics.

A treacherous eunuch has taken advantage of his position to act as emperor. He has seized control and disrupted the government, deceived the ruler and flouted the law. He recognizes no higher authority, turns his back on the favors the emperor has conferred on him, and interferes with the inherited institutions. I beg Your Majesty to order an investigation so that the dynasty can be saved.

When Emperor Taizu [i.e., Hongwu] first established the laws and institutions, eunuchs were not allowed to interfere in any affairs outside the palace; even within it they did nothing more than clean up. Anyone who violated these rules was punished without chance of amnesty, so the eunuchs prudently were cautious and obedient. The succeeding emperors never changed these laws. Even such arrogant and lawless eunuchs as Wang Zhen (WAHNG JUHN) and Liu Jin (LEE-oh JIN) were promptly executed. Thus the dynasty lasted until today.

How would anyone have expected that, with a wise ruler like Your Majesty on the throne, there would be a chief eunuch like Wei Zhongxian, a man totally uninhibited, who destroys court precedents, ignores the ruler to pursue his selfish ends, corrupts good people, ruins the emperor's reputation as a Yao (YOW) or Xun (SHUN), and brews unimaginable disasters? The entire court has been intimidated. No one dares denounce him by name. My responsibility really is painful. But when I was supervising secretary of the office of scrutiny for war, the previous emperor personally ordered me to help Your Majesty become a ruler like Yao and Xun. I can still hear his words. If today out of fear I also do not speak out, I will be abandoning my determination to be loyal and my responsibility to serve the state. I would also be turning my back on your kindness in bringing me back to office after retirement and would not be able to face the former emperor in Heaven.

I shall list for Your Majesty Zhongxian's twenty-four most heinous crimes. Zhongxian was originally an ordinary, unreliable sort. He had himself castrated in middle age in order to enter the palace. He is illiterate, unlike those eunuchs from the directorate of ceremonial. Your Majesty was impressed by his minor acts of service and plucked him out of obscurity to confer honors on him....

Our dynastic institutions require that rescripts be delegated to the grand secretaries. This not only allows for calm deliberation and protects from interference, but it assures that someone takes the responsibility seriously. Since Zhongxian usurped power, he issues the imperial edicts. If he accurately conveys your orders, it is bad enough. If he falsifies them, who can argue with him? Recently, men have been forming groups of three or five to push their ideas in the halls of government, making it as clamorous as a noisy market. Some even go directly into the inner quarters without formal permission. It is possible for a scrap of paper in the middle of the night to kill a person without Your Majesty or the grand secretaries knowing anything of it. The harm this causes is huge. The grand secretaries are so depressed that they ask to quit. Thus Wei Zhongxian destroys the political institutions that had lasted over two hundred years. This is his first great crime....

One of your concubines, of virtuous and pure character, had gained your favor. Zhongxian was afraid she would expose his illegal behavior, so conspired with his cronies. They said she had a sudden illness to cover up his murdering her. Thus Your Majesty is not able to protect the concubines you favor. This is his eighth great crime....

Questions to Consider

1. Discuss how this document reflects the power politics of the Ming dynasty.
2. Discuss how a similar document might have been phrased if it had been written from the perspective of a eunuch and not the palace scholar-bureaucrat.

From Patricia Buckley Ebrey, *Chinese Civilization: A Sourcebook*, 2nd ed. (New York: Free Press, 1993), pp. 263–266.

ated their status by their sons' success in the examination system. Poor boys, whose work was needed on their parents' farms, were far less likely to devote years to exam preparation. In spite of the system's theoretical openness to boys of all backgrounds, in reality only the rich had the chance to study and enter government service. By the sixteenth century, there were approximately 100,000 students preparing for exams at any given time.

As time passed, Ming rulers became resistant to innovation. Yet even this resistance had a positive aspect, in that it generated an aura of stability through most of the 1500s, when Chinese culture was a model for East Asia. Sixteenth-century European visitors were impressed by Chinese courtesy, respect for law, confidence, and stately ceremonies. They saw material prosperity in the bustling markets, stone-paved roads, and beautiful homes of Ming officials. They noted with awe the breadth of literacy and the availability of books written in vernacular language comprehensible to many readers. The elaborate Ming examination system, with its proclaimed principle of advancement on merit, often evoked favorable surprise. European commentators were lavish in their praise of Chinese justice, an attitude that would change greatly several centuries later.

Ming Society, Scholarship, and Culture

Market towns and commercial networks had been growing in China since the Song dynasty (see Chapter 10). As the population rebounded following its decline during the Yuan dynasty, market towns expanded. The distance between market towns shortened, and commercial links were improved. At the same time, other forms of social interaction developed, especially kinship (lineage) groups and community associations pledging to do good deeds and lead moral lives. Community orientation did not necessarily require that all people be treated equally, but rather humanely. During the Ming era, for instance, women became less visible to the larger society. They were to stay inside the house; widows were not supposed to remarry but rather continue to live with the family of their deceased husband; and the practice of foot binding spread throughout the country, even among commoners. The ideal of the exemplary Confucian woman was institutionalized in the form of written accounts of virtuous widows and of arches built in front of the homes of women widowed before they were 30 who reached the age of 60 without remarrying. Though Ming law, ironically, offered a financial incentive to widows' families to marry them off—if she remarried, a widow's dowry could be kept by her late husband's family, who would also earn a "bride price" from her next husband's family—widows deemed virtuous did not remarry. Morality tales written during the Ming, while likely exaggerated for didactic effect, portrayed virtuous widows as committing suicide or self-mutilation to show grief or prove their loyalty to dead husbands.

Under Ming rule, legal recognition of **concubinage** also encouraged the sale of young virgins from poor families to families of generally higher status. While women's official legal status, especially that of widows, was lowered because of stricter adherence to Confucian norms, it can also be said that women's independence was encouraged by the same ideology. New Confucian regulations and standards encouraged education for girls as well as boys. Young women, who read the more than 50 works extolling female obedience through accounts of the lives of virtuous women, were also given access to other reading material that could easily have challenged the official vision of a woman as a person confined to a household.

Even foot binding can be seen from several perspectives. The practice mutilated the foot in order to enhance a woman's desirability; mothers bound their daughters' feet to improve their marriage prospects and thus, perhaps, spare their daughters a life of hard physical labor. Farm women often did not have bound feet, as their labor was needed. On the one hand, it could be said that a life of field work liberated a woman from bound feet; on the other, bound feet usually freed a woman from backbreaking field work. Nowhere else in Asia was foot binding practiced, and yet women had subordinate status there as in most parts of the world. Thus, foot binding was a painful, mutilating practice but was itself not a cause of women's second-class status.

The Ming respect for learning and literacy was evident in officially commissioned works as well as popular works. Numerous official works were published, including vast multivolume collections, 1500 local histories, and famous medical works like *The Outline of Herb Medicine*, which took 30 years to complete. The Yongle emperor ordered the compilation of all existing literature, that is, an encyclopedia of all knowledge. It has been surmised that these works added up to more printed works than all the manuscript books throughout the world at that time. (This was also, of course, a half-century before Gutenberg

---

concubinage—A legal relationship of a man and a secondary wife, who usually did not have the rights and protection of a primary wife. Concubines were often obtained by rich men to produce sons.

printed his first book.) The **Yongle Encyclopedia** was produced by over 2000 scholars, who arranged material taken from more than 7000 works, by subject, into over 22,000 chapters bound into half that number of volumes. Although the encyclopedia was too unwieldy to print and distribute, more accessible intellectual developments—not only for the use of the emperor and his officials—were encouraged by the increased printing of books and by the growth of education in private academies that prepared students for public examinations.

During the first half of the Ming, the state considered Zhu Xi (JOO SHEE) Confucianism (see Chapter 10) as orthodox. Zhu Xi's interpretations were reflected in the exam system. Other scholars' views became increasingly important in the sixteenth century, the most important of which was that of the soldier, poet, and philosopher Wang Yang-ming (WAHNG yahng-MING; 1472–1528), who taught that knowledge is intuitive and inseparable from experience. Wang believed anyone could be a sage and could practice self-cultivation even while doing other tasks. In later centuries, Wang Yang-ming's ideas inspired reformers and revolutionaries in China, Japan, and Korea.

Ming literature, which embraced romantic notions, evolved in ways similar to scholarship. Written in colloquial language accessible to larger numbers of readers, novels, based on orally transmitted tales, described ordinary life. Three of the best-known Chinese novels date from the sixteenth century. *Journey to the West* (also known as *Monkey*) is a rollicking semisatirical tale about a Buddhist monk traveling to India with his pig and a monkey that had led an earlier human life. The erotic novel *Golden Lotus* recounts the romantic adventures of a merchant, his wife, and his concubines. Perhaps the best-read work is *The Water Margin* (also known as *All Men Are Brothers*), the story of an outlaw band who, like Robin Hood's merry men, broke the law in the name of what they saw as greater justice. Travel literature and adventures found great acceptance among the merchant classes; farmers read treatises on improving their agricultural practices; and students and scholars could cram for exams with study guides. Thousands of titles were available for a wide range of tastes.

Playwrights from the south dominated Chinese drama, which had a golden age of its own during the Ming period. Plays sometimes were as long as ten acts, developing intricate plots and subplots with unexpected endings. Music became more prominent on the stage as solos, duets, and even entire choirs alternated with the spoken word in performances.

Ming artists and architects produced great quantities of high-quality works. The horizontal lines of the Forbidden City, the imperial family's area of temples and palaces constructed from 1403 to 1424, illustrate the period's values of balance and formalism. In Ming painting, naturalistic landscapes were a favorite topic of literati painters Shen Zhou (SHEN JOH; 1427–1509) and his most talented pupil, Wen Zhengming (WEN juhng-MING; 1470–1559). The great later Ming painter Dong Qichang (DONG chee-CHAHNG; 1555–1636) was noted for the formal discipline of his brush strokes.

This subtle work, Whispering Pines on a Mountain Path, *painted by Tang Yin (1470–1523) embodies the artistic ideals of the Ming dynasty.*

Yongle Encyclopedia—Compilation of all known scholarship by Yongle emperor's team of scholars in the fifteenth century.

The period's major artistic achievement was its porcelains, mostly produced at the Ming imperial kilns at Jingdezhen (JING-duh-JEN). While blue pottery had been produced earlier, it so characterized these kilns that Ming pottery is often assumed (incorrectly) to all be blue. Ming porcelain was emulated in Japan and Holland, and it was a major Chinese export item.

The blue-and-white pattern on the Ming jar (sixteenth century) is usually associated with the era, but as we can see in the vase at the right red was an equally vivid color in Ming culture. Carved red lacquer ware was produced in palace workshops.

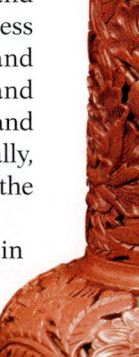

The Ming and the Sixteenth-Century World

The Ming's great voyages of exploration and its expansion toward the southwest were completed by the end of the fifteenth century. Though official maritime trade was limited to the ports of Ningbo for Japan, Fuzhou (foo-JOH) for the Philippines, and Guangzhou (gwahng-JOH) for Indonesia, extralegal trade carried on by Japanese, Chinese, Korean, Dutch, Portuguese and Spanish "pirates" enriched Chinese consumers' access to exotic goods. China exported mainly pottery and silk, importing Southeast Asian woods, spices, and food, New World foods like corn, sweet potatoes, and peanuts, and silver from both Mexico and, especially, Japan. The Ming economy became monetized with the huge influx of silver.

The population had expanded from 85 million in 1400 to 310 million by 1650, fueling a rise in the number and size of market towns, particularly in the heavily populated south. Crowded conditions led many to emigrate to Indonesia and the Philippines, where they functioned as cultural and commercial intermediaries. Domestic trade grew alongside foreign trade. Portuguese traders, banned in 1517, were permitted to operate from Macao after 1557. Soon, other European traders were knocking on China's door. They were accompanied by missionaries, at first mostly Jesuits who impressed the Ming imperial court with their scholarly ways and technical expertise in science, medicine, shipbuilding, calendar-making, and mathematics. The primary goal of the Jesuits and other Christian missionaries was to convert the Chinese to their religion, but the court was most impressed by their secular knowledge. Jesuits hoped to influence the top rulers by wearing the clothes of Confucian gentlemen and by speaking Chinese. Matteo Ricci, the best known among them, was extraordinarily erudite, but neither he nor other Christians won over many converts.

A European View of Asia

Matteo Ricci's Journals

A Chinese View of Ricci

Exciting new ideas and products were entering China, and much of the world looked to China as the source of both luxuries and everyday items. China continued to be the center of trade in Eurasia and was one leg of a triangle of trade whose other two legs were the Spanish colonies in the Philippines and in the western hemisphere (the trans-Pacific vessels were called "Manila Galleons"). But governance began to fall apart at the end of the sixteenth century, and the Ming's sophisticated global commerce could not save it from the effects of its shoddy economic mismanagement at home.

Corruption, waste, bureaucratic inertia, and conservatism prevailed at every level of government. The emperor Wanli (wahn-LEE; r. 1573–1619) was known as particularly ineffective, especially in the last decades of his reign. Thousands of his imperial family members lived off the revenues paid by a decreasing number of tax-paying peasants (rich landowners managed to remove themselves from the tax rolls). Peasant discontent with these injustices, combined with the imperial government's inability to respond to weather catastrophes in the 1620s (a "little ice age"), led to tenant uprisings and urban riots. Foreign issues exacerbated the Ming's economic worries at home. In the 1630s, Japan severely restricted its foreign trade, and Japanese silver supplies were rapidly being depleted. Struggles between Chinese and Spanish immigrants in the Philippines cut off access to China's other source of silver—that brought to Asia by the Manila Galleon.

The decline of the military also undermined the Ming. It was badly equipped and, in general, poorly led. The army suffered a serious drop in morale as disorder increased throughout the country: Pirates ravaged the coasts, and Mongol attacks brought near-anarchy along the Great Wall. The Chinese helped defend the Koreans against Japanese attacks in the 1590s, but that was the Ming army's last major stand against an outside threat.

Local governors and commanders, rather than the imperial government, had some success in dealing with these threats. There were even some women among these local leaders. The famous female general Qin Liangyu (CHIN lee-ahng-YOO; 1574–1648) put down local rebellions in southwestern China and later fought the Manchus at the end of the Ming dynasty. Known for her bravery and strength of character, she was also a refined woman who wrote elegant poetry. Meanwhile, the central administration nearly ceased to function. The highly formalized system was insufficiently flexible to deal with new challenges. Moreover, some emperors were puppets of eunuch ministers who pursued policies that were increasingly frivolous and unrealistic.

In the summer of 1644, after attempting to kill his oldest daughter to prevent her inevitable rape, mutilation, and death at the hands of rebels, the last Ming emperor, Chongzheng (chong-JUHNG; r. 1627– 1644), hanged himself in his imperial garden, leaving a pitiful note to indicate his shame in meeting his ancestors. An insurgent government had already formed to the west in Sichuan, another rebel army was approaching Beijing, and only a few Portuguese mercenaries and some imperial guards remained nominally loyal. But neither of the Chinese countermovements would succeed. As the Ming regime collapsed, Manchu forces crossed the northern border into Ming territories and began the Qing (Ching) dynasty in 1664.

KOREA: THE MAKING OF A CONFUCIAN SOCIETY

■ *How were Confucian ideas adopted and modified in the early Chosŏn dynasty?*

For fifteen centuries, kingdoms on the Korean peninsula had produced a blend of indigenous and Chinese culture, arts, religions, and statecraft. At the end of the fourteenth century, King T'aejo (TAI-joh), founder of the Chosŏn dynasty, and his successors, especially the fourth Chosŏn king, the brilliant King Sejong (SEH-jong; r. 1418–1450), both enhanced Korean culture and effectively used Chinese governance and political theory. T'aejo continued the practice of sending tribute missions to China, adopted Chinese-style state ministries, and made Confucian learning the basis for government and hence for the exams taken by many candidates for bureaucratic posts. In spite of T'aejo's respect for the Ming, the Ming refused to recognize the Korean dynasty as legitimate until the third Chosŏn king, T'aejong (TAI-jong; r. 1400–1418).

Unlike in China, in Korea only the sons of the hereditarily elite class, the yangban (YAHNG-bahn), undertook Confucian study and self-cultivation in preparation for a prestigious government post. (The term *yangban* meant "of the two branches," the branches being civil and military.) Other talented young men interested in technical positions as medical doctors, law clerks, scribes, astronomers, and translators came from the hereditary *chung'in* (CHOONG-een) or middle class and took different types of technical exams. In addition, there were nonexam routes to official jobs in Korea. As in China, a comprehensive history of the preceding dynasty was commissioned as a way of asserting one's own dynasty's legitimacy. While Chosŏn Korea became as Confucianized as China, Koreans were also interested in preserving their own culture, arts, religion, and language. Diverging from China in the fifteenth century, they devised a new syllabary called **han'gul** (HAHN-gool), to better represent Korean literature.

The Early Years of the Chosŏn Dynasty

In addition to setting up Chinese-style government ministries, King T'aejo made a number of other changes when he came to power. He created a capital with a Chinese-style palace at Hanyang, now the modern city of Seoul. He set up a military controlled by the throne, replacing the armed militias of powerful families. He handed out **Rank Lands** to officials recruited from the yangban class through Confucian examinations. These Rank Lands were intended to be used as

---

han'gul—Indigenous Korean script, invented by King Sejong.

Rank Lands—Lands granted to yangban officials as pay. They became hereditary, thereby making yangban hereditary aristocracy.

Chosŏn Korea	
1392–1910	Chosŏn dynasty
1418–1450	Reign of King Sejong
1501–1570	Yi T'oegye, Confucian scholar
1592, 1598	Invasions by Japan
1627, 1630	Invasions by Manchus

pay during the lifetime of the official, but because the lands tended to become hereditary, they were replaced in the 1450s with salaries. T'aejo also made permanent grants of land to "merit subjects," people who had helped him in his rise to power. Merit lands and the power that went with them were often resented, however, by other yangban without such privileges.

Free and unfree farmers lived on the lands granted to officials or merit subjects. As many as one-third of the farmers were slaves in the Chosŏn period. Actors and entertainers, butchers and hide tanners, and women entertainers called *kisaeng* (kee-SANG)—a Korean version of the Japanese *geisha* (GAY-shah)—were considered to be "lowborn" people as well. Free peasants paid a very low tax on their output (just one-tenth and later one-twentieth of their harvest), but together with local tribute taxes, labor service, military duty, and other requirements, the total tax burden was heavy. Nevertheless, some free but not initially rich peasants eventually became wealthy landholders called commoner-landlords. By the beginning of the seventeenth century, new crops were grown for the expanding urban market. Improved farming technology and irrigation were used by some farmers involved in the production of these commercial crops, and in time, some became wealthy enough to get out of debt and buy enough land to be landlords themselves. The demographic structure of the countryside shifted from one with rich, elite people on top and poor commoners or slaves on the bottom, to a more complicated structure that had some yangban, some rich commoner-landlords, some small peasants, some tenants, and some unemployed homeless people. While the development of the countryside was good for overall economic growth in Korea, the resulting rural stratification would eventually lead to peasant discontent and uprisings.

Chosŏn society was officially divided into four statuses, roughly equivalent to the Chinese status groups (scholars, farmers, artisans, and merchants). In Korea, the yangban were on top followed by farmers, artisans, and the lowborn. In effect, the biggest divide was between the yangban and everyone else. Artisans were, at first, either government employees or government slaves. About 2800 lived in Seoul and 3500 elsewhere in Korea. In addition to doing work for the state, they also took private orders, and in time, these played a more important role in their professions. Eventually, most artisans became independent. Merchants, too, were more restricted than elsewhere in Asia in the early Chosŏn era. Money was used less commonly, and cotton cloth was a major unit of exchange. By the seventeenth century, however, merchants developed a lively commercial scene. They sold new commercial products produced by artisans and farmers—ginseng, cotton, and tobacco, the latter a New World product, were the most common cash crops—and increasing quantities of imported goods. Rows of shops selling a variety of products joined the official Six Licensed Stores that had been permitted since the early years of the dynasty.

In addition to divisions by class and status, Koreans were divided by gender. Women were subordinate to men, and this was particularly true in family law. Inheritance and succession were in the male line, so men with land or any valuables would often have a secondary wife or concubine, believing that could enhance their chances of having a son. Sons of concubines, though educated alongside their "legitimate" brothers, were barred from taking the civil service exams; they could, however, take the specialized exams for the *chung'in*.

Yangban women were more restricted than women of other classes in this period, though no women had rights of inheritance or the ability to decide such family matters as where they would live. Wives had to go along with their husbands and their parents-in-law. Women's most important virtue was preservation of their "chastity." This led to the prohibition of premarital contact with one's fiancée, of a woman having sexual relations with any man other than her husband, and of the remarriage of widows. Some impoverished widows were unable to avoid remarriage, but as in China, it was strongly discouraged. Also, as in China, chastity was encouraged through didactic writings and laws and with rewards. In 1152, *The Register of Licentious Women* stated that when a married woman did some "lustful deed" her position in society should be demoted to that of a sewing woman, a sort of servant. Moreover, her children were to be barred from office. During the Chosŏn dynasty, this sentiment intensified. By the end of the dynasty, yangban women were confined to their homes, had lost ritual duties in ancestral rites, and were not allowed to inherit property. The emphasis on chastity was to have repressive effects on women in Korean society until the end of the twentieth century.

The most effective king of the Chosŏn dynasty was Sejong. Under his rule, Korean borders were extended northward to the present borders. Though Korea was itself in the subordinate position toward China in its tribute system, Sejong established a parallel system with the ruler of the Japanese island of Tsu from whom he required tribute (this relationship eventually played a very significant role in Japanese international trade). A great patron of scholarship, Sejong embodied the **Neo-Confucian** (see Chapter 10) ideal of the scholar-king. He gathered the top scholars of his day

---

Neo-Confucianism—Chinese Confucian school of thought, originated in eleventh century; adopted throughout East Asia; focus on *li* ("principle") and *qi* ("matter" or "energy").

King Sejong of Korea (1418–1450), a member of the Chosŏn dynasty. During his reign, Korea reached the height of cultural achievements, and the modern boundaries of the country were fixed. Sejong is also credited with the creation of the Korean phonetic, or han'gul, alphabet.

in a "Hall of Worthies" and commissioned them to create a Korean writing system because, as he wisely noted, the Chinese characters Koreans had been using did not fit the Korean language. Their efforts produced han'gul, which Sejong called "proper sounds to instruct the people." The king then established an Office for Publication, which put out numerous Buddhist texts, geographies, histories, and didactic works of various kinds, including books on medical science and farming. The publication office occasionally used movable copper type, and a number of books were printed with it between 1403 and 1484. Other "Worthies" made advances in mathematics and invented musical instruments, a rain gauge, clocks, and military weapons.

The new han'gul alphabet stimulated cultural expression, particularly in literature and philosophy. Some of these works were prose compositions on simple subjects, but poetry, stressing love of nature, personal grief, and romantic love, was especially popular. Many of the Chosŏn lyric poets were women. The government also sponsored professional painters, most of whom painted landscapes. Confucian gentlemen—often referred to as *literati*—also painted, did calligraphy, and wrote poetry, but always as amateurs. Since artisans were professional artists, it was less appropriate for a gentleman of the yangban class to be a professional artist; it was expected, however, that he would cultivate his skills at the same level as a professional. As in China and Japan, skilled amateurs of this era preferred black ink paintings, sometimes with subdued colors. Other aspects of Korean painting differentiated it from Chinese styles, including humor that made use of bold calligraphy, chromatic contrasts, and an emphasis on vertical expressions rather than on depth.

Among all of the arts, the Chosŏn era is best known for its ceramics. The early Chosŏn blue-green pottery contrasted with the white porcelain produced by the government by the middle of the fifteenth century. The difference was not only one of color. The blue-green ceramics were simple but imaginative and intended for commoners. The white porcelain was made for the aristocratic yangban class.

The sixteenth century was a time of great growth in scholarship as well. One of Korea's best-known philosophers of Neo-Confucianism, Yi T'oegye (YEE TO-eh-ghee-EH; 1501–1570) was a strong supporter of Zhu Xi's learning. Yi T'oegye launched a debate about the relative importance of *i* (EE; Chinese *li*, meaning "principle") and *ki* (KEE; Chinese *qi*, "material force" or "energy"), and other philosophers weighed in. Neo-Confucian scholars have debated this point since the twelfth century. What is interesting about this debate is that many of the philosophers involved went on to establish their own schools. The boys in those schools were fiercely loyal to their teachers. Eventually, this loyalty led to intense school rivalry and the development of factions. The early sixteenth century saw a proliferation of

This Chosŏn era bottle is punchŏng *ware. The attention to detail on an object of daily use indicates the level of Korean sophistication.*

private academies and the increasing role—and factionalism—of men educated in those academies who were advising at the national level.

Korea faced a serious crisis at the hands of Japan in the 1590s. In 1592, soon after consolidating his control over a previously divided Japan,

Toyotomi Hideyoshi (TOH-yoh-TOH-mee HEE-deh-YO-shi), Japan's hegemonic military overlord at the time, extended his ambitions to a desire for continental conquest. He took his soldiers, well trained though exhausted from years of conflict in Japan, and invaded Korea with a force of 200,000 soldiers supported by 9000 sailors. Hideyoshi hoped to use Korea as the first stage of his ultimate conquest of Ming China. The official Chosŏn military was no longer effective, and peasants, merchants, yangban, and other ordinary Koreans rose up to defend Korea against an invader armed with guns that the Koreans did not possess. The Chosŏn king was useless, and after he and his high officials fled Seoul, that city's slaves set fire to many government buildings, especially the one where the lists of slaves were kept. The Ming sent soldiers in support of their tributary partner, but it was naval warfare that saved Korea. The hero of the Korean defense was Admiral Yi Sunsin (YEE soon-SHEEN; 1545–1598) who maneuvered his copper-clad ships into narrow waterways where he trapped the invading forces and cut their supply lines. The odd appearance of Yi's armored boats, used almost 300 years before armored vessels were used in the American Civil War, earned them the name "turtle boats." Hideyoshi's forces retreated, but when the terms of the peace treaty were not carried out, the war began again. Again Admiral Yi was called into action. The war was going well for the Koreans, and the Japanese forces withdrew as soon as Hideyoshi died in Japan (of natural causes). The impact on Korea, in spite of its victory, was enormous. The seven years of war diminished Korea's wealth and inflicted terrible hardships on its people. There are few buildings in Korea dating from before the 1590s; unlike other parts of Asia, few ancient Buddhist temples remain. King Kwanghaegun (kwahng-HAI-goong; r. 1608–1623) made determined efforts to rebuild the country, but he was also concerned about maintaining careful foreign relations with new rival continental forces—the Ming dynasty in China and the rising Manchus north of Korea in Manchuria. His successors were not so fortunate or skillful at negotiating. Twice, in 1627 and again in 1636, the Manchus invaded Korea when it appeared the Chosŏn king would side with the Ming. Thousands of Koreans, held hostage by the Manchus, suffered great cruelty and privation before they could be ransomed. Many Korean families rejected female members who had been sexually violated and therefore dishonored. This attitude reflected the intensification of a Neo-Confucian emphasis on female chastity in Chosŏn Korea. When the Manchus conquered China and established the Qing dynasty in 1644, the Koreans had to submit to them until the 1890s. For a long time, Koreans, who had favored the Ming, resented being in a tributary relationship with the Qing.

JAPAN: THE ERA OF SHŌGUNS AND WARRING STATES

■ *How were art, culture, and religion central to the creation of Japanese identity?*

Like Korea and China, Japan had a monarch, the *tennō* (TEN-noh) or emperor, whose dynasty had already reigned for almost a millennium by the fourteenth century. But the emperor's court had not held real power since the late twelfth century, although it had twice attempted in the thirteenth and fourteenth centuries to reassert its authority in the political and economic realms. Instead, military lords and their samurai supporters had created a political system in the eastern town of Kamakura that in many ways resembled medieval European feudalism (see Chapter 10). The Kamakura system was not entirely stable, and internal and external pressures, including the Mongol invasions in the late thirteenth century, undermined the dominance of the shōgun's government.

Renewed warfare in the fourteenth century ended in 1336 with a shaky balance of power among dozens of provincial lords and a new overlord, Ashikaga Takauji (ah-shee-KAH-gah tah-kah-OO-jee), invested with the title of **shōgun** in 1338. Because the Ashikaga set up their shogunal court in the Muromachi (MOO-roh-MAH-chee) section of Kyoto (kee-OH-toh), the period from 1338 to 1568 is called the Muromachi period. The balance of power had actually ended before the end of the Muromachi period, when succession disputes and a struggle for power among newly emerging provincial forces began a 130-year-long Warring States period in 1467. During this period, coalitions of samurai with initially tiny land-

shōgun—The supreme military overlord in Japan from 1185 to 1868.

Japan	
1338–1568	Muromachi period
c. 1368–1443	Zeami Motokiyo, playwright
1467–1600	Warring States period
1568–1582	Oda Nobunaga begins unification, attacks Buddhists
1588	Toyotomi Hideyoshi's Sword Hunt
1600	Tokugawa victory at Sekigahara
1637–1638	Shimabara revolt

Korea was part of the Chinese tribute system throughout the Chosŏn dynasty. Japan also traded with China and Korea, but was able to circumvent the more restricted measures of the tribute system because of its maritime separation from the continent.

holdings, supported by villagers whose crops they used to support their troops, fought their samurai neighbors for increasingly larger areas of control. By the mid-sixteenth century, the largest of these warrior lords came to be known as *sengoku daimyō* (SEN-goh-koo DAI-mee-oh) or Warring States lords, and it is from those ranks that three powerful warriors, Oda Nobunaga (OH-dah NOH-boo-NAH-gah; 1534–1582), Toyotomi Hideyoshi (1536–1598), and Tokugawa Ieyasu (toh-koo-GAH-wah EE-eh-YAH-soo; 1544–1616), brought Japan under unified control.

Villages and Towns: The Base of Samurai Power

Villages provided most of the wealth for the rise of these powerful **daimyō** from among the hundreds of small-scale samurai lords. Not all samurai lords survived the warfare of the sixteenth century. Those who

daimyō—A military lord, served by samurai.

enjoyed good relations with villagers, often by being part-time samurai-farmers themselves, were more likely to mobilize the villages' output for their own benefit. Oppressed villagers could run away from their land, and land was worthless without peasants to farm it. Thus, in many areas of Japan, villagers were granted a large degree of autonomy and gradually developed methods of self-government. This does not mean, however, that sixteenth-century villages were democratic entities. Local government varied from village to village; some allowed all families a voice in a village council, while others had a hereditary village headman. Still others were run from the local Shintō shrine or Buddhist temple association.

Just as villages were not run democratically despite their freedom from constant control by warriors or aristocrats, so, too, families were not run democratically. Though women had been able to inherit and make important personal decisions in earlier centuries, inheritance was increasingly in male hands. Village men and women all participated in festivals, and women were responsible for spring planting and often for marketing products. No farm could run without both men and women, as each had necessary chores. But by the Muromachi and Warring States eras, even farm women had to take a back seat to their husbands in ceremonial and political participation in village associations. Wives and daughters of samurai and *daimyō* in the Warring States era had a much more dangerous life than farm women. They were expected to be skilled at defending themselves and their families' interests, but they were also frequently married off by powerful fathers and other relatives in order to cement alliances with other warlords. In those treacherous times, when military alliances shifted frequently, marriage was often not a safe haven for samurai-class women; husbands wondered if their wives were spies on behalf of their fathers or brothers, and many wives were involuntarily divorced, used as hostages, or in a few cases, even executed. Of course, life was hard for male samurai warriors, too; but the decline in the official status of elite women from the early medieval era was quite clear.

The heads of the largest extended families in the villages (families with multiple generations and married cousins or siblings living under one roof) were often samurai-farmers, serving as local notables who settled village disputes and oversaw some of the farming activities of their less fortunate neighbors. Some villages were more independent and powerful than others, particularly those villages, organized around Pure Land (see Chapter 10) temples, which became increasingly militant in the defense of both their faith and their livelihoods during the Warring States period. The first of the "three great unifiers," Oda Nobunaga, found these villages to be one of the greatest challenges to his rise to dominance. After ending the

Muromachi **shogunate** in 1568, he conquered and forced the submission of other *daimyō* lords. But the Pure Land villagers refused to surrender, believing their faith would keep them strong against their enemies' military power. Oda Nobunaga attacked the Buddhists with extreme violence. His forces killed 20,000 men, women, and children in one brutal struggle in 1574. Three years earlier, he had attacked the 700-year-old temple community at Mt. Hiei (HEE-ay), founded by Saichō, burning 300 monastic buildings, including residences, libraries with irreplaceable treasures, and prayer halls.

As a symbol of his power, Oda Nobunaga built the enormous Azuchi (ah-ZOO-chee) Castle (1576–1579). He filled it with art intended to glorify his rule. It was lavishly painted by the great master Kanō Eitoku (KAH-noh AY-to-koo; 1543–1590), using fine colors and gold leaf. Despite his self-aggrandizement, however, Oda Nobunaga was cut down in a most ordinary way—he was assassinated by one of his subordinates in 1582. Nobunaga's assassination afforded Hideyoshi (a man of humble origins who had not yet been awarded the surname Toyotomi at that time) the opportunity to seize power. Intercepting a message not meant for him, Hideyoshi learned that Nobunaga had been killed. Hideyoshi mobilized his forces secretly to attack the perpetrator. This began Hideyoshi's march to power throughout Japan. He conquered rival military leaders and, recognizing that other rural samurai-farmers might become great leaders as he had, decided to neutralize their potential power. In 1588, he issued the famous "Sword Hunt" edict, disarming all villagers and, in the process, gaining them merit in the afterlife:

> *The farmers of the various provinces are strictly forbidden to possess long swords, short swords, bows, spears, muskets, or any form of weapon. . . . So that the . . . swords collected shall not be wasted, they shall be [melted down and] used . . . in the forthcoming construction of the Great Buddha. This will be an act by which the farmers will be saved in this life, needless to say, and in the life to come. . . . If farmers possess agricultural tools alone and engage [themselves] completely in cultivation, they shall [prosper] unto eternity.*

In 1591, Hideyoshi followed up with the Edict on Changing Status, which stipulated that samurai, farmers, and merchants all remain in the status group into which they were born. The same year he carried out surveys of land and its productivity so that he could tax his own lands and gain information about the wealth of other *daimyō* lords. The growth of cities and towns in the seventeenth century shows that the prohibition on mobility was never as rigidly applied as Hideyoshi, and his successors in the Tokugawa shogu-

nate, intended. He got the emperor to name him "regent," an old title from the Heian period, which had no meaning except as a sign of the emperor's recognition. Hideyoshi was never shōgun.

Though Hideyoshi's edicts applied to lands under his own direct control, they were copied by other *daimyō*. Hideyoshi and the *daimyō* lords moved the samurai from the countryside and housed them in barracks around their castles. Merchants and artisans moved nearby to supply the samurai and their lords. In time, these towns, called "castle-towns," became Japan's main cities. Hideyoshi and the *daimyō* built castles, roads, drainage ditches, bridges, port facilities, temples, and countless other structures. Most of the labor force came from the countryside. *Daimyō* ordered farmers to work on their own urban construction projects and on those demanded by Hideyoshi. For example, Hideyoshi requisitioned from his *daimyō* approximately 250,000 workers to build his grand castle at Fushimi (foo-SHEE-mee). After completing their projects, many of these workers settled in the new castle-towns, in spite of Hideyoshi's edict forbidding farmers to permanently change their status.

Art and Culture in Medieval Japan

Hideyoshi's period was an era of grand and colorful art. Like Oda Nobunaga, Hideyoshi used architectural monuments as symbols of his power. Castles and temples, decorated in the most ornate and at times even ostentatious styles, were built by legions of conscripted laborers. The bold and lavish paintings of Kanō Eitoku and his followers, patronized by the rich and powerful, continued to dominate painting for several decades into the next century. The Europeans, with their exotic clothing, appearance, and strange objects of daily life, were another popular theme in artwork patronized by urban connoisseurs.

Townsfolk, whether merchants, samurai, or the highest level elite were not the only ones to patronize and enjoy artistic production. From the fourteenth to the sixteenth century, itinerant storytellers, many of them originally monks and nuns, traveled throughout Japan, to villages and mansions alike, creating what one historian has called a "national literature" that transcended regional and class boundaries. These performances included song, dance, recitation, the playing of stringed instruments, the use of puppets, and the showing of pictures to accompany the text or songs.

Urban elites built permanent theaters to present plays with human actors or puppets. In the Muromachi period, **Nō** (NOH) plays, which had religious and often historical themes and the refined, spare sen-

---

shogunate—The government headed by the shōgun.

Nō—A dramatic form developed in Japan in the fourteenth century; inspired by Buddhist themes.

sibility of Zen, were created by master playwrights like the actor-playwright-critic Zeami Motokiyo (zeh-AH-mee MOH-toh-KEE-yo; c. 1363–1443). Nō developed from thirteenth-century religious rites into a sophisticated theatrical form by the fourteenth century. In the seventeenth century, new forms like puppet plays and kabuki (kah-BOO-kee) plays with human actors emerged (see Chapter 20).

The tea ceremony, intended to be refined, intimate, and meditative, was another artistic form that

Document: *Sotoba Komachi*, a Fourteenth-Century Japanese Nō Play

Kan'ami (1333–1384), father of the great playwright Zeami, pioneered the transformation of simple plays and complex court dances into the sophisticated dramatic form of the Nō. Zen aesthetics, Pure Land salvation, and shamanistic spirit possession come together in these dramas. The spare stage and tranquility of action of most of a Nō play culminates in a wild dance, as the main actor is transformed into the tormented soul of another. In this play, Komachi, a poet who had actually lived in the Heian period, is an old woman, no longer the famous beauty of her day. She comes upon two priests who inform her she is sitting on a stupa (*sotoba* in Japanese), whereupon she is possessed by the spirit of a man whose soul cannot cease to be reborn in worldly torment because it is consumed by desire due to the young Komachi's toying with his love. She had told him that if he called on her 100 times, she would consent to see him, but he died after 99 visits, unrequited. The excerpts here are from her conversation with the Buddhist priests at the beginning of the play and from her frenzied comments, as well as those of the Chorus which advances the action of the play, at the end.

KOMACHI: How sad that once I was proud.
   . . . Golden birds in my raven hair
   When I walked like willows nodding, charming
   As the breeze in spring.
   The voice of the nightingale
   The petals of the rosewood, wide stretched. . . .
   I was lovelier than these.
   Now I am foul in the eyes of the humblest creatures
   . . . The wreck of a hundred years . . .
FIRST PRIEST: . . .That old beggar woman sitting on a sacred stupa. We should warn her to come away.

Following some discussion between the priests and the old woman about Buddhist spiritual matters, the priests ask the old woman her name. All three, as well as the Chorus, lament the evanescence of life. Suddenly, Komachi turns into her spurned lover. At times, she speaks as though she is the lover, at other times as herself. The Chorus also speaks as the lover.

KOMACHI: An awful madness seizes me
   And my voice is no longer the same.
   Hey! Give me something you priests!
FIRST PRIEST: What do you want?
KOMACHI: To go to Komachi!
FIRST PRIEST: What are you saying? You *are* Komachi!
KOMACHI: No. Komachi was beautiful.
   Many letters came, many messages. . .
   But she made no answer, even once. . .
   Age is her retribution now
   Oh, I love her! . . .
CHORUS: I came and went, came and went
   One night, two nights, three . . .
   I came and carved my mark upon the pillar.
   I was to come a hundred nights,
   I lacked but one . . .
KOMACHI: It was his unsatisfied love possessed me so . . .
   In the face of this I will pray
   For life in the worlds to come . . .
   Before the golden, gentle Buddha I will lay
   Poems as my flowers
   Entering in the Way . . .

Questions to Consider

1. Nō plays were intended as entertainment for samurai and *daimyō*. Why do you think their content was so strongly religious?
2. What Buddhist principles are evident in this excerpt?
3. Why do you think a fourteenth-century playwright would use a tenth-century event as the theme of his play?

From Kan'ami Kiyotsugu, "Sotoba Komachi," in Donald Keene, ed., *Anthology of Japanese Literature* (New York: Grove Press, 1955).

became more popular in the harsh times of the Warring States period. Beautiful teapots and cups were manufactured in Japan or imported as luxury items from China or Korea. Hideyoshi had studied with the greatest tea master of his day, Sen no Rikyō (SEN no REE-kee-oo), but for reasons historians still cannot understand, ordered this important artist to commit suicide in 1591.

Architecture was another art that developed during the three centuries of the Muromachi period and Warring States period. Ashikaga shōguns, especially the third, Yoshimitsu (YOH-shee-MEE-tsoo), and sixth, Yoshimasa (YOH-shee-MAH-sah), built remarkable religious retreats of a modest size which blended with their surroundings. The Temple of the Golden Pavilion (the photo at the beginning of this chapter), though rebuilt following a fire after World War II, and the Temple of the Silver Pavilion, which still stands, are the finest examples of Muromachi architecture. Later buildings might be grandiose, as were the castles of Oda Nobunaga and Toyotomi Hideyoshi, or beautiful as well as functional, like Himeji (Hee-MAY-jee) castle, built by *daimyō* during the Warring States period.

Japan was very much part of the international commercial world during the Muromachi and Warring States periods. Arts were freely imported and exported to the rest of Asia. As we have seen, the Ming tried to control the volume of trade, but freebooting merchants from China, Japan and Korea, called "Japanese pirates" by the Ming, got around the Ming restrictions. Hideyoshi imposed some restrictions of his own. In 1587, attempting to allay Ming concerns about piracy, Hideyoshi suppressed many of the Japanese who had been involved in uncontrolled trade. But Hideyoshi's other foreign policy initiatives were decidedly a failure. His invasions of Korea were disastrous not only for Korea but also for his own ability to establish long-lasting rule by his family in Japan. Indeed, though the invasions were immediately terminated when he died in 1598, he had so weakened his closest supporters by sending them to war in Korea that other powerful men, rivals to his child heir Hideyori (HEE-deh-YOH-ree), were able to defeat the boy's supporters and take over Japan in 1600. An additional result of Hideyoshi's disastrous foreign adventurism was the policy of the Tokugawa shōguns to minimize and strictly control foreign relations.

Himeji Castle, completed in the early seventeenth century, is the finest extant example of late Warring States era castle construction. Like other such castles, it sits atop a hill and its stone base is capable of defending against the cannon that began to be used in the late sixteenth century. The lovely living quarters at the top were vulnerable to fire, but manifested the glory of the daimyō *who commanded the castle.*

Christians presented a related problem. Europeans had been arriving in the islands since a shipwreck in 1543 in which three Portuguese came ashore with arquebuses. These early muskets would soon alter the course of warfare, for Nobunaga and a few other *daimyō* used firearms to great tactical advantage. Thereafter, Portuguese ships began arriving in greater numbers, bringing not only new products, as noted above, but also Jesuit missionaries, starting in 1549. Some *daimyō* converted to Christianity to facilitate trade and often forced their samurai to convert as well. By the 1580s, as many as 200,000 residents of the island of Kyūshū had adopted the foreign faith. Hideyoshi first noticed the divisive role played by Christians in 1586 while fighting his rivals on that island. He issued two edicts, one to expel missionaries and one to limit the propagation of Christianity, but neither edict was effectively carried out. A few years later, Hideyoshi treated Jesuits cordially and offered land in Kyoto to the rival order of Franciscans. Hideyoshi's first expulsion and limitation edicts were apparently not intended to be applied generally but rather were directed at a small group of troublesome Jesuits in Nagasaki who encouraged destruction of Shintō shrines and Buddhist temples and served as currency brokers. Later, however, Hideyoshi became convinced that missionaries were the leading edge of Iberian colonialism and executed several missionaries and converts. But few other actions were taken, as trade was too valuable to jeopardize by offending the Iberians at that time. The systematic expulsion of Christians would come later, under the Tokugawa.

The Road to Sekigahara

In 1590, Tokugawa Ieyasu received a highly productive territory, the Kantō plain in eastern Japan, in exchange for his military assistance to Hideyoshi. The Kantō, which had been the home of the Minamoto shōguns in the Kamakura period (see Chapter 10) and is today the heartland of Japan, was Japan's most productive rice producing area. Tokugawa Ieyasu selected a tiny farming village along Edo creek to build a castle-town, which he called Edo. By 1610, Edo had 5000 houses; by 1620, it had 150,000 residents; and by 1700, with over a million inhabitants, the little fishing village had become the world's largest city. As Hideyoshi and Nobunaga had done, in the 1590s Ieyasu mobilized peasants to clear forests; to cut timber to construct castles, barracks, temples, and buildings for mercantile activities; to lay out roads and canals; and to build bridges and docks. He needed skilled workers of all kinds. He exhausted natural resources, especially lumber, an environmental problem that would have be dealt with later in the Tokugawa period.

Ieyasu was one of five regents appointed by Hideyoshi on his deathbed to administer the realm until his son Hideyori came of age. Soon, tensions among the five erupted into a renewal of warfare. Ieyasu and his allies created an army of 80,000 men and challenged the supporters of Hideyori at the battle of Sekigahara (SEH-kee-gah-HAH-rah) in the fall of 1600. Victory in this battle established Tokugawa hegemony and allowed Tokugawa Ieyasu to reward his followers and punish his opponents by either eliminating or reducing their domains. Hideyori and his family were moved to one of the Toyotomi castles, at Osaka, where they remained until the Tokugawa eliminated them in 1615. Tokugawa Ieyasu asked the emperor to declare him shōgun, which he did in 1603. His wealthy domain in the Kantō, his use of natural and human resources, and his military effectiveness led to his victory.

Tokugawa Ieyasu was not known for his kindness, though he was a strong leader. Like his predecessors, Ieyasu manipulated the marriages of women in his family for his own ends. As we have seen, *daimyō* women were expected to act as spies for their fathers or brothers, leading to their husbands' distrust of them. Ieyasu himself was the victim of manipulation at the hands of Nobunaga, whose daughter he married. Hideyoshi forced his sister to divorce her first husband to marry Ieyasu, whereupon the sister's distraught first husband committed suicide. Ieyasu married his granddaughter to Hideyori, son of Hideyoshi; Ieyasu's forces went on to execute the granddaughter's little son (and Ieyasu's own great-grandson) in 1615. The status of women was entirely dependent on their social status, with *daimyō* women the only ones used as marriage pawns. Fortunately, though women's status would remain low during the Tokugawa period, women of other classes were not placed in that kind of jeopardy, and the worst excesses, the use of women as hostages through forced marriages, were terminated with the end of the battles for unification in Japan.

The Early Tokugawa Years

Ieyasu faced some difficult problems in the first years of the Tokugawa shogunate (1600–1868). Even simple public safety was an early problem, as samurai whose *daimyō* had been defeated at the battle of Sekigahara in 1600 roamed the streets of Japan's towns with little to do but make trouble. These masterless samurai, called rōnin (ROH-neen), continued to emerge in times of turmoil in the next several hundred years. For the most part, however, the Tokugawa managed to control them within a few years by offering them alternate forms of employment and amusement. Another problem con-

Edicts by Tokugawa Ieyasu

cerned the shogunate's relationship to the loyal *daimyō*. What Ieyasu and his next two successors, his son Hidetada (HEE-deh-TAH-dah; r. 1606–1623) and grandson Iemitsu (EE-eh-MEE-tsoo; r. 1623–1651), did was move the *daimyō* around the country to form layers of protection from those they believed least trustworthy; proclaim a code of conduct for the *daimyō* in 1615; take over control of roads, mines, ports, and international relations; and set up a control system called the "alternate attendance system."

Tokugawa Japan, 1600–1800

The alternate attendance system had many unanticipated effects, which are discussed in Chapter 20, but it also achieved its primary goal of controlling the *daimyō*. To be a *daimyō* in the Tokugawa era, a lord had to possess a domain that produced at least 10,000 *koku* of rice (a *koku* is a unit of measurement; one *koku* fed approximately one person for one year). Each *daimyō* had to maintain a mansion in the shōgun's capital at Edo in addition to his castle in his home domain. He had to live in the mansion every other year (hence, he *attended* the shōgun in *alternate* years), and his wife and children had to live permanently in Edo, thus making sure he would not raise the banner of rebellion while back at home in his own castle. The alternate attendance system, requiring the movement across the whole country of vast numbers of samurai in the retinues of the *daimyō*, was extremely expensive, as was the maintenance of two homes and two staffs. The impoverishing of the *daimyō* also kept them from rising up against the Tokugawa.

Another area brought under regulation by the first three Tokugawa shōguns was foreign affairs. Some *daimyō*—such as the *daimyō* of Tsu in Korean trade—were involved in foreign relations, but the Tokugawa tried to control it. Ieyasu welcomed trade but not evangelism. Most Europeans wanted both, but the Dutch claimed that religious propagation was not their goal. The English made a similar claim. But unable to compete with Dutch traders, the English abandoned Japan by 1623. The Japanese were finding it more difficult to conduct business as silver supplies began to run low, but trade continued many years into the seventeenth century. Evangelism was another story. Ieyasu's son Hidetada increased

A Japanese View of European Missionaries

pressure to suppress the Christians in Japan. The end of all missionary activity, and indeed, the closing of Japan to all international contacts excepts those by the Chinese, the Koreans, and the Dutch, was precipitated by a revolt at Shimabara in which Christian banners were raised in 1637–1638, reminding the fearful Tokugawa of the Buddhist-inspired village revolts of the Warring States period.

By the end of the 1630s, peasant starvation and overwork, exacerbated by poor weather due to a devastating El Niño pattern, was at the heart of peasants joining rōnin in demands against the state. Revolts broke out in many places, but the most severe was the Shimabara (SHEE-mah-BAH-rah) revolt. Laying siege to the peasants and rōnin holed up at Shimabara, the Tokugawa starved out 37,000 villagers. The stringent regulation of foreign trade began after this revolt. Japan continued to have a high volume of trade through the rest of the seventeenth century, but its trading partners were limited to the three it could be confident would not try to smuggle in forbidden Christian texts. Japan's foreign policy was then called a *sakoku* (SAH-koh-koo) or closed-country policy, but it would be more accurate to call it a strictly regulated foreign policy.

---

sakoku—Policy of limiting Japan's foreign and trade relations to China, Korea, and the Netherlands from 1640 to 1853. Literally, "closed country."

The shrine at Nikko is one of several built after the death of Tokugawa Ieyasu to legitimate the shogunate's power by designating its founder as a Shintō deity. The ornate construction contrasts with the simplicity of medieval architecture.

By 1650, the Tokugawa had established control of Japan's foreign policy, brought the *daimyō* under their control, and created a regulated society. They continued their control of Japanese politics—the emperor was honored by the Tokugawa but had no power—until the middle of the nineteenth century (see Chapter 24). For the next 200 years, Japan was at peace, and the arts, commerce, scholarship, and the people's livelihood flourished.

SOUTHEAST ASIA: STATES WITHIN A REGION

■ *How did cultural blending influence Southeast Asian civilizations?*

Situated on the main sea route between East Asia and the Indian Ocean and divided geographically into diverse subregions, Southeast Asia had long been an area of contending states. Although each of these regions had been influenced for centuries by the cultures of India and China, they developed a strong sense of separate cultural identities and statehood. Wars in defense of independence or attempted conquest of neighboring states were, as a result, fairly common.

In the thirteenth century, the powerful land-based Khmer (KMEHR) state, which had dominated southern and central mainland Southeast Asia for four centuries, began to decline. Its very wealth and power were, ironically, factors leading to its decline. With great agricultural wealth derived from its sophisticated irrigation system, Khmer built 20,000 shrines, 102 hospitals, and other monuments. The state supported 300,000 priests and monks. These expenditures sapped the state, as did wars against the neighboring Chams and the encroaching Thais. In the fourteenth century, the Mongols in China encouraged the Thais to move into Khmer territory. The Mongols, who temporarily received tribute from mainland Southeast Asia and parts of Java, seriously disrupted all existing governments. Throughout Southeast Asia, there were ruinous petty wars, often based on Hindu-Buddhist conflicts, each side of which suffered individually under Muslim expansion. Finally, Muslim regimes replaced many traditional Hindu states in Indonesia, which also felt the effects of European empire building, first by the Portuguese and then by the Dutch. Before 1650, however, the total European impact on the mainland was negligible.

Tracing the political interactions among the nations and empires making up the region we now know as Southeast Asia may often seem confusing. Here, what is most significant is that we recognize the important regional influences, such as the roles of religion and trade networks.

Southeast Asia	
1050	Beginnings of Burmese unification
1283–1317	Rama Khamheng, king of Thailand
1280s	Mongol invasions
1402	Founding of Malacca
1407–1418	Ming invasion of Vietnam
1418	Founding of Le dynasty in Vietnam

Burma and the Thais

In the first millennium C.E., the region of present-day Burma remained an ethnically diverse region, divided into a number of small principalities. Around 1050 a process of political unification began under the Burmese, a group of people who moved to the south from the Tibetan frontier about 900 years earlier. This movement was shattered by the Mongol invasions of the 1280s. The process of unification recommenced after the invasions, but it took till the sixteenth and seventeenth centuries for the Tongoo kingdom to unify most of Burma.

Advancing to the south during the Mongol invasions were the Thais, a group of people from Yunnan, in China. The Mongols' destruction of Burma and the threat to the Khmer helped the expansion of Ayuthaya (AH-yoo-TAI-ya), the Thai state, but it was not the only reason for the rise of the Thais. The weakening of these two other states offered opportunities for expansion to the Thais, who had already begun to penetrate the region centuries earlier. Arriving in Khmer and Burma, the Thais—whose name "Thai" meant "free"—also absorbed the richness of the Indian civilization that had for centuries influenced Southeast Asia. In the late thirteenth century, the Thai monarch, Rama Khamheng (RAH-mah KAHM-heng; r. 1283–1317), the head of the small Thai principality of Sukhothai (SOO-koh-THAI), extended Thai power after deciding to establish an independent Thai state. Under Sukhothai rule, the Thai people were given a cultural and political identity derived from several sources in the region. The idea of a divine monarch was borrowed from the Khmer. Burma provided principles of law and Theravada Buddhism. The Thai alphabet was created by Rama Khamheng, based on

Thai Statue

South Indian script. In the fifteenth century, the Thai kingdom moved its capital to the agricultural center of the country and brought the various Thai principalities under the king's control. This centralized monarchical system lasted into the nineteenth century.

Under the Tongoo King Bayinnaung (BAI-in-NOWNG) in the 1550s and 1560s, Burma briefly absorbed Laos (LAH-ohs) and conquered Siam (now Thailand) with an army estimated at 500,000, the largest ever assembled in Southeast Asia. Bayinnaung's capital at Pegu was a nucleus of Buddhist culture, a thriving commercial center, and the site of his wondrous palace, which was roofed in solid gold. But his successor wasted resources in unsuccessful wars on its neighbors. Later, the Thai state gained supremacy, humbling Cambodia and Burma after 1595 and profiting from a commercial alliance with the Dutch.

Document   A Traveller's Account of Siam

This description is by a Ma Huan, translator and interpreter for the fourth expedition of eunuch maritime navigator Zheng He, from 1413–1415. The account tells us as much about Chinese attitudes as about "Xian Luo," known to Europeans as Siam, and now known as Thailand.

. . . Travelling from Chan city towards the south-west for several days and nights with a fair wind, the ship comes to the estuary at New Street Tower and enters the anchorage; then you reach the capital.

The country is a thousand *li* in circumference, the outer mountains [being] steep and rugged, [and] the inner land wet and swampy. The soil is barren and little of it is suitable for cultivation. The climate varies—sometimes cold, sometimes hot.

The house in which the king resides is rather elegant, neat, and clean. The houses of the populace are constructed in storeyed form; in the upper [part of the house] they do not join planks together [to make a floor], but they use the wood of the areca-palm, which they cleave into strips resembling bamboo splits; [these strips] are laid close together and bound very securely with rattans; on [this platform] they spread rattan mats and bamboo matting, and on these they do all their sitting, sleeping, eating, and resting.

As to the king's dress: he uses a white cloth to wind round his head; on the upper [part of his body] he wears no garment; [and] round the lower [part he wears] a silk-embroidered kerchief, adding a waist-band of brocaded silk-gauze. When going about he mounts an elephant or else rides in a sedan-chair, while a man holds [over him] a gold-handled umbrella . . . [which is] very elegant. The king is a man of the So-li race, and a firm believer in the Buddhist religion.

In this country the people who become priests or become nuns are exceedingly numerous; the habit of the priests and nuns is somewhat the same as in the Central Country; and they, too, live in nunneries and monasteries, fasting and doing penance. . . .

It is their custom that all affairs are managed by their wives; both the [illegible text] of the country and the common people, if they have matters which require thought and deliberation—punishments light and heavy, all trading transactions great and small—they all follow the decisions of their wives, [for] the mental capacity of the wives certainly exceeds that of the men.

If a married woman is very intimate with one of our men from the Central Country, wine and food are provided, and they drink and sit and sleep together. The husband is quite calm and takes no exception to it; indeed he says 'My wife is beautiful and the man from the Central Country is delighted with her'. The men dress the hair in a chignon, and use a white head-cloth to bind round the head [and] on the body they wear a long gown. The women also pin up the hair in a chignon, and wear a long gown.

Questions to Consider

1. Would the role of Thai women in decision-making have been surprising to a Chinese observer of the Ming dynasty?
2. Did Ma Huan find Thailand exotic? What kinds of exchanges do you think the Ming and Thailand would have made under the tribute system? In this description of Thailand in the fifteenth century can you see cultural or social similarities with any other parts of East Asia during approximately the same time period?

From Ma Huan, *Ying-yai Sheng-lai: The Overall Survey of the Ocean's Shores (1433)*, trans. Feng Ch'eng Chun, intro. by J. V. G. Mills (Cambridge: Cambridge University Press, 1970).

under King Trailok (1448–1488), who was more successful in creating an efficient army and establishing a civil administration. By the end of the fifteenth century, the Vietnamese, along with the Thais, momentarily controlled the mainland region of Southeast Asia. Rather than encouraging trade, however, Vietnam's ruling dynasty based its rule on a Confucian approach to national wealth. Stating that commerce was "peripheral," the powerful monarch Le Thanh Tong (leh tahng tong; r. 1460–1497) focused on agriculture, stating: "Concentrate all our forces on agriculture, expand our potential."

Maritime Southeast Asia

The kingdom of Majapahit (mah-JAH-pah-heet), like the Thai state, was able to consolidate its position on the Indonesian island of Java due to Mongol pressure on its neighbors. From the late thirteenth century, Majapahit extended its hegemony over most of the islands of Indonesia, dominating trade and developing a sophisticated and artistic culture. In 1402, Malacca (mah-LAH-ka) declared itself an independent state, and one by one, other Indonesian rulers involved in maritime trade converted to Islam and abandoned Majapahit. Expanding into Indonesia in a gradual and generally peaceful manner, Islam achieved a great success in the fourteenth and fifteenth centuries. Sufi Muslim missionaries were drawn to the area by the expanding India-China trade, particularly when Chinese interests waned in the decade after 1424. Many

Shwemawdaw Pagoda, Pegu.

Vietnam

Under Chinese rule for a millennium, Vietnam was the Southeast Asian country that was, at the same time, most Sinified and most ardently committed to independence from China. Vietnam used Chinese script, borrowed institutions of government, and adopted Buddhism from Chinese missionaries. Political independence from China was followed by the two countries' continuing tributary relationship and Vietnam's careful study of Confucian scholarship. The Mongol attacks were repulsed by the Vietnamese, but the Ming did briefly rule Vietnam early in the fifteenth century. In 1418, Le Loi (LEH LO-ee), an aristocratic landholder, led an army to push out the Ming. But he and his successors in the Le dynasty adopted Chinese methods; they then succeeded in dominating their Southeast Asian neighbors. These nations were all in decline; indeed, Burma was still broken into a number of principalities. An exception was the Thai polity

The trade routes across the Indian Ocean served as an arena for the interaction of Chinese, Indian, Arab, and Southeast Asian cultures as well as Hindu, Buddhist, and Muslim religions and eastern and western goods and products.

local rulers embraced Islam to gain independence from the great Hindu state of Majapahit; others sought a share of Indian commerce. The Muslims were tolerant of the Hindu-Buddhist culture of the new converts, and daily practices, rituals, arts, and music, even those contrary to Muslim rules, were allowed to continue. Foreigners, among them the large number of immigrant Chinese and merchants from Egypt, Persia, Arabia, and western India, were accepted. The Muslims mixed easily with the populations of the port cities. As the power of the Majapahit Empire weakened, the influence of Islam grew. Muslim sailors–either pirates or traders, depending on the circumstances–came to control the various straits between the islands and set up their own states.

The indigenous population adopted Islam, as the local princely families intermarried with Muslims in alliances uniting the power and legitimacy of the local nobility with the wealth of the Muslim merchants. From this base in Indonesia, Islam spread throughout present-day Malaysia, the Molucca Islands, and some of the islands of the Philippines. Only Bali remained relatively untouched by the Islamic advance.

The rising Muslim commercial center of Malacca, on the Malay coast opposite Sumatra, best illustrates the entry of Islam into Southeast Asia. Founded in 1402 and by 1404 part of the Ming tribute system, its rulers converted to Islam and built an empire of commercial vassal states in the region. Despite the sultan's profession of Islam, Malacca continued to use the structure of Hindu-Buddhist princely courts. Malacca was multicultural. For example, in 1462, the Arab navigator Ibn Majid described the people of Melaka (Malacca) as follows:

> They have no culture at all. The infidel marries Muslim women while the Muslim takes pagans to wife. You do not know whether they are Muslims or not. They are thieves for theft is rife among them and they do not mind.
> The Muslim eats dogs for meat for there are no food laws.
> They drink wine in the markets and do not treat divorce as a religious act.

Malacca was the busiest port in Asia, linking China and the Moluccas with India and Africa. Its growing success paralleled Muslim expansion through western Indonesia to the Philippines in the sixteenth century.

Arrival of the Europeans

The Portuguese arrived in maritime Southeast Asia in the early sixteenth century. Butchering its Muslim population, they took the port of Malacca in 1511 and held it for the next 130 years. By 1550, the profits from the trade through Malacca were four times Portugal's internal revenues. But Portuguese rule was arbitrary and cruel and turned increasing numbers of Southeast Asians to convert to Islam to facilitate joining a trade network apart from the Portuguese. Mainland governments in Southeast Asia generally maintained their independence against the Europeans. Portuguese missionaries, at first active in Vietnam, were expelled by the end of the period. Portuguese traders and mercenary soldiers served everywhere, but they were usually controlled. Some were enslaved in Burma; only in weakened Cambodia and Laos did they acquire significant political influence. By the seventeenth century the Portuguese were giving way to the Dutch, who courted the Vietnamese in only partially successful efforts to monopolize trade with Siam and Burma.

Well before 1650, Europeans were becoming very active in Indonesia. The Portuguese used Malacca as a base for dominating trade in the region, but Muslim rulers in nearby states forcefully ejected them from Java and Sumatra and limited their operations in the Molucca Islands. In the late 1500s Spain acquired a foothold in the Philippines. The Spanish established a colonial capital at Manila and sent in missionaries to convert the country to Christianity. The missionaries eventually exerted even greater control over people's daily lives than the Spanish colonial officials in Manila. With the creation of the colony of the Philippines, the triangular trade of the Manila Galleon embraced Mexico, the Philippines, and Japan.

Dutch trading companies merged into the United East India Company in 1602, and initially sought trade, not territory or the conversion of souls, in Southeast Asia. They took control of the Moluccas and expelled the Portuguese in 1641. Soon after that, the Dutch concluded a long war in Java by forcing upon the sultans a treaty that guaranteed a Dutch commercial monopoly in return for native political autonomy. Thereafter, however, Dutch plantation agriculture began undermining Indonesian economies. By the second half of the century, the Dutch had replaced the Muslims as the most powerful merchants in the region. From then on, Europe's demands for the spices and riches of the region would be satisfied by the merchants of Amsterdam. Later, the Dutch would take complete political control of Indonesia.

CONCLUSION

The years after the Mongol conquest of China, which had created a massive Eurasian commercial network, saw the development of diverse nations and cultures. Yet each was tied in some important ways to the others. In China, the tribute system tried to arrange states hierarchically by their proximity and conformity to China's Confucian order. The Confucian emphasis on hierarchy moderated by benevolence (see Chapter 2) was replicated in the obeisance of subordinate states in return for China's protection. The Ming rulers began by trying to expand the tribute system but ended up increasingly inward-directed. At the same time, the people of China began to lay claim to a national culture that defined their identity as Chinese.

In Korea, the Chosŏn dynasty rested under the immediate gaze of its immense neighbor and struggled, in the middle of the period, with calamitous foreign invasions. But, just as the Chinese during the Ming dynasty, the Korean people as a whole gradually laid claim to Korean culture. Japan was part of the East Asian commercial world but, unlike Korea, was only tangentially part of the China-centered tribute system, and even that involvement continued for only part of the late medieval period. Japan was further differentiated from Korea and Vietnam by being relatively uninfluenced by Confucianism in this period; Buddhism dominated both the popular and the elite culture in medieval Japan.

Southeast Asia, both maritime and mainland, was part of international trading networks. These networks attracted many religions and cultures to the region. For hundreds of years, Southeast Asians have borrowed eclectically from many traditions, enhancing the multicultural nature of the region.

Suggestions for Web Browsing

You can obtain more information about topics included in this chapter at the websites listed below. See also the companion website that accompanies this text, http://www.ablongman.com/brummett, which contains an online study guide and additional resources.

Imperial China: The Ming
http://www.fordham.edu/halsall/eastasia/eastasiasbook.html#Imperial%20China

Map and images pertaining to the Ming dynasty, 1368–1644; a part of the Internet East Asian History Sourcebook.

Chinese History
http://sun.sino.uni heidelberg.de/igcs

Internet guide to Chinese studies covers all periods and all topics in Chinese history.

Japanese Samurai
http://www.samurai-archives.com

Extensive collection of biographies of important samurai and daimyō in medieval and early modern Japan.

Masterpieces of the Kyoto National Museum
http://www.kyohaku.go.jp/

Numerous images, with descriptions, of the artworks of Japan, Korea, and China.

History of Korea
http://www.lifeinkorea.com/Information/history1.cfm

Text and images documenting the Koryŏ and Chosŏn dynasties of Korea.

Literature and Film

An abridged version of the Chinese classic *Monkey, Journey to the West,* trans. David Kherdian (Shambhala, 2000), offers students a chance to think about Ming era popular beliefs. For a translation of *The Romance of the Three Kingdoms* see Moss Roberts, trans. *Three Kingdoms: A Historical Novel* (University of California Press, 1991).

Films include *China's Forbidden City,* produced for the History Channel, A&E TV Network (1997); *Rise of the Dragon: The Genius That Was China, Part One,* produced by John Merson and David Roberts (Coronet Film & Video, 1990); *Japan: Memoirs of a Secret Empire, The Way of the Samurai,* the first of a four-part series on the Tokugawa period produced by Lyn Goldfarb for PBS (2004).

Classic movies by some of Japan's premier filmmakers deal with the Warring States period. See, for example, *Kagemusha,* by Akira Kurosawa (20th Century Fox, 1980) and *Ugetsu Monogatari,* by Kenzo Mizoguchi (Daiei Studios, 1953).

Suggestions for Reading

Fine general histories of early modern China include Charles O. Hucker, *China's Imperial Past* (Stanford University Press, 1975), and the *Cambridge History of China,* Vol. 7 (Cambridge University Press, 1988) and Vol. 8 (Cambridge University Press, 1998), which cover the Ming. Ray Huang, *1587, A Year of No Significance* (Yale University Press, 1981), is noteworthy for its penetrating case study of late Ming weaknesses. For complete coverage of Chinese technology and engineering, see Joseph Needham, *Clerks and Craftsmen in China and the West* (Cambridge University Press, 1970). Dorothy Ko, *Teachers of the Inner Chambers* (Stanford University Press, 1994), is an excellent treatment of women.

On Korea, see Carter J. Eckert et al., *Korea Old and New* (Harvard University Press, 1990); Andrew C. Nahm, *Introduction to Korean History and Culture* (Holly International, 1993); and James Palais, *Politics and Policy in Traditional Korea* (Council of East Asian Studies, 1991). Yung-Chung Kim, *Women of Korea* (Ewha Women's University, 1982), provides a readable and informative treatment of women of the period.

A wealth of material on medieval and early modern Japan has come out in the last several decades. Among these fine studies are Conrad Totman, *Early Modern Japan* (University of California Press, 1993); Jeffrey P. Mass, *Origins of Japan's Medieval World* (Stanford University Press, 1997); Hitomi Tonomura, *Community and Commerce in Late Medieval Japan* (Stanford University Press, 1992); Andrew Goble, *Kenmu: Go-Daigo's Revolution* (Harvard University Press, 1996); and Hitomi Tonomura, Anne Walthall, and Wakita Haruko, eds., *Women and Class in Japanese History* (University of Michigan, 1999). These are also fine studies: John W. Hall et al., *Japan Before Tokugawa* (Yale University Press, 1981), and John W. Hall and Takeshi Toyoda, *Japan in the Muromachi Age* (Cornell University Press, 2001). Two excellent biographies that mirror the time are Mary Elizabeth Berry, *Hideyoshi* (Harvard University Press, 1989), and Conrad Totman, *Tokugawa Ieyasu: Shogun* (Heian International, 1983).

The most comprehensive treatment of Southeast Asia may be found in Nicholas Tarling, ed., *Cambridge History of Southeast Asia,* 2 Vols. (Cambridge University Press, 1992). Anthony Reid, *Southeast Asia in the Age of Commerce, 1450–1680* (Yale University Press, 1995), covers separate cultures and attempts a synthesis of the whole region in terms of commerce. Fine general works include D. R. Sardesai, *Southeast Asia: Past and Present* (Westview Press, 2003), and George Coedes, *The Making of Southeast Asia,* 2nd ed. (Allen & Unwin, 1983). Treatments of individual countries may be found in Michael Aung-Thwin, *Pagan: The Origins of Modern Burma* (University of Hawaii Press, 1985); David K. Wyatt, *Thailand: A Short History,* 2nd ed. (Yale University Press, 2003); David P. Chandler, *A History of Cambodia,* 3rd ed. (Westview, 2000); Barbara W. Andaya and Leonard Y. Andaya, eds., *A History of Malaysia,* 2nd ed. (Macmillan, 2000); and John David Legge, *Indonesia,* 3rd ed. (Prentice Hall, 1980). Barbara W. Andaya, *Other Pasts: Women, Gender and History in Early Modern Southeast Asia* (University of Hawaii Press, 2001) is excellent.

CHAPTER 14

European Cultural and Religious Transformations

The Renaissance and the Reformation 1300–1600

CHAPTER CONTENTS

- Social Upheaval
- The Italian Renaissance
  - **DISCOVERY THROUGH MAPS:** *The Lagoon of Venice*
  - **DOCUMENT:** *Machiavelli,* The Prince: *On Cruelty and Mercy*
- Italian Renaissance Art
- The Northern Renaissance
- The Crisis in the Catholic Church: 1300–1517
- Luther and the German Reformation
- Henry VIII and the Anglican Reformation
- Protestantism from Switzerland to Holland: Zwingli and Calvin
  - **DOCUMENT:** *Anne Ayscough (Mrs. Thomas Kyme), English Protestant Martyr*
- Reform in the Catholic Church

1300

1300s Classical revival, humanism (Petrarch, Boccaccio)

1305–1377 Babylonian Captivity of the church; papacy under French influence

1320–1384 John Wycliffe

1348 Black Death begins to devastate Europe

1350

1378–1417 Great Schism of the Catholic Church

1400

1400s *Quattrocento,* Italian Renaissance (Ghiberti, Brunelleschi, Donatello, Masaccio, Piero della Francesca, Mantagna, Verrocchio, Botticelli)

1414 Council of Constance

1415 John Hus, Bohemian reformer, burned at the stake

1434–1494 Medici family rules Florence

1450

1450s Movable type used in printing

1453 Constantinople falls to Turks

1483–1546 Martin Luther

1500

c. 1500 Northern Renaissance begins (Erasmus, More, Rabelais, von Hutten, Montaigne, Cervantes, Shakespeare, van Eyck, Dürer, Bosch, Holbein, Brueghel)

c. 1500–1530 High Renaissance in Italy (Bramante, da Vinci, Raphael, Michelangelo, Castiglione)

1509–1564 John Calvin, leader of Reformation in Geneva

1517 Luther issues Ninety-Five Theses

1524–1525 German Peasant Revolt

1527 Sack of Rome; Venice becomes center of Renaissance art (Giogione, Titian)

1545–1563 Council of Trent

c. 1530–1600 Mannerist style popular (Tintoretto, Cellini)

Each of the world's civilizations has had a moment when a combination of stability, wealth, and confidence allowed its thinkers, artists, and artisans to create expressions of that civilization's values which not only pleased their contemporaries, but served as models for future generations. These moments are sometimes called "Golden Ages." The two parts of the Han dynasty in China (206 B.C.E.–8 C.E. and 23 C.E.–228 C.E.); the Classical Mayan civilization in Mexico and Central America in the first millennium of the Common Era; the early part of the Tokugawa Shogunate in Japan in the sixteenth through the early eighteenth centuries; and in Africa Great Zimbabwe (1290–1410), the Swahili city-states on the east coast of the continent (fourteenth century), and Benin and Mali in the fourteen and fifteenth centuries: All set standards of excellence for their citizens.

In the Mediterranean world the Hellenic accomplishments in the middle part of the fifth century B.C.E., the Hellenistic variations on Hellenic themes to the end of the first century B.C.E., and the Roman and Byzantine consolidation and transmission of those intellectual and artistic qualities formed the classical basis of European civilization. That precious legacy was enriched by the magnificent accomplishments of the Islamic world from 900–1100. The work of Arab thinkers, artists, and scientists was transmitted through Spain and into Italy in translations to become part of the Western heritage.

In each of the Golden Ages cited above, there was a certain well-being in which philosophical and artistic creation took place. Yet this was not the case for the Italian and Northern Renaissance during the fifteenth and sixteenth century. This period of European history began in crisis: recession, famine, plague, and war; it ended amid similar crises: war, revolutionary economic change, and religious ferment. In spite of, but in part because of these crises, Europe during the centuries of Renaissance and Reformation developed the individualism that marked this Golden Age of European history.

SOCIAL UPHEAVAL

■ *What were the most significant reasons for the great social crises in European society in the fourteen and fifteenth centuries?*

The period from 1300 to 1600 in Europe was one of the most disruptive in its history. Among the most significant challenges to European stability were economic depression and the devastation caused by the **Bubonic Plague**. The combination of these two forces provoked an upheaval that changed European society.

Economic Depression and Bubonic Plague

In the three centuries preceding 1300, European agricultural methods had improved, crops were more productive, arable land increased, and the population probably doubled between 1000 and 1300. But the beginning of the fourteenth century saw changing weather patterns bringing drought, famine, and widespread starvation and unemployment. Overpopulation and unsanitary lifestyles contributed to the factors that rendered Europe more vulnerable to the plague which killed probably one-third of Europe's population—around 25 million people—between 1347 to 1350 and continued to reappear sporadically until the seventeenth century.

Called the Black Death because of the discoloring effects it had on the body (especially the lymph nodes), the plague was carried by fleas on infected rats and had worked its way through the trade routes of Asia and India to Europe. Cities were particularly devastated; Florence's population fell from 114,000 to 50,000, London's from 60,000 to 40,000. The outbreak of the Hundred Years' War between France and England in 1337 (see Chapter 15) added to the destruction in both those nations. The Black Death had a very significant formative effect on the development of European history.

Many looked for spiritual explanations for the plague's devastation: that God was punishing a sinful humanity, or perhaps that there was no God at all. Many blamed the Jews for the plague and sought their expulsion from cities throughout Europe. Others found their scapegoats for problems—ranging from the plague, crop failures, economic crises, and religious upheaval—in their searches for witches in the next two centuries. Over 100,000 of these unfortunates were prosecuted during this period, and many were executed by strangling, drowning, burning, or beheading. Seventy percent of those killed were women, nearly half of whom were older single women or widows.

The Plague's Effect on European Society

By devastating the population of Europe, the Plague fundamentally changed the social patterns in Europe. A lack of rural workers effectively ended the remnants of the feudal structure in many places on the continent. Wage payments replaced the centuries-old payments in kind. In the cities in the late fourteenth and early fifteenth century, urban skilled craftsmen and the guilds that gave them security in an earlier age now became beneficiaries of higher prices paid for their goods, and their economic good fortune resulted in increased power and participation in urban politics. The church was also an economic beneficiary of the era; despite the decline of its revenues from its agricultural holdings, its wealth was vastly increased from donations and bequests from those wishing to increase their chances of a heavenly reward. But for those not in the guilds, life in the cities became increasingly difficult as the social problems of urban growth outran the resources of the Catholic Church to deal with them.

The beginning of the sixteenth century marked the beginning of another economic downturn that spread suffering throughout Europe. Economic dislocation accompanying the early development of capitalism added to the strains of transitioning between medieval and modern times, especially for the peasantry. The sixteenth century also marked the end of the relatively favorable situation women had enjoyed in the Middle Ages. The new emphasis on wage labor and competition from men limited their opportunities for outside work. Although women could find some part-time employment as field laborers, this paid very little.

A new global economy brought high rates of inflation and shifting trade routes. The decline of the importance of the Hanseatic League in the Baltic and North Seas, the Mediterranean, and the routes connecting the two hurt the economy of central Europe. Later, the shifting of work to laborers in the surrounding villages—the cottage industry—ruined many old guild industries while swelling the ranks of the urban unemployed. Large-market agriculture weakened the peasants' traditional rights, subjected them to rents beyond their resources, and drove them from the land into the towns, where they joined the idle and the impoverished.

Bubonic Plague—An infectious and usually fatal disease caused by the bacterium *Yersinia pestis*, which is carried and spread by the rat flea. Characteristics include high fever and swollen lymph nodes (buboes).

The poor and out-of-work often increasingly directed their anger against the Church because it was a visible source of authority, and it was rich. For society at large the profit motive overshadowed the church's canon law, which stressed compassion for the weak and the poor and a **"just price."**

In the midst of all of this economic and social upheaval, there began in Italy a cultural movement that touched only the elites but had consequences that would affect the development of Western civilization: It would come to be called the Renaissance, or the "rebirth."

"just price"—A medieval theory of economics supported by the Christian church. The church maintained that a just price should set the standards of fairness in all financial transactions. According to this theory, making interest on any loans was considered improper and labeled as *usury*.

THE ITALIAN RENAISSANCE

■ *Why is this period in Europe's history called a Renaissance—a "rebirth"?*

This cultural rebirth or Renaissance did not take place in a vacuum. Prior to the twelfth century, almost all learning in Europe was under the control of the church, and medieval art and literature reflected the church's influence. Latin was the European language of diplomacy, scholarship, and serious literature. But in the later medieval period the number of literate men and women in secular society began to increase, and the popularity of literature written in the vernacular, or commonly spoken languages of Europe, gained more and more popularity and acceptance, especially in the forms of poetry and song.

This map illustrates Europe in the time of the Italian and Northern Renaissance, as well as some of the cities that served as centers for artistic and humanist activities during the period.

Literary Precedents

Dante and Chaucer provided a bridge between the medieval and Renaissance worlds. Dante Alighieri (DAHN-teh ah-lig-hi-EH-ree; 1265–1321) was the author of the *Divine Comedy*, one of the great masterpieces of world literature. Combining a deep religious impulse with classical and medieval literature, Dante composed an allegory of medieval man (Dante) journeying through earthly existence (hell) through conversion (purgatory) to a spiritual union with God (paradise). Dante's work is regarded both as a culmination of the medieval intellectual tradition and at the same time as a composition of such unique brilliance that it should be considered one of the first creative works of the Renaissance.

DOCUMENT
Dante, *Divine Comedy*

Geoffrey Chaucer (c. 1340–1400), the author of *Canterbury Tales*, wrote an English vernacular account of the journey of 29 pilgrims to the shrine of St. Thomas á Becket at Canterbury. His personality profiles and stories satirized contemporary English customs and lifestyles, and his work solidly established the vernacular as a legitimate literary form of expression in England.

Another voice of the transition was one of the most gifted vernacular poets of the fourteenth century was a woman—Christine de Pizan (pi-ZAHN; 1365–c. 1430), who wrote to support her children after her husband's death. She authored more than ten volumes of poetry and prose, and her allegorical work—*The Book of the City of Ladies*—presented a defense of women's significance in society and a plea for greater compassion to their burdens.

The Italian Setting for the Development of Humanism

In Italy during the fourteenth century, a growing number of literate and artistic individuals began to call themselves *humanists*—citizens of a modern world that would perfect itself through the recovery, study, and transmission of the cultural heritage of Greece and Rome. They believed themselves to be the initiators of a new era—a renaissance (rebirth) of the culture and values of classical antiquity. But this culture historians call the Italian Renaissance did not come into being without tremendous influence from its medieval past—in fact, many historians consider the Renaissance to be more of a natural maturation of medieval society than a radical break with traditional culture. Yet most students of the period agree that the heritage of the past, in combination with a newly found passionate concern with Greece and Rome and emerging political and economic patterns, produced a distinctly different culture.

During the fourteenth and fifteenth centuries, after recovering from the effects of the Black Plague, the city-states of northern and central Italy experienced a tremendous growth in population and expanded to become small territorial states. Eventually five such states emerged: the duchy of Milan; the Papal States, in which the restored authority of the popes crushed the independence of many smaller city-states in central Italy; the republics of Florence and Venice; and the kingdom of Naples. Selling or leasing their country holdings, Italian nobles moved to the cities and joined with the rich merchants to form an urban ruling class. By 1300 nearly all the land of northern and central Italy was owned by profit-seeking urban citizens who produced their goods for city markets. In the large export industries, such as woolen cloth (the industry employed 30,000 in Florence), a capitalistic system of production, in which the merchants retained ownership of the raw material and paid others to finish the product, brought great profits. More great wealth was gained from commerce, particularly the import-export trade in luxury goods from the East.

So much wealth was accumulated by these merchant-capitalists that they turned to money-lending and banking. From the thirteenth to the fifteenth centuries, Italians monopolized European banking (Florence alone had 80 banking houses by 1300). These economic and political successes made the Italian upper-class groups strongly assertive, self-confident, and passionately attached to their city-states. Even literature and art reflected their self-confidence.

Political leaders and the wealthy merchants, bankers, and manufacturers conspicuously displayed their wealth and that of their cities by patronizing the arts and literature. Artists and scholars were provided with governmental, academic, and tutorial positions and enjoyed the security and protection offered by their patrons and the advantage of working exclusively on commission. Among the most famous patrons were members of the Medici family, who ruled Florence for 60 years (1434–1494). Renaissance popes were lavish patrons who made Rome the foremost center of art and learning by 1500.

Humanism and the Classical Revival: Petrarch and Boccacio

Historians are not able to agree on an exact meaning of the Renaissance term known as *humanism*. But they generally agree that humanism consisted of the study and popularization of the Greek and Latin classics and the culture those classics described. The humanists, students of the classics as well as advocates of the Roman concept of a liberal education (or *studia humanitatis*), promoted an education in "humanistic studies," but also advocated civic patriotism and social betterment.

Discovery Through Maps

The Lagoon of Venice

Maps can be designed to illustrate much more than merely the physical features of a geographical area. They may also be designed to serve as vehicles to enhance the image of a particular state—to serve as propaganda. For instance, examine this cartographic rendering of the Lagoon of Venice and the neighboring regions of Friulli and Istria, one of a series of magnificently designed maps painted by Ignazio Danti (1536–1586), a mathematician, astronomer, geographer, and Dominican priest and bishop—another example of the idealized "Renaissance man." Danti was commissioned by Pope Gregory XIII to make a number of maps of ancient and modern Italy, many of which are presently on display in the Vatican Museum in Rome. Danti's map of the Lagoon of Venice depicts an idealized land and seascape that features a bustling harbor, replete with sailing vessels both mythical and contemporary to the sixteenth century. Over the harbor the sun radiates its glory on the land and sea, and a formal inscription in Latin gives testimony to the ancient significance of the harbor and past glories.

The primary purpose of this map was certainly not to provide geographical assistance, but rather to promote the power and glory of the Republic of Venice. Such a map provided its observers with a sense of the historic significance of the Lagoon, its almost mythical role in the history of the Italian peninsula, and the opulence and splendor of one of the most significant republics of Renaissance Italy.

Questions to Consider

1. What seem to be the most significant features emphasized in this map of the Lagoon of Venice? Why does the artist appear to focus most of his attention on the sea rather than the land itself?
2. What effects do you think this map would have had on its viewers in the sixteenth century? What impressions do you believe Danti wanted to impart to his contemporaries who studied this map?
3. Why do you think Danti portrayed such a variety of vessels from different eras and subjects drawn from both pagan mythology and Christian tradition in the harbor?

The classic example of the Renaissance nobleman, statesman, and patron of the arts was the Florentine Lorenzo de' Medici, known as Lorenzo the Magnificent. Under his patronage and guidance, Florence became the leading city of the Italian Renaissance, renowned for the splendor of its buildings and lavish support for the arts.

The humanists were also the founders of modern historical research and linguistics. Humanism was not an anti-Christian movement, and most humanists remained religious, but the church bureaucracy and the extreme authority claimed by the popes received their strongest criticism.

"Father of humanism" is a title given to Francesco Petrarca (frahn-CHEHS-koh peh-TRAHR-kah), better known as Petrarch (1304–1374), by later Italian humanists because he was the first to play a major role in making people conscious of the attractions of classical literature. He wrote Latin epic poetry and biography in addition to his famous and innovative love sonnets to a married woman named Laura, whom Petrarch admired romantically. Petrarch's works held to his Christian values, but displayed much more of a secular orientation and an involvement with the society and social issues of the day.

DOCUMENT
Petrarch, Letter to Cicero

Another celebrated early humanist was the Florentine Giovanni Boccaccio (gee-oh-VAH-nee boh-KAH-chee-oh; 1313–1375), a student and friend of Petrarch's who began his career as a writer of poetry and romances. But his masterpiece was the *Decameron*, a collection of one hundred stories told by three young men and seven young women, as they sought to avoid the Black Plague in the seclusion of a country villa. The *Decameron* offers a wealth of anecdotes, portraits of flesh-and-blood characters, and vivid glimpses of Renaissance life.

The *Decameron* was both the high point and the end of Boccaccio's career as a creative artist. Largely through the influence of Petrarch, whom he met in 1350, Boccaccio gave up writing in Italian and turned to the study of antiquity. He began to learn Greek, composed an encyclopedia of classical mythology, and visited monasteries in search of manuscripts. By the time Petrarch and Boccaccio died, the study of the literature and learning of antiquity was growing throughout Italy.

Classical Revival and Philosophy

The recovery and assimilation of Greek and Roman learning was a consuming passion of the humanists. The search for manuscripts became a mania, and before the middle of the fifteenth century, original works, unedited by the church, of most of the important Latin authors had been found. In addition to these Latin works, precious Greek manuscripts were brought to Italy from Constantinople after it fell to the Turks in 1453, and many Greek scholars were welcomed to Italy, in particular to Florence, where the Medici gave their support to a gathering of Florentine

A miniature portrait of Petrarch from his illuminated manuscript of Remedies Against Fortune. *In keeping with a classical tradition, Petrarch composed many letters—which he edited for publication—that were in effect literary essays expressing his own attitudes and humanistic concerns.*

humanists which came to be called the Academy. Under the leadership of the humanists Marsilio Ficino (mar-SEE-lee-oh fee-CHEE-noh) (1433–1499) and Pico della Mirandola (PEE-koh de-lah mee-RAHN-doh-lah; 1463–1494), the Academy focused its study on the works of Plato, and placed particular emphasis on Plato's admiration of human reason and free will. The influence of Aristotle still remained strong among Scholastic thinkers during the Renaissance, especially at the University of Padua, where the study of natural science, logic, and metaphysics continued to be emphasized. Scholasticism was the dominant school of thought in the West from the ninth through seventeenth centuries, drawing its inspiration from Aristotle, St. Augustine, and the declared truths of the church (see Chapter 9).

A growing number of women were well educated, read the classics, and wrote during the Renaissance.

Document — Machiavelli, *The Prince:* On Cruelty and Mercy

Niccoló Machiavelli, born into an impoverished branch of a noble family of Florence, began his pubic life as a diplomat in the service of the Florentine republic. When the Medici family returned to dominate Florence in 1512, Machiavelli was imprisoned and tortured for his supposed plot against the Medici family. He then retired to the countryside to write his most famous works. Machiavelli's best known work is *The Prince* (1532), which presents a description of how a prince might best gain control and maintain power. His ideal prince is calculating and ruthless in his quest to best those who would destroy him in his effort to establish a unified Italian state. The following excerpts from this famous work describe how a prince must decide how, when, and if a prince should use cruelty or mercy to accomplish his aims:

From this arises an argument: whether it is better to be loved than to be feared, or the contrary. I reply that one should like to be both one and the other: but since it is difficult to join them together, it is much safer to be feared than to be loved when one of the two must be lacking. For one can generally say that about men: that they are ungrateful, fickle, simulators and deceivers, avoiders of danger, greedy for gain; and while you work for their good they are completely yours, offering you their blood, their property, their lives, and their sons, as I said earlier, when danger is far away; but when it comes nearer to you they turn away. And that prince who bases his power entirely on their works, finding himself stripped of other preparations, comes to ruin; for friendships that are acquired by a price and not by greatness and nobility of character are purchases but are not owned, and at the proper moment they cannot be spent. And men are less hesitant about harming someone who makes himself loved than one who makes himself feared because love is held together by a chain of obligation which, since men are a sorry lot, is broken on every occasion in which their own self-interest is concerned; but fear is held together by a dread of punishment which will never abandon you.

A prince must nevertheless make himself feared in such a manner that he will avoid hatred, even if he does not acquire love: since to be feared and not hated can very well be combined; and this will always be so when he keeps his hands off the property and the women of his citizens and his subjects. And if he must take someone's life, he should do so when there is proper justification and manifest cause; but, above all, he should avoid the property of others; for men forget more quickly the death of their father than the loss of their patrimony. Moreover, the reasons for seizing their property are never lacking; and he who begins to live by stealing always finds a reason for taking what belongs to others; on the contrary, reasons for taking a life are rarer and disappear sooner. . . .

I conclude, therefore, returning to the problem of being feared and loved, that since men love at their own pleasure and fear at the pleasure of the prince, a wise prince should build his foundation upon that which belongs to him, and not upon that which belongs to others: he must strive only to avoid hatred, as has been said.

Questions to Consider

1. Comment on Machiavelli's speculations about the nature of man, and the ways in which a prince should capitalize on the reality of human character as he analyses it. Is he overly cynical, or is he a realist?
2. Does Machiavelli's advice seem out of date given the realities of politics and the quest for power in the modern world?
3. What principles of conduct does Machiavelli advise a prince to cultivate? Is his prince a complete despot, or a more crafty and manipulative, yet ethical, student of man's nature?

From Peter Bondanella and Mark Musa, eds., *The Portable Machiavelli* (New York: Viking Press, 1979), pp. 135–136.

Most of these women were daughters or wives of wealthy aristocrats who could afford private tutoring in liberal studies, since the universities were for the most part still inaccessible to females. But in the works of most humanists—echoing their classical precedents—there is little that supports the participation of women on equal footing with males in scholarly or civic activities. Some historians even maintain that Renaissance women were more restricted in their intellectual pursuits than they had been in the late Middle Ages. Still, some noble women gained great reputation and respect for their political wisdom and intelligence. Battista Sforza (SFOHR-zah), wife of the Duke of Urbino in the fifteenth century, was well known for her knowledge of Greek and Latin and admired for her ability to govern in the absence of her husband. Her contemporary, Isabella d'Este, wife of the Duke of Mantua, was renowned for her education and support of the arts, and for assembling one of the finest libraries in Italy.

ITALIAN RENAISSANCE ART

■ *How did Italian Renaissance artists differ from their medieval predecessors?*

Fourteenth- and fifteenth-century Italy produced innovations in art that culminated in the classic High Renaissance artistic style of the early sixteenth century. These innovations were the products of a new

Giotto, St. Francis Receiving the Stigmata *(c. 1295). Both a painter and architect, Giotto is credited as the first great genius of Italian Renaissance art. Like his medieval predecessors, his subjects were mainly religious, but his human subjects were portrayed as full of life and emotion. One of his favorite subjects was St. Francis of Assisi, who here receives the wounds of Jesus's crucifixion—the stigmata.*

Major Artists of the Italian Renaissance and Their Works

c. 1266–1337	Giotto: *Life of the Virgin, Life of St. Francis, Life of St. John the Baptist*
1401–1428	Masaccio: *Tribute Money, Trinity, St. Peter*
1447–1510	Botticelli: *Judith and Holofernes, St. Sebastian, The Birth of Venus*
1452–1519	Da Vinci: *Adoration of the Magi, The Last Supper, La Gioconda* (Mona Lisa)
1475–1564	Michelangelo: Ceiling of the Sistine Chapel, *Moses, Pietá, David*
c. 1477–1576	Titian: *The Venus of Zerbine, The Allegory of Marriage, Venus and Adonis*

society centered in rich cities, the humanistic and more secular spirit of the times, a revived interest in the classical art of Greece and Rome, and the creativity of some of the world's most gifted artists.

From Giotto to Donatello

The new approach in painting was first evident in the work of the Florentine painter Giotto (JOT-toh; c. 1266–1337). Earlier Italian painters had copied the stylized, flat, and rigid images of Byzantine paintings and mosaics, Giotto observed from life and painted a three-dimensional world peopled with believable human beings moved by deep emotion. He humanized painting much as Petrarch humanized thought and St. Francis, whose life was one of his favorite subjects, humanized religion. Giotto initiated a new epoch in the history of painting, one that expressed the religious piety of his lay patrons, but also their delight in the images of everyday life.

Masaccio, Expulsion from Eden. *Masaccio's mastery of perspective creates the illusion of movement as the angel drives Adam and Eve from Paradise.*

In his brief lifetime the Florentine Masaccio (mah-SAH-chee-oh; 1401–1428) completed the revolution in technique begun by Giotto. As can be seen in his few surviving paintings, Masaccio was concerned with the problems of perspective, and the modeling of figures in light and shade (*chiaroscuro;* CHAH-roh-SKOO-roh). He was also the first Renaissance artist to paint nude figures (Adam and Eve, in his *Expulsion from Eden*), reversing the tradition of earlier Christian art.

Inspired by Masaccio's achievement, most *quattrocento* (quah-troh-CHEN-toh; Italian for "the 1400s" or "fifteenth century") painters constantly sought to improve technique. But the Florentine Sandro Botticelli (sahn-DROH boh-tah-CHEH-lee; 1447–1510) proceeded in a different direction, abandoning the techniques of straightforward representation of people and objects and trying instead to inspire the viewer's imagination and emotion through close attention to strikingly beautiful portraiture and decorative backdrop landscapes.

New directions were also being taken in sculpture, and it, like painting, reached stylistic maturity at the beginning of the *quattrocento*. The Florentine Donatello (1386–1466) produced truly freestanding statues based on the realization of the human body as a coordinated mechanism of bones and muscles; his *David* was the first bronze nude made since antiquity.

Botticelli, The Birth of Venus. *The last great Florentine painter of the early Renaissance, Botticelli did most of his best work for Lorenzo de' Medici and his court. In* The Birth of Venus, *Botticelli blends ancient mythology, Christian faith, and voluptuous representation.*

The High Renaissance, 1500–1530: Leonardo da Vinci, Raphael, and Michelangelo

The painters of the High Renaissance had learned the solutions to such technical problems as perspective space from the *quattrocento* artists. The artists of the earlier period had been concerned with movement, color, and narrative detail, but painters in the High Renaissance attempted to eliminate nonessentials and concentrated on the central theme of a picture and its basic human implications.

The three greatest High Renaissance painters were Leonardo da Vinci, Raphael, and Michelangelo. Leonardo da Vinci (1452–1519) was brilliant in a variety of fields: engineering, mathematics, architecture, geology, botany, physiology, anatomy, sculpture, painting, music, and poetry. Because he loved the process of experimentation more than seeing all his projects through to completion, few of the projects da Vinci started were ever finished. He was a master of soft modeling in light and shade and of creating groups of figures perfectly balanced in a given space. One of his most famous paintings is *La Gioconda*, known as the Mona Lisa, a portrait of a woman whose enigmatic smile captures an air of tenderness and humility. Another is *The Last Supper*, which he painted on the walls of the refectory of Santa Maria delle Grazie in Milan. In this painting da Vinci experimented with the use of an oil medium combined with plaster, which unfortunately was unsuccessful. The painting quickly began to disintegrate and has been restored several times.

Raphael (1483–1520) was summoned to Rome in 1508 by Pope Julius II to aid in the decoration of the Vatican. His **frescos** there display a magnificent blending of classical and Christian subject matter and are the fruit of careful planning and immense artistic

---

fresco—A type of wall painting in which water-based pigments are applied to wet, freshly laid lime plaster. The dry-powder colors, when mixed with water, penetrate the surface and become a permanent part of the wall. The Italian Renaissance was the greatest period of fresco painting.

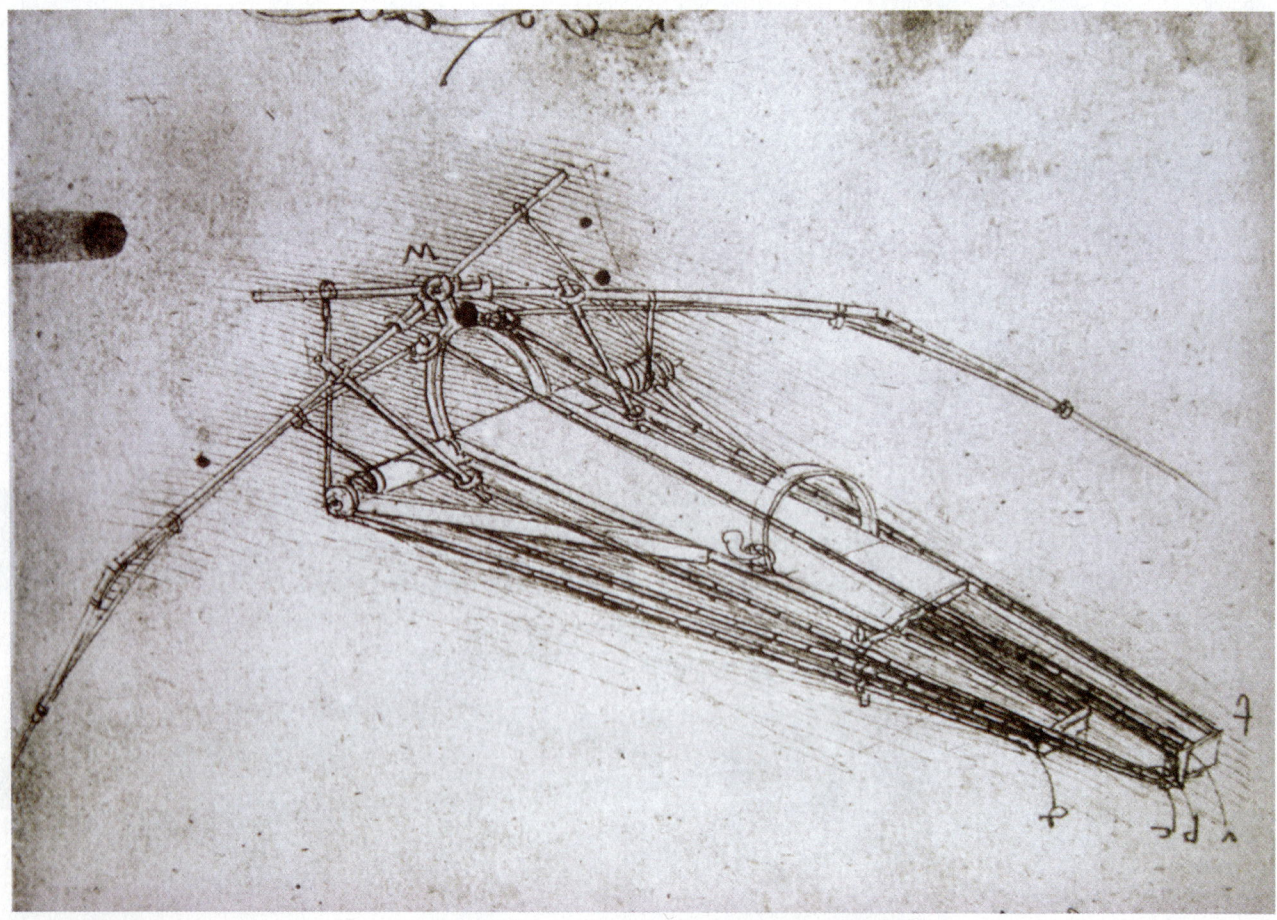

Leonardo da Vinci, Drawing of a Flying Machine. *One of the artist's later designs for a flying machine, which modern engineers speculate could have worked, although it was much too heavy. Da Vinci was convinced that a successful flying machine had to be modeled after the wings of bats and birds, as his numerous sketches of these animals show.*

knowledge. Critics consider him the master of perfect design and balanced composition.

The individualism and idealism of the High Renaissance have no greater representative than Michelangelo Buonarroti (MEE-kel-AHN-je-loh boo-na-ROH-ti; 1475–1564). Stories of this stormy and temperamental personality have helped shape our definition of a genius. His great energy enabled him to paint for Julius II in four years the entire ceiling of the Vatican's Sistine Chapel, an area of several thousand square yards, and his art embodies a superhuman ideal. With his unrivaled genius for rendering the

Raphael, Madonna of the Meadow *(c. 1505/1506)*. *Raphael's painting in oil on canvas is a classic example of a composition based on the figure of a pyramid. The scene is formally balanced yet features the interaction of the figures. The infants portrayed are John the Baptist (left) and Jesus.*

High Renaissance art, Mannerist artists sought to express their own inner vision in a manner that evoked shock in the viewer. Typical are the paintings of Parmigianino (par-me-zhian-NI-no), whose *Madonna with the Long Neck* (1535) purposely shows no logic of structure.

THE NORTHERN RENAISSANCE

■ *How did the Northern Renaissance differ from the Italian Renaissance?*

The Italian Renaissance, by seeking meaning in the classical world, had placed human beings once more in the center of life's stage and infused thought and art with humanistic values. These stimulating ideas spread north to inspire other humanists, who absorbed and adapted the Italian achievement to their own particular national circumstances.

Throughout the fifteenth century, hundreds of northern European students studied in Italy. Though their chief interest was the study of law and medicine, many were influenced by the intellectual climate of Italy with its new enthusiasm for the classics. When these students returned home, they often carried manuscripts—and later printed editions—produced by classical and humanist writers. Both literate laymen and devout clergy in the north were ready to welcome the new outlook of humanism, although these north-

Michelangelo, David. *To Michelangelo, the Florentine painter, sculptor, poet, and architect, sculpture was the noblest of the arts. The large marble statue of the biblical David was commissioned in 1501 to stand in Florence as a symbol of the city, its government, and its culture.*

human form, he devised a wealth of expressive positions and attitudes for his figures in scenes from Genesis. Michelangelo also excelled as poet, engineer, and architect and was undoubtedly the greatest sculptor of the Renaissance. The glorification of the human body was Michelangelo's great achievement. His statue of *David*, commissioned in 1501 when he was 26, expressed his idealized view of human dignity and majesty. He also became chief architect of St. Peter's in 1546, designed the great dome, and was still actively creative as a sculptor when he died, almost in his ninetieth year, in 1564.

From about 1530 to the end of the sixteenth century, Italian artists responded to the stresses of the age in a new style called *Mannerism*. Consciously revolting against the classical balance and simplicity of

Cellini, Saltcellar of Francis I. *The utilitarian purpose of the condiment dish is subordinate to its lavish decoration. Neptune, god of the sea, guards the boat-shaped salt container while a personification of Earth watches over the pepper. Figures around the base represent the four seasons and the four parts of the day. The intricacy of the design is a showcase for the sculptor's virtuosity.*

Major Figures in the Northern Renaissance and Their Works

c. 1395–1441	Jan van Eyck (painter): *Man with the Red Turban, Wedding Portrait*
c. 1466–1536	Desiderius Erasmus (humanist and scholar): *The Praise of Folly, Handbook of the Christian Knight*
1471–1528	Albrecht Dürer (painter): *Adam and Eve, The Four Apostles, Self-Portrait*
1478–1535	Sir Thomas More (humanist and diplomat): *Utopia*
c. 1483–1553	François Rabelais (writer): *Gargantua and Pantagruel*
1488–1523	Ulrich von Hutten (humanist and poet)
1547–1616	Miguel de Cervantes (writer): *Don Quixote*
1564–1616	William Shakespeare (playwright and poet): *Julius Caesar, Romeo and Juliet, King Lear*

ern humanists were more interested in religious reform than their Italian counterparts.

The Influence of Printing

Very important in the diffusion of the Renaissance and later in the success of the Reformation was the invention of printing with movable type in Europe. The essential elements—paper and block printing—had been known in China since the eighth century. During the twelfth century, the Spanish Muslims introduced papermaking to Europe; in the thirteenth, Europeans, in close contact with China (see Chapter 10), brought knowledge of block printing to the West. The crucial step was taken in the 1440s at Mainz, Germany, where Johann Gutenberg (YOH-hahn GOOT-en-berg) and other printers invented movable type by cutting up old printing blocks to form individual letters. Gutenberg used movable type for papal documents and for the first printed version of the Bible (1454).

Soon all the major countries of Europe possessed the means for printing books. Throughout Europe, the price of books sank to one-eighth of their former cost and came within the reach of many people who formerly had been unable to buy them. In addition, pamphlets and controversial tracts soon began to circulate, and new ideas reached a thousand times more people in a relatively short span of time. In the quickening of Europe's intellectual life, it is difficult to overestimate the effects of the printing press.

Humanism in France, Germany, Spain, and England

One of the best-known French humanists was François Rabelais (frahn-SWAH RAH-be-lay; c. 1483–1553), who is best remembered for his novel *Gargantua and Pantagruel*. Centering on figures from French folklore, this work relates the adventures of Gargantua and his son Pantagruel, genial giants of tremendous stature and appetite. Rabelais satirized his society while putting forth his humanist views on educational reform and inherent human goodness. He made powerful attacks on the abuses of the church and the

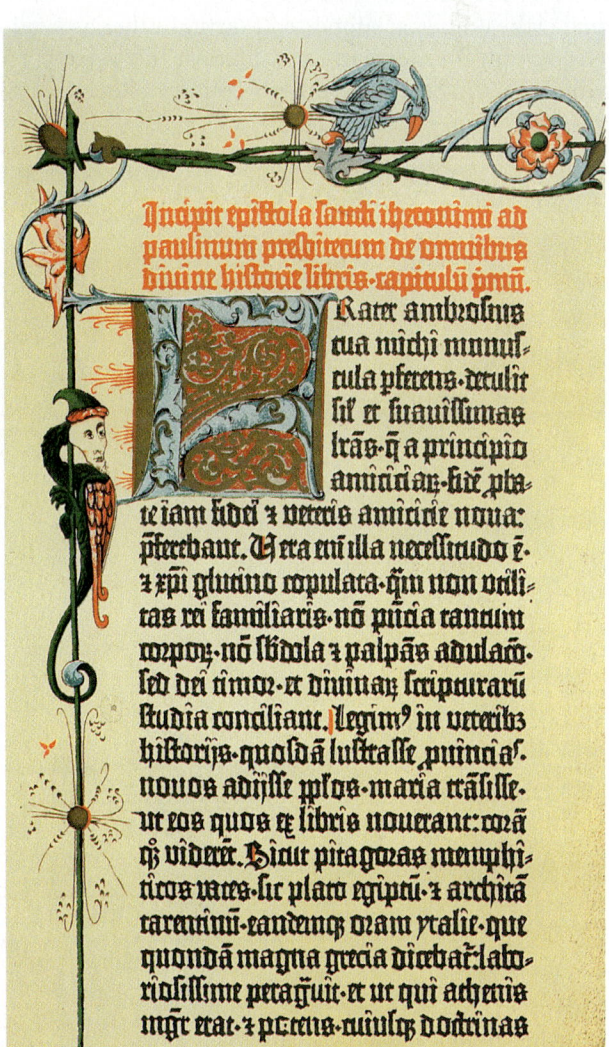

Facsimile copy of a page from the Gutenberg Bible, the Book of Genesis. With the development of printing, learning was no longer the private domain of the church and those few persons wealthy enough to own hand-copied volumes.

hypocrisy and repression he found in contemporary political and religious practice.

Another notable northern humanist was the French skeptic Michel de Montaigne (mee-SHEL de mohn-TANYE; 1533–1592). At age 38, he gave up the practice of law and retired to his country estate and well-stocked library, where he studied and wrote. Montaigne developed a new literary form and gave it its name—the *essay*. In 94 essays he set forth his personal views on many subjects: leisure, friendship, education, philosophy, religion, old age, death. He advocated open-mindedness and tolerance—rare qualities in the sixteenth century, when France was racked by religious and civil strife.

Montaigne, *Essays*

One of the most outstanding German humanists was Ulrich von Hutten (HOO-ten; 1488–1523). His idealism combined a zeal for religious reform and German nationalist feelings. This member of an aristocratic family, who wanted to unite Germany under the emperor, supported Martin Luther as a rallying point for German unity against the papacy, to which he attributed most of his country's ills.

In the national literatures that matured during the northern Renaissance, the transition from feudal knight to Renaissance courtier finds its greatest literary expression in a masterpiece of Spanish satire, *Don Quixote de la Mancha*, the work of Miguel de Cervantes (1547–1616). By Cervantes's time, knighthood and ideals of chivalry had become archaic in a world of practical concerns. Cervantes describes the adventures of Don Quixote (ki-HOH-te), a knight who is a representative of an earlier age. Don Quixote appears to be ridiculous old man who desires the great days of the past and has a series of misadventures in his attempts to recapture past glories. But Cervantes's real objective was to expose the inadequacies of chivalric idealism in a world that had acquired new and intensely practical aims. He did so by creating a sad but appealing character to serve as the personification of an outmoded way of life.

The reign of Queen Elizabeth I (1558–1603) was the high point of the English Renaissance and produced an astonishing number of gifted writers. Strongly influenced by the royal court, which served as the busy center of intellectual and artistic life, these writers produced works that were intensely emotional, richly romantic, and often wildly creative in combination with traditional poetic allusions to classical times.

The dominant figure in Elizabethan literature is William Shakespeare (1564–1616). His rich vocabulary and poetic imagery were matched by his turbulent imagination. He was a superb lyric poet, and numerous critics have judged him the foremost sonnet writer in the English language.

Shakespeare wrote 37 plays—comedies, histories, tragedies, and romances. His historical plays reflected the patriotic upsurge experienced by the English after the defeat of the Spanish Armada in 1588. For his comedies, tragedies, and romances, Shakespeare was content, in a great majority of cases, to borrow plots from earlier works. His great strength lay in his creation of characters and in his ability to translate his knowledge of human nature into dramatic speech and action. Today his comedies still play to enthusiastic audiences, but it is in his

Michel de Montaigne, author of the Essays. *Montaigne retired from the business world while in his thirties to reflect on and write about humanity's problems.*

tragedies that the poet-dramatist runs the gamut of human emotion and experience.

Shakespeare possessed in abundance the Renaissance concern for human beings and the world around them. His plays deal first and foremost with the human personality, passions, and problems.

Northern Painting

Before the Italian Renaissance began to influence the artistic circles of northern Europe, the painters of the Low Countries—modern Belgium, Luxembourg, and the Netherlands—had been making significant advances on their own. Outstanding was the Fleming Jan van Eyck (YAHN van AIK; c. 1395–1441), who painted in the realistic manner developed by medieval miniaturists. Van Eyck also perfected the technique of oil painting, which enabled him to paint with greater realism and attention to detail. In his painting of the merchant Arnolfini and his wife, for example, he painstakingly gives extraordinary reality to every detail, from his own image reflected in the mirror in the background to individual hairs on the little dog in the foreground.

The first German painter to be influenced deeply by Italian art was Albrecht Dürer (1471–1528) of Nuremberg. Dürer made several journeys to Italy, where he was impressed both with the painting of the Renaissance Italians and with the artists' high social status—a contrast with northern Europe, where artists were still treated as craftsmen, not men of genius. His own work is a blend of the old and the new and fuses the realism and symbolism of Gothic art with the style and passion of the Italian artists. In his own lifetime and after, Dürer became better known for his numerous engravings and woodcuts, produced for a mass market, than for his paintings.

Another famous German painter, Hans Holbein the Younger (1497–1543), chiefly painted portraits and worked abroad, especially in England. His memorable portraits blend the realism and concern for detail characteristic of all northern painting with Italian dignity.

Two northern painters who remained completely isolated from Italian influences were Hieronymus Bosch (hai-ROH-ni-muhs BAHSH; 1480–1516) and Pieter Brueghel (BROI-gel) the Elder (c. 1525–1569).

Jan van Eyck, Wedding Portrait. *The painting of a merchant named Arnolfini and his pregnant bride is extraordinary for its meticulously rendered realistic detail. Van Eyck painted exactly what he saw—he "was there," as his signature on the painting says (Johannes de Eyck fuit hic). The painting is also filled with symbolism; the dog, for instance, stands for marital fidelity.*
Jan van Eyck, *The Wedding Portrait,* 1434. NG 186. © National Gallery, London.

Hieronymous Bosch, Hell, *from* The Garden of Earthly Delights *(1503/1504). Part of a three-paneled altarpiece (a triptych) depicting the dreams that affect people in a pleasure-seeking world. The panel pictured here displays the horrors that await those sent to hell, where they spend their days tortured by half-human monsters, devils, and demons in a fantastic landscape.*

Brueghel retained a strong Flemish flavor in his portrayal of the faces and scenes of his native land. He painted village squares, landscapes, skating scenes, and peasants at work and at leisure just as he saw them, with an expert eye for detail.

Very little is known about the Dutch master Bosch other than that he belonged to one of the many puritanical religious sects that were becoming popular at the time. This accounts for his most famous painting, *The Garden of Delights,* a triptych whose main panel is filled with large numbers of naked men and women partaking in the sins of the flesh. The smaller left panel, by contrast, depicts an idealized Garden of Eden, while the right panel portrays a nightmarish hell filled with desperate sinners undergoing punishment. Bosch was a stern moralist whose obsession with sin and hell reflects the fears of many of his contemporaries—concerns that contributed to the religious movement known as the Reformation.

Erasmus, Thomas More, and Northern Humanism

The most influential of the northern humanists was Desiderius Erasmus (c. 1466–1536). Dutch by birth, he passed most of his long life elsewhere—in Germany, France, England, Italy, and especially Switzerland. He corresponded with nearly every prominent writer and thinker in Europe and personally knew popes, emperors, and kings. He was *the* scholar of Europe, and his writings and translations of the classics, and the works of the church fathers, as well as a new Latin translation of the New Testament, were eagerly read everywhere.

Perhaps the most famous and influential work by Erasmus was *The Praise of Folly*, a satire written in 1511 at the house of the English humanist Sir Thomas More. This influential work poked fun at and ridiculed a broad range of political, social, economic and religious evils of the day. Erasmus' scholarship and the objects of his literary attention typify the central concerns of the northern humanists. They were interested not only in the classics, but in the Bible and early Christian writings. Their primary focus of reform was not civil society and the state, but morality and a return to the simplicity of early Christianity.

The most significant figure in English humanism was Sir Thomas More (1478–1535), a good friend of Erasmus. More is best known for his *Utopia*, the first important description of an ideal state since Plato's *Republic*. In this work, More criticized his age through his portrayal of a fictitious sailor who contrasts the ideal

More, *Utopia*

Portrait of Erasmus *by Hans Holbein the Younger. Erasmus's scholarly achievements include a Greek edition of the New Testament and editions of the writings of St. Jerome and other early church fathers. Erasmus is best known, however, for his popular works, especially* The Praise of Folly.

the Complutensian Bible between 1502–1517, under the supervision of Cardinal Ximenes (HE-men-es). Similar texts in Greek, Latin, and Hebrew were printed on the same page for most of the books of the Bible to assure a proper translation of scripture. In other places, humanism's questioning of authoritative documents, such as Lorenzo da Valla's linguistic research that indicated that the Donation of Constantine was a forgery, emboldened critics of the church to press their case for change. Unfortunately for the church, it went through one of its most stormy periods between 1300 and 1500, and there was much to criticize.

THE CRISIS IN THE CATHOLIC CHURCH: 1300–1517

■ *What factors led to the erosion of church authority from 1300 to 1517?*

The power of the medieval papacy reached its height during the pontificate of Innocent III (1198–1216), who exerted his influence over kings and princes without serious challenge. The church seemed unrivaled in its prestige, dignity, and power. Yet that dominance was challenged on several fronts, and over the next two centuries, the power of the medieval church was diminished and transformed.

Religious Diversity in the Western World

Boniface VIII

Papal power was threatened by the growth of nation-states, whose monarchs challenged the church's temporal power, the papal bureaucracy's maintenance of a separate judicial structure for those under the pope's authority, and the privilege to collect **tithes** destined for Rome. In addition, the papacy became regularly criticized by reformers who questioned the legitimacy of papal authority and its secular power in place of the biblical example of simplicity and otherworldliness in matters of belief. The bourgeoisie, the middle-class workers and craftsmen of the towns whose attitudes were much more pragmatic than those of the rural peasantry of an earlier age, fostered an outlook of growing skepticism, national patriotism, and religious self-reliance.

life he has seen in Utopia (the "Land of Nowhere") with the harsh conditions of life in England. In Utopia, the evils brought on by political and social injustice were overcome by the holding of all property and goods in common. More's economic outlook was a legacy from the Middle Ages, and his preference for medieval collectivism over modern economic individualism was consistent with his preference for a church headed, in medieval style, by popes rather than by kings. This view prompted Henry VIII, who had appropriated the pope's position as head of the Church of England, to execute More, who had been one of Henry's most trusted advisers and officials, for treason.

Erasmus and More transmitted humanist values and research skills throughout Northern Europe. Through their writings they contributed to the increasing demand for reform of the Catholic Church: However, neither man sought the breakup of the church. In some places, such as Spain, the new humanistic linguistic and research skills were used to produce

---

tithes—Contribution of a tenth of one's income to the Church. Tithing dates to the Old Testament and was adopted by the Western Christian church in the sixth century and enforced in Europe by secular law from the eighth century.

Pope Boniface VIII (1294–1303) was an outspoken advocate of papal authority and a strident opponent of any monarch who dared to attempt to tax the church without papal consent. The powerful and popular kings of England, Edward I, and France, Philip IV the Fair, attempted to tax the church and limit the authority of papal courts, and in response Boniface boldly declared in the papal bull *Unam Sanctam* (OO-nam SANK-tam; 1302) that all temporal matters, and even rulers, were ultimately subject to the spiritual power wielded by the pope. Philip demanded that the pope be brought to trial by a general church council. In 1303 French officials and their allies broke into Boniface's summer home at Anagni, roughed the old man up, and attempted to arrest him and take him to France to stand trial, but the pope was rescued by his supporters. Boniface died a month later, perhaps from the shock and physical abuse he suffered during the attack.

DOCUMENT
Boniface VIII, Unam Sanctum

CASE STUDY
Role and Authority of the Pope

The Avignon Papacy

Philip's success was as complete as if Boniface had actually been dragged before the king to stand trial. Two years after Boniface's death, a French archbishop was chosen pope; he never went to Rome but instead moved the papal headquarters to Avignon (AH-vin-yahn), a city on the southern border of France, on land technically owned by the papacy, but where the popes and the papal court remained under strong French influence from 1305 to 1377. During this Avignon papacy, also called the Babylonian Captivity of the church, papal prestige suffered enormously. Most Europeans believed that Rome was the only proper capital for the church. Moreover, the English, Germans, and Italians accused the popes and the cardinals, the majority of whom now were also French, of being instruments of the French king.

The Avignon papacy also gave credence to critics who attacked the fiscal and moral corruption of the church bureaucracy and the very obvious lack of spiritual dedication of the Avignon popes. Increasing their demands for income from England, Germany, and Italy and living in splendor in a newly built fortress-palace, the Avignon popes expanded the papal bureaucracy, added new church taxes, and collected the old taxes more efficiently. These actions provoked denunciation of the wealth of the church and a demand for its reform.

Wycliffe and Hus

With the abuses of the church at Avignon all too obvious, reformers began to call for not only an end to corruption, but change in church teaching and structure. In England, a professor of philosophy and theology at Oxford, John Wycliffe (WIK-lif; c. 1320–1384), attacked not only church abuses but also certain of the church's doctrines. He also worked for the English royal government of Richard II as a cleric attached to foreign missions and was employed to write pamphlets justifying the Crown's seizure of Church property.

Wycliffe was strongly influenced by the writings of St. Augustine and emphasized the primacy of the Bible in the life of a Christian. He believed that God directly touched each person and that the role of the popes was of minor importance. In fact, he asserted, the kings had a higher claim on their subjects' loyalty, and the monarchs themselves were accountable only to God, not the pope. Wycliffe believed that the church is the community of believers, and not the Catholic hierarchy. He even went so far as to question the validity of some of the sacraments. Toward the end of his life, the Roman Church launched a counterattack, and after his death he was declared a heretic. In 1428 his remains were taken from consecrated ground and burned, and his ashes were thrown into a river. In the church's eyes, this act condemned his soul to perpetual wandering and suffering and destroyed the possibility that Wycliffe's followers could preserve any parts of his body as relics. But the influence of his writings took root in England through a group he helped organize called the "poor priests," later known as the Lollards, who were likewise condemned and outlawed, but they continued an underground church that surfaced in the sixteenth century.

In Bohemia, where a strong reform movement linked with the resentment of the Czechs toward their German overlords was under way, Wycliffe's opinions were popularized by Czech students who had studied with him at Oxford. In particular, his beliefs influenced John Hus (c. 1369–1415), a teacher in Prague and later rector of the university there. Hus's attacks on the abuses of clerical power led him to conclude that the true church was composed of a universal priesthood of believers and that Christ alone was its head. In 1402, after becoming the dominant figure at his university, he started to give sermons in the Czech language that soon attracted congregations as large as 3000 people. He preached that the Bible is the only source of faith and that every person has the right to read it in his own language. Like Wycliffe, Hus preached against clerical abuses and the claim of the church to guarantee salvation. This message became more explosive because it was linked with his criticism of the excesses of the German-dominated church at a time of a growing Czech nationalist movement.

In his preaching he openly acknowledged his debt to Wycliffe and refused to join in condemning him in

1410. Hus was later excommunicated and called to account for himself at the Council of Constance in 1415. Even though he had been given the assurance of safe passage, he was seized and burned at the stake as a heretic, and his ashes were thrown into the Rhine. His death led to the Hussite wars (1419–1437), in which the Czechs withstood a series of crusades against them. They maintained their religious reforms until their defeat by the Habsburgs in the Thirty Years' War.

The Great Schism of the Roman Catholic Church

In response to pressure from churchmen, rulers, scholars, and commoners throughout Europe, the papacy returned to Rome in 1377, it seemed for a time that its credibility would be regained. However, the reverse proved true. In the papal election held the following year, the **College of Cardinals** elected an Italian pope. A few months later the French cardinals declared the election invalid and elected a French pope, who returned to Avignon. During the Great **Schism** (1378–1417), as the split of the church into two allegiances was called, there were two popes, each with his college of cardinals and capital city, each claiming complete authority, each sending out papal administrators and collecting taxes, and each excommunicating the other. The nations of Europe gave allegiance as their individual political interests influenced them.

The Great Schism continued after the original rival popes died, and each group elected a replacement. Doubt and confusion caused many Europeans to question the legitimacy and holiness of the church as an institution.

The Conciliar Movement

Positive action came in the form of the Conciliar Movement. In 1395 the professors at the University of Paris proposed that a general council, representing the entire church, should meet to heal the schism. A majority of the cardinals of both factions accepted this solution, and in 1409 they met at the Council of Pisa,

College of Cardinals—Cardinals are the highest-ranking churchmen serving under the pope in the Catholic Church. Collectively, they constitute the Sacred College of Cardinals, and their duties include electing the pope, acting as his principal counselors, and aiding in governing the church.

Schism—Literally a split or division (from the Greek *schizein* = to split). The word is usually used in reference to the Great Schism (1378–1417), when there were two, and later three, rival popes, each with his own College of Cardinals.

deposed both popes, and elected a new one. But neither of the two deposed popes would give up his office, and the papal throne now had three claimants.

The intolerable situation necessitated another church council. In 1414 the Holy Roman Emperor assembled at Constance the most impressive church gathering of the period. By deposing the various papal claimants and electing Martin V as pope in 1417, the Great Schism was ended and a single papacy was restored at Rome.

The Conciliar Movement represented a reforming and democratizing influence in the church. But the movement was not to endure, even though the Council of Constance had decreed that general councils were superior to popes and that they should meet at regular intervals in the future. Taking steps to preserve his authority, the pope announced that to appeal to a church council without having first obtained papal consent was heretical. Together with the inability of later councils to bring about much-needed reform and with lack of support for such councils by secular

Religious Reforms and Reactions

1415	John Hus, Bohemian reformer, burned at the stake
1437–1517	Cardinal Ximenes carried out reforms of Spanish Catholic Church
c. 1450	Revival of witchcraft mania in Europe
1452–1498	Savonarola attempted religious purification of Florence
1483–1546	Martin Luther
1484–1531	Ulrich Zwingli, leader of Swiss Reformation
1491–1556	Ignatius Loyola, founder of Society of Jesus (Jesuits)
1509–1564	John Calvin, leader of Reformation in Geneva
1515–1582	St. Teresa of Avila, founder of Carmelite religious order
1517	Luther issues Ninety-Five Theses
1521	Luther declared an outcast by the Imperial Diet at Worms
1534–1549	Pontificate of Paul III
1545–1563	Council of Trent
1561–1593	Religious wars in France

rulers, the restoration of a single head of the church enabled the popes to discredit the Conciliar Movement by 1450. Not until almost a century later, when the Council of Trent convened in 1545, did a great council meet to reform the church. But by that time the church had already irreparably lost many countries to Protestantism.

While the popes refused to call councils to effect reform, they failed to bring about reform themselves. The popes busied themselves not with internal problems but with Italian politics and patronage of the arts. The issues of church reform and revitalization were largely ignored.

Political Challenges

During the fifteenth century major issues of contention between Rome and the various leaders of Europe dealt with the control of taxes and fees, the courts, the law, and trade. The Catholic Church owned vast properties and collected fortunes in tithes, fees, and religious gifts, controlling, by some estimates, between a fifth and a fourth of Europe's wealth. Impoverished secular rulers looked enviously at the church's wealth. Because the Atlantic states of England, France and Spain were more unified, they were better able to deal with Rome than states of the fragmented Holy Roman Empire.

No longer able to prevail over secular rulers by its religious authority alone after 1300, the papacy fared badly in an era of power politics in foreign relations. Free Italian cities, such as Venice and Florence, had helped build a new balance-of-power diplomacy after the 1450s. But the French invasion at the end of the fifteenth century made the peninsula an arena for desperate struggle between the Habsburg and French Valois (Val-WAH) dynasties that would last until 1559. The Papal States became a political pawn. The papacy's weaknesses were exploited by the troops of Charles V when they sacked Rome in 1527.

Spiritual and Intellectual Developments

The Roman Catholic Church faced more than just social and political challenges by 1500. At the lowest level, popular religion remained based on illiterate believers who worshipped for the magical or practical earthly benefits of the sacraments and the cults of the saints. In their short and grim lives they were far from the political intrigue and sophisticated theological disputes that would trigger the Reformations and much closer to beliefs in the existence of witches, ghosts, phantom grunting swine, and demons who might lurk around the next corner. Arguments between Augustinian and Dominican monks meant little, and dedication to the opinions of the pope in faraway Rome was weak. Of much greater concern was how to avoid going to Hell, a possibility that was constantly in evidence during this time of fragile life and early death.

At the elite levels, during the fifteenth century, humanist reformers believed that abuses in the Catholic Church resulted largely from misinterpretation of Scripture by late medieval Scholastic philosophers and theologians (see p. 274). Northern humanists like Erasmus and Sir Thomas More ridiculed later Scholastics as pedantic (see p. 412).

Intellectual conflict was not new in Europe. But the means of communicating the nature and extent of the disagreements after the 1450s was new. The printing presses, after their European introduction in the 1350s, produced 6 million publications in more than 200 European towns by 1500. There were better-educated people with a thirst to read these books, which dealt largely with religious themes, and the result was the force of mobilized public opinion.

Some of these readers responded to critics, such as the Augustinian monks, who saw the Scholastics as presumptuous and worldly. Following the teachings of St. Augustine, they believed humans to be such depraved sinners that there could be saved not through "good works," as the Church taught, but only through personal repentance and faith in God's mercy. **Augustinians** accepted only Scripture as religious truth; they believed that faith was more important than the Scholastics' manipulated power of reason. And it was to the Augustinians that Martin Luther would turn to pursue his search for understanding.

LUTHER AND THE GERMAN REFORMATION

■ *Why did the most important fracture in Christendom occur in Germany?*

Martin Luther had no intention of striking the spark that launched more than a century of European conflict. Born in 1483, the son of an ambitious and tough Thuringian peasant turned miner and small businessman, he was raised by his parents under a contradictory regime of Christian love and the attendant harsh physical discipline that would affect his way of dealing with the world after 1521. Like many young boys of his time, he enjoyed the sometimes earthy and profane humor of his peasant society. Unlike many of his friends, he, as did St. Augustine 1200 years earlier, distrusted his own passionate

Martin Luther

Augustinians—Founded in 1256, a religious order dedicated to following of St. Augustine's life and teaching.

nature and became obsessed with fear of the devil and an eternity in hell. Until 1517 Luther's pursuit of his salvation was an intensely personal one, with little regard to the larger context of upheaval in which he lived.

The Search for Salvation

Martin Luther found great comfort in the teachings of the humanists and the Augustinians. After four years of studying the law, he disappointed his father by entering an Augustinian monastery at age 22, following what was to him a miraculous survival in a violent thunderstorm. As a monk, however, Luther was tormented by what he saw as his sinful nature and the fear of damnation. Then, in his mid-thirties, he read St. Paul's Epistle to the Romans and found freedom from despair in the notion of justification by faith: "Then I grasped that the justice of God is that righteousness by which through grace and sheer mercy God justifies us through faith. Thereupon, I felt myself to be reborn and to have gone through open doors into paradise."[1]

As an Augustinian, Luther entered into abstract religious debates that became more spirited because of the widespread problems of the church in central Europe. The buying and selling of church offices and charging fees to give comfort through a variety of theologically questionable ceremonies to superstitious parishioners disturbed him. But the practice that outraged Luther and brought him openly to oppose the Roman Catholic Church was the sale of indulgences. Theologically, these were shares of surplus grace, earned by Christ and the saints and available for papal dispensation to worthy souls after death. Originally, indulgences were not sold or described as tickets to heaven. By the sixteenth century, however, papal salesmen regularly peddled them as guarantees of early release from purgatory.

Luther's immediate adversary in 1517 was a **Dominican** monk named Johan Tetzel (TET-zel), commissioned by the Pope Leo X and Archbishop Albert of Mainz to sell indulgences. At the papal level, this was part of a large undertaking by which Pope Leo X hoped to finance completion of St. Peter's Basilica in Rome: The Archbishop of Mainz received 50 percent of the money for his own purposes. Tetzel used every appeal to crowds of the country people around Wittenberg (vit-en-BERG), begging them to aid their deceased loved ones and repeating the slogan "A penny in the box, a soul out of purgatory."[2] Luther and many other Germans detested Tetzel's methods and his Roman connections. He also rejected Tetzel's Dominican theology, which differed from Augustinian beliefs.

Dominicans—St. Dominic established this religious order in 1215 to go out into the world to teach and preach the word of God.

Lucas Cranach, Martin Luther and His Friends. *That Martin Luther (left) and other Protestant reformers did not suffer the same fate as John Hus a century earlier was largely due to the political support of rulers such as the Elector Frederick of Saxony (center).*

There are moments in history when the actions of a single person will link all of the prevailing and contrasting currents of an era into an explosive mixture. In Wittenberg on October 31, 1517, Martin Luther issued his Ninety-Five Theses, calling for public debate—mainly with the Dominicans—on issues involving indulgences and basic church doctrines.

This document was soon translated from Latin into German and published in all major German cities. The Theses denied the pope's power to give salvation and declared that indulgences were not necessary for a contrite and repentant Christian. Number 62, for example, stated that the "true treasure" of the Church was the "Holy Gospel of the Glory and Grace of God," and number 36 indicated that Christians truly desiring forgiveness could gain it without "letters of pardon." The resulting popular outcry forced Tetzel to leave Saxony, and Luther was almost immediately hailed as a prophet, directed by God to expose the pope and a grasping clergy.

His message was so well received because it satisfied those who wanted a return to simple faith; it also appealed to those, like the humanists, who fought church abuses and irrational authority. Luther's message provided an outlet for German resentment against Rome, and it gave encouragement to princes seeking political independence. The ensuing controversy, which soon raged far beyond Wittenberg, split all of western Christendom and focused and strengthened the social, economic, and political contradictions of the time.

Luther was soon in trouble. Although Rome was not immediately alarmed, the Dominicans levied charges of heresy against their Augustinian competitor. Having already begun his defense in a series of pamphlets, Luther continued in 1519 by debating the eminent theologian John Eck (1486–1543) at Leipzig (LEIP-zig). There Luther denied the **infallibility of the pope** and church councils, declared the Scriptures to be the sole legitimate doctrinal authority, and proclaimed that salvation could be gained only by faith. That same year a last effort at reconciliation failed completely, and in June 1520 Luther was excommunicated by the pope.

Charles V, only recently crowned emperor and aware of Luther's increased following among the princes, afforded the rebellious monk an audience before the **Imperial Diet** at Worms in 1521 to hear his defense of statements against church teachings and papal authority. If Luther recanted, he could perhaps escape his excommunication and execution. After much discussion, when the Orator of the Empire finally asked if he was prepared to recant, Luther responded:

> Your Lordships demand a simple answer. Here it is, plain and unvarnished. Unless I am convicted of error by the testimony of Scripture or (since I put no trust in the unsupported authority of Pope or of councils, since it is plain that they have often erred and often contradicted themselves) by manifest reasoning I stand convicted by the Scriptures to which I have appealed, and my conscience is taken captive by God's word, I cannot and will not recant anything, for to act against our conscience is neither safe for us, nor open to us. On this I take my stand, I can do no other. God help me. Amen."[3]

The Diet finally declared him an outcast. Soon afterward, as he left Worms, Luther was secretly detained for his own protection in Wartburg (VART-burg) Castle by Elector Frederick of Saxony, his secular lord. He would not burn at the stake, as did John Hus, because he enjoyed substantial political and popular support. His message had been spread by the 300,000 copies of his 30 works printed between 1517 and 1520, and he was a German hero.

The Two Kingdoms: God and the State

At Wartburg Luther set his course for the rest of his life as he began organizing an evangelical church distinct from Rome. Although he denounced much of the structure, formality, and ritual of the Catholic Church, Luther spent much of his time after the Diet of Worms building a new church for his followers. It reflected his main theological differences with Rome but kept many traditional ideas and practices. The fundamental principle of the Lutheran creed was that salvation occurred through faith that Christ's sacrifice alone could wash away sin. This departed from the Catholic doctrine of salvation by faith and good works, which required conformance to prescribed dogma and participation in rituals. The Catholic Mass became the Lutheran Communion, involving all who attended services and requiring no priestly blessing to transform the bread and wine into Christ's body and blood, which in Lutheran theory automatically "coexisted" with the wafer and the wine. Other changes included church services in German instead of Latin, an emphasis on preaching, the abolition of monasteries, and the curtailment of formal ceremonies foreign to the personal experiences of ordinary people. The Lutheran Church claimed to be a "priesthood of all believers" in which each person could receive God directly or through the Scriptures. To that end, Luther translated the Bible from Latin into German and composed the sermons that would be repeated in hundreds of Lutheran pulpits all over Germany and Scandinavia.

He took off his clerical habit in 1523 and two years later married a former nun, Katherine von Bora, who bore him six children, raised his nieces and nephews, managed his household, secured his income, entertained his colleagues, and served as his supportive companion. Luther's ideas on marriage and Christian equality promised women new opportunities, which

---

infallibility of the pope—The belief that popes cannot be wrong in matters of faith and doctrine.

Imperial Diet—A meeting of the political and religious leaders of the various member states of the Holy Roman Empire.

were only partly realized. He stressed the importance of wives as marriage partners for both the clergy and the **laity**. Contrary to Catholic doctrine, he even condoned divorce in cases of adultery and desertion. During the 1520s, his views drew numerous women to Wittenberg, where they found refuge from monasteries or their Catholic husbands. Some Lutheran women became wandering preachers, but they evoked protests from male ministers and legal prohibitions from many German municipal councils, including those of Nuremberg and Augsburg. Although first teaching that women were equal to men in opportunities for salvation and in their family roles, in his later writings, Luther described them as subordinate to their husbands and not meant for the pulpit.

Lutheranism recognized two main human spheres of human obligation: The first and highest was to God; the other involved a subordinate loyalty to earthly governments, which also existed in accordance with God's will. Luther's idea of "two kingdoms," one of God and one of the world, fit well with contemporary political conditions, winning him support from German and Scandinavian rulers while connecting his movement to dynastic nationalism. Luther's political orientation was clearly revealed in 1522 and 1523 during a rebellion of German knights. When Lutheran support was not forthcoming, the rebellion was quickly crushed. Luther took no part in the struggle but was embarrassed by opponents who claimed his religion threatened law and order.

DOCUMENT
Sermon at the Castle Pleissenberg

Another example of Luther's political and social conservatism was provided by a general revolt of peasants and discontented townsmen in 1524 and 1525. Encouraged by Lutheran appeals for Christian freedom, the rebels drew up petitions asking for religious autonomy. At first Luther expressed sympathy for the requests, particularly for each congregation's right to select its own pastor. Then, as violence erupted throughout central Germany in April and May 1525, imperial and princely troops crushed the rebel armies, killing an estimated 90,000 insurgents. Luther had advised rebel leaders to obey the law as God's will; when they turned to war, he penned a virulent pamphlet, *Against the Thievish and Murderous . . . Peasants*. In it he called on the princes to "knock down, strangle, . . . stab, . . . and think nothing so venomous, pernicious, or Satanic as an insurgent."[4]

There was soon a struggle for religious control in Germany between the emperor and the Lutheran princes. When Catholics sought to impose conformity in Imperial Diets during the late 1520s, Lutheran leaders drew up a formal protest (hence the appellation *protestant*). After this Augsburg Confession (1530) was rejected, the Lutheran princes organized for defense in the Schmalkaldic League. Because Charles V was preoccupied with the French and the Turks, open hostilities were minimized, but a sporadic civil war dragged on until after Luther's death in 1546. It ended with the Peace of Augsburg in 1555, when the imperial princes were permitted to choose between Lutheranism and Catholicism in their state churches, thus increasing their independence of the emperor. In addition, Catholic properties confiscated before 1552 were retained by Lutheran principalities, which provided a means for financing their policies. Although no concessions were made to other protestant groups, such as the Calvinists, this treaty shifted the European political balance against the Empire and the church.

Outside Germany, Lutheranism furnished a religious stimulus for developing national monarchies in Scandinavia. There, as in Germany, rulers welcomed not only Lutheran religious ideas but also the chance to acquire confiscated Catholic properties. They appreciated having ministers who preached obedience to constituted secular authority. In Sweden, Gustavus Vasa (goos-TA-vus VAH-sah; 1523–1560) used Lutheranism to lead a successful struggle for Swedish independence from Denmark. In turn, the Danish king, who also ruled Norway, issued an ordinance in 1537 establishing the national Lutheran Church, with its bishops as salaried officials of the state. Throughout Eastern Europe, wherever there was a German community, the Lutheran church spread—for a brief time even threatening the supremacy of the Catholic Church in Poland and Lithuania.

HENRY VIII AND THE ANGLICAN REFORMATION

■ *What were the political considerations impelling Henry VIII to create the Anglican Church?*

England was affected by the same economic and social crises and changes of the fourteenth and fifteenth centuries as the rest of Europe. But unlike central Europe, England was one of the new Atlantic states characterized by national monarchies, centralized authority, and greater independence from the papacy. The Tudor dynasty adapted itself to the new conditions after the Hundred Years' War with France and the devastating War of the Roses, which destroyed much of the traditional nobility.

Legitimate Heirs and the True Church

During this time of difficult transition, it was necessary that each monarch raise a strong and healthy heir

---

laity—The community of believers in the Christian Church, served by the clergy, the trained and specialized leaders of the community.

to ensure the continuity of the dynasty and the strength of England. Henry VIII (1509–1547) became the heir to the English throne when his older brother Arthur died in 1502. It had not been expected that he would be king, and his education ran to that of a true Renaissance man. He showed talent in music, literature, philosophy, jousting, hunting, and theology. Not only did he become the king of England on his father's death in 1509, but he also soon married the woman who had been his brother's wife, Catherine of Aragon (1485–1536), thus continuing the dynastic alliance with Spain. Catherine was a cultured, strong, respected woman and devoted wife: she successfully conducted a war against Scotland when Henry was campaigning in France.

Henry was a devout Roman Catholic, who gained the title "Defender of the Faith" from the pope for a pamphlet he wrote denouncing Luther and his theology. However, his immediate problem in the 1520s was the lack of a male heir. After 11 years of marriage, he had only a sickly daughter and an illegitimate son. His queen, after four earlier pregnancies, gave birth to a stillborn son in 1518, and by 1527, when she was 42, Henry had concluded that she would have no more children. His only hope for the future of his dynasty seemed to be a new marriage and a new queen. This, of course, would require an annulment of his marriage to Catherine. In 1527 he appealed to the pope, asking for the annulment.

Normally, the request would probably have been granted; the situation, however, was not normal. Because she had been the wife of Henry's brother, Catherine's marriage to Henry had necessitated a papal dispensation, based on her oath that the first marriage had never been consummated. Now Henry professed concern for his soul, tainted by "living in sin" with Catherine. He also claimed that he was being punished, citing a passage in the Book of Leviticus that predicted childlessness for the man who married his dead brother's wife. The pope was sympathetic and certainly aware of an obligation to the king, who had strongly supported the church. However, granting the annulment would have been admission of papal error, perhaps even corruption, in issuing the earlier dispensation. Added to the Lutheran problem, this would have doubly damaged the papacy. A more immediate concern for Henry was Catherine's nephew. As the aunt of Charles V, whose armies occupied Rome in 1527, she was able to exert considerable pressure on the pope to refuse an **annulment**.

Holbein's portrait of Henry VIII, painted in 1542, shows a man sure of himself in his royal setting. He had by this time broken with Rome, married six times in pursuit of a legitimate male heir, and turned England into a major naval power. What the portrait does not show is all of the suffering and discord he left in his wake.

When the pope delayed a decision, Henry began to rally his support at home. During the three years after 1531, when Catherine saw him for the last time, Henry took control of affairs. Sequestering his daughter Mary (1516–1558) and his banished wife in separate castles, he forbade them from seeing each other. The king forced the clergy into proclaiming him head of a separate, English church "as far as the law of Christ allows," extracted from Parliament the authority to appoint bishops, and designated his willing tool Thomas Cranmer (1489–1556) as archbishop of Canterbury. In 1533 Cranmer pronounced Henry's marriage to Catherine invalid; at the same time, he legalized his union with Anne Boleyn (bo-LIN), a lady of the court who was carrying his unborn child, the future Elizabeth I. Henry even forced his daughter Mary to accept him as head of the church and to admit the illegality of her mother's marriage—by implication acknowledging her own illegitimacy. Parliament also ended all payment of revenues to Rome.

Now, having little other choice, the pope excommunicated Henry, making the breach official on both sides. On his side, Henry divided up the Church's properties—some 25 percent of the wealth of the realm—to distribute to the gentry to consolidate his domestic support. In 1539 Parliament completed its

---

annulment—A religious or political judgment that a marriage was/is not valid, and hence no longer existed/exists.

seizure of monastery lands and the wealth of pilgrimage sites such as Canterbury Cathedral. Meanwhile, Catholics such as the former chancellor and humanist Sir Thomas More (see p. 412), who refused to swear allegiance to the new order, were executed.

There had already been a strong underground resistance movement present in England even before Henry came to power. English theologians, beginning with John Wycliffe and his followers, played an active role in the intellectual and theological debates of the High Middle Age. During the fifteenth and first part of the sixteenth centuries there was an active underground church, the Lollards, in which lay people—especially women—played an important role. William Tyndale's (1494–1536) skillful translation of the New Testament, a work marked by Lutheran influences, served as the basis for the English Bible published in 1537, which made scripture available to all literate English-speaking people. This popular Protestantism was not at all close to the new Anglican Church, which brought about little change in doctrine or ritual. The Six Articles, Parliament's declaration of the new creed and ceremonies in 1539, reaffirmed most Catholic theology except papal supremacy.

Radical Protestants and Renewed Catholics

In his later years, after the decapitation of Anne Boleyn on charges of adultery in 1536 (the year that Catherine of Aragon also died), Henry grew increasingly suspicious of popular Protestantism, which was buttressed by reformist movements spreading into England and Scotland from the Continent. Further, he refused to legalize clerical marriage, which caused great hardships among many Anglican clergymen, including some bishops, and their wives and lashed out indiscriminately at those people such as the protestant Anne Ayscough who dared to question him.

In the decade after Henry's death in 1547, religious fanaticism brought social and political upheaval. For six years, during growing political corruption, extreme protestants ruled the country and dominated the frail young king, Edward VI (1547–1553), born of Henry's third wife Jane Seymour—who died in childbirth. His government was controlled by the Regency Council, dominated first by the duke of Somerset and then, after 1549, by his rival, the duke of Northumberland. The same mix of political opportunism and religious change continued as the council members enriched themselves and pursued their ambitions. At the same time, a radical form of Protestantism swept through many parishes. The government sought political support by courting the religious radicals: it repealed the Six Articles, permitted priests to marry, replaced the Latin service with Cranmer's English version, and adopted the Forty-Two Articles, the expression of extreme Protestantism.

When Edward died in 1553, Mary Tudor came to the throne and tried to restore Catholicism through harsh persecutions, which earned her the name "Bloody Mary" from Protestant historians. The new queen possessed many of the same admirable qualities of her mother, Catherine of Aragon: dignity, intelligence, compassion, and a strong moral sense. Her religious obsession, however, eventually cost her the support of a substantial number of her subjects. Her hopeless love for her Catholic husband, Philip II of Spain—who married her in 1554—led to her being seen as a puppet of Spanish diplomacy. She restored the Catholic Church service, proclaimed papal authority in her realm, and forged an alliance with Spain. In putting down the protestants, she burned 300 of them at the stake—among whom were Cranmer, two other bishops, and 55 women. Mary died pitifully, rejected by her husband and people, but steadfast in her hope to save English Catholicism. Leaving no heir, she was compelled to name Elizabeth, her half-sister, as her successor.

PROTESTANTISM FROM SWITZERLAND TO HOLLAND: ZWINGLI AND CALVIN

■ *Why were the protestants in the Rhine Valley so much more radical in their approaches than Luther or the Anglicans?*

A very different variety of church reforms took place in Switzerland and France. The leaders of these reforms were conscious of the state but not dominated by it, as the Anglicans were. Like the Lutherans, they were also concerned for the salvation of their souls, but in a much more doctrinal and often vindictive way. Calvinism was the most popular and the most conservative of the reforms, but there were many others, including multiple forms of **Anabaptism**. These movements went farther than Lutheranism and Anglicanism in rejecting Catholic dogma and ritual. Generally, they were opposed to monarchy, but their position did not become very apparent until they were deeply involved in religious wars after 1560, when they often found themselves under attack by both the Catholics and the Lutherans.

Anabaptism—A Protestant faith that holds that baptism and church membership come only when one is an adult. Anabaptists also tend to believe in a strict separation of church and state.

Document: Anne Ayscough (Mrs. Thomas Kyme), English Protestant Martyr

Anne Ayscough, the daughter of Sir William Ayscough, received a good education and became remarkably independent at a time when the normal expectation was that a woman's role was to look after the house and be able to entertain guests. She read voraciously, especially Tyndale's version of the New Testament, and participated vigorously in the theological controversies of her time. She did not like the papacy, nor did she much like Henry's VIII's pet theologians and their version of English Catholicism—the Anglican Church. Duty to her family forced her to marry a Catholic husband, but soon he was not pleased when she set out to spread the Gospels by reading from the Bible to the peasants—a practice later forbidden by the law of 1543. For Anne the issues were quite clear: "[T]he papists were the agents of Antichrist and would always be opposed to the Saints of God. . . . " In standing upon her own righteousness and excluding from her heart all love of her enemies, Anne Ayscough was very much a child of her age. In 1545 she was called to London to face charges of heresy. She was then tortured—the only woman in English history put on the rack, tried, and found guilty for her refusal to believe that the wafer literally becomes the body of Christ in the communion, a process called transubstantiation.

On the eve of her execution, she wrote: "O friend most dearly beloved in God, I marvel not a little what should move you to judge in me so slender a faith as to fear death, which is the end of all misery. In the Lord I desire you not believe of me such weakness. For I doubt it not but God will perform his work in me, like as he hath begun. I understand the Council is not a little displeased, that it should be reported abroad that I was racked in the Tower. They say now that what they did there was but to frighten me; whereby I perceive they are ashamed of their uncomely doings and fear much lest the King's majesty should have information thereof. Wherefore they do not want any man to tell it abroad. Well, their cruelty God forgive them."

At the same time, she wrote Henry VIII: "I Anne Ayscough, of good memory, although God hath given me the bread of adversity and the water of trouble (yet not so much as my sins have deserved), desire this to be known unto your Grace. Forasmuch as I am by the law condemned for an evil-doer, here I take heaven and earth to record that I shall die in my innocence. And according to what I have said first and will say last, I utterly abhor and detest all heresies. And as concerning the Supper of the Lord, I believe so much as Christ hath said, therein, which he confirmed with his most blessed blood, I believe so much as he willed me to follow, and I believe so much as the Catholic church of him doth teach. For I will not forsake the commandment of his holy lips. . . ."

And as she was taken out to be executed, her final prayer was written down: "O Lord, I have more enemies now than there be hairs on my head. Yet, Lord, let them never overcome me with vain words, but fight thus, Lord, in my stead, for on thee cast I my care. With all the spite they can imagine they fall upon me, which am thy poor creature. Yet, sweet Lord, let me pay no heed to them which are against me, for in thee is my whole delight. And, Lord, I heartily desire of thee, that thou wilt of thy most merciful goodness forgive them that violence which they do and have done unto me. Open also thou their blind hearts, that they may hereafter do that thing in thy sight, which is only acceptable before thee, and to set forth thy verity aright, without all vain fantasy of sinful men. So be it, O Lord, so be it."

Anne Ayscough was burned at the stake with four companions on July 16 1546. Already viewed as a heroine by many in England, she became the best known English martyr.

Questions to Consider

1. What was there in Anne Ayscough's views that provoked such a harsh response from the leaders of the English Church, such as putting her on the rack?
2. Why were heretics burned at the stake and not, for example, hanged, or decapitated?
3. What qualities earn a person such as Anne Ayscough the accolade of being a "martyr?" What is a martyr? Whom would you consider to be martyrs during the twentieth century?

From Derek Wilson, *A Tudor Tapestry: Men, Women and Society in Reformation England* (London: Heinemann, 1972), pp. 164, 229–232.

Ulrich Zwingli

Popular Protestantism arose early in Switzerland, where many of the same difficult conditions found in the German states favored its growth. During the late medieval period, the country prospered in the growing trade between Italy and Northern Europe. Busy Swiss craftsmen and merchants in Zurich, Bern, Basel, and Geneva suffered under their Habsburg overlords and by papal policies, particularly the sale of indulgences. In 1499 the Confederation of Swiss Cantons won independence from the Holy Roman Empire and the Habsburgs. To many Swiss, this was also the first step in repudiating outside authority.

The Swiss Reformation began in Zurich, shortly after Luther published his Theses at Wittenberg. It was led by Ulrich Zwingli (OOL-rikh ZWING-lee; 1484–1531), a scholar, priest, and former military chaplain, who persuaded the city council to create a regime of clergymen and magistrates to supervise government, religion, and individual morality. Zwingli agreed with Luther in repudiating papal in favor of scriptural authority. He simplified services, preached justification by faith, attacked monasticism, and opposed clerical celibacy. More rational than Luther, he was also more interested in practical reforms, going beyond Luther in advocating additional grounds for divorce and in denying any mystical conveyance of grace by baptism or communion; both, to Zwingli, were only symbols. These differences proved irreconcilable when Luther and Zwingli met to consider merging their movements in 1529.

As Zwingli's influence spread rapidly among the northern cantons, religious controversy separated north from south, rural from urban, and feudal overlords—both lay and ecclesiastical—from towns within their dominions. When, in the 1520s, Geneva repudiated its ancient obligations and declared its independence from the local bishop and the count of Savoy, the city became a hotbed of Protestantism, with preachers streaming in from Zurich. Zwingli was killed in the religious war of 1531, after which it was decided in the Second Peace of Kappel that each Swiss canton could choose its own religion.

John Calvin

Hoping to ensure the dominance of Protestantism in Geneva after the religious wars, local reformers invited John Calvin (1509–1564) to Geneva. Calvin arrived from Basel in 1536. He was an uncompromising French reformer and a formidable foe of the ungodly, but a caring colleague and minister to humble believers. His preaching, based on his study of theology in Paris and law in Orleans, ultimately won enough followers to make his church the official religion. From Geneva, the faith spread to Scotland, Hungary, France, Italy, and other parts of Europe after the early 1540s.

In Basel he had published the first edition of his *Institutes of the Christian Religion* (1536), a theological work that transformed the general Lutheran doctrines into a rational legal system based around the concept of predestination. It also earned Calvin his invitation to Geneva. His original plan for a city government there called for domination by the clergy and banishment of all dissidents. This aroused a storm of opposition from Anabaptists—who believed in adult baptism and separation of church and state—and from the more worldly portion of the population, and Calvin was forced into exile. He moved on to Strasbourg where he associated with other reformers who helped him refine his ideas. Calvin's second regime at Geneva after 1541 involved a long struggle with the city council. His proposed ordinances for the Genevan Church gave the clergy full control over moral and religious behavior, but the council modified the docu-

Margaret of Navarre, a supporter of Protestantism, was the author of the Heptameron, *a collection of tales modeled on Boccaccio's* Decameron.

ment, placing all appointments and enforcement of law under its jurisdiction.

Although recognizing the Bible as supreme law and the *Institutes* as a model for behavior, the Geneva city council did not always act on recommendations from the Consistory, Calvin's supreme church committee. For the next 14 years Calvin fought against public criticism and opposition in the council. He gradually increased his power, however, through support from the protestant refugees who poured into the city. His influence climaxed after a failed "revolt of the godless" in 1555. From that year until his death in 1564, he dominated the council, ruling Geneva with an iron hand, within the letter, but not the spirit, of the original ordinances.

Particularly in the later period, the Consistory apprehended violators of religious and moral law, sending its members into households to check every detail of private life. Offenders were reported to secular magistrates for punishment. Relatively light penalties were imposed for missing church, laughing during the service, wearing bright colors, dancing, playing cards, or swearing. Religious dissent, blasphemy, mild heresies, and adultery received heavier punishments, including banishment. Witchcraft and serious cases of heresy led to torture, and then execution—sometimes as many as a dozen or more a year. Michael Servetus (SEHR-vee-tus; 1511–1553), a Spanish theologian-philosopher and refugee from the Catholic Inquisition, was burned for heresy in Calvin's Geneva because he had denied the doctrine of the trinity.

Calvin accepted Luther's insistence on justification by faith; like Luther, he saw Christian life as a constant struggle against the devil, and he expected a coming divine retribution, an end-time, when God would redress the evils that were increasing on every side. Calvin also agreed with Luther in seeing God's power as a relief for human anxiety and a source of inner peace. Both reformers believed man to be totally depraved, but Calvin placed greater emphasis on this point, at the same time emphasizing God's immutable will and purpose. If Calvinism, to human minds, seemed contradictory in affirming man's sinful nature and his creation in God's image, this connection only proved that God's purposes were absolutely beyond human understanding. For depraved humans, God required faith and obedience, not understanding.

DOCUMENT
Calvin on Predestination

God's omnipotence was Calvin's cardinal principle. He saw all of nature as governed by a divinely ordained order, discernible to man but governed by laws that God could set aside in effecting miracles as he willed. Carried to its logical conclusion, such ideas produced Calvin's doctrine of predestination.

By predestination we mean the eternal decree of God, by which he determined with himself whatever he wished to happen with regard to every man. All are not created on equal terms, but some are preordained to eternal life, others to eternal damnation; and, accordingly, as each has been created for one or other of these ends, we say that he has been predestined to life or to death....[5]

In Calvin's grand scheme, as laid out precisely in the *Institutes*, his church served to aid the elect in honoring God. The human purpose was not to win salvation—for this had already been determined—but to honor God and prepare the elect for salvation. As communities of believers, congregations were committed to constant war against Satan. They also functioned to spread the Word (Scripture), educate youth, and alleviate suffering among the destitute.

Calvin was particularly ambivalent in his views on government. Ministers of the church were responsible for advising secular authorities on religious policies and resisting governments that violated God's laws. He believed that all rulers were responsible to God and subject to God's vengeance. But throughout the 1540s, when he was hoping to gain the support of monarchs, he emphasized the Christian duty of obedience to secular authorities. Even then, however, he advised rulers to seek counsel from church leaders, and he ordered the faithful, among both the clergy and the laity, to disregard any government that denied them freedom in following Christ. Although willing to support any political system that furthered the true faith, Calvin always preferred representative government.

Another ambiguity in Calvin's social thought involved his attitude toward women. Unlike Catholic theologians, he did not cast women in an inferior light. In his mind, men and women were equally full of sin, but they were also equal in their chance for salvation. As he sought recruits, he stressed women's right to read the Bible and participate in church services. At the same time he saw women as naturally subordinate to their husbands in practical affairs, including the conduct of church business.

Before the Peace of Augsburg, Calvinism was strongest in France, the reformer's own homeland, where the believers were known as *Huguenots*. Calvinism made gains elsewhere but did not win political power. In Italy, the duchess of Ferrara installed the Calvinist church service in her private chapel and protected Calvinist refugees. Strasbourg in the 1530s was a free center for protestant reformers such as Matthew Zell and his wife Katherine, who befriended many Calvinist preachers, including Martin Bucer (BOOT-sur), a missionary to England during the reign of Edward VI. In the same period, John Knox spread the Calvinist message in Scotland.

More extreme than Calvinism were many divergent protestant splinter groups, each pursuing its own "inner lights." Some saw visions of the world's end, some advocated a Christian community of shared wealth, some opposed social distinctions and economic inequalities, some—these Anabaptists—repudiated infant baptism as a violation of Christian responsibility, and some denied the need for any clergy. Most of the sects emphasized biblical literalism and direct, emotional communion between the individual and God. The majority of them were indifferent or antagonistic to secular government, many favored pacifism and substitution of the church for the state.

Women were prominent among the sects, although they were usually outnumbered by men. These women were known for their biblical knowledge, faith, courage, and independence. They helped found religious communities, wrote hymns and religious tracts, debated theology, and publicly challenged the authorities. Some preached and delivered prophecies, although such activities were suppressed by male ministers by the end of the century. More women than men endured torture and suffered martyrdom. Their leadership opportunities and relative freedoms in marriage, compared to women of other religions, were bought at the high price of hardship and danger.

Persecution of the sects arose largely because of their radical ideas. But Catholics and other protestants who opposed them usually cited two revolutionary actions. The first came when some radical preachers took part in the German peasants' revolt of the 1520s and shared in the savage punishments that followed. The second came in 1534 when a Catholic army besieged Münster (MIUN-ster).

Thousands of recently arrived Anabaptist extremists had seized control and expelled dissenters from this German city near the southern Netherlands. Following their radical theology, the "regime of saints" took private property, allowed polygamy, and planned to convert the world. John of Leyden (LI-den), a former Dutch tailor who claimed divine authority, headed a terrorist regime during the final weeks before the city fell. Those who survived the fall of the city suffered horrible tortures and then execution.

Among the most damaging charges against the Münster rebels were their alleged sexual excesses and the dominant role played by women in this immorality. Such charges were mostly distortions. The initiation of **polygamy,** justified by references to the Old Testament, was a response to problems arising from a shortage of men, hundreds of whom had fled the city. Many other men were killed or injured in the fighting. Thus, the city leaders required women to marry so that they could be protected and controlled by husbands. Most Anabaptist women accepted the requirement as a religious duty. Although some paraded through the streets, shouting religious slogans, the majority prepared meals, did manual labor on the defenses, fought beside their men, and died in the fighting or at the stake. Most of the original, Catholic, Münster women, however, fiercely resisted forced marriage, choosing instead jail or execution.

Like Calvin later in Geneva, the Anabaptist regime of John of Leyden closely monitored and controlled private life and public behavior. Their theocratic state found its laws in Scripture. In looking at the laws of the city, capital punishment was applied in the following cases:

> *Whoever curses God and his holy Name or his Word shall be killed (Lev. 24).*
>   *No one shall curse governmental authority (Ex. 22, Deut. 17), on pain of death.*
>   *Both parties who commit adultery shall die (Ex. 20, Lev. 20, Matt. 5).*
>   *. . . Whoever disobeys these commandments and does not truly repent, shall be rooted out of the people of God, with ban and sword, through the divinely ordained governmental authority.*[6]

For more than a century, memories of Münster plagued the protestant sects in general. Although most did not go to the extremes of "the saints," they were almost immediately driven underground throughout Europe, and their persecution continued long after they had abandoned violence. In time, they dispersed over the Continent and to North America as Mennonites, Quakers, and Baptists, to name only a few denominations. Given their suffering and oppression, voices of the radicals were among the first raised for religious liberty. Their negative experience with governments made them even more suspicious of authority than the Calvinists were. In both the Netherlands and England, they participated in political revolutions and helped frame the earliest demands for constitutional government, representative institutions, and civil liberties.

With the exception of Henry VIII's political reformation, the reformers, going back to Wycliffe and Hus and moving on through Luther and Calvin and the Anabaptists, did not believe that they were creating something new. Instead, they were trying to reclaim the purity of the early church.

---

polygamy—A type of marriage in which a husband has more than one wife.

REFORM IN THE CATHOLIC CHURCH

■ *How successful was the Catholic Church in dealing with the problems that faced it?*

The era of the Protestant Reformation was also a time of rejuvenation for the Roman Catholic Church. This revival was largely caused by the same conditions that had sparked Protestantism. Throughout the fifteenth century, many sincere and devout Catholics had recognized a need for reform, and they had begun responding to the abuses in their church long before Luther acted at Wittenberg. Almost every variety of reform opinion developed within the Catholic Church. Erasmus, More, and other Christian humanists provided precedents for Luther, but none followed him out of the Catholic Church. In a category of his own was Savonarola (sa-vo-na-RO-la; 1452–1498), a Dominican friar, puritan, and mystic who ruled Florence during the last four years before his death. This "Catholic Calvin" consistently railed against the worldly living and sinful luxuries he found: His criticisms of the pope and the clergy were

This map illustrates the geographical patterns of the Protestant Reformation. Lutheranism spread through German-speaking areas along the Baltic Sea but rarely crossed the Rhine River. The spread of Calvinism defies linguistic explanation.

much more severe than Luther's. At the other extreme of the Church was Cardinal Ximenes (1437–1517) in Spain, who carried out his own Reformation by disciplining the clergy, compiling the Complutensian Bible—eliminating many of the errors made by medieval copyists and instilling a new spirit of dedication into the monastic orders.

After the protestant revolt began, the primary Catholic reformer was Alessandro Farnese (far-NAY-se), Pope Paul III (1534–1549). Coming into office at a time when the church appeared ready to collapse, Paul struggled to overcome the troubled legacy of his Renaissance predecessors and restore integrity to the papacy. Realizing that issues raised by the protestants would have to be resolved and problems within the church corrected, he attacked the indifference, corruption, and vested interests of the clerical organization. In pursuing these reforms he appointed a commission, which reported the need for correcting such abuses as the worldliness of bishops, the traffic in benefices (church appointments with guaranteed incomes), and the transgressions of some cardinals. Their recommendations led Paul to call a church council, an idea that he continued to press against stubborn opposition for more than ten years.

When Paul died in 1549, he had already set the Roman Church on a new path, although his proposed church council, the Council of Trent, had only begun its deliberations. Perhaps his greatest contribution was his appointment of worthy members to the College of Cardinals, filling that body with eminent scholars and devout stewards of the church. As a result of his labors, the cardinals elected a succession of later popes who were prepared, intellectually and spiritually, to continue the process of regeneration.

The spirit of reform was reflected in a number of new Catholic clerical orders that sprang up in the early sixteenth century. Some of these worked with the poor, ministered to the sick, and taught. Among the better known were the Carmelites founded by St. Teresa of Avila (1515–1582) whose determination and selfless devotion became legendary. She inspired mystical faith and reforming zeal in written works such as *Interior Castle* and *The Ladder of Perfection*.

Rules for Thinking with the Church

The most significant of the new orders was the Society of Jesus, whose members are known as Jesuits. Organized along military lines, with their founder, the Spaniard Ignatius Loyola (1491–1556) as general and the pope as commander in chief, the Jesuits were an army of soldiers, sworn to follow orders and defend the faith. As preachers, teachers, confessors,

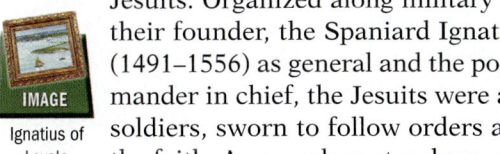
Ignatius of Loyola

organizers, diplomats, and spies, they took the field everywhere, founding schools and colleges, serving as missionaries on every continent, and working their way into government wherever possible. Their efforts were probably most responsible for the decided check that Protestantism received after the 1560s, as they zealously defended Catholicism in France, pushed the protestants out of Poland, and reclaimed southern Germany. Jesuit missions also helped Spain and Portugal develop their global empires.

Pope Paul's reform initiatives were given form by the great multinational church council, the first since 1415, which met in three sessions between 1545 and 1563 in the northern Italian city of Trent. Devoting much attention to the external struggle against Protestantism, the council also sought to eliminate internal abuses by ordering changes in church discipline and administration. It strictly forbade absenteeism, false indulgences, selling church offices, and secular pursuits by the clergy. Bishops were ordered to supervise their clergies—priests as well as monks and nuns—and to fill church positions with competent people. The Council of Trent also provided that more seminaries be established for educating priests while instructing the clergy to set examples and preach frequently to their flocks.

Rejecting all compromise, the Council of Trent retained the basic tenets of Catholic doctrine, including the necessity of good works as well as faith for salvation, the authority of church law and traditions, the sanctity of all seven sacraments, the use of only Latin in the Mass, and the spiritual value of indulgences, pilgrimages, veneration of saints, and the cult of the Virgin. The council also strengthened the power of the papacy. It defeated all attempts to place supreme church authority in any general council. When the final session voted that none of its decrees were valid without papal approval, the church became more than ever an absolute monarchy.

The full significance of Trent became evident after the 1560s when the Catholic reaction to Protestantism acquired a new vigor and militancy. Having steeled itself from within, the church and its shock troops, the Jesuits, went to war against protestants and other heretics. The new crusade was both open and secret. In Spain, Italy, and the Netherlands, the Inquisition more than ever before became the dreaded scourge of protestants and other heretics. Jesuit universities, armed with the Index of Forbidden Works, trained scholars and missionaries who would serve as priests and organizers in protestant countries such as England. Many died as martyrs, condemned by protestant tribunals, while others suffered similar fates meted out by pagans whom they sought to convert in America and Asia. But

The devotional works and personal example of St. Teresa of Avila, mystic and visionary, inspired the rebirth of Spanish Catholicism. In 1970 she was proclaimed a doctor of the church, the first woman to be so honored. The sculpture here, The Ecstasy of St. Teresa *(1645–1652), is by the Italian baroque artist Giovanni Bernini.*

Protestantism made no more significant gains in Catholic lands after Trent. Indeed, after Trent, the Catholic Church became a global church.

CONCLUSION

In could be argued that Europe's Golden Age of the Renaissance was no more than a recapitulation of that which had gone before. By resurrecting the gifts of the Greeks and Romans and learning from the science and history of the Arabs, the elites who participated in the movement were, in fact, reactionaries. But in looking back, they invented new and demanding methods of research, and the most important legacy they revived was the old Greek message that "Man Can Know." This individual liberation could be seen immediately in the artistic and architectural works as well as in the writings of Lorenzo da Valla and Machiavelli. The new humanism was not necessarily intellectually superior to the best of the scholastic thinking. However, it allowed new questions to be posed in critical ways.

Christianity had always been a religion in ferment, and the authorities in Rome and Constantinople after the Seventh Ecumenical Council had sought to stamp out those who were not in accord with orthodoxy. Luther, in many ways, echoed the thoughts of John Wycliffe and John Hus. He succeeded where they failed because of the more favorable political context he found himself in.

In many ways, the Protestant Reformation and Catholic Counter-Reformation helped create the modern world. By breaking the religious monopoly of European Catholicism, Lutheranism and Anglicanism assisted the growth of northern European national monarchies. Later, the Puritan values and "work ethic" of Calvinism helped justify the profit-seeking activities of the middle classes. Even the Catholic Church itself was transformed by the various protestant challenges. After the Council of Trent, the Catholic Counter-Reformation checked the spread of Protestantism, and the Roman Church emerged strengthened to protect and advance itself. Because the Reformation and Counter-Reformation occurred at the same time of the development of the state system (see Chapter 16), faith came to play an integral, and often dangerous, role in politics until 1648.

Because these momentous changes coincided with the beginnings of the European explorations around the world (see Chapter 15), and the construction of Portuguese, Dutch, Spanish, French, and English empires, protestant and Catholic missionaries were able to spread their messages around the globe. Political and economic imperialism were accompanied by a religious imperialism. The Christians had no doubt they were saving the heathen from hell, but this well-intentioned zealousness had mixed, and sometimes destructive, results to the peoples of Asia, Africa, and the Americas touched by European expansion.

Suggestions for Web Browsing

You can obtain more information about topics included in this chapter at the websites listed below. See also the companion website that accompanies this text, **http://www.ablongman.com/brummett**, which contains an online study guide and additional resources.

Italian Renaissance Art Project
http://www.italian-art.org

> One of the very best and most comprehensive sites for reproductions of the major paintings, works of sculpture, and architecture from the Renaissance. An amazing resource of the study of Renaissance art.

Web Museum, Paris: Italian Renaissance (1420–1600)
http://www.ibiblio.org/wm/paint/tl/it-ren/

> A useful site for anyone interested in the art of the Italian Renaissance, especially the work of Leonardo da Vinci, Raphael, and Michelangelo.

Florence in the Renaissance
http://www.mega.it/eng/egui/epo/secrepu.htm

> A history of the Florentine Republic, with details about the city's influence on Renaissance culture.

Sistine Chapel
http://www.christusrex.org/www1/sistine/0-Tour.html

> Photo collection depicting all facets of the Sistine Chapel, including images of Michelangelo's ceiling.

Michelangelo
http://www.michelangelo.com/buonarroti.html

> Featuring the works of the artist beautifully illustrated and annotated. An outstanding site.

The Louvre
http://www.paris.org/Musees/Louvre

> Website for one of the world's greatest museums offers many paths to some of the most beautiful Renaissance art in existence.

Medieval and Renaissance Women's History
http://womenshistory.about.com/od/medieval/

> Site serves as a directory for a wide variety of discussions and references about Renaissance women painters, writers, and women of social standing.

Creative Impulse: Renaissance
http://history.evansville.net/renaissa.html

> The University of Evansville's outstanding series of sites on Western civilization includes this compendium of art, history, and descriptions of daily life and culture. Includes one of the very best compilations of other sites dealing with the Renaissance.

Medieval and Renaissance Fact and Fiction
http://www.angelfire.com/mi/spanogle/medieval.html

> A useful guide to Web resources for students interested in the history, culture, and literature of the Renaissance.

Northern Renaissance ArtWeb
http://www.msu.edu/~cloudsar/nrweb.htm

A collection of links for exploring the artists and literature of the Northern Renaissance.

Internet Medieval History Sourcebook: Protestant and Catholic Reformations
http://www.fordham.edu/halsall/sbook1y.html

Extensive online source for links about the Protestant and Catholic Reformations, including primary documents by or about precursors and papal critics, Luther, and Calvin and details about the Reformations themselves.

Martin Luther
http://www.wittenberg.de/e/seiten/personen/luther.html

This brief biography of Martin Luther includes links to his Ninety-Five Theses and images of related historical sites.

Tudor England
http://englishhistory.net/tudor.html/

Site detailing life in Tudor England includes biographies, maps, important dates, architecture, and music, including sound files.

Lady Jane Grey
http://www.ladyjanegrey.org/

A biography of the woman who would be queen of England for nine days, and a general history of the time.

Literature and Film

One of the best novels dealing with the Renaissance is Irving Stone, *The Agony and the Ecstasy: A Biographical Novel of Michelangelo* (New American Library, 1996). An outstanding account of the past and present of Florence is given by Mary McCarthy in *The Stones of Florence* (Harvest Books, 2002). There are also many excellent videos available on the art and architecture of the Renaissance. Some of the more notable are *The Art of the Western World: Early and High Renaissance: Realms of Light* (Kultur Video, 1994); *Leonardo Da Vinci: Renaissance Man to the World* (Madacy Entertainment, 1997); *The Art of Renaissance Science: Galileo and Perspective*, by Joseph W. Dauben for Science Television (1991); and *Florence: Cradle of the Renaissance* (Museum City Video, 1992).

The politics of the time provide a rich resource for novels. The activities of this time attracted the best attentions of Alexandre Dumas. Writing about events in France, he published *The Two Dianas*, (dealing with the time of Francis I), *The Page of the Duke of Savoy* (touching the time of the Emperor Charles V), *Ascanio* (France in the middle of the century), and *Marguerite de Valois* (touching the civil wars)—and this is only an incomplete list. Mark Twain wrote about the time of Edward VI in *The Prince and the Pauper*. More recently, Robin Maxwell sheds some light on the reign of Henry VIII in *The Secret Diary of Anne Boleyn: A Novel* (Scribner, 1998).

Filmmakers have been equally attracted to the period, especially the English scene. *A Man for All Seasons* (Columbia/Tristar, 1966), directed by Fred Zinnemann, is a fine telling of the story of Sir Thomas More. Queen Elizabeth has been the subject of films throughout the twentieth century, including *Elizabeth* (Umvd, 1998), directed by Shekhar Kapur, and indirectly in Academy Award winner *Shakespeare in Love* (Miramax, 1998), directed by John Madden. A film dealing with the period after Henry VIII is *Lady Jane* (Paramount, 1985), directed by Trevor Nunn. The 1933 film, *The Private Life of Henry VIII* (AAE Films), directed by Alexander Korda, is worth seeing. From the continent, *The Return of Martin Guerre* (Fox Lorber, 1982), directed by Daniel Vigne, does justice to Natalie Zemon Davis's fine monograph. The film of the life of *Martin Luther* (VCI Home Video, 1953) is a revealing look at the reformer.

Suggestions for Reading

Johnathan Zophy, *A Short History of Renaissance and Reformation Europe*, 2nd ed. (Prentice Hall, 1998) and John Hale, *The Civilization of Europe in the Renaissance* (Scribner, 1994) are both excellent introductions to the period. Jacob Burckhardt, *The Civilization of the Renaissance in Italy*, 2 Vols. (Torchbooks, 1958), first published in 1860, inaugurated the view that the Italian Renaissance of the fourteenth and fifteenth centuries was a momentous turning point in the history of Western civilization. The editors of this edition maintain that Burckhardt's major interpretations remain valid. Donald R. Kelley, *Renaissance Humanism* (Twayne, 1991), and Brian P. Copenhaver, *Renaissance Philosophy* (Oxford University Press, 1992) are excellent surveys. Katharina M. Wilson, ed., *Women Writers of the Renaissance and Reformation* (University of Georgia Press, 1987), is an excellent study of a neglected subject. John White, *Art and Architecture in Italy, 1250–1400*, 3rd ed. (Yale University Press, 1993) is an excellent overview. See also Charles Seymour Jr., *Sculpture in Italy, 1400–1500* (Yale University Press, 1994). Ross King, *Brunelleschi's Dome* (Walker, 2000), is an excellent account of the construction of the famous Florentine's work. Also, Silvio Bedini, *The Pope's Elephant* (Penguin, 2000), is a delightful account of Pope Leo X and his court.

A fascinating study of the attitudes of the Christian laity during the Reformation period can be found in Keith Thomas, *Religion and the Decline of Magic: Studies in Popular Beliefs in Sixteenth and Seventeenth Century England* (Oxford University Press, 1997). A useful context to the religious upheavals of the time is given by John Bossy, *Christianity in the West, 1400–1700* (Oxford University Press, 1985). On the impact of John Hus, see Thomas A. Fudge, *The Magnificent Ride: The First Reformation in Hussite Bohemia* (Ashgate Publishing, 1998). The general background of the Reformation is covered well in Steven E. Ozment, *Protestants: The Birth of a Revolution* (Doubleday, 1992). Brad S. Gregory, *Salvation at Stake: Christian Martyrdom in Early Modern Europe* (Harvard University Press, 2000), is a distinguished work of scholarship that takes the martyrs of the time at their word. Richard Marius, *Martin Luther: The Christian Between God and Death* (Belknap Press of Harvard University Press, 1999), is a superb new study of Luther to 1526. The context for the English Reformation is provided by Richard H. Britnell in *The Closing of the Middle Ages: England, 1471–1529* (Blackwell, 1997). Ulrich Gabler gives a thorough background of Ulrich Zwingli's place in history in his *Huldrych Zwingli: His Life and Work* (Clark, 1995).

William J. Bouwsma, *John Calvin* (Oxford University Press, 1988), is a scholarly portrayal of Calvin's human side, emphasizing his inner conflict against the humanistic trend of his time. On the "left wing" of Protestantism, Anthony Arthur's *The Tailor-King: The Rise and Fall of the Anabaptist Kingdom of Münster* (St. Martin's Press, 1999) is a first-rate history of the radical Reformation city-state in northern Germany. John C. Olin places the Catholic response in perspective in *The Catholic Reformation: From Savonarola to Ignatius Loyola* (Fordham University Press, 1993). R. Po-chia Hsia, *The World of Catholic Renewal 1540–1770* (Cambridge University Press, 1998), is an innovative study of the history of the Catholic Church from the run up to the Council of Trent to the suppression of the Jesuits.

CHAPTER 15

The Development of the European State System, 1300–1650

CHAPTER CONTENTS

- Politics in an Age of Crisis, 1300–1500
  - **DOCUMENT:** *The Trial of Joan of Arc*
  - **DISCOVERY THROUGH MAPS:** *A Pilgrim's Map of Canterbury*
- The Religious-Political Fusion
- Wars of Religions: The Spanish Habsburgs' Quest for European Hegemony, 1556–1598
- Orthodox Europe: Russian Consolidation and Ottoman Expansion
- The Austrian Habsburgs' Drive for Superiority and the Thirty Years' War
  - **DOCUMENT:** *Simplicissimus on the Horrors of the Thirty Years' War*

1300

1305–1377 Babylonian Captivity of the church; papacy under French influence

1337–1453 Hundred Years' War between England and France

1350

1356 Golden Bull regulates the election of German emperors

1450

1455–1485 Wars of the Roses in England

1479 Ferdinand and Isabella begin joint rule in Spain

1492 Spain conquers Granada, unifies Spanish nation

1500

1526 Ottomans defeat Hungarians at Mohacs

1550

1556–1598 Reign of Philip II of Spain

1560s Ivan the Terrible wages war against disobedient boyars

1561–1593 Religious wars in France

1564 Start of Dutch Revolt

1571 Spanish and Venetian navy defeat Ottomans at Lepanto

1587 Dutch Republic formed

1588 English defeat Spanish Armada

1600

1618–1648 Thirty Years' War

1648 Peace of Westphalia

For the greater part of the period between 1300 and 1500, Europe was militarily and economically inferior to other world civilizations. Europeans were no match for the Turkish armies, did not possess the wealth of China or India, and lacked the centralized efficiency of the Incas. From 1500 to 1650, however, the balance of military and economic power began to change, and Europe began its global expansion, a process that would continue until 1914.

Three influences contributed to this expansion. We have already discussed two of them: the changes in European thought coming out of the Renaissance and the Reformation (see Chapter 14). The third factor in the increase in European power came in the development of the nation-state system.

State structures began to be seen during the origins of modern civilizations, and the variety of state systems throughout history ranges from despotism, to empire, to religious states, to city-states, to loose federations. These states all share the same qualities: they have defined boundaries, possess the power to tax, and monopolize force. As one of the most influential analysts of the origins and dominance of the nation-state system, Charles Tilly, once noted "war made the state, and the state made war." In the thirteenth century, the most successful form of the state, the nation-state emerged, largely sparked by political opposition to the claims of papal power.

Until 1789, the typical European nation-state was inhabited in large part by people of a similar ethnic and linguistic background (the nation) and led by a king or queen who embodied the state. Tilly indicates that the nation-state succeeded because of its capacity to profit from the rise of capitalism and to mobilize the resources within its boundary to fight wars. Some scholars find the approach of linking the changes in military technology to state development to be simplistic. But it cannot be denied that as the age of gunpowder warfare arrived in the fifteenth century, a new infrastructure was demanded to support the standing army and arms factories needed to compete in the international state system. This military efficiency combined with the scientific advances coming out of the new ways of thinking and religious zeal helped propel Europe to a world force.[1]

POLITICS IN AN AGE OF CRISIS: 1300–1500

■ *How did the crisis posed by the Black Death and its consequences change European politics?*

Europe saw many changes during the final two centuries of the late Middle Ages, some disastrous, some constructive. The suffering produced by the Black Death (bubonic plague), famine, and economic depression took a massive toll on the population (see Chapter 14) and was compounded by a number of destructive wars. Underway at the same time, however, were political changes that would have lasting effects on the growth and expansion of European power.

England and France: The Hundred Years' War

Nation-making in both England and France was greatly affected by the long conflict that colored much of both nations' history during the fourteenth and fifteenth centuries. The Hundred Years' War (1337–1453) had its origins in a fundamental conflict between the English kings, who claimed much of French territory as theirs, and the French monarchs, whose ultimate goal was a centralized France under the direct rule of the monarchy at Paris.

Another cause was the clash of French and English economic interests in Flanders. This region was falling more and more under French control, to the frustration of both the English wool-growers, who supplied the great Flemish woolen industry, and the

A fifteenth-century portrait of Joan of Arc in battle dress. After leading the French to victory at Orléans in 1429, she was captured by the English, tried and convicted of witchcraft and heresy, and burned at the stake in 1431. The French king, Charles VII, whose kingdom she had helped save, did nothing to rescue her.

Medieval Politics, 1300–1500

1337–1453	Hundred Years' War between France and England
1356	Golden Bull regulates the election of German emperors
1386	Unification of Poland and Lithuania
1454	Treaty of Lodi brings peace to Italian city-states
1455–1485	Wars of the Roses: civil war in England
1479	Marriage of Ferdinand of Aragon and Isabella of Castile
1492	Spain conquers Granada, unifies Spanish nation
1494	France invades Italy

English king, whose income came in great part from duties on wool.

The first years of warfare witnessed impressive English victories. With no thought of strategy, the French knights charged the enemy and then engaged in hand-to-hand fighting. But the English had learned more effective methods. Their greatest weapon was the longbow. Six feet long and made of yew wood, the longbow shot steel-tipped arrows that were dangerous at 400 yards and deadly at 100. The usual English plan of battle called for the knights to fight dismounted. Protecting them was a forward wall of bowmen just behind a barricade of iron stakes planted in the ground to slow the enemy's cavalry charge. By the time the French cavalry reached the dismounted knights, the remaining few French were easily killed.

The revival of the French military effort and a rebirth of national spirit is associated with Joan of Arc, who inspired a series of French victories. Moved by inner voices that she believed divine, Joan persuaded the

Document: The Trial of Joan of Arc

Joan of Arc (1412?–1431) is without doubt one of the most remarkable figures in European history. At the age of 13, Joan was hearing the voices of her "saints," who instructed her to come to the aid of the heir to the French throne and win for him a victory over the English at Orléans. The victory was won, Charles became king, and promptly turned his back on Joan, who was captured by the English and put on trial as a witch, a heretic, and a transvestite, since she now preferred to wear men's clothes even off the battlefield.

The following firsthand accounts were recorded by men who were witness to her trial and ultimate condemnation and execution:

Joan was dressed in men's clothes, that is, a tunic, a cape, and a short robe and other men's clothes, a costume that on our orders she had previously put aside, and had taken on women's clothes. And so we interrogated her to learn when and for what reason she had once more assumed men's clothes: "I did it on my own will," Joan declared; "I took it again because it was more lawful and convenient than to have women's clothes because I am with men; I began to wear them again because what was promised me was not observed, to wit that I should go to mass and receive the body of Christ and be freed from these irons.... I would rather die than stay in these irons; but if it is permitted for me to go to mass, and if I could be freed of these irons, and if I could be put in a decent prison and if I could have a woman to help me [her expression, *avoir femme*, is written on the minutes but not on the official transcript of the trial], I would be good and do what the church wishes."

"Since Thursday, have you heard the voices of St. Catherine and St. Margaret?" [Cauchon asked.]

"Yes."

"What have they told you?"

"God has expressed through St. Catherine and St. Margaret His great sorrow at the strong treason to which I consented in abjuring and making a revocation to save my life, and said that I was damning myself to save my life."

In the margin of the account, the author of this account wrote: "A deadly reply."

Shortly before her execution, another account of a conversation with Joan was recorded by a Dominican monk who visited her very shortly before her death:

The day that Joan was abandoned to secular judgment and delivered to be burned, I found myself in the morning in the prison with Friar Martin Ladvenu, whom the bishop of Beauvais had sent to tell her of her coming death and to induce her to true contrition and penance, and also to hear her confession, which Ladvenu did very carefully and charitably. And when he announced to the poor woman the death that she was to die that day, which her judges had ordered, and when she had understood and heard the hard and cruel death that was coming, she began to cry out sorrowfully and pitiably to tear and pull her hair. "Alas! That they treat me so horribly and cruelly that my body, clean and whole, which was never corrupted, should be today consumed and reduced to ashes! Ah! I would prefer to be beheaded seven times than to be burned like that! Alas! If I had been in an ecclesiastical prison to which I submitted myself, and if I had been guarded by men of the church, not by my enemies and adversaries, it would not have turned out for me as miserably as it has. Ah! I protest before God, the Great Judge, the great wrongs and grievances that they have done me." She then made marvelous complaint in that place of the oppression and violences that had been done to her in prison by the jailers and by the others they had made enter against her.

After these complaints, the bishop arrived, to whom she said immediately: "Bishop, I die because of you." He began to remonstrate with her, saying: "Ah, Joan, take it patiently, you will die because you have not held to what you promised us and because you return to your first witchcraft." And the poor Maid answered him: "Alas! If you had put me in the prison of a church court and handed me over to the hands of competent and agreeable ecclesiastical caretakers, this would not have happened to me. That is why I complain of you before God." That being done, I went outside and heard no more.

Questions to Consider

1. Do you feel that these accounts of Joan's actions and thoughts as she approached her execution are trustworthy? Do you think that the recorders are unbiased, or swayed toward or against her?

2. What image of Joan is created by these accounts? Does she seem to be a deluded peasant girl, a mystic visionary, or a rational martyr?

3. Are these firsthand accounts of value in illuminating Joan as a historical figure, or do they add to Joan's status as an almost mythological symbol of French resistance to the English?

From Regine Pernoud and Marie Veronique Clin, *Joan of Arc: Her Story,* trans. Jeremy duQuesnay Adams (St. Martin's Press, 1998), pp. 132–133.

Discovery Through Maps

A Pilgrim's Map of Canterbury

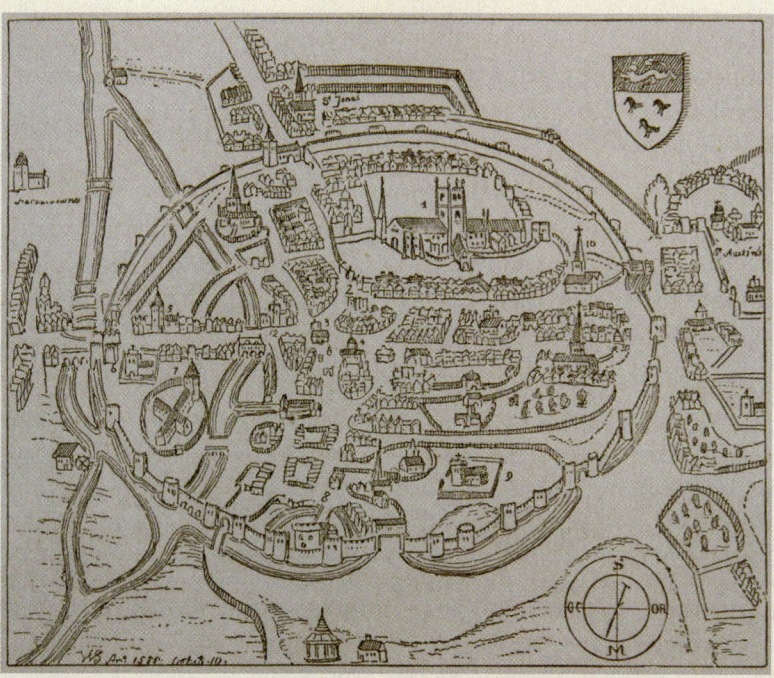

This medieval fifteenth-century map of Canterbury is in many ways a precursor of our modern tourist maps that indicate the "must see" sights of a visitor's destination. Canterbury was an English tourist attraction as early as the Roman occupation of the island—Julius Caesar and the Emperor Claudius were early visitors. But Canterbury's great fame as a pilgrimage site began when the Archbishop of Canterbury, the most influential bishop in the English Catholic Church, was killed in the cathedral by knights who claimed they were sent to conduct the assassination by the King of England, Henry II. The Archbishop, Thomas à Becket, immediately became regarded as a martyr for the cause of religious freedom. King Henry himself visited Canterbury as a pilgrim, asking forgiveness for his sins and walking barefoot to the shrine of the man he may have ordered murdered. Thomas was quickly made a saint, and the site of his murder became a destination for medieval pilgrims seeing forgiveness for their sins.

Such a pilgrimage is described by Geoffrey Chaucer in his Canterbury Tales. Chaucer prefaces this work by describing how he joined near London with a group of 29 pilgrims on their way to Canterbury to visit Thomas à Becket's shrine. To ward off the boredom of the trip, the pilgrims agree to tell tales (two on the way to Canterbury and two on the journey back), and whoever told the best tale was to be rewarded with a supper paid for by the others. Chaucer's resultant stories still remain as one of the greatest works of English literature.

Canterbury's popularity as a pilgrimage site continued throughout the Middle Ages. Although the most famous landmark remained the cathedral, the church of St. Dunstan attracted the increased attention of pilgrims in the late sixteenth century, since that church became the final resting place of the head of Sir Thomas More (1478–1535). This noted English lawyer, scholar, and humanist served as King Henry VIII's chancellor before refusing to deny the legitimacy of the king's first marriage and later failing to recognize Henry as the head of the church in England in place of the pope. More was imprisoned, refused to change his position, was put on trial, and was convicted of treason. He was beheaded in London, but his head found its final resting place in Canterbury. Henry VIII went on to confiscate much of the wealth of Canterbury, including donations of pilgrims over the centuries, in order to increase revenue. He also discouraged pilgrimage to the shrines, but Canterbury's popularity as a visitor's site has maintained its popularity to the present day.

Questions to Consider

1. How would this map serve the purposes of a visitor unfamiliar with the city of Canterbury?
2. Do you think the lack of great detail would be of concern to viewers of this map?
3. The twelve sites named and numbered on the map are almost all churches. Why do you think that is the case?

French ruler to allow her to lead an army to relieve the besieged city of Orléans. Clad in white armor and riding a white horse, she inspired confidence and a feeling of invincibility in her followers, and in 1429 Orléans was rescued from what had seemed certain conquest. Joan was captured by the enemy, found guilty of bewitching the English soldiers, and burned at the stake. But her martyrdom seemed a turning point in the long struggle.

France's development of a permanent standing army and the greater use of gunpowder also began to transform the art of war. English resistance crumbled as military superiority now turned full circle; the English longbow was outmatched by French artillery. Of the vast territories they had once controlled in France, the English retained only Calais when the war ended in 1453.

The Hundred Years' War exhausted England and fueled discontent with the monarchy in Parliament and among the common people. Baronial rivalry to control both Parliament and the crown erupted into full-scale civil war known as the Wars of the Roses (1455–1485); the white rose was the symbol of the Yorkists, and the red rose the House of Lancaster. Thirty years of bloody civil war ended in 1485 with the victory of Henry Tudor over his rivals. His victory at Bosworth Field enabled him to become Henry VII, the first of the Tudor dynasty. Henry VII (1485–1509) proved to be a popular and effective monarch, bringing national unity and security to the English people.

The Hundred Years' War left France with a new national consciousness and royal power that was stronger than ever. Shortly after the war, Louis XI (1461–1483) continued the process of consolidating royal power. Astute and tireless, yet completely lacking in scruples, Louis XI earned himself the epithet the "universal spider" because of his constant intrigues. In his pursuit of power he used any weapon—violence, bribery, treachery—to obtain his ends. The "spider king" devoted his reign to restoring prosperity to his nation and to reducing the powers of the noble families still active and ambitious after the long war. Like Henry VII in England, Louis XI was one of the "new monarchs" who worked for the creation of a subject-sovereign relationship in their kingdoms, replacing the old feudal ties of personal fidelity.

Spain: Ferdinand and Isabella and the Reconquista

Spain became strongly centralized under an assertive and aggressive monarchy in 1479, when Isabella of Castile and Ferdinand of Aragon began a joint rule that united the Iberian peninsula except for Navarre, Portugal, and Granada. The "Catholic Majesties," the title the pope conferred on Ferdinand and Isabella, set out to establish effective royal control in all of Spain.

Ferdinand and Isabella believed that the church should be subordinate to royal government. By tactful negotiations, the Spanish sovereigns induced the pope to give them the right to make church appointments in Spain and to establish a Spanish court of **Inquisition** largely free of papal control. The Spanish Inquisition confiscated the property of many *conversos* (Jews and Muslims who had converted to Christianity to avoid persecution) and terrified the Christian clergy and laity into accepting royal absolutism as well as religious orthodoxy. Although the Inquisition greatly enhanced the power of the Spanish crown, it also caused many people to flee Spain and the threat of persecution. About 150,000 Spanish Jews, mainly merchants and professional people, fled to the Netherlands, England, North Africa, and the Ottoman Empire. Calling themselves Sephardim (su-faer-DUIM), many of these exiles retained their Spanish language and culture into the twentieth century.

Inquisition—A special Roman Catholic court directed to search out and punish heretics, believers in doctrines other than those prescribed by the Church.

The uniting of Castile and Aragon, represented here by Isabella and Ferdinand, provided the foundation for the dominant Spanish state in the sixteenth century.

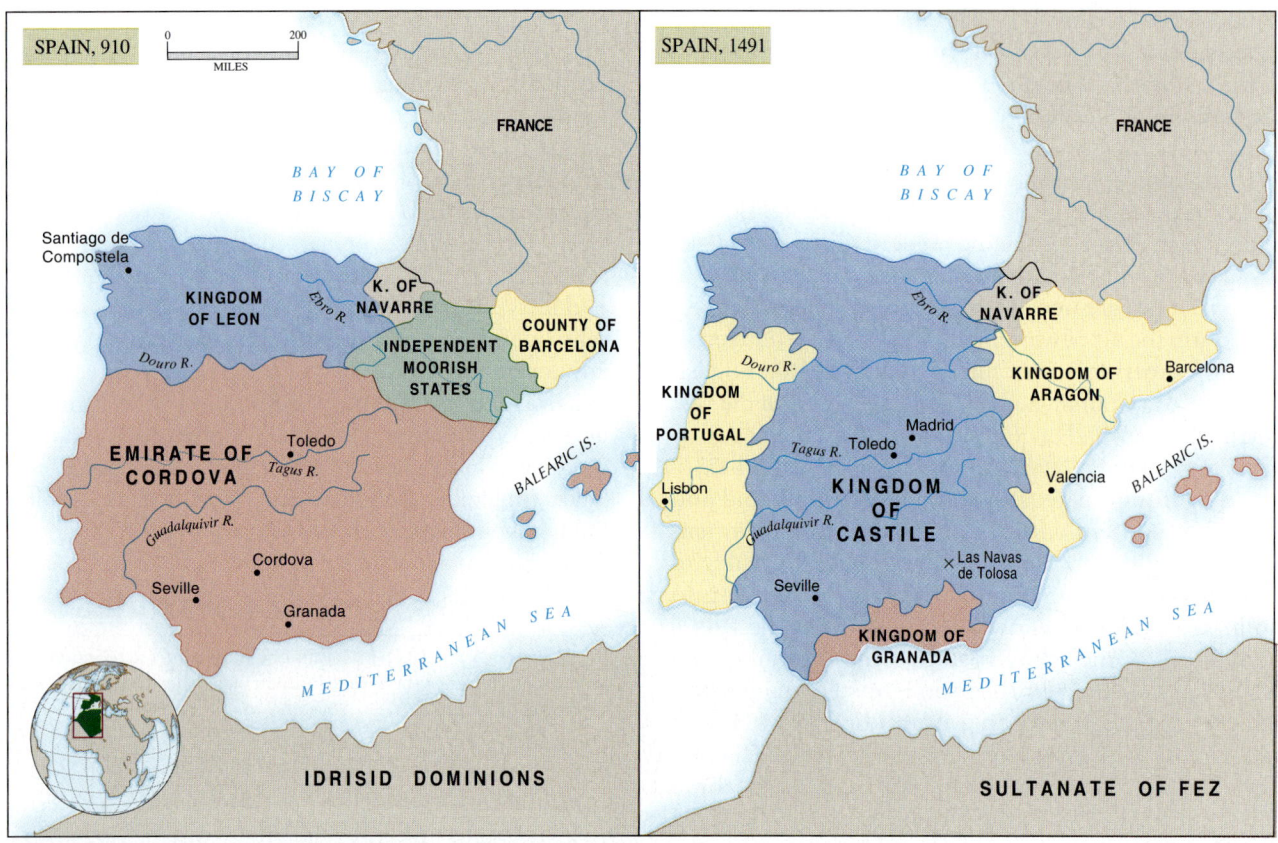

The progress of nation-building in Spain was linked to the Reconquista, the effort to expel the Muslims from the peninsula—in 1492 the kingdom of Granada, the East Muslim stronghold in Spain, fell to the Spanish.

Another manifestation of Spanish absolutism, defined by Isabella herself as "one king, one law, one faith," was the intentional neglect of the Cortes of Castile and Aragon. These representative assemblies, having emerged in the twelfth century, never were allowed by the monarchy to take an effective position as legislative bodies.

One of the most dramatic achievements of the Catholic Majesties was the completion of the *Reconquista* in 1492 with the defeat of Granada, the last Moorish state on the Iberian Peninsula. This occurred in same year that Columbus claimed the New World for Spain. Before Ferdinand died in 1516, a dozen years after Isabella, he seized the part of Navarre that lay south of the Pyrenees. This acquisition, together with the conquest of Granada, completed the unification of the Spanish nation-state.

Portugal

The western part of the Iberian Peninsula, Portugal, had a different historical evolution than did Spain. There was never a classic feudal tradition in the country, in which kings gave grants of land and positions to their vassals; rather the country was dominated by strong regional barons against whom the kings would struggle during the thirteenth century. But during the fourteenth century the centralizing power of monarchy began to impose its will over the country, and the Avis dynasty would rule Portugal from 1384 to 1580.

As will be shown in Chapter 16, the Portuguese were the first Europeans to venture out into the Atlantic in search of new business and resources. The person most known for this adventure was Prince Henry (1394–1460), the Navigator. He established an observatory where advances in navigation and ship making were made. In 1411, he crossed the Straits of Gibraltar and captured the Moroccan city of Ceuta (SIU-ta). During his life his sailors took the Azores and penetrated as far south as Senegal. In response to the economic stimulus of new markets and resources, Portugal doubled its population between 1400 and 1600 and established a global trading empire, however briefly. Then in 1580, during the reign of the Spanish Habsburg, Philip II, Spain incorporated Portugal into its realm.

Central Europe 1300–1521

Central Europe at this time included the Holy Roman Empire, Italy, and the Catholic nations of Poland, the Czech lands of Bohemia and Moravia, and Hungary. The history of this region was largely one of conflict:

political (Empire-Papacy), ethnic (German-Slav), or religious (Orthodox-Catholic). The region was, however, tied together by economics. It comprised an economic zone anchored on the west by the Rhine river, the primary route of the overland trade from the Mediterranean to the North Sea and beyond to the Baltic Sea and Russia. The cities of the **Hanseatic League** dominated the northern portions of this trade route, trading primarily in beer, wool, wood, and grain. Until the opening of the Atlantic trade routes in the sixteenth century, this zone experienced comparative economic well-being and important cultural exchange, despite the plague and wars.

The Holy Roman Empire

In the late Middle Ages, the Holy Roman Empire lapsed progressively into political disunity. In 1273 the imperial crown was given to the weak Count Rudolf of the House of Habsburg. During the remainder of the Middle Ages, the Habsburgs had amazing success in territorial acquisition; Rudolf himself acquired Austria through marriage, and, thereafter, the Habsburgs ruled their holdings from Vienna.

While the empire grew, however, its authority over its constituent states weakened. In 1356 the German nobility won significant victory in their efforts to avoid the creation of a powerful monarchy. **The Golden Bull,** a document that served as the political constitution of Germany until early in the nineteenth century, established a procedure by which seven German electors—three archbishops and four lay princes—chose the emperor. The electors and other important princes were given rights that made them virtually independent rulers, and the emperor could take no important action without the consent of the imperial feudal assembly, the Diet, which met infrequently. The empire, including 2000 independent lesser nobles, 66 autonomous cities, over 100 imperial counts, 30 secular princes, and 70 quasi-independent bishoprics was loosely governed by the Imperial Diet.

Despite the absence of political unity with the Empire, the Habsburg family managed to vastly expand its power in the fifteenth century. They achieved this primarily through successful marriage alliances and not by battle. Most marriage contracts among royal families involved a clause in which, in the case of the death of one of the participants in the marriage, all of the holdings of that person would pass to the survivor. The Habsburgs started this period of marital expansion in 1477 when Frederick III, largely ineffectual in the face of attacks by the Hungarians, arranged the marriage of his son Marximilian I to Maria of Burgundy—whose family laid claim to the lands of northeastern France and the Low Countries. Their marriage produced one son, Philip.

When Frederick died, Maximilian picked up his deceased father's Austrian lands, and then put together a marriage alliance between his son Philip and the daughter of the Spanish king, Juana. Although their marriage ended sadly, they produced a number of children, three of whom became important: Charles, Ferdinand, and Maria. Charles (1516–1556) became Holy Roman Emperor in 1519 and controlled the family's central and western holdings—including Spain and its world empire. Ferdinand headed the eastern part of the Empire, and Maria was married off to the king of Hungary, Louis II. When Louis was killed by the Turks at Mohacs in 1526, Maria Habsburg received her late husband's holdings.

The Hapsburgs' rise to power was not unnoticed at the time, and a phrase made the rounds, *Bella gerant alii, tu felix Austria nube* ("Let the others fight wars; you lucky Austrian, marry"[2]).

Because of his long reign and political skill, the Austrian monarch Frederick III (r. 1440–1493) started the successful policy of favorable marriage alliances that led to the Habsburgs ruling over a world empire in the sixteenth century.

Hanseatic League—A commercial league of mostly German cities extending from the English Channel to the eastern end of the Baltic Sea that was active between the thirteenth and seventeenth centuries.

Golden Bull—A document issued from the Holy Roman Emperor King Charles IV in 1356 that served as the political constitution of the German speaking lands until the nineteenth century.

Switzerland

In 1291, citizens in the German-speaking parts of the Alps began the drive to separate themselves from the Habsburg-dominated Empire. In 1291 the three cantons that controlled the access to Italy through the Saint Gothard Pass made an alliance to protect their independence. Fourteen years later they fought off the Habsburgs at the battle of Mortgaten, thus beginning the history of the country of Switzerland.

Because of its location on the overland route between the Mediterranean and the Rhine road to the North Sea, the region became rich. In addition, the Swiss artisans became known throughout Europe for the quality of their weapons. As we saw in Chapter 14, the region became touched by the currents of the Reformation during the career of Ulrich Zwingli.

Italy

After 1300, the middle and southern parts of the Italian peninsula gained a bit of distance from the Germans. In southern Italy, the Angevin dynasty asserted itself, while in the center the papacy worked to extend its holdings. Between Rome and the Alps, the rich and powerful city-states of Genoa, Milan, and Florence joined with Venice to construct their own diplomatic and political structures.

The years between 1300 and 1500 were not stable: As one authority notes, it was a time of threatened cities, kingdoms without kings, feudal holdings in transition to becoming principalities. Throughout the fourteenth and early fifteenth centuries the area was marked by intra-city conflicts fought using mercenary forces known as the **condotierri** (kon-do-TIER-ree). These mercenaries, many of them Spanish, fought for pay and would change sides in mid-battle if a better offer was made by their opponents. Economic developments shifted the political center of gravity during the 1400s to the northern cities from the Kingdom of Sicily and the Papal States.

As we saw in Chapter 14, in the northern Italian cities, new, bourgeois elites led by families such as the Medici accumulated great wealth from the wool business and banking to sponsor the great artists and thinkers of the middle classes. In 1454 they tired of their ongoing conflicts and at the Treaty of Lodi worked out a way of getting along, including exchanges of ambassadors with extraterritoriality. Unfortunately, all of the new peace was destroyed when the French invaded in 1494, and Italy became an object of and no longer a subject in European diplomacy. Incipient steps toward some sort of Italian sovereignty would have to wait nearly four centuries before being realized.

condotierri—Mercenaries employed by the Italian city-states during the conflicts of the fourteenth and fifteenth centuries.

The Catholic Frontier: Poland, Bohemia, and Hungary

East of the empire and north of the Italian peninsula, the frontiers of the Roman Catholic zone were to be found. In the tenth century, three peoples along the frontier accepted Roman Catholic Christianity: the Poles (966), the Czechs (864), and the Hungarians (1000). They joined a singular religious community that stretched from the Bug River to the Straits of Gibraltar to Iceland. Common threads uniting this community were the Latin language and a belief in papal authority. Irish and German missionaries had carried the Roman faith to this frontier area, and they were followed and sustained by a Germanic population movement, the *Drang nach Osten* ("drive to the east"). The royal families of the Poles, Czechs, and Hungarians intermarried with those of France, Luxembourg, and Austria and they participated fully in all of the major events and movements of the Western tradition. As converts to Catholicism, they proudly saw themselves, in Oscar Halecki's words, as the borderlands of civilization—facing Orthodox and even Turkish and Mongol attacks.[3]

Unlike the centralizing tendencies in western Europe where kings became stronger than their nobles, in east Central Europe—especially in Poland and Hungary—the nobles jealously guarded their authority in the fourteenth and fifteenth centuries, leading to weakened central power.

The church played a key role in both the uniting of the countries and the formation of the national identity, lending its legitimacy by converting the royal family in each country. In the course of the tenth century the Polish Piasts (895–1306), the Bohemian Přemyslids (PSHEM-ui-sleds; 895–1306), and the Hungarian Arpads (896–1310) formed the dynasties that would rule their respective countries until 1300. The Poles, Czechs, and Hungarians suffered from the Mongol invasions in the 1240s but recovered quickly within a generation. Each of their states had close commercial and cultural ties with the Germans, and—sometimes went to war with them.

The cities of Poland and Hungary tended to be dominated by Germans and Jews, the bulk of the indigenous people living as serfs. In Bohemia, however, urban life was dominated by the Czech people, still with a healthy representation of Germans and Jews. The Czechs would be the only people of eastern Europe to share fully in the urban lifestyle of Central Europe. The three countries had their individual legal traditions—the Hungarians, for example, refer to their Golden Bull of 1222 as the equivalent to the English Magna Carta in terms of its guarantees of liberties.

The region did not suffer as heavily from the Black Plague as western Europe, and as a result Poland, Bohemia, and Hungary experienced a golden age of cultural and economic development in the fourteenth century. There were universities established at Prague (1348), Krakow (1364), and Pecs (1369) and scholars from those schools participate in the humanist movement in the fifteenth century. Even with their economic and cultural progress, the three states argued over a number of issues as their respective kings sought to expand their influences and fought over regions such Silesia.

During that fourteenth century, the originating dynasties died out in Hungary and Bohemia. Foreign kings such as the Angevin Louis the Great of Hungary (1342–1382), and the Luxembourger Charles the Great of Bohemia (1333–1378) were elected by the powerful nobles and bourgeoisie of the area. The last Piast, Casimir the Great of Poland (1333–1370) led his country through its golden age, but after his death the Poles resorted to a system of elective kingship.

This well-being of the fourteenth century, however, would not last long because of the expansion of Russia to the east, Sweden to the north, and the Ottoman Empire to the south. Internal problems also would lead to a weakening of the realms. Elective kings in Poland and Hungary frittered away their central powers to satisfy the demands of the nobles who elected them. The weakening of central power hit its peak in Poland, where successive royal elections cut the powers of the monarchy until the installation of the **Liberum Veto**, an act that allowed one member of the nobility, the *szlachta* (SCHLOK-tah), to block a king's program by his negative vote.

In 1386 Poland united with Lithuania—the last pagan country in Europe—and became the largest state in Europe. Invasions from the east and the west, however, eroded the strength of this state. The Poles had earlier added to their own problems in 1225 when they invited the crusading order of the Teutonic knights into Poland to aid in the combat against the indigenous Baltic peoples to the north, the Prus. The Teutonic knights, out of work after failed crusades in the Eastern Mediterranean, slaughtered the Prus, established their own state based around present-day Kaliningrad (Koenigsberg), and called it Prussia. They proved a considerable threat to the Poles and were not defeated until the battle of Tannenberg in 1410. Later the Teutons would turn their territory of West Prussia over to the Poles and keep East Prussia as a fief of the Polish crown. Poland would face competition and eventual destruction by Russia, Prussia, Sweden, and Austria in the seventeenth and eighteenth centuries.

The Bohemians became the richest part of the Catholic orbit and went on to challenge the Germans politically, economically, and religiously. The Golden Bull of 1356 made the Bohemian king one of the seven electors of the Holy Roman Empire. We have already discussed the religious controversy between the Czechs and the Germans during the late fourteenth century. The creation of the Hussite Church after Jan Hus's immolation led to four crusades being preached by the Catholic Church against the forces at Prague. The Czechs successfully defended themselves under leaders such as John Žižka (ZHISH-kah) and they would continue to progress, growing economically and politically until the seventeenth century—when they were defeated in the first phase of the Thirty Years' War.

The Hungarians experienced a brilliant fifteenth century under János Hunyadi (YAWN-nosh HOON-ia-dee) and his son and successor Mathias Corvinus. As Magyar aristocrats, they ended the period of foreign kings. János Hunyadi, by his wealth and military prowess, paved the way for his son Mathias to be elected king in 1458, who came to be known as Mathias Corvinus. During his 32-year reign, Mathias established close ties with the Italian Renaissance cities, especially Florence. Scholars and artists at his court participated fully in the cultural movements of the

Matthias Corvinus was a true "renaissance man." He was a patron of the arts, supporter of artists and writers, and a collector of books and manuscripts. He was also one of the pioneers in introducing printing to Central and Eastern Europe.

Liberum Veto—In order to guard against the potential power of a strong central monarchy, the Polish nobles in 1652 installed the Liberum Veto, an act that allowed one member of the nobility to block the king's program by his single negative vote in the noble assembly.

time. He founded a printing press and had one of the most important libraries in Europe. Although he was unable to increase his central power in competition with the Czechs and the Poles, he did manage to capture Vienna. After he died in 1490 from unknown causes, the Hungarian magnates went back to electing foreign kings. The Hungarians became disunited and were finally defeated by the Ottoman Turks at the battle of Mohacs (1526). Hungary was divided into three zones, the larger part controlled directly by the Ottomans.

THE RELIGIOUS-POLITICAL FUSION

■ *The framers of the American Constitution demanded a total separation of church and state. What examples can you find in the wars of religion between 1517 and 1648 to support their belief in a separation of faith and politics?*

Religious Diversity in Western Europe

The papacy's political power had been in a continual decline since the thirteenth century. In Central Europe, local elites fought the Catholic clergy and the excluded lower classes for political control. In the Atlantic states of England, France, and Spain, the monarchs became increasingly independent of the Pope's demands. The French invasion at the end of the fifteenth century made the Italian peninsula an arena for desperate struggle between the Habsburg and French Valois dynasties that would last until 1559. The Papal States became a political pawn. The papacy's weaknesses were exploited by the troops of Charles V when they sacked Rome in 1527. Protestant leaders such as Martin Luther profited from the disarray in the Catholic world, and his followers combined religion and politics in a new and explosive way that Catholic leaders quickly learned to emulate. The result would be a series of religious-political conflicts that would last until 1648.

Protestant Politics

The rise of the Protestants finally liberated the nation-state from any claim of authority by the church. As we saw in Chapter 14, Luther spelled out that humans have two obligations: first and most importantly, loyalty to God and second, loyalty to the earthly government. Luther's positions on church-state relations found biblical support in the words of Christ: "Therefore, render unto Caesar, that which is Caesar's and unto God, that which is God's" (Matthew 22:21).

Luther immediately gained support from German and Scandinavian rulers and in every city along the Baltic coast where there was a German-speaking majority—including in Poland and present-day Estonia. Luther supported the repression of the protesting German knights and the crushing of the Peasant's Revolt in 1524–1525. In addition, Luther said little about the Protestant princes' taking the considerable wealth of the Catholic Church

The religious split between Lutherans and Catholics soon took the form of military alliances. Lutheran princes organized for defense in the **Schmalkaldic League** and were not immediately challenged because Emperor Charles V had to deal with the French and Turkish threats. A low-intensity, sporadic civil war dragged on in the empire until after Luther's death in 1546. It ended with the Peace of Augsburg in 1555, when the imperial princes were permitted to choose between Lutheranism and Catholicism in their state churches, thus increasing their independence from the emperor. In addition, Catholic properties confiscated before 1552 were retained by Lutheran principalities, which provided a means for financing their policies.

Henry VIII's Break with Rome

In England, the conflict between the church and state had little if anything to do with differences over religious doctrine. As we saw in Chapter 14, Henry VIII (r. 1509–1547) broke from the church because he needed a legitimate male heir. When Henry's wife Catherine of Aragon failed to provide him with an heir, he sought in 1527 to have his marriage to her annulled so he could remarry. For political reasons, however, the Pope refused to grant an annulment, and Henry forced the clergy into proclaiming him head of a separate, English church.

The Anglican Church was essentially the same as the Catholic Church, with the exception that the English monarch served as the head of the church, the clergy could marry, and English replaced Latin as the official language of the church. Henry also extracted from Parliament the authority to appoint bishops, and Parliament ended all payment of revenues to Rome. In 1539 Parliament completed its seizure of monastery lands and the wealth of pilgrimage sites such as Canterbury Cathedral. While Henry's break from the church left a legacy of turmoil and strife that would last for another 150 years, his actions placed both temporal and spiritual authority in the

---

Schmalkaldic League—A defensive alliance of Lutheran princes organized in 1531 under the leadership of Philip the Magnanimous of Hesse to defend themselves against the Catholic powers of the Holy Roman Empire.

hands of the monarchy, strengthening the power of the English state.

Calvinist Variations

Calvin on Predestination

Calvin viewed politics as a theocratic exercise—the laws of God become the laws of the state. His plans for a city government in Geneva called for domination by the clergy—full control over moral and religious behavior—and banishment of all dissidents. Though met with grudging opposition, he gradually increased his power through support from the Protestant refugees who poured into the city. His influence climaxed after a failed "revolt of the godless" in 1555. From that year until his death in 1564, he dominated the council, ruling Geneva with an iron hand, within the letter, but not the spirit, of the original ordinances. As we saw in Chapter 15, he imposed a religious totalitarianism over Geneva, and religious police held the power to investigate every detail of private life.

In advising people from outside of Geneva, he said that political authorities had to consult with the church on policies. He also said, however, that it was the duty of Christians to obey the state in secular matters. When he discussed how governments should be run, he advocated the concept of representative government.

Many of the divergent Protestant splinter groups up and down the Rhine saw different lessons in scripture. The majority of them were indifferent or antagonistic to secular government; many favored pacifism and substitution of the church for the state.

The legacy of the Protestant Reformation on politics was mixed. Luther, Henry VIII, Calvin, and the Protestant radicals all advocated different combinations of the church and the state. Between 1517 and 1564, however, political life in Europe became revolutionized. The change from the concept of Christendom in 1300 to communities based on faith and allegiance imposed by the state brought with it much death, suffering, and destruction.

WARS OF RELIGIONS: THE SPANISH HABSBURGS' QUEST FOR EUROPEAN HEGEMONY, 1556–1598

■ *Did Philip II of Spain use the powers of the state to spread the influence of the Catholic Church, or did he use the Church for political gain?*

After the 1560s, religious fanaticism, both Protestant and Catholic, combined with pragmatic politics to form a combustible mixture. Sometimes religious conflict caused the reshaping of the old political system to justify movements against royal authority. More often, it popularized centralized monarchies, whose rulers promised to restore order by wielding power. Despite pious declarations, kings and generals in this period conducted war with little regard for moral principles; indeed, as time passed they steadily subordinated religious concerns to dynastic ambitions or national interests. This change, however, came slowly and was completed only in 1648 after Europe was thoroughly exhausted by the human suffering and material destruction of religious wars.

Until the end of the sixteenth century, Spain, led by Philip II, attempted to impose its will over the Continent. When he took power in 1556, he looked across the Pyrenees and across the Mediterranean and saw a Europe split by religious strife and still threatened by the presence of the Ottoman Empire. In Central Europe, the Peace of Augsburg ended a short war in Germany and sought to bring an accord between the Catholics and Lutherans. Even before Calvin died in 1564, however, his movement was spreading rapidly throughout the Continent. The Council of Trent launched a formidable counteroffensive, led by the Jesuits and supported by the Spanish and Austrian Habsburgs, against all Protestants. England remained on the verge of religious civil war after the death of Queen Mary, while France plunged into three decades of conflict after the extinction of the Valois line to the throne in 1559. Religious conflict broke out in the Spanish Netherlands, and in eastern Europe, militant Catholicism reversed the gains made by Protestants in the previous half-century. Philip saw opportunity in

War and Politics in the Age of Philip II

1556–1598	Reign of Philip II of Spain
1558–1603	Reign of Elizabeth I of England
1561–1593	Religious wars in France
1566	Revolt in the Netherlands
1571	European forces defeat Turks at Lepanto
1572	Massacre of St. Bartholomew's Eve in Paris
1581	Dutch United Provinces declare independence from Spain
1587	Dutch Republic formed
1588	English defeat Spanish Armada

this tumultuous setting where the politics of religion dominated the scene in Europe.

The Era of Spanish Habsburg Dominance

Although it was a relatively underdeveloped and sparsely populated country of 8 million people, Spain, under Philip II (1556–1598), was the strongest military power in Europe. Seven centuries of resistance against the Moors (see Chapter 9) had formed a chivalric nobility that excelled in the military arts, if not also in business. This tradition, in addition to the promise of empire, saw the rigidly disciplined Spanish infantry absorb neighboring Portugal and fan out around the world as conquistadores, bringing back silver in seemingly unlimited quantities from the Americas. Working in tandem with the army was the Spanish Church, whose courts of the Inquisition, which had earlier banished the Jews, were now being used to eliminate the few remaining Moors and Spanish Protestants.

Philip willingly took on the Habsburgs' global burdens of maintaining Catholic orthodoxy, fighting the Turks, and imposing his will on his troublesome European neighbors. He considered this responsibility a part of his inheritance from his father, Charles V, whose long reign ended in 1556 when he abdicated his imperial throne and entered a monastery. At that time, Charles split his Habsburg holdings. His brother Ferdinand acquired control of Austria, Bohemia, and Hungary and became Holy Roman Emperor in 1556. Philip received Naples, Sicily, Milan, the Netherlands, Spain, and a vast overseas empire, which was much more lucrative than the traditional imperial domain in Central and eastern Europe. Indeed, the division of Habsburg lands appeared to be a blessing for Philip, allowing him to shed his father's worrisome "German problem" and concentrate more effectively on his Spanish realm.

Philip was a slightly built, somber, hardworking man. He was totally absorbed by the tasks of running a worldwide empire and rarely broke away to enjoy the luxurious life offered by his position. He seldom delegated authority, and his councilors served more as advisers than as administrators. Philip labored endlessly, reading and annotating official documents and dominating the *Cortes* (the traditional assembly of estates) of Castile. He married each of his four wives—Maria of Portugal, Mary of England, Elizabeth of France, and Anne of Austria, his niece—for political reasons; except for Mary, they bore his children but ate at his table only during official banquets. Elizabeth was his favorite, as were her daughters, who received some of his few open shows of tenderness and loving concern.

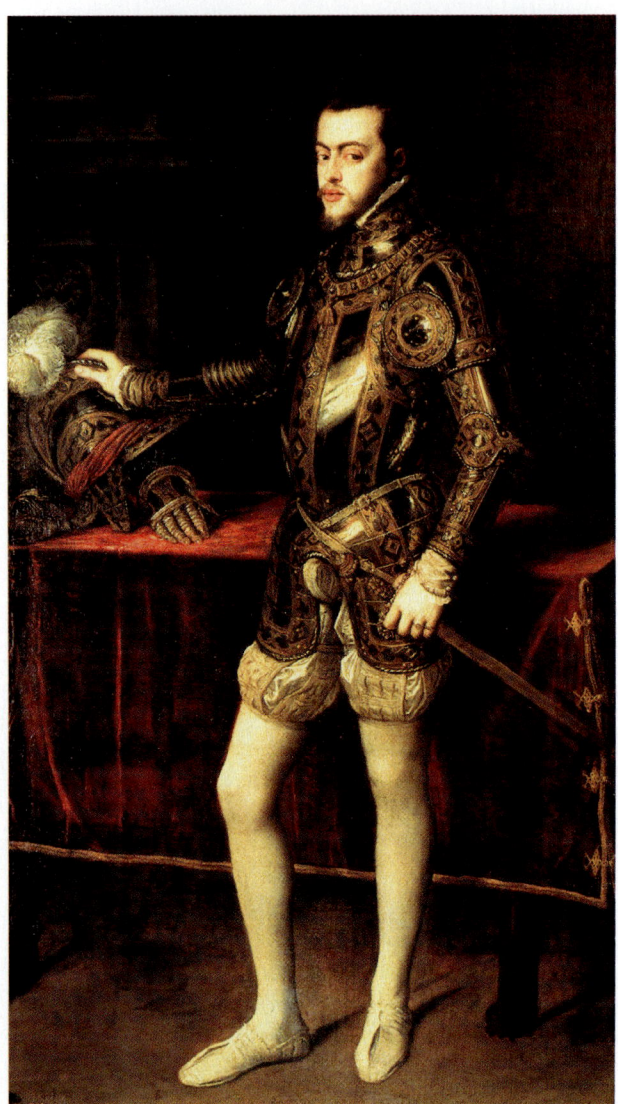

Philip II dominated the European scene during the second half of the sixteenth century. Even though he worked hard to assure Spanish Habsburg dominance, he failed to defeat the Dutch and the British and left Spain in an exhausted condition.

Philip took advantage of his role as defender of the Catholic faith. Although the church was wealthy and had unleashed the Inquisition to wipe out dissent, Philip used it to enforce Spanish traditions, arouse patriotism, and increase his popularity to strengthen the state. He was by no means a tool of the papacy: indeed, he defied more than one pope by denying jurisdiction over Spanish ecclesiastical courts, opposing the Council of Trent on clerical appointments, and fighting the Jesuits when they challenged his authority. He saw the Catholic Church as an arm of his government, and not vice versa.

Throughout his long reign, Philip continually encountered limitations to his authority. Spain had only recently been unified, and powerful nobles opposed him and his viceroys in their local councils. An overworked and overextended bureaucracy and a weak financial, communications, and industrial infrastructure placed the victories gained by the army and the state on a weak foundation. The backward Spanish sociopolitical system caused Philip many economic problems. Tax-exempt nobilities, comprising under 2 percent of the people, owned 95 percent of nonchurch land; the middle classes, overtaxed and depleted by purges of Jews and Moriscos (Spanish Muslims), were diminished; and the peasants were so exploited that production of food, particularly grains, was insufficient to feed the population. State regulation of industry and trade further limited revenues and forced primary reliance on precious metals from the Americas to fill the treasury, which ultimately produced a ruinous inflation. When his income failed to meet expenses, Philip borrowed at rising interest rates from Italian and Dutch banks. In 1557 and 1575 Philip had to suspend payments, effectively declaring national bankruptcy.

Revolt in the Netherlands

Philip's centralized rule encouraged some unity in Spain; the Netherlands, however, with its own traditions, was immediately suspicious of its foreign king who tried to enforce Catholic conformity. The Netherlands ("Low Countries") at the time also included modern Belgium, Luxembourg, and small holdings along 200 miles of marshy northern coast, an area not open to easy conquest. The geographical setting promoted strong local nobilities but also relatively independent peasants and townsmen. Even in medieval times, cities were centers of rapidly expanding commerce: of the 300 walled towns in 1560, some 19 had populations of over 10,000. (At the same time, England had only three or four of that size.) Antwerp was the commercial hub of northern Europe, serving as the crossroads of the Hanseatic League and the Italian-English trade axis. The combination of geography and wealth created a

The inherent logic of balance-of-power politics is readily evident in this map showing the extent of Habsburg—both Spanish and Austrian—holdings.

spirit of independence in religious affairs, as Lutherans, Calvinists, and Anabaptists were found in great numbers. Charles V had attempted sporadically to suppress the Protestants and had even burned a few notable heretics. But his status as a native son allowed him to maintain a tenuous stability in the region.

Anabaptist Torture in Muenster

Charles's daughter, Margaret of Parma (1522–1586) served as Philip's first regent for the Netherlands. She was sensitive to the religious complexities of her task; Philip, however, ordered a crackdown on the Protestants. Margaret introduced the Inquisition to fight heresy, a policy that forced leading nobles to leave her council and provoked vocal protests from her subjects. As the Inquisition did its work and executed prominent Protestants, the protests became loud and violent. Finally the so-called Calvinist Fury erupted in 1566, terrorizing Catholics and desecrating 400 churches. Most of the people in the Netherlands were shocked by the excesses of the radicals and voiced their support for Margaret.

Philip's response was to send the duke of Alva to the Netherlands with 10,000 Spanish troops, a great baggage train, and 2000 camp followers to establish order. Alva removed Margaret from her regency and clamped a brutal military dictatorship on the country. By decree, he centralized church administration, imposed new taxes, and established a special tribunal, soon dubbed the Council of Blood, to stamp out treason and heresy. During Alva's regime between 1567 and 1573, at least 8000 people were killed, including the powerful counts of Egmont and Horne. In addition, the Catholic terror deprived 30,000 people of their property and forced 100,000 to flee the country.

By 1568 Alva's excesses had provoked open rebellion—the first national liberation struggle, led by William of Orange (1533–1584), nicknamed William the Silent. Constant early defeats left him impoverished and nearly disgraced, but in 1572 the port of Brielle fell to his privateers, the "sea beggars," an event that triggered revolts throughout the north. Soon thereafter, William cut the dikes near Zeeland and mired down a

In his 1564 rendering of the biblical account of The Massacre of the Innocents *(1566–1567; Matthew 2:16), Pieter Brueghel the Elder anticipated well the horrors of violence that would befall the Netherlands.*

weary Spanish army. The continuing war was marked by savage ferocity, such as the sack of Antwerp by mutinous Spanish soldiers (1576). At the Spanish siege of Maestricht (MICE-treeschte) in 1579, women fought beside their men on the walls, and Spanish soldiers massacred the population, raping women first before tearing some limb from limb in the streets. That same year, in the Pacification of Ghent, Catholics and Protestants from the 17 provinces united to defy Philip, demand the recall of his army, and proclaim the authority of their traditional assembly, the States General.

Unfortunately for the rebel cause, this unity was soon destroyed by religious differences between militant northern Calvinists and Catholic southerners, particularly the many powerful nobles. The Spanish commander Alexander Farnese exploited these differences by restoring lands and privileges to the southern nobles. He was then able to win victories that induced the ten southern provinces to make peace with Spain in 1579. The Dutch, now alone, proclaimed their continued resistance to Spanish persecution and, in 1581, declared their independence from Spain. They persisted after William of Orange was assassinated in 1584, but meanwhile, the Spanish continued their war on heresy, butchering, burning, and burying alive Protestants who would not renounce their faith. The conflict lasted until a truce was negotiated in 1609.

Religious Wars in France

Although frustrated in the Netherlands, Philip did not face his father's French problem. According to the Treaty of Cateau-Cambrésis (KA-tow kam-BRAY-sees) in 1559, France gave up claims in Italy and the Netherlands. This humiliating surrender to the Habsburgs marked a definite turning point in French history. With its government bankrupt, its economy nearly prostrate, and its people disillusioned, France lost its leverage in foreign affairs as civil wars encouraged by Philip wasted the country during the next four decades.

Beneath the prevailing religious contention was another bitter struggle between the haves and have-nots. High prices, high rents, and high taxes drove the lower classes to riot and rebel against urban oligarchies, noble landlords, and government tax collectors. The social unrest continued sporadically throughout the sixteenth century. It brought no improvement of conditions for suffering peasants and town artisans, but it did frighten the wealthy nobles, merchants, and bankers whose mildly divergent interests were unified by threats from below.

By the 1560s Calvinism had become a major outlet for the frustrations of the discontented. Although outlawed and persecuted earlier, the movement grew rapidly during the decade. It converted approximately 15 percent of the population, most of whom were of the lower urban middle class; however, the leadership came mainly from the nobility, 40 to 50 percent of whom accepted Calvinism. Their motives varied—although many were sincerely religious, most pursued political ends. Even among the lesser nobles, the Calvinist side promised military employment, political prominence, and a way for taking advantage of popular discontent. The movement's potential popular support was particularly appealing to contenders for the throne among the high nobility. In 1559 the Huguenots held a secret synod in Paris that drew representatives from 72 congregations and a million members. A distinct minority, they were nevertheless well-placed and well organized with articulate spokesmen and competent military leaders.

Religious, political, and social forces combined when France suffered the loss of King Henry II in 1559, who left his crown to his sickly 15-year-old son, Francis II. His young queen was Mary Stuart (later Mary, Queen of Scots), whose uncles, the brothers Guise, took actual control of the government. They were opposed by noble families from the Huguenot camp. Francis II died in 1560, and the crown passed to his 9-year-old brother Charles. At that time, however, the real power behind the throne was Charles's mother, Catherine de Medici. Single-minded, crafty, and ready to use any means, she was determined to save the throne for one of her three sons, none of whom had produced a male heir. Exploiting the split between the Guises—the champions of the Catholic cause—and their enemies, she assumed the regency for Charles. She then attempted, through reforms of the church, to reconcile the differences between Catholics and Protestants. In this endeavor she was unsuccessful, but she kept her tenuous control, using every political strategy, including a squadron of noble women who solicited information by seducing powerful nobles.

Religious war erupted in 1561; supported by substantial Spanish financial and military interventions, it lasted through eight uneasy truces until 1593. Fanaticism evoked the most violent and inhumane acts on both sides, as destructive raids, assassinations, and torturous atrocities became commonplace. Catherine maneuvered through war and uneasy peace, first favoring the Guises and then the Bourbons. In 1572, fearing that the Huguenots were gaining supremacy, she joined a Guise plot that resulted in the murder of some 10,000 Huguenots in Paris. This Massacre of St. Bartholomew's Eve was a turning point in decisively dividing the country. The final "war of the three Henries" in the 1580s involved Catherine's third son, Henry III, who became king upon the death of Charles in 1574. The king's rivals were Henry of Guise and the

DOCUMENT
Massacre of St. Bartholomew

Protestant Henry of Navarre. When the other two Henries were assassinated, Henry of Navarre proclaimed himself king of France in 1589. Spain would have little to fear from France for the next half-century.

Elizabethan England, 1558–1603

For most of the sixteenth century, Spain built its European foreign policies on the base of an English alliance. Despite Henry's breaking his marriage with Catherine of Aragon, the Spanish ambassadors did not give up their efforts to keep England in their camp. For the better part of his reign, Philip had to deal with England's most outstanding monarch, Elizabeth I, who ruled a country that was, as the earl of Essex put it, "little in territory, not extraordinarily rich and defended only by itself."[4]

Elizabeth, a superb image maker, projected the picture of a country united behind a national church, even as her government suppressed Catholicism, put down a northern rebellion, and avoided serious troubles with Scotland and Ireland. Elizabeth dealt with potential dangers from the great Catholic powers by playing them against each other. Such successes were seen as the natural result of her brilliance and courage. This image only partly reflected reality. The "Protestant Queen" detested most of the Protestants, especially those founded on the heretical traditions of the **Lollards.** Her support for Scottish and Dutch rebels went against her fervent belief in absolute monarchy. Her celebrated coy approach in encouraging but ultimately denying prospective royal suitors, despite the diplomatic advantages of the practice, often ran counter to her emotional inclinations, throwing her into momentary rages against her advisers.

But she had learned her lesson well from Tudor politics—to compromise and discount personal feelings for the larger interests of her realm. Consequently, England became her family and her primary interest. She was especially skilled at judging people, dealing with foreign diplomats in their own languages, and projecting her charisma in public speeches. With these notable talents, she brought the English people a new sense of national pride, often expressed in Shakespeare's plays. In the second half of the sixteenth century—in contrast to France—England gave the impression of having achieved relative peace and prosperity.

Elizabeth's earliest immediate danger emerged in Scotland, where Mary of Guise was regent for her daughter Mary Stuart, queen of both France and Scotland. French troops in Scotland supported this Catholic regime. Because Mary Stuart was also a direct descendant of Henry VII of England, she was a leading claimant for the English throne and a potential rallying symbol for Catholics who hoped to reestablish their faith in England. These expectations were diminished in 1559 when a zealous Calvinist named John Knox (1505–1572), fresh from Geneva, led a revolt of Scottish nobles. Aided by English naval forces, the Scots broke religious ties with Rome, established a Presbyterian (Calvinist) state church, and, with Elizabeth's help, drove out the French soldiers.

Another serious problem loomed in Ireland, where Spanish and papal emissaries used old grievances over taxes and religion to arouse uprisings against English rule. James Maurice, an Irish leader in the southwest, began a series of revolts in 1569. Eight years later, the pope helped raise troops and money for him on the Continent. An expedition in 1579 to aid the Irish rebels was ruthlessly suppressed, but fighting dragged on for four more years. In 1601 a more serious Irish rebellion aided by 3000 Spanish troops cost Elizabeth a third of her revenues. Although never directing a successful Irish policy, as has been true of all of her successors up to the present, she managed to escape catastrophe by her stubborn persistence.

Her innate pragmatism was most beneficial in quieting English sectarian strife. She despised **Puritans** and favored rich vestments for the clergy, but she thoroughly understood the practical necessity of securing Protestant political support. Moving firmly but slowly, Elizabeth re-created a nominal Protestant national church, but one similar to her father's. The queen's policy lessened religious controversy and persecution but failed to end either completely.

Elizabeth also faced a serious danger from abroad. In 1568, after Mary Stuart was forced into exile by her Protestant subjects, she was received in England by her royal cousin. Although kept, for all intents and purposes, a prisoner, she became involved in a series of Catholic plots, which appeared even more dangerous after the pope excommunicated Elizabeth in 1570. Philip of Spain aided the plotters but still hoped to enlist Elizabeth's cooperation in creating a Catholic hegemony in Europe.

Despite all her troubles, Elizabeth's reign showed marked economic improvement. By careful—some said stingy—financial management, her government reduced debt and improved national credit. A new coinage helped make London the financial center of Europe, especially after the Spanish destruction of Antwerp. Monopolies granted to joint stock companies promoted foreign trade and brought wealth into the country. By the end of her reign in 1603, England, despite festering social and religious problems, was the most prosperous state in Europe.

Lollards—Followers of John Wycliffe who spread his doctrines both openly and secretly throughout England in the fifteenth and sixteenth centuries.

Puritans—Those English protestants in the 1500s and 1600s who found the theology and worship services of the Church of England to be not in accord with Holy Scripture.

Lepanto and the Armada

Philip's wars against Turkey—including the destruction of the Turkish fleet at Lepanto off the western coast of Greece—promoted his image as the Catholic champion, boosted Spanish morale, and revived the traditional national pride in defending the faith. When Cyprus, the last Christian stronghold in the eastern Mediterranean, fell to the Turks in 1570, Philip responded to the pope's pleas and formed a Holy League to destroy Turkish naval power. Spanish and Venetian warships, together with smaller squadrons from Genoa and the Papal States, made up a fleet of over 200 vessels that drew recruits from all over Europe. In 1571 the Holy League's fleet and the Turkish navy clashed at Lepanto, off the western coast of Greece. Christian Europe scored a major victory over the Ottoman Empire, which would never pose a naval threat again. The Spanish king could bring all of his resources to bear in northwest Europe.

Philip's diplomatic efforts, particularly his marriage to Mary Tudor in 1558, his next marriage to Elizabeth of Valois in 1560, and his clumsy efforts to court Queen Elizabeth, brought no lasting influence over English or French policies. Indeed, English captains were preying on Spanish shipping in the Atlantic, and Dutch privateers, with English and Huguenot support, were diminishing the flow of vital supplies to northern Europe. In 1580, after nine years of frustration in the Netherlands, Philip launched the first phase of his new offensive policy, using military force to validate his claim to the Portuguese throne. As king of Portugal, he gained control of the Portuguese navy and Atlantic ports, where he began assembling an oceangoing fleet, capable of operations against the Dutch and English in their home waters.

Philip's last hope for an easy solution to his problems was dashed in 1587. Pressed by the pope and the English Catholic exiles, he had tried for years to use

This detail from a painting by artists in the school of Tintoretto dealing with the Battle of Lepanto presents the decisive battle for the control of the Mediterranean in a splendid light.

Mary Stuart to overthrow Elizabeth, regain England for Catholicism, and seize control of the country. But Mary's complicity in a plot against the English queen's life was discovered, and Elizabeth finally signed a death warrant. Mary's execution confirmed Philip's earlier decision that England had to be conquered militarily. In pursuing this end, Philip planned a "great enterprise," an invasion of England blessed by the pope.

The Spanish strategy depended on a massive fleet, known as the Invincible Armada. It was ordered to meet a large Spanish army in the southern Netherlands and land this force on the English coast. But in 1588, when the Armada sailed for Flanders, Dutch ships blocked the main ports, preventing the Spanish galleons from entering the shallow waters. Philip's project was then completely ruined when the smaller and more maneuverable English ships, commanded by Charles Howard and captained by privateers such Sir Francis Drake and Sir John Hawkins, scattered the Armada in the English Channel. Retreating through the North Sea, the Spanish fleet was then battered by a severe storm, called the "Protestant wind," and forced to make a miserable return to Spain.

DOCUMENT
John Hawkins Reports on the Spanish Armada

Philip II's Failure in Europe

Contrary to English expectations, the defeat of the Armada brought no immediate shift in the international balance of power. Spain retained its military might, built new ships, and defended its sea-lanes. On the ground, the Spanish infantry would not suffer defeat until 1643 at the battle of Rocroi (ruh-KWAH). In fact, all the major combatants were exhausted, a factor that largely explains the Bourbons' acquisition of the French crown and continued Dutch independence. Lingering wars brought new opportunities for France and the Netherlands, but only more exhaustion for England and Spain.

During the last decade of Philip's life, his multiple failures foreshadowed the decline of his country. He encountered rebellion in Aragon, quarreled with Pope Clement VIII over recognizing the Bourbons (see following), and sent two more naval expeditions against England, both of which were scattered by storms. Before he died in 1598, he turned over the Netherlands to his favorite daughter Clara Isabella Eugenia and her husband, Archduke Albert, an Austrian Habsburg. He had also made peace with France. He left Spain bankrupt for the third time during his reign, having wasted the country's considerable resources and sacrificed its future to his dynastic pride. His son Philip III (r. 1598–1621), no match for his father, presided in a lazy, extravagant, and frivolous way over the beginning of the long decline of the Spanish Empire.

England experienced similar difficulties. Though sea raids on Spanish shipping continued and brought in badly needed money, all of Elizabeth's grand projects failed, such as in 1596 when the earl of Essex plundered Cadiz but missed the Spanish treasure fleet. Conflicts in France, the Netherlands, and Ireland drained her treasury, and Parliament delayed in granting her funds to continue fighting. Social and religious tensions surfaced at the turn of the seventeenth century, and the Puritans proved to be an especially irritating group for the aging queen. At her death in 1603, she left no successors, and the Stuarts took the English throne.

The Dutch declaration of independence in 1581 reflected more concern for aristocratic privilege and national survival than democratic principles, but it served as a basis for holding the northern Netherlands together. After finding no acceptable French or English person to be their king, the Dutch created a republic in 1587 and tenaciously persevered to sign a truce with Spain in 1609. As time passed, their growing maritime trade and naval power guaranteed their security.

The post-Armada stalemate most benefited the French. With the death of the last Valois claimant in 1589, the Bourbon Protestant king of Navarre was proclaimed king of France as Henry IV. This act threw the Catholic Holy League into a fanatical antiroyalist frenzy and encouraged Philip's military intervention in France to support his daughter's claim to the throne. But English aid and Henry's willingness to turn Catholic—he is said to have claimed that "Paris is worth a mass"—led to Philip's withdrawal and the Peace of Vervins in 1598. To pacify his Huguenot allies, Henry issued the Edict of Nantes, which guaranteed them some civil and religious rights and permitted them to continue holding more than a hundred fortified towns. Henry had at last gained peace for his exhausted country.

ORTHODOX EUROPE: RUSSIAN CONSOLIDATION AND OTTOMAN EXPANSION

■ *In the last part of the sixteenth century, the Ottoman Empire was at its peak and Muscovite Russia was in a state of crisis. By 1700 the Turks were in a state of decline and the Russians were on the verge of becoming a major power. How do you account for the differences in the developments of the two empires?*

Russian Autocracy

As we saw in Chapter 6, Ivan III had claimed the Byzantine heritage of the Russian state and used his marriage to the niece of the last ruler of Byzantium to proclaim himself as the tsar (Russian for caesar), and he adopted the use of the two-headed eagle as the symbol for the

Russian throne. His grandson, Ivan IV (1533–1584), later surnamed "the Terrible," tried to take the next step toward the imposition of a truly imperial, autocratic rule. Ivan was three years old when his father died, and during the next decade he learned to distrust the aristocratic boyars, who showed him, his mother, and his tutors no respect as they took advantage of his youth. Once he took power in the late 1540s, he began a series of reforms to put the Russian state on a modern footing. He published a new law code, brought together representatives of the Russian population—the **Zemski Sobor** (ZIEM-ski so-BOR)—to reform the administration of the land, saw his forces take Kazan and Astrakhan, and opened trade with the West.

Ivan "the Terrible"

As would be the case with the monarchies in western and Central Europe, Ivan faced the opposition of his nobles, the boyars, to his plans to strengthen the state. After 1560 he launched a full-scale war against them. He declared most of Russia, including Moscow, to be under a martial law, enforced by a group of special forces called the *oprichniki* (oh-PREACH-nee-kee), masked men of legendary cruelty dressed in black, riding black horses, carrying broomsticks topped with dog skulls. He wanted to replace the old independent boyar class with a service nobility loyal to him. To that end he and his *oprichniki* drove 12,000 families from their lands in the dead of winter. To those who opposed him, Ivan responded with an inventive cruelty that gained him his name. As the terror increased, he lost control of himself, accidentally killing his beloved son and heir to the throne. Finally he achieved his goals, and the terror diminished. When he died in 1584, he was succeeded by another son Fedor, who was totally unequipped to face the challenge of a devastated and discontented land.

For a time Fedor ruled with the advice of his brother-in-law, Boris Godunov, a competent and ambitious boyar. For seven years the country recovered from the trauma through which it had been put by Ivan IV; however, in 1591 Ivan's last son, Dmitri, died under mysterious circumstances, and when Fedor died in 1598 without an heir, the Rurik line of rulers came to an end. Boris presented himself as the next tsar and received the acclaim of the nobles and church. However, Russia felt the effects of the same famine, economic failure, and discontent that preceded the Thirty Years' War in Central Europe. Boris's policies failed to bring the country back to even minimal prosperity. At the same time, plots against him spread throughout the country, and when he died in 1605, there was no agreed-on successor. Eight years of civil war and Polish intervention, known as the "time of troubles," devastated Russia. Finally, the Russians reunited to drive the Poles out and call a zemski sobor in 1613 to choose a new ruling family, the Romanovs.

Between 1613 and 1676, the first two Romanov tsars, Michael and Alexis, integrated most aristocrats into the state nobility and achieved some degree of stability. As in Prussia, the nobles and the government were reconciled in their common exploitation of the serfs through the Code of 1649, which established serfdom, and the primitive agricultural economy encouraged aristocratic independence. Russian ignorance and

Adan Olearius: A Foreign Traveler in Early Russia

Zemski Sobor—A meeting of representatives of the Russian population—an assembly of the land—to reform the state in the 1550s and then to approve the choice of the Romanovs as the ruling family in 1613.

In the second part of his reign, Ivan the Terrible lapsed into periods of insanity from time to time. In one of these periods he killed his favorite son and heir. Il'ya Repin captured this tragedy in a nineteenth century painting.

technical deficiencies, along with a conservative-minded nobility, made the country stagnant in comparison with Western states.

The Balkans

As we saw in Chapter 6, the nations of the Balkans took advantage of the reduced status of the Byzantine Empire and the rise of the Italian city-states to consolidate their power in the thirteenth and fourteenth centuries. The Second Bulgarian Empire, the Empire of Stephan Dushan in Serbia, and even Skanderbeg's Albania enjoyed their golden ages in the fourteenth and fifteenth century.

But after 1345, the Ottoman Turks began their biannual incursions into Europe. It was the Byzantines themselves who had invited the Turks to cross the Dardanelles during one of their periodic dynastic disputes. Three hundred years later the Ottomans would be at the gates of Vienna.

The advancing Turks found no obstacle in the weakened government at Constantinople, and as they proceeded up the rivers of the Balkans they found not much in the way of opposition from the Bulgarians, Slavs, and Romanians. In a time of economic difficulties and religious controversies, there was a considerable degree of class conflict in the area. In addition, instead of uniting against the Ottomans, the various Slavic princes squabbled with each other, mirroring the civil wars in the Byzantine world, until it was too late.

The Ottomans were nothing if not patient, and they took advantage of the conflicts within the Balkans. They understood that they did not have enough troops in the 1350s and 1360s to militarily take the area—so they advanced diplomatically, signing treaties, establishing tribute payments, and then rearming for the next advance. Then in 1362 they took Adrianople, present-day Edirne, and from there they proceeded in a measured matter through Macedonia, then to take Sofia in 1384, then Nis 1386, and southward to take Salonika in 1387. Finally on June 15, 1389, Sultan Murad I defeated the Serbian and Bosnian forces at Kosovo and effectively sealed Ottoman control over the Balkans for the next 500 years. The taking of Constantinople in 1453 completed the conquest. Only Montenegro, of all of the Balkan region, would be able to escape Ottoman rule.

An Ambassador's Report on the Ottoman Empire

Thereafter the Balkans would experience a different historical development from the rest of Europe. The Ottomans ruled through a theocratic model (see Chapter 6)—all were slaves of the sultan who was, himself, the shadow of God. *Sharia* law was to be followed by Muslims, based on the Koran and other religious writings. There was no secular state.

The nations of the Balkans were ruled either as core provinces or as vassal states. In the core, the different regions were under the command of a governor—who had his miniature version of the Istanbul government. He delegated power to various regional and district authorities, while combining military and civilian authority. Then there were the vassal states—Moldavia, Wallachia, Transylvania, and Ragusa-Dubrovnik (ra-GOOZ-a dew-BROV-nik)—who were allowed to rule themselves in return for loyalty to the sultan and extensive payments in money and grain.

In the core provinces, those who were not Muslims, but followers of a religion of the book—the Bible or the Torah—were governed theocratically, also, through the *millet* system. As Peter Sugar noted, "These were parallel organizations, and each was independent within the limits of its own competence. The Ottomans had no concept corresponding to national lines of differentiation . . . but of religions. . . . The purpose of the . . . system was simply to create a secondary imperial administrative and primary legal structure for the *dhimmis* (non-Muslims in a protected position)." The chief rabbi in Istanbul had his own courts and law enforcers for Jews, as did the leaders of each Christian division—Armenian Catholics, Roman Catholics, and Orthodox Christians. The Phanariote Greeks who dominated the Orthodox structure became extremely powerful in the Balkans during Ottoman rule.

The Ottoman armies remained the most important part of the sultan's government. Before going into Europe, the military was characterized by valiant, independent volunteer horsemen, who fought when there was a war and went home when there was none. Once the empire began to expand in Europe, Sultan Orkhan began to divide the new land among his soldiers, to be given to them for their lifetime. This rewarded the forces for their work but did not create, for the moment, a hereditary service nobility. Orkhan also created a new, slave-based army, the janissaries.

As the empire grew larger, the Ottomans needed more fighters and bureaucrats. They instituted in the core area an arrangement to supply soldiers and bureaucrats, the **devshirme** (dev-SHIR-ma) system. Ottoman officials would go to villages throughout the Balkans and select male children whom they would take from their families and enroll in Ottoman service. The boys thus chosen would be given examinations to determine where they would serve the sultan, whether as janissaries or officials at the highest levels. This levy of Christian male children was carried on between the end of the fourteenth century and the beginning of the seventeenth system, and historians estimate that

---

devshirme—The Ottoman levy of Christian male children in the Balkans. More than 200,000 young boys were taken from their families to serve in the Ottoman army or bureaucracy.

around 200,000 sons were taken from their families during that time. Most of the boys taken came from the Slavic Orthodox populations.

The Balkans participated in none of the formative developments of modern European civilization. They did not experience the Renaissance or the Reformation, the Capitalist and Scientific Revolutions, nor the Enlightenment and Industrialization. The splendor of Constantinople was paid for by the exactions—human and materials—taken from the Balkans peoples. When the region reentered European affairs in the nineteenth century it lagged behind Central and western Europe.[5]

THE AUSTRIAN HABSBURGS' DRIVE FOR SUPERIORITY AND THE THIRTY YEARS' WAR

■ *Why was the Thirty Years' War the most destructive military conflict in Europe until the First World War in the twentieth century?*

By 1600 the Spanish Habsburgs' golden age had ended, but the potent mixture of religious and political competition among dynasties and nations would continue with even greater intensity. Philip had taken on too much and had failed to impose his will. Now, in their turn, his cousins in Central Europe—the Austrian Habsburgs—would attempt to impose their dominance in Europe. Religious passions remained at a high pitch as increasing numbers of Calvinists and Lutherans on one side and proponents of the Catholic Counter-Reformation on the other still dreamed of the complete victory of their faith and their realms. It was a dangerous time of disruption, frustration, and fanaticism.

Europeans faced severe economic depression, along with intensified conflict in every sphere of human relations. The first few decades of the seventeenth century brought a marked decline to the European economy, even before the advent of open warfare. Prices continued to fall until about 1660, reversing the inflation of the 1500s. International trade declined, as did Spanish bullion imports from Central and South America. Heavy risks on a falling market caused failures among many foreign trading companies; only the larger houses, organized as joint-stock companies, were able to survive. A climate change, bringing on colder weather, reduced the growing season and agricultural production, and the hard times in the countryside were felt in the cities, where urban craftspeople saw their wages drop.

Tensions accompanying economic depression added to those arising from continuing religious differences. The most dangerous area for religious conflict was in Central Europe, which had directly experienced an increasingly militant Counter-Reformation since the Peace of Augsburg. Although the European power balance in 1618 resembled that of the 1500s, it was much less fixed. The power of the Habsburgs of Vienna drove even normally competitive states to come together in alliances. Underneath the facade of their sixteenth-century dominance there was a sense of vulnerability. Spain was weakening and there were other states—France, the Netherlands, and Sweden—which were growing more powerful. Under these circumstances European opposition against Austrian Habsburg dominance became almost inevitable.

The Bohemian and Danish Phases of the Thirty Years' War: The Habsburgs' High Tide to 1630

The Thirty Years' War, fought between 1618 and 1648, was a culmination of all these related religious and political conflicts. Almost all of western Europe except England was directly involved and suffered accordingly. Central Europe was hit particularly hard, as can be seen in an account by a soldier writing under the name Simplicissimus, suffering population declines that would take two centuries to replace.

Despite the devastation, neither Protestantism nor Catholicism won decisively. What began as a religious war in Bohemia and the German principalities turned into a complex political struggle involving the ambitions of northern German rulers, the expansionist

War and Politics in the Age of Austrian Habsburg Dominance

1589–1610	Reign of Henry IV of France, beginning of Bourbon dynasty
1598	Edict of Nantes guarantees Protestant rights in France
1611–1632	Reign of Gustavus Adolphus in Sweden
1618–1648	Thirty Years' War
1624–1642	Cardinal Richelieu holds power in France
1643	Spanish infantry suffers first defeat at Battle of Rocroi
1648	Peace of Westphalia
1649	Independence of the United Provinces

Document: Simplicissimus on the Horrors of the Thirty Years' War

The Protestant and Catholic armies that ranged throughout Central Europe destroyed entire villages, cities, and districts. Battles were the least of the problems for the unfortunate peasants caught in the way. Accompanying the armies were thousands of camp followers who took what they wanted and destroyed the rest. In some instances it took two centuries for the devastated regions to regain their population levels and recover from the damage done by the competing forces. This account of disaster and suffering by Hans von Grimmelshausen (c. 1622–1676), the son of a German innkeeper who was left an orphan and carried away by soldiers during the Thirty Year's War, gives vivid testimony to the horrors of war. Writing under the name of Simplicissimus, he describes the arrival of an army in his home and the activities of the invaders. These ring as true for his day as they do for recent wars such as those in the Balkans, where destruction for destruction's sake and rape are common fare.

The first thing that the riders did was to stable their horses. After that, each one started to his own business which indicated nothing but ruin and destruction. While some started to slaughter, cook and fry, so that it looked as though they wished to prepare a gay feast, others stormed through the house from top to bottom as if the golden fleece of Colchis were hidden there. Others again took linen, clothing and other goods, making them into bundles as if they intended on going to market; what they did not want was broken up and destroyed. Some stabbed their swords through hay and straw as if they had not enough pigs to stab. Some shook the feathers out of the beds and filled the ticks with ham and dried meat as if they could sleep more comfortably in these. Others smashed the ovens and windows as if to announce an eternal summer. They beat copper and pewter vessels into lumps and packed the mangled pieces away. Bedsteads, tables, chairs, and benches were burned, although many stacks of dried wood stood in the yard. Earthenware pots and pans were all broken, perhaps because our guests preferred roasted meats, or perhaps they intended to eat only one meal with us. Our maid had been treated in the stable in such a way that she could not leave it any more—a shameful thing to tell! They bound the farm-hand and laid him on the earth, put a clamp of wood in his mouth and emptied a milking churn full of horrid dung water into his belly. This they called the Swedish drink, and they forced him to lead a party of soldiers to another place, where they looted men and cattle and brought them back to our yard. Among them were my dad, my mum and Ursula.

The soldiers now started to take the flints out of their pistols and in their stead screwed the thumbs of the peasants, and they tortured the poor wretches as if they were burning witches. They put one captive peasant into the bake-oven and put fire on him. Then they tied a rope around the head of another one, and twisted it with the help of a stick so tightly that blood gushed out through his mouth, nose and ears. In short everybody had his own invention to torture the peasants, and each peasant suffered his own martyrdom.... What happened to the captive women, maids and daughters I do not know as the soldiers would not let me watch how they dealt with them. I only very well remember that I heard them miserably crying in corners here and there, and I believe that my mum and Ursula had no better fate than the others.

In the midst of this misery I turned the spit and did not worry as I hardly understood what all this meant. In the afternoon I helped to water the horses and found our maid in the stable looking amazingly disheveled. I did not recognize her but she spoke to me with pitiful voice:

"Oh, run away, boy, or the soldiers will take you with them. Look out, escape! Can't you see how evil...."

More she could not say.

Questions to Consider

1. What military roles do the physical abuse and rape mentioned by Simplicissimus play in the securing of an area? Are they just instances of bestial behavior or do they reflect military strategy?
2. In considering recent instances of conflict—for example, Yugoslavia, the Palestinian conflict, and Indonesia—do you find that the nature of warfare has changed significantly in the past four centuries?
3. Do you believe that if the local peasantry in the account you have just read had had their own weapons against the occupying army that their villages and property would have been saved?

Mark A. Kishlansky, ed., *Sources of the West: Readings in Western Civilization*, 4th edition, Longman Publishers, New York, 2001, pp. 15–18.

ambitions of Sweden, and the efforts of Catholic France to break the "Habsburg ring."

Despite the general decline of Habsburg supremacy in Spain, the early years of the war before 1629, usually cited as the Bohemian (1618–1625) and Danish (1625–1629) phases, brought a last brief revival of Habsburg prospects. The new Habsburg emperor, Ferdinand II, a fanatical Catholic, was determined to intensify the Counter-Reformation, set aside the Peace of Augsburg, and literally wipe out Protestantism in Central Europe. For a time he almost succeeded.

Ferdinand's succession came amid severe political tension. Spreading Calvinism, in addition to the aggressive crusading of the Jesuits, had earlier led to the formation of a Protestant league of German princes in 1608 and a Catholic league to counter it the next year. The two alliances had almost clashed in 1610. Meanwhile, the Bohemian Protestants had extracted a promise of toleration from their Catholic king, Rudolf II (1576–1612). In 1618 the Bohemian leaders, fearing that Ferdinand would not honor that promise, threw two of his officials out a window after heated discussions—an incident known as the **defenestration of Prague.** When Ferdinand mobilized troops, the Bohemians refused to recognize him and gave their throne to Frederick, the Protestant elector of the Palatinate, in western Germany.

defenestration of Prague—The end of negotiations between Bohemia and the Holy Roman Empire in 1618; the Bohemian representatives were so angry with the representatives of the Holy Roman Emperor that they threw them out the window.

In the short Bohemian war that followed, Frederick was quickly overwhelmed. In 1620 Ferdinand deployed two strong armies, one from Spain and the other from Catholic Bavaria, and scattered the Bohemian forces at the battle of the White Mountain, near Prague. Ferdinand gave the Bohemian lands to Maximillian of Bavaria, distributed the holdings of Bohemian Protestant nobles among Catholic aristocrats, and proceeded to stamp out Protestantism in Bohemia. Of the some 3.2 million Bohemians in 1618, mostly Protestants, all that remained 30 years later were less than 1 million people, all Catholics.

War began again in 1625 when Christian IV (r. 1588–1648), the Lutheran king of Denmark, invaded Germany. As duke of Holstein and thus a prince of the empire, he hoped to revive Protestantism and win a kingdom in Germany for his youngest son. Unlike Frederick in Bohemia, Christian had support from the English, the Dutch, and the North German princes. Their help was not enough. Ferdinand dispatched his new general, Albert von Wallenstein, to crush the Protestants in a series of overpowering campaigns. By 1629 Christian had to admit defeat and withdraw his forces, thus ending the Danish conflict with another Protestant debacle. Their successful campaigns of the 1620s gave the Habsburgs almost complete domination in Germany. In 1629 Ferdinand issued his Edict of Restitution, restoring to the Catholics all properties lost since 1552. This step seemed to be only the first step toward eliminating Protestantism

By the simplicity and starkness of his portrayal, the French artist Jacques Callot captured, in a series of 24 etchings, the senseless tragedy of the Thirty Years' War (1633). The dangling bodies in this plate dramatize the tenuousness of life in turbulent times.

completely and creating a centralized Habsburg empire in Central Europe.

The Swedish and French Phases and the Balance of Power, 1630–1648

Fearing the Counter-Reformation and the growing Habsburg power behind it, threatened European states resumed the war in 1630. As the war rapidly spread and intensified, religious issues were steadily subordinated to power politics. This transformation could be seen in the phases of the conflict usually designated as the Swedish (1630–1635) and the French (1635–1648) because these two countries led successive and ultimately successful anti-Habsburg coalitions. By 1648 the Dutch Republic had replaced Spain as the leading maritime state and Bourbon France had become the dominant European land power.

Protestant Swedes and French Catholics challenged Ferdinand's imperial ambitions for similar political reasons. Although Gustavus Adolphus (r. 1611–1632), the Swedish king, wanted to save German Lutheranism, he was also determined to prevent a strong Habsburg state on the Baltic from restricting his own expansion and interfering with Swedish trade. A similar desire to liberate France from Habsburg encirclement motivated Cardinal Richelieu, the powerful minister of Louis XIII. Richelieu offered Gustavus French subsidies, for which the Swedish monarch promised to invade Germany and permit Catholic worship in any lands he might conquer. Thus, the Catholic cardinal and the Protestant king compromised their religious differences in the hope of achieving mutual political benefits.

Gustavus invaded Germany in 1630, while the Dutch attacked the Spanish Netherlands. With his mobile cannons and his hymn-singing Swedish veterans, Gustavus and his German allies won a series of smashing victories, climaxed in November 1632 at Lützen, near Leipzig, where Wallenstein was decisively defeated. Unfortunately for the Protestant cause, Gustavus died in the battle. A stalemate for the next three years led to the 1635 Peace of Prague and a momentary compromise between the emperor and the German Protestant states.

The situation now demanded that France act directly to further its dynastic interests. Thus, a final French phase of the war began when French troops moved into Germany and toward the Spanish borders. The French also subsidized the Dutch and Swedes and an army of German Protestant mercenaries. The Paris government continued limiting Protestantism within its borders but gladly allied with Protestant states against Spain, Austria, Bavaria, and their Catholic allies. The war that had begun in religious controversy had now become pure power politics, completing the long political transition from medieval to modern times.

For 13 more years, the seemingly endless conflict wore on. France's allies, the Swedes and northern Germans, kept Habsburg armies engaged in Germany, while French armies and the Dutch navy concentrated on Spain. In 1643 the French beat the Spaniards in the decisive battle at Rocroi, in the southern Netherlands. Next they moved into Germany, defeating the imperial forces and, with the Swedes, ravaging Bavaria.

For all practical purposes, the war was over, but years of indecisive campaigning and tortuous negotiations delayed the peace. Finally, a horde of diplomats met at Westphalia in 1644. Even then, Spain and France could reach no agreement for four years, but a settlement for the empire, the Treaty of Westphalia, was finally completed in 1648.

The Peace of Westphalia

The peace agreement at Westphalia signaled a victory for Protestantism and the German princes while almost dooming Habsburg imperial ambitions: France moved closer to the Rhine by acquiring Alsatian territory; Sweden and Brandenburg acquired lands on the Baltic; and the Netherlands and Switzerland gained recognition of their independence. The emperor was required to obtain approval from the Imperial Diet for any laws, taxes, military levies, and foreign agreements—provisions that nearly nullified imperial power and afforded the German states practical control of their foreign relations. German religious autonomy, as declared at Augsburg, was also reconfirmed, with Calvinism now permitted along with Lutheranism. In addition, Protestant states were conceded all Catholic properties taken before 1624.

In its religious terms the treaty ended the dream of reuniting Christendom. Catholics and Protestants now realized that major faiths could not be destroyed. With this admission, a spirit of toleration would grad-

Sweden's warrior-king Gustavus Adolphus is portrayed here at the battle of Breitenfeld in 1631.

ually emerge. Although religious uniformity could be imposed within states for another century, it would not again be a serious issue in foreign affairs until the end of the twentieth century.

The Peace of Westphalia is particularly notable for confirming the new European state system. Henceforth states would customarily shape their policies in accordance with the power of their neighbors, seeking to expand at the expense of the weaker and to protect themselves—not by religion, law, or morality, but by alliances against their stronger adversaries. Based on the works of the Dutch jurist Grotius, the treaty also instituted the international conference as a means for registering power relationships among contending states, instituted the principle of the equality of all sovereign states—as seen today in the General Assembly of the United Nations—and put into practice the tools of modern diplomacy such as extraterritoriality and diplomatic immunities.

Both Spain and Austria were weakened, and the Austrian Habsburgs shifted their primary attention from Central to southeastern Europe. German disunity was perpetuated by the autonomy of so many of the microstates. France emerged from this time as the clear winner, the potential master of the Continent. The war also helped England and the Netherlands. No matter the condition of the surviving states, their future relations would be based on the pure calculus of power, both military and economic.

CONCLUSION

Despite almost constant political and religious conflict, the years between 1300 and 1650 saw the nation-state system firmly established in Europe, particularly in the Atlantic states of Spain, France, and England.

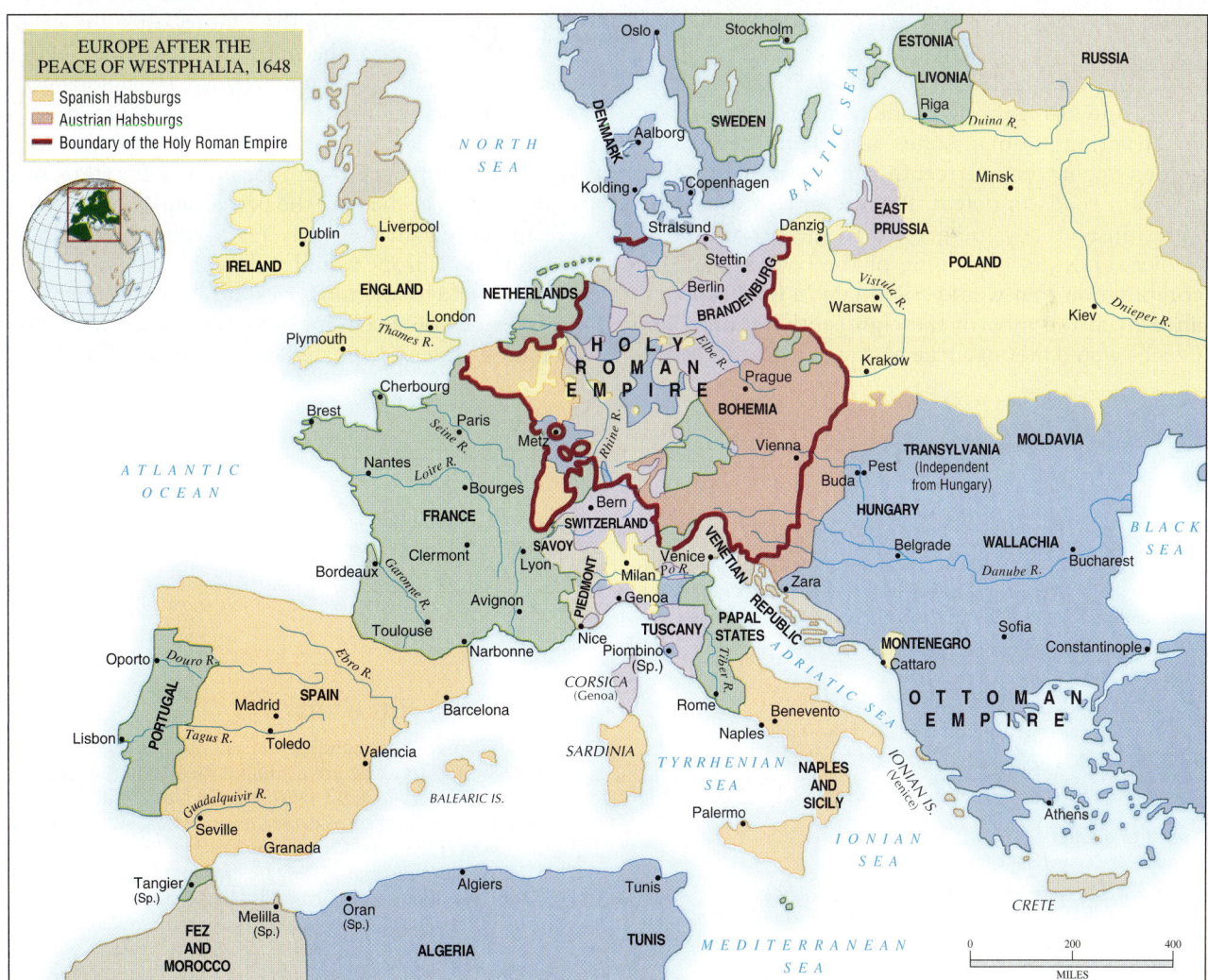

Exhausted Europeans finally agreed to put an end to the Thirty Years' War with the Treaty of Westphalia. This agreement put an end to Habsburg ambitions in Central Europe, marked the emergence of France as the major continental power, and removed religion as a factor in interstate relations. It also laid the foundations for modern international law.

Each of these three countries evolved in different ways. The political evolution of both England and France was affected by the Hundred Years' War. In England, the power of Parliament was increased, and the upsurge in the power of the nobility led to the Wars of the Roses, which ended finally with the accession of the Tudor dynasty; in France, royal power was consolidated under Louis XI, and his abilities in government made possible further progress in national unification. Nation-making in Spain was unique, since the ambitions of the monarchy were combined with the religious fervor of the Reconquista and then the Inquisition. Not until the end of the fifteenth century was the task of Spanish unification completed.

In Central and eastern Europe, state building proceeded in a haphazard and often tragic way. In the last two centuries of the Middle Ages, the Holy Roman Empire remained divided and weak; there, national unification would not be achieved until the nineteenth century. In Italy, the attempt at building a unified structure after 1454 suffered a defeat with the French invasions of a half-century later. The Italian peninsula would remain split into competing areas, also, until the nineteenth century. Poland, the Czech lands, and Hungary all made strong starts toward constructing national states, and then after a brief golden age in the fourteenth century they followed different roads to defeat. Poland opted for elective kingship and saw the growth in the powers of its nobles, and the weakening of the central state—a combination that would culminate in its disappearance from the map in the eighteenth century. The Czechs would mount a true national liberation movement against German dominance in the fifteenth century and withstand numerous attacks. However, they fell victim to Habsburg aggression in the seventeenth century. Hungary, after a shining moment under king Mathias Corvinus in the fifteenth century would be conquered by the Turks in 1526.

In eastern Europe, the Russians under Ivan III attempted to construct a strong central state, before facing chaos in the later years of his rule, and then Polish invasion during the Time of Troubles. The Romanovs slowly began to restore central power thereafter. The Balkans nations fell under the domination of the Ottoman Turks in the fourteenth and fifteenth centuries and would pursue a totally different road to state development.

The 130 years after Luther's stand at Wittenberg was an era of wrenching change for Europe. At the opening of the period, most people in their villages were still imbued with the individual, medieval concern for salvation, which gave meaning to the religious issues of the Protestant Reformation and Catholic Counter-Reformation. In the century after the Peace of Augsburg (1555), the nature of state and society changed. Initially, long and exhaustive religious wars and civil wars dominated the Continent. Later, secular political concerns became increasingly evident. But whether the wars were for faith or for state, or a combination of the two, the period until the Treaty of Westphalia ended the Thirty Years' War was the bloodiest century Europe would endure until the twentieth. Finally, in 1648, the modern state structure emerged. Europeans now lived, for better or worse, in a world of nation-states dominated by secular concerns.

Suggestions for Web Browsing

You can obtain more information about topics included in this chapter at the websites listed below. See also the companion website that accompanies this text, **http://www.ablongman.com/brummett,** which contains an online study guide and additional resources.

End of Europe's Middle Ages
http://www.ucalgary.ca/applied_history/tutor/endmiddle/

This site is developed to aid students of the late Middle Ages by providing collected links and access to primary sources.

Tudor England
http://tudor.simplenet.com/

Site detailing life in Tudor England includes biographies, maps, important dates, architecture, and music, including sound files.

The Thirty Years' War
http://www.pipeline.com/~cwa/TYWHome.htm
http://en.wikipedia.org/wiki/Thirty_Years'_War
http://www.historylearningsite.co.uk/thirty_years_war.htm

Images and explanations of Europe's bloodiest conflict, until 1914.

Peace of Westphalia
http://www.yale.edu/lawweb/avalon/westphal.htm

Complete text of the peace treaties that together made up the Treaty of Westphalia (1648), which ended the Thirty Years' War.

Literature and Film

Several recent and outstanding translations and/or editions of later medieval literature are available: Geoffrey Chaucer, *The Canterbury Tales in Modern English,* ed. Neville Coghill (Penguin, 2000); Dante Alighieri, *The Divine Comedy,* trans. Allen Mandelbaum (Knopf, 1995); and Giovanni Boccaccio, *Decameron,* trans. G. H. McWilliam (Penguin, 1996) are outstanding presentations.

This is a rich period for novels. The activities of this time attracted the best attentions of Alexandre Dumas. Writing about events in France, he produced *The Two Dianas* (dealing with the time of Francis I), *The Page of the Duke of Savoy* (touching the time of the Emperor Charles V), *Ascanio* (France in the middle of the century), and *Marguerite de Valois* (touching the civil wars), and this is only an incomplete list. Mark Twain wrote about the time of Edward VI in *The Prince and the Pauper* (1881). More recently, Robin Maxwell sheds some light on the reign of Henry VIII in *The*

Secret Diary of Anne Boleyn: A Novel (Scribner, 1998), and Reay Tannahill's *Fatal Majesty: A Novel of Mary Queen of Scots* (Griffin, 2000) offers another recent discussion of the tragic queen.

Some excellent video explorations of the late medieval period are *Siena: Chronicle of a Medieval Commune* (Metropolitan Museum of Art, 1988); *Landmarks of Western Art: The Medieval World* (Kultur Video, 1999); *Living in the Past: Life in Medieval Times* (Kultur Video, 1998); and *Medieval Warfare* (1997; Kultur Video, 3 tapes).

Filmmakers have been equally attracted to the period, especially the English scene. (All of the following are available in VHS.) Fred Zinnemann's *A Man for all Seasons* (Columbia, 1966) is a fine telling of the story of Sir Thomas More. Queen Elizabeth has been the subject of films throughout the twentieth century, including Shekhar Kapur's *Elizabeth* (Channel Four Films, 1998), and indirectly in *Shakespeare in Love* (Miramax, 1998). A film dealing with the period after Henry VIII is Trevor Nunn's *Lady Jane* (Paramount, 1986). The 1933 film, Alexander Korda's *The Private Life of Henry VIII* (London Film Productions) is worth seeing as is *Mary Queen of Scots* (Charles Jarrett, director, Universal Pictures, 1971). On the continent, *The Return of Martin Guerre* (Daniel Vigne, director, European International, 1982) does justice to Natalie Zemon Davis's fine monograph. The film of the life of Martin Luther (Louis de Rochemont Associates, 1953) is a revealing look at the reformer.

Suggestions for Reading

For the spirit of the age see David Nirenberg, *Communities of Violence: Persecution of Minorities in the Middle Ages* (Princeton University Press, 1996). See also S. Harrison Thomson, *Czechoslovakia In European History* (Frank Cass and Co. Ltd., 1965); Lonnie R. Johnson, *Central Europe: Enemies, Neighbors, Friends* (Oxford University Press, 1996); Daniel Herlihy, *The Black Death and the Transformation of the West* (Harvard University Press, 1997); and Richard Kieckhefer, *Magic in the Middle Ages* (Cambridge University Press, 2000). See also C. H. Haskins, *The Rise of Universities* (Cornell University Press, 1965).

Valuable sources of English history include Bell Henneman, ed., *The Medieval French Monarchy* (Krieger, 1973); C.B. Bouchard, *Strong of Body, Brave and Noble: Chivalry and Society in Medieval France* (Cornell, 1998); Nigel Saul, ed., *The Oxford History of Medieval England* (Oxford, 2001); and P.S.P. Goldberg, ed., *Women in Medieval English Society* (Sutton, 1997). See also Edmund King, *Medieval England, 1066–1485* (Salem House, 1989). Bernard T. Reilly, *The Medieval Spains* (Cambridge University Press, 1993), and Richard Fletcher, *Moorish Spain* (University of California Press, 1993), are excellent surveys.

On later medieval society, see Philip Ziegler, *The Black Death* (Sutton, 1998); Christopher Allmand, *The Hundred Years' War* (Cambridge University Press, 1988); Norman Cantor, *In the Wake of the Plague: The Black Death and the World It Made* (Free Press, 2001); Jonathan Sumption, *The Hundred Years' War: Trial by Battle* (University of Pennsylvania Press, 1999); and Daniel Waley, *Later Medieval Europe: From St. Louis to Luther* (Longman, 1985).

Geoffrey Parker, *The Grand Strategy of Philip II* (Yale University Press, 1998), is the best study of the construction of the Spanish world empire. It is still important to read Fernand Braudel's *The Mediterranean and the Mediterranean World in the Age of Philip II*, 2 vols. (Harper Torchbook, 1976), translated by Siân Reynolds, for its lessons both about the age and about how to understand history in a broader context. The classic treatment of the Armada is Garrett Mattingly, *The Armada* (Houghton Mifflin, 1988).

For the Dutch rebellion see James D. Tracy's, *Holland Under Habsburg Rule* (University of California Press, 1990). Simon Schama, *The Embarrassment of Riches: An Interpretation of Dutch Culture in the Golden Age* (Knopf, 1987), and Charles R. Boxer, *The Dutch Seaborne Empire* (Penguin, 1989), depict the republic at the apex of its struggle for power and wealth. Guido Marnef, *Antwerp in the Age of Reformation* (Johns Hopkins University Press, 1996), gives the texture and detail of this extraordinary time.

French society and politics during the whole era are ably treated in Mack P. Holt, *The French Wars of Religion, 1562–1629* (Cambridge University Press, 1995), a new study of the chaotic period preceding Richelieu, with considerable emphasis on social history. Henry Heller, *Iron and Blood: Civil Wars in Sixteenth-Century France* (McGill-Queen's University Press, 1991), describes the catastrophic religious wars. For a re-creation of life just beneath the religious and political conflict see Natalie Zemon Davis's classic, *The Return of Martin Guerre* (Harvard University Press, 1984).

A revealing survey of English social history is J. A. Sharpe, *Early Modern England: A Social History, 1550–1760*, 2nd ed. (Arnold, 1997). On the growing social and political awareness of English women in the sixteenth and seventeenth centuries, see Katherine A. Henderson and Barbara McManus, *Half Humankind: Contexts and Texts of the Controversy About Women in England, 1540–1640* (University of Illinois Press, 1985), and Mary Prior, ed., *Women in English Society, 1500–1800* (Methuen, 1985). Excellent general interpretations of Elizabethan England are presented in Arthur Bryant, *The Elizabethan Deliverance* (St. Martin's Press, 1982), and David B. Quinn and A. N. Ryan, *England's Sea Empire, 1550–1642* (Allen & Unwin, 1983). Biographies worth consulting include Anne Somerset, *Elizabeth I* (Knopf, 1991), and J. Mary Wormald, *Mary, Queen of Scots* (Philip & Sons, 1988). A noteworthy special work on Elizabethan women is Susan Cahn, *The Transformation of Women's Work in England, 1500–1600* (Columbia University Press, 1987). Wallace T. MacCaffrey, *Elizabeth I, War and Politics 1588–1603* (Princeton University Press, 1992), is the best general survey of her reign.

On the less developed absolutism in eastern Europe, see Robert James Weston Evans, *The Making of the Habsburg Monarchy, 1550–1700* (Oxford University Press, 1984); see also Norman Davies, *A History of Poland*, Vol. 1 (Columbia University Press, 1981). A useful study of Prussian history in this period is Otis Mitchell, *A Concise History of Brandenburg-Prussia to 1786* (University Press of America, 1980). Development of the Romanov state is ably described in Otto Hoetzsch, *The Evolution of Russia* (Harcourt Brace, 1966), and W. Bruce Lincoln, *The Romanovs* (Dial, 1981).

Ronald G. Asch, *The Thirty Years' War, the Holy Roman Empire and Europe, 1618–1648* (St. Martin's Press, 1997), is a brief up-to-date survey with a good appreciation of the historiographical conflicts surrounding this event that adds to, but does not replace, Cicely V. Wedgewood's classic *The Thirty Years' War* (Anchor Books, 1961). Joseph Polisensky discusses the by-products of the war in *War and Society in Europe, 1618–1648* (Cambridge University Press, 1978). Michael Roberts, *Sweden's Age of Greatness* (St. Martin's Press, 1973), gives good coverage of both the political and military events in this conflict.

GLOBAL ISSUES

TECHNOLOGICAL EXCHANGE

How does technology move from one culture to another?

First trial of Maxim machine gun by English troops in Africa, 1887.

Technology has played a decisive role in human history, but its movement between cultures is often overlooked. Indeed, while American society tends to stress the creative genius of individual inventors such as Thomas Edison and the Wright brothers, technological innovations such as the light bulb and the airplane rest on a vast body of knowledge that stretches both back in time and around the world. It is, in fact, a universal tendency for individuals and societies to build on past discoveries, whatever their place of origin.

Traditionally, most world cultures have been open to beneficial new technologies originating from other cultures. Between 800 and 1300 C.E. Islamic civilization became dominant in the sciences in part because it eagerly absorbed the scientific knowledge of other civilizations such as Greece, Persia, and India. Caliphs and wealthy patrons sponsored medical centers, observatories, and libraries that translated foreign scientific treatises and undertook their own scientific investigations. Their efforts helped Muslim scientists make advances in mathematics, astronomy, medicine, and navigation. During this era, Arabic became the language of science, and both technological innovations and classical learning flowed from the Islamic world to Europe, where they helped stimulate the Renaissance.

Technology has often moved from its culture of origin to new cultures only to undergo further development there and then be transmitted on to other cultures and even back to its culture of origin, which was the case with gunpowder technology. A range of societies had experimented with explosives, but it was the Chinese who first invented gunpowder in the mid-ninth century C.E., initially only to make fireworks for religious and entertainment purposes. It would take another three centuries before they applied this technology to warfare, with the invention of rockets, bombs, and mortars. In the thirteenth century, the invading Mongols, in turn, helped to spread gunpowder technology from China across Asia to the Islamic world and Europe. Muslims and Christians alike were quick to recognize the potential of this new technology. When two English nobles in Spain witnessed the battle of Tarifa in 1340, they observed an Arab army fielding cannons against a Spanish force. They took that knowledge back with them to England, where it was immediately put to use in their wars with the French.

The Europeans, in fact, were so quick to embrace and develop gunpowder technology that it was the Portuguese and not the Chinese who first introduced muskets to East Asia in the early sixteenth century. The Japanese quickly accepted the new technology and begun manufacturing their own muskets. In a very short time, they were making guns equal to, if not better than, those made by the Europeans. This trend, however, would not last. In the seventeenth century, the samurai, the warrior class of Japan, opposed production of guns because they recognized that guns would endanger their exclusive status in Japanese society.

The Japanese only changed their view about guns out of necessity some 200 years later when a relatively small British force defeated China in the Opium War during the 1840s and Matthew Perry's warships anchored in Edo Bay in 1853. The Meiji emperor's embrace of modernization came out of the realization that Japan had to rapidly assimilate Western weapons of war if it wanted to fend off Western domination. Japanese scientists and officers studied English, French, and German military science, and the government poured money into the armament industry. Foreigners were admitted as teachers and technicians, and Japanese students were sent to American and European universities. The Imperial University, established in 1886, set up a faculty of engineering with departments specifically for explosives and shipbuilding. Japan's embrace of Western technology paid dividends when it defeated first China in the Sino-Japanese War of 1894–1895 and then Russia in the Russo-Japanese War of 1905.

Given the military and economic advantages offered by many technologies, it should not be surprising that many nations have sought to secure their own technologies and acquire or even steal the "protected" technologies of other nations. The Chinese closely guarded the secrets of silk and porcelain production for centuries until spies finally managed to carry those secrets abroad and break the Chinese monopoly. In the nineteenth century, Europeans may have eagerly sold the finished products of their technologies in the Americas, Asia, and Africa, but they generally kept the most advanced technologies for themselves, particularly weapons. Hilaire Belloc's famous couplet stated the truth bluntly: "Whatever else we have got / The Maxim gun and they have not."

The Europeans also sought to ensure that the manufacture of finished products—and thus the industry and profits—remained in their home countries. The colonized peoples of Africa and Asia, then, became the consumers of finished products and were prevented from developing their own manufacturing capabilities—a legacy that continues to challenge many countries in the developing world today.

Over the last two centuries one way some countries have sought to protect valuable technologies and encourage inventiveness in their people is through the issuing of patents, which give inventors an exclusive monopoly on the production of their invention for a number of years. Patented technologies are generally honored in the developed world, but cases of counterfeiting and piracy are rampant in the developing world. Of course, patent or no patent, if a business or individual is to have any chance of protecting a technology, it must recognize its value in the first place. This wasn't the case of the American company Western Electric and the transistor. American scientists had invented the transistor, but American electronics companies still relied on vacuum tubes in their products and were not prepared to apply the new technology in their manufacturing. Instead, a Japanese firm, Tokyo Telecommunications, recognized the importance of transistors and bought the rights from Western Electric when it sold its patent in 1954. Within a few years, the Japanese company had designed a transistor radio, and, after changing its name to Sony, it became a world leader in mass-producing electronics products.

Today, the dominant new economic technologies of our times are embodied in the Internet and information technology (IT). While these technologies have been exchanged freely around the world, their benefits have not reached all people. Because of the costs of achieving connectivity, a "digital divide" has emerged in which access to the Internet, for example, is often limited to urban elites in developing countries. On the other hand, some new technologies such as cell phones have opened up communications and business opportunities in remote areas of the world and are often even more ubiquitous in developing countries than they are in the West.

With advances to communication and transportation technology making the world smaller and smaller by the day, it seems certain the rate of technological exchange between cultures will only accelerate in the future.

Questions

1. What reasons might a culture have for rejecting a new technology coming from another culture?
2. Can you think of any situations in which counterfeiting and piracy of a technology would be morally acceptable?
3. Why is technological exchange inevitable?

CHAPTER 16

Global Encounters
Europe and the New World Economy, 1400–1650

CHAPTER CONTENTS

- The Iberian Golden Age
- The Portuguese and Africa

  DISCOVERY THROUGH MAPS: *Savage Pictures: Sebastian Munster's Map of Africa*

  DOCUMENT: *Portuguese Encounters with Africans*

- The Growth of New Spain
- Iberian Systems in the New World

  DOCUMENT: *Disease and the Spanish Conquest*

- Beginnings of Northern European Expansion

1300

1394–1460 Prince Henry the Navigator

1400

1400s Iberian navigators develop new naval technology; Spain and Portugal stake claims in Asia, Africa, and the Americas; Atlantic slave trade begins

1492 Christopher Columbus reaches San Salvador

1498 Vasco da Gama rounds Cape of Good Hope, reaches India

1500

1513 Vasco de Balboa reaches Pacific Ocean

1519 Hernando Cortés arrives in Mexico, defeats Aztecs

1520 Ferdinand Magellan rounds South America

1600

c. 1600 Second phase of European overseas expansion begins

1609 Henry Hudson establishes Dutch claims in North America; English East India Company chartered

1620 Pilgrims land at Plymouth

During the fifteenth century, European nations began a process of exploration, conquest, and trade, affecting almost all areas of the world. Their activities were mirrored in other parts of the world as Asian and Arab states took the lead in expanding their trading networks and their connections with each other. The processes were furthered by improved navigational technology and the resulting expansion of trade that encouraged long sea voyages by Arabs, Japanese, and Chinese. Likewise, sea power, rather than land-based armies, was the key to Europe's becoming a significant force in various parts of the world, especially the Americas and Africa.

European endeavors overseas were obviously related—both as cause and as effect—to trends set in motion as Europe emerged from the medieval era. The Crusades and the Renaissance stimulated European curiosity; the Reformation produced thousands of zealous missionaries seeking converts in foreign lands and refugees searching for religious freedom; and the monarchs of emerging sovereign states sought revenues, first by trading in the Indian Ocean and later by exploiting new worlds. Perhaps the most permeating influence was the rise of European capitalism, with its monetary values, profit-seeking motivations, investment institutions, and consistent impulses toward economic expansion. Some historians have labeled this whole economic transformation the Commercial Revolution. Others have used the phrase to refer to the shift in trade routes from the Mediterranean to the Atlantic. Interpreted either way, the Commercial Revolution and its accompanying European expansion helped usher in a modern era, largely at the expense of Africans and Amerindians.

Europe's Commercial Revolution developed in two quite distinct phases. The first phase involved Portugal and Spain; the second phase, after 1600, was led by the Netherlands, England, and to some extent France. The second fostered a maritime imperialism based more on trade and finance than the more directly exploitative systems of the first phase.

THE IBERIAN GOLDEN AGE

■ *What motivated the Portuguese and Spanish to develop global commercial networks?*

Portugal and Spain, the two Iberian states, launched the new era in competition with each other, although neither was able to maintain initial advantages over the long term. Portugal lacked the manpower and resources required by an empire spread over three continents. Spain wasted its new wealth in waging continuous wars while neglecting to develop its own economy. In 1503 Portuguese pepper cost only one-fifth as much as pepper coming through Venice and the eastern Mediterranean. Within decades, gold and silver from the New World poured into Spain. Iberian bullion and exotic commodities, flowing into northern banks and markets, provided a major stimulus to European capitalism. This early European impact abroad also generated great cultural diffusion, promoting an intercontinental spread of peoples, plants, animals, and knowledge that the world had never seen before. But it also destroyed Amerindian states and weakened societies in Africa.

Conditions Favoring Iberian Expansion

A number of conditions invited Iberian maritime expansion in the fifteenth century. Muslim control over the eastern caravan routes, particularly after the Turks took Constantinople in 1453, brought rising prices in Europe. At the same time, the sprawling Islamic world lacked both unity and intimidating sea power, and China, after 1440, had abandoned its extensive naval forays into the Indian Ocean. Because Muslim and Italian rivals prevented the Iberian states from tapping into the spice trade in the eastern Mediterranean and the gold trade in West Africa, Portugal and Spain sought alternative sea routes to the East, where their centuries-old struggle with Muslims in the Mediterranean might be continued on the ocean shores of sub-Saharan Africa and Asia.

During the 1400s, Iberian navigators became proficient in new naval technology and tactics. They adopted the compass (which came from China through the Middle East), the **astrolabe,** and the triangular **lateen sail** that gave their ships the ability to take advantage of winds coming from oblique angles and cut weeks off longer voyages. They also learned to tack against the wind, thus partly freeing them from hugging the coast on long voyages. This skill was important because prevailing winds and ocean currents made it impossible for Portuguese sailors to go farther south than Cape Bojador (bo-hyah-DOR) and still return home. In 1434, a Portuguese seafarer learned that it was possible to sail west toward the Canary Islands and catch trade winds that allowed ships to proceed home. This discovery opened up a new era of exploration.

The Iberians, especially the Portuguese, were also skilled cartographers and chartmakers. But their main advantages lay with their ships and naval guns. The stormy Atlantic required broad bows, deep keels, and complex square rigging for driving and maneuvering fighting ships. Armed with brass cannons, such ships could sink enemy vessels without ramming or boarding at close range. They could also batter down coastal defenses. Even the much larger Chinese junks were no match for the European ships' maneuverability and firepower.

A strong religious motivation augmented Iberian naval efficiency. Long and bitter wars with the Muslim Moors had left the Portuguese and Spanish with an obsessive drive to convert non-Christians or destroy them in the name of Christ. Sailors with Columbus recited prayers every night, and Portuguese seamen were equally devout. Every maritime mission was regarded as a holy crusade.

For two centuries Iberians had hoped to expand their influence in Muslim lands by launching a new Christian crusade in concert with Ethiopia. The idea

Portuguese and Spanish Exploration and Expansion

1470–1541	Francisco Pizarro
1474–1566	Bartolomé de Las Casas
1479	Treaty of Alcacovas
1494	Treaty of Tordesillas
1509–1515	Alfonso de Albuquerque serves as eastern viceroy of Portugal
1510–1554	Francisco de Coronado
1510	Portuguese acquire Goa, in India
1531	Pizarro defeats Incas in Peru
c. 1550	Spanish introduce plantation system to Brazil
1565	St. Augustine founded; first European colony in North America

astrolabe—An instrument used in navigation for calculating latitude.

lateen sail—A triangular sail that is set at a 45-degree angle to the mast and takes advantage of winds coming from oblique angles.

originated with twelfth-century crusaders in the Holy Land; it gained strength later with Ethiopian migrants at Rhodes, who boasted of their king's prowess against the infidels. Thus arose the myth of "Prester John," a mighty Ethiopian monarch and potential European ally against Mongols, Turks, and Muslims. In response to a delegation from Zar'a Ya'kob, the reigning emperor, a few Europeans visited Ethiopia after 1450. These and other similar contacts greatly stimulated the determination to find a new sea route to the East that might link the Iberians with the legendary Ethiopian king and bring Islam under attack from two sides.

"The Land of Prester John"

This dream of war for the cross was sincere, but it also served to rationalize more worldly concerns. Both Spain and Portugal experienced dramatic population growth between 1400 and 1600. The Spanish population increased from 5 to 8.5 million; the Portuguese population more than doubled, from 900,000 to 2 million, despite a manpower loss of 125,000 in the sixteenth century. Hard times in rural areas prompted migration to cities, where dreams of wealth in foreign lands encouraged fortune seeking overseas. Despite the obvious religious zeal of many Iberians, particularly among those in holy orders, a fervent desire for gain was the driving motivation for most migrants.

The structures of the Iberian states provided further support for overseas expansion. In both, the powers of the monarchs had been recently expanded and were oriented toward maritime adventure as a means to raise revenues, divert the Turkish menace, spread Catholic Christianity, and increase national unity. The Avis dynasty in Portugal, after usurping the throne and alienating the great nobles in 1385, made common cause with the gentry and middle classes, who prospered in commercial partnership with the government. In contrast, Spanish nobles, particularly the Castilians, were very much like Turkish aristocrats, who regarded conquest and plunder as their normal functions and sources of income. Thus, the Portuguese and Spanish political systems worked in different ways toward similar imperial ends.

Staking Claims

During the late fifteenth century, both Portugal and Spain staked claims abroad. Portugal gained a long lead over Spain in Africa and Asia. But after conquering Granada, the last Moorish state on the Iberian peninsula, and completely uniting the country, the Spanish monarchs turned their attention overseas. The resulting historic voyage of Columbus established Spanish claims to most of the Western Hemisphere.

The man most responsible for Portugal's ambitious exploits was Prince Henry (1394–1460), known as "the Navigator" because of his famous observatory at

Using ships like these broad-beamed carracks, the Portuguese controlled much of the carrying trade with the East in the fifteenth and sixteenth centuries.

Sagres (SAH-greesh), where skilled mariners planned voyages and recorded their results. As a young man in 1415, Henry directed the Portuguese conquest of Ceuta (see-YOO-tah), a Muslim port on the Moroccan coast, at the western entrance to the Mediterranean. This experience imbued him with a lifelong desire to divert the West African gold trade from Muslim caravans to Portuguese ships. He also shared the common dream of winning Ethiopian Christian allies against the Turks. Such ideas motivated him for 40 years as he sent expeditions down the West African coast, steadily charting and learning from unknown waters.

Before other European states began extensive explorations, the Portuguese had navigated the West African coast to its southern tip. Henry's captains claimed the Madeira Islands in 1418 and the Azores in 1421. A thousand miles to the west of Portugal, these uninhabited islands were settled to produce, among other things, wheat for bread-starved Lisbon.

By 1450 the Portuguese had explored the Senegal River and then traced the Guinea coast during the next decade. After Henry's death in 1460, they pushed south, reaching Benin in the decade after 1470 and Kongo, on the southwest coast, in 1482. Six years later, Bartolomeu Dias rounded southern Africa, but his disgruntled crew forced him to turn back. Nevertheless, King John II of Portugal (1481–1495) was so excited by the prospect of a direct route to India that he named Dias's discovery the "Cape of Good Hope."

Spain soon challenged Portuguese supremacy. The specific controversy was over the Canary Islands, some of which were occupied by Castilians in 1344 and others by Portuguese after the 1440s. The issue, which produced repeated incidents, was ultimately settled in 1479 by the Treaty of Alcacovas (ahl-KAHS-ko-vahsh), which recognized exclusive Spanish rights in the Canaries but banned Spain from the Madeiras, the Azores, the Cape Verdes, and West Africa. Spanish ambitions were thus temporarily frustrated until Columbus provided new hope.

Christopher Columbus (1451–1506), a Genoese sailor with an impossible dream, had been influenced by Marco Polo's journal to believe that Japan could be reached by a short sail directly westward. Although he underestimated the distance by some 7000 miles and was totally ignorant of the intervening continents, Columbus persistently urged his proposals on King John of Portugal and Queen Isabella of Spain, who was captivated by Columbus's dream and became his most steadfast supporter until her death in 1504. Having obtained her sponsorship, Columbus sailed from Palos, Spain, in three small ships on August 3, 1492. He landed on San Salvador in the West Indies on October 12, thinking he had reached his goal. In three more attempts he continued his search for an Asian passage. His voyages touched the major Caribbean islands, Honduras, the Isthmus of Panama, and Venezuela. Although he never knew it, he had claimed a new world for Spain.

VIDEO
Christopher Columbus and the Round World

Columbus's first voyage posed threats to Portuguese interests in the Atlantic and called for compromise if war was to be averted. At Spain's invitation, the pope issued a "bull of demarcation," establishing a north-south line about 300 miles west of the Azores. Beyond this line all lands were opened to Spanish claims. The Portuguese protested, forcing direct negotiations, which produced the Treaty of Tordesillas (tor-dhai-SEE-lyahs) in 1494. It moved the line some 500 miles farther west. Later explorations showed that the last agreement gave Spain most of the New World but left eastern Brazil to Portugal.

Motivated by a desire to find a sea route to India that bypassed the overland caravan routes controlled by Muslim states, Prince Henry the Navigator was a leading figure in promoting Portuguese explorations down the West African coast. Ironically he seldom left Portugal himself. When he died in 1460, his sailors had reached the Canary Islands, but by the end of that century, Vasco da Gama had sailed from Portugal to India.

The Developing Portuguese Empire

Through the first half of the sixteenth century, the Portuguese developed a world maritime empire while maintaining commercial supremacy. They established trading posts around both African coasts and a falter-

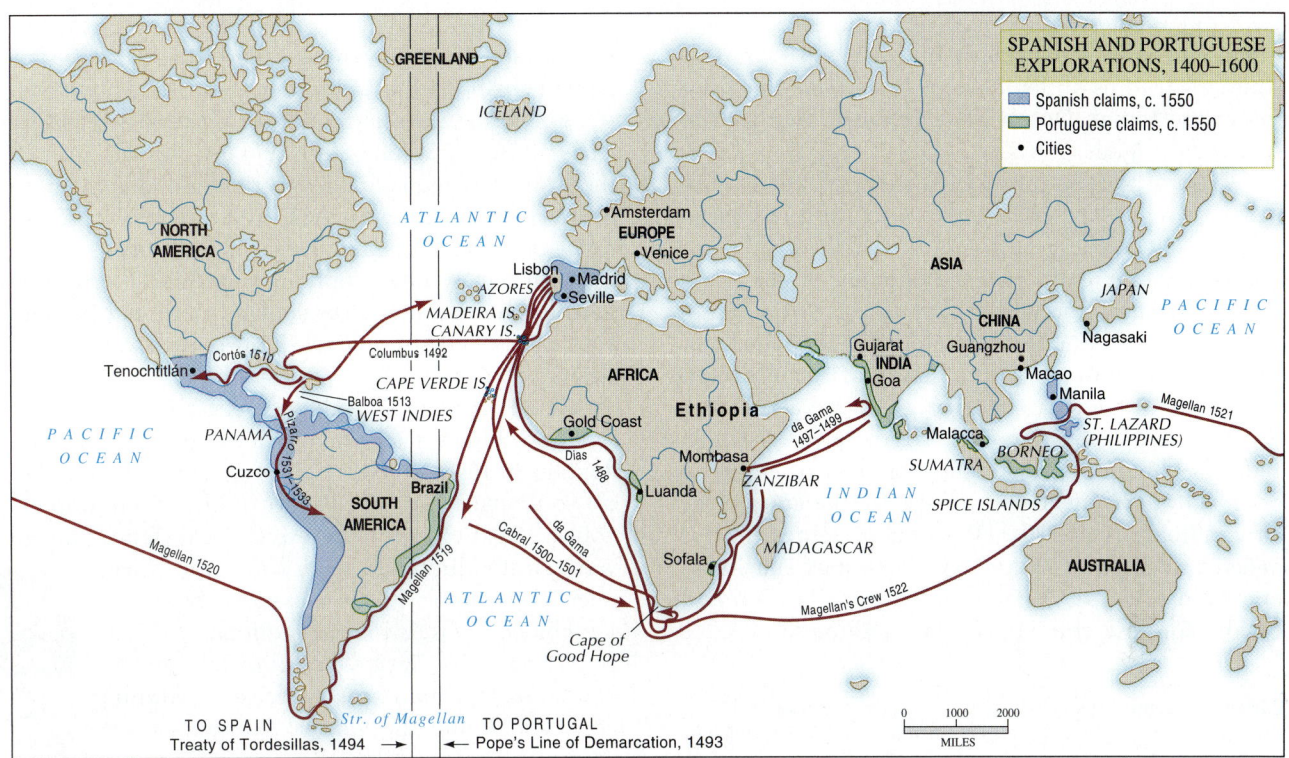

From the mid-fifteenth to the mid-sixteenth centuries, Portugal and Spain took advantage of new naval technology and tactics to become the leading seafaring nations in the world.

ing colony in Brazil, but their most extensive operations were in southern Asia, where they gained control of shipping routes and dominated the Indian Ocean spice trade.

Two voyages at the turn of the sixteenth century laid the foundations for the Portuguese interests in the Americas and the Orient. In 1497 Vasco da Gama (1469–1524) left Lisbon, Portugal, in four ships, rounding the Cape of Good Hope after 93 days on the open sea. While visiting and raiding the East African ports, da Gama picked up an Arab pilot, who brought the fleet across the Indian Ocean to Calicut (KAL-i-kut), on the western coast of India. When he returned to Lisbon in 1499, da Gama had lost two ships and a third of his men, but his cargo of pepper and cinnamon returned the cost of the expedition 60 times over. Shortly afterward, Pedro Cabral (1468–1520), commanding a large fleet on a second voyage to India, bore too far west and sighted the east coast of Brazil. The new western territory was so unpromising that it was left unoccupied until 1532, when a small settlement was established at São Vicente. In the 1540s it had attracted only some 2000 settlers, mostly men, although a few Portuguese women came after the arrival of the lord protector's wife and her retinue in 1535. The colony served mostly as a place to send convicts, and by 1600 it had only 25,000 European residents.

Brazil was neglected in favor of extensive operations in the Indian Ocean and Southeast Asia, where the Portuguese sought to gain control of the spice trade by taking over flourishing port cities, places strategically located on established trade routes. The most striking successes were achieved under Alfonso de Albuquerque, eastern viceroy from 1509 to 1515. He completed subjugation of the Swahili city-states and established fortified trading posts in Mozambique and Zanzibar. After a decisive naval victory over an Arab fleet (1509), Albuquerque's force captured Hormuz (hor-MOOZ) six years later, thus disrupting Arab passage from the Persian Gulf. In 1510 the Portuguese acquired Goa on the west coast of India; it became a base for aiding Hindus against Indian Muslims and conducting trade with Gujerat (goo-ja-RAHT), a major producer of cloth. The next year a Portuguese force took Malacca, a Muslim stronghold in Malaya, which controlled trade with China and the Spice Islands, through the narrow straits opposite Sumatra (soo-MAH-trah). Although a Portuguese goal was to spread the Christian faith at the expense of Islam, the expulsion of Muslim traders had the opposite effect. These traders moved to the Malaysian peninsula and founded new Muslim states.

The Indian Ocean had previously been open to all traders, but the Portuguese network left no room for competitors, and rival traders, especially Muslims, were squeezed out of their previous settlements. Portuguese officials financed their operations from two sources, customs duties and a tax levied on ships trading in the Indian Ocean. All ships were required to stop at Portuguese ports and take a **cartaz.**

The Portuguese presence was largely felt on the ocean; it had very little impact on the land-based empires and trading networks of the Ottomans, the Safavids, the Mughuls, and the Chinese. On the Asian mainland, for instance, the Portuguese were mostly supplicants because they had to interact with well-established and more powerful states. They acquired temporary influence in Laos and Cambodia but were expelled from Vietnam and enslaved in Burma. In China their diplomatic blunders and breaches of etiquette offended Ming officials, who regarded the Portuguese as cannibals. In 1519 a Portuguese representative angered the Chinese by, among other things, starting to erect a fort in Canton harbor without permission and buying Chinese children as slaves. Chinese officials responded by jailing and executing a group of Portuguese emissaries who had been visiting Beijing. After being banished from Chinese ports in 1522 and 1544, the Portuguese cooperated with Chinese smuggling rings off South China before Chinese officials granted them strictly regulated trading rights in Macao (mah-KOU) in 1554. Although the Chinese generally had little interest in European goods, the Portuguese served a useful purpose by supplying the Chinese economy with Indian manufactures such as cloth and Indonesian spices and silver from the Americas reexported through Europe.

The Portuguese developed an extensive relationship with Japan. The connection was established accidentally in 1542 when three Portuguese traders landed off southern Japan after a storm blew their ship off course. At the time Japanese *daimyo* (feudal lords) were contending with each other for power, and Portuguese traders prospered by selling matchlock muskets to rival factions.

The Jesuit priests who followed the merchants in 1549 had great success in winning converts. While the *daimyo* Nobunaga was gaining mastery over his opponents, he

A Japanese View of European Missionaries

cartaz—A license issued by the Portuguese that permitted non-Portuguese traders to operate in areas of the Indian Ocean controlled by the Portuguese.

In the sixteenth century a Japanese artist depicted the Portuguese as "Southern Barbarians" in a decorative screen.

encouraged the Catholics because they were useful allies against Buddhist sects opposing him. By the 1580s, the Catholics were claiming as many as 150,000 adherents. However, as Japan became unified in the late sixteenth century, Nobunaga's successors began regarding Christians as a divisive threat. They perceived the arrival of Spanish Franciscan friars in 1592 as an additional danger because they had recently scored major successes in winning converts in the Philippines. Japanese officials issued a series of anti-Christian edicts that led to the persecution and killing of thousands of Christians. Following the suppression of a Christian peasant revolt in 1637–1638, the Japanese government expelled all Europeans except for a small contingent of Dutch traders who were confined to a small island in the Nagasaki harbor.

Long before this expulsion, the Portuguese Empire had begun to decline. It did not have the special skills or fluid capital required by a global empire and had become dependent on the bankers and spice brokers of northern Europe for financing. This deficiency was magnified by Albuquerque's failure to recruit women from home who might have produced a Portuguese governing elite in the colonies. To make matters worse, the home population dropped steadily after 1600. Thus the relatively few Portuguese men overseas mated with local women. Most were concubines, prostitutes, or slaves—regarded generally as household pets or work animals. These conditions contributed largely to a decided weakening of morale, economic efficiency, and military power. After the turn of the seventeenth century, the Portuguese lost ground to the Omani Arabs in East Africa, the Spanish in the Philippines, and the Dutch in both hemispheres. Despite a mild later revival, their empire never regained its former glory.

THE PORTUGUESE AND AFRICA

■ *How did Africans respond to the opportunities offered by trade with the Portuguese?*

The Portuguese came to Africa as traders rather than settlers. Their original goal was to find a way around Muslim middlemen who controlled the trans-Saharan caravan trade and to gain direct access to the fabled goldfields of West Africa. Muslim kingdoms of the Sudan, such as Mali, Kanem-Bornu, and the Hausa states, dominated trade in the West African interior and were reluctant to open up their trade to Europeans. Therefore, the Portuguese concentrated their efforts on establishing commercial bases along the West African coast.

The Portuguese in West Africa

Africa was not of primary importance to the Portuguese, especially after they opened up sea routes to Asia. Thus, they selectively established links with African states where they could trade for goods of value such as gold, which could be traded anywhere in the world, and slaves, which were initially taken to southern Portugal as laborers. The first bases of operation for Portuguese seafarers were at Cape Verde, Arguin (ahr-GWEEN), and Senegambia.

Portuguese Travelers in Africa

Although the Portuguese conducted hit-and-run raids for slaves and plunder, they soon learned that if they expected to sustain a profitable trade in gold, they could not afford to alienate African rulers. When the Portuguese arrived on the Gold Coast (present-day Ghana) in 1471, they found Akan states carrying on a vigorous trade to the north through Muslim Dyula traders. Still hoping to develop trade links with the kingdom of Mali, the Portuguese sent several envoys with Dyula traders to Mali in the late fifteenth century. However, Mali's king sent a clear signal about his lack of interest in ties with Portugal by informing the envoy that he recognized only three kings beside himself—the rulers of Yemen, Cairo, and Baghdad.

From that point on, the Portuguese concentrated on establishing a profitable relationship with Akan leaders, exchanging firearms (that could not be obtained through Mali), copper and brass objects, textiles, slaves, and later cowrie shells for gold. From their fort at Elmina ("the mine"), established in 1482, the Portuguese exported close to half a ton of gold annually for the next half century. Because the Akan required slave labor to clear forests for arable agricultural land, the Portuguese brought slaves from the region of Benin and Kongo. It took several more

	The Portuguese and Africa
1482	Portuguese establish Fort Elmina on Gold Coast; Portuguese reach kingdom of Kongo
1506–1543	Reign of Nzinga Mbemba, king of Kongo
1506	Portuguese seize Sofala
1571	Portuguese establish colony of Angola
1607	King of Mutapa kingdom signs treaty with Portugal
1698	Portuguese driven from East African coast by Omani Arabs

centuries before Akan states actively participated in selling rather than buying slaves.

The Portuguese also initiated contacts with the kingdom of Benin, located in the forests of southwestern Nigeria. The kings of Benin, called *obas,* had governed their land since the eleventh century. When the Portuguese arrived, Benin possessed a formidable army and was at the peak of its power. Edo, the walled capital, was a bustling metropolis with wide streets, markets, and an efficient municipal government. The huge royal palace awed Europeans who chanced to see it, although the Portuguese—and later the Dutch—were generally prohibited from living in the city. The few European visitors who gained entrance were amazed by Benin's metalwork, such as copper birds on towers, copper snakes coiled around doorways, and beautifully cast bronze statues.

The first Portuguese emissary who arrived at oba Ozuola's court in 1486 was sent back to Lisbon with gifts, including a Maltese-type cross. The cross excited the Portuguese who interpreted it as a sign that Benin was near Prester John's kingdom and that its inhabitants would be receptive to conversion to Christianity. However, when Ozuola admitted Catholic missionaries to his kingdom in the early 1500s in the hope of securing Portuguese muskets, the Portuguese made acceptance of Christianity a precondition for receiving arms. Although the missionaries converted several of Ozuola's sons and high-ranking officials, their influence ended at Ozuola's death.

Portugal believed that it could manipulate Benin's rulers to extend Portuguese trade over a much wider area, but the obas did not regard trade with the Portuguese as a vital necessity and did not allow them to establish a sizable presence in the kingdom. The obas controlled all transactions, and Portuguese traders duly paid taxes, observed official regulations, and conducted business only with the obas' representatives.

The Portuguese traded brass and copper items, textiles, and cowrie shells for pepper, cloth, beads, and slaves. Because Benin did not have access to sources of gold, the Portuguese took the slaves from Benin and traded them for gold with the Akan states, which needed laborers for clearing forests for farmland. However, in 1516, Benin decided to curtail the slave trade and offered only female slaves for purchase.

Although effectively limited in Benin, Portuguese traders openly operated among nearby coastal states, where they gained some political influence. They were particularly successful in the small kingdom of Warri, a Niger delta vassal state of Benin. Shortly after 1600, the Warri crown prince was educated in Portugal and brought home a Portuguese queen. Warri supplied large numbers of slaves, as did other nearby states, which were now competing fiercely with one another. Before long, even Benin would accept dependence on the slave trade in order to control its tributaries and hold its own against Europeans.

Benin artists cast brass plaques that adorned the oba's palace walls. The plaques depicted important events in Benin's history, including the engagement with the Portuguese. The two Portuguese soldiers in this plaque are notable for their long wavy hair and military uniforms.

The Portuguese and the Kongo Kingdom

Farther south, near the mouth of the Congo River, the Portuguese experienced their most intensive involvement in Africa. There, Portuguese seafarers found the recently established Kongo kingdom of several million people, ruled by a king who was heavily influenced by the queen mother and other women on his royal council. Although the Kongo initially perceived the Europeans as water or earth spirits, Kongo's king, Nzinga Nkuwu, soon came to regard them as a potential ally against neighboring African

IMAGE
Loango, Capital of the Kingdom of the Congo

Discovery Through Maps

Savage Pictures: Sebastian Munster's Map of Africa

Voyages of exploration in the fifteenth and sixteenth centuries greatly expanded European knowledge of the rest of the world. However, mapmakers who knew very little about the geography and peoples of continents such as Africa still tended to rely on outdated information or stereotypical representations. Thus, when Sebastian Munster (1489–1552 C.E.), a professor of Hebrew and mathematics at Basel, the home of Switzerland's oldest university, developed an interest in maps, he turned to Ptolemy (90–168 C.E.), a celebrated astronomer, geographer, and mathematician of Alexandria, Egypt, whose theories about the universe influenced the European and Arab worlds for many centuries. When Ptolemy's *Guide to Geography* was published in Florence around 1400, it was the first atlas of the world.

Ptolemy's view of the world heavily influenced Munster when he began drawing his own world atlas. First published in 1544, Munster's *Cosmographia Universalis* went through 46 editions and was translated into six languages. It was the first collection to feature individual maps of Europe, Asia, the Americas, and Africa.

Munster's map of Africa relied not only on Ptolemy but also on Portuguese and Arab sources. However, it still contained many errors. The map identified the source of the Nile far to the south and, based on the assumption that the Senegal was connected to the Niger River in West Africa, showed a river flowing westward to the Atlantic.

The *Cosmographia* was also a descriptive geography, providing an accompanying narrative and drawings of prominent figures, the customs and manners of societies, and the products, animals, and plants of regions. Munster's Africa map depicted a lone human figure that bore no resemblance to Africans and a large elephant at the southern end of the continent. His rendering of Africa conformed to Jonathan Swift's satirical lines:

So Geographers in Africa-Maps
With Savage-Pictures fill their Gaps;
And o'er unhabitable Downs
Place Elephants for want of Towns.

Questions to Consider

1. Why do you think Muster chose to rely on Ptolemy's views rather than on more recent information?
2. Compare the portrayal of Africa in Munster's map with that in Abraham Cresque's Catalan map. Why does Cresque's map contain so much more detail than Munster's?

states. In the 1480s he invited the Portuguese to send teachers, technicians, missionaries, and soldiers. His son, Nzinga Mbemba (1506–1543), who converted to Catholicism in 1491, consolidated the control of the Catholic faction at his court, making Portuguese the official language and Catholicism the state religion. He encouraged his court to adopt European dress and manners while changing his own name to Don Afonso. Many friendly letters subsequently passed between him and King Manuel of Portugal.

This mutual cooperation did not last long. While the Portuguese were prepared to assist Afonso's kingdom, their desire for profits won out over their humanitarian impulses. Portuguese traders, seeking slaves for their sugar plantations at São Tomé (SAH-o TO-mai) and Principe, ranged over Kongo. By 1530 some 4000 to 5000 slaves were being taken from Kongo annually. No longer satisfied with treaty terms that gave them prisoners of war and criminals, the traders ignored the laws and bought everyone they could get, thus creating dissension and weakening the country. Driven to despair, Afonso wrote to his friend and ally Manuel: "There are many traders in all corners of the country. They bring ruin. . . . Every day, people are enslaved and kidnapped, even nobles, even members of the King's own family."[1] Such pleas brought no satisfactory responses. For a while, Afonso tried to curb the slave trade; however, he was shot by disgruntled Portuguese slavers while he was attending Mass in 1430. Afonso's successors were no more successful, and Portuguese slavers operated with impunity throughout Kongo and in neighboring areas.

The Portuguese crown also turned its attention to the Mbundu kingdom to the south of Kongo. In 1520 Manuel established contact with the Mbundu king, Ngola. However, when the Portuguese government agreed to deal with Ngola through Kongo, São Tomé slavers were given a free hand to join with Mbundu's rulers to attack neighboring states. Using African mercenaries known as pombeiros equipped with firearms and sometimes allied with feared Imbangala warriors, the slavers and their allies began a long war of conquest. In 1571 the Portuguese crown issued a royal charter to establish the colony of Angola, situated on the Atlantic coast south of the Kongo kingdom. Although Portugal had ambitious plans to create an agricultural colony for white settlement and to gain control over a silver mine and the salt trade in the interior, Angola was never a successful venture. Few settlers immigrated, and Angola remained a sleepy outpost, consisting of a handful of Portuguese men, even fewer Portuguese women, a growing population of Afro-Portuguese, and a majority of Africans. The colony functioned primarily as a haven for slavers. By the end of the sixteenth century, 10,000 slaves were flowing annually through Luanda (loo-AHN-dah), Angola's capital.

The Portuguese in East Africa

Portuguese exploits in East Africa were similar to those in Kongo and Angola. The Swahili city-states along the coast north of the Zambezi (zam-BEE-zee) River were tempting targets for Portuguese intervention because they were strategically well located for trade with Asia. However, because they rarely engaged in wars with each other or supported sizeable militaries, they could not effectively defend themselves against a ruthless Portuguese naval force that sacked and plundered city-states from Kilwa to Mombasa. At Mombasa Portuguese sailors broke into houses with axes, looted, and killed before setting the town afire. The sultan of Mombasa wrote to the sultan of Malindi: "[They] raged in our town with such might and terror that no one, neither man nor woman, neither the old or the young, nor even the children, however small, was spared to live."[2]

DOCUMENT

"Of the Coasts of East Africa and Malabar"

Although a few city-states such as Malindi (mah-LEEN-dee) escaped the wrath of the Portuguese by becoming allies, the Portuguese usually relied on coercion to keep the city-states in line. They constructed fortified stations from which they attempted to collect tribute and maintain trade with the interior. An early station at Mozambique became the main port of call for vessels on the Asia route. In the 1590s the Portuguese built a fort at Mombasa, hoping to intimidate other cities and support naval operations against Turks and Arabs in the Red Sea. Although the Portuguese dominated trade in gold and ivory along the East African coast, they could not control the whole coastline and Swahili merchants continued to trade with their traditional partners. However, local industries such as ironworking and weaving virtually disappeared under Portuguese rule. When Omani Arabs expelled the Portuguese from the Swahili coast in 1698, the Swahili did not lament their departure. A Swahili proverb captured Swahili sentiment: "Go away, Manuel [the king of Portugal], you have made us hate you; go, and carry your cross with you."[3]

On the southeast coast the Portuguese were drawn to the Zimbabwean plateau by reports of huge gold mines. The Portuguese needed gold to finance their trade for spices in the Indian Ocean, while Shona kingdoms desired beads and cotton cloth from India. The Portuguese seized Sofala in 1506, diminishing the role of Muslim traders and positioning themselves as the middlemen for the gold trade with the coast. After establishing trading settlements along the Zambezi River at Sena and Tete, the Portuguese developed a close relationship with the Karanga kingdom of Mutapa, which received Portuguese traders and Catholic missionaries. This relationship soured when the king of Mutapa ordered the death of a Jesuit missionary in 1560. In the 1570s the Portuguese retaliated

Document: Portuguese Encounters with Africans

The Portuguese had very specific objectives in Africa. They usually established amicable relations with stronger states, while they were more likely to coerce weaker states such as the Swahili city-states in East Africa. When Vasco da Gama dealt with the ruler of Kilwa, an island off the East African coast, he showed little patience for the subtleties of diplomacy and quickly resorted to threats to achieve his aims. This document records an exchange between da Gama and the King of Kilwa.

In the case of the Kingdom of the Kongo, the Portuguese were dealing with a state that clearly defined its interests and did not regard Portugal as a superior nation. Kongo's king, Don Afonso, who converted to Catholicism, wrote a series of letters to the king of Portugal in 1526. These letters demonstrate the complex relationship between the Kongolese leadership and the Portuguese. Afonso complains about Portuguese involvement in the slave trade but also conveys a request for doctors and apothecaries to treat illnesses.

KING IBRAHIM OF KILWA: Good friendship was to friends like brothers are and that he would shelter the Portuguese in his city and harbor ... to pay tribute each year in money or jewelry was not a way to a good friendship, it was tributary subjugation ... to pay tribute was dishonor ... it would be like to be a captive ... such friendship he did not want with subjugation ... because even the sons did not want to have that kind of subjugation with their own parents.

VASCO DA GAMA: Take it for certain that if I so decide your city would be grounded by fire in one single hour and if your people wanted to extinguish the fire in town, they would all be burned and when you see all this happen, you will regret all you are telling me now and you will give much more than what I am asking you now, it will be too late for you. If you are still in doubt, it is up to you to see it.

KING IBRAHIM: Sir, if I had known that you wanted to enslave me, I would not have come and I would have fled into the forest, for it is better for me to be a fox but free, than a dog locked up in a golden chain.

From Chapurukha M. Kusimba, *The Rise and Fall of Swahili States* (Walnut Creek: AltaMira Press, 1999), pp. 161–162.

Moreover, Sir, in our Kingdom there is another great inconvenience which is of little service to God, and this is that many of our people [*naturaes*], keenly desirous as they are of the wares and things of your Kingdoms, which are brought here by your people, freed and exempt men; and very often it happens that they kidnap even noblemen and the sons of noblemen, and our relatives, and take them to be sold to the white men who are in our Kingdoms; and for this purpose they have concealed them, and others are brought during the night so that they might not be recognized.

And as soon as they are taken by the white men they are immediately ironed and branded with fire, and when they are carried to be embarked, if they are caught by our guards' men the whites allege that they have brought them but they cannot say from whom, so that it is our duty to do justice and to restore to the freemen their freedom, but it cannot be done if your subjects feel offended, as they claim to be.

And to avoid such a great evil we passed a law so that any white man living in our Kingdoms and wanting to purchase goods in any way should first inform three of our noblemen and officials of our court ... who should investigate if the mentioned goods are captives or freemen, and if cleared by them there will be no further doubt nor embargo for them to be taken and embarked. But if the white men do not comply with it they will lose the aforementioned goods. ...

[1526] Sir, Your Highness has been kind enough to write to us saying that we should ask in our letters for anything we need, and that we shall be provided with everything, and as the peace and health of our Kingdom depend on us ... it happens that we have continuously many and different diseases which put us very often in such a weakness that we reach almost the last extreme; and the same happens to our children, relatives and natives owing to the lack in this country of physicians and surgeons who might know how to cure properly such diseases.

And to avoid such a great error and inconvenience, since it is from God in the first place and then from your Kingdoms and from Your Highness that all the good and drugs and medicines have come to save us, we beg of you to be agreeable and kind enough to send us two physicians and two apothecaries and all the necessary things to stay in our kingdoms. ...

From Basil Davidson, *African Past* (Boston: Little, Brown and Co., 1964), pp. 192–194.

Questions to Consider

1. Why did the Portuguese treat the kings of Kongo and Kilwa in different ways?
2. What do the letters from the King of the Kongo reveal about the involvement of his people and the Portuguese in the slave trade?

by sending several expeditionary forces up the Zambezi to seize control over the gold-producing areas. The Portuguese believed the gold came from rich mines, when, in reality, African peasants recovered most of the gold from riverbeds during the winter months. In any event, these adventures ended disastrously as drought, disease (especially malaria), and African resisters decimated the Portuguese forces.

A series of internal rebellions and wars with neighboring states, however, forced Mutapa's rulers to turn to the Portuguese for assistance. In 1607 they signed a treaty that ceded control of gold production to the Portuguese. For the rest of the century the Portuguese regularly intervened in Mutapa's affairs until the forces of Mutapa and a rising power, Changamire, combined to expel the Portuguese from the Zimbabwean plateau. Along the Zambezi River the Portuguese crown granted huge land concessions **(prazos)** to Portuguese settlers *(prazeros)* who ruled them as feudal estates. Over time, the *prazeros* loosened their ties with Portugal's officials and became virtually independent. In the absence of Portuguese women, *prazeros* intermarried with Africans and adopted African culture.

The tale of Prester John, the mythical Ethiopian Christian monarch who held the Muslims at bay, had long captivated Portugal's monarchs. Thus, they initially responded positively when the astute Ethiopian empress Eleni made diplomatic overtures. Eleni, the daughter of a Muslim king, had married the Ethiopian emperor Baeda Maryam and converted to Christianity. After his death in 1478, she remained an influential figure as regent during the reigns of two of her sons and two grandsons. Recognizing that the interests of both Ethiopia and Portugal would be served by defeating Muslim states on the Red Sea coast, she wrote Portugal's king in 1509 proposing an alliance against the Ottoman Turks. She reasoned that the combination of Ethiopia's army and Portugal's sea forces would be very potent. However, the Portuguese, disappointed that Ethiopia did not meet their grand expectations of a kingdom ruled by Prester John, were reluctant to sign a pact.

After Eleni's death in 1522, her projected alliance was not completed for several decades. In 1541, the army of Muslim leader Ahmad Gran of the kingdom of Adal had come close to conquering Ethiopia. This time, the Portuguese responded to Ethiopian appeals by dispatching 400 Portuguese musketeers who helped to defeat the Muslims. The following year, however, Muslim forces, augmented by Turkish soldiers, rallied and defeated the Portuguese contingent, killing its commander, Christopher da Gama, Vasco's son. When the Ethiopians eventually pushed the Muslims out, they enticed some of the Portuguese soldiers to stay on by granting them large estates in the countryside. Subsequent Ethiopian rulers called on descendants of the Portuguese in their conflicts with the Turks.

The Portuguese impact on Africa was not as immediately disastrous as Spanish effects on the New World. The Portuguese did not have the manpower or arms to dictate the terms of trade with most African states. However, they did inflict severe damage in Kongo, Angola, Zimbabwe, and the Swahili city-states. Their most destructive involvement was the slave trade.

By the end of the sixteenth century the Portuguese had moved an estimated 240,000 slaves from West and Central Africa; 80 percent were transported after 1575. These trends foreshadowed much greater disasters for African societies in the seventeenth and eighteenth centuries as the Atlantic slave trade expanded (see Chapter 19).

THE GROWTH OF NEW SPAN

■ *What factors contributed to the Spanish conquest of Amerindian societies?*

While Portugal concentrated on Asian and African trade, Spain won a vast empire in America. Soon after 1492, Spanish settlements were established in the West Indies, most notably on Hispaniola (ees-pah-nee-O-lah) and Cuba. By 1500, as the American continents were recognized and the passage to Asia remained undiscovered, a host of Spanish adventurers—the **conquistadora**—set out for the New World with dreams of acquiring riches. From the West Indies they crossed the Caribbean to eastern Mexico, fanning out from there in all directions, toward Central America, the Pacific, and the vast North American hinterlands.

In Mexico the Spaniards profited from internal problems within the Aztec Empire. By the early 1500s, the Aztecs ruled over several million people in a vast kingdom that stretched from the Gulf of Mexico to the Pacific Ocean and from present-day central Mexico to Guatemala. However, unrest ran rampant among many recently conquered peoples, who were forced to pay tribute and taxes and furnish sacrificial victims to their Aztec overlords.

In 1519 Spanish officials in Cuba, excited by reports of a wealthy Amerindian civilization from two

---

prazo—A land grant from the Portuguese crown to a Portuguese settler (*prazero*) in the Zambezi river valley in Mozambique that gave the settler control over tribute and labor service from local residents.

conquistadora—The Spanish soldiers who conquered Mexico and Peru.

expeditions to the Yucatán (yoo-kah-TAHN) peninsula, dispatched Hernando Cortés (1485–1574) with 11 ships, 600 fighting men, 200 servants, 16 horses, 32 crossbows, 13 muskets, and 14 mobile cannons. Before marching against the Aztec capital, he destroyed 10 of his 11 ships to prevent his men from turning back. He had the good luck to secure two interpreters. One was an Amerindian woman, Malitzin, later christened Doña Marina, who became a valuable interpreter and intelligence gatherer as well as bearing Cortés a son. As Cortés's band marched inland, he added thousands of Amerindian warriors to his small force. He easily enlisted Amerindian allies, such as the Cempoala who had suffered under Aztec rule. By contrast, the loyalty of the Tlaxcalan (tlash-KAH-lahn) was secured only after Cortez's force demonstrated the superiority of its firearms, steel swords, and armor and horses (that the Aztecs initially thought were deer).

DOCUMENT
Cortez to King Charles V of Spain

The Aztec emperor Moctezuma II's initial view of the Spaniards was shaped by an Aztec belief that the Spaniards were representatives of the white-skinned and bearded Teotihuacán (tay-o-tee-wah-KAHN) god, Quetzalcoatl (KAT-SAL-KWA-tel), who had been exiled by the Toltecs in the tenth century C.E. He forbade human sacrifice and had promised to return from across the sea to enforce his law. However, as reports of Spanish victories came to his attention, Moctezuma had second thoughts as Cortés approached the Aztec capital, Tenochtitlán (te-noch-teet-lahn), a city of more than 150,000 people. Thus, Moctezuma warily welcomed Cortés as a guest in his father's palace. Although surrounded by a host of armed Aztecs, Cortés seized the ruler and informed him that he must cooperate or die. The bold scheme worked temporarily. But when Cortés left the capital to return to the coast, his commander attacked an unarmed crowd at a religious festival, killing many Aztec notables. The massacre touched off a popular uprising. Cortés returned with reinforcements, but when he placed Moctezuma on a wall to pacify the Aztecs, they renounced their former ruler as a traitor and stoned and killed him. Neither the Aztecs nor the Spaniards showed any mercy in the fierce fighting that followed. The Aztecs ultimately drove a battered band of terrified Spaniards from the city in the narrowest of escapes. Later, having regrouped and gained new Amerindian allies, Cortés wore down the Aztecs in a bloody siege during which some Spanish prisoners were sacrificed in full view of their comrades. The outcome of the fighting was in doubt when a smallpox epidemic, accidentally introduced by a Spanish soldier, broke out, killing many thousands of Aztecs who had no immunity to the disease. Finally, in August 1521, some 60,000 exhausted and half-starved defenders surrendered.

DOCUMENT
From the "Account of Alva Ixtlilxochitl"

As the inheritors of the Aztec empire, the Spaniards found the Aztec's hierarchical system suited to their needs. They replaced an urbanized Aztec elite with their own and gave privileged positions to Amerindian allies such as the Tlaxcalans. The Spanish ruled from Tenochtitlán, rebuilt as Mexico City, which became the capital of an expanding Spanish empire.

Although *conquistadora* steadily penetrated the interior, the fierce Mayas of Yucatán and Guatemala put up a determined resistance until the 1540s. By then, Spanish settlements had been established throughout Central America. The first colony in North America was founded at St. Augustine, on Florida's

An illustration from the Codex Azacatitlán of the Spanish arriving in Mexico. Standing next to Cortés is Malitzin, the Aztec woman who served as his interpreter.

east coast, in 1565. Meanwhile, numerous expeditions, including those of Hernando de Soto (1500–1542) and Francisco de Coronado (1510–1554), explored what is now California, Arizona, New Mexico, Colorado, Texas, Missouri, Louisiana, and Alabama. Spanish friars established a mission at Santa Fe in 1610, providing a base for later missions. All these new territories, known as New Spain, were administered from Mexico City after 1542.

The viceroyalty of Mexico later sponsored colonization of the Philippines, a project justified by the historic voyage of Ferdinand Magellan (1480–1521). Encouraged by the exploits of Vasco de Balboa (1479–1519), who had crossed Panama and discovered the Pacific Ocean in 1513, Magellan sailed from Spain in 1520, steered past the ice-encrusted straits at the tip of South America, and endured a 99-day voyage to the Philippines. He made an unwise choice by intervening in a conflict between two sheikdoms, and he lost his life in a battle with the inhabitants of Mactan Island. Many of Magellan's crew died after terrible suffering from **scurvy.** This illness explains why only one of Magellan's five ships completed this first circumnavigation of the world. However, the feat established a Spanish claim to the Philippines. It also prepared the way for the first tiny settlement of 400 Mexicans at Cebu in 1571. By 1580, when the Philippine capital at Manila had been secured against attacking Portuguese, Chinese, and Moro fleets, the friars were beginning conversions that would reach half a million by 1622. The colony prospered in trade with Asia but remained economically dependent on annual galleons bearing silver from Mexico. Because the Spanish were excluded from China, they relied on a community of Chinese merchants in Manila to trade the silver in the Chinese market for luxury items such as porcelain, silk, and lacquer ware.

The Development of Spanish South America

As in Mexico, the Spanish exploited unique opportunities as well as epidemics in their process of empire building in Peru. Just before they arrived, the recently formed Inca state had been torn apart by a succession crisis. When the emperor Huayna Capac and his heir apparent suddenly died of smallpox in 1526, the claim of his son Huascar (was-KAR) to the throne was contested by Atahualpa, a half-royal son who had been Huayna Capac's favorite. Their conflict, which soon destroyed nearly every semblance of imperial unity, was a major factor in the surprisingly easy triumph of a handful of Spanish freebooters over a country of more than ten million people, scattered through Peru and Ecuador in hundreds of mountain towns and coastal cities.

Francisco Pizarro (1470–1541), the son of an illiterate peasant, was the conqueror of Peru. After two earlier exploratory visits, he landed on the northern coast in January 1531 with a tiny privately financed army of 207 men and 27 horses. For more than a year he moved south, receiving some reinforcements as he plundered towns and villages. Leaving a garrison of 60 soldiers in a coastal base, he started inland in September 1532 with a Spanish force of fewer than 200. About the same time, word came that Altahualpa's forces had defeated Huascar's in battle and were poised to capture the imperial capital, Cuzco. Pizarro now posed as a potential ally to both sides. At Cajamarca he met and captured Altahualpa, slaughtering some 6000 unarmed retainers of the Inca monarch. He next forced Altahualpa to fill a room with 26,000 pounds of silver and over 13,000 pounds of gold. Then, having collected the ransom, Pizarro executed his royal prisoner and proclaimed Manco, the young son of Altahualpa's dead brother, as emperor.

Thus, upon arriving in Cuzco with their puppet ruler, the Spaniards were welcomed as deliverers and quickly secured tentative control of the country. Manco, after suffering terrible indignities from the Spaniards, organized a rebellion in 1536. Although his army of 60,000 heavily outnumbered Pizarro's 200 Spaniards, they could not score a decisive victory. Manco and his supporters retreated to the northwest to a mountain outpost at Vilacamba where an independent Inca kingdom survived until the Spanish captured and executed the last Inca emperor in 1572.

Although the *conquistadora* had triumphed over the Incas, political anarchy still reigned in Peru as the *conquistadora* split into two factions led by the Pizarro and Almagro families. When Pizarro was assassinated in his palace in 1542, it touched off a bloody civil war that raged for six years.

The period was marked by an obsessive Spanish rape of the country, along with cruel persecution of its Amerindian population, and by ruthless contention, involving every degree of greed and brutality, among the conquerors. Meanwhile, marauding expeditions moved south into Chile and north through Ecuador into Colombia. Expeditions from Chile and Peru settled in Argentina, founding Buenos Aires. Relationships between *conquistadora* and Amerindian women were common, and they

---

scurvy—A disease contracted on voyages of longer than a month because sailors' diets lacked sufficient quantities of vitamins B and C.

produced a new *mestizo* population in Paraguay. Despite this dynamic activity, there was no effective government at Lima, the capital, until the end of the sixteenth century.

Along with brutality, Spaniards in the post-conquest era also demonstrated unprecedented fortitude and courage. Pizarro's Spaniards were always outnumbered in battle. They faced nearly unendurable torments, including scorching heat, disease-carrying insects, air too thin for breathing, and cold that at times could freeze a motionless man into a lifeless statue. Amid the terrible hardships of this male-dominated era, both Amerindian and Spanish women played significant roles. As in Mexico, Amerindian women were camp-following concubines who prepared food and bore children; in addition to traditional feminine tasks, some Spanish women fought beside the men when necessary. Ines Suarez achieved distinction by donning armor and leading the defense of Santiago, Chile, shortly after its founding in 1541. Some women were present on all the pioneering ventures, and others were direct participants in the terrible sacrifices of the civil wars.

To govern Mexico and Peru the Spanish established two viceroyalties that by 1600 contained over 200 towns with a Spanish and mestizo population of 200,000. By then, the empire was in decline. Peruvian silver, the main source of Spanish wealth, was either running out or requiring very expensive mining operations; the Amerindian labor force was depleted, and African slaves were both scarce and expensive. Spain's deteriorating home economy and waning sea power presented even more serious problems.

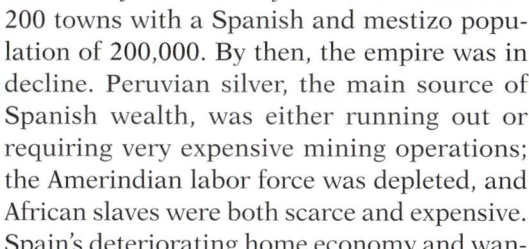

MAP
European Empires in Latin America, 1660

shock, and inhumane treatment. This tragic catastrophe was accompanied by a decided change in the racial composition of Iberian America as an influx of African slaves, along with continued Spanish and Portuguese immigration, led to a variegated racial mixture, ranging through all shades of color between white and black. Fortunately, the

The arrival of the Spanish and Portuguese in America led to a mixing of three cultures: European, African, and Amerindian. This painted wooden bottle, done in Inca style and dating from about 1650, shows the mix. The three figures are an African drummer, a Spanish trumpeter, and an Amerindian official.

Amerindian population began recovering in the mid-1600s, and their cultures, combining with Iberian and African, formed a new configuration, to be known later as Latin American.

The General Nature of Regimes

Iberian regimes in America faced serious problems. Their vast territories, far greater than the homelands, contained nearly impassable deserts, mountains, and dense rain forests. Supplies had to be moved thousands of miles, often across open seas. Communications were difficult, wars with indigenous peoples were frequent, and disease was often rampant. Such conditions help explain, if not justify, the brutality of Iberian imperialism.

DOCUMENT
New Laws for the Treatment and Preservation of the Indians

With all their unique features, Iberian overseas empires were similar to Roman or Turkish provinces: they were meant to produce revenues. In theory, all Spanish lands were the king's personal property. The Council of the Indies, which directed the viceroys in Mexico City and Lima, advised him on colonial affairs. The highborn Spanish viceroys were aided (and limited) by councils *(audiencias)*, made up of aristocratic lawyers from Spain. Local governors, responsible to the viceroys, functioned with their advisory councils *(cabildos)* of officials. Only the rich normally sat in such bodies; poor Spaniards and mestizos had little voice, even in their own taxation. Most taxes, however, were collected by Amerindian chiefs *(caciques)*, still acting as rulers of Amerindian peasant villages.

IBERIAN SYSTEMS IN THE NEW WORLD

■ *What role did Amerindian and African labor play in the Spanish and Portuguese economic systems?*

European expansion overseas after the fifteenth century brought revolutionary change to all the world's peoples, but the Iberian period before 1600 was unique in its violence and ruthless exploitation. Not only were highly organized states destroyed in the New World, but whole populations were wiped out by European diseases,

mestizo—A person of Spanish and Indian descent.

cabildos—Town councils whose members were usually appointed by the governor.

cacique—An Amerindian chief who assisted the Spanish in collecting taxes from his subjects.

Portuguese Brazil was less directly controlled than the Spanish colonies. It languished for years under almost unrestricted domination of 15 aristocratic "captains" who held hereditary rights of taxing, disposing lands, making laws, and administering justice. In return, they sponsored settlement and paid stipulated sums to the king. This quasi-feudal administration was abandoned in 1548. When Philip II became king of Portugal in 1580, he established municipal councils, although these were still dominated by the hereditary captains.

Iberian Economies in America

Both the philosophies and the structures of the Iberian states limited colonial trade and industry. Most Spanish and Portuguese immigrants were disinclined toward productive labor. With few exceptions, commercial contacts were limited to the homelands; Mexican merchants fought a steadily losing battle to maintain independent trade with Peru and the Philippines. Local trade grew modestly in supplying the rising towns, some crafts developed into large-scale industrial establishments, and a national transport system, based on mule teams, became a major Mexican industry. So did smuggling, as demand for foreign goods rose higher and higher.

Agriculture, herding, and mining silver, however, were the main economic pursuits. The early gold sources soon ran out, but silver strikes in Mexico and Peru poured a stream of wealth back to Spain in the annual treasure fleets, convoyed by warships from Havana to Seville. Without gold to mine, many Spanish aristocrats acquired conquered Amerindian land, raising wheat, rice, indigo, cotton, coffee, and sugarcane. Cattle, horses, and sheep were imported and bred on ranches in the West Indies, Mexico, and Argentina. Brazil developed similar industries, particularly those related to brazilwood (for which the country was given its name), sugar, livestock, and coffee. Although Iberian economic pursuits in America were potentially productive, revealing numerous instances of initiative and originality, they were largely repressed by bureaucratic state systems.

Before 1660, plantations (large estates that used servile labor to grow crops) were not typical for agriculture in Iberian America, although they were developing in certain areas. The Spanish tried plantations in the Canaries, later establishing them in the West Indies, the Mexican lowlands, and Central America and along the northern coasts of South America. Even in such areas, which were environmentally suited for intensive single-crop cultivation, it was not easy to raise the capital, find the skilled technicians, and pay for the labor the system required.

The Spanish initially dealt with the labor problem in Mexico and Peru by forcing Amerindians on the labor market with taxation, but so many died from the devastating impact of European diseases that the Spanish turned to Africans for slave labor. Besides being separated from their families and societies, Africans slaves were mobile and could be shipped anywhere (see p. 563). By the 1550s, some 3000 African slaves were in Peru, working in gold mines and on cattle ranches and participating in a variety of unskilled and skilled occupations in the capital, Lima. At the end of the century, Africans, although replaced in the mines by Amerindians, continued to labor on coastal plantations and serve in elite households. Some 75,000 slaves were in the

Amerindian slaves work a Spanish sugar plantation on the island of Hispaniola. Spanish treatment of the Amerindians was often brutal.

Spanish colonies by 1600; more than 100,000 more arrived in the next four decades.

Portugal established sugar plantations on its Atlantic islands (Madeira, Cape Verde, and São Tomé). São Tomé was uninhabited when the Portuguese settled on it in 1485. Because the island is situated on the equator and receives abundant rainfall, it was an ideal setting to begin sugar production a half century later. São Tomé was also near Angola, a primary source of slaves. This experience created a direct link between the production of sugar and African slave labor. São Tomé also witnessed the resistance of slaves, who, much like the Maroons in Jamaica, fled the sugar plantations for the safety of the mountainous interior.

São Tomé, Cape Verde, and Madeira were the models when the Portuguese introduced the plantation system into northern Brazil around 1550. Like the Spanish, the Portuguese initially recruited Amerindian labor, but after a smallpox epidemic in the 1560s killed off many Amerindians, they began to rely on African slaves as the primary laborers on plantations. By the early 1600s, 30,000 Africans were annually being brought to Brazil. After 1650, as Dutch, British, and French possessions in the Caribbean islands were drawn into the sugar economy, they, as well as Portuguese Brazil, became the largest importers of unfree labor from Africa.

Some slaves were brutally oppressed as laborers in the mines, and others sweated on Spanish or Brazilian plantations. Slaves were also teamsters, overseers, personal servants, and skilled artisans. Particularly in the Spanish colonies, a good many earned their freedom, attaining a social status higher than that of Amerindian peasants. Free blacks, both men and women, operated shops and small businesses. Prostitution was common among black and **mulatto** women, a profession that went hand-in-hand with the sexual exploitation of female slaves as concubines and breeders.

Iberian Effects on Amerindian Life

The Spanish and Portuguese brought terrible disaster to most Amerindians. Having seen their gods mocked and their temples destroyed, many accepted Christianity as the only hope for survival, as well as salvation, while toiling for their Iberian masters. Some died from overwork, some were killed, and others simply languished as their cultures disintegrated. The most dangerous adversity was disease—European or African—to which Amerindians had no immunities.

---

mulatto—A person of European and African descent.

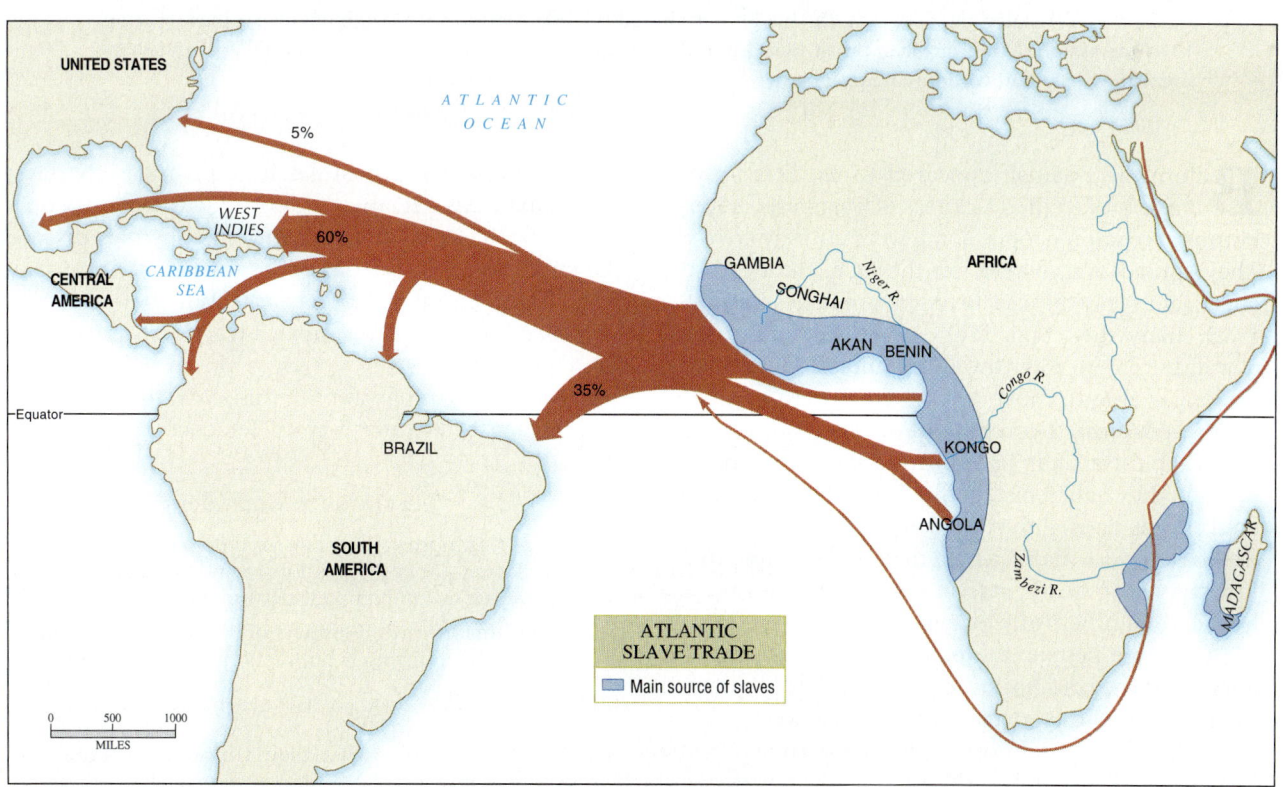

Africans were forcibly captured in raids and kidnappings in the interior of Africa and taken to the coast. After they were sold to European traders, the slaves were transported across the Atlantic to work on sugar plantations in the New World.

Epidemics arrived with Columbus and continued throughout the sixteenth century. Smallpox on Hispaniola in 1518 left only 1000 Amerindians alive there. Cortés's men carried the pox to Mexico, where it raged while he fought his way out of Tenochtitlán. From Mexico the epidemic spread through Central America, reaching Peru in 1526. It killed the reigning emperor and helped start the civil war that facilitated Pizarro's conquest. Following these smallpox disasters in the 1540s and 1570s, a wave of measles, along with other successive epidemics, continued depleting the population.

Depopulation of Amerindians was caused in part by their enslavement, despite disapproval by the Catholic Church and the Spanish government. The worst excesses came early. Original settlers on Hispaniola herded the Arawaks to work like animals; they soon became extinct. A whole indigenous population of the Bahamas—some 40,000 people—were carried away as slaves to Hispaniola, Cuba, and Puerto Rico. Cortés captured slaves before he took Tenochtitlán; other Amerindians, enslaved in Panama, were regularly sent to Peru. Before Africans arrived in appreciable numbers, the Portuguese organized "Indian hunts" in the forests to acquire slaves.

Another more common labor system in the Spanish colonies was the **encomienda.** This system was instituted in Mexico by Cortés as a way of using Amerindian caciques to collect revenues and provide labor. It was similar to European feudalism and manorialism, involving a royal grant that permitted the holder *(encomendero)* to take income or labor from specified lands and the people living on them. Many

---

encomienda—A system of control over land and Indian labor granted to a Spanish colonist *(encomendero)*.

Document: Disease and the Spanish Conquest

Diseases introduced by Europeans had a devastating impact on indigenous societies in the New World. This account of the impact of a smallpox epidemic among the Aztecs appeared in the Florentine Codex, an invaluable history of the Aztecs published in the mid-sixteenth century. Written in Nahuátl, the Aztec language and translated into Spanish, the books were based on information gathered by Aztec scribes under the supervision of a Franciscan priest Bernadino de Sahagún. This story of the smallpox epidemic drew on eyewitness accounts of individuals who lived through the Spanish conquest.

Before the Spanish appeared to us, first an epidemic broke out, a sickness of pustules. . . . Large bumps spread on people, some were entirely covered. They spread everywhere, on the face, the head, the chest, etc. The disease brought great desolation; a great many died of it. They could no longer walk about, but lay in their dwellings and sleeping places, no longer able to move or stir. They were unable to change position, to stretch out on their sides or face down, or raise their heads. And when they made a motion, they called out loudly. The pustules that covered people caused that covered people caused great desolation. very many people died of them, and many just starved to death; starvation reigned, and no one took care of others any longer.

On some people, the pustules appeared only far apart, and they did not suffer greatly, nor did many of them die of it. But many people's faces were spoiled by it, their faces and noses were made rough. Some lost an eye or were blinded.

This disease of pustules lasted a full sixty days; after sixty days it abated and ended. When people were convalescing and reviving, the pustules disease began to move in the direction of Chalco. And many were disabled or paralyzed by it, but they were not disabled forever. . . . The Mexica warriors were greatly weakened by it.

And when things were in this state, the Spaniards came, moving toward us from Tetzcoco.

Questions to Consider

1. What was more responsible for the Spanish conquest of the Aztecs—Spanish weapons, armor, horses or the diseases that accompanied the Spanish?
2. What was the overall impact of diseases such as smallpox on the indigenous populations of the Americas?

From James Lockhart, *We People Here: Nahuatl Accounts of the Conquest of Mexico* (Berkeley: University of California Press, 1993), pp. 180–182.

encomenderos lashed and starved their Amerindian laborers, working men and women to exhaustion or renting them to other equally insensitive masters. Amerindian women on the *encomiendas* were generally used as wet nurses, cooks, or maids or as sex slaves by the owners and the caciques, who served as overseers.

The *encomienda* system was slowly but steadily abandoned after the 1550s largely because of the efforts of a former *conquistadore* and *encomendero*, Bartolomé de Las Casas (1474–1566). A Dominican friar, he protested the cruel treatment of Amerindians and persuaded Charles V that they should hold the same rights as other subjects. His efforts led to the New Law of 1542, which ended existing *encomiendas* upon the death of their holders, prohibited Amerindian slavery, and gave Amerindians full protection under Spanish law. Most of these provisions, however, were rescinded when the law evoked universal protest and open rebellion in Peru. Although later governors gradually eliminated *encomiendas*, many Amerindians were put on reservations and hired out as contract laborers under the direction of their caciques and local officials *(corrigodores)*. This practice eliminated some of the worst excesses of the *encomiendas*, but corrupt officials often exploited their wards, particularly in Peru.

DOCUMENT
From "In Defense of the Indians"

Such physical hardships were matched by others of a psychological nature, which were almost equally damaging to Amerindians. The Spaniards insisted on forcing Christian conversion even while they raped and destroyed, as Pizarro did before executing Atahualpa. Except when they used Amerindian authorities to support their regimes, the Spaniards went out of their way to insult, shame, and degrade their unfortunate subjects. In the new social milieu, Amerindians were constantly reminded of their lowly status, unworthy of human consideration. For example, Cortés, who had multiple Amerindian mistresses, passed off Malitzin to one of his captains; Pizarro forced Manco, while still an ally, to give his young Inca queen to the conqueror. Such indignities, repeated by the hundreds among both Spanish and Portuguese, left many Amerindians demoralized to the point of utter despair.

Their distress was alleviated to some extent by missions, established by the Dominican and Jesuit religious orders. These afforded Amerindians the most effective protection and aid. Las Casas led the way in founding such settlements, where Amerindians were shielded from white exploitation, instructed in Christianity, and educated or trained in special skills. The prevailing philosophy in the missions stressed patient persuasion. Large mission organizations developed in Brazil, Venezuela, Paraguay, and upper California. But even the Amerindians protected by the missions died rapidly in this alien way of life.

Moved by the simplicity and gentle nature of the Amerindians, Bartolomé de Las Casas launched a vigorous campaign to ensure their protection. His Apologetic History of the Indies *(1566) is an indictment of the Spaniards' harsh treatment of the Amerindians.*

Although most Amerindians were demoralized by their misfortunes, some resisted. In Yucatán and Guatemala, where the Mayas did not believe the Spaniards were gods, bloody fighting lasted until the 1540s. About that time, the Spanish put down a revolt on the Mexican Pacific coast with great difficulty. As the silver mines opened in northern Mexico into the 1590s, the Chichimecs, relatives of the Apaches of North America, conducted a border war, using horses and captured muskets. In Peru an Inca rebellion, led first by Manco, was subdued only in 1577. The most stubborn resistance came from the Araucanians of southern Chile, who fought the Spaniards successfully until the close of the sixteenth century.

The full Iberian impact on Amerindian culture is difficult to assess, although there can be no denying that it was disastrous. A conservative estimate of Amerindian population losses puts the proportion at 25 percent during the era to 1650, but some recent figures place losses much higher, up to 95 percent of the pre-1492 total of 100 million. Signs of mental deterioration were also evident in prevalent alcoholism, which began among Amerindians shortly after the conquest.

Spanish Colonial Society and Culture

Spanish colonial society was stratified but somewhat flexible. A small elite of officials and aristocrats contended over politics, policy toward subject peoples, and foreign trade. Merchants and petty officials were on a lower social level but above mestizos, mulattoes, and **zambos.** Amerindians were considered incompetent wards of the home government, and African slaves were legally designated as beneath the law, but there were numerous individual exceptions. Many Amerindians went from their rural homes to the towns, mines, or **haciendas;** some caciques enjoyed wealth and privilege; and a few established Amerindian families retained their nobility as early Spanish allies. Similarly, some African slaves were overseers, privileged personal servants, and involved in urban crafts such as tailoring, shoemaking, carpentry, and blacksmithing; others acquired freedom and became prosperous merchants; still others escaped slavery, organized free communities, and successfully defended their independence.

Women in Spanish American society were a numerical minority. They played ambiguous roles, reflecting the traditional ideal of male superiority. They were excluded from male contacts throughout childhood, not allowed to join in dinner conversations, educated in cloistered schools to become wives and mothers, married in their teens to further family interests, and legally subordinated to their husbands. Most could not serve in public office or qualify as lawyers. Those who did not marry, particularly women of the upper classes, usually entered convents. There was, however, another side to the story. Spanish law guaranteed a wife's dowry rights, a legal protection against the squandering of her wealth, and leverage to limit her husband's activities. The courts recognized separations and at times even granted annulments in cases of wife abuse. Women, particularly widows, operated businesses. Some were wealthy, powerful, and even cruel *encomenderas*, supervising thousands of workers. Whatever their special roles, Iberian matrons defended religion, sponsored charities, dictated manners, and taught their children family values. They civilized the empires conquered by their men.

zambo—A person of African and Indian descent.
hacienda—An estate or plantation belonging to elite families.

Both the unique environment and the mix of peoples shaped Spanish colonial culture toward a new distinctive unity. From southwestern Europe came its aristocratic government, disdain for manual labor, a preference for dramatic over precise expression, and ceremonial Catholic Christianity. From Amerindian traditions came characteristic foods, art forms, architecture, legends, and practical garments like the poncho and serape, as well as substantial vocabulary. From Africa came agricultural knowledge, crafts, and animal husbandry. By 1650 this characteristic colonial culture was being preserved in its own universities, such as those at Lima and Mexico City, both founded more than a century earlier.

BEGINNINGS OF NORTHERN EUROPEAN EXPANSION

■ *What were the experiences of the Dutch, French, and British with their colonies of European settlement?*

European overseas expansion after 1600 entered a second phase, comparable to developments at home. As Spain declined, so did the Spanish Empire and that of Portugal, which was unified with Spain by a Habsburg king after 1580 and plagued with its own developing imperial problems. These conditions afforded opportunities for the northern European states. The Dutch between 1630 and 1650 almost cleared the Atlantic of Spanish warships while taking over most of the Portuguese posts in Brazil, Africa, and Asia. The French and English also became involved on a smaller scale, setting up a global duel for empire in the eighteenth century.

The Shifting Commercial Revolution

Along with this second phase of expansion came a decisive shift in Europe's Commercial Revolution. Expanding foreign trade, new products, an increasing supply of bullion, and rising commercial risks created new problems, calling for energetic initiatives. Because the Spanish and Portuguese during the sixteenth century had depended on quick profits, weak home industries, and poor management, wealth flowed through their hands to northern Europe, where it was invested in productive enterprises. Later it generated a new imperial age.

European markets after the sixteenth century were swamped with a bewildering array of hitherto rare or unknown goods. New foods from America included potatoes, peanuts, maize (Indian corn), tomatoes, and fish from Newfoundland's Grand Banks. In an era without refrigeration, imported spices—such as pepper, cloves, and cinnamon—were valued for making spoiled

Marketplace at Antwerp. In the sixteenth century, Antwerp was the leading city in international commerce. As many as 500 ships a day docked in its bustling harbor, and as many as 1000 wagons arrived each week carrying the overland trade.

foods palatable. Sugar became a common substitute for honey, and the use of cocoa, the Aztec sacred beverage, spread throughout Europe. Coffee and tea from the New World and Asia would also soon change European social habits. Similarly, North American furs, Chinese silks, and cottons from India and Mexico revolutionized clothing fashions. Furnishings of rare woods and ivory and luxurious oriental carpets appeared more frequently in the homes of the wealthy. The use of American tobacco became almost a mania among all classes, further contributing to the booming European market.

Imported gold and, even more significant, silver probably affected the European economy more than all other foreign goods. After the Spaniards had looted Aztec and Inca treasure rooms, the gold flowing from America and Africa subsided to a respectable trickle; but 7 million tons of silver poured into Europe before 1660. Spanish prices quadrupled, and because most new bullion went to pay for imports, prices more than tripled in northern Europe. Rising inflation hurt landlords who depended on fixed rents and creditors who were paid in cheap money, but the bullion bonanza ended a centuries-long gold drain to the East, with its attendant money shortage. It also increased the profits of merchants selling on a rising market, thus greatly stimulating northern European capitalism.

At the opening of the sixteenth century, Italian merchants and moneylenders, mainly Florentines, Venetians, and Genoese, dominated the rising Atlantic economy. The German Fugger banking house at Augsburg also provided substantial financing. European bankers, particularly the Fuggers and the Genoese, suffered heavily from the Spanish economic debacles under Charles V and Philip II. As the century passed, Antwerp, in the southern Netherlands, became the economic hub of Europe. It was the center for the English wool trade as well as a transfer station, drawing southbound goods from the Baltic and Portuguese goods from Asia. It was also a great financial market, dealing in commercial and investment instruments. The Spanish sack of the city in 1576 ended Antwerp's supremacy, which passed to Amsterdam and furthered Dutch imperial ventures.

Meanwhile, northern European capitalism flourished in nearly every category. Portuguese trade in Africa and Asia was matched by that of the Baltic and the North Atlantic. Northern joint-stock companies pooled capital for privateering, exploring, and commercial venturing. The Dutch and English East India companies, founded early in the seventeenth century, were but two of the better-known stock companies. In England common fields were enclosed for capitalistic sheep runs. Throughout western Europe, domestic manufacturing, in homes or workshops, was competing with the guilds. Large industrial enterprises, notably in mining, shipbuilding, and cannon casting, were becoming common. Indeed, the superiority of English and Swedish cannons caused the defeat of the Spanish Armada and Catholic armies in the Thirty Years' War.

The Dutch Empire

By 1650 the Dutch were supreme in both southern Asia and the South Atlantic. Their empire, like that of the Portuguese earlier, was primarily commercial; even their North American settlements specialized in fur trading with the Indians. They acquired territory where necessary to further their commerce but tried to act pragmatically in accordance with Asian cultures rather than by conquest. An exception was their colony in Java, where the Dutch drive for monopolizing the spice trade led them to take direct control of the island. Unlike the Spanish and the Portuguese, the Dutch made little attempt to spread Christianity.

Dutch involvement in the Indian Ocean was the direct result of the Spanish absorption of Portugal in 1580. The Spanish restricted the flow of spices, especially pepper, to Northern Europe, and Dutch seafarers set out to control the sources of the trade. Systematic Dutch naval operations commenced in 1595 when the first Dutch fleet entered the East Indies. Dutch captains soon drove the Portuguese from the Spice Islands. Malacca, the Portuguese bastion, fell after a long siege in 1641. The Dutch also occupied Sri Lanka (SHREE-lahn-KAH) and blockaded Goa, thus limiting Portuguese operations in the Indian Ocean. Although largely neglecting East Africa, they seized all Portuguese posts on the west coast north of Angola. Across the Atlantic, they conquered and held part of Brazil for a few decades, drove Spain from the Caribbean, and captured a Spanish treasure fleet. Decisive battles off the English Channel coast near Kent (1639) and off Brazil (1640) delivered final blows to the Spanish navy. What the English began in 1588, the Dutch completed 50 years later.

Five Dutch trading companies initially conducted trade with Asia, but the Dutch state decided their competition with each other cut into profits and established the Dutch East India Company. Chartered in 1602 and given a monopoly over all operations between the Cape of Good Hope in South Africa and the Strait of Magellan, it conserved resources and cut costs. In addition to its trade and diplomacy, the company sponsored explorations of Australia, Tasmania, New Guinea, and the South Pacific.

The Dutch Empire in the East was established primarily by Jan Pieterszoon Coen, governor-general of the Indies for two periods between 1619 and 1629 and founder of the company capital at Batavia in northwestern Java. At first he cooperated with local rulers in return for a monopoly over the spice trade. When this involved him in costly wars against local sultans as well as their Portuguese and English customers, Coen determined to control the trade at its sources. In the ensuing numerous conflicts and negotiations, which outlasted Coen, the Dutch acquired all of Java, most of Sumatra, the spice-growing Moluccas (mol-U-kuz), and part of Sri Lanka. They began operating their own plantations, overseen by Dutch settlers and worked by thousands of slaves brought in from such diverse areas as East Africa, Bengal, Persia, and Japan. The plantations produced cinnamon, nutmeg, cloves, sugar, tea, tobacco, and coffee, but it was pepper that reaped the highest profits. In the seventeenth century 7 million pounds of pepper were shipped to Europe annually.

Although commercially successful in Asia, the Dutch were not able to found flourishing colonial settlements. Many Dutchmen who went to the East wanted to make their fortunes and return home; those willing to stay were usually mavericks, uninterested in establishing families but instead pursuing temporary sexual liaisons with female slaves or servants. For a while after 1620 the company experimented with a policy of bringing European women to the Indies, but such efforts were abandoned when the venture failed to enlist much interest at home or in the foreign stations. Consequently, the Dutch colonies in Asia, as well as those in Africa, the Caribbean, and Brazil, remained primarily business ventures with less racial mixing than in the Iberian areas.

After resuming war with Spain in 1621, the Dutch formed the West India Company, charged with overtaking the diminishing Spanish and Portuguese holdings in West Africa and America. The company wasted no time. It soon supplanted the Portuguese in West Africa; by 1630 it had taken over the slave trade with America. After driving the Spanish from the Caribbean, the Dutch

Dutch Exploration and Expansion

1576	Sack of Antwerp; Amsterdam becomes commercial hub of Europe
1595	First Dutch fleet enters East Indies
1609	Henry Hudson explores Hudson River
1621	Dutch form West India Company
1624	Dutch found New Amsterdam on Manhattan Island
1641	Dutch drive Portuguese out of Malacca

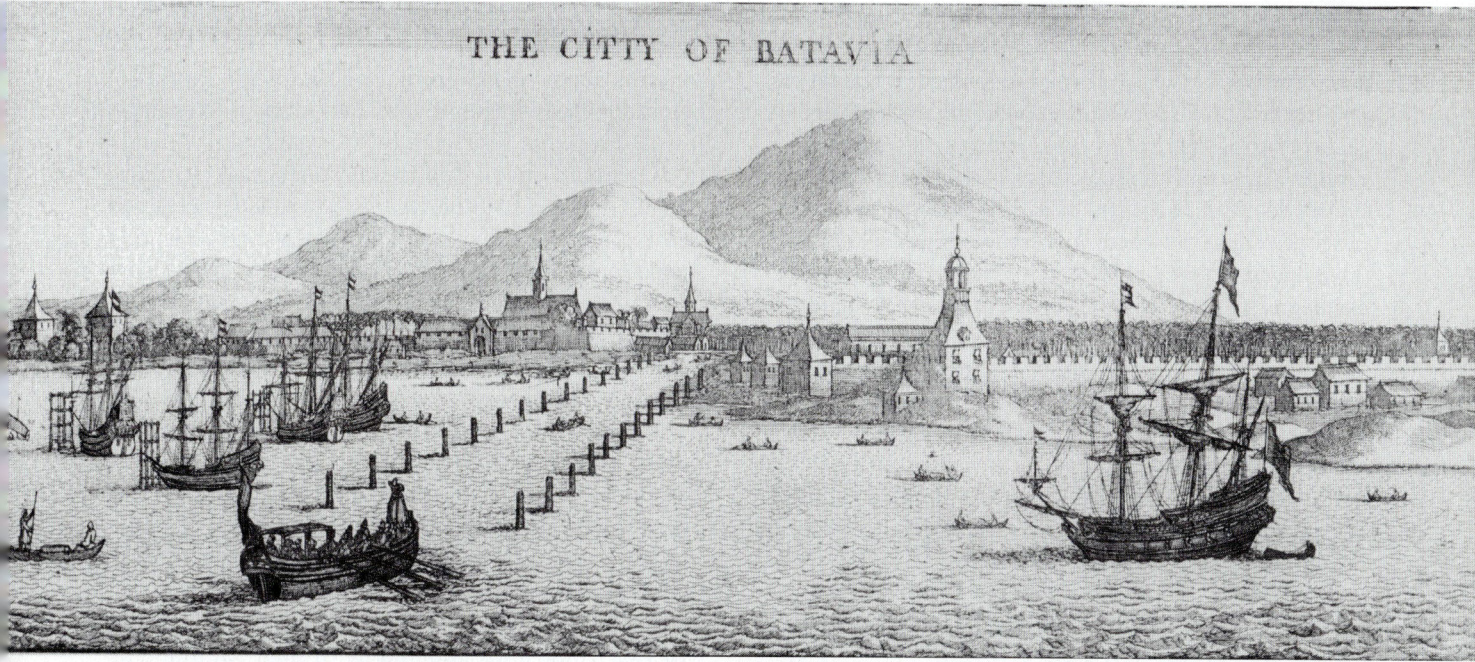

Batavia (present-day Djakarta), on the island of Java, became the headquarters of the Dutch East India Company when the Dutch ousted the Portuguese and took command of the East Indies trade in the seventeenth century.

invited other European planters to the West Indies as customers, keeping only a few bases for themselves. The company then launched a successful naval conquest of Brazil, from the mouth of the Amazon south to the San Francisco River. In Brazil the Dutch learned sugar planting, passing on their knowledge to the Caribbean and applying it directly in the East Indies.

Dutch settlements in North America never amounted to much because of the company's commercial orientation. In 1609 Henry Hudson (d. 1611), an Englishman sailing for the Dutch, explored the river (ultimately named for him) and established Dutch claims while looking for a northwest passage. Fifteen years later the company founded New Amsterdam on Manhattan Island; over the next few years it built a number of frontier trading posts in the Hudson valley and on the nearby Connecticut and Delaware Rivers. Some attempts were made to encourage planting by selling large tracts to wealthy proprietors **(patroons)**. Agriculture, however, remained secondary to the fur trade, which the company developed in alliance with the Iroquois tribes. This arrangement hindered settlement; in 1660 only 5000 Europeans were in the colony.

The French Empire

French exploration began early, but no permanent colonies were established abroad until the start of the seventeenth century. The country was so weakened by religious wars that most of its efforts, beyond fishing, privateering, and a few failed attempts at settlement, had to be directed toward internal stability. While the Dutch were winning their empire, France was involved in the land campaigns of the Thirty Years' War. Serious French empire building thus had to be delayed until after 1650, during the reign of Louis XIV.

Early French colonization in North America was based on claims made by Giovanni da Verrazzano (1485–1528) and Jacques Cartier (1491–1557). The first, a Florentine mariner commissioned by Francis I in 1523, traced the Atlantic coast from North Carolina to Newfoundland. Eleven years later Cartier made one of two voyages exploring the St. Lawrence River. These French expeditions duplicated England's claim to eastern North America.

French colonial efforts during the sixteenth century were dismal failures. They resulted partly from French experiences in exploiting the Newfoundland fishing banks and conducting an undeclared naval war in the Atlantic against Iberian treasure ships and trading vessels after 1520. In 1543 Cartier tried unsuccessfully to establish a colony in the St. Lawrence valley. No more serious efforts were made until 1605, when a French base was established at Port Royal, on Nova Scotia. It was meant to be a fur-trading center and capital for the whole St. Lawrence region. In 1608, Samuel de Champlain (1567–1635), who had been an aide to the governor of the Nova Scotia colony, acted for a French-chartered company in founding Quebec on the St. Lawrence. The company brought in colonists, but the little community was disrupted in 1627 when

patroon—An owner of a landed estate granted by the Dutch West India Company in New York and New Jersey.

British troops took the town and forced Champlain's surrender. Although when Champlain came back as governor the fort was returned to France by a treaty in 1629, growth was slowed by the company's emphasis on fur trading, the bitterly cold winters, and skirmishes with Indians. Only a few settlers had arrived by Champlain's death in 1635, and just 2500 Europeans were in Quebec as late as 1663. Nevertheless, Montreal was established in 1642, after which French trapper-explorers began penetrating the region around the headwaters of the Mississippi.

Elsewhere, the French seized opportunities afforded by the decline of Iberian sea power. They acquired the isle of Bourbon (BOOR-bon), later known as Réunion, in the Indian Ocean (1642) for use as a commercial base. In West Africa they created a sphere of commercial interest at the mouth of the Senegal River, where they became involved in the slave trade with only slight opposition from the Dutch. Even more significant was the appearance of the French in the West Indies. They occupied part of St. Kitts in 1625 and later acquired Martinique, Guadeloupe, and Santo Domingo. Fierce attacks by Carib Indians limited economic development before 1650. However, by the late eighteenth century, Santo Domingo had become the crown jewel of France's Caribbean possessions. Possessing half of the Caribbean's slave population, the island was the largest producer of sugar in America, and—after coffee was introduced in 1723—the world's largest coffee producer until the Haitian revolution of 1791.

British and French Exploration and Colonization

1485–1528	Giovanni da Verrazzano
1491–1557	Jacques Cartier
1497–1498	John Cabot establishes English claims in North America
1567–1635	Samuel de Champlain founds Quebec
1605	French establish base at Port Royal, in Nova Scotia
1607	First English colony in North America founded at Jamestown
1627	British conquer Quebec
1629	Puritans settle near Boston
1632–1635	English Catholics found colony of Maryland
1642	Montreal established

The English Empire

In terms of power and profit, English foreign expansion before 1650 was not impressive. Like French colonialism, it was somewhat restricted by internal political conditions, particularly the poor management and restrictive policies of the early Stuart kings, which led to civil war in the 1640s. A number of circumstances, however, promoted foreign ventures. The population increased from 3 to 4 million between 1530 and 1600, providing a large reservoir of potential indentured labor; religious persecution encouraged migration of nonconformists; and holders of surplus capital were seeking opportunities for investment. Such conditions ultimately produced a unique explosion of English settlement overseas.

During the sixteenth century, English maritime operations were confined primarily to exploring, fishing, smuggling, and plundering. English claims to North America were registered in 1497 and 1498 by two voyages of John Cabot, who explored the coast of North America from Newfoundland to Virginia but found no passage to Asia. For the next century, English expeditions sought such a northern passage, both in the East and in the West. All of them failed, but they resulted in explorations of Hudson Bay and the opening of a northeastern trade route to Russia. From the 1540s, English captains, including the famous John Hawkins of Plymouth, indulged in sporadic slave trading in Africa and the West Indies, despite Spanish restrictions.

After failures in Newfoundland and on the Carolina coast, the first permanent English colony in America was founded in 1607 at Jamestown, Virginia. For a number of years the colonists suffered from lack of food and other privations, but they were saved by their leader, Captain John Smith (1580–1631), whose romantic rescue by the Indian princess Pocahontas (1595–1617) is an American legend. Jamestown set a significant precedent for all English colonies in North America. By the terms of its original charter, the London Company, which founded the settlement, was authorized to supervise government for the colonists, but they were to enjoy all the rights of native Englishmen. Consequently, in 1619 the governor called an assembly to assist in governing. This body would later become the Virginia House of Burgesses, one of the oldest representative legislatures still operating.

Shortly after the founding of Jamestown, large-scale colonization began elsewhere. In 1620 a group of English Protestants, known as Pilgrims, landed at Plymouth. Despite severe hardships, they survived, and their experiences inspired other religious dissenters against the policies of Charles I. In 1629 a number of English Puritans formed the Massachusetts Bay Company and settled near Boston, where their charter gave them the rights to virtual self-government. From this first enclave, emigrants moved out to other areas in present-day Maine, Rhode Island, and Connecticut. By 1642 more than 25,000 people had migrated to New England, laying the foundations for a number of future colonies. Around the same time (1632–1635), a group of English Catholics, fleeing Stuart persecution, founded the Maryland colony. These enterprises firmly planted English culture and political institutions in North America.

Life in the English settlements was hard during those first decades, but a pioneering spirit and native colonial pride was already evident. Food was scarce, disease was ever-present, and conflicts with Amerindians were not uncommon. Yet from the beginning, and more than in other European colonies, settlers looked to their future in the new land because they had left so little behind in Europe. Most were expecting to stay, establish homes, make their fortunes, and raise families. The first Puritans included both men and women; a shipload of "purchase brides" arrived in 1619 at Jamestown to lend stability to that colony. This was but the first of many such contingents, all eagerly welcomed by prospective husbands. In addition, many women came on their own as indentured servants.

Anglo-American colonial women faced discrimination but managed to cope with it pragmatically. They were legally dependent on their husbands, who controlled property and children; a widow acquired these rights, but it was not easy to outlive a husband. Hard work and frequent pregnancies—mothers with a dozen children were not uncommon—reduced female life expectancies. Nevertheless, many women developed a rough endurance, using their social value to gain confidence and practical equality with their husbands, although some did this more obviously than others. This independent spirit was exemplified by Anne Hutchinson (1591–1643), who was banished from Massachusetts for her heretical views and founded a dissenting religious settlement in Rhode Island. Another freethinker was Anne Bradstreet (c. 1612–1672), who, although painfully aware that men considered her presumptuous, wrote thoughtful poetry.

The English government considered the rough coasts and wild forests of North America less important in this period than footholds in the West Indies and Africa, where profits were expected in planting and slave trading. Therefore, a wave of English migrants descended on the West Indies after the Dutch opened the Caribbean. In 1613 English settlers invaded Bermuda, and by the 1620s others had planted colonies on St. Kitts, Barbados, Nevis, Montserrat (mawn-suh-RAHT), Antigua (ahn-TEE-gwah), and the Bahamas. Tobacco planting was at first the major enterprise, bringing some prosperity and the promise of more. The white population expanded dramatically, especially on Barbados, which was not subject to Carib Indian attacks. There, the English population increased from 7,000 to 37,000 in seven years. As yet, there were few African slaves on the English islands, although some were already being imported for the sugar plantations.

This is an anonymous engraving made around 1776 of the Mohawk chief and diplomat Tiyanoga. He was an ally for the British and known to them as "King Hendrick." In this portrait, one can see the influence of European trade goods in Tiyanoga's dress. His shirt is made of linen or calico, and his mantle and breechcloth of English wool duffels.

Meanwhile, English slaving posts in West Africa were beginning to flourish, and English adventurers were starting operations in Asia. Captain John Lancaster took four ships to Sumatra and Java in 1601, returning with a profitable cargo of spices. But expansion outside of the Caribbean was difficult because the Dutch were uncooperative. In the Moluccas, for example, they drove out the English in the 1620s, after repeated clashes. The English fared better in India. By 1622 the British East India Company, which had been chartered in 1600, had put the Portuguese out of business in the Persian Gulf. Subsequently, the English established trading posts on the west coast of India at Agra, Bombay, Masulipatam, Balasore, and Surat. The station at Madras, destined to become the English bastion on the east coast, was founded in 1639. The East India Company prospered from the trade in Indian cotton and silk cloth for the English and European markets.

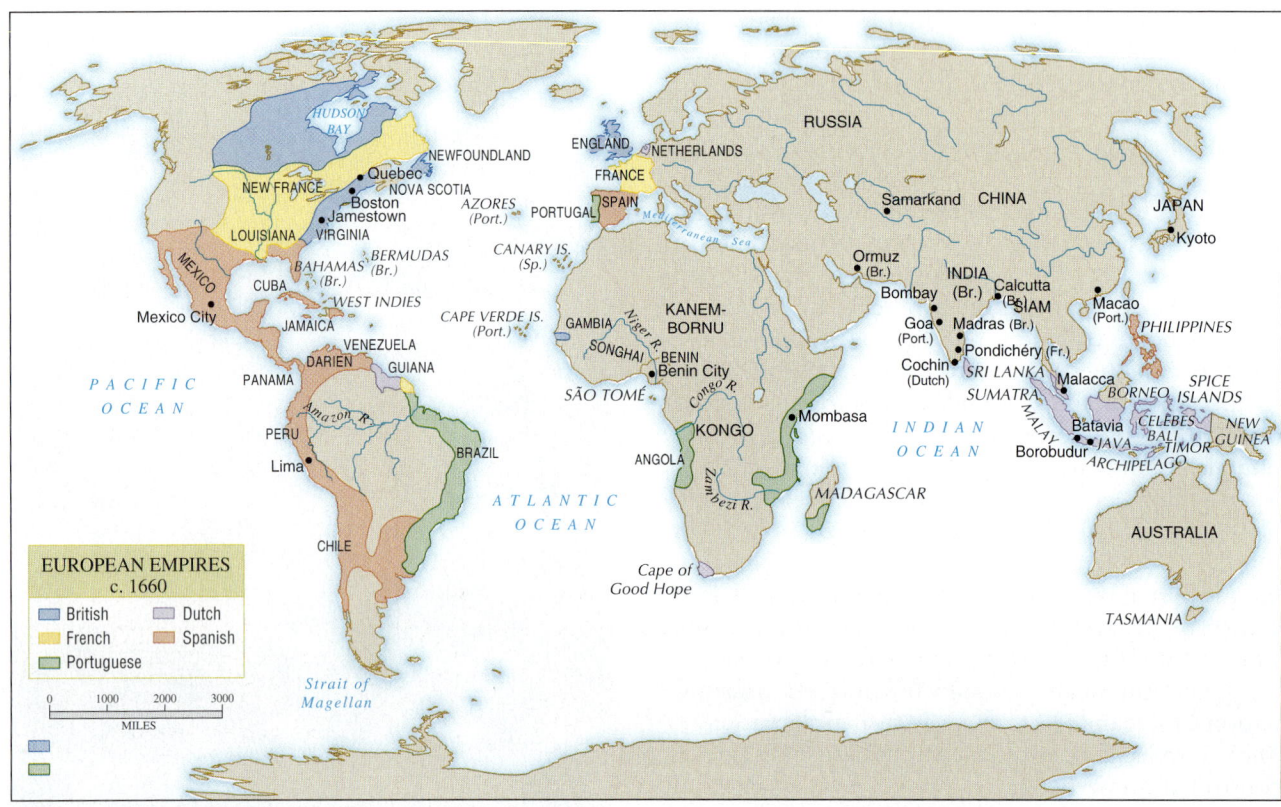

By the late 1600s the Portuguese and Spanish, the pioneers in global exploration, had been displaced in many regions by the English, French, and Dutch.

CONCLUSION

Between 1450 and 1650, the era of the early Commercial Revolution, Europeans faced outwards toward a new world and, following precedents set by earlier Eurasian empires, initiated their own age of oceanic expansion. In the process they stimulated capitalistic development, found a sea route to Asia, became more familiar with Africa, began colonizing America, and proved the world to have a spherical surface. For most of the period Spain and Portugal monopolized the new ocean trade and profited most from exploiting American gold and silver. Only after 1600, when leadership shifted toward the Dutch, French, and English, did European colonialism show signs of developing in new directions.

Overseas expansion exerted a tremendous effect on European culture and institutions. Spain's political predominance in the sixteenth century was largely bought with Amerindian treasure, and Spain's eventual decline was mainly caused by the squandering of wealth on war rather than on investment and the influx of American bullion, which inflated Spanish money and discouraged Spanish economic development. Northern European capitalism, developing in financial organization, shipbuilding, metalworking, manufacturing, and agriculture, brought a new vitality to northern economies in response to Spanish and Portuguese purchasing power. Economic advantages also contributed to Protestant victories in the Thirty Years' War.

By the late seventeenth century, the Europeans had experienced mixed results in their encounters with societies around the world. In the Indian Ocean, where they engaged well-established states, such as in China, Japan, and India, they usually had to respect their laws and authority and even do their bidding and had little impact on land-based trading networks. The Portuguese were run out of China twice before they came to respect Chinese law, and other Europeans fared worse. All were ultimately excluded from Japan. Southern India was not entirely open, as the Portuguese found by the end of the period. In the main, Turks, Arabs, Chinese, Japanese, Thais, and Vietnamese felt superior to Europeans and were usually able to defend their interests with effective action.

Where they dealt with smaller states and city-states, such as in Indonesia and East Africa, Europeans were more likely to directly intervene or dominate their affairs. Sri Lanka and the Spice Islands of the Malay archipelago, which were vulnerable to sea attack, came under domination, direct or indirect, and were exploited by the Portuguese and the Dutch.

In the New World the European impact was both dramatic and tragic. Portuguese captains and Spanish *conquistadora*, as well as diseases such as smallpox, nearly destroyed indigenous peoples and subjected most of the survivors to terrible hardships, indignities, cultural deprivations, and psychological injuries. However, the Portuguese and Spanish in America generated a new cultural synthesis, blending European, Amerindian, and African elements to produce a richness and variety not present in any of the parent cultures. This integration was largely accomplished by racial mixing, which created a new Latin American stock in the Western Hemisphere.

The European impact on Africa was less apparent at the time but perhaps more damaging in the long run than what happened to the Amerindians of Latin America. When the Portuguese began exploring the African coastline, they were more concerned with scoring quick profits through gold exports than with establishing stable, long-term relationships with African states. Moreover, with the exception of Angola or landed estates along the Zambezi River, the Portuguese did not have the manpower or resources to conquer or influence the political affairs of African states. However, as the Atlantic slave trade increased, the Portuguese and African states, especially along the Atlantic and Indian Ocean coasts, became bound up in a destructive process that would run its tragic course over the next few centuries.

Suggestions for Web Browsing

You can obtain more information about topics included in this chapter at the websites listed below. See also the companion website that accompanies this text, **http://www.ablongman.com/ brummett**, which contains an online study guide and additional resources.

Age of Discovery
http://www.win.tue.nl/cs/fm/engels/discovery/#age

An excellent collection of resources that includes text, images, and maps relating to the early years of European expansion.

Internet Medieval History Sourcebook: Exploration and Expansion
http://www.fordham.edu/halsall/sbook1z.html

Extensive online source for links about Western exploration and expansion, including primary documents by or about da Gama, Columbus, Drake, and Magellan.

Columbus Navigation Home Page
http://www1.minn.net/~keithp/

Extensive information regarding the life and voyages of Christopher Columbus.

Internet African History Sourcebook
http://www.fordham.edu/halsall/africa/africasbook.html

Extensive online source for links about African history, including primary documents about the slave trade and by people who opposed it, supported it, and were its victims.

Literature and Film

Two major documentary series marked the quincentennial of Columbus's 1492 voyage in different ways. *Columbus and the Age of Discovery* (1991) is a seven-part series that primarily treats European exploration and expansion in the New World, while *500 Nations* (1995) is an eight-part series that examines Native American history before and after the arrival of Europeans. *Conquistadores* (2001) is Michael Wood's presentation of European explorers/conquerors such as Cortés and Pizarro.

Mexican writer Carlos Fuentes has written a major epic, *Terra Nostra*, trans. Margaret Peden (Farrar, Straus, and Giroux, 1976) and a collection of short stories and novellas, *The Orange Tree*, trans. Alfred MacAdam (Farrar, Straus, and Giroux, 1994), with Spanish exploration and conquest of the New World as their backdrop. James Lackhart's *We People Here: Nahuatl Accounts of the Conquest of Mexico* (University of California Press, 1993) presents indigenous Indian narratives of the Spanish conquest compiled by a Franciscan priest in the sixteenth century.

Suggestions for Reading

Several excellent works, which cover the subject of European exploration and colonization, are Geoffrey V. Scammell, *The First Imperial Age: European Overseas Expansion, 1400–1700* (Unwin Hyman, 1989); Anthony Pagden, eds., *European Encounters with the New World* (Yale University Press, 1993); and Nicholas Canny and Anthony Pagden, *Colonial Identity in the Atlantic World* (Princeton University Press, 1989). European encounters with other peoples are treated in Urs Bitterli, *Cultures in Conflict: Encounters Between European and Non-European Cultures, 1492–1800* (Stanford University Press, 1989), and Stuart Schwartz, ed., *Implicit Understandings: Observing, Reporting, and Reflecting on the Encounters between Europeans and Other Peoples in the Early Modern Era* (Cambridge University Press, 1994).

Books on the Iberian New World are Tzvetan Todorov, *The Conquest of America* (Harper&Row, 1984) and Mark A. Burkholder, *Colonial Latin America* (Oxford University Press, 1989). Works on Columbus include Felipe Fernandez-Armesto, *Columbus* (Oxford University Press, 1992), and John Yewell, Chris Dodge, and Jan De Surey, *Confronting Columbus: An Anthology* (McFarland, 1992).

For a penetrating study of Latin American social conditions, see Louisa Hoberman and Susan M. Socolow, eds., *Cities and Society in Colonial Latin America* (University of New Mexico Press, 1986).

Luis Martin, *Daughters of the Conquistadores* (Southern Methodist University Press, 1989) documents the significant role of women in the grueling process of colonization. Good coverage of the Spanish campaigns in Peru is provided in Susan Ramirez, *The World Upside Down: Cross-Cultural Contact and Conflict in Sixteenth-Century Peru* (Stanford University Press, 1996).

On political, economic, and social conditions, see Leslie B. Simpson, *The Encomienda in New Spain*, 3rd ed. (University of California Press, 1982). Edward Murguca, *Assimilation, Colonialism, and the Mexican American People* (University Press of America, 1989), depicts the racial and cultural synthesis in colonial Mexico.

A respected work on Portuguese exploration and colonization is A. J. R. Russell-Wood, *A World on the Move: The Portuguese in Africa, Asia and America, 1415–1808* (St. Martin's Press, 1992). On the Portuguese in Asia, see Michael Pearson, *The Indian Ocean* (Routledge, 2003).

A sound treatment of Dutch imperial development is Charles R. Boxer, *The Dutch Seaborne Empire* (Penguin, 1989). French colonialism in America is covered in William J. Eccles, *France in America* (Michigan State University Press, 1990), and the British Empire in William R Lewis, Nicholas Canny, P. J. Marshall, and Alaine Low, eds., *The Origins of Empire: British Overseas Enterprise to the Close of the Seventeenth Century* (Oxford University Press, 1998).

CHAPTER 17

Politics in the First Age of Capitalism, 1648–1774

Absolutism and Limited Central Power

CHAPTER CONTENTS

- Capitalism and the Forces of Change
- Social Crises during the Capitalist Revolution
  - **DOCUMENT:** *Conditions Among Eighteenth-Century French Peasants*
- Louis XIV, the Sun King: The Model for European Absolutism
  - **DOCUMENT:** *Louis XIV to His Son*
- The Gravitational Pull of French Absolutism
- Holland and England: Limited Central Power
- Breaking the Bank: Diplomacy and War in the Age of Absolutism: 1650–1774
  - **DISCOVERY THROUGH MAPS:** *The Elegant Destruction of Poland*
- Economic Challenges
- Louis XV and the Decline of European Absolutism: 1715–1774

1550

1587 Dutch Republic formed

1588–1679 Thomas Hobbes, author of *Leviathan* (1651), which provided secular, contractual justification for absolutism

1600

1603–1625 Reign of James I of England, beginning of Stuart dynasty

1619–1683 Jean Baptiste Colbert, finance minister for Louis XIV

1640–1688 Reign of Frederick William the Great Elector of Prussia

1642–1648 English Civil War

1643–1715 Reign of Louis XIV of France, the Sun King

1648 Peace of Westphalia

1649–1653 French Civil War, the Fronde, revolt of the nobility against absolutism

1650

1688 Glorious Revolution in England

1689–1725 Reign of Peter the Great of Russia

1700

1707 Act of Union between England and Scotland

1713 Peace of Utrecht

1713–1740 Reign of Frederick William I of Prussia

1715–1774 Reign of Louis XV of France

A century and a half of European turmoil came to an end in 1648. As we saw in Chapter 15, the new political system after the Treaty of Westphalia would be based on *raison d'état,* calculated policies to further the growth of the individual states. State structures took one of two forms thereafter: either the absolutist model perfected by Louis XIV of France or the limited central power approach found in the Netherlands and England. During this time, however, politics and diplomacy—with the numerous "Balance of Power wars"—were not the most important developments.

Capitalism—an economic system based on private ownership of property, individual risk taking, and market determination of the prices of goods—became the basis of the economy, and by implication, political power. Rich states with great resources and comparatively efficient bureaucracies grew stronger while nations such as Poland, which remained mired in its medieval political and economic structure, literally disappeared from the map.

France and England—after gaining domination over Holland—extended their influence and markets around the globe as Spain entered a period of relative stagnation. These two states probed for advantage with the powers of Africa and Asia in the late seventeenth and eighteenth centuries. The peoples of the Americas also became caught up in the Europeans' global economic and political competition.

CAPITALISM AND THE FORCES OF CHANGE

■ *What role do economics and politics play in determining the success or failure of a state?*

Dynamic economic and social forces challenged all European governments, no matter what their form, in the seventeenth and eighteenth century. Every part of Europe, from Britain to Russia, to the colonies around the world, and every social class, from peasants to the most tradition-bound nobles, felt the insecurity and restlessness inherent in the economic and social transformation. Governments with sufficient flexibility survived these changes; those that could not adapt were weakened or destroyed.

Expanding Capitalism

The primary force driving change was an energetic capitalistic economy developing so rapidly that it could hardly be controlled or even predicted. **Capitalism** generated new economic pursuits that developed almost spontaneously outside established institutions. It also created unprecedented increases in the volume of trade by dealing both in precious goods and in bulk commodities. Eastern Europe and the Baltic supplied grains, timber, fish, and naval stores while western Europe supplied manufactures for its outlying regions and overseas trade. Dutch, English, and French merchant-bankers controlled shipping and credit. Plantation agriculture in the tropics, particularly the cultivation of Caribbean sugar, produced the greatest profits for overseas commerce. The African slave trade, along with its many supporting industries, also became an integral part of the intercontinental economic system. The New World economy widened European horizons while contributing to European wealth. New foods such as potatoes, yams, lima beans, tapioca, and peanuts became part of the European diet. Tropical plantation crops such as rice, coffee, tea, cocoa, and sugar ceased to be luxuries.

These new markets and resources contributed greatly to the development of modern capitalistic institutions. As the volume rose, great public banks chartered by governments replaced earlier family banks like the Fuggers of Augsburg. The Bank of Amsterdam (1609) and the Bank of England (1694) are typical examples. Such banks, holding public revenues and creating credit by issuing notes, made large amounts of capital available for favored enterprises and the state.

The Rise of Capitalism

1600	English East India companies formed
1602	Dutch East India Company
1609	Bank of Amsterdam opens
c. 1688	Lloyds of London begins operation
1694	Bank of England is chartered
1698	London Stock Exchange opens
1724	Paris Bourse is established

Building on this seventeenth-century foundation, four new conditions produced the commercial boom in the century and a half after Westphalia. First, government demand for goods reached astronomical heights as huge standing armies and navies required mountains of food, clothing, arms, and ammunition. Second, a rising European population created another expanding market, demanding bulk commodities, while the increasing average life span allowed businessmen to amass more profits for investment over the course of their lives. Developing plantation agriculture in tropical colonies provided a third stimulus to foreign trade. Finally, Brazilian gold and diamond strikes stimulated the growth of capitalistic enterprises after the 1730s by driving up prices and creating greater profits.

European Population Density, c. 1600

The resulting economic changes brought promising but sometimes disturbing results. As wealth increased beyond all expectations, investment and production rose accordingly in textiles, coal, iron, and shipbuilding. With enterprises growing larger, partnerships and **joint-stock companies** began replacing individually owned companies, as had happened earlier in foreign trade. At the same time, specialization became common in new phases of wholesaling and retailing operations.

Expansion and increasing complexity were accompanied by a steady monetary inflation. Wages, for example, increased far less than food prices, thus depressing the condition of workers. Nobles on the Continent who received fixed fees from their peasants, and English landlords who had leased their fields on long-term contracts were hurt badly. Conversely, landowners who rented to short-term tenants or received payment in kind, profited, as did other capitalistic investors, who became wealthy from the general

---

capitalism—An economic system based on private ownership of property, individual risk taking, and market determination of the price of goods.

joint-stock companies—A business or other enterprise in which the ownership is divided among a number of stock holders who jointly share the profits and the risks.

Capitalist agriculture, shown here in the rolling and spinning of tobacco, demanded a large and dependable supply of labor. Slaves or indentured servants in the North American colonies did the hard work that returned a profit for European investors.

increase in the cost of goods. At times, their profits soared in a wildly speculative "boom and bust" market.

International trade was the most obvious indicator of European business prosperity. An even larger trade with overseas areas encouraged the formation of East India Companies in Austria and Prussia as clones of their older and better-known English, Dutch, and French counterparts. The resulting trade in sugar, silk, cotton, tobacco, and various luxury products generated whole new European industries. Perhaps more of an impact came from the African slave trade, centered in Liverpool and Bordeaux (bor-DOH), which reached its peak during the eighteenth century. Altogether, the total foreign trade of Britain and France increased by some 450 percent. The Dutch, in imperial decline, experienced a notable decrease.

The Growth of Free Enterprise

Prosperity threatened government attempts to control the economy. As opportunities for profit increased, capitalists searched for profits outside state-sponsored enterprises and even beyond the legal limits set by governments and traditions. Some of these endeavors were deliberate efforts to evade the law; others—perhaps most—were responses to opportunity. This rising free enterprise capitalism, as distinct from mercantilist state capitalism, was evident in every phase of the pre-1789 economy.

A growing demand for food encouraged the trend in capitalist agriculture: the large-scale trading of agricultural goods as commodities in national and international markets. Soaring food prices lured surplus capital into land and improvements. This trend was most typical of England, but the agricultural boom, on a slightly smaller scale, extended to France, the Dutch Republic, the Low Countries, Prussia, and even the wine producers of Italy and Spanish Catalonia. Wherever it developed, capitalistic agriculture emphasized efficiency and profits, which usually required procedures that did not fit in with the traditional cooperative methods and servile labor of rural villages.

Four Englishmen pioneered the movement. Jethro Tull (1674–1741) carefully plowed the land planted in neat rows using a drill he invented and kept the plants well cultivated as they grew to maturity. Viscount Charles Townshend (1674–1738), nicknamed "Turnip

Townshend," specialized in restoring soil fertility by such methods as applying clay-lime mixtures and planting turnips in **crop rotation.** Robert Bakewell (1725–1795) attacked the problem of scrawny cattle. Through selective breeding, he was able to increase the size of meat animals and also the milk yields from dairy cows. Another Englishman, Arthur Young (1741–1820), an ardent advocate for the new agriculture, made lecture tours throughout Europe and recorded his observations. He popularized the advantages of well-equipped farms and economical agricultural techniques and did much to free European agriculture from the less productive methods of the past.

New agricultural techniques demanded large capital investment and complete control of the land. Common fields, where villagers shared customary rights, could not be cultivated with the new methods. The land needed to be drained, irrigated, fertilized, and cultivated by scientific methods. Selective stock-breeding could not be practiced with an unregulated community herd. Landlords and investors who wanted to use the new methods brought about a devastating destruction of traditional society by trying to fence or enclose their acres. By outright purchase, foreclosure, suit, fraud, or even legislation, they tried to free their lands from old manorial restrictions, particularly from traditional rights to community use of the commons.

The gentry used their political dominance to improve their economic position, especially in the countryside. Although English manorial fees and services were abolished in the seventeenth century, many villages had retained their medieval rights to pasturage and fuel gathering on the commons. These rights were lost to enclosures. From 1750 until the end of the century, 40,000 to 50,000 small farms disappeared into large estates under the **Enclosure Acts.** Some of the peasants forced from the land went to the cities, some became agricultural laborers at pitifully poor wages, and others went into parish poorhouses, which were soon overflowing. This movement was strongest in England but also was seen on the Continent. Inflation and buyouts in France, particularly in the north, drove many peasants from the land, but they were so important as taxpayers that the government managed to restrict the movement. Consequently, French landlords were still complaining about manorial restrictions until 1789. But in England, the gentry—unlike many of their colleagues on the Continent—had already embraced capitalism and were powerful in Parliament: They were able to pass 2000 enclosure laws between 1760 and 1800.

In industry the movement toward free enterprise produced the so-called domestic system, which involved contractual arrangements between capitalistic brokers and handworkers. Brokers supplied materials to the workers in their homes and later collected the products, to be sent through another stage of finishing or sold directly on the market. The system became common in industries where demand was high, profits were large, and capital was available. Domestic manufacturing moved early to the country, away from the regulations imposed by city guilds. The advantages and disadvantages were those associated with unregulated industry. Contracts were freely negotiated and prices were usually low, but capitalists and consumers faced considerable risks. Workers, particularly women and children, were easier to exploit than the guilds were.

Domestic industry was common all over western Europe after 1500, reaching a climax of growth in the eighteenth century. Although most typical of England, it also developed rapidly in northern France, the Low

---

crop rotation—The practice of planting different crops in successive seasons on the same plot of land so as to preserve the soil's fertility. Otherwise, if the same crop is planted year after year on the same plot of land the soil will become exhausted, and the land will have to lie fallow for at least a year to recover its fertility.

Enclosure Acts—A series of laws passed after 1760 that favored capitalist agriculture. Common lands were divided up, farming plots were combined, poor peasants lost the right to scavenge in the former common lands, and gates had to be installed at the boundaries around farms. The end result was to drive poor peasants off the land.

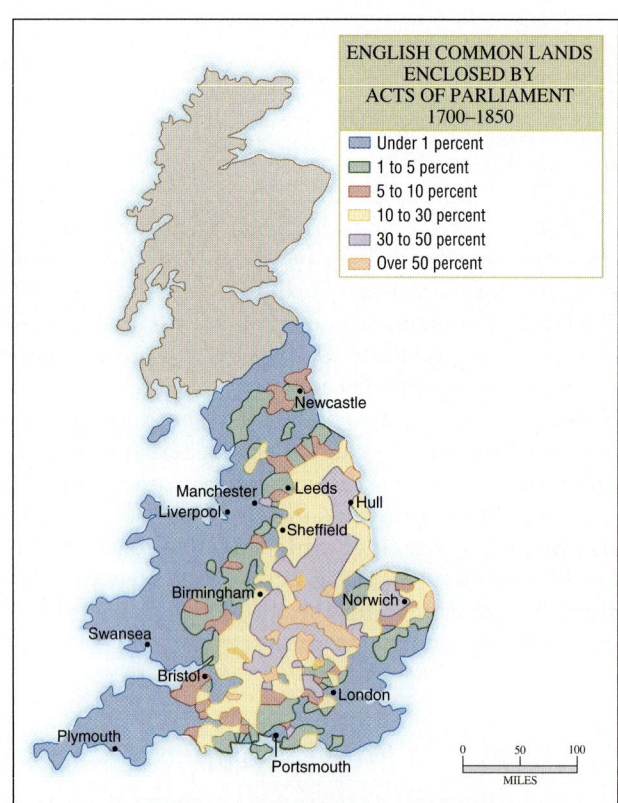

As the English gentry rose to political dominance after 1685, they used their strength in parliament to push through the Enclosure Acts, shutting the peasantry out from access to common lands.

The individual, human skills needed to perform the art of stocking frame work knitting came to be done by machines by the beginning of the nineteenth century.

Countries, and southern Germany. It was involved in all essential processes of the woolen industries, notably spinning, weaving, fulling, and dyeing. The system also spread among other textile industries, such as linens and cottons, which provided a decided stimulus to the trend in the 1700s. Other affected industries were silk, lace, leather, paper, glass, pottery, and metals. By 1750, English domestic manufacturing employed over 4 million workers.

The career of Ambrose Crowley illustrates the domestic system in the infant English iron industry. Crowley started as a blacksmith who worked as a guildsman in Greenwich, where he accumulated a little capital. Around 1680 he moved to a small Durham village and built a domestic organization for the large-scale production of hardware. By 1700 the village had become a thriving town of 1500 workers. Crowley, who rented them their houses and supplied some of their tools as well as ore and fuel, employed most of them. The village produced nails, locks, bolts, hammers, spades, and other tools, which Crowley marketed elsewhere. A wealthy and respected citizen, he was knighted in 1706.

British industry benefited from the political system in place. Because most guild monopolies had passed with the seventeenth century, domestic industry faced few legal obstacles, but it did experience frequent functional crises. Despite widespread business prosperity, wages failed to keep up with the steady inflation. Between 1756 and 1786 wages rose by 35 percent but food prices increased by more than 60 percent. Workers also had to accept periodic unemployment, even in good times. They were thus inclined to resist the wage system and agitate for state intervention against low wages and high prices. Their bitter discontent was expressed in violent riots, most notably in 1765 and 1780.

Joint-stock companies were drastically reoriented in the late seventeenth century. Companies such as the Dutch and English East India Companies pooled the resources of many investors. In the late seventeenth century, exchanges for buying and selling stock—or **stock exchanges**—were becoming common, as were maritime insurance companies such as Lloyds of London, which began operations about 1688. Originally, joint-stock companies were exclusive monopolies, both in their areas of operation and in their limited number of stockholders. They were generally criti-

stock exchanges—Places where stocks—certificates representing the ownership of a part of a company or enterprise—were bought and sold.

cized, and their trading rights were regularly violated by competitors and smugglers. Under pressure, the British East India Company and similar firms steadily liberalized their policies until ultimately most stocks were sold on the open market. Sales of stock greatly increased opportunities for investment and multiplied the number of joint-stock companies. By 1715 more than 140 existed in England. This situation also encouraged a huge, speculative bull market on stock exchanges, which sprang up in taverns and coffeehouses all over western Europe. The London Stock Exchange opened in 1698 and the Paris Bourse in 1724; both were involved in the mania of speculation that collapsed the South Sea and Mississippi Companies in 1719–1720. Despite these disasters, such institutions become necessary to the private sector of Europe's economy in the early 1700s.

Banking performed a similarly necessary role. In a sense, the banks of Sweden, Amsterdam, and London were examples of state operation; their directors were often government advisers, authorized to perform semiofficial functions such as issuing notes and financing public debts. In another sense, however, these institutions became integral parts of the free market economy, providing the necessary credit for business enterprise while creating their own nonofficial commercial methods and institutions. Moreover, smaller banks developed within the private monetary and credit systems. The first English country bank was founded as a private enterprise in 1716 at Bristol; by 1780 there were 300 in the country.

Major insurance companies, banks, and stock exchanges formed an integrated institutional system, functioning in a free international market. Their standardized procedures became so complicated that ordinary people could not understand them. That strange new world of business enterprise, unlike the political world, was not controlled directly by anyone, not even by the power of concentrated capital. Goods and credit, commodity prices and wages, monetary values and stock quotations all interacted according to their own laws, which could be studied but not accurately predicted. Participants in this system learned that the number of losers could and often did outnumber the winners.

SOCIAL CRISES DURING THE CAPITALIST REVOLUTION

- *Capitalism rewards those who are the most efficient. What happened to those people—noble and peasant—who were unable to compete in the capitalist market?*

The Aristocracy and the Commoners

Ignoring the mass discontent and middle-class frustrations, the old regimes continued to depend largely on local authorities, military officers, and bureaucrats, drawn almost exclusively from nobilities and wealthy commoners. Governments therefore legalized privilege, conferring social status, political power, and fabulous wealth on a small elite while dooming the masses to grinding poverty. The system cut across class lines. Most of the clergy and nobles were as poor as some peasants, and the great majority of the urban middle classes were denied the leisured comfort of the wealthy bankers and merchants.

The aristocratic nature of the old regimes derived partly from encroachments on royal prerogatives by European nobilities after the Peace of Westphalia. Temporarily checked by such strong monarchs as Louis XIV and Peter the Great, the nobles retained or regained political power in the Habsburg domain, Germany, and Poland. Early in the eighteenth century, they did the same in Sweden, Spain, Russia (after Peter's death), and particularly in Louis XV's France.

Europe's old regimes were topped by official ruling classes of high clergy and nobles. Combined, these two privileged orders accounted for less than 2 percent of the total European population; the great magnates, who enjoyed real wealth and power, were concentrated in only 5000 families, among some 4 million titled aristocrats. Most of the true elite lived in city mansions and palaces, far away from their broad acres in the country. For their high incomes, tax immunities, and numerous honors, they contributed almost nothing beyond decoration to church and state.

France provides a good illustration of the system. There the church owned 20 percent of the land and collected returns equal to half those from royal estates. Some of the monies supported education, social work, and charities, but most went to 11,000 of the 130,000 members of the clergy, particularly to 123 bishops and 28 archbishops. Some of their annual incomes exceeded the equivalent of $1 million—the equal of what top-ranking CEOs earn today—but many of the overworked lower clergy existed on $100 a year. Among the 400,000 nobles, only 1000 families were represented at Versailles, where their members held numerous honorific appointments requiring no work. Titled nobles held 20 percent of the land, most by feudal tenures, which permitted them to collect numerous customary fees from their peasants. From all such sources, high French nobles probably averaged an annual equivalent of well over $100,000. Many, including some of the royal **intendants,** were former wealthy nonnobles who had bought their titles or offices.

---

intendants—Officials working for the king.

Fantastic hairstyles, like that shown in this engraving, were one of the ways in which members of the French upper class displayed their extravagance.

Conspicuous consumption was typical of the high European nobility, such as the Fitzwilliamses in Ireland, the Newcastles in England, the Schonbrüns (SHOUN-brun) in Bohemia, the Radziwills (RODZH-veel) in Poland, and the Esterhazys (ES-ter-haz-ee) in Hungary. Prince Esterhazy owned about 10,000 acres, including 29 estates, 160 market towns, and 414 villages; his annual revenues exceeded the equivalent of $400,000. With such wealth, the magnates built elaborate city dwellings and sumptuous country retreats, filling them with priceless handcrafted furniture, rich tapestries, and fine works of art. While most people scratched for food, the high nobles enjoyed meats, fruits, and rare delicacies that were literally unknown among common people. Generally, the top aristocrats lived lavishly in a fantasy world, marred only by the dull ceremonies accompanying their brilliant but busy social activities.

Beneath this aristocratic superstructure lived millions of European commoners, 80 percent of whom were peasants. Except in Sweden, where they could protest to the parliament, they were unrepresented in government. Three-fourths were landless, and many were serfs, bound to their villages, not only in Russia, Poland, and Prussia but also in Denmark. Among city-dwellers, only 11 percent were merchants, shopkeepers, artisans, and professionals. This proportion was higher in the Netherlands, England, and northern Italy, but generally lower elsewhere, particularly in eastern Europe. At the bottom of urban society was the mass of indigent poor, barely able to survive. Commoners of all economic levels paid most of the taxes. They were subject to legal discrimination in favor of the nobility, from whom they were also separated by differences in education, speech, manners, dress, and social customs.

This general pattern was evident in the French **Third Estate.** Including some 26 million people, it was more varied in its extremes than the first two estates, the clergy and nobles. At the top were about 75,000 wealthy bankers and merchants who had not bothered to buy titles. Another 3 million urban dwellers consisted largely of shopkeepers, lawyers, doctors, craftsmen, and street people, these last being most prevalent in Paris and port cities. The great mass of commoners in France, as in Europe generally, was the 23 million rural peasants. Most held some property rights to their lands, but many were tenants and about a million were still serfs in 1789. Almost all peasants, serf or free, paid fees to their local nobles. Government taxes were irregular but heavy everywhere; the *taille* (TIE-yeh), or main land tax, fell heaviest on the class that was least able to pay. French peasants lived better than serfs in eastern Europe or the starving farm laborers of England, but life in a French village was a constant struggle for survival.

The Challenge of Population Growth

Europe experienced a population explosion in the eighteenth century. The number of people there increased more than 58 percent, from about 118 million in 1700 to 185 million a century later; some 50 million of this increase came after 1750. Population growth during the era was much higher in Europe than in Asia or Africa; in fact, in percentage terms it had never been as rapid before and has never been exceeded since. In the past, historians have emphasized rising life expectancy (falling death rates) as the cause. They have attributed this lower mortality to an improved social environment, involving such conditions as cleaner clothes and dishes, made possible by the new textile and pottery industries; better water and sewage facilities, following wider use of iron piping; and better medical treatment, particularly in reducing infant mortality. However, other recent

---

Third Estate—Under the social system of pre-1789 France, society was divided by function: The first estate—the clergy—prayed; the second estate—the nobles—fought; and the third estate—the rest of society—worked. Established in the tenth century, the Estate System was an anachronism by the eighteenth century.

studies have suggested that a major cause for population growth was rising fertility in response to more productive agriculture and increasing food supplies, which also encouraged rural people to marry earlier and have more children to work the land. Whatever the cause, population expansion triggered major social changes, including rising economic demand, the growth of cities, an increasing labor surplus, vagabondage, and extensive migration.

Nearly every part of Europe experienced this tremendous expansion between 1650 and 1800. The English population rose from 5 million to over 9 million; that of Russia increased from 17 to 36 million; and the French population rose from 21 to 28 million. Other areas, which had earlier seen declines, posted gains: The Spanish population rose from 7.5 million to 11 million, while that of Italy expanded from 11 to 19 million. The increased number of people who could not afford to remain in their ancestral homes either migrated overseas or moved to urban areas, where 10 percent of Europe's population lived by 1800.

People moved in all directions. Some, like the Swiss and Irish, became foreign mercenaries. Others, like 300,000 French Huguenots (hyu-ge-NO), moved to escape religious persecution: 40,000 of them settled in England, and 20,000 of the most skilled went to Prussia. Both the Prussian and Russian governments regularly imported specialized craftsmen. German peasants by the thousands also went east to acquire land in Hungary or Russia. And the New World enticed many. In the eighteenth century, more than 750,000 English and 100,000 Irish settlers arrived in North America, the largest national contingents of a European migration to the Americas that numbered more than 2 million people.

Cities grew rapidly in the West, the main area of commerce—both domestic and foreign—and finance. Most affected were the English towns and cities, where populations generally increased faster than those of rural areas. The scope and significance of the trend may be quickly illustrated by a few figures. London's population rose from 400,000 to over 800,000 between the Peace of Utrecht (1713) and the French Revolution (1789). Other English cities, such as Bristol, Norwich, Liverpool, Leeds, Halifax, and Birmingham, which had been country towns in the 1600s, became medium-sized cities of between 20,000 and 65,000 inhabitants. On the Continent, the population of Paris reached 750,000 by 1789, and the number of residents in Bordeaux, Nantes, Le Havre, and Marseilles (mar-SEIL-e) all increased appreciably. Farther east were other expanding cities—Hamburg, Frankfurt, Geneva, Vienna, Berlin; the last two each had more than 100,000 inhabitants in the eighteenth century. In no city did the basic services of police, health, and employment keep pace with the increase in population.

Cities, of course, were the breeding grounds of ideas and contention. There were books and newspapers, coffeehouses, sailors from foreign lands, and varied populations, exchanging views and challenging prejudices. Violent spectacles, such as animal baiting and cockfighting, provided common amusements. Urban life was not only exciting, it was also more impersonal, dangerous, and frustrating. Using every kind of trick and deceit, a large criminal element flourished in the streets. Mobs were easily formed and more easily aroused, particularly in London and Paris, which regularly faced riots in the eighteenth century. Unlike the relatively placid inhabitants of rural villages, city-dwellers thrived on danger, diversity, and unpredictability. One person in three in the cities was unemployed in the eighteenth century. While the unemployed men sought relief in the proliferating gin

William Hogarth cast a critical and unsparing eye on the desperate conditions of the poor in London during the eighteenth century. In Gin Lane *(1751) he depicted the alcoholism that allowed the poor to escape momentarily the misery of their lives.*

mills of London, many women had no choice but to practice prostitution to feed their children.

Oppressive Conditions for Women

Post-1648 society was especially oppressive to women, whose general prospects declined despite some slight gains among those in the upper classes. Poor widows were hit hardest, as suggested by the number starving in English workhouses. Women died, on the average, five years younger than men, a fact explained largely by the high proportion that died in childbirth. A significant factor was malnutrition, because poor women lacked calcium in their diets and were therefore subject to hemorrhaging. For most women among the rural and urban poor, life was a nightmare of deprivation, suffering, and struggling to survive.

This situation was particularly true for poor country women, as noted by the British writer Arthur Young, who described a French peasant woman of 28 years who appeared to be 60 or 70. Capitalistic agriculture depressed farm wages, forcing farm laborers to leave the villages in search of work. Women had to stay and eke out support for the children by domestic spinning or weaving. Some went to work in the fields for lower pay and longer hours than men. As work opportunities diminished, thousands took to the roads, carrying their babies and begging for food. Many died with their children by the roadsides; others joined criminal gangs of robbers or smugglers. The hardiest and the most determined reached the cities, where the best hope for a displaced peasant woman was employment as a cook or maid with a well-to-do family.

In the cities a poor woman's life was not much better than in the villages. The lucky few in household service were paid much less than men, assigned cramped quarters, fed leftovers, and frequently exploited sexually by their masters. Alternate employment was extremely limited because women were denied membership in most craft guilds. A few could find work outside the guilds, spinning, weaving, sewing, or working leather in starvation-wage sweatshops. Others took dirtier and heavier jobs in the metal trades and in the coalfields, both above and below the ground. Another option, reluctantly chosen by many women, was prostitution. This ancient profession was growing rapidly in every large city, with 50,000 known female prostitutes in London and more than 40,000 in Paris by the late 1700s. Social degradation, venereal disease, and continuous harassment marked their lives as civil authorities allowed them to operate but subjected them to periodic imprisonment.

A vast social chasm separated poor women from those of the wealthy classes; yet even at the top, another broad gulf divided the sexes. Royal and noble women exercised considerable political power, but except for numerous ruling monarchs, they operated as satellites of the men they manipulated. Among both aristocratic women and those of the wealthy middle class, many were withdrawn from meaningful work as mothers and homemakers to become social ornaments for the husbands. Legally, upper-class wives remained subordinated to their husbands in the disposition of property and rights to divorce; the double standard of marital fidelity remained supreme, both socially and legally. Indeed, despite their improved education and their artistic and literary pursuits, women were still regarded as childlike, irresponsible, and passion-ruled by such eminent eighteenth-century men as Rousseau, Frederick the Great, and Lord Chesterfield.

The Prevalence of Human Misery

A significant base for popular discontent against governments after Westphalia was an ever-prevalent misery among the ever-growing numbers of the poor. The various wars destroyed crops, ruined cities, created hordes of starving refugees, and depopulated whole provinces. Armies contributed to prevailing diseases, such as smallpox, typhus, and malaria. Lack of sanitation and the presence of horse manure on roads and streets attracted swarming flies, which spread typhoid and infantile diarrhea among thousands of children. While epidemics of plague spread throughout Central Europe, rickets and tuberculosis reflected malnutrition among half the workers, who could not achieve marginal proficiency. Mortality rates were appalling: Half of the children died before they reached 6 years old, one woman in five died in childbirth, and life expectancy was only about 28 years. For a large proportion of Europeans, unemployment, homelessness, grinding poverty, and hunger were inevitable. Indeed, horrible reality could be escaped only on rare affordable occasions in alcohol.

Although sometimes exciting, life in the cities was also miserable for the urban poor, who made up 20 to 40 percent of city populations. Many had come in from the country, seeking survival. Without homes, friends, or steady work, they lived as best they could, toiling at transitory menial jobs, begging, stealing, or selling themselves as prostitutes. Only a social notch higher were the apprentices and journeymen of the decaying craft guilds, who also faced real hardships. The discipline, particularly for apprentices, was difficult; hours were long; and wages were barely enough to buy food. Crowded into filthy quarters, without adequate light, air, or bathing facilities, they lived dull lives conditioned by ignorance, squalor, disease, and crime. Bad as these conditions were, they might always get worse, for as the guilds faced competition,

Document: Conditions Among Eighteenth-Century French Peasants

British writer Arthur Young made these observations just before the French Revolution. He saw better conditions elsewhere but was appalled at the backward state of French agriculture and the great gap in living standards between the nobility and the lower classes in the country.

SEPTEMBER 1ST. To Combourg. The country has a savage aspect; husbandry not much further advanced, at least in skill, than among the Hurons, which appears incredible amidst enclosures; the people almost as wild as their country, and their town of Combourg one of the most brutal filthy places that can be seen; mud houses, no windows, and a pavement so broken, as to impede all passengers, but ease none; yet here is a château, and inhabited. Who is this Mons. de Chateaubriand, the owner, that has nerves strung for a residence amidst such filth and poverty? Below this hideous heap of wretchedness is a fine lake, surrounded by well-wooded enclosures. Coming out of Hédé, there is a beautiful lake belonging to Mons. de Blossac, Intendant of Poitiers, with a fine accompaniment of wood. A very little cleaning would make here a delicious scenery. There is a [Château de Blossac], with four rows of trees, and nothing else to be seen from the windows in the true French style. Forbid it, taste, that this should be the house of the owner of that beautiful water; and yet this Mons. de Blossac has made at Poitiers the finest promenade in France!...

SEPT. 5TH. To Montauban. The poor people seem poor indeed; the children terribly ragged, if possible worse clad than if with no clothes at all; as to shoes and stockings they are luxuries. A beautiful girl of six or seven years playing with a stick, and smiling under such a bundle of rags as made my heart ache to see her. They did not beg, and when I gave them anything seemed more surprised than obliged. One-third of what I have seen of this province seems uncultivated, and nearly all of it in misery....

JULY 11TH. Pass [Les] Islettes, a town (or rather collection of dirt and dung) of new features, that seem to mark, with the faces of the people, a country not French.

JULY 12TH. Walking up a long hill, to ease my mare, I was joined by a poor woman, who complained of the times, and that it was a sad country. Demanding her reasons, she said her husband had but a morsel of land, one cow, and a poor little horse, yet they had a *franchar* (42 lb.) of wheat, and three chickens, to pay as a quit-rent to one seigneur; and four *franchar* of oats, one chicken and 1 *sou* to pay to another, besides very heavy *tailles* and other taxes. She had seven children, and the cow's milk helped to make the soup. But why, instead of a horse, do not you keep another cow? Oh, her husband could not carry his produce so well without a horse; and asses are little used in the country. It was said, at present, that *something was to be done by some great folks for such poor ones, but she did not know who nor how,* but God send us better, *car les tailles et les droits nous écrasent* [because the *tailles* and other taxes are crushing us]. This woman, at no great distance, might have been taken for sixty or seventy, her figure was so bent, and her face so furrowed and hardened by labour; but she said she was only twenty-eight. An Englishman who had not travelled cannot imagine the figure made by infinitely the greater part of the countrywomen in France; it speaks, at the first sight, hard and severe labour. I am inclined to think, that they work harder than the men, and this, united with the more miserable labour of bringing a new race of slaves into the world, destroys absolutely all symmetry of person and every feminine appearance....

Questions to Consider

1. Young writes just before the French Revolution—what do you see in the first paragraph of the selection that would provoke a violent reaction?
2. Young was an agricultural reformer in England. How did he characterize the nature of the methods used by the French peasants in preparing their land?
3. What was the effect of the rural situation in France on women?
4. It is alleged that peasants have little understanding of the economic and political system in which they find themselves. Did the woman with whom Young talked on July 12th comprehend why her life was so hard?

From Arthur Young, *Travels in France*, ed. Constantia Maxwell (Cambridge: Cambridge University Press, 1929), pp. 107 ff.

many shops were forced to close, leaving their journeymen to become wandering artisans among the vagabonds on the roads.

Most of these pitiful derelicts were products of the century's most serious social challenge, rural poverty. Despite a general prosperity lasting until about 1770, European peasants suffered severely from ravaging armies and increasing agricultural specialization. High agricultural prices turned aristocrats into aspiring capitalists, willing to gouge their peasants in seeking greater profits. Some nobles, particularly on the Continent, revived and enforced their old manorial rights to fees and services. Others moved in an opposite direction by eliminating the peasants' medieval rights and using hired labor to work their lands. Either way, the peasants lost a substantial amount of their livelihood and were likely to become criminals, vagrants, or part of an alienated subculture. They ceased to be assets to the state—as either taxpayers or soldiers—becoming instead potentially dangerous and expensive liabilities.

Although faring better than the serfs of eastern Europe, western peasants still faced terrible conditions. Some in France were reduced from tenants to laborers when merchants bought up land to profit from rising food prices. Under Louis XV, some 30,000 rural vagrants thronged French roads. About 35 percent of the peasants who had managed to acquire land were still paying manorial fees and services to local lords in accordance with feudal law. Earlier, these exactions had hurt the peasants' pride more than their chances for survival; when the practice was stepped up during the depression of the 1780s, many lost their lands.

Responses to the plight of the urban and rural poor were crude and cruel. It was felt that the way to eliminate vagrancy was through punishment. The approach was similar to the brutal beating of military delinquents, the condemning of criminals to galley slavery, or the confinement of debtors on rotting prison ships. For the poor, similar punitive solutions were sought in the British parish workhouses and the French "beggar depots." At the end of the century, the English workhouses held 100,000 inmates, compared with 230,000 in the French depots. Both systems, like others all over Europe, perpetuated abominable living conditions while denying hope for the unfortunate victims. In England, the workhouses were favored by some large landowners, who welcomed cheap labor supplied by the state. Other taxpayers opposed the cost of improving the workhouses and tried to push vagrants into other parishes. Even a pregnant woman or one with a sick child might be given a few pennies and turned away.

Ultimately, the governments built larger workhouses for fewer parishes, attempting to spread the cost of poverty relief. Such policies destroyed the initiative of the poor and conditioned them to seek public assistance. The simmering pressure of the discontent of the multitudes could be denied for a while, but in the 1770s and 1780s across Europe, mass outbreaks of violence and finally revolution would be the price to be paid. (See Chapter 18.)

Protests, Riots, and Rebellions

Injustice and misery among women and the poor were obvious sources of discontent, but even more dangerous for old regimes were changing attitudes among the higher classes. A general spirit of change and hope, coupled with the chaotic confusion and inefficiency of most monarchies, aroused general feelings of dissatisfaction, particularly among members of the lower middle class and lesser nobles, who were too numerous to be absorbed into the established system. Even some favored aristocrats showed a casual indifference to royal authority and a stubborn determination to defend their privileges. Potential middle-class rebels, particularly lawyers, were well equipped to voice grievances, which they did often by the late 1700s. Although lacking education and opportunities to register direct protests, city workers and peasants sometimes did express their despair in sporadic riots and futile local uprisings.

Because their testimony must be taken from official records, often from the statements of tortured captives, no one can accurately describe peasant attitudes on the Continent at that time. They surely varied from place to place, as did the conditions. Where life was hardest, they regularly resorted to individual acts of violence, such as killing animals or burning outbuildings. Generally, they lacked long-range political objectives but could be aroused en masse by immediate threats to their well-being. Seventy-three peasant rebellions occurred in eighteenth-century Europe, notoriously in Poland (1730s), Bohemia (1775), and in Russia, the great Pugachev (poo-gah-CHOV) revolt (1773–1775). Suffering English farm laborers rioted six times between 1710 and 1772. Although generally more docile, French peasants precipitated violent upheavals in 1709, 1725, 1740, 1749, and 1772. In his writings, Arthur Young recognized their surly attitudes and contempt for authority. In 1789, when they could express grievances to delegates headed for the **Estates-General,** they were universally bitter against feudal exactions and government taxes.

Urban workers were usually more aggressive and perhaps better informed than peasants but more

---

Estates-General—A national meeting in France of representatives of the three estates to present petitions to the king.

confused by the complexities of their problems. While their numbers increased with the size of cities, they became alienated from the upper classes by periodic unemployment and inflation. Rioting among workers and the idle poor of the cities was thus common, notably in London and Paris. Such outbreaks, however, were more violent than politically significant. Workers did recognize two potential enemies: the capitalist, who contracted for labor and influenced government to eliminate welfare, and the guild, which exploited the journeyman in favor of the master. To combat these enemies, workers occasionally organized in England and France. The organizations were weak, however, and their efforts usually failed for want of leadership.

Middle-class discontent, like that of some peasants, arose more from thwarted expectations than from terrible suffering. Upward mobility, from middle class to aristocracy, was a by-product of economic prosperity all over Europe, particularly in England and France. The movement took many forms—purchase of land and titles, marriage, even reward for personal services of lawyers, doctors, tutors, or governesses. This middle-class struggle for respectability was individually competitive, as long as opportunities were open. But in time, room at the top became limited, as old regimes stabilized and more of the middle class sought to climb the social ladder. At this point, ambitious middle-class outsiders became dangerously hostile to the system.

Most dissenting action came from men, but women were also represented among the malcontents. They were regularly involved in local uprisings against the high cost of bread, the introduction of machines to depress labor, and rising taxes. In 1770 a mob of Parisian women left their workplaces to protest the deportation of their vagrant children to the colonies. Such actions were not yet aimed directly against old regimes, but later (as we shall see in Chapter 18) other French and English women would go further to champion women's rights, along with the "rights of man."

More dangerous to monarchical establishments than outside opposition was aristocratic opposition from within. Gains by the nobles in Sweden, Spain, Austria, and even France increased their confidence and whetted their appetites for more power. As old regimes wavered, nobles at the top were frantically determined to maintain their positions; indeed, they professed to believe that they were more legitimate rulers than the kings. This was partly an effort to combat middle-class influence, for nobles were often heavily in debt and feared legal reforms that might require them to pay. At the same time, most lesser nobles resented the court cliques; a few even dreamed of helping the middle classes change the system. Noble opinions were indeed varied, promising weakening support for royal authority but refusing cooperation with kings in curtailing privileges. On this last point, nearly all nobles were in total agreement.

LOUIS XIV, THE SUN KING: THE MODEL FOR EUROPEAN ABSOLUTISM

■ *Why did most European countries follow the absolutist trend of government between 1650 and 1789? What advantages and disadvantages do an absolutist government bring to a state?*

The word **absolutism,** which is applied to regimes such as that of Louis XIV (1638–1715, r. 1643–1715), is somewhat misleading. Despite his grandiose role-playing, Louis faced problems arising from preindustrial technology, diverse ethnic groups, local customs, traditional rights, and nobles who still commanded formidable followings, both regionally and nationally. But he was helped by the post-1648 obsession for security and by economic growth.

Absolutism: France, England, and Russia, 1600–1700

Foundations of Absolutism

The prevailing respect for power was most clearly revealed in theoretical justifications for absolute monarchy. Some of these, such as the arguments advanced by Bishop Jacques Bossuet (BOS-siu-ay), employed the older idea of "divine right," claiming that rulers were agents of God's will. The most influential secular justification for absolutism came from the English philosopher Thomas Hobbes (1588–1679), whose political treatise, *Leviathan,* appeared in 1651. Unlike Bossuet, he did not see God as the source of political authority. According to Hobbes, people created governments as a protection against themselves because human life was naturally "poor, nasty, brutish, and short." Forced by human nature to surrender their freedoms to the state, people have no rights under government except obedience. Monarchs were therefore legitimately entitled to absolute authority, limited only by their own deficiencies and by the power of other states.

Neither Hobbes nor Bossuet described the workings of the monarchy of Louis XIV. Louis and his colleagues functioned within institutional systems carried over from the medieval past. Their success or failure depended on their ability to shape old feudal struc-

---

absolutism—The political system in which the ruler has total power, with no limitations.

tures into centralized states. In this process, none succeeded completely in eliminating aristocratic influence and local tradition as limits to royal authority. Their proclaimed absolutism reflected a trend, rather than an accomplished fact. But one goal that Louis and other monarchs across Europe shared was a desire to dominate and control their nobles, many of whom came from families with far more distinguished lineages than those of the kings. To these nobles, the king was simply *primus inter pares* (PREE-moos in-ter pa-REES) or "first among equals." Centralizing kings could not tolerate such familiarity.

The attempted absolutism of Louis XIV followed a long monarchical tradition of French kings trying to centralize power. Francis I in the early sixteenth century had increasingly subordinated the feudal nobility and created a centralized administration. Henry IV and his chief minister, the duke of Sully (suil-EE; 1560–1641) produced a balanced budget and a treasury surplus in little more than a decade. At the same time, Henry ended the nobles' control of hereditary offices and council seats. This centralization was temporarily disrupted in 1610 when Henry was assassinated, but the queen, Marie de' Medici (MEH-de-chee; 1573–1642) served as a regent for her young son Louis XIII until 1617 when he, at the age of 15, seized power to rule for himself. For the next thirteen years, after he restored her to his council, they continued their duel for power. Marie favored a pro-Spanish and Catholic policy, while Louis—following the advice of the Cardinal Richelieu (REESH-e-lieu; 1585–1642)—saw the Habsburgs and the papacy as the main threats to French interests.

Cardinal Richelieu finally came out the winner in this contest for power, and Marie de' Medici was banished from France in 1631. Richelieu worked ceaselessly to increase the king's powers over the nobles: he organized a royal civil service, restricted the traditional local courts, brought local government under central control, outlawed dueling, prohibited fortified castles, stripped the Huguenots of their military defenses, and developed strong military and naval forces loyal only to the king. His policies were carried on after his death by his colleague, Cardinal Mazarin (1602–1661), who, for all intents and purposes, ran the government until his death, when the 23-year-old Louis XIV could finally take direct control of the state. During the time of Mazarin's supervision, a civil war, the Fronde (1649–1653), was waged by some of the highest-ranking French nobles against the king. More than once, Louis barely escaped being captured by the rebel forces.

The memories of the Fronde and the impact of the lessons he received from Mazarin prepared Louis well to be an absolute monarch. His personal political convictions were clearly revealed in a characteristic statement: "All power, all authority resides in the hands of the king, and there can be no other in his kingdom than that which he establishes. The nation does not form a body in France. It resides entirely in the person of the king."[1] Louis also claimed authority over the French church and the religion of his subjects, enforcing that authority in contention with both Protestants and the papacy. The king was involved in a long struggle with the pope over revenues. In 1685 he revoked the Edict of Nantes, by which in 1598 Henry IV had granted freedom of worship to Protestant Huguenots. The new law subjected Protestants to torture or imprisonment. Luckily for them, but not for France, some 300,000 escaped to other lands, taking with them valuable skills and knowledge.

During his long reign, Louis worked at projecting an image of himself to France as a "Grand Monarch," a figure worthy of awe well as worship. But the reality of his personal life at court was marked by a casual, frivolous, morality. Louis shared his bed with numerous

Louis XIV in Robes of State *(1701), by court painter Hyacinthe Rigaud. The portrait captures the splendor of the Grand Monarch, known as the Sun King, who believed himself to be the center of France as the sun was the center of the solar system.*

Document: Louis XIV to His Son

This memoir, designed to instruct a young prince who never became king, nevertheless provides revealing insights into Louis's personal rationalizations for his one-dimensional view of government.

I laid a rule on myself to work regularly twice every day, and for two or three hours each time with different persons, without counting the hours which I passed privately and alone, nor the time which I was able to give on particular occasions to any special affairs that might arise. There was no moment when I did not permit people to talk to me about them, provided that they were urgent; with the exception of foreign ministers who sometimes find too favourable moments in the familiarity allowed to them, either to obtain or to discover something, and whom one should not hear without being previously prepared.

I cannot tell you what fruit I gathered immediately I had taken this resolution. I felt myself, as it were, uplifted in thought and courage; I found myself quite another man, and with joy reproached myself for having been too long unaware of it. This first timidity, which a little self-judgment always produces and which at the beginning gave me pain, especially on occasions when I had to speak in public, disappeared in less than no time. The only thing I felt then was that I was King, and born to be one. I experienced next a delicious feeling, hard to express, and which you will not know yourself except by tasting it as I have done....

All that is most necessary to this work is at the same time agreeable: for, in a word, my son, it is to have one's eyes open to the whole earth; to learn each hour the news concerning every province and every nation, the secrets of every court, the mood and the weaknesses of each Prince and of every foreign minister; to be well-informed on an infinite number of matters about which we are supposed to know nothing; to elicit from our subjects what they hide from us with the greatest care; to discover the most remote opinions of our own courtiers and the most hidden interests of those who come to us with quite contrary professions. I do not know of any other pleasure we would not renounce for that, even if curiosity alone gave us the opportunity....

I gave orders to the four Secretaries of State no longer to sign anything whatsoever without speaking to me; likewise to the Controller, and that he should authorise nothing as regards finance without its being registered in a book which must remain with me, and being noted down in a very abridged abstract form in which at any moment, and at a glance, I could see the state of the funds, and past and future expenditure.

The Chancellor received a like order, that is to say, to sign nothing with the seal except by my command, with the exception only of letters of justice, so called because it would be an injustice to refuse them, a procedure required more as a matter of form than of principle.... I let it be understood that whatever the nature of the matter might be, direct application must be made to me when it was not a question that depended only on my favour; and to all my subjects without distinction I gave liberty to present their case to me at all hours, either verbally or by petitions....

Regarding the persons whose duty it was to second my labours, I resolved at all costs to have no prime minister; and if you will believe me, my son, and all your successors after you, the name shall be banished for ever from France, for there is nothing more undignified than to see all the administration on one side, and on the other, the mere title of King....

Questions to Consider

1. Given Louis' experience with the Cardinal Mazarin, who virtually kept the reins of power, why do you think he tells his son to have no prime minister? How does having a prime minister correlate with absolutist?
2. How would you characterize Louis' management style? A hands-off delegator of power or a micro-manager?
3. What do you think Louis finds most enjoyable about his job?

From *A King's Lesson in Statecraft: Louis XIV: Letters to His Heirs,* in Harry J. Carroll et al., eds., *The Development of Civilization,* Vol. 2 (Glenview, Ill.: Scott, Foresman, 1970), pp. 120–121.

women, each of whom was designated in her time as the "head mistress"—and rarely his wife, the Spanish *infanta*. He shared none of his power with them and was extremely wary of their efforts to extract political favors.

The Functioning of French Absolutism

To symbolize his life-giving presence in the council chamber, Louis had a rising sun painted on his official chair. He constantly strove to inspire awe of the monarchy, as was evidenced by his great palace at Versailles, a short distance from Paris. It was set in 17,000 beautifully landscaped acres. The parks and buildings, surrounded by a 40-mile wall, contained 1400 fountains, 2000 statues, and innumerable rooms decorated with marble columns, painted ceilings, costly draperies, mirrored walls, and handcrafted furniture.

The most striking characteristic of the government of Louis XIV was the decided contrast between central and local functions. In the provinces he had to contend with entrenched local authorities and legal structures, which remained despite his attempts at centralization. They constituted an obstacle that hindered the enforcement of royal edicts and the collection of revenues. At Versailles the situation was quite different. There, Louis was the final authority and arbiter of fashion. Theoretically, he made all major decisions. He was the supreme lawgiver, the chief judge, the commander of all military forces, and the head of all administration.

The aristocracy through which Louis funneled his power dominated France with clear distinctions precisely defined by law. The rest of French society consisted of unprivileged taxpaying commoners, including merchants, craftsmen, and, above all, peasants. Most peasants owed dues and services to their landlords, although they were no longer bound to the soil as serfs. Commoners, including middle-class townspeople, paid most of the taxes, which were used to finance frequent wars and extravagant royal courts.

In France during the reign of Louis XIV, an alliance paired royal government with wealthy merchant-bankers in the king's attempt to gain the most money he could from the capitalists to support his ambitious plans. The result was a system of national economic regulations known as **mercantilism**, which had originated earlier but was adopted generally by European governments through the late

---

mercantilism—Governmental regulation of all aspects of the economy.

With access to Louis XIV being necessary to gain power in France, the king was surrounded by ambitious courtiers and courtesans, such as the witty and beautiful Athénaïs de Montespan.

seventeenth century. The trend was accentuated by the expansion of overseas trade, the expenses incurred in wars, and the economic depression of the middle 1600s.

Louis's comptroller of finance, Jean-Baptiste Colbert (1619–1683), installed mercantilism at the expense of Dutch overseas commerce. He created a comprehensive system of tariffs and trade prohibitions, levied against foreign imports. French luxury industries—silks, laces, fine woolens, and glass—were subsidized or developed in government shops. The state imported skilled workers and prescribed the most minute regulations for each industry. Colbert also improved internal transportation by building roads and canals. He chartered overseas trading companies, granting them monopolies on commerce with North America, the West Indies, India, Southeast Asia, and the Middle East. In all of this, he tried

The Reign of Louis XIV

1638	Birth of Louis XIV
1643	Louis ascends to the throne under the aegis of Cardinal Mazarin
1649–1653	Revolt of the nobles in the Fronde
1661	Death of Mazarin: Louis takes personal control
1661–1685	First phase of rule: Colbert installs mercantilism, Louvois reforms army
1670–1713	Four wars of Louis XIV
1685	Revocation of Edict of Nantes
1715	Death of Louis XIV

to harness the energies of capitalism—but ultimately failed.

"Bullionism" was one of the system's basic principles. It sought to increase precious metals within a country by achieving a "favorable balance of trade," in which the monetary value of exports exceeded the value of imports. The result was, in a sense, a national profit. This became purchasing power in the world market, an advantage shared most directly by the government and favored merchants. Louis's advisers believed state economic regulation to be absolutely necessary for gaining a favorable balance. They used subsidies, chartered monopolies, taxes, tariffs, harbor tolls, and direct legal prohibitions to encourage exports and limit imports. For the same purpose, French state enterprises received advantages over private competitors. Because Colbert viewed the world market in terms of competing states, he emphasized the importance of colonial expansion. He regarded colonies as favored markets for French products and as sources of cheap raw materials.

Louis's able minister of war, the Marquis de Louvois (lou-VWAH; 1641–1691), revolutionized the French army. In addition to infantry and cavalry, he organized special units of supply, ordnance, artillery, engineers, and inspectors. Command ranks, combat units, drills, uniforms, and weapons were standardized for the first time in Europe. Louvois also improved weaponry by such innovations as the bayonet, which permitted a musket to be fired while the blade was attached. By raising military pay, providing benefits, and improving conditions of service, the war minister increased the size of the army from 72,000 to 400,000, a force larger than all belligerents put together at any one time during the Thirty Years' War. Louvois also improved and expanded the navy. In addition to a Mediterranean galley fleet based at Toulon, the overseas forces by 1683 consisted of 217 warships, operating from Atlantic ports and served by numerous shipyards. The new navy was also part of Colbert's grand strategy for building an enormous overseas dominion. In the last decades of the seventeenth century, the French Empire extended to North America, Africa, and Asia.

Madame de Maintenon, shown here with her niece, exercised considerable influence in the court of Louis XIV.

---

bullionism—A theory that states that wealth is to be found only in precious metals, and trade policy should guarantee a favorable balance of trade to insure a continuous increase in the amount of precious metals held by the state.

THE GRAVITATIONAL PULL OF FRENCH ABSOLUTISM

■ *Why did most European states admire and try to imitate French absolutism?*

The popular image of Louis XIV as the Sun King symbolized his position in France but also implied that the French system exerted an influence on other European states. Like all such symbolism, the idea was only partly true. As much as it was a response to the French example, royal authority was accepted because it promised efficiency and security, the greatest political needs of the time. Yet, French wealth and power certainly generated European admiration and imitation. Countries across the Continent imitated various aspects of the political theater created by Louis in Versailles and also copied the economic and military policies of the Sun King.

The Germanic Satellites

Among the most obvious satellites of the French sun were the numerous German principalities of the Holy Roman Empire. The 1648 Treaty of Westphalia recognized more than 300 sovereign states in the empire. Without serious responsibilities to the emperor and with treasuries filled with the proceeds of confiscated church properties, their rulers struggled to increase their prerogatives and dabble in international diplomacy. Many sought French alliances against the Habsburg emperor; those who could traveled to France and attended Louis's court. Subsequently, many a German palace became a miniature Versailles. Even the tiniest states were likely to have standing armies, state churches, court officials, and economic regulations. The elector of Brandenburg demonstrated the ultimate deference to the French model. Although sincerely loyal to his wife, he copied Louis XIV by taking an official mistress and displaying her at court without requiring her to perform the duty usually associated with the position.

Scandinavia

The era of the Sun King also witnessed an upsurge of royal authority in Scandinavia. After an earlier aristocratic reaction against both monarchies, Frederick III (r. 1648–1670) in Denmark and Charles XI (r. 1660–1697) in Sweden broke the power of the nobles and created structures similar to the French model. Frederick in 1661 forced the assembled high nobility to accept him as their hereditary king. Later royal edicts proclaimed the king's right to issue laws and impose taxes. A similar upheaval in Sweden (1680) allowed Charles to achieve financial independence by seizing the nobles' lands. Both kingdoms developed thoroughly centralized administrations. Sweden, particularly, resembled France with its professional army, navy, national church, and mercantilist economy. Although Swedish royal absolutism was limited by the nobles in 1718, the Danish system remained into the nineteenth century.

Spain and Portugal: Irregular Orbits

Unlike the Scandinavian and German states, most European governments resembled Louis's system more in their direction of development than in their specific institutions. As agricultural economies became commercialized, changing the developing interests of monarchs and commoners, rulers sought to be free of their feudal councils and exercise more authority. Some states during this period had not developed as far in this direction as France had; others were already finding absolutism at least partly outmoded. Although all felt the magnetic pull of French absolutism, their responses varied according to their traditions and local conditions.

The process is well illustrated by a time lag in the Spanish and Portuguese monarchies. United by Spanish force in 1580 and divided again by a Portuguese revolt in 1640, the two kingdoms were first weakened by economic decay and then nearly destroyed by the costs of the Thirty Years' War and their own mutual conflicts, which lasted until Spain accepted Portuguese independence in 1668. Conditions deteriorated further under the half-mad King Alfonso VI (r. 1656–1668) in Portugal and the feeble-minded Charles II (r. 1665–1700) in Spain.

The nobilities, having exploited these misfortunes to regain their dominant position in both countries, could not be easily dislodged. In Portugal not until the 1680s did Pedro II (r. 1683–1706) restore a semblance of royal authority. His successor, John V (r. 1706–1750), aided by new wealth from Brazilian gold and diamond strikes, centralized the administration, perfected mercantilism, and extended control over the church. In Spain similar developments followed the War of the Spanish Succession and the granting of the Spanish crown to Louis XIV's Bourbon grandson, Philip V (r. 1700–1746). Philip brought to Spain a corps of French advisers, including the Princesse des Ursins (pran-SESS days ur-SAN), a spy for Louis XIV. Philip then followed French precedents by imposing centralized ministries, local intendants, and economic regulations.

The Habsburgs

Aristocratic limits on absolutism, so evident in the declining kingdoms of Portugal and Spain, were even more typical of the Habsburg monarchy in eastern Europe. The Thirty Years' War had diverted Habsburg attention from the Holy Roman Empire to lands under the family's direct control. By 1700 the Habsburgs held the archduchy of Austria, a few adjacent German areas, the kingdom of Bohemia, and the kingdom of Hungary, recently conquered from the Turks. This was a very large domain, stretching from Saxony in the north to the Ottoman Empire in the southeast. It played a leading role in the continental wars against Louis XIV after the 1670s.

Leopold I (r. 1657–1705) was primarily responsible for strengthening the Austrian imperial monarchy during this period. In long wars with the French and the Turks, Leopold modernized the army, not only increasing its numbers but also instilling professionalism and loyalty in its officers. He created central administrative councils, giving each responsibility for an arm of the imperial government or a local area. He staffed these high administrative positions with court nobles, rewarded and honored like those in France. Other new nobles, given lands in the home provinces, became political tools for subordinating the local estates. Leopold suppressed Protestantism in Bohemia and Austria while keeping his own Catholic Church under firm control. In 1687 the Habsburgs were accepted as hereditary monarchs in Hungary, a status they had already achieved in Austria and Bohemia.

In the eighteenth century Maria Theresa (r. 1740–1780) confronted Leopold's problems all over again. When she inherited her throne at the age of 22, her realm, lacking both money and military forces, faced threats from Prussia. In the years after Leopold's time, the nobles had regained much of their former power and were rebuilding their dominions at the expense of the monarchy. Known as "Her Motherly Majesty," Maria was a religious and compassionate woman, but she put aside this gentle image to hasten much needed internal reforms. Count Haugwitz (HOG-vitz), her reforming minister, rigidly enforced new laws that brought provincial areas under more effective royal control.

Despite its glitter and outward trappings, the Habsburg Empire was not a good example of absolutism. Its economy was almost entirely agricultural and, therefore, dependent on serf labor. This situation perpetuated the power of the nobles and diminished revenues available to the crown. In addition, subjects of the monarchy comprised a mixture of nationalities and languages—German, Czech, Magyar, Croatian, and Italian, to name only a few. Lacking ethnic unity, the various areas persisted in their localism. Even the reforms of Leopold and Maria Theresa left royal authority existing more in name than in fact. Imposed on still functioning medieval institutions, the Habsburg regime was a strange combination of absolutist theory and feudal fact.

Poland: The Last Medieval State

While Habsburg absolutism wavered in an irregular orbit around the French sun, Poland stood completely outside of the France-centered political and economic system. Local trade and industry were even more insignificant in its economy, the peasants were more depressed, and land-controlling lesser nobles—some 10 percent of the population—grew wealthy by supplying grain for Western merchants. Nobles avoided military service and most taxes; they were lords and masters of their serfs. More than 50 local assemblies dominated their areas, admitting no outside jurisdiction. The national diet (council), which was elected by the local bodies, chose a king who had no real authority. In effect Poland was 50 small and independent feudal estates.

Absolutism in Prussia

The rise of the Hohenzollerns (HO-hen-zol-lerns) was among the most striking political developments of the era. These relatively unimportant nobles, who once occupied a castle on Mount Zollern in southern Germany, pursued their ambitious policies through marriage, intrigue, religious factionalism, and war. By the early seventeenth century, they held lands scattered across northern Germany. The Thirty Years' War was almost disastrous for the Hohenzollerns but conditioned them to austerity, perseverance, and iron discipline.

Two reigns laid permanent foundations for the later monarchy. Frederick William (r. 1640–1688), called "the Great Elector," used his small but well-trained army to win eastern Pomerania at the end of the Thirty Years' War. In the near-anarchy that prevailed in Germany immediately after Westphalia, he reformed the administration in Brandenburg, created a strong army of 30,000 soldiers, intimidated the nobles in Prussia and Cleves, and won central control over all three areas. His son Frederick I (r. 1688–1713) exploited Russia's victory over Sweden to annex western Pomerania. As a reward for fighting France, he was also recognized as "King in Prussia" by the Peace of Utrecht in 1713.

After Utrecht, Prussia became a drill yard, with the monarch Frederick William I (r. 1713–1740) as drillmaster. This crusty soldier-king demanded hard work and absolute obedience from his subjects. He once told a group of them, "We are king and master and can do what we like." On another occasion he proclaimed, "I need render account to no one as to the matter in which I conduct ... affairs."[2] With such unabashed absolutism, he reorganized the government under the so-called **General Directory**,

---

General Directory—The efficient, centralized organization of the Prussian state in 1722.

Unlike most of their colleagues in the Holy Roman Empire, the electors of Brandenburg showed a single-minded drive over the centuries to expand from their bases in Berlin and Königsberg to become a major European power at the end of the eighteenth century.

established a civil service for local administration, created a royal supreme court, taxed the nobles, required the nobles to train for professional military careers, and built an army of 80,000, considered the best trained and best equipped in Europe. At the end of his reign, the Hohenzollern monarchy was ready for military expansion.

Frederick William I held high hopes for his son Frederick II (r. 1740–1786). The young prince, however, reacted against his Spartan training, secretly seeking escape in music, art, and philosophy. When caught after attempting flight to France, he was forced to witness the beheading of his accomplice and best friend. More years of severe training and discipline brought him in line with his father's wishes but robbed the future king of the capacity for personal feeling. In later years, while retaining his cultural interests and mingling freely with writers and artists, he developed no lasting relationships, particularly not with women. He married early to escape his father's household, and then ignored his wife, Elizabeth, subjecting her to a courteous but cold formality. Neither she nor any of his frequent but temporary mistresses could influence his judgment. Neither did he confide in his family after the old king died. Wilhelmina, the sister who had shared his youthful enmity against their father, lost his confidence as they both matured. Such was the price he paid to become a superb administrator, a master of Machiavellian diplomacy, and—as we shall see—the greatest soldier of his day.

In 1780, the Prussia of Frederick II, called "the Great," was regarded as a perfectly functioning absolute monarchy. Stretching some 500 miles across northern Germany between the Elbe and Niemen Rivers, its flourishing population had grown from 750,000 in 1648 to 5 million. For 23 years, between 1740 and 1763, it had waged nearly continuous war, with 200,000 men often in the field. Consequently, the government ran as precisely as an efficient army. Like any good commander, Frederick claimed all ultimate authority. He required rigid discipline and deference to superiors from civilian officials as well as from military officers. Prussian nobles were honored over merchants or nonnoble

This portrait of Frederick II of Prussia adorns the lid of a snuffbox. A patron of the arts and sciences as well as an able military leader and administrator, Frederick devoted himself to strengthening his country's military power while he also engaged in the study of philosophy, history, and poetry.

officials and were permitted complete mastery over their serfs. Frederick's mercantilism stressed tariff protection for agriculture, encouraged industry with government subsidies, imported artisans, and sought economic self-sufficiency as a means of achieving military superiority.

Russian Autocracy

A new era in Russian history began with Peter I, "the Great" (r. 1682–1725). When he was 10 years old, Peter's half-sister Sophia staged a palace coup, in which her troops looted the palace, killing many of Peter's maternal uncles. For seven years, while Sophia ruled as regent for Peter and his handicapped half-brother, Ivan, the young co-tsar lived in fear and insecurity. Later, Peter roamed the quarter reserved for foreigners, without discipline or much formal education. He recruited and drilled his own guard regiments and learned about boats and Western ways. When he was 16, his mother arranged his marriage to a young noblewoman. From the beginning this was a mismatch; after impregnating his wife, Peter abandoned her within three months. He was now a young giant, weighing 230 pounds and standing 6 feet 8 inches tall, with a temper to match. Fortunately, he also had a sharp mind and boundless energy. Perhaps unfortunately for Russia, he despised Moscow, the traditions of the Russian court, and the culture of his country. In his efforts to westernize Russia, he would drive a wedge between the elites of the country and the masses that would last through the twentieth century.

After 1689 Peter took control of the country and his life. When Sophia failed in an attempt to become sole ruler, he forced her into a convent, although his brother Ivan remained co-tsar until his death in 1696. Peter amused himself with mistresses and wild drinking parties but continued his pursuit of Western knowledge. His difficulties in wars with the Turks convinced him that he must modernize his army and build a navy. In 1697 he traveled incognito as a member of a great embassy to Poland, Germany, the Netherlands, and England. He worked as a common ship carpenter in the Netherlands, learning Dutch methods firsthand. Back in Moscow, Peter crushed a rebellion of his palace guards with savage cruelty, began extensive reforms, and conducted new wars against the Turks and Swedes in efforts to gain "a window on the sea." He achieved this goal in 1703 when he founded St. Petersburg as his

DOCUMENT
Lomonosov to Peter the Great

IMAGE
Winter Palace at St. Petersburg

Larger than life for the era in which he lived, the 6-foot 8-inch Tsar Peter the Great remains one of the most controversial figures in Russian history. Liberals see him as a positive force for opening his country to the West. Conservatives see him as a negative factor in Russian history for the same reason.

CASE STUDY
Reflections on the Accomplishments of Peter the Great

future capital on the Baltic. That same year Peter met Marfa Skavronska (ska-vron-SKA), a Lithuanian peasant girl who became his mistress, campaign companion, and, after the tsarina's death in a convent, his wife.

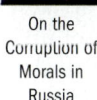
DOCUMENT
On the Corruption of Morals in Russia

Peter's reforms enforced Russian absolutism, in fact as well as in theory. He centralized the government, replacing all representative bodies with an appointed council and appointed ministries. Royal military governors assumed local authority. The Chancery of Police maintained order and collected information from an elaborate spy network. By forcing his nobles to shave their beards and don European-style attire, he conditioned them to accept change and become living symbols of his power over them. They were now required to serve in the army, the government, or industry. Peter also officially abolished the office of patriarch as head of the state church, substituting a synod of bishops, dominated by a secular official, the procurator, who represented the tsar. In copying European mercantilism, Peter established factories, mines, and shipyards, importing technical experts along with thousands of laborers. He levied tariffs to protect native industries and taxed almost everything, including births, marriages, and caskets. As revenues increased, he improved the army and navy, both of which were expanded, professionalized, and equipped with efficient Western weapons.

Before and after Peter's time, Russian absolutism reached into the forested wastes of Siberia. Russian Cossacks and fur traders explored this enormous territory between 1580 and 1651. During the seventeenth century, it remained a vast game preserve, exploited by the Russian government for its fur. Agents responsible to the Siberian Bureau in Moscow or St. Petersburg governed the relatively peaceful native peoples, collecting tribute from them in furs and a percentage from the profits of chartered companies. Given the financial succession of the tightly regulated fur trade, the government discouraged settlement in Siberia. In the eighteenth century, however, restrictions were lightened and western Siberia, between the Ob and Yenesei Rivers, began

From 1696 to 1725 Peter the Great allowed his country only one year of peace. For the rest of his time he radically changed the form and nature of his government in order to pursue war. At the end he had achieved his much desired "Window on the West" on the Baltic.

attracting colonists; convicts and political prisoners were transported there as well. Some 400,000 settlers had arrived by 1763, but Siberia was largely undeveloped until the late nineteenth century.

After his death in 1725, Peter's policies continued to affect Russian politics through the eighteenth century. In reaction, the nobles worked constantly to regain their former freedom from the state, while the "old believers," Orthodox Christians who refused to recognize seventeenth-century religious reforms, maintained an underground existence. Another striking characteristic of the period was the prominence of female rulers. Of the seven monarchs between 1725 and 1801, only three were men, and they reigned for just six and a half disastrous years. The four tsarinas were Catherine I (r. 1725–1727), Peter's camp-following second wife and the first Russian empress; Anna Ivanovna (r. 1730–1740), daughter of Peter's half-brother, Ivan; Elizabeth (r. 1741–1762), daughter of Peter and Catherine I; and Catherine II (r. 1762–1796), known as "the Great." All tried to continue Peter's policies of turning his country away from its roots toward western Europe. Anna Ivanovna allowed the Baltic Germans too much power, thus alienating their Russian subjects. Elizabeth avoided this mistake while further consolidating the central government and winning new respect in western Europe for Russian military power. She laid the foundations for the long and successful reign of Catherine the Great, whose role as an "enlightened despot" will be discussed in Chapter 18.

HOLLAND AND ENGLAND: LIMITED CENTRAL POWER

■ *What social and economic factors impelled Holland and England to pursue the political model of limited central power?*

In the century between the Dutch rebellion and the British **Glorious Revolution,** constitutional government took root in the Netherlands and survived and prospered in England. The Dutch profited from the declining fortunes of the Spaniards and established global trading dominance. Protected by its island geography and strengthened by its traditions, England carried on a sometimes bloody argument about its political structure. In both countries, rapidly developing commerce and increasing social mobility encouraged a direct transition from feudalism to constitutional government, without a prolonged intermediate stage of centralized monarchy.

The Dutch Experiment

The Dutch blazed the trail to modernity in Europe in the first half of the seventeenth century, a period described as a time of an "Embarrassment of Riches."[3] They staged the first modern national liberation struggle; conducted the first modern guerrilla war; set up the first modern republic; established the first modern banks, insurance companies, and stock markets; created the first modern capitalist agriculture; and were among the first to practice the recycling of resources. After a long and tenacious struggle against the Spaniards, they went on to establish a global trading network (see Chapter 16) that gave them the highest quality of life in Europe. Unfortunately, their lack of military power led to their being dominated by the English in the 1660s. But their precedent-setting contributions established the foundations of modern political and economic life in the West.

The internal Dutch power balance shifted during the early seventeenth century. Republicans, representing the great urban merchants, supported religious toleration, limited central authority, and peace. The monarchists, representing a majority of the urban lower classes and the nobles, especially the House of Orange, wanted a Calvinist state church, strong stadtholders (provincial governors), a large army, and an aggressive foreign policy against the Habsburgs. Until 1619 the republicans held power, but their leader, John Oldenbarnveldt (OL-den-barn-feldt; 1547–1619), was ultimately overthrown and executed after a royalist uprising. Between 1619 and the Peace of Westphalia, the country was ruled by domineering stadtholders, who conducted the war against Spain and acquired a status approaching that of European kings.

In the mid-seventeenth century the Dutch enjoyed prosperity and power far beyond their limited population base and territory. During the interval between the decline of Spain and the rise to dominance of modern France and England, the Dutch enjoyed naval, commercial, and colonial supremacy. This predominance, of course, could only be temporary. The Netherlands had not enough people nor defensible boundaries to afford long-term competition with France in Europe or with England overseas. But even as a secondary power, which it was destined to become after 1650, it remained economically progressive, culturally advanced, and a pioneer in developing constitutional government. Because of its liberal system, it became the refuge for many of Europe's finest scientists and philosophers.

Glorious Revolution—This event took place in 1688 and ended the Stuart dynasty's rule in England.

Jan Steen, who graphically portrayed daily life in Holland, gave a vivid presentation of *The Fish Market at Leiden (1625–1626)* in the seventeenth century. Note the variety of dress and activities Steen portrays.

The English Debate

Between the death of Queen Elizabeth in 1603 and the Glorious Revolution in 1688, the English carried on a fundamental debate about the nature of government. At its base were the questions of the control of property, the role of law, the nature of the state, and the notion of sovereignty. The Stuart dynasty and its allies upheld the centrality of the monarch as the fundamental principle of government. Arrayed against them were individuals who saw the nation's will as expressed through Parliament as the primary principle of government. The Stuarts saw their legitimacy in birth and "the natural order of things," whereas the parliamentary forces referred to four centuries of legal traditions and practices.

Crown vs. Parliament

James, a cousin of Elizabeth and the son of Mary Stuart, had learned his lessons well in 36 years as king of Scotland. He was rational and learned and a fervent believer in monarchical divine right. He also hated parliaments and Presbyterians but recognized the need for taking what "can be" over what "should be" in political affairs. During his English reign (1603–1625), James maintained a shaky stability while tentatively pursuing unpopular policies that led to his being not very successful with Parliament. The problems here were mostly financial, involving rejection of his revenue proposals. Outside the political arena in the first part of the seventeenth century, the religious climate became more radical. English Protestants suspected first James and then his successor, Charles, of being pro-Catholics.

James's political skills were not to be found in his successor, Charles. After enduring many stormy debates with Parliament, he accepted the Petition of Right in 1628. This document affirmed ancient English rights by securing parliamentary approval of taxes, abolishing arbitrary imprisonment, ending the quartering of soldiers with citizens, and prohibiting martial law in peacetime. But Charles's cooperative attitude was only temporary. From 1629 to 1640 he ruled without Parliament, alienating much of English society, particularly the Puritan church reformers and the gentry. The king's personal rule cut him off from an understanding of what the parliamentary forces really wanted and deepened the suspicions of Charles's opponents. When his archbishop tried to force the Anglican prayer book on the Scottish kirk ("church"), the Scots rebelled and invaded England in 1640. Charles was forced to conclude a humiliating peace by paying the invaders to withdraw.

DOCUMENT
On the Divine Right of Kings

After agreeing to buy off the Scots, Charles called Parliament to raise the money and secure his future finances. When it insisted on debating other issues, this "Short Parliament" was dismissed after it sat for little more than three weeks. The government then resorted to forceful measures: It imprisoned dissidents, imposed more illegal taxes, forced loans from merchants, and impressed men for the army, measures that made the situation only worse. Desperate for funds and facing mounting public hostility, the king called what would become known as the "Long Parliament," because it sat through 20 years of constitutional debate and civil war. Finally, in January 1642, he left the capital for York, and Parliament took the unprecedented action of declaring, without royal approval, its legal authority over national military forces.

The ensuing civil war would last another seven years; the government would alternate between a republic and a monarchy, but the prospects for English absolutism were doomed forever. The parliamentary forces made alliance with the Scots, organized their forces into a national army, and enlisted popular support by appeals to radical Protestantism. In 1646, after defeating the royalists decisively at Marston Moor (1644) and Naseby (1645), they accepted Charles from the Scots, who had taken him prisoner. After four long years, the war now seemed to be over. Almost immediately, however, new conflicts arose between Parliament and its army. Conservative Presbyterians in Parliament, fearful of radical Protestantism in the ranks, were anxious to demobilize the army. Most officers, including the leading commanders Oliver Cromwell (1599–1658) and Lord Fairfax (1612–1671), supported the men and their demands for back pay.

Some rebels in the army advocated truly democratic reforms. Their most striking proposals originated with a civilian group known as **"Levellers"** because they advocated reforms to favor the common people. They were led by the former army officer "honest John Lilburne" (1614–1657). As it turned out, the radical dream was only a side issue in maneuvers for power among the Presbyterian Parliament, the conservative army officers, and the radical soldiers. When Charles escaped in November and began negotiations with the Scots, the officers suppressed the mutineers, shooting some of the Leveller leaders and imprisoning others. Although Charles managed to renew the war, he lost his last battle at Preston in August 1648. Again, the officers professed to consider the radical program while they tried unsuccessfully to extract a promise from Charles to free protestant churches from state control. Finally resorting to force, they again outlawed the Levellers while purging Parliament of 143 Presbyterian opponents. The remaining "Rump Parliament," under the dominance of Oliver Cromwell, then abolished the House of Lords, executed the king after a perfunctory trial, and declared England a republic.

For the next 11 years, Cromwell's military regime was able to perpetuate itself in different forms. At first, the Rump and a Council of State, dominated by Cromwell, governed the country while crushing all resistance in Scotland and Ireland. In 1653 more contention between Rump politicians and the council resulted in dissolution of the token Parliament and creation of a thinly veiled dictatorship. A new constitution, the Instrument of Government, written by Cromwell's henchmen, assigned him extensive powers as Lord Protector. Two years later, Cromwell finally dismissed the Instrument's impotent Parliament and instead ruled through military governors. His regimes during the **interregnum** were able to

DOCUMENT
Cromwell Abolishes the English Monarchy

England: From Stuart Ambition to Parliamentary Power

1603	James VI of Scotland becomes James I of England
1625	Charles I becomes king of England
1628	Petition of Right
1629	Charles I dissolves Parliament
1640	Short Parliament; Long Parliament convenes
1642–1648	Civil war
1649	Charles I executed
1649–1660	Various attempts at a Puritan Commonwealth
1660	Charles II restored to the English throne
1670	Secret Treaty of Dover between France and England
1685	James II becomes king of England
1688	Glorious Revolution
1689	William II and Mary II come to the throne of England
1702–1714	Queen Anne, the last of the Stuarts
1714	George I of Hanover becomes king of England

---

levellers—A group during the English civil war that advocated total economic, social, political, and religious equality.

interregnum—The period of time between kings.

The English Civil War led to the beheading of a monarch, seen by the parliamentary forces as guilty of exercising extra-constitutional powers. Ironically, Oliver Cromwell—shown here dissolving the Long Parliament—in his role as Lord Protector generated heated opposition to his rule from people who believed him also to be overreaching his authority.

increase trade and raise respect for England abroad, but they were never popular, a fact attested to by the continued life of the radical movements, which enlisted popular support and required government countermeasures until after the mid-1650s. Despite ultimate radical failures, the period of the civil war and the interregnum, which ended two years after Cromwell's death in 1658, brought significant changes to England.

Restoration and "Glorious" Revolution

The period from 1660 to 1688 would be marked by increasingly severe struggles between the Stuarts and Parliament. Initially, almost everyone welcomed the new ruler, Charles II (1660–1685), called back from exile in France and restored to the throne, with his lavish court and his mistresses. But Charles, the cleverest politician of the Stuart line, exploited this common desire for normality to avoid the terms of his restoration, which bound him to rule in cooperation with Parliament. Charles cleverly manipulated the English political system to get what he wanted in the first, comparatively relaxed, years of the Restoration. However, political opposition against him began to harden, precipitating a crisis by 1681. In the last part of his reign, he dismissed four Parliaments and governed without the legislative branch, taking advantage of the strong desire among the propertied classes to avoid another civil war. The Whig opposition, however, which represented the desires of the lesser landowners and their business allies in the cities, had forced a resignation from Charles II's first minister, imprisoned the second, excluded the king's Catholic supporters from public office, and provided individuals with legal security against arbitrary arrest and imprisonment.

Charles's brother James II (1685–1688) proved to be an even more determined absolutist. Like Charles, he was an admirer of Louis XIV. While Charles concealed his Catholic sympathies, his brother was openly Catholic. When James' wife gave birth to a prince who was widely regarded as a potential Catholic king, parliamentary leaders and Protestant aristocrats met and offered the crown to the former heir Mary Stuart, the Protestant daughter of James by an earlier marriage. Mary accepted the offer with the provision that her husband, William of Orange, be co-ruler. William landed at Dover with an efficient Dutch army and forced James to flee into exile. This "Glorious Revolution" ultimately pushed England far in the direction of limited monarchy.

DOCUMENT
The English Bill of Rights

After William forced James into exile in France, he accepted Parliament's conditions for his kingship, enacted as the Bill of Rights. This declaration provided that the king could not suspend laws; no taxes would be levied or standing army maintained in peacetime without the consent of Parliament; sessions of Parliament would be held frequently; freedom of speech in Parliament would be assured; subjects would have the right of petition and be free of excessive fines, bail, or cruel punishments; the king would be a protestant.

Other parliamentary acts supplemented the Bill of Rights and consolidated the Revolution. In 1689 the Mutiny Act required parliamentary approval for extending martial law more than one year. In 1693, when Parliament failed to renew the customary Licensing Act, the country achieved practical freedom of the press. Finally, in the Act of Settlement in 1701, Parliament prescribed a protestant succession to the throne and barred the monarch from declaring war, removing judges, or even leaving the country without parliamentary consent. The Glorious Revolution permanently limited the English monarchy, guaranteed important legal rights, and helped popularize the ideal, if not the practice, of popular sovereignty.

Whigs and Tories

After 1688, the landed gentry—functionally a lower aristocracy of landed capitalists with a variety of economic interests—gained almost complete control of the House of Commons. From their base in the Whig alliance, they shaped state policy through a prime minister and a cabinet system that became responsible to Parliament, not the king. The gentry made government a closed system, putting members of their class into most of the public offices, lucrative positions in the Anglican Church, and commissioned ranks in the army and navy. These privileges were shared only with the few remaining nobles (220 in 1790) who sat in the House of Lords.

After the reign of William and Mary, English leaders looked to the German principality of Hanover for the next monarchs. The first two Hanoverian kings, George I (r. 1714–1727) and George II (r. 1727–1760), relied on their chief advisors (prime ministers) to work with Parliament. Sir Robert Walpole (1676–1745) first held this post, managing a Whig political machine. Walpole insisted that the entire ministry (cabinet) should act as a body; single members who could not agree were expected to resign. Later he learned the practicality of resigning with his whole cabinet when they could not command a parliamentary majority. This pragmatically developed system of cabinet government and ministerial responsibility provided the constitutional machinery needed to apply the principles of the Glorious Revolution while permitting Parliament to avoid awkward conflicts with royal authority.

English politics, so dynamic in the mid-1600s, became stagnant by the end of George II's reign in 1760. The next Hanoverian king, George III (r. 1760–1820), imposed his personality and policies more directly on British politics than did his predecessors. First, he alienated many commercial and colonial interests by opposing an aggressive policy toward France. Then, he began implementing powers never claimed by his Hanoverian predecessors, who had been virtual captives of Whig politicians. In only a few years, using lavish bribes and patronage (methods developed earlier by Walpole), George's ministers eroded Whig influence and gained control of Parliament. By 1770 they had filled the House of Commons with their supporters, known as "the King's Friends" (Tories). During George's first 12 years as the head of government, his policies made domestic enemies and produced a determined opposition party. This trouble at home was less serious, in the long run, than that provoked in the American colonies. George Grenville (1712–1770), the king's chief minister after 1763, devised a comprehensive plan to settle problems in North America left after the Seven Years' War, which sparked the movement leading to the American Revolution.

BREAKING THE BANK: DIPLOMACY AND WAR IN THE AGE OF ABSOLUTISM: 1650–1774

■ *In the century and a half after 1650 there were outbursts of European war every 20 years or so. Why were the various states so ready to fight, and not negotiate?*

Because of dynastic and colonial rivalries, Europeans were constantly involved in conflicts during the age of absolutism. Fighting took place overseas in America, Africa, and Asia—not only against non-Europeans but also in global wars among European colonial powers. At the same time, wars raged on the Continent as dynastic states competed for predominance. While Spain, Sweden, and Poland were declining, Prussia, Russia, and Austria were becoming first-class powers.

Along with England and its dominance overseas, the last three exerted major influences on the European balance of power.

From Westphalia to Utrecht: The Dominance of France

France was the strongest and most threatening military power in Europe from the Peace of Westphalia (1648) to the Treaty of Utrecht (1713). Louis XIV first dreamed of expanding French frontiers to the Rhine; later, he coveted the Spanish crown. Colbert also helped him plan the conquest of a large overseas empire in America, Africa, and Asia. The diplomacy of other European states in the era centered largely on their common efforts to unite against French expansion.

Russian policy was one important exception to this general trend. In early wars with the Turks, Peter the Great took Azov, on the Black Sea. His main target in the later Great Northern War (1709–1721) was Sweden, but his preparatory diplomacy failed when his allies, Denmark and Poland, were quickly defeated by the Swedish warrior-king Charles XII (r. 1697–1712). The Swedes next invaded Russia. They were met with a "scorched earth" withdrawal before being annihilated at Poltava (1709). The war ended in 1721 with Sweden exhausted and Peter gaining a section of the Baltic coast, where he had already begun building his new capital at St. Petersburg.

The three Anglo-Dutch naval wars between 1652 and 1674 showed the balance-of-power principle in one of its more intricate applications. Conflicting commercial and colonial interests of the two maritime states were the immediate issues. At the same time, both belligerents were increasingly aware of danger from a powerful and aggressive France. The Dutch were most directly affected because French expansion toward the northern Rhine threatened the survival of the Netherlands as a nation. To deal with this problem, the Dutch tacitly accepted English maritime supremacy while preparing for an Anglo-Dutch alignment against Louis XIV. Ultimately, the French menace was more decisive than naval action in ending Anglo-Dutch hostilities.

After 1670 Louis was the prime mover in European diplomacy. He fought four major wars, each with overseas campaigns. In the first, Louis claimed the Spanish Netherlands (Belgium). Thwarted by the Dutch and their allies, he next bought off Charles II of England in the Treaty of Dover and attacked the Dutch directly. Frustrated again by a combination of enemies, he tried in the 1690s to annex certain Rhineland districts. This time, almost all of Europe allied against him and forced him to back down. The climax to these repeated French efforts came between 1701 and 1713, in the War of the Spanish Succession, when Louis sought to secure the Spanish throne for his grandson Philip. Although he finally succeeded in this project, the victory was a hollow one.

In this most destructive of Louis's wars, women played a major part behind the scenes. In England during the early years, Sarah Churchill, wife of the English supreme commander, the duke of Marlborough, consistently pressured Queen Anne (r. 1702–1714) and members of Parliament for vigorous prosecution of the war. On the other side, at the Spanish court and elsewhere on the continent, Mary of Modena, in exile with her husband, the deposed James II of England, exerted all of her influence to bolster support for France. Other women were most instrumental in bringing peace. Among them were Madame de Maintenon (men-te-NON) and Princesse des Ursins, who helped persuade Louis to drop the idea of uniting the French and Spanish Bourbon monarchies. In England after about 1709, Anne, a patient and plodding monarch, but one with at least some common sense, freed herself from Sarah Churchill's influence and guided her ministers toward the Peace of Utrecht.

Louis could not overcome all of the power balanced against him. As France became stronger, it invariably provoked more formidable counteralliances. At first, Louis faced Spain, the Netherlands, Sweden, and some German states. In the last two wars, England led an alliance that included almost all of western Europe. In this anti-French alignment, Anglo-Dutch commercial rivalry and other traditional prejudices, such as Anglo-Dutch hatred of Spain, were subordinated to the balance-of-power principle.

The Treaty of Utrecht (1713) ushered in a period of general peace, lasting some 30 years. Philip V, Louis's grandson, was confirmed as king of Spain, with the provision that the thrones of France and Spain would never be united. Since Spain had been declining for a century and France was drained financially, the Bourbon succession promised little for French ambitions in Europe. In fact, Spain had surrendered the southern Netherlands (Belgium) and its Italian holdings (Naples, Milan, and Sardinia) to the Austrian Habsburgs. In addition, Savoy was ceded to Sicily, which was subsequently traded (in 1720) to Austria for Sardinia. The duke of Savoy was also recognized as king, as was Frederick I of Prussia. The House of Savoy would unify Italy in the nineteenth century, and the Hohenzollerns would accomplish the same for Germany.

By the Treaty of Utrecht, almost all the participants except Britain lost more in the wars than they gained. The Dutch had borne the cost of most land fighting against the French; France had been demoralized by a three-front war and a Huguenot uprising, for which it received no tangible compensation except the retention of Alsace; and Spain lost heavily to the Austrian Habsburgs. Britain, by contrast, received the North American properties of Newfoundland and Nova Scotia from France in addition to French acceptance of British claims to the Hudson Bay area. Britain also retained the Mediterranean naval bases at Gibraltar and Minorca it had taken from Spain. Even more important commercially were the concessions permitting Britain to supply Spanish America with slaves and to land one shipload of goods each year at Porto Bello in Panama. These stipulations helped Britain become the leading colonial power in Europe.

From Utrecht to Paris: An Unstable Balance

The balance of European power wavered dangerously in the eighteenth century. Prussia and Russia—and even Habsburg Austria—attained great military potential, and each was tempted by power vacuums in Poland and the Ottoman Empire. The situation was complicated by the difficulty in determining which of the Eastern states was the most serious threat and therefore the logical object of counteralliances. To confuse matters further, both Britain and France were absorbed in their growing colonial rivalry, in which Britain was the obvious frontrunner. Major conflicts were on the way.

By 1730, it was apparent that France and Britain would soon clash over their conflicting colonial ambitions. Both empires were rapidly increasing their wealth and populations. In the Caribbean, French sugar production had surpassed that of the British, while French slavers were not only supplying their own islands but also challenging British trading privileges in Spanish America, as defined at Utrecht. On the other side of the world, the British and French were also scrambling to obtain influence among the petty rulers of southern India. The two powers, each with Native American allies, were fighting sporadic little wars in North America. In the preliminary diplomatic testing, French size and military force in Europe were balanced against British financial resources, naval power, and a larger American colonial population.

The Treaty of Utrecht confirmed the expansion of French power in Europe after the half century of wars of Louis XIV, the increased strength of Brandenburg Prussia, and the decline of the Habsburg Empire.

Discovery Through Maps: The Elegant Destruction of Poland

After the century and a half of continent-wide upheaval caused by the Reformation, Counter-Reformation, wars of religion, and Thirty Years' War, Europeans sought to impose stability through international law and absolutism. Concepts like "balance of power," *"raison d'état,"* and reason replaced the passions of the religious wars of the sixteenth and the first half of the seventeenth centuries.

This did not mean that peace came to Europe—far from it. War came to be more organized, professional, and limited as state competition took on not only a military but also an economic dimension. In the new arena of 1648 politics, state relations were conducted with almost mathematical precision. States took stock of their strength in terms of population, economic strength, and military power. They ranked themselves and their neighbors and then attacked when it seemed possible, in search of national interest, not religious truth. The wars of Louis XIV sought to gain France its "natural boundaries" of the Pyrenees and the Rhine. The Prussians sought to unify their diverse holdings in north-central Europe. Peter the Great led Russia into war against its neighbors in search of a "Window on the West."

In the last third of the eighteenth century Poland paid the price for its inability to adapt to the modern world. Since the fourteenth century the Polish nobility had tenaciously fought the attempts by their kings to assemble a strong army, preferring often to lose the first battle against invaders while waiting for the nobles to come to the country's defense. Poland after the seventeenth century fell under the influence of the Russians and the Prussians, and not until the 1770s did the Poles try to reform their institutions. It was too late. National interests led Prussia, Russia, and Austria to partition the country in 1772. After the French Revolution broke out, the Russians and Prussians partitioned the country again in 1793 and then, after a doomed national resistance, removed Poland as a state from the map of Europe. The Polish nation remained divided among the three partitioning powers until 1918.

This engraving by Le Mire is a rather caustic commentary on what was, after all, the murder of a nation-state. Here we have the monarchs of Russia, Prussia, and Austria regally carving up Poland while the Polish king, Stanislaus Poniatowski, grabs his crown to keep from losing that too. Le Mire captures the "civilized" nature of post-1648 state relations, in which *raison d'état* imposed no moral or ethical limits.

Questions to Consider

1. What had Poland done to deserve being carved up by these monarchs?
2. Do you think the artist is celebrating the occasion he portrays, or is he being sarcastic?
3. What role does the angel play in this scene? What were the religious faiths of the Prussians, Russians, and Austrians?

Conflict began in 1739 over British trade in Spanish America. An English captain testified before Parliament that Spanish authorities had boarded his vessel and cut off his ear, which he displayed wrapped in cotton. The "War of Jenkins's Ear" soon spread, with France immediately offering support to Spain. Frederick of Prussia, meanwhile, seized Silesia, part of the family holdings of the Habsburg heiress Maria Theresa, who had just succeeded to the Austrian throne. France and Spain now aligned with Frederick, along with the German states of Saxony and Bavaria. Fearful of France, Britain and the Netherlands, now allied with Hanover, joined Austria in 1742. By 1745, Prussia had almost knocked Austria out of the war, but fighting dragged on overseas in North America and India until 1748. The resulting Peace of Aix-la-Chapelle (ex la sha-PELLE) left Frederick with Silesia and the colonial positions of Britain and France about the same as they had been in 1739.

The agreements at Aix-la-Chapelle brought no peace but only a short truce of eight years. During the cessation of hostilities, France and Britain prepared to renew their global conflict. At the same time, Maria Theresa, having learned some lessons in international politics and having effected some necessary internal reforms, joined with Tsarina Elizabeth of Russia to negotiate an alliance against Frederick. The Austro-Russian alliance also included Sweden and some German states. Maria Theresa's greatest coup, however, was recruiting France, the old Habsburg enemy, possibly with help from Madame de Pompadour, Louis XV's mistress, who despised Frederick. Prussia was now effectively isolated, but so was Britain, which was more concerned about colonial issues than aggression on the Continent. Britain, therefore, formed a new alliance with Prussia against France, Russia, and Austria. This swapping of alliances, the famous diplomatic revolution of the 1750s, was another notable attempt at balance-of-power politics in both the European and world theaters.

Beginning in 1756, war raged relentlessly on three continents—Europe, North America, and Asia (India). Known in American history as the French and Indian War, the conflict in Europe is called the Seven Years' War. Attacked on all sides by three major powers, Frederick marched and wheeled his limited forces, winning battles but seeing little prospect for ultimate victory. He tried without success to buy Madame de Pompadour's influence for peace. Later he described his nearly hopeless predicament, comparing himself to a man assaulted by flies: "When one flies off my cheek, another comes and sits on my nose, and scarcely has it been brushed off then another flies up and sits on my forehead, on my eyes, and everywhere else."[4]

Frederick was saved and the war won by the narrowest of margins when a new pro-Prussian tsar, Peter III, recalled the Russian armies from the gates of Berlin and withdrew from the war. Austria then sued for peace, leaving Frederick with Silesia.

The end of the Seven Years' War in 1763 confirmed the status of Prussia and Russia as great powers and prepared for a new diplomatic order in eastern Europe. Despite its great losses, Prussia gained enormously in prestige—its internal damage would not be revealed until the nineteenth century—and Russia regained the military reputation it had achieved under Peter I without winning any striking victories. Austria lost prestige and military strength but managed to retain its respectability. The Ottoman Empire and Poland were the real losers in the postwar decades. In 1772 Poland lost half its territory to the Russians, Prussians, and Austrians in a three-way partition, despite Maria Theresa's protestations of remorse. In 1793 and 1795, Poland was eliminated entirely in two final partitions. The Ottoman Empire, meanwhile, lost the Crimea and most of the Ukraine to the aggressive expansionist policies of Catherine the Great of Russia.

Much more significant than the war's effects on eastern Europe was its impact on Anglo-French colonial rivalry. Britain gained even more than it had at Utrecht, while French colonial hopes were all but destroyed. By the Peace of Paris (1763), France lost to Britain the St. Lawrence valley and the trans-Appalachian area east of the Mississippi. Spain also ceded Florida to Britain, receiving Louisiana west of the Mississippi from France as compensation. In the West Indies, France gave up Granada, Dominica, and St. Lucia. The French kept their main trading stations in India but were not permitted to fortify them or continue their political ties with local rulers. Meanwhile, the British East India Company not only extended its political influence but also acquired Bengal. The Peace of Paris made Britain's the largest, wealthiest, and most powerful empire in the world. At the end of the last round of warfare, however, all of Europe's governments were economically exhausted. The balance-of-power warfare between kings was soon to be challenged by a new kind of ideological war in the French Revolution, a war between peoples believing in opposing ideas.

ECONOMIC CHALLENGES

■ *Why were the European states—both absolutist and limited-power—unable to respond successfully to the challenges and opportunities provided by capitalism?*

Floating atop the dynamic changes of Europe, the governments, especially on the Continent, continued in the first half of the eighteenth century to act in a "business as usual" manner. Regimes did not adapt to changing conditions, and the result was increasing political weakness and misuse of power. By midcentury, the aristocratic social structure acquired the sanctity of tradition, the confidence of long experience, and the insensitivities of old age. Although no longer as typically cruel or exploitative as in the past, its governing classes had become extremely selfish and unresponsive to the larger needs of the countries that supported them in such a rich manner and incapable of understanding the potential opportunities presented by the changes of the century.

The Failure of State Controlled Economies

Eighteenth-century monarchs faced many problems in competing with traditional local authorities, but they encountered even more pressing difficulties in enforcing mercantilist regulations. In the sixteenth century, merchant-bankers had accepted the system because they shared common interests with kings in combating the Catholic Church and the feudal nobilities. As time passed, however, monarchical states became increasingly more paternalistic and ordered, while capitalism developed spontaneously toward more freedom from state control.

Bureaucrats and Smugglers

The development, as well as the success, of mercantilism varied widely from East to West. In Prussia and Russia reforms were imposed through state control and worked well, compared with previous attempts; state-imported craftsmen and tools from western Europe continued to improve the economies of both monarchies. Habsburg efforts met with less success because the empire was unable to impose regulations effectively on the aristocracy. Meanwhile, most continental states in western Europe could not easily keep their controlled manufactures competitive in the world market.

In France, government regulations favored luxury goods over bulk commodities, which limited French participation in world trade. Reliance on urban guilds created another limitation. These medieval monopolies were given the responsibility for enforcing thousands of minute regulations in every aspect of industry. Government inspectors then sought to monitor the regulatory actions of the guilds. The system, which suffered from vested interests, local politics, corruption, and bureaucratic confusion, provoked periodic confrontations, particularly when it was extended into the countryside. In 1770 the guilds and the French government attempted to stop the domestic production of printed cotton cloth (calicoes). More than 16,000 people died in the resulting violent conflicts and subsequent executions. On one day in Valence, 631 offenders were sentenced to the galleys, 58 were put to torture on the wheel, and 77 were hanged. Yet despite all such efforts, printed calicoes continued to be made and sold illegally.

Difficulties in industry were mild compared with those in foreign trade and public finance. France and England attempted the careful control of external commerce, but the increased volume and consequent promise of rich profits from such enterprise encouraged widespread smuggling. No government of a coastal state was sufficiently wealthy to police a long and irregular coastline. Moreover, the coast guards, port authorities, and customs officials charged with enforcing trade restrictions were usually so corrupt that they were ineffective. Thus, despite feeble efforts to stop it, illegal trade flowed with growing pressure through rotten and fragile mercantilist sieves, violating increasingly complicated commercial laws. To meet this problem, governments resorted to private contractors, often granting immunity from the laws as payment for enforcing the regulations. The resulting monopolies assumed and usually abused government authority.

British controls were probably more successful than the French or the Spanish, but they were extremely costly in the long run. A great body of officials—more than 1250 in London alone—cost the government more than the amounts they were supposed to save in revenues. In the second half of the eighteenth century, the government imposed stricter controls over the trade of the American colonies. As a result, smugglers took over much of the English coastline, and the colonies were pushed toward armed rebellion.

Smuggling was big business in the colonies, where it exceeded legal trade in the 1700s. West Indian planters of all nationalities conducted illicit commerce with English colonial merchants. New England timber and manufactures were regularly exchanged for French molasses, which was then made into rum and smuggled into Europe. Half the trade of Boston in 1750 violated British laws; Rhode Island and Pennsylvania merchants grew rich supplying the French during the Seven Years' War; and 80 percent of all tea used in the English colonies before 1770 came in free of duties. In addition, large quantities of tobacco were landed illegally in England with the connivance of Virginia and Carolina planters.

Smuggling was just as common in Europe, where every seacoast swarmed with illegal traders. Families grew wealthy in the business, and fathers trained their sons to maintain their enterprises. Contraband runners and government agents engaged in a continual civil war, using intelligence operations, pitched battles, and prepared sieges. Systematic enforcement was almost impossible because officials were bribed or personally involved, witnesses refused to testify, and juries often acquitted offenders caught in the act. During their classic era after the Seven Years' War, English smugglers operated openly in almost all English west coastal ports, including Bristol and Liverpool. On the other side of the country, desperate smuggling cliques roamed Kent, Sussex, and East Anglia. One of these, the notorious Hawkhurst gang of 500 armed men, forced farmers to store smuggled goods. The booty was then moved under armed convoys from depot to depot and on to waiting London merchants. When the government attempted to stop this traffic, a near civil war resulted, but smuggling was not appreciably curtailed.

The Crisis in Public Finance

Public finance was a serious problem even for Britain, the most commercially advanced state in Europe. In 1700, after war with France, the state debt reached 13 million pounds sterling and was secured by the Bank of England. The public debt continued to rise, despite the government's efforts in the 1720s to eliminate it with profits from its overseas trading monopoly, the South Sea Company. Unfortunately, following a wild speculation in South Sea stock, the venture failed. Succeeding colonial wars with France drove the debt still higher. By 1782 it had risen to 232 million pounds. Britain was very wealthy and, therefore, could easily carry this tremendous burden, but the debt nevertheless contributed to internal political unrest.

The most obvious weaknesses involved the abuse of state powers or the inability to use them for the public good. Early absolute monarchs had promised to correct abuses in state churches. Such establishments now held great wealth but continued to persecute thousands of dissenting subjects for their religious beliefs. Some kings had vowed to bring their states economic prosperity and security. Under mercantilism, their state enterprises and monopolies favored wealthy patrons and throttled trade. Even state military systems were controlled by aristocratic officers, many of whom bought their commissions and commanded local private armies. Even royal provincial agents and judges often existed beside and shared authority with thousands of lingering manorial courts and local officials, operating under the authority of local feudal lords.

The causes of the financial crisis could also be found in the political inefficiency took many other forms. Laws were a perplexing mix of variable local customs, feudal presumptions, and royal decrees. Provincial tolls were imposed on trade within states; on the Rhine River alone there were 38 toll stations between Basel and Rotterdam. Coinage, as well as weights and measures, sometimes differed in adjoining provinces. Overlapping authorities confused courts and officials about their jurisdictions. Public servants avoided responsibilities, fearing they would be blamed for error, a situation that produced bureaucratic delay and elaborate red tape. Every form of bribery, fraud, and distortion characterized governments at every level. Such evils were difficult to combat because legalized privilege was so common.

LOUIS XV AND THE DECLINE OF EUROPEAN ABSOLUTISM: 1715–1774

■ *Why did French absolutism become an ineffective and corrupt form of government?*

The absolutists and their supporters in France—perhaps 2 percent of the population—made an inadequate response to the economic and social pressures of the time. After his death in 1715, Louis XIV was succeeded by his 5-year-old great-grandson. Known as "the Well-Beloved," the new king reigned as Louis XV until 1774 but never ruled as a Sun King, partly because of his personal weaknesses, but largely because the inflexible institutions of absolutism could not contain or direct the dynamic changes of the eighteenth-century world. In middle age, with most of his royal prerogatives still intact, Louis was openly pessimistic about the future of his dynasty. He might easily have delivered the famous prophecy, stated by his mistress Madame de Pompadour (1721–1764), but usually attributed to him: *"Après moi, le déluge"* (a-pre mwa le DAY-loozh; "After me, the Flood"). France, the model of absolutist government for Europe, faced a severe crisis, as did the other governments that imitated the French example.

Such royal cynicism reflected the old regime's knowledge that it could do little to control the revolutionary developments of the time. Two centuries of war and foreign expansion had changed the basic way of life for most people and generated high expectations, particularly among the expanding urban middle classes—around 8 percent of the population—who benefited most by the worldwide explosion of foreign trade. Encouraged by the philosophies of the Enlightenment (see Chapter 18), they became more aggressive in improving their position, gaining social recognition, and demanding personal happiness outside the limits imposed by typical monarchical states and their privileged social orders.

Old Regime Monarchs

FRANCE

1715–1774	Louis XV
1774–1792	Louis XVI

HABSBURGS

1711–1740	Charles VI
1740–1780	Maria Theresa
1780–1790	Joseph II

PRUSSIA

1713–1740	Frederick William I
1740–1786	Frederick the Great
1786–1797	Frederick William II

RUSSIA

1730–1740	Anna
1741–1762	Elizabeth
1762	Peter III
1762–1796	Catherine II

GREAT BRITAIN

1714–1727	George I
1727–1760	George II
1760–1820	George III

Facing such challenges, those states could not respond effectively. They had earlier promised pragmatic compromise, whereby centralized government would maintain the interests of wealthy merchant-bankers and landed aristocrats. By the mid-eighteenth century, the system could no longer satisfy its supporters, nor could it absorb any more of the lesser nobles or the excluded middle class as each group grew more numerous. Indeed, with their expensive wars, ballooning debts, outmoded laws, passive bureaucrats, and corrupt officials, the absolute monarchies generally displayed striking political weaknesses and obvious misuses of the powers they managed to wield.

Despite all efforts at centralization, Louis XIV left a chaotic system of councils and committees, each with its own expanding network of officials and clerks, whose conflicting claims to authority were barely less perplexing than their complicated procedures. During the next reign the selling of offices became a main source of revenue and patronage. There was no body comparable to the English Parliament for registering public opinion; the French Estates-General was last called in 1614. Government was most deficient in handling revenues, which it attempted to do without budgets, precise accounting, or standard assessments. French local government was even more chaotic. Late medieval districts, with their bailiffs and seneschals, coexisted with largely ceremonial provincial governors and royal intendants who struggled to placate other officials and influence local government after the seventeenth century. Some 360 different legal codes and 200 customs schedules applied in different parts of the country. Attempts to achieve uniformity invariably provoked strong reactions from local interests.

The French government, like some others, was severely damaged by the laziness of King Louis XV, who hated the tedium of governing and was more interested in beautiful women. Well into the 1740s, he left most power in the hands of an able minister, Cardinal Fleury (fleu-REE), who had maintained peace and reasonable stability since Louis was a boy. Even in his early reign, however, "mistress power" enlisted the king's fancy; later it influenced his policies. Louis's Polish queen endured a series of rivals who were installed in the palace near the king's bedchamber, granted titles, showered with costly gifts, and paraded by Louis in public. The best known of them was Jeanne-Antoinette Poisson (PWA-sohn), of nonnoble parentage, who became Madame de Pompadour. She received 17 estates, had a personal staff of 50 attendants, enjoyed nearly unlimited access to the royal treasury, and advised Louis on public policy, particularly during the Seven Years' War. A later famous royal mistress, Madame Du Barry (1743–1793), was another woman of nonnoble origin who played the palace game better than the noble ladies at court, whom she overcame in a series of backbiting struggles for Louis's favor. Until he died in 1774, she reveled in her power, jewels, and luxurious houses. Such behavior earned France a reputation for "petticoat governance."

Other European kings squandered fortunes on mistresses, palaces, courts, and idle aristocrats, thus contributing to their common problem of rising public debt. Their financial difficulties also arose from their military expenses in attempting to protect colonial possessions and play the game of dynastic power politics in Europe. In the late 1700s, each of the great continental powers (France, Russia, and Austria) kept standing armies of 250,000 men. Rulers might have borne such heavy expenses if they could have governed by brute force, as former emperors had done, but they were prevented from doing so by their dependence on an international market, which supplied their vital material needs only in exchange for goods, bullion, or credit. Ultimately, they were forced to borrow, putting their states at the mercy of bankers and their own credit ratings. Such financial accountability, almost unknown in the ancient world, placed a serious restriction on monarchical policies in this era.

For France, where the economy was less expansive and commanded less foreign credit, the problem was more serious. Badly weakened by Louis XIV's wars, France averted financial disaster in the 1720s and 1730s only because of Fleury's peaceful foreign policy and reduced military spending. After 1742, however, deficits mounted steadily while France fought three major wars. In 1780, the French debt was so large that interest payments absorbed over half the annual income of approximately $33.8 million. Admittedly, the French debt was not excessive in comparison with Britain's. What the French lacked, however, was the Dutch capital that poured into England. Without adequate foreign credit, France was thrown back on its own resources, which caused a tripling of taxes between 1715 and 1785. The ensuing tax burden, in addition to the growing anxiety of wealthy government creditors, created the most serious threat to the Old Regime in France.

Necker Concealing the Deficit (Cartoon, 1789)

Even with that, the absolutist governments tried to impose central control—sanctioned by God— over the society, economy, church, culture, and military systems during this time. This system of government responded to the perceived need for stability and order after a century of religious wars. As absolutism was the system of government in France under Louis XIV—Europe's strongest power—it tended to be copied by almost all of the European states of the era. However, the structural weaknesses of a centralized control over a continent undergoing the revolutionary social and economic changes of the Capitalist Revolution became evident. The incapacity of the kings to impose their theoretical power led to massive corruption. The aristocracy could not or would not serve as transmitters of royal power, and across Europe, the nobles began a drive to reclaim the power they had lost to centralizing kings. Wars and the luxurious tastes of the monarchs drained the state treasuries and spread misery to the expanding populations. By the middle of the eighteenth century the absolutist system had come to be known as the *ancien régime*—the Old Regime—and it did not work any more.

The Dutch and the English went against the absolutist trends of the day, with differing results. The Netherlands emerged under the political, financial, military dominance of the British, while England proceeded to build a world empire. But in each case, these examples of limited government provided a different political alternative for those who had become disaffected with absolutism. When the British succeeded in ousting the Stuarts in 1688, the resulting political and theoretical doctrines established the precedent for the American Revolution a century later.

The limited central powers proved better able to ride the waves of change that swept the globe in the seventeenth and eighteenth century. Even though the political process was not marked by idealism in England, the diversity of the goals of the political elites provided a suitable framework to absorb the demographic, financial, and social changes that affected the country during the century.

CONCLUSION

The most important occurrence of the century and a half between the Treaty of Westphalia and the outbreak of the French Revolution was the Capitalist Revolution. This revolution developed so rapidly that it could hardly be controlled or even predicted. The absolutist governments tried to ride the waves of economic growth and even control them through schemes such as mercantilism. But the economic changes came so fast that, linked with a vastly expanding population, no matter how the kings might try, they could not control the new economic pursuits that developed almost spontaneously outside of established institutions.

Suggestions for Web Browsing

You can obtain more information about topics included in this chapter at the websites listed below. See also the companion website that accompanies this text, **http://www.ablongman.com/ brummett,** which contains an online study guide and additional resources.

Internet Modern History Sourcebook: The Early Modern World
http://www.fordham.edu/halsall/mod/modsbook03.html

Online source for numerous documents about the expanding global power of the Dutch and the British.

Trade Products in Early Modern History
http://www.bell.lib.umn.edu/Products/Products.html

University of Minnesota site chronicles the development of global trade, in particular, by the Dutch and the British, as they search for a variety of products, from beaver to tulips, from coffee to tobacco.

Age of the Sun King (*L'Age d'Or*)
http://www.geocities.com/Paris/Rue/1663/index.html

Extensive site describing, with text and images, the world of France under Louis XIV.

Internet Modern History Sourcebook: The *Ancien Régime*
http://www.fordham.edu/halsall/mod/hs1000.html#ancien

Extensive online source for links about the ancien régime, including primary documents by or about Louis XIV and Cardinal Richelieu and the enlightened despotism of Catherine the Great and Frederick II.

Frederick the Great of Prussia
http://members.tripod.com/~Nevermore/king.html

Extensive site on the king of Prussia and his times.

The Glorious Revolution of 1688
http://www.thegloriousrevolution.com

The site includes a range of documents and images regarding the important legal and political precedents set in motion by the Glorious Revolution of 1688.

Literature and Film

Most of the novels listed here have also served as the bases of major films: Alexandre Dumas captured the drama of this period in his *The Three Musketeers* (1844), *The Man in the Iron Mask* (originally published as part of the *Vicomte de Bragelonne*, 1848–1850), and *The Count of Monte Cristo* (1844). Victor Hugo contributed *The Hunchback of Notre Dame* (1831), which takes place at the beginning of this period. Sir Walter Scott wrote *Rob Roy* (1817) and *The Pirate* (1822). A later author, Rafael Sabatini, wrote a fine swashbuckler of a book with titled *Captain Blood* (1922). Daniel Defoe captured the spirit of the English Civil War with *Memoirs of a Cavalier: Or a Military Journal of the Wars in Germany and the Wars in England from the Year 1632 to the Year 1648* (1722). He also added to the canon with *Moll Flanders* (1722). Henry Fielding's *The History of Tom Jones, a Foundling* (1749), is a rollicking view into some of the social realities in England in the eighteenth century. More recently, Nancy Mitford and Amanda Foreman have made a fine reassessment of *Madame Pompadour* and her world (New York Review of Books, 2001).

An opulent portrayal of many different aspects of eighteenth century life is Stanley Kubrick's film masterpiece *Barry Lyndon* (Hawk Films, 1975).

Suggestions for Reading

Dynamic European economic growth is strongly emphasized in Fernand Braudel, *Civilization and Capitalism, Vol. 2: The Wheels of Commerce* (Harper & Row, 1986). See also Gunnar Persson, *Pre-Industrial Economic Growth, Social Organization, and Technological Progress in Europe* (Blackwell, 1988).

For a view of the development of French absolutism to the depths of the Old Regime, see Emmanuel Le Roy Ladurie, *The Ancien Régime: A History of France, 1610–1774*, trans. Mark Greengrass (Blackwell, 1998). A general treatment of absolutism is found in John Miller, *Absolutism in Seventeenth-Century Europe* (St. Martin's Press, 1990). A revisionist views of absolutism is found in Nicholas Henshall, *The Myth of Absolutism* (Longman, 1992).

French political and social affairs are studied in Roger Mettam, *Power and Faction in Louis XIV's France* (Blackwell, 1987). Changes in the European class structure are treated in George Rude, *Europe in the Eighteenth Century: Aristocracy and the Bourgeois Challenge* (Harvard University Press, 1985) and Colin Mooers, *The Making of Bourgeois Europe* (Verso, 1991). Some obvious social threats to European monarchies are described in M. S. Anderson, *War and Society in Europe of the Old Regime, 1618–1789* (St. Martin's Press, 1988); and Frederick Krantz, *History from Below: French and English Popular Protest, 1600–1800* (Blackwell, 1988). On negative conditions affecting European women, see Marilyn Boxer and Jean H. Quatgaert, *Connecting Spheres: Women in the Western World* (Oxford University Press, 1987).

On French government and classes see Guy Chaussinand-Nogaret, *The French Nobility in the Eighteenth Century* (Cambridge University Press, 1985). On the role of eighteenth-century French women, see Joan Landes, *Women and the Public Sphere in the Age of the French Revolution* (Cornell University Press, 1988).

Jonathan I. Israel, *The Dutch Republic and the Hispanic World* (Oxford University Press, 1986), and Charles R. Boxer, *The Dutch Seaborne Empire* (Penguin, 1989), discuss the world trading empire of the Dutch. Social backgrounds are treated in Sherrin Marshall, *The Dutch Gentry, 1500–1650: Family, Faith, and Fortune* (Greenwood, 1987). On the decisive conflict with the English, see J. R. Jones, *The Anglo-Dutch Wars of the Seventeenth Century* (Addison-Wesley, 1996). Simon Schama provides a brilliant view into the seventeenth century in the Netherlands in *An Embarrassment of Riches: An Interpretation of Dutch Culture in the Golden Age* (Vintage, 1997).

On the reigns of the first two Stuart monarchs and the English civil war, see Maurice Ashley, *The English Civil War* (St. Martin's, 1990), and Derek Hirst, *Authority and Conflict in England, 1603–1658* (Harvard University Press, 1986). A recent book on the radical fringe is David Petegorsky, *Left-Wing Democracy in the English Civil War: Gerrard Winstanley and the Digger Movement* (Alan Sutton, 1997). For a broad selection of contemporary accounts of the civil war, see John Eric Adair, *By the Sword Divided: Eyewitness Accounts of the English Civil War* (Alan Sutton, 1998).

Among the best treatments of Charles II and his problems are Kenneth H. D. Haley, *Politics in the Reign of Charles II* (Blackwell, 1985). On James II and the Glorious Revolution, see John Childs, *The Army, James II, and the Glorious Revolution* (St. Martin's, 1981) and K. Merle Chacksfield, *The Glorious Revolution, 1688* (Wincanton, 1988).

CHAPTER 18

New Ideas and Their Political Consequences

The Scientific Revolution, the Enlightenment, and the French Revolutions

CHAPTER CONTENTS

- Revolution in Science: The Laws of Nature
  DISCOVERY THROUGH MAPS: *The Heliocentric Cosmos of Copernicus*
  The Widening Scope of Scientific Discovery
- The Sciences of Society: The "Age of Reason"
- The Failure of Monarchical Reform
- The French Revolution: The Domestic Phase, 1789–1799
  DOCUMENT: *Declaration of the Rights of Man and Citizen*
  DOCUMENT: *Olympe de Gouges on the Rights of Women*
- The French Revolution: The Napoleonic Phase, 1799–1815

1450
1473–1543 Nicolaus Copernicus

1550
1564–1642 Galileo Galilei

1650
1690 John Locke, *An Essay Concerning Human Understanding, Second Treatise on Civil Government*

1750
1740–1780 Reign of Maria Theresa of Austria

1740–1786 Reign of Frederick II of Prussia

1751–1772 Denis Diderot, *Encyclopédie*

1762 Jean-Jacques Rousseau, *Émile; The Social Contract*

1762–1796 Reign of Catherine the Great of Russia

1780–1790 Reign of Joseph II of Austria

1789 Tennis Court Oath: storming of the Bastille; *Declaration of the Rights of Man* issued, women's march on Versailles

1790 French Constitution put in effect; National Constituent Assembly Dissolved; *Declaration of Rights of Women* issued

1793 Louis XVI executed; "Reign of Terror"

1795 National Convention establishes Directory to govern France; National Convention dissolved

1799 Napoleon seizes power

1805 British navy defeats French and Spanish navies at Trafalgar

1807 French gain control of continent

1808 Overthrow of Spanish Monarchy by Napoleon sets in train Latin American revolutions

1812 Napoleonic forces fail in their invasion of Russia

1815 Napoleon defeated at Waterloo

In order to understand the universe, sophisticated astronomical observations, mathematical systems, and engineering principles were established in ancient Babylonia, Egypt, China, and India. Later, in Mesoamerica and sub-Saharan Africa, the elites of the local communities charted the stars and devised complex hydraulic systems. Muslim scientists wrote learned treatises on subjects as diverse as disease and chemistry and contributed the numbering systems used by all countries today.

In the Western tradition, the Ionian Greeks, the Hellenistic Greeks, and the Romans produced theories about the paths of the stars, the functioning of the human body, the qualities of the earth, and all of the plants and animals found on it. During the thousand years after the end of the ancient world, scholars in the church took advantage of the work of the Greeks and the Romans and also of Arab scientists to try to understand all that God created.

The Polish scholar Copernicus, through his research on the nature of the universe at the beginning of the sixteenth century, served unknowingly as the bridge between the medieval-theological and the modern, scientific ways of thinking. Following him, scientists such as Isaac Newton worked in the areas of physiology, biology, optics, chemistry, and mathematics to establish the natural laws governing the universe.

The Englishman John Locke asked the same fundamental questions about the universe and its people and applied scientific reason to society, politics, and religion in an attempt to improve the world. He symbolized the age, and it is his words and his ideas, flowing through Jefferson's pen, that began the American Declaration of Independence. Enlightenment thinkers applied the test of reason to their own political and social institutions in France, and found them wanting. By August 1789, the *ancien régime* (ahn-SIEN ray-ZHEEM) had disappeared.

527

REVOLUTION IN SCIENCE: THE LAWS OF NATURE

■ *Why did religious figures resist accepting the findings of scientists in the sixteenth and seventeenth centuries?*

Far removed from the religious upheavals of the early sixteenth century, the Polish astronomer and Aristotelian scholar Nicolaus Copernicus (ko-PER-ni-cus; 1473–1543) investigated the old geocentric view of the cosmos that assumed that the sun, the planets, and the stars all circled the earth, which lay at the center of the universe. He had pursued this question out of a purely intellectual interest and an admiration for Ptolemy. In preparation for his work Copernicus had studied at the great centers of Renaissance learning—Bologna, Rome, and Padua—and when he returned to Poland, he set out to affirm and perfect the Ptolemaic system. His research, however, led him to disprove Ptolemy's assertions, and shortly before his death he published *On the Revolutions of the Heavenly Spheres* in Nuremberg in 1543. His rediscovered heliocentric theory—Aristarchus had arrived at the same conclusion philosophically in the third century B.C.E.—postulated the sun as the center, around which the planets moved, a theory directly opposed to the traditional Ptolemaic explanation accepted by most Christians for the rhythm of day and night and the apparent movement of heavenly bodies. The Catholic Church, in the floodtide of the Counter-Reformation, attacked his findings as heretical (and later placed his book on the Roman Catholic Church's Index of Forbidden Books in 1616); Luther and Melanchton (me-LANK-ton) also ridiculed him, as did the English scientist Francis Bacon.

DOCUMENT
On the Revolution of the Heavenly Spheres

Copernicus offered his idea as a mathematical theory. By the end of the century, however, Tycho Brahe (TEE-co BRA-hey; 1546–1601), a Danish astronomer, aided by his sister, Sophia (1556–1643), had recorded hundreds of observations that pointed to flaws in the Ptolemaic explanation. Brahe even attempted, without much success, to find a compromise between the Ptolemaic and Copernican systems by postulating that the planets moved about the sun while the latter orbited the earth. This proposition raised even more problems and therefore met with little acceptance.

Brahe's data were used by his one-time assistant, the German mathematician Johannes Kepler (yoh-HAN-nes KEP-ler; 1571–1630) to support the Copernican theory. While working mathematically with Brahe's records on the movement of Mars, Kepler was ultimately able to prove that the planet moved not in a circular orbit but in an ellipse. He also discovered that the paces of the planets accelerated when they approached the sun. From this he concluded that the sun might emit a magnetic force that directed the planets in their courses. The idea was not yet confirmed by a mathematical formula, but that would soon be achieved by Newton, using Kepler's hypothesis. Even in his own time, however, Kepler's laws of planetary motion almost completely undermined the Ptolemaic theory. In their work, Kepler and Brahe proceeded from positions that reflected their theology as much as their scientific thinking.

During the early seventeenth century, growing acceptance of the heliocentric theory precipitated an intellectual and political crisis affecting European society, particularly the Catholic Church. Medieval Catholicism had accepted Aristotle on physics and Ptolemy on astronomy. The church now saw its reputation and authority being challenged by the new ideas. Both Copernicus and Brahe had evaded the issue by purporting to deal only in mathematical speculations. Kepler and others of his time became increasingly impatient with this subterfuge. The most persistent of these scientific rebels was the Italian mathematician-physicist Galileo Galilei (1564–1642).

In 1609 Galileo made a telescope, with which he discovered mountains on the moon, sunspots, the satellites of Jupiter, and the rings of Saturn. Galileo discovered more facts to verify the Copernican theory. But, as he wrote to Kepler:

> Up to now I have preferred not to publish, intimidated by the fortune of our teacher Copernicus, who though he will be of immortal fame to some, is yet by an infinite number (for such is the multitude of fools) laughed at and rejected.[1]

He also knew that he was writing at a time when the church increasingly demanded obedience to its views.

In 1616, after having published his findings and beliefs, he was forced by the church—which had originally supported his research—to promise that he would "not hold, teach, or defend" the heretical Copernican doctrines. After another publication, he was again hauled before a church court in 1633 and forced to make a public denial of his doctrines. Galileo was thus defeated—he would not be pardoned by the church until 1992—but heliocentric theory would win common acceptance by the end of the century.

DOCUMENT
Galileo to the Grand Duchess Christina

The discovery process begun by Copernicus would be replicated in every other scientific area, as scientists continued to build on the discoveries to add their own hypotheses to push forward the frontiers of knowledge.

Discovery Through Maps

The Heliocentric Cosmos of Copernicus

From the first person who walked across the mountain pass that had delimited the world to the first to see the views from satellites hovering thousands of miles above the equator, humans have drawn new maps to express their changing perspectives. Nothing made Europeans rethink their perspectives more than the discoveries of the Polish scientist Copernicus. He was not the first to postulate a sun-centered cosmic system. Among others, the Hellenistic Greeks in Alexandria had advanced the concept of the sun at the center of our planetary system with the planets revolving around it in the third century B.C.E.

Ptolemy, another Greek astronomer, disagreed and embellished on Aristotle's theory that the earth was at the center of the universe. This fit in nicely with the emerging Christian Church's theology. After all, if God created man in his image, why would God place him anywhere else but the center of the system? A tidy closed universe came to be the conventional wisdom, with the earth surrounded by crystallized rings containing the moon, sun, planets; hovering outside the last ring were, of course, God and the angels.

Medieval observers noted obvious flaws in this explanation, but the clever thinkers of the church devised satisfactory refutations of the contradictions. In the 1490s Nicolaus Copernicus left his home in Torun and journeyed to the Polish university town of Krakow, where he became caught up in the debate about the nature of the universe. In the next decade in Krakow and then at the University of Bologna he pursued his study of astronomy. He returned to a post at a church in Frauenburg, where, for the next 30 years, he worked on making the church's view on the nature of the universe simpler, yet mathematically precise.

The more he worked, the less he could defend Rome's position, and finally in 1543, in a book dedicated to Pope Paul III, he advanced his hypothesis of a sun-centered (heliocentric), not human-centered (homocentric) universe. It was criticized by the church and by Martin Luther and was considered suspicious by most of the astronomers of the time. But by the end of the century the Copernican hypothesis had been verified, and Europeans began to look to charts such as this one by Andreas Cellarius portraying the heliocentric cosmos. The universe had been turned upside down.

Questions to Consider

1. Why did Copernicus's ideas about the Cosmos spark such a wide-ranging debate? What difference did it make if the universe was seen as earth- or sun-centered?

2. What fundamental ideas in your life are being debated today, and what will be the effect on you if one of these ideas is overturned?

3. In your view, what is the nature of the relationship between science and society? Should scientists be limited by community values, or should there be an absolute freedom to find the basic laws and functions of the universe?

The Widening Scope of Scientific Discovery

In the two centuries after Copernicus advanced the heliocentric theory, European scientists laid the theoretical foundations for the study of physiology, astronomy, physics, chemistry, and biology.

- *Astronomy:* The astronomer-mathematician Pierre Laplace (1749–1827) demonstrated that apparent inconsistencies, such as comets, are also governed by mathematical laws and developed the nebular hypothesis, which maintains that our sun, once a gaseous mass, threw off the planets as it solidified and contracted.

- *Biology:* Antonie van Leeuwenhoek (1632–1723) discovered protozoa, bacteria, and human spermatozoa. Robert Hooke (1635–1703), an Englishman, described the cellular structure of plants.

- *Chemistry:* Robert Boyle (1627–1691) was the first to distinguish between chemical compounds and mixtures. On the basis of his many experiments he devised a crude atomic theory, superseding the "four elements" and "four humors" of medieval alchemists and physicians. Boyle also investigated fire, respiration, fermentation, evaporation, and the rusting of metals. Joseph Priestley (1733–1804) isolated ammonia, discovered oxygen, and generated carbon monoxide. Along with the discovery of hydrogen (1766) by the Englishman Henry Cavendish (1731–1810), Priestley's work furnished an explanation of combustion. Antoine Lavoisier (1743–1794) proved that combustion is a chemical process involving the uniting of oxygen with the substances consumed. He also showed that respiration is another form of oxidation. Such discoveries led him to define the law of conservation: "Matter cannot be created or destroyed." Much of the credit for Lavoisier's scientific success should go to his wife, Marie-Anne (1758–1836), who assisted with all his major experiments, took notes, kept records, illustrated his books, and published her own papers. After he died on the guillotine during the French Revolution, she edited and published a compilation of his works.

- *Physics:* Galileo defined the law of falling bodies, demonstrating that their acceleration is constant, no matter what their weight or size. His experiments also revealed the law of inertia: a body at rest or in motion will remain at rest or continue moving (in a straight line at constant speed) unless affected by an external force. In addition, he showed that the path of a fired projectile follows a parabolic curve to earth, an inclination explained later by the law of gravitation. Galileo made additional notable discoveries through his studies of the pendulum, hydrostatics, and optics. His work was clarified by two professors at the University of Bologna, Maria Agnesi (1718–1799) in mathematics and Laura Bassi (1700–1778) in physics. Christiaan Huygens (1629–1695), along with Newton, developed a wave theory to explain light. Otto von Guericke (1602–1668) proved the material composition of air. His experiments showed that air could be weighed and that it could exert pressure, both properties in accordance with Newton's law.

- *Physiology:* Anatomist Andreas Vesalius (1514–1564), in *On the Fabric of the Human Body* (1543), gave detailed drawings of the body. William Harvey (1578–1657) described the human circulatory system, tracing the flow of blood from the heart through the arteries, capillaries, and veins and back to the heart.

New Ways of Thinking

As it was developed in the seventeenth century, scientific research involved a combination of two approaches, each depending on reason, with differing applications. The deductive approach started with self-evident truths and moved toward complex propositions, which might be applied to practical problems. It emphasized logic and mathematical relationships. The inductive approach started with objective knowledge of the material world, from which proponents of induction sought to draw valid general conclusions. In the past, the two procedures had often been considered contradictory. Early European astronomers were dependent on both kinds of reasoning.

René Descartes (ruh-NAY DAY-cart; 1596–1650), the French philosopher-mathematician, initiated a new critical mode of deduction. In his *Discourse on*

Method (1627), Descartes rejected every accepted idea that could be doubted. He concluded that he could be certain of nothing except the facts that he was thinking and that he must, therefore, exist. From the basic proposition *"Cogito, ergo sum"* ("I think, therefore I am"), Descartes proceeded in logical steps to deduce the existence of God and the reality of both the spiritual and material worlds. He ultimately conceived of a unified and mathematically ordered universe that operated as a perfect mechanism. In Descartes' universe, supernatural processes were impossible; everything could be explained rationally, preferably in mathematical terms.

Descartes' method was furthered by discoveries in mathematics, and the method in turn popularized study of the subject. Descartes' work coincided with the first use of decimals and the compilation of logarithmic tables, which reduced, by half, the time required to solve intricate mathematical problems. Descartes himself developed analytical geometry, permitting relationships in space to be expressed in algebraic equations. Using such equations, astronomers could represent the movements of celestial bodies mathematically. Astronomers were further aided later in the century when Isaac Newton (1642–1727) in England and Gottfried Wilhelm Leibniz (LAIB-nitz; 1646–1716) in Germany independently perfected differential calculus, the mathematics of infinity, variables, and probabilities.

Another great early contributor to the theory of scientific methodology was the Englishman Francis Bacon (1561–1626). He participated actively in both the tumultuous politics and intellectual debates of his time. Bacon entered Parliament after finishing his studies at Cambridge and had a successful political career, rising to the post of Lord Chancellor in 1618, before being forced to resign 1621 after admitting to accepting a bribe. At the same time, Bacon conceived of a system of thought that advocated the use of reason for interpreting human sensory experiences. His approach emphasized the use of systematically recorded facts derived from experiments to produce tentative hypotheses. When these were tested and verified by continued experiments, he believed they would ultimately reflect fundamental laws of nature. Bacon's ideas, outlined in his *Novum Organum* (1626), were the first definitive European statement of inductive principles.

The inductive approach became even more effective with the invention and perfection of scientific instruments. Both the telescope and the microscope came into use at the start of the seventeenth century. Other important inventions included the thermometer (1597), the barometer (1644), the air pump (1650), and the accurate pendulum clock (1657). With such tools, scientists were better able to study the physical world.

The Newtonian Universe

Great as the contributions of Galileo and Kepler were, their individual discoveries had not been united into one all-embracing principle that would describe the universe as a unit. Both Copernicus and Galileo—the first through mathematical speculation and the second through observation—had been dimly aware of a universal force in material nature. But the final proof was established later by Isaac Newton, who was born the year the English Civil War broke out, entered Cambridge at the time of the Restoration, and became a professor of mathematics at Cambridge University in the 1660s.

The notion of gravitation occurred to Newton in 1666, when he was only 24 and away from Cambridge because of a renewed outbreak of the plague. According to his later account, he was sitting in a contemplative mood under an apple tree when a falling apple roused him to wonder why it, and other objects, fell toward the center of the earth and not sideways or

Isaac Newton's discovery and expression of the universal principles underlying gravity confirmed the basic premise of modern science: that all nature is governed by laws.

upward. A flash of insight suggested to him a drawing power in matter that was related to quantity and distance. In his *Principia* (1687)—the same year he defended the sovereign rights of Cambridge University against King James II—Newton expressed this idea precisely in a mathematical formula. The resulting law of gravitation states that all material objects attract other bodies inversely—according to the square of their distances, and directly—in proportion to the products of their masses. Hundreds of observations soon verified this principle and at the same time increased the credibility of scientific methods.

Newton had not only solved the astronomical problems defined by Kepler and Galileo but had also confirmed the necessity of combining the methods advocated by Descartes and Bacon. Although the *Principia* used mathematical proofs, these were tested by observation. Newton insisted that final conclusions must rest on solid facts; he further contended that any hypothesis, no matter how mathematically plausible, must be abandoned if not borne out by observation or experimentation.

Newton also confirmed the basic premise of modern science that all nature is governed by laws. Indeed, his own major law was applicable to the whole universe, from a speck of dust on earth to the largest star in outer space. The magnitude of this idea—the concept of universal laws—was exciting and contagious. He presented this vision as an explanation of how God worked:

> *The Deity ... endures for ever and is everywhere present, and by existing always and everywhere. He constitutes duration and space.... (He) governs all things and knows all things that are, and can be done ... Who, being in all places, is more able by His will to move the bodies within His boundless uniform sensorium, and thereby to form and reform the parts of the Universe, then we are by our will to move the parts of our body.*[2]

Within decades, his universal principles had spread throughout the Western world and had been applied in every area.

The Popularity of Science

Science, long suspect among the leaders of society and particularly the church, had now become respectable by the end of the seventeenth century. Scientists were now invited to the best salons, and scientific academies gained public support as they sprang up all over Europe. The most famous were the Royal Society of London, chartered in 1662, and the French Academy of Science, founded in 1664. Most academies published journals that circulated widely. Scientists and would-be scientists carried on voluminous correspondence, developing a cosmopolitan community with its own language, values, and common beliefs.

Rising enthusiasm on the public fringes of the scientific community was matched by a fervor among national monarchs as well as hundreds of other nobles, wealthy merchants, and progressive craftsmen. Support for academies was merely one form of public endorsement. Kings endowed observatories, cities founded museums, well-to-do women helped establish botanical gardens, and learned societies sponsored well-attended lectures. Scientists became respected heroes. Giordano Bruno (gi-or-DAN-oh BRU-noh), the Italian philosopher-scientist, was burned for heresy in 1600 by the Inquisition, and Galileo was hounded by persecutors through his most productive years, but at the end of the century Newton received a well-paying government position. He was lionized and knighted during his lifetime, and when he died in 1727, he was buried at Westminster Abbey.

THE SCIENCES OF SOCIETY: THE "AGE OF REASON"

■ *Why were those in power in Europe threatened by the test of reason?*

On the same boat that carried Princess Mary of Holland to England in February 1689 after the Glorious Revolution (see Chapter 17), a more modest person traveled. In his bags John Locke carried the manuscripts of two works that he had written during his six years in exile in Amsterdam. Born in 1632, Locke, as a youth, had lived through all of the turmoil of the English civil war. His father was an ardent Puritan, a notary who served as a captain in the army that defended Parliament. At Oxford, Locke was interested for a while in all of the arguments of the Cromwell years, but he soon tired of the constant disputes and welcomed the calm of the Restoration. Deeply affected by the works of Descartes, he continued his studies in medicine and the development of his own philosophy.

He even began to work with Lord Ashley, the count of Shaftesbury, whose unsuccessful plots against the Stuarts led him to seek exile in Holland—the place of refuge for all Europe—and with him went Locke. Amsterdam was the center of European thought in those days, made more intellectually alive by the influx of French Huguenots, Jews, Bohemian refugees, and others. Locke pursued his studies there in an atmosphere that was violently against the Catholic Church and absolutism. He became close to William of Orange, the leader of the Dutch, and gave him a copy of a work justifying the revolt of Parliament. This work was finally published in 1690 as the

After his study of medicine and exile in the Netherlands, John Locke laid the foundations for modern democratic government, including the American Declaration of Independence, in his writings.

Second Treatise on Civil Government. Its goals were to destroy absolute monarchy and to refute the theory of divine right.

Locke's *Second Treatise* attempted to support the new English political system by grounding it on the natural laws of psychology, economics, and politics. This justification of the Glorious Revolution of 1688 became the clarion call and rationale for every revolution for the next three centuries. In passing from his studies of Descartes, medicine, and the natural world to espousing the right of revolution in the Western world—based on natural law, Locke charted the transition from the Scientific Revolution to the Enlightenment and beyond.

The Age of Reason: English and Dutch Phases

In the seventeenth and eighteenth centuries, most Western thinkers understood that they lived in a new intellectual age, one that historians later called the Age of Reason. This new age did not herald a monolithic approach to the world; rather, it reflected the particular conditions of each country in which it was found. But its principles were based on Newtonian science, which dominated thinking at the start of the eighteenth century. This reasoning sought to create a science of man that would solve human problems, just as other sciences were beginning to reveal secrets of nature. At first the movement was confined to scholars, theologians, and conservative men of affairs, who opposed any threat to existing institutions. But after about 1760, as new ideas were conceived and spread in print among the middle classes, the movement generated a more radical version that logically supported the need for social and political change.

The most fundamental concepts of the Enlightenment, held by its conservative and radical proponents alike, were faith in nature and belief in human progress. Nature was seen as a complex of interacting laws governing the universe. The individual human being, as part of that system, was designed to act rationally. If free to think, the doctrine assumed, people would naturally seek happiness for themselves; reason would show them that this goal could best be attained through the well-being of others. Accordingly, both human virtue and happiness required freedom from needless restraints, including many imposed by the state or the church. Enlightenment thinkers also passionately believed in education as the path toward future improvement. Indeed, they thought society could become perfect if people were given opportunities and were free to use their reason.

The early conservative Enlightenment movement was centered in England. It was largely a product of the Glorious Revolution, when a group of Whig politicians, having secured control of Parliament, and thereby Parliament's control of the king, tried to consolidate its hold on power and avoid further political disturbance. (The Whigs were a political movement in the late seventeenth, eighteenth, and nineteenth centuries that sought to favor the power of Parliament over that of the throne.) Newton himself identified with this group. He hoped that his system of nature would influence the public to respect political authority and strengthen belief in a God who ruled the stars and the solar system, as well as human beings.

At the same time, a secret society including the intellectual and business elites of England, the Masonic movement, encouraged by the Whig government, began organizing and pleading the cause of

English limited monarchy on the Continent, where France was a major rival and a wartime enemy until 1713. By then, the early English Enlightenment had reached maturity and was beginning to spread abroad.

A new radical version of the Enlightenment movement soon developed on the Continent. Under the later Stuart kings, many dissident English thinkers fled to Holland, and some stayed on after the Glorious Revolution. They collaborated with French Huguenots, who themselves had fled France after Louis XIV revoked the Edict of Nantes in 1685. This latter group included Pierre Bayle (1647–1706), the French skeptic. Both French and English dissidents, led by the Anglo-Irish freethinker John Toland (1670–1772), were also influenced by Baruch Spinoza (spin-O-tsah; 1632–1677), a Jewish intellectual and the greatest Dutch philosopher.

Spinoza accepted Newton's astronomy but denied Newton's contention that God controlled nature as a separate force. He taught that God exists in all of nature and in the farthest reaches of the universe: This is the underlying foundation of **Pantheism** ("All God"). The ideas of Toland and Spinoza were used to develop arguments against both state churches and monarchies. They were spread slowly over the Continent by an underground press, financed by the radical Dutch **Huguenots** and many antiestablishment Masonic lodges.

The French *Philosophes* and the Radical Enlightenment

The Enlightenment remained largely moderate as it permeated French high society. Its leading proponents were known as ***philosophes*** (fil-o-SOFS), although the term cannot be literally translated into English as "philosophers." The *philosophes* were mostly writers and intellectuals who analyzed the evils of society and sought reforms in accordance with the principles of right reason and existing institutions. Their most supportive allies were ***salonières*** (sa-lo-nee-AIRS), socially conscious and learned women such as the Marquise du Châtelet (shat-e-LAY; 1706–1749), Voltaire's mistress, who translated Newton, and Madame de Tencin (tan-SEN), whose natural son, Jean d'Alembert (da-lem-BEHR; 1717–1783), was assistant editor of Diderot's *Encyclopédie*. The *salonières* regularly entertained *philosophes* in their salons, at the same time sponsoring their literary works, artistic creations, and new political ideas. By midcentury the *salonières*, their salons, and the *philosophes* had made France once again the intellectual center of Europe.

Two leading lights among the *philosophes* were the Baron de Montesquieu (mon-tes-KEU; 1688–1755), a judicial official as well as a titled nobleman, and François-Marie Arouet (ar-ou-EH), better known as Voltaire. Montesquieu was among the earliest critics of absolutist society. His *Persian Letters* (1721), purportedly from an Oriental traveler describing irrational European religious customs and behavior, delighted a large reading audience. His other great work, *The Spirit of Laws* (1748), expressed his main political principles, including checks and balances as safeguards of liberty.

More than any of the *philosophes*, Voltaire personified the skepticism of his century toward traditional religion and the injustices of the ***ancien régime*** (Old Regime). His early exile in England converted him to Newtonian science and freedom of expression. With a caustic pen, he turned out hundreds of histories, plays, pamphlets, essays, and novels, as well as an estimated correspondence of 10,000 letters, including many to Frederick the Great of Prussia and Catherine the Great of Russia. Always, he employed his wry wit in crusading for rationalism and reform of abuses. Even in his own time, his reputation became a legend among kings as well as literate commoners.

Voltaire had many disciples, imitators, and critics among the *philosophes*, but his only rival in successfully spreading the Enlightenment was a set of books, the French *Encyclopédie*, edited by Denis Diderot (1713–1784). Begun in 1751 and completed in 1772, it contained 28 volumes and more than 70,000 articles on every conceivable subject, many of which emphasized the supremacy of the new science, decried superstition, expounded the merits of human freedom, exposed the evils of the slave trade, and denounced unfair taxes. It featured thousands of treatises on practical subjects dealing with agriculture, industry, and medicine, as well as others on art, architecture, literature, and philosophy. Authors included tradesmen and mechanics, along with professors and scientists.

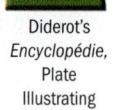

Diderot's *Encyclopédie*, Plate Illustrating Agriculture

The last volumes of the *Encyclopédie* appeared just as the Enlightenment was discernibly splitting away from its earlier moderation. Unlike Newton's God, who not only supervised nature but also might

---

Pantheism—The belief that an impersonal God is manifest in all things throughout the universe, which is governed by immutable natural laws.

Huguenots—French Protestants, many of whom fled persecution in Catholic France and resettled in England and Holland. Their views on the social contract for government influenced Enlightenment thinkers such as Locke and Rousseau.

philosophes—Literally "philosophers"; writers and intellectuals in eighteenth-century France who used reason to question the political and social conditions of their time.

salonières—A group of educated, aristocratic women in eighteenth-century France who supported and sponsored Enlightenment and its leading thinkers.

ancien régime—Literally "old regime"; the political governing structure in Europe before the French Revolution and the reforms of the nineteenth century. Its characteristics included the divine right of monarchs and the placement of nobles and clergy above commoners.

decree miracles, the new God of Spinoza, an impersonal deity of immutable natural laws, was steadily gaining credibility. More extreme French materialists such as the Baron Paul Henri d'Holbach (dol-BAK; 1723–1789), Claude Helvetius (el-ve-SIUS; 1771), Julien de la Mettrie (duh-lah may-TREE; 1709–1751), and Étienne de Condillac (ay-TIEN duh-kon-dee-YAK; 1715–1780) went further than Spinoza, using Newton's law and Locke's psychology to deny any reality except matter, reduce all thought to mere sensation, deny the soul's existence, and disclaim knowledge of any deity. At the other extreme, another argument subordinated reason to feeling as a way to truth and emphasized the natural goodness of human beings, which had been perverted in the past by inhumane institutions. Such new versions of the Enlightenment, although pointing in different directions, were easily used against authorities by popular journalists, who appealed first to an alienated middle class and later, in the 1780s, to an awakening world of cafés, workshops, and city streets, particularly in Paris.

Perhaps the best known *philosophe* and the forerunner of many later radicals was that eccentric proponent of Romantic rebellion, Jean-Jacques Rousseau (roos-SOH; 1712–1778). Although believing in the general objectives of the Enlightenment, Rousseau distrusted reason and science. He gloried in human impulse and intuition, trusting emotions rather than thought, the heart rather than the mind. This emphasis was also true of his social criticism. His early rejections by polite society encouraged both contempt for old regimes and professed admiration for "noble savages," who lived completely free of law, courts, priests, and officials. In his numerous writings, Rousseau spoke passionately as a rebel against all established institutions. The most famous of his works, *The Social Contract* (1762) protested against corrupt governments. It began with the stirring manifesto: "Man is born free, but today he is everywhere in chains." In short, human beings are born with inalienable rights and the ideal state, based on contract, exists as a guarantor and protector of those rights, and not the destroyer of them—as was the case with the Old Regime.

Enlightenment Thought and Women

Few Enlightenment thinkers, however, said "woman is born free." In fact, the Enlightenment thinkers disagreed on the place of women in the natural order of things. Although a few of them advocated extending the doctrine to include females, such voices were in the minority. Nevertheless, some women, even before the issue was raised forcefully during the French Revolution, staked their claims under the widely acclaimed laws of nature.

Although she was a monarchist and a follower of Descartes rather than Locke, Mary Astell (1666–1731) claimed legal equality for women on the basis of their innate rationality in her *Serious Proposal to the Ladies* (1694). This clarion call was not repeated for decades, but its echoes were manifest in the writings of English women such as Mary Montague (mon-ta-GEU; 1689–1762), Catherine Macaulay (1731–1791), and Mary Wollstonecraft (1759–1797) during the eighteenth century. In France a number of *salonières*, including Madame de Puisseux (PWEE-zeuh; 1720–1798) and Madame Gaçon-Dufour (1753–1835), wrote books defending their sex. Outside the salons, between 1761 and 1775, the *Journal des Dames,* a magazine edited by women, preached freedom, progress, and women's rights.

Before the French Revolution, the question of women's status in society did not concern many leading philosophers. Rousseau represented most of them when he described the ideal woman's proper role as housekeeper, mother, and quiet comforter of her husband, who was responsible for her protection and moral instruction. A few thinkers disagreed. Both Hobbes and Locke mildly questioned the idea that women were naturally subordinate to men. D'Alembert thought female limitations resulted from women's degradation by society, and Montesquieu saw absolute monarchy as the cause for women's lack of status. But the Marquis de Condorcet (mar-KEE duh-kon-dor-SAY; 1743–1794) was the only *philosophe* who made a special plea for feminine equality. In his *Letter of a Bourgeois of New Haven* (1787), he claimed that women's rationality entitled them to full citizenship, including the right to vote and hold public office. For the most part, however, his voice went unheard.

International Responses to the French Enlightenment

In the late eighteenth century, the French Enlightenment exerted a powerful influence on Western civilization. Many young upper-class Englishmen visited France to complete their education. Among them were three leading British thinkers: Adam Smith (1723–1790), the Scottish father of modern economics; David Hume (1711–1776), the best-known Scottish skeptic; and Jeremy Bentham (1748–1832), the founder of **utilitarianism.** Another famous English rationalist was the historian Edward Gibbon (1737–1794), whose *Decline and Fall of the Roman Empire* markedly criticized early Christianity, among many other things. Many English political radicals after 1770—including Joseph Priestley (1733–1804), Richard Price (1723–1791), and

---

utilitarianism—A social philosophy that holds that one should strive to achieve the greatest good for the greatest number of people.

Thomas Paine (1737–1809)—were greatly affected by French thought. Paine, who figured prominently in the American and French Revolutions, was also a leader in English radical politics.

The reforming doctrines of the radical Enlightenment spread into Central and Southern Europe and also reached the New World. A leading spokesman in Germany was Moses Mendelssohn (men-del-SOHN; 1729–1786), who wrote against dogmatism and in favor of natural religion. In Italy the humanist philosopher Cesare Beccaria (CHAY-sar-ay be-KAR-ee-ah; 1738–1794) made the first real study of the economic and social causes of crime and pleaded for humanitarian legal reforms. His ideas directly contributed to legal and penal reform throughout the world.

The Enlightenment was popular among the upper classes in such absolutist strongholds as Prussia, Russia, Austria, Portugal, and Spain. French ideas were read widely in Spanish America and Portuguese Brazil. In the English colonies Locke and the *philosophes* were avidly followed by Thomas Jefferson (1743–1826), Mercy Warren (1728–1814), Abigail Adams (1744–1818), and Benjamin Franklin (1706–1790). Franklin was a full-fledged participant in both the Scientific Revolution and the Enlightenment. Between 1749 and 1752, he carried out fundamental research that proved that lightning was another form of electricity and encouraged the work of others through establishing the American Philosophical Society for Promoting Useful Knowledge, based in Philadelphia. Later, he went on to play an important role in the establishment of the United States of America based on the principles of the Age of Reason.

Faith or Reason?

For such early thinkers as Descartes and Spinoza, the major theoretical problem was reconciling the mechanistic, self-regulating universe with the traditional belief in an all-powerful God. Descartes solved this problem for himself by dividing all reality between mind and matter. According to Descartes, both realms were governed by a divine will, but they appeared disconnected to human beings. Through science, human reason could accurately comprehend material reality; through faith and theology, the mind might know, directly from God, truths beyond the world that is apparent to the senses. Thus Descartes, a loyal Catholic, sought to reconcile the old and the new. In contrast, his Dutch pupil, Spinoza, saw mind and matter as dual parts of nature, which was one with God. This pantheistic theory revealed God directly in every natural process, leaving no need for theology or supernatural revelation.

Another early school of religious theory tried to reconcile scientific law with God's free will by subordinating the former to the latter. Newton believed God could set the laws aside and perform miracles if they were needed. Locke, by contrast, argued that some apparent miracles, as described in the Bible, were actually explicable by laws not known at the time of occurrence.

The most popular religious belief among participants in the late Enlightenment was **Deism.** This belief involved a clear break with traditional Christianity, although most Deists accepted Jesus Christ as a great moral teacher. Deists believed in God as an impersonal force, the "master clockwinder" of the universe. Although some accepted the idea of an afterlife, Deists attached no significance to emotional faith as a means to salvation. They based all moral reliance on the individual's reason and conscience. Their common convictions also included rejection of miracles, disbelief in Christ's divinity or his virgin birth, and direct communion with God without need for church or clergy. Nature was the Deists' church, and nature's laws were their Bible. Their number included John Toland, Thomas Woolston (1679–1731), and Thomas Paine in England; Voltaire, Diderot, and d'Alembert in France; and Thomas Jefferson, Ethan Allen (1738–1789), and Elihu Palmer (1764–1806) in the English American colonies.

CASE STUDY

The Conflict Between Science and Religion

Rationalist leaders of the Enlightenment were in almost perfect agreement on one point: They championed religious freedom of conscience. In addition, most were participants in a continuing struggle against alleged abuses of organized religion. Hundreds of their writings, especially those of Voltaire and the *philosophes,* depicted churches and priests as part of a vast conspiracy aimed at perpetuating tyranny. Their crusade for separating church and state was thus particularly threatening to absolutism.

The Economic Critique: The Physiocrats and Adam Smith

Natural law, a basic concept of the Enlightenment, was applied most consistently and effectively in economic arguments against absolutism. The **physiocrats** (fee-zee-oh-KRATS), a group of economic thinkers in eighteenth-century France made effective critiques of mercantilism. Their leading spokesman was François Quesnay (kuh-NAY; 1694–1774), the personal physician to Louis XV, who also wrote for the *Encyclopédie.*

Deism—The belief that views God as an impersonal force that created the universe and the natural laws that govern it (see also Pantheism). Deists do not believe in the supernatural or miraculous and hold reason and conscience to be the foundation of morality, not emotional faith.

physiocrats—A group of economic thinkers in eighteenth-century France who critiqued mercantilism.

Originally, Quesnay and his followers opposed the comptroller of finance Jean-Baptiste Colbert's (KOL-bair) policy of subordinating agriculture to government-controlled industry. This narrow emphasis later developed into a comprehensive theory based on natural law. Quesnay, for example, compared the circulation of money to the circulation of blood. He likened mercantilist controls to tourniquets, which shut off a life-giving flow. Quesnay also denounced the mercantilist theory of bullionism, arguing that prosperity depended on production, not gold and silver in the royal treasury. According to another physiocrat, Robert Turgot (tur-GOH; 1720–1781), selfish profit-seeking in a free market would necessarily result in the best service and the most goods for society.

The most influential advocate of the new economic theory was a leader in the Scottish Enlightenment, Adam Smith, a professor of moral philosophy at Glasgow University, who had visited France and exchanged ideas with the physiocrats. In 1776 Smith published *An Inquiry into the Nature and Causes of the Wealth of Nations,* in which he set forth his ideas. The work has since become the Bible of classical economic liberalism, extolling the doctrine of free enterprise or **laissez-faire** (lay-SAY fehr) economics.

Smith was indebted to the physiocrats for his views on personal liberty, natural law, and the role of the state as a mere "passive policeman." He argued that increased production depended largely on division of labor and specialization. Because trade increased specialization, it also increased production. The growing volume of trade, in turn, depended on each person's being free to pursue individual self-interest. In seeking private gain, each individual was also guided by an "invisible hand," also known as the law of supply and demand, in meeting society's needs. As he wrote:

> It is not from the benevolence of the butcher, the brewer, or the baker that we expect our dinner, but from their reward to their own interests. We address ourselves not to their humanity, but to their self-love.

Smith regarded all economic controls, by the state or by guilds and trade unions, as injurious to trade. He scoffed at the mercantilist idea that the wealth of a nation depended on achieving a surplus of exports, amassing bullion, and crippling the economies of other countries. In Smith's view, trade should work to the benefit of all nations, which would follow if trade were free. In such a natural and free economic world, the prosperity of each nation would depend on the prosperity of all. He also saw colonies as potential economic drains on a colonial power.

---

laissez-faire—Literally "leave it alone," the economic doctrine of free enterprise and open markets advocating non-intervention by the state, more commonly, "hands off."

The Political Critique of the Old Regime

Although proponents of the moderate Enlightenment were not revolutionaries and most favored monarchy and an aristocratic social order, they were avid reformers. In this role they developed a tightly organized philosophy, purportedly based on scientific principles and contradicting every argument for absolute monarchy as it generally existed in the eighteenth century. The case against absolutism, as presented by the *philosophes* and their foreign sympathizers, condemned divine right monarchy, hereditary aristocracies by birth, state churches, and mercantilism. Each was found to be irrational, unnatural, and therefore basically unsound.

The thinkers in the Enlightenment saw the arbitrary policies of absolute monarchs as violations of innate rights, which are required by human nature. The most fundamental part of this nature was reason, the means by which people learned and realized their potential. Learning, as described by Locke in his *Essay Concerning Human Understanding* (1690), consisted entirely of knowledge gained through the senses, interpreted by reason, and stored in memory. Locke admitted no internal sources of knowledge; he insisted that the mind at birth is like a blank piece of paper (*tabula rasa*) on which experience writes.

Later thinkers took this idea further than Locke wanted to go, seeing the absence of innate ideas as an indication that moral judgments were only the mind's response to pleasure or pain. Whether this was true or whether the mind was guided by what the Scottish moderate Thomas Reid called "common sense," the individual was primarily a thinking and judging being who required maximum freedom to operate effectively. The best government, therefore, was the government that ruled least. This argument for human freedom was the heart of the anti-absolutist case.

Political freedom, like religious freedom, depended ultimately on government, the source of most restrictions or coercion. For this reason political principles in the case against absolutism were fundamental to all others. They were developed in two main categories: ideas concerning individual rights and ideas concerning the organization of government. Both categories involved efforts that were directed at securing individual freedom against unnatural abuses of authority.

According to Locke and most political theorists of the Enlightenment, government existed to maintain order, protect property, defend against foreign enemies, and protect the natural rights of its people. This idea contradicted the divine right theory, which was held by most reigning monarchs in the seventeenth and eighteenth centuries. Locke, along with many other Enlightenment thinkers including Rousseau, answered the divine right doctrine with the opposing theory of a social contract.

Locke agreed with Hobbes that the base of power was the people. But instead of seeing people as nasty and brutish, Locke saw that an existence in a free and equal society would bring out the best in human beings, as long as their property was defended and they lived in a state of reason. Locke asserted that people voluntarily came together to form governments for the protection of their basic rights, and it was the consent of the people—and that alone—that gave legitimacy to a government. He did not invent the concept of the social contract—the Huguenots in France had discussed it a century earlier. Hobbes had used the contract idea to justify royal authority; Locke turned Hobbes's argument around in his *Second Treatise on Government*, contending that political systems were originally formed by individuals for defense of their natural rights to life, freedom, and property, against local or foreign enemies. Such individuals voluntarily ceded to government the responsibility for protecting their natural rights. In this transaction, government's authority was derived from the governed. It was not absolute but was limited to performing the functions for which it was constituted. When its authority was used for other purposes, the contract was broken and the people were justified in forming another government.

As insurance against abuses of political authority, theorists of the Enlightenment generally advocated the separation of powers. Locke, for example, proposed that kings, judges, magistrates, and legislatures should share authority and thus check one another. Spinoza also stressed the need for local autonomy and a locally based militia to guard against power concentrated in a central government. Montesquieu, although somewhat skeptical about natural laws and Locke's version of the social contract, advocated the separation of powers in his *Spirit of the Laws*, as did most of the other *philosophes*.

Political freedom and guarantees for human rights were common goals, but ideas concerning the ideal form of government varied considerably. The majority of the *philosophes* were not necessarily opposed to monarchy, despite their rejection of the divine right principle. Voltaire and Montesquieu believed that rule by a "benevolent despot," aided by an aristocracy of integrity and talent, was the most likely way to attain desirable reforms. A few monarchs

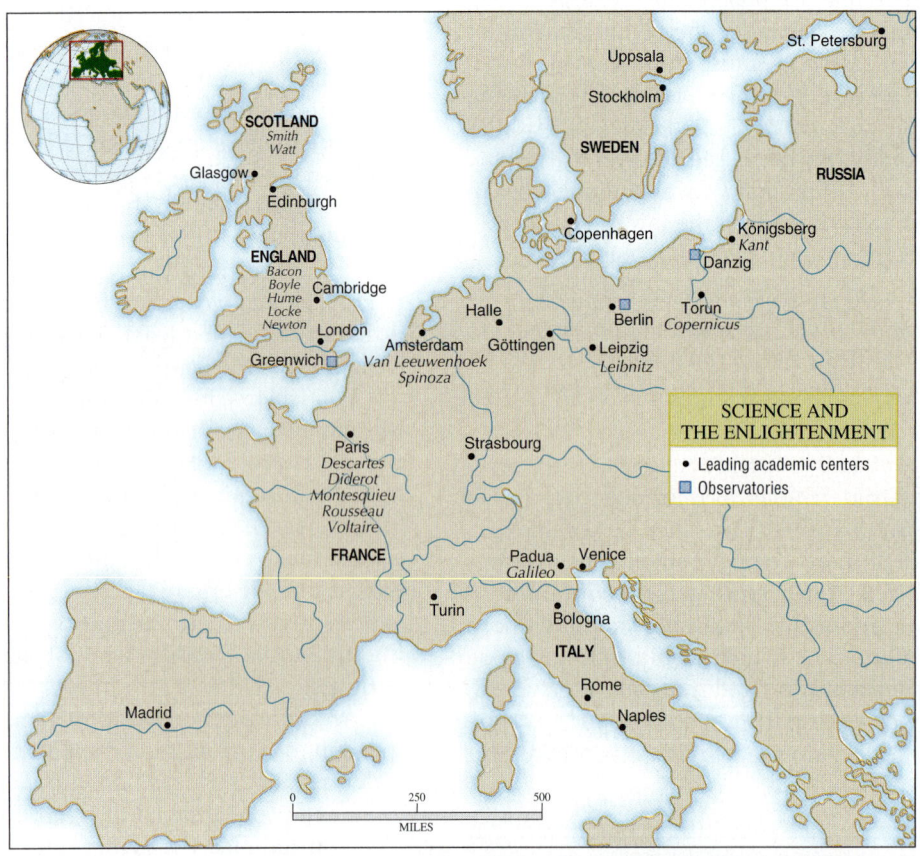

Scientific advances and Enlightenment contributions came from all parts of Europe, from Königsburg in East Prussia to Glasgow in Scotland.

were inspired by this revived Platonic ideal of the philosopher king, but the results of their policies did not always match their principles.

Perhaps the most popular form of government, particularly during the early Enlightenment, was constitutional monarchy on the English model. Locke, of course, was the recognized spokesman for the Glorious Revolution and the limited English monarchy established by Parliament. Both Voltaire and Diderot were very much impressed with the English system as they understood it. Montesquieu praised it as a practical balance of traditional forces, which secured liberty without sacrificing order.

These differences over forms of government were inconsequential compared with the points of political agreement among thinkers of the Enlightenment. All of them rejected the idea of divine right monarchy and considered monarchs to be the public servants of their peoples and to be obligated to maintain natural rights for all. These rights to life, liberty, and property, as construed by the *philosophes* and their friends abroad, seriously threatened absolutist systems.

It was Locke who made the most forceful political statement. In a state of nature, said Locke, people have two powers: to do what is necessary for the preservation of their rights and to respect the rights of others. These two powers naturally devolved into the legislative and the executive functions; of the two, the legislative function was the more important, for it was here where people maintained their dignity. The executive power was inferior to that of the legislature. It could not enslave or destroy any right or go against the foundations of the laws of nature. If it did so, the people had the right to overthrow it.

THE FAILURE OF MONARCHICAL REFORM

- *Why were the "enlightened" despots unable to implement reforms that matched their philosophical ideals?*

As old regimes faltered after the middle of the eighteenth century, an urgent need to respond to the problems of the day challenged the rulers of major European states. Neither the nobles nor the clergy, despite their high social status and political power, could provide the necessary leadership because they were committed to protecting their privileges, particularly immunity from taxation, which threatened the financial security of most countries. Responding to the literature of the Enlightenment, action by the enlightened despots did bring some curtailment of mercantilism, peasant exploitation, and government repression and seemed to offer a belated "best hope" for solving the problem. This hope, however, soon proved to be inadequate.

"Enlightened Despotism": Frederick of Prussia, Catherine of Russia, and Joseph of Austria

Some eighteenth-century kings earned recognized historical reputations—some generated by themselves—as "enlightened despots." Perhaps the major figure in this "monarch's age of repentance" was Frederick II of Prussia, known as "the Great," who became a model ruler during the second half of his reign. An avowed admirer of Voltaire, Frederick, in his writings, popularized the ideal monarch as the "first servant of the state," the "father of his people," and the "last refuge of the unfortunate."[3] "Old Fritz," as his subjects called him, was slavishly committed to his principles. He left his bed at five each morning and worked until dark, reading reports, supervising, traveling, listening to complaints, and watching every aspect of government.

Under Frederick, Prussia was considered the best-governed state in Europe. Within only a few years it recovered economically from the terrible ravages of war, largely through the state's aid in distributing seed, livestock, and tools. Frederick lessened the burdens of serfs on crown estates, imported new crops, attracted skilled immigrants, opened new lands, and tried to promote new industries, such as silk and other textiles. He codified the law and reorganized the courts, along with the civil service. Following ideas he had learned from French philosophy, he established civil equality for Catholics, abolished torture in obtaining confessions from criminals, decreed national compulsory education, and took control of the schools away from the church. Until he died in 1786, Frederick worked diligently at improving Prussia.

Frederick's contemporary, Catherine II of Russia, was also known in her time as an enlightened despot and as "the Great." Having learned the politics of survival at the Russian court, she had conspired with palace guards to kill her erratic husband, Peter, and have herself declared tsarina in 1762. She was a ruthless Machiavellian in foreign affairs, with far more lovers than many male monarchs. She also was a sensitive woman who appreciated the arts, literature, and the advantages of being considered enlightened. She corresponded with Voltaire and gave Diderot a pension. The latter even stayed at her court for a year, meeting with her daily for private discussions on intellectual subjects, including how to improve her empire.

Catherine's reign brought considerable enlightenment and social progress to St. Petersburg society. She

Catherine the Great's Constitution

subsidized artists and writers, permitted publication of controversial works, established libraries, patronized galleries, and transformed the capital city with beautiful architecture. Catherine also founded hospitals and orphanages, notably those providing foundling children with improved education, one of her main interests. During the decade after 1775, she tried to start a national system of elementary and secondary schools. In that same year she began a reorganization of local government, including the cities, one of many administrative reforms that literally demilitarized civil administration in the empire by turning it over to her partners in assassination, the nobility. She secularized church land, restricted the use of torture, and won acclaim for her much publicized orders to a royal commission charged with modernizing and codifying Russian laws.

Detail of Catherine's Palace in Pushkin

Catherine's program, however, like Frederick's, was limited in scope and significance. Almost every reform had been attempted or suggested earlier and enhanced royal authority. For example, rigid state control and political indoctrination of the curriculum were fixed in the new educational system. Local government after 1775 was controlled by aristocratic landowners, while aristocrats in the commission sabotaged the much heralded legal reforms. Such deference to the aristocracy was typical of Catherine's later internal policies following the disastrous peasant revolt of the 1770s. The nobles' hysteria forced her to issue a charter giving them freedom from taxes, release from compulsory government service, and guaranteed ownership of their serfs. The reaction thus begun was continued during the French Revolution, when Catherine reversed most of her earlier stated liberal opinions and imposed severe censorship. Her political legacy was a rigid autocracy, based on support from an aristocratic elite infected by Western liberal ideals.

The most radical of the would-be benevolent despots was Joseph II (1780–1790), the son of Maria Theresa and her successor as Habsburg ruler of Austria. He was intelligent and well educated; indeed, Catherine considered him to be one of the reform leaders of her generation. He was also completely converted to the principles of the new philosophers. "I have made philosophy the legislator of my empire," he wrote to a friend in 1781, shortly after his accession.[4] During his whole reign, he fancied himself a royal voice of reason, fighting for human progress against ignorance, superstition, and vice.

Joseph's reign was an explosion of reform effort that threatened to destroy much of the old aristocratic Habsburg structure. He proposed to simplify Catholic services, abolish the monasteries, take over church lands, remove religion from education, and grant civil equality to Protestants and Jews. Attacking the ancient landed establishment head on, he planned to tax the nobles, abolish entail of their lands, and free the serfs. With increasing revenues, he hoped to finance national education, balance the budget, and improve opportunities for industry and trade. The whole undertaking would be consolidated and regulated under a comprehensive code of laws.

Despite their theoretical benefits, Joseph's endeavors aroused a storm of protest, lasting through the reign and bringing him practical failure. For all of his interest in progress, Joseph was a hardheaded and narrow-minded autocrat, determined to build a state on an Enlightenment model. His administrative reforms were aimed not only at higher efficiency but also at centralized government over all the multinational Habsburg territories. His attempted unification of administration seriously alienated the Hungarians and provoked revolts in the Low Countries, Bohemia, and the Tyrol. Peasants were angry because he subjected them to compulsory military service, the clergy harangued against him, and the nobles conspired to hinder the conduct of government at every level. He died in 1790, painfully aware of his unfulfilled ideals.

Even though Catherine II spoke of governing Russia in accordance with Enlightenment principles, the condition of the Russian peasant reached its lowest point during her reign.

The French Dilemma

The last Bourbon kings in France before the Revolution, Louis XV and his grandson Louis XVI (1774–1792), responded halfheartedly to these reforming ideas. Although he was almost indifferent to affairs of state and dozed through his council meetings, Louis XV abolished serfdom on royal lands, tried twice to tax the nobles, and attempted to curtail the special privileges of the traditional courts, particularly the most aristocratic *parlement* (par-le-MON) court of Paris. Each attempt led to years of controversy between the government and the nobles; in each instance Louis ultimately gave up the fight.

Louis XVI was well-meaning but poorly educated, lazy, and shy. Avoiding government business, he spent his happiest hours in a workshop, tinkering with locks. His child bride, the frivolous Habsburg princess Marie Antoinette, furnished him with no wisdom or practical support. Although dimly aware of problems, Louis was no more successful than his grandfather: the clamor of the nobles forced him to abandon proposals for eliminating the more undeserved pensions and levying a very modest tax on all landed property.

Antoinette (1755–1793), was unpopular in her own right. Louis's lapse of leadership led first to discord in top echelons of authority before May 1789 and then to mob action in July of that year. The outbreak of widespread violence in the cities and countryside dominated all subsequent political decisions.

Between Louis's succession in 1774 and 1789, his finance ministers faced continuously rising national deficits. The debt ultimately reached an equivalent of $6 billion (in 2004 dollars), with interest payments absorbing half of annual revenues. French financial support of the American revolutionary wars against the English brought diplomatic success, but added to the financial problems.

Because loans to cover shortfalls were becoming almost impossible to raise, the government in 1787 and 1788 sought help from Assemblies of Notables (prominent nobles and high churchmen). But these bodies refused gifts or taxes without audits of royal accounts and other fiscal reforms. Louis then forced the courts *(parlements)* to register new laws authorizing more taxes and loans. The crisis was intensified by poor harvests caused by spring floods in 1788,

THE FRENCH REVOLUTION: THE DOMESTIC PHASE, 1789–1799

France, Revolution, and Europe: 1789–1815

■ *What group played the most important role in bringing an end to the* ancien régime *in France?*

The structural problems of France and the inequities found in that country came under the critical examination of the Enlightenment thinkers throughout the eighteenth century. Very few of the governmental, social, or religious institutions withstood the test of reason successfully. However, viewed from the outside, France in 1789 was the center of Europe, the most populous and cultured state of the time, with its thousand-year-old social, political, and economic structure. Its fragility was soon to be revealed.

Versailles and the Estates-General: May–June 1789

The process of revolution, by default, proceeded quickly toward its long-delayed climax during the summer of 1789. Louis XVI, who had succeeded his grandfather in 1774, was intelligent but lacked initiative. He managed in one way or another to alienate most of his subjects through indecision and bad political judgment; his extravagant Austrian queen, Marie

France, the model of an absolutist state and the foremost model of an "old regime," shocked and then threatened its neighbors with its thoroughgoing revolution in the five years after 1789.

followed by devastating hailstorms in July 1788 that destroyed the second planting. France endured the second coldest winter of the century in 1788–1789. Merchants holding stocks of grain drove the price of bread up to the highest level in 75 years. By the spring of 1789, the country was seething with unrest, and the government was out of money once again.

With no other recourse, Louis now bowed to the Notables and agreed to call the **Estates-General,** the nation's medieval representative assembly, which had not met since 1614. The Notables saw the Estates-General meeting as a way to leverage more advantages from the king in return for their support in ending the financial crisis. By blindly pursuing their narrow interests in the decade before 1789, they lit the fuse leading to the revolutionary explosion that destroyed their millennium-old position of superiority in French society.

During the spring of 1789, amid feverish excitement but little open hostility among the estates, electors of each order—the clergy (the First Estate); the nobles, a diverse group of which perhaps 5 percent were in the truly ancient families (the Second Estate); and the commoners (the Third Estate)—met in local assemblies across the country to select representatives. A few women participated among the clergy and nobles, but the 4.3 million electors in the Third Estate were all males, aged 25 or older, who paid the head tax. They, nevertheless, included most peasants, urban craftsmen, merchants, and professionals, comprising a much larger number of voters than those holding the parliamentary franchise in Britain.

After the delegates were elected, they compiled lists of reform proposals, the *cahiers* (kai-YEAS). The Third Estate requested a national legislature, a jury system, freedom of the press, and equitable taxes; there was no mention of overthrowing the monarchy or eliminating the aristocracy. The delegates themselves were not revolutionaries—most were moderate reformers. Of the more than 1100 delegates in the three orders, about 90 of 285 nobles were more or less sympathetic to the views of the bourgeoisie and 205 of 308 clergy were from nonnoble families. The 621 members of the Third Estate included 380 lawyers, 85 businessmen, and 64 landowners; 267 were officeholders.

Once the Estates-General convened on May 5 at Versailles, the economic question—the issue that had led the king to call the Estates-General—was instantly forgotten. The Third Estate insisted that voting should be by head rather than by chamber—which had traditionally been the case, because it had more members than the other two estates combined. Voting by head had already been adopted in some regional assemblies, and the principle had been requested in a large majority of the *cahiers*. During weeks of wrangling on this issue, some members of the clergy joined the Third Estate.

Estates-General—France's medieval representative assembly, consisting of the First Estate (the clergy), the Second Estate (the nobles), and the Third Estate (the commoners).

Locked out of their meeting hall on the king's orders, aroused delegates to the Estates-General, primarily members of the Third Estate, convened at a nearby indoor tennis court, where they swore the historic "Tennis Court Oath." The painting is by Jacques-Louis David.

On June 17, the Third Estate declared itself the national legislature and invited members of the other estates to attend its sessions. Two days later, most of the clergy voted to accept the invitation. Then, on June 20, when members found their meeting hall closed, ostensibly to prepare for the king's upcoming address, delegates of the Third Estate moved a half-mile to an indoor tennis court (*jeu de paume;* zhu de POM-e), where they solemnly swore not to disband until they had produced a French constitution. Later, after defying a royal order to reconvene separately, they declared themselves the National Constituent Assembly of France—a group legally elected to write a constitution.

At this point the delegates had declared—and won—a revolution in principle, but their full understanding of the process or even their commitment to it would develop only with time. Few members among the middle-class majority were merchants seeking free trade. Many were landowners, officeholders, or judges; many others were disappointed at not yet becoming nobles. Liberal aristocrats were willing to give up some privileges, including their manorial fees and tax immunities, in return for enlightened reforms that would improve the administration of government.

Die-hard support for the Old Regime was concentrated primarily among the relatively impoverished local "nobles of the sword" and the traditional peasants from remote communities. Sensing what was to come, however, there were many other nobles who chose to leave France, to become émigrés.

Suffering and Explosion in Paris and the Provinces: July–August 1789

Another factor, however, was already exerting its powerful influence. Economic depression in the late 1780s, particularly rising bread prices in the cities, prompted unrest and violence among more than 20 million French workers and peasants. This unfocused force of frustration and violence would, for the next five years, constantly overwhelm the plans and goals of the various governments' leaders.

Although grudgingly accepting the National Assembly on June 27, Louis tried to placate the nobles by bringing 18,000 troops to the vicinity of Versailles. Middle-class members of the Assembly, nearly panicking in fear of military intervention and a bloody response, appealed for popular support. In Paris, the forces of public order were in a confused state as many of the soldiers, especially among the *gardes-françaises* (gardz fran-SAEZ), who were supposed to protect stocks of grain and weapons, refused to follow the orders of their officers. As the contradictory rumors swirled in from Versailles on the morning of July 14, Parisians broke into military storerooms and took an estimated 30,000 rifles and cannons with little or no resistance. Later that day, an estimated 100,000 Parisian shopkeepers, workers, and women demolished the Bastille in Paris, as well as similar buildings in other cities in France. The significance of the action was not in the prisoners they liberated—a small group of obscure nobles. The Bastille—a medieval fortress—had served as the most visible symbol of the Old Regime, and its fall clearly demonstrated the rapidly growing popular defiance. Paris became an independent city with its own middle-class council and its own National Guard.

Meanwhile, other urban uprisings and peasant violence in the country consolidated the Assembly's position. As for the king, he had completely lost control and even comprehension of events, as can be seen by the entry he made in his journal for July 14, the day of the fall of the Bastille: *"Rien"* (ree-EN; "Nothing.").

The most dramatic action of the Assembly occurred on the night of August 4, 1789. By then, order had been restored in the cities, but peasants all over France were still rising against their lords—burning, pillaging, and sometimes murdering—in desperate efforts to destroy records of their manorial obligations. Faced with this violence, known as the Great Fear, the Assembly ultimately chose to grant concessions. Consequently, on that fateful night, nobles and clergy rose in the Assembly to renounce tithes, serfdom, manorial duties, feudal privileges, unequal taxes, and the sale of offices. The Old Regime, which had evolved over ten centuries, legally disappeared in a few hours. This was the real French Revolution.

Moderate Phase of the Revolution: August 1789–September 1791

To define its political principles and set its course, the Assembly issued the *Declaration of the Rights of Man and Citizen* on August 26. Intended as a preamble to a new constitution, it proclaimed human "inalienable rights" to liberty, property, security, and resistance to oppression. It also promised free speech, press, and religion, consistent with public order. Property was declared inviolate unless required for "public safety," in which case the owner was to receive "just compensation." All (male) citizens were to be equal before the law and eligible for public office on their qualifications. Taxes were to be levied only by common consent. Other accents on civil equality and property rights indicated the document's middle-class orientation.

DOCUMENT
Declaration of the Rights of Man and the Citizen

A climax to the summer upheaval came in October. Louis tried to delay taking official action to carry out the Assembly's decrees of August 4, and he was anxiously awaiting the arrival of a trusted regiment from Flanders. Meanwhile, angry Parisians marched and rioted in the streets. Two months later, on October 5, after the Flanders regiment had arrived, some 6000 women, many of them armed, marched to Versailles, accompanied by the National Guard under Lafayette. It was symbolic of the disconnection between Louis XVI and the events of his country that no preparation had been made to anticipate the arrival of this group. He had been out hunting, and, to his surprise, he was met by a deputation of six women who presented their demands. In the face of this confrontation, the king signed the decrees of August 4. Other women entered the hall where the Assembly was sitting, disrupted proceedings, and forced an adjournment. The next day, October 6, after a mob stormed the palace and killed some guards, the king and his family returned to Paris as virtual prisoners, their carriage surrounded by women carrying pikes on which were impaled the heads of the murdered bodyguards.

Shortly after the march on Versailles, the Assembly achieved some political stability by declaring martial law, to be enforced by the sometimes dependable National Guard. During the next two years, the Assembly's leaders followed the Enlightenment principles and the statements of the *Declaration* in attempting to reorganize France. Because most came from the middle class, with a preponderance of lawyers and a sprinkling of nobles, they were committed to change but also determined to keep order, protect property, and further their own special interests. Thus, as they achieved their goals, they became increasingly satisfied and conservative. Good harvests and the lowering of food prices also favored them.

One thing remained constant during the revolutionary year of 1789: France was bankrupt. And this financial distress remained one of the new government's most immediate concerns. The Assembly attempted to solve the problem by seizing church properties and using them as a base for new issues of paper currency, the *assignats* (AHS-seen-yat). Members also voted to eliminate tithes, largely in an attempt to placate Catholic peasants. Some would have gone further, but many were reluctant to abolish the state church completely, believing that it could be controlled and used to help defend property. Consequently, the Assembly decreed a "Civil Constitution of the Clergy," which made all clericals salaried public servants, abolished all archbishoprics, and reduced the number of bishoprics. Monastic orders were simply dissolved. Incumbent churchmen were required to swear loyalty to the nation, but only seven bishops and half the clergy conformed. The remainder became bitterly hostile to the government and exerted great influence, particularly among the peasants.

Understandably, the Assembly's economic policies were aimed at winning middle-class support. It therefore assured payment to holders of government bonds, secured not only by impending sales of confiscated church lands but also by lands taken from nobles who had fled the country. Most of this property was sold to middle-class speculators, who resold it to wealthy land-grabbers and social climbers; very little of it was ever acquired by peasants. The Assembly also abolished all internal tolls, industrial regulations, and guilds, thus throwing open to all the chance to work in the arts and crafts. It banned trade unions and decreed that wages be set by individual bargaining. Except for a few remaining controls on foreign trade, the Assembly applied the doctrines of Adam Smith and the physiocrats, substituting free competition for economic controls.

The Assembly dashed some of the high hopes held by French women. The early Revolution enlisted many, not only from the poor rioting Parisians of the shops and markets but also from those of the middle class, whose salons were political centers. Other women were already prominent in the political clubs of the era, forming women's patriotic societies and proposing female militias. In addition, some women were involved in a strong feminist movement, a cause taken up by the Friends of Truth, an organization that regularly lobbied the Assembly for free divorce, women's education, and women's civil rights. Its pleas, however, were largely ignored. Two women, Claire "Rose" Lacombe and Pauline Leon (po-LEEN LAY-on), who had struggled to survive the economic hardships of 1788 led the most important women's club, the Society of Republican Revolutionary Women. Lacombe was an actress; Leon was the daughter of a chocolate maker who tried to keep the family business going. Together, they often appeared before the Assembly, stating their case to improve women's place in society and, when war broke out, demanding the right to bear arms. The royalist Olympe de Gouges (OH-lamp duh GOOZHE) also fought for the cause through her manifestos and arguments before the assembly. However, it was not a promising epoch for women. The Society of Republican Revolutionary Women was shut down because of its radical leadership and programs: de Gouges, along with other women leaders, died by the guillotine in 1793.

The Assembly's Enlightenment ideology clashed with its rising conservatism on the issue of policy toward the French West Indies (see Chapter 21). News from France in 1789 brought violent altercations on Santo Domingo and Martinique, where planters, merchants, poor whites, mulattoes, and slaves evaluated the Revolution according to their diverse interests. Planters in the Assembly differed on trade policies and colonial autonomy but concurred in their fanatic defense of slavery and their opposition to civil rights for free mulattoes. Meanwhile, mulattoes in France

Document: Declaration of the Rights of Man and Citizen

This moderate middle-class document of the French Revolution was inspired by the American Declaration of Independence. Notice, however, that it differs slightly in its precise mention of property rights.

The National Assembly recognizes and declares, in the presence and under the auspices of the Supreme Being, the following rights of man and citizen.

1. Men are born and remain free and equal in rights. Social distinctions can be based only upon the common good.

2. The aim of every political association is the preservation of the natural and imprescriptible rights of man. These rights are liberty, property, security, and resistance to oppression. . . .

3. Liberty consists in the power to do anything that does not injure others; accordingly, the exercise of the natural rights of each man has no limits except those that assure to the other members of society the enjoyment of these same rights. These limits can be determined only by law.

4. The law can forbid only such actions as are injurious to society. Nothing can be forbidden that is not forbidden by the law, and no one can be constrained to do that which it does not decree.

5. Law is the expression of the general will. All citizens have the right to take part personally, or by their representatives, in its enactment. It must be the same for all, whether it protects or punishes.

6. No man can be accused, arrested, or detained, except in the cases determined by the law and according to the forms which it has prescribed. Those who call for, expedite, execute, or cause to be executed arbitrary orders should be punished; but every citizen summoned or seized by virtue of the law ought to obey instantly. . . .

7. The law ought to establish only punishments that are strictly and obviously necessary, and no one should be punished except by virtue of a law established and promulgated prior to the offense and legally applied.

8. Every man being presumed innocent until he has been declared guilty, if it is judged indispensable to arrest him, all severity that may not be necessary to secure his person ought to be severely suppressed by law.

9. No one should be disturbed on account of his opinions, even religious, provided their manifestation does not trouble the public order as established by law.

10. The free communication of thoughts and opinions is one of the most precious of the rights of man; every citizen can then speak, write, and print freely, save for the responsibility for the abuse of this liberty in the cases determined by law.

11. The guarantee of the rights of man and citizen necessitates a public force; this force is then instituted for the advantage of all and not for the particular use of those to whom it is entrusted.

12. For the maintenance of the public force and for the expenses of administration a general tax is indispensable; it should be equally apportioned among all the citizens according to their means.

13. All citizens have the right to ascertain, by themselves or through their representatives, the necessary amount of public taxation, to consent to it freely, to follow the use of it, and to determine the quota, the assessment, the collection, and the duration of it. . . .

14. Society has the right to require of every public agent an account of his administration.

15. Any society in which the guarantee of the rights is not assured, or the separation of powers not determined, has no constitution.

16. Property being a sacred and inviolable right, no one can be deprived of it, unless a legally established public necessity evidently requires it, under the condition of a just and prior indemnity.

Questions to Consider

1. What themes of the Enlightenment do you find see reflected in this declaration?
2. Does this document strike you as a conservative, liberal, or radical statement?
3. What role does private property play in the construction of the new society?

From Mark A. Kishlansky, ed., *Sources of the West: Readings in Western Civilization*, Volume II, fourth edition, Longman Publishers, New York and London, pp. 115–117.

Document: Olympe de Gouges on the Rights of Women

Olympe de Gouges's (1745–1793) father was a butcher and her mother took in washing. As a child, she had no advantage except for her beauty, which brought her marriage to a rich man close to the age of her father. She soon became a widow and had enough money to go to Paris in 1788, where she tried to enter the public debates of the time. However because of her lack of education, she wrote badly, and was not taken seriously.

Another reason she was not taken seriously by French men was because of her radical feminist views, even though she was a royalist. Nonetheless, she wrote more than 30 pamphlets and manifestos, including the *Declaration of the Rights of Woman*. She was a courageous woman who spoke her mind, especially during the time of mass executions of the Committee of Public Safety. She soon joined the ranks of the victims and was guillotined in 1793, at the age of 48.

Man, are you capable of being just? It is a woman who poses the question; you will not deprive her of that right at least. Tell me, what gives you sovereign empire to oppress my sex? Your strength? Your talents? Observe the Creator in his wisdom; survey in all her grandeur that nature with whom you seem to want to be in harmony, and give me, if you dare, an example of this tyrannical empire.

Declaration of the Rights of Woman and the Female Citizen

For the National Assembly to decree in its last sessions, or in those of the next legislature.

Preamble Mothers, daughters, sisters [and] representatives of the nation demand to be constituted into a national assembly. Believing that ignorance, omission, or scorn for the rights of woman are the only causes of public misfortunes and of the corruption of governments, [the women] have resolved to set forth in a solemn declaration the natural, inalienable, and sacred rights of woman in order that this declaration, constantly exposed before all the members of the society, will ceaselessly remind them of their rights and duties; in order that the authoritative acts of women and the authoritative acts of men may be at any moment compared with and respectful of the purpose of all political institutions; and in order that citizens' demands, henceforth based on simple and incontestable principles, will always support the constitution, good morals, and the happiness of all. Consequently, the sex that is as superior in beauty as it is in courage during the suffering of maternity recognized and declares in the presence and under the auspices of the Supreme Being, the following Rights of Woman and of Female Citizens.

Article 1 Woman is born free and lives equal to man in her rights. Social distinctions can be based only on the common utility.

Article 2 The purpose of any political association is the conservation of the natural and imprescriptible rights of woman and man; these rights are liberty, property, security, and especially resistance to oppression.

Article 3 The principle of all sovereignty rests essentially with the nation, which is nothing but the union of woman and man; no body and no individual can exercise any authority which does not come expressly from it [the nation].

Article 4 Liberty and justice consist of restoring all that belongs to others; thus, the only limits on the exercise of the natural rights of woman are perpetual male tyranny; these limits are to be reformed by the laws of nature and reason. . . .

Article 7 No woman is an exception: she is accused, arrested, and detained in cases determined by law. Women, like men, obey this rigorous law. . . .

Article 11 The free communication of thoughts and opinions is one of the most precious rights of woman, since the liberty assures the recognition of children by their fathers. Any female citizen thus may say freely, I am the mother of a child which belongs to you, without being forced by a barbarous prejudice to hide the truth; [an exception may be made] to respond to the abuse of this liberty in cases determined by the law. . . .

Article 13 For the support of the public force and the expenses of administration, the contributions of woman and man are equal; she share all the duties [*corvees*] and all the painful tasks; therefore, she must have the same share in the distribution of positions, employments, offices, honors and jobs [*industrie*]. . . .

Article 15 The collectivity of women, joined for tax purposed to the aggregate of men, has the right to demand an accounting of his administration from any public agent. . . .

Article 17 Property belongs to both sexes whether united or separate; for each it is an inviolable and sacred right; no on can be deprived of it, since it is the true patrimony of nature, unless the legally determined public need obviously dictates it, and then only with a just and prior indemnity.

Questions to Consider

1. What are the major differences between the *Declarations of the Rights of Man and Citizen* and the *Declaration of the Rights of Woman and the Female Citizen*?
2. What points made by Olympe de Gouges seem to you to be applicable to the drive for women's equal rights today?
3. In your opinion, why did male French revolutionaries pay so little attention to the efforts of their female counterparts?

Mark A. Kishlansky, ed., *Sources of the West: Readings in Western Civilization*, Volume II, fourth edition, Longman Publishers, New York and London, pp. 115–117.

spread their pamphlets and petitioned the Assembly, supported by the *Amis des Noirs* (ah-MEE day nwha; "Friends of the Blacks"), whose supporters also angrily attacked slavery in the Assembly hall. The chamber was left divided and nearly impotent. It first gave the island governments complete control over their blacks and mulattoes; then, yielding to the radicals, it granted political rights to mulattoes born of free parents. This was only a temporary solution to a difficult political and social problem.

After two years of tedious controversy, the Assembly finally produced the Constitution of 1791, which made France a limited monarchy. It assigned the law-making function to the single-chambered Legislative Assembly, which would meet automatically every two years. Louis became a figurehead, allowed to select ministers and temporarily veto laws but denied budgetary control or the right to dismiss the legislature. He had fewer powers than the new American president, George Washington, and he could also be legally deposed. In addition, the constitution created an independent and elected judiciary and completely reorganized local government on three levels—departments, districts, and communes—with elected officials relatively free of supervision from Paris. Despite implications in the *Declaration*, only male citizens who paid a specified minimum of direct taxes acquired the vote; millions could not vote. Property qualifications were even higher for deputies to the Assembly and national officials. Women were made "passive citizens," without the vote, but marriage became a civil contract, with divorce open to both parties. Other individual rights under a new law code were guaranteed to all citizens, including Jews, according to the principles of the *Declaration*.

On September 30, 1791, the Assembly dissolved itself after mandating that no present member of the Assembly was to be eligible for election to the new legislative body. It had passed more than 2000 laws that combined to end feudalism, serfdom, an irrational provincial system, conflicting courts, sale of offices, and absolute monarchy itself. It had not, however, made all citizens equal, even before the law, a point repeatedly emphasized by radical agitators and their followers among the angry street people of Paris.

The Drift Toward Radicalism: September 1791–June 1793

For more than a year before the new constitution was completed, the moderate conservative Assembly, which wanted to protect property rights and middle-class advances, had come under the increasing pressure of radicals, who wanted to carry out fundamental political and social reforms. Despite all efforts of the National Guard, unrest in the country and mob action in the cities disturbed the uneasy peace. Particularly in Paris after the spring of 1790, radical members of the Assembly played on popular fears and suspicions, encouraged by condemnations of the Revolution from émigré nobles and foreign royalists. Tensions within France were further aggravated by secret efforts by the king and queen to enlist foreign support. In June 1791, when the king—who opposed the state loyalty oath imposed on the clergy—and his family were caught trying to flee the country, the situation deteriorated. People in favor of a republic called for Louis to be removed. Angry crowds gathered, and the Guard fired on them, killing 15 people. The resulting wave of discontent would continue to intimidate national lawmakers, shaping their policies for the next three years.

In this charged atmosphere, the new and inexperienced Legislative Assembly met on October 1, 1791. Its prospects during the fall were not promising. The sullen king continued his secret plotting with foreign supporters while a 20 percent drop in the value of *assignats*, the Revolutionary government's currency, alarmed middle-class investors. Public opinion in the cities became more radical as the popular press mounted a virulent and often vulgar campaign against Louis and the Assembly, and crowds in Paris and the port cities cursed the government. On the other side, opponents of the Revolution began to act against it. Full-scale revolts threatened to erupt among Catholic peasants in Vendée (von-DAY), Avignon (ah-veen-YON), Brittany, and Mayenne. The divisions and apprehensions in the country were naturally reflected in the Assembly.

At first, the delegates formed themselves into three groups whose location in the meeting hall provided the political vocabulary for the future: conservatives to the right of the podium, moderates in the center, and liberals to the left. In Paris in 1791 the delegates on the right supported the limited monarchy; the undecided—roughly half of the delegates—were in the center; and on the left was a diverse group split by their geographical origins—for example, the **Girondins** (ZHEE-rohn-DAN) from the southwest of the country and the **Jacobins** from Paris—and political goals, and united only by their distrust for the king and his supporters. A majority could agree only on their repudiation of the Declaration of Pillnitz (August 1791), in which the Austrian and Prussian rulers threatened military intervention if Louis XVI were not properly treated.

The Girondists exploited this foreign threat in emotional appeals that rallied the center behind a war to

---

Girondins—Radical members of the National Assembly (seated on the left) from the southwest of France.

Jacobins—Radical members of the National Assembly (seated on the left) from Paris.

"save the Revolution." Debate gave way to action as the country slipped toward armed conflict during the spring of 1792. The stage was set in February, when Austria and Prussia formed an alliance, a move accented in March when the young and aggressive Francis II (1768–1835) succeeded his comparatively liberal father as Holy Roman Emperor. Louis and his queen, Marie Antoinette, were now hopeful for a war that might set them free. The Girondins savored their newfound dominance, which gave them control of the ministry in March. The Jacobins, under Georges-Jacques Danton (1759–1794) and Maximilien Robespierre (maks-e-MIL-i-en rob-es-PEE-er; 1758–1794), argued against entering a war, noting that, in France's economic condition, war would harm the Revolution and end government economic aid for the common people.

There was a moment of general elation when France declared war on Austria and Prussia in April. But despair soon set in when it became obvious that revolutionary enthusiasm was no match for Austrian and Prussian military discipline. There were too few trained French recruits, led by too few dependable officers, and the armies soon retreated in disorder amid mass desertions from an invasion of the Austrian Netherlands (in present day Belgium). Only the enemy's caution and concern about a Russia advance from the east prevented a complete French disaster. Despair, however, turned to mass determination in July, when the Prussian duke of Brunswick, who commanded the invading armies, issued a threat to destroy Paris if the French royal family was harmed.

In the wake of the military collapse and the Prussian threat, the Girondist rabble-rousers in the Assembly began to lose their support and came under the attack of Danton, the Jacobin deputy prosecutor for the **Paris Commune.** Danton was an enormous brute of a man with a voice of commanding power who mesmerized angry street audiences when he denounced the king as a traitor to France and those who did not share Jacobin views as fools, or worse. On August 10 an incited throng of Parisians, women as well as men, broke into the palace, terrorized the royal family, massacred the Swiss guards, and looted the premises. There followed the Jacobin-directed "September Massacres," in which, under the continual pressure of the mob, the Paris Commune seized power from the Legislative Assembly, deposed the king, and executed some 2000 suspected royalists and priests who did not support the Revolution. As there was no longer a king, it was necessary to call for a new national constitutional convention with members elected by universal male suffrage to prepare the way for a new government. The Jacobin pogrom spread throughout France, even after September 22, when the new National Convention declared France a republic.

Two days earlier, a revitalized French army defeated the Prussians at Valmy, in northern France. This victory fused radicalism with nationalism as French armies began successful advances in the Austrian Netherlands, the Rhineland, and Savoy. Confirmed by their victory in November, the Convention declared universal revolutionary war by promising "fraternity to all peoples who wish to recover their liberty" and ordered inhabitants of occupied countries to accept revolutionary principles. Led by Danton, the lawyer Robespierre—a fanatical follower of Rousseau—and Jean-Paul Marat (mah-RAH; 1743–1793)—the publisher of a violent paper that consistently denounced traitors—the radical Jacobins were now riding a rising tide. But the Girondists, despite their continued enthusiasm for the war, were now the conservatives of the Convention. They had become mainly the spokesmen for wealthy middle-class provincials, who advocated clemency for the king. On this major issue, the execution of Louis XVI, the Jacobins finally triumphed by one vote—despite foreign ambassadors' bribes—and Louis was decapitated on January 21, 1793. Marie

As revolutionary justice condemned an increasing number of people to death after 1791, the guillotine provided an efficient means to decapitate the guilty. The advocates of using the guillotine proclaimed it to be humane because the only thing the condemned would feel would be a "slight breeze at the back of the neck." Here the head of Louis XVI is being shown to the crowd.

Paris Commune—The city government of Paris in Revolutionary France.

Antoinette followed her husband to the guillotine nine months later on October 16, 1793.

Early French military advances had alarmed European capitals, but the execution of Louis XVI and his queen proved to be the decisive factor in turning all of Europe against France. Britain, Austria, Prussia, Spain, the Netherlands, and Sardinia formed the First Coalition in February and March 1793. Coalition forces soon expelled French troops from the Austrian Netherlands and Germany, after which France was invaded at a half-dozen places around its borders. In the ensuing military crisis, the Convention initiated a nationwide effort to raise a new levy of 300,000 men from quotas assigned to every unit of local government. Lazare Carnot (kar-NO; 1753–1823), the republic's minister of war, reorganized the armed forces by opening promotion to all ranks and meshing volunteers with old-line units. His efforts, along with a national patriotic response, brought a hard-won but belated stability.

As in the previous year, threats from abroad generated an internal crisis during the spring of 1793. Execution of the king spurred full-scale civil war in Brittany and the Vendée as peasant armies, led by royalist émigrés and supplied by British ships, fought regular battles against troops of the Republic. Meanwhile in Paris, worsening hunger among the poor widened the breach between Jacobins and Girondins. Again, furious mobs entered the Convention hall, protesting food prices and demanding price controls. Such a measure was pushed through the Convention in April by the *Enragés* (ahn-razh-AY), an extremist faction of the Jacobins led by the radical journalist Jacques Hébert (AY-behr; 1755–1794). When the Girondins staged uprisings in Marseilles, Lyons, Bordeaux, and Toulon, left-wing Jacobins in the Paris Commune called another armed mob into the Convention on May 31, 1793, and purged that body of any remaining Girondists. Others throughout France, wherever the Convention still retained authority, were arrested or driven into hiding.

The Jacobin Republic

The Convention was now a "rump" council of the most extreme Jacobins. Their power was secured after July 12 when Charlotte Corday (1768–1793), a young Girondist sympathizer, came to Paris from Caen and murdered Marat. He had been an adored leader of the *Enragés*, and his death infuriated the street people, including a contingent of revolutionary women who cursed Corday as they followed her to the guillotine. The general anti-Girondist mania brought the Convention under the domination of Robespierre, who remained in power until the late spring of 1794. During that time, revolutionary France, in a convulsion of

Jacques-Louis David, The Death of Marat *(1793). David's painting extols Marat as a martyr of the Revolution.*

patriotic violence, reorganized itself, suppressed internal strife, drove out foreign invaders, and catapulted the radical Jacobin party to a pinnacle of power.

The regime achieved its success largely through rigid dictatorship and terror. The 12-member **Committee of Public Safety,** headed first by Danton, and after July by Robespierre, decided security policies. Subordinate committees were established for the departments, districts, and communes. These bodies deliberately forced conformity and used neighbors to inform on neighbors and sons and daughters to testify against their parents. Suspected traitors were brought to trial before revolutionary tribunals, with most suspects receiving quick death sentences. Between September 1793 and July 1794 some 25,000 victims were dragged to public squares in carts—the famous *tumbrels* (toom-BREL)—and delivered to the

---

Committee of Public Safety—A 12-member group that decided security policies for the Jacobin administration.

guillotines. Ultimately, the **Reign of Terror,** or simply the Terror, as this period came to known, destroyed most of the revolutionaries, including the Girondists (September 1793), the Dantonists (April 1794), and Robespierre himself (July 1794).

While it lasted, the Jacobin dictatorship was remarkably efficient in its war efforts, as it mobilized all of France to fight and changed the nature of European warfare. The Convention made all males between 18 and 40 eligible for military service, a policy known as the *levée en masse* (le-VAY on MAHSS; "mass conscription"), which ultimately produced a force of 800,000, the largest standing army ever assembled in France. Its officers were promoted on merit and encouraged to exercise initiative. Soldiers were lionized in public festivals and provided with special entertainments, while 300 civilian commissars monitored morale and combat readiness. Between 1793 and 1795, these French citizen armies put down all internal rebellions while fighting a series of remarkably successful campaigns against foreign invaders as well. They regained all lost French territory, annexed Belgium, and occupied other areas that extended to the Rhine, the Alps, and the Pyrenees, thus gaining in two years the "natural frontiers" that Louis XIV had dreamed about. By 1794 Prussia and Spain had left the coalition and the Netherlands had become a French ally. Only Britain, Austria, and Sardinia remained at war with France.

Despite their stated beliefs in free enterprise as an ideal, the Jacobins created a war economy, which operated under extensive controls. Government agencies conscripted labor and took over industries, directing them to produce large quantities of uniforms, arms, medical supplies, and equipment. In Paris alone, 258 forges made 1000 gun barrels a day. Reacting to bread riots and the revolutionary women's condemnation of monopolists and speculators, the Convention imposed price controls, rationing, and fixed wages while issuing currency without reference to bank reserves or market demand. The government also punished profiteers, used the property of émigrés to relieve poverty, sold land directly to peasants, and freed the peasants from all compensatory payments to their old lords.

Many other changes reflected a strange combination of reason and fanaticism. The regime prohibited all symbols of status, such as knee breeches, powdered wigs, and jewelry. It abolished titles; people had to be addressed as "citizen" or "citizeness." Streets were renamed to commemorate Revolutionary events or to honor revolutionary heroes. The calendar was reformed by dividing each month into three weeks of ten days each and giving the months poetic new names; July, for example, became Thermidor (hot) to avoid referring to the tyrant Julius Caesar. The Revolution took on a semireligious character in ceremonies and fêtes, which featured attractive young women as living symbols of reason, virtue, and duty. Along with these changes came a strong reaction against Christianity: churches were closed and religious images destroyed. For a while, "Worship of the Supreme Being" was substituted for Roman Catholicism, although, in 1794, religion became a private matter.

Colonial problems, which had confounded the National and Legislative Assemblies, were met head-on by the Jacobin Convention. The grant of citizenship to free blacks and mulattoes of the islands in 1792 had drawn the mulattoes to the government side, but their armies, enlisted by the governors, faced determined insurrection from royalists and resentful escaped slaves. Sometimes, the two anti-Convention forces were united with support from Spain or the British. In the late spring of 1793, the late spring of 1793, the governor of Santo Domingo issued a decree freeing all former slaves and calling on them to join against foreign enemies. His strategy narrowly averted a British conquest. The chamber responded by freeing all slaves in French territories and giving them full citizenship rights. Later, Napoleon would reimpose slavery in the colonies, where it would last until 1848.

Unfortunately, the revolutionary women in France were not so successful. At first, they were welcomed as supporters by the radical Jacobins, until the latter gained power; then, the Jacobins regarded revolutionary women as troublemakers. In October 1793, the Convention refused to hear a group of women who wanted to protest violations of the Constitution. During the next six months, the government repressed women's societies and imprisoned their leaders. Although the Jacobin legislature denied women the vote, it did improve their education, medical care, and property rights.

Because they regulated the economy and showed concern for the lower classes, the Jacobins have often been considered as forerunners of socialism. The Constitution of 1793, which was developed by the Convention but suspended almost immediately because of the war, does not support this interpretation. It did provide public assistance for the poor and aided the unemployed in seeking work, but it also guaranteed private property, included a charter of individual liberties, confirmed the Constitution of 1791's emphasis on local autonomy, and provided for the Central Committee, appointed by the departments. The greatest difference, in comparison with the Constitution of 1791, was the right to vote, which was granted to all adult males. Although the Jacobin constitution indi-

---

Reign of Terror—The period, roughly from September 1793 to July 1794, in which the Jacobin Dictatorship executed some 25,000 people by the guillotine.

cated a concern for equality of opportunity, it also revealed its authors as eighteenth-century radical liberals who followed Rousseau rather than Locke.

Conservative Counter-Revolution and the End of the Terror

The summer of 1794 brought a conservative reaction against radical revolution. With French arms victorious everywhere, rigid discipline no longer seemed necessary, but Robespierre, still committed to Rousseau's "republic of virtue," was determined to continue the Terror. When he demanded voluntary submission to the "general will" as necessary for achieving social equality, justice, and brotherly love, many practical politicians among his colleagues doubted his sanity. Others wondered if they would be among those next eliminated to purify society. They therefore cooperated to condemn him in the Convention. In July 1794, his enemies sent him to the guillotine with 20 of his supporters, amid great celebration.

Robespierre's fall ended the Terror and initiated a revival of the pre-Jacobin past. In 1794, the Convention eliminated the Committee of Public Safety; the next year, it abolished the revolutionary tribunal and the radical political clubs and freed thousands of political prisoners. It also banned women from attendance in the Convention hall, an act that symbolized the return to a time when women's political influence was confined to the ballroom, the bedroom, and the salon. Indeed, as the exiled Girondists, émigré royalists, and nonconforming priests returned to France, Parisian politics moved from the streets to the drawing rooms of the elite, such as that of the former courtesan Madame Tallien (TAL-lee-en; 1773–1835), which became a center of high-society gossip and political intrigue. Outside Paris, by the summer of 1795, armed reactionary "white" terrorists roamed the countryside, seeking out and murdering former Jacobins. Everywhere, the earlier reforming zeal and patriotic fervor gave way to conservative cynicism.

Before it dissolved itself in 1795, the Convention proclaimed still another constitution and established a new political system known as the Directory, which governed France until 1799. The new government was headed by an executive council of five members (directors) appointed by the upper house of a bicameral (two-house) legislature. Assemblies of electors in each department selected deputies to the two chambers. These electors were chosen by adult male taxpayers, but the electors themselves had to be substantial property owners. Indeed, they numbered only some 20,000 in a total population of more than 25 million. Government was thus securely controlled by the upper middle classes, a condition also evident by the return to free trade.

The Directory was conspicuously conservative and antidemocratic, but it was also antiroyalist. A Bourbon restoration would have also restored church and royalist lands, which had been largely acquired by wealthy capitalists during the Revolution. Politicians who had participated in the Revolution or voted for the execution of Louis XVI had even greater reason to fear restoration of the monarchy. In pursuing this antiroyalist path at a time when royalist principles were regaining popularity, the government had to depend on the recently developed professional military establishment. More than once between 1795 and 1797, army action protected the government against royalists and radicals. The Directory also encouraged further military expansion, hoping to revive patriotic revolutionary fervor. Except for young military officers such as Napoleon Bonaparte, bureaucrats, members

The French Revolutions

1787–1789	Bad weather cuts down on grain harvest, drives up bread prices
August 1788	Louis XVI announces meeting of Estates-General to be held May 1789
May 5, 1789	Estates-General convenes
June 1789	Third Estate declares itself the National Assembly, Oath of the Tennis Court
July 14, 1789	Storming of the Bastille, revolution of peasantry begins
June 1791	Louis XVI and family attempt to flee Paris, are captured and returned
April 1792	France declares war on Austria
January 1793	Louis XVI executed
1793–1794	Reign of Terror
1799	Napoleon overthrows the Directory and seizes power
1804	Napoleon proclaims himself emperor of the French
September 1812	French army reaches Moscow, is trapped by Russian winter
1813	Napoleon defeated at Leipzig
June 15, 1815	Napoleon is defeated at Waterloo and exiled to island of St. Helena

of the landowning middle classes, merchants in large cities, and some professionals, the majority of people in 1796 were worse off than they had been two decades before. But the Directory paid little attention to the majority of people and protected its own.

THE FRENCH REVOLUTION: THE NAPOLEONIC PHASE, 1799–1815

■ *What influence did Napoleon have on European history?*

Even as a student, Napoleon considered himself a man of destiny, and he worked hard to construct the image he wanted to project to the future. As soon as the ship carrying him to exile in St. Helena set sail in 1815, his partisans and detractors began a debate over his career that continues to the present day. Whatever the viewpoint of the participants in that debate, all agree that few people have as decisively affected their times and set in motion developments that so profoundly altered the future as did Napoleon Bonaparte.

Napoleon the Corsican

Revolutions favor the bright, the ambitious, and the lucky. Napoleon Bonaparte (1769–1821) had all three qualities in abundance. He was born on Corsica to a low-ranking Florentine noble family in 1769, the year after control of that island passed from Genoa to France. At the age of 10, he was placed by his father in the military academy at Brienne (bree-EN). Six years later, he received his officer's commission. At the beginning of the French Revolution, he was a 20-year-old officer, doomed to a mediocre future by his family's modest standing and the restrictions of the Old Regime. Ten years later, he ruled France. The Revolution gave him the opportunity to rise rapidly, the result of his intelligence, ability, charm, and daring.

Napoleon arrived at the right time—a generation earlier or later, the situation would not have allowed him to gain power. He took advantage of the gutting of the old officer class by the revolutionary wars and the destruction of what was left of the older by the Jacobins to rise quickly to a prominent position from which he could appeal to the Directory. That self-interested group of survivors asked the Corsican to break up a right-wing uprising in October 1795. The following year, the Directory gave Napoleon command of the smallest of the three armies sent to do battle with the Austrians.

The two larger forces crossed the Rhine on their way to attack the Habsburgs while, as a diversionary

This heroic portrait by Antoine-Jean Gros shows Napoleon at the age of 27, a time when he was leading his troops at the battle of Arcola in northern Italy in November 1796.

move, Napoleon's corps went over the Alps into Italy. Contrary to plan, the main forces accomplished little while Napoleon, intended as no more than bait, crushed the Sardinians and then the Austrians in a series of brilliant campaigns. As he marched across northern Italy he picked off Venice and was well on the road to Vienna when the Austrians approached him to make peace. Without instructions from his government, Napoleon negotiated the Treaty of Campo Formio (FORM-ee-oh; 1797) and returned home a hero.

After considering an invasion of Britain in the first part of 1798—a cross-Channel task he deemed impossible—Napoleon set out, with the Directory's blessing, to strike at Britain's economy by attacking its colonial structure. He would invade Egypt, expose the weakness of the Ottoman Empire, and from there launch an attack on India. The politicians were as much impressed by this grand plan as they were relieved to get the increasingly popular Napoleon out of town. He successfully evaded the British fleet in the Mediterranean, landed in Egypt, and took Alexandria and

Cairo in July. The British admiral Horatio Nelson (1758–1805), however, found the French fleet and sank it at Aboukir on August 1, 1798. Even though their supply lines and access to France were cut off, Napoleon's forces fought a number of successful battles against the Turks in Syria and Egypt.

The fact remained that the French armies were stranded in Egypt and would be forced to remain there until 1801, when a truce allowed them to come home. This development would normally be regarded as a defeat, yet when Napoleon abandoned his army in August 1799, slipped by the British fleet, and returned to Paris, he was given a frenzied, triumphant homecoming. In public appearances, he adopted a modest pose and gave addresses on the scientific accomplishments of the expedition, such as the finding of the Rosetta Stone, a discovery that provided the first clue in the deciphering of Egyptian hieroglyphics.

Napoleon, his brothers, and the Abbé Sieyès (ab-AY see-YES)—the former vicar general and author of the important 1789 pamphlet "What Is the Third Estate?"—sought to take advantage of the political crisis surrounding the Directory. The Second Coalition, led by Russia and Great Britain, threatened France from the outside, while a feverish inflation ravaged the economy domestically. Various political factions courted Napoleon, whose charisma made him seem the likely savior of the country. In the meantime, he and his confederates planned their course. They launched a clumsy, though successful, coup in November 1799 and replaced the Directory with the Consulate. The plotters shared the cynical belief that "constitutions should be short and obscure" and that democracy meant that the rulers rule and the people obey.

The takeover ended the revolutionary decade. France remained, in theory, a republic, but nearly all power rested with the 31-year-old Napoleon, who ruled as First Consul. Still another constitution was written and submitted to a vote of the people. Only half of the eligible voters went to the polls, but an overwhelming majority voted in favor of the new constitution: 3,011,007 in favor versus 1,562 against.

New Foundations

Ten years of radical change made France ready for one-man rule, but of a type much different from that exercised by the Bourbon monarchy. The events of 1789 had overturned the source of legitimate political power. Now it came not from God but from the people. The social structure of the Old Regime was gone and with it the privileges of hereditary and created nobility. The church no longer had financial or overt political power. The old struggles between kings and nobles, nobles and bourgeoisie, peasants and landlords, and Catholics and Protestants were replaced by the rather more universal confrontation between rich and poor.

There had been three attempts to rebuild the French system in the ten years of revolution: the bourgeois-constitutional efforts to 1791, the radical programs to 1794, and the rule to 1799 by survivors who feared both the right and the left. Although each attempt had failed, each left valuable legacies to the new France. The first attempt established the power of the upper middle classes; the second showed the great power of the state to mobilize the population; and the third demonstrated the usefulness of employing former enemies in day-to-day politics.

Ever the pragmatic tactician, Napoleon used elements from the Old Regime and the various phases of the Revolution to reconstruct France. He built an autocracy far more powerful than Louis XVI's government. He took advantage of the absence of the old forms of competition to central power from the nobility and the feudal structure that had been destroyed in the name of liberty, equality, and brotherhood. He used the mercantile policies, military theories, and foreign policy goals of the Old Regime, the ambitions of the middle class, and the mobilization policies of the Jacobins. All he asked from those who wished to serve him was loyalty. Defrocked priests, renegade former nobles, reformed Jacobins, small businessmen, and enthusiastic soldiers all played a role. His unquestioning acceptance of the ambitious brought him popularity because ten years of constant change had compromised most politically active people in some form of unprincipled, immoral, or illegal behavior.

Napoleon built his state on the *philosophes*' conception of a system in which all French men would be equal before the law. The Revolution destroyed the sense of personal power of a sovereign and substituted what the British historian Lord Acton would later in the century call the "tyranny of the majority." The French state accordingly could intervene more effectively than ever before, limited only by distance and communication problems.

The mass democratic army created by the total mobilization of both people and resources was one of the best examples of the new state system. A revolutionary society had fought an ideological war, and the experience changed the nature of combat forever. Because advancement and success were based on valor and victory, rather than bloodlines or privilege, the army profited from the new social structure and sought to preserve and extend it. The army best symbolized the great power of the French nation unleashed by the Revolution. Many of the economic and diplomatic problems that preceded the Revolution remained, but Napoleon's new state structure provided inspired solutions.

Taking advantage of his military supremacy, Napoleon gained breathing space for his domestic reforms by making peace with the Second Coalition by March 1802. He then set about erecting the governing structure of France, which remained virtually intact into the 1980s. He developed an administration that was effective in raising money, assembling an army, and exploiting the country's resources. His centralized government ruled through prefects, powerful agents in the provinces who had almost complete control of local affairs and were supported by a large police force. He then established a stable monetary policy based on an honest tax-collecting system, backed by up-to-date accounting procedures. The Bank of France that he created remains a model of sound finance.

Napoleon knew that the country he ruled was overwhelmingly Catholic and that national interest dictated that he come to terms with the papacy. Through the Concordat of 1801 with Pope Pius VII, the pope gained the right to approve the bishops whom the First Consul appointed to the reestablished Catholic Church. The state permitted seminaries to be reopened and paid priests' salaries. Pius regained control of the Papal States and saw his church recognized as the religion of the majority in France. The church thus resumed its position of prominence, but without its former power and wealth.

Napoleon viewed education as a way to train useful citizens to become good soldiers and bureaucrats, and he pursued the development of mass education by trying to increase the number of elementary schools, secondary schools, and special institutes for technical training. The schools were to be used to propagandize the young to serve the state through "directing political and moral opinion." Overarching the entire system was the University of France, which was more an administrative body to control education than a teaching institution. Napoleon had neither the time nor the resources to put mass education in place during his lifetime, although he did gain immediate success in training the sons—but rarely the daughters—of the newly arrived middle classes to become state functionaries.

Perhaps his greatest accomplishment came in the field of law. Building on reforms begun ten years earlier, he assembled a talented team of lawyers to bring order to the chaotic state of French jurisprudence. At the time he took power, the country was caught in the transition from 366 separate local systems to a uniform code. By 1804 the staff had compiled a comprehensive civil law code (called the **Code Napoléon**

Code Napoléon—A civil law code instituted by Napoleon's administration in 1804. It formed the basis for many legal systems throughout Europe.

after 1807) that was a model of precision and equality when compared to the old system. The code ensured the continuation of the gains made by the middle classes in the previous decade and emphasized religious toleration and abolition of the privileges held under the old order. Unfortunately, the code perpetuated the inferior status of women in the areas of civil rights, financial activities, and divorce. Nonetheless, it has served as the basis for law codes in many other countries.

The price France paid for these gains was rule by a police state that featured censorship, secret police, spies, and political trials, which sent hundreds to their deaths and thousands into exile. Order did prevail, however, and for the first time in a decade, it was safe to travel the country's roads. Napoleon also reduced the "representative assemblies" to meaningless rubber stamps. Liberty, equality, and brotherhood meant little in a land where the First Consul and his police could deny a person's freedom and right of association because of a perceived intellectual or political conflict.

To consolidate all of the changes, Napoleon proclaimed himself emperor in December 1804. Fifteen years after the outbreak of the Revolution, France had a new monarch. In a plebiscite, the nation approved the change by 3,572,329 to 2,579. As Napoleon took the crown in his hands from Pope Pius VII, who had come from Rome for the occasion, and crowned himself, the First French Republic came to an end.

Napoleon as Military Leader

War had been France's primary occupation since 1792, and, on the whole, it had been a profitable enterprise. The French had gained much land and money, as well as the opportunity to export the Revolution. Napoleon's reforms helped make his country even stronger in battle. At the end of 1804, Napoleon embarked on a series of campaigns designed to show France's invincibility. A key to French success was the emperor himself, who employed his own remarkable genius in leading his strong and wealthy country.

Napoleon brought intellectual strength, sensitivity to mood and opportunity, and bravery to the task of making war. He had been trained in the most advanced methods of his day, and he had better, more mobile artillery and more potent powder to blow holes through the enemy's lines. He worked well with a talented command staff, to which he gave much responsibility to wield their divisions as conditions dictated. Finally, he was the ultimate leader. Whether as lieutenant, general, First Consul, or emperor, Napoleon inspired masses of soldiers in a dramatic way. At the same time, he mobilized the home front through the use of the press and skillfully written dispatches.

Beneath this image making, the supreme commander was extremely flexible in his use of resources, always changing his tactics. He was pragmatic, moved rapidly, and lived off the land. He won the loyalty of his men by incentives and rewards, not brutal discipline. He set many military precedents, among them the use of ideological and economic warfare, as well as the rapid simultaneous movement of a large number of military columns. These columns could quickly converge on a given point with devastating results, breaking the will of the enemy. Finally, he personally led his troops into battle, exposing himself to incredible dangers with little regard for his own safety.

His nemesis was Great Britain, and during 1803 and 1804, he prepared a cross-Channel invasion. But the inability of the French navy to control the Channel and the formation of the Third Coalition (Great Britain, Russia, Austria, and Sweden) forced him to march eastward. In October 1805 Admiral Nelson and the British ended Napoleon's hopes of dominating the seas by destroying the joint French-Spanish fleet at the battle of Trafalgar.

France did far better on land, gaining mastery over the Continent by the end of 1807. Napoleon totally demoralized the Third Coalition in battles at Ulm (October 1805) and Austerlitz (December 1805). He then annihilated the Prussians, who had entered the conflict in the battles at Jena and Auerstadt (October 1806). He occupied Berlin, where he established the **Continental System,** a blockade of the Continent that was an effort to defeat Britain by depriving it of trade with the rest of Europe. Finally, in June 1807, he defeated the Russians at the battle of Friedland and forced Tsar Alexander I to sign the Tilsit Treaty in July. This treaty, ratified on a raft anchored in the middle of the Nieman River, brought the two major land powers of Europe together in an alliance against Britain.

At the beginning of 1808, Napoleon stood supreme in Europe, leading France to a dominance it had never experienced before and has not experienced since. Several of his relatives occupied the thrones of neighboring countries. The rest of the continent appeared to be mere satellites revolving around, this time, a Napoleonic sun.

Napoleon's Revolution in Europe

As he achieved his military goals, Napoleon set in motion a chain reaction of mini-revolutions that had a profound impact on the rest of the century. British sea power stood in the way of France's total domination of the Continent. Even though the British economy suffered under the impact of the Continental System (exports dropped by 20 percent, with a resultant cutback in production and rise in unemployment), the damage was not permanent. The Continental System inadvertently contributed to Britain's economic development by forcing it to industrialize quickly as it sought new markets and methods. Safe behind their wall of ships, the British turned out increasing quantities of goods as they passed through the early phases of industrialization.

Napoleon's armies carried French ideological baggage and institutional reforms across the Continent. Even though the emperor consolidated the Revolution in a conservative way in France, he broke apart his opponents' fragile social and governmental structures when he marched across the Rhine. Napoleon consciously spread the messages of liberty, equality, and brotherhood with all of the antifeudal, antiprivilege, and antirepressive themes inherent in the revolutionary triad. Where the French governed directly, they used the Code Napoléon and the reformed administrative practices.

The French presence triggered a hostile wave of nationalistic resentments. Many Europeans saw Napoleon as an imperialist, and the people he had "emancipated" began to realize that they had exchanged an old form of despotism for a new one. By posing as the champion of the Revolution, Napoleon sowed the seeds of the opposition that would work against him later, especially in Prussia. With the exception of the Poles, who had labored under Russian dominance and now served Napoleon well, the rest of Europe reacted against the French yoke.

The most significant rebellion took place in Portugal and Spain. Napoleon's entry into those countries to topple the passive Bourbons and strengthen the leaky Continental System was uncharacteristically shortsighted. The emperor had a serious fight on his hands in the Peninsular War that followed. Guerrilla uprisings soon broke out, supported by a British expeditionary force and supplies. These bloody wars tied down 200,000 to 300,000 French troops over a period of five years and drained the French treasury. The invasion of Spain also prompted a series of uprisings in the New World that gave birth to modern Latin American history (see Chapter 21).

The social and political changes the French triggered in Germany were equally profound. When he redrew the map of Europe after his victories, Napoleon destroyed the remnants of the Holy Roman Empire and, in so doing, erased 112 states of that ancient league. Only six of the former 50 free cities retained their status. Further, by changing the territorial

Continental System—An economic system Napoleon imposed on Europe to prevent countries from trading with Great Britain.

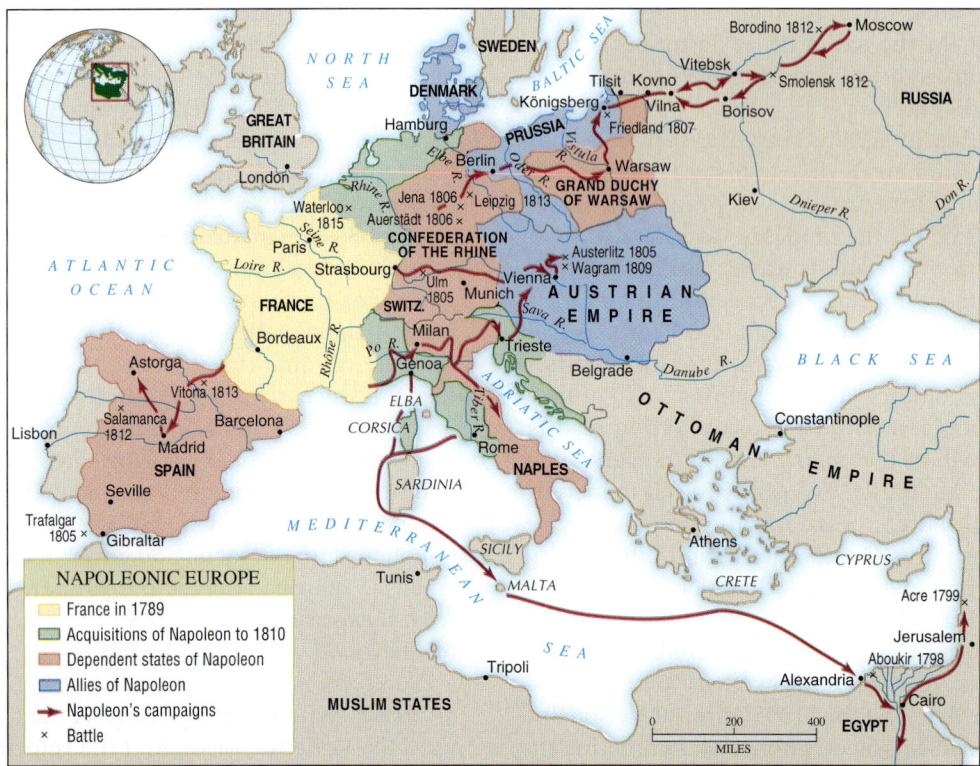

Napoleon combined the military advances of the ancien régime *and the unleashed democratic forces of the Revolution to achieve in ten years what Louis XIV had failed to accomplish in a half century: the domination of Europe.*

arrangements of other areas, he reduced the number of German political units from more than 300 to 39. All over Germany, a wave of nationalism stirred the politically conscious population and prepared the way for the liberation movement.

Napoleon's Downfall

Opposition to Napoleon grew in both Austria and Russia. After the valiant but unsuccessful campaigns against the French in 1809, culminating in the bloody battle of Wagram, Vienna became a docile, though unreliable, ally. Napoleon's marriage to Marie Louise, the daughter of Francis I of Austria, proved to be only a tenuous tie between the French emperor and the Habsburgs. In Russia the Tilsit Treaty had never been popular, and the economic hardships brought on by the Continental System made a break in the alliance virtually inevitable. By the end of 1810 France and Russia prepared to go to war against each other.

The emperor prepared carefully for his attack on Russia. Food supply would be a major problem for the 611,000 troops—half of them non-French—in the first and second lines of the invasion because his forces would be too large to live off the land. Furthermore his army took with them over 200,000 animals, which required forage and water. The invasion force delayed its march until late June to ensure that the Russian plains would furnish sufficient grass to feed the animals.

The Russian campaign was both a success and a failure for Napoleon. The French did gain their objective—the city of Moscow—but the Russians refused to surrender. Shortly after the French occupied Moscow, fires broke out, destroying three-fourths of the city. After spending 33 days in the burned shell of the former capital waiting in vain for the tsar, who was 400 miles north in St. Petersburg, to agree to peace, Napoleon gave orders to retreat. He left the city on October 19. To remain would have meant having his lines cut by winter and being trapped with no supplies. His isolation in Moscow would have encouraged his enemies in Paris. Leaving the city, as it turned out, condemned most of his men to death. As the remnants of Napoleon's forces marched west in October and November, they were forced to retrace virtually the same route they had used in the summer. They suffered starvation, attacks by partisans, and the continual pressure of Russian forces. Thousands perished daily, and by the end of November, only about 10,000 of the original force had made their escape from Russia.

Russia, which had stood alone against the French at the beginning of 1812, was soon joined by Prussia, Austria, and Britain in 1813 and 1814 in what came to be known as the War of Liberation. While British armies under the duke of Wellington (1769–1852) helped clear the French forces out of Spain, the allied troops pushed Napoleon's forces westward. A combination of Napoleon's genius and the difficulties in coordinating the allied efforts prolonged the war, but in October 1813, the French suffered a decisive defeat at Leipzig in the Battle of the Nations, one year to the day after Napoleon had fled Moscow.

The allies sent peace offers to Napoleon, but he refused them. After Leipzig the Napoleonic Empire rapidly disintegrated, and by the beginning of 1814, the allies had crossed the Rhine and invaded France. At the end of March, the Russians, Austrians, and Prussians took Paris. Two weeks later, Napoleon abdicated his throne, receiving in return sovereignty over Elba, a small island between Corsica and Italy.

Napoleon arrived in Elba in May and established rule over his 85-square-mile kingdom. He set up a mini-state, complete with an army, a navy, and a court. He soon exhausted the possibilities of Elba and in February and March 1815 he eluded the British fleet and returned to France to begin his campaign to regain power "within one hundred days." His former subjects, bored with the restored Bourbon Louis XVIII, gave him a tumultuous welcome. Napoleon entered Paris, raised an army of 300,000 men, and sent a message to the allies gathered to make peace at Vienna that he desired to rule France and only France. The allies, who were on the verge of breaking up their alliance, united, condemned Napoleon as an enemy of peace, and sent forces to France to put him down once and for all.

At the battle of Waterloo on June 18, 1815, the duke of Wellington, supported by Prussian troops under Field Marshall Gebhard von Blücher (fon BLOOK-er; 1749–1819), narrowly defeated Napoleon. The vanquished leader sought asylum with the British, hoping to live in exile in either England or the United States. But the allies, taking no chances, shipped him off to the bleak South Atlantic island of St. Helena, 5000 miles from Paris. Here he set about writing his autobiography. He died of cancer in 1821 at the age of 51.

Even with the brief flurry of the One Hundred Days, Napoleon had no hope of re-creating the grandeur of his empire as it was in 1808. The reasons for this are not hard to determine. Quite simply, Napoleon was the heart and soul of the empire, and after 1808, his physical and intellectual vigor began to weaken. Administrative and military developments reflected this deterioration as Napoleon began to appoint sycophants to positions of responsibility.

Further, by 1812, the middle classes, on which he depended, began suffering the economic consequences of his policies. The Continental System and continual warfare made their effects deeply felt through decreased trade and increased taxes. Even though some war contractors profited, the costs of Napoleon's ambitions began to make Frenchmen long for peace.

The Empire of Napoleon in 1812

Outside France, the growth of nationalistic resistance on the Continent worked against the dictator, who first stimulated it by exporting the call for liberty, equality, and brotherhood. Equally important, the 25 years of French military superiority disappeared as other nations adopted and improved on the new methods of fighting. Finally, the balance-of-power principle made itself felt. France could not eternally take on the whole world.

CONCLUSION

Copernicus asked the fundamental questions about whether or not the earth moved, repeating a process of inquiry that in the West went back to the Ionian Greeks: similar inquiries were to be found in India, China, and Egypt. When, after extensive mathematical calculations, he established the heliocentric theory, his findings were published, to be read and challenged. As others improved on his findings and established the natural laws that defined the motion of the planets, scientific inquiries became widely admired in some parts of Europe and widely attacked by Christian churches in others. The surprising discoveries of astronomers produced a new view of the individual's place in the universe; their perspective was apparently proved mathematically by Sir Isaac Newton in the law of gravitation. His laws, along with the other laws of science, suggested that human reason operated effectively only when it was interpreting sensory experience. Material reality was accepted by some thinkers as the only reality. Therefore, the natural laws affecting human society were also considered basically materialistic. Respect for Enlightenment philosophy, many of whose early participants contributed to the Scientific Revolution, was largely derived from the successes and popularity of science.

Within this political context, the eighteenth-century Age of Reason brought a new vision of the future to European civilization. Its proponents thought they had discovered a simple way to achieve perpetual human happiness. They sought to deliver people from irrational restraints so that they might act freely in accordance with a universal human nature. On the one hand, their writings promised that pursuit of self-interest would benefit society; on the other, it promised that a free human reason would produce sound moral judgments. In other words, individual freedom furthered the operation of natural laws. Believing they had learned these laws, eighteenth-century rationalists thought they had found the secret of never-ending progress.

Although the *philosophes* and their prototypes outside of France were not revolutionaries, their ideas promised to undermine absolutism in all of its phases. Deism questioned the necessity of state churches and clergies. The physiocrats, Adam Smith, and other early economic liberals demonstrated the futility of mercantilism. The Enlightenment's political principles substituted the social contract for divine right while emphasizing the natural human rights of political freedom and justice.

This reasonable search for natural law, and the demand that all things must stand the test of reason came at a time when colonial wars had forced France to go deeper into debt. Louis XVI's fiscal problems forced him to call the Estates-General—the representatives of the French people—in May 1789 to meet for the first time in 175 years. The subject of debate passed quickly from discussion of debt to considerations of social and political reform of the *ancien régime*. The old system collapsed under the weight of these considerations and, two months later, plunged into the maelstrom of revolution from which it emerged only ten years later, again under the control of a single leader—this time the Corsican-born Napoleon, who, thereafter, carried out his own version of the French revolution that touched all of Europe and much of the Western world.

Suggestions for Web Browsing

You can obtain more information about topics included in this chapter at the websites listed below. See also the companion website that accompanies this text, **http://www.ablongman.com/brummett,** which contains an online study guide and additional resources.

Galileo Project
http://es.rice.edu/ES/humsoc/Galileo/

A hypertext source of information about the life and work of Galileo Galilei and the science of his time.

Internet Modern History Sourcebook: The Scientific Revolution and the Enlightenment
http://www.fordham.edu/halsall/mod/modsbook09.html

Extensive online source for links about the Scientific Revolution and the Enlightenment, including primary documents by or about Copernicus, Kepler, Galileo, Descartes, Adam Smith, and John Locke.

Catherine the Great
http://members.tripod.com/~Nevermore/CGREAT.HTM

A treasure trove of materials on the Enlightened Empress.

Eighteenth-Century Fashion
http://www.marquise.de/en/1700/index.shtml

A virtual guided tour of European fashion during the rococo period.

French Revolution
http://otal.umd.edu/~fraistat/romrev/frbib.html

Lists several major websites and a selected general bibliography dedicated to the French Revolution.

Marie Antoinette
http://www2.lucidcafe.com/lucidcafe/library/95nov/antoinette.html

A short biography of the queen, with related Web sites offering portraits, genealogy, and life at Versailles.

Napoleon
http://www.napoleonseries.org/

Site provides extensive bibliographic and general historical information about Napoleon and his times.

Military History: Napoleonic Wars (1800–1815)
http://www.cfcsc.dnd.ca/links/milhist/nap.html

Canadian Forces College site lists links on the biographies of Napoleon and Nelson, campaigns and battles, museums, naval operations, and reenactments.

The Congress of Vienna
http://members.aol.com/varnix/congress/

A good collection of documents and images from the Congress that put Europe back together again.

Literature and Film

Alexander Pope captured the spirit of the age his *Essay on Man* (1733). Jonathan Swift used satire for political criticism in *Gulliver's Travels* (1726). Voltaire's *Candide* (1759) is a fine critique of contemporary society. Daniel Defoe's *Robinson Crusoe* (1719) is a pathbreaking novel. Johann Wolfgang von Goethe's *The Sorrow of Young Werther* (1774) set the stage for modern romantic novels. See Neal Stephenson's three-volume series on the Scientific Revolution, *The Baroque Cycle*, beginning with *Quicksilver* (2003–2004)

Milos Forman's film *Amadeus* (Warner, 1984) is superb. Gérard Corbiau's *Farinelli: Il Castrato* (Columbia/Tristar, 1995) gives splendid insights into the society of the time. Marvin Chomsky captures eighteenth-century Russia in his film *Catherine the Great* (A & E Entertainment, 1995).

Two panoramic novels stand head and shoulders above the rest for this period, Charles Dickens's *A Tale of Two Cities* (1859) and Leo Tolstoy's *War and Peace* (1864–1869). There are several film versions of each. Rafael Sabatini's *Scaramouche: A Romance of the French Revolution* (1921) is a good, epic, read. Two recent historical novels deserve attention, Sandra Gulland's trilogy on

Josephine (Touchstone, 2002) and Floyd Kemske's novel on Talleyrand, *The Third Lion* (Catbird, 1997).

Abel Gance's silent film *Napoleon* (Universal, 1927) is a cinematic classic. *Danton* (Home Vision Entertainment, 1982) gives a good visual context for the most radical part of the revolution. Felix de Rooy's *Desiree* (1984) casts Napoleon in a sensitive light.

Suggestions for Reading

A useful survey of scientific achievements during the period is A. Rupert Hall, *The Revolution in Science, 1500–1750* (Longman, 1983).

A good survey of the Enlightenment is presented in Robert Anchor, *The Enlightenment Tradition* (University of Pennsylvania Press, 1987). Steven Nadler, *Spinoza: A Life* (Cambridge University Press, 1999) is a fine biography. French and American colonial women who played roles in the Enlightenment are ably credited in Joan B. Landes, *Women and the Public Sphere in the Age of the French Revolution* (Cornell University Press, 1988).

François Furet gave a powerful reinterpretation of the whole revolutionary epoch in *The French Revolution, 1770–1814*, trans. Antonia Nevill (Blackwell, 1996). A fundamental examination of the nature of the Revolution is provided in T. C. W. Blanning, *The French Revolution: Class War or Culture Clash?* (St. Martin's Press, 1998).

On the significance of class hostilities and mob psychology, see Peter M. Jones, *The Peasantry in the French Revolution* (Cambridge University Press, 1988) and the classic George F. E. Rude, *The Crowd in the French Revolution* (Greenwood, 1986). The role of the revolutionary army is well depicted in Jean-Paul Bertaud, *The Army of the French Revolution: From Citizen Soldiers to Instrument of Power* (Princeton University Press, 1988). An important reconsideration of the 1792–1794 period is Patrice L. R. Higonnet, *Goodness Beyond Virtue: Jacobins During the French Revolution* (Harvard University Press, 1998).

Jean Tulard's *Napoleon: The Myth of the Saviour* (Weidenfeld & Nicolson, 1984) is a good study among the many on the French emperor. The military arts of the era are well described in Gunther Rothenberg, *The Art of Warfare in the Age of Napoleon* (Indiana University Press, 1978).

CHAPTER 19

Africa, 1650–1850

CHAPTER CONTENTS

- The Atlantic Slave Trade
  DOCUMENT: *A Slave's Memoir*
- The End of the Slave Trade in West Africa
- Islamic Africa
- Africans and European Settlement in Southern Africa
- **DOCUMENT:** *"Song of the Afflicted"*
- **DISCOVERY THROUGH MAPS:** *The Myth of the Empty Land*
- African State Formation in Eastern and Northeastern Africa

1550

c. 1581–1663 Queen Njinga, ruler of Ndongo kingdom, Angola

1650

1632–1667 Reign of Ethiopian Emperor Fasilidas

1672–1727 Reign of Moroccan Sultan Mulay Ismail

1685 Portuguese invade kingdom of Kongo

1700

1713 British obtain right to sell slaves in Spanish ports

c. 1717 Death of Asante King Osei Tutu, West Africa

1725 Fulani Muslims launch jihad in Futo Jalon, West Africa

1750

1779 First Xhosa-European war in eastern Cape, South Africa

1780s Peak decade of transatlantic slave trade

1800

1816 Shaka becomes king of Zulu people

1834 Beginning of Great Trek of Afrikaners

1840 Zanzibar becomes center for Omani Arab rule

1850

1868 Suicide of Tewodros II of Ethiopia

The mid-seventeenth to the mid-nineteenth centuries was a period of sometimes gentle and sometimes violent change in the states and societies of Africa. These states faced a set of challenges prompted by both external interventions and internal transformations. The internal upheavals took the forms of regional conflicts, the formation of new kingdoms, the expansion of Islam, migrations, and economic shifts. The external threats primarily came from the intrusion of Dutch and British settlers in southern Africa and a dramatic upswing in the Atlantic slave trade.

Arabs in North Africa and the Middle East had long maintained a slave trade with Africans in the interior of West Africa and on the East African coast. Europeans had also been involved for several centuries in a slave trade with Africans along the West and Central African coasts, but in the eighteenth century as the demand increased for slaves to work on the sugar plantations in the Americas, Portuguese, British, Dutch, and French slavers bought many more slaves from African states that rarely allowed European traders to intrude in their affairs. In the seventeenth century alone, around six million Africans were sold into the transatlantic slave trade. Although the slave trade was destructive, the transatlantic trade opened up exchanges with the Americas in crops such as cassava, peanuts, and maize that benefited African agriculture and increased African populations. In the late eighteenth century, as European nations entered the industrial age, European traders began shifting away from trading for slaves to trading for commodities such as palm oil and palm kernels.

The European presence and influence in Africa was largely limited to coastal areas. However, at the southern tip of Africa, where Europeans could survive in a temperate climate, the Dutch and British established colonies. Dutch settlers primarily engaged in subsistence pastoralism, while the British were interested in commercial farming. But both required land that they conquered from indigenous Africans.

These centuries also saw the political map of Africa being redrawn as some older states that participated in the transatlantic slave trade declined and many new ones were created throughout the continent. In northeastern Africa the long-established kingdom of Ethiopia saw its monarchy weakened and nobles assert their autonomy.

In East Africa the kingdoms of Buganda and Rwanda developed. Holy wars contributed to the spread of Islam and the emergence of Muslim kingdoms across the West African Sudan. And, in southern Africa in the early eighteenth century, the Zulu and Basotho, responding to changing trade patterns and increased conflict, established major kingdoms.

THE ATLANTIC SLAVE TRADE

■ *What factors contributed to the creation and the growth of the Atlantic slave trade?*

Throughout the seventeenth century Europeans became increasingly active in the Atlantic slave trade, which combined to create a huge international complex of enterprises involving the economies of four continents. The western Saharan coast was the setting for the beginning of the Atlantic slave trade in 1441. To win the favor of Prince Henry the Navigator, a Portuguese sea captain kidnapped one man and one woman who were sold into the Mediterranean slave market. The slave trade reached its peak three centuries later as a major component in the rapidly expanding capitalism of northern Europe. Because it was conducted in partnerships between Africans and Europeans, the trade was a less obvious short-term danger to African interests than the migrating Dutch settlers in South Africa, but it posed a more serious long-term threat.

The full historical significance of the slave trade can best be understood if it is viewed in its broader setting. Europe's economy at the time derived large profits from bulk plantation commodities such as sugar, tobacco, and coffee. The most productive European plantations, which were located in the West Indies, depended primarily on slave labor from West Africa. Thus, slaving ports, such as Liverpool and Bristol in England and Bordeaux and Nantes in France, became thriving centers of a new prosperity. Related industries—such as shipbuilding, sugar refining, distilling, and textile and hardware manufacturing—also flourished. All contributed much to the development of European capitalism and ultimately to the Industrial Revolution.

Northern Europe's commercial impetus reached West Africa in the middle of the seventeenth century. The Portuguese, after losing the whole Atlantic coast to the Dutch, won back only Angola. For a while, the Dutch nearly monopolized the trade. After seizing Elmina on the Gold Coast in 1637, the Dutch West India Company was taking almost 7000 slaves a year a decade later. In the 1630s the English also established footholds on the Gold Coast at Cormantin and Cape Castle; by 1700 they had seven other posts in the area. The French, meanwhile, acquired St. Louis on the Senegal in the north, which allowed them to control most trade as far south as the Gambia River. In the resulting triangular competition, the Dutch faced constant pressure from their two rivals but maintained their dominance from a dozen strong Gold Coast forts.

CASE STUDY *Portuguese Travelers in Africa*

By 1700 England was challenging Dutch predominance. Having defeated the Dutch at sea in the late 1600s, Britain next defeated France in the War of the Spanish Succession. At the ensuing Peace of Utrecht in 1713, Britain obtained the right to sell 4800 slaves each year in Spanish ports. Another advantage after 1751 was the British shift from a monopolistic chartered company to an association of merchants, which increased incentives by opening opportunities for individual traders. Finally, in the continuing Anglo-French colonial wars of the eighteenth century, the British fleet consistently hampered French operations. For these reasons, by 1785, the British were transporting thousands more slaves from West Africa than all of their competitors combined.

Despite this regional competition among Europeans, they conducted trade locally as a black-white partnership, largely on African terms. Africans leaders, who refused to grant any European nation a monopoly over the slave trade in their territories, were adept at playing one European group off another. Europeans, largely confined to their fortified settlements, recognized that they could easily be excluded from trade if they did not establish amicable working relationships with Africans. Hence, they learned to rely on African rulers who not only enforced their authority but also eagerly took profits from regular port fees, rents on the **barracoons** or slave stockades, and a contracted percentage on the sale of slaves.

MAP *African Empires in the Western Sudan*

Europeans also turned to a class of Westernized blacks and Afro-Europeans who served as critical intermediaries and power brokers between Europeans and

---

barracoons—Slave stockades on the African coast. Barracoons were generally run by Europeans and supplied by African rulers, who leased the land for the buildings to the Europeans. Slaves were held in the stockades until shipped across the Atlantic to European colonies.

This drawing is the layout of a European slave-trading center in West Africa in the mid-eighteenth century.

Africans. Many adopted European dress, and a few were lionized in Europe or became Christian missionaries. Some found work as guides, clerks, or interpreters, while others developed trading networks or participated actively in the slave trade. For example, Mae Aurelia Correia, the African wife of a Portuguese army captain posted to Portuguese Guinea, supplemented her husband's meager wages by venturing into the slave trade as well as by establishing peanut plantations that relied on slave labor. Most European traders were not so successful. Plagued by an unhealthy climate and surrounded by suspicious inhabitants, they led short and dreary lives in their remote exiles.

Most slaves awaiting shipment in West African barracoons had been kidnapped or taken in war by other rival tribes, although some were sold by their tribe or family to pay off debts, as punishment for breaking laws, or in times of famine and hunger. Only a few were seized directly by white raiders. Slaves were usually forcibly marched to the coast in gangs, chained or roped together, and worn down by poor food, lack of water, unattended illnesses, and brutal beatings. Once in the barracoons, where they might stay for several months, they were stripped and examined for physical defects by ship doctors and then displayed before captains who were looking to buy their cargoes. The bargaining was hard and complex as slaves were exchanged for cloth (Indian textiles were preferred because they were durable and their colors did not run in hot climates), manufactured goods, bar iron, agricultural implements, alcohol, and firearms and gunpowder.

About twice as many men as women were enslaved and shipped abroad. The traditional explanation for this imbalance is that men brought the highest prices in overseas markets because they could cope with the physical demands imposed on plantation laborers. But recent research has shown that women were just as likely to be assigned the harshest field work and that they fetched roughly the same prices as men. An important reason more women slaves were kept in Africa was that they were more desired as domestic slaves in royal households, as concubines, and as agricultural laborers, and that they were less likely to resist. The British Royal African Company reinforced this imbalance by issuing a standing order to their ship captains to purchase two males for every female.

After spending time in the barracoons, slaves met a worse nightmare during the notorious **Middle Passage,** the voyage that typically took a month from

---

Middle Passage—The collective name applied to the shipment of African slaves across the Atlantic throughout the time of the Atlantic slave trade. The voyage at sea generally took one to two months, depending on the destination, and most slaves were confined within the ship's hold. Mortality rates for the slaves ranged as high as 20 percent.

Africa to Brazil and two months to the Caribbean and the United States. Slaves were separated according to age and gender. Women usually huddled together on a ship's open deck. To prevent rebellions, male slaves were chained together in pairs, in lower decks, each person allotted a space 16 inches wide by 30 inches high. Children, who made up about 10 percent of slaves, were placed in separate quarters.

The treatment of slaves was abominable. White crews frequently resorted to threats of violence and lashings to control slaves. Slaves who contracted diseases were frequently thrown overboard. When slaves refused to eat, a special device, the *speculum oris* or "mouth opener," was used to force-feed them. Some slaves jumped into the sea while being exercised. In 1694 the British captain of the *Hannibal* commented on the despondency of slaves in these conditions: "The negroes are so wilful and loth to leave their own country, that they have often leap'd out of the canoes, boats and ships, into the sea, and kept under water till they were drowned to avoid being taken up and saved by our boats...."[1]

Through the early seventeenth century, the cramped and unsanitary conditions and poor diets of slaves on board led to mortality rates of as many as 20 percent on each voyage. Most died from the dehydration caused by gastrointestinal illnesses such as dysentery and communicable diseases such as smallpox and fevers. With improved diets and quicker crossings, the mortality rate dropped to less than 10 percent by the end of the eighteenth century. European crews on these voyages did not fare any better. Because of diseases such as malaria and yellow fever that they contracted off the African coast, their mortality rate was almost as high as the slaves.

Over 300 slave mutinies took place during the Middle Passage. Most occurred shortly after ships left the African coast. Most of them failed, and rebels were punished with savage brutality. In 1797 women slaves on the *Thomas* rebelled a few days before the ship was due to land in Barbados. As they were exercising on deck, they seized guns from an unlocked musket closet and took control of the ship. After freeing the rest of the slaves, they were no closer to freedom because none of them knew how to sail the ship. The ship drifted for more than a month until a British warship captured the slaves and resold them into slavery.

The harsh conditions of the Middle Passage did not shake the Christian faith of slave ship captains, who stood to pocket from 2 to 5 percent of the proceeds from slaves they sold. "This day," British slave trader John Newton confided to his journal in 1752, "I have reason . . . to beg a public blessing from Almighty God upon our voyage. . . ." After four voyages, however, Newton underwent a dramatic conversion and left slaving for the ministry. His legacy is his moving hymn of atonement, "Amazing Grace."

DOCUMENT
"A Defense of the Slave Trade"

The era after the Peace of Utrecht has been termed the slave century. Between 1600 and 1700, when the slave-trading companies were mostly state-chartered monopolies, some 1.5 million slaves were carried across the Atlantic. During the next century when much more trade was being conducted by individual captains outside the forts, more than 6 million slaves were taken to the Americas. With higher prices for slaves on Caribbean sugar plantations fueling demand, the trade peaked in the 1780s when 750,000 Africans were taken from West and Central Africa.

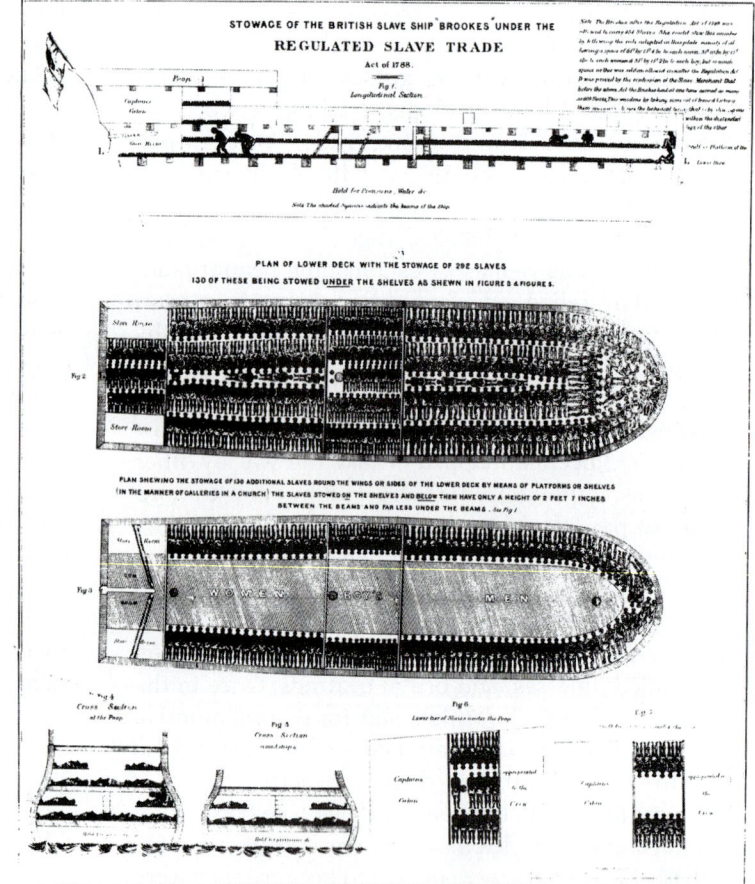

This diagram shows how slaves were packed into cargo holds for the notorious Middle Passage to the Americas. The plan was a model of efficiency as slave traders sought to maximize profits by filling their ships up to and beyond capacity.

Document   A Slave's Memoir

Kidnapped into slavery when he was eleven, Olaudah Equiano was taken by British slavers first to Barbados and then to Virginia. Sold to a Quaker businessman from Philadelphia, he eventually purchased his freedom. In later life, he became an antislavery campaigner in England, and he published a best-selling autobiography in the late 1780s that dramatized the horrors of the slave trade.

The first object which saluted my eyes when I arrived on the coast was the sea, and a slave ship which was then riding at anchor and waiting for its cargo. These filled me with astonishment, which was soon converted into terror when I was carried on board. I was immediately handled and tossed up to see if I were sound by some of the crew, and I was now persuaded that I had gotten into a world of bad spirits and that they were going to kill me. Their complexions too differing so much from ours, their long hair and the language they spoke (which was very different from any I had ever heard) united to confirm me in this belief. Indeed such were the horrors of my views and fears at the moment that, if ten thousand worlds had been my own, I would have freely parted with them all to have exchanged my condition with that of the meanest slave in my own country. When I looked around the ship too and saw a large furnace or copper boiling and a multitude of black people of every description chained together, every one of their countenances expressing dejection and sorrow, I no longer doubted my fate; and quite overpowered with horror and anguish, I fell motionless on the deck and fainted. When I recovered a little I found some black people about me, who I believed were some of those who had brought me on board and had been receiving their pay; they talked to me in order to cheer me, but all in vain. I asked them if we were not to be eaten by those white men with horrible looks, red faces, and loose hair. They told me I was not, and one of the crew brought me a small portion of spirituous liquor in a wine glass, but being afraid of him I would not take it out of his hand.

The stench of the hold while we were on the coast was so intolerably loathsome that it was dangerous to remain there for any time, and some of us had been permitted to stay on the deck for the fresh air; but now that the whole ship's cargo were confined together it became absolutely pestilential. The closeness of the place and the heat of the climate, added to the number in the ship, which was so crowded that each had scarcely room to run himself, almost suffocated us. This produced copious perspirations, so that the air soon became unfit for respiration from a variety of loathsome smells, and brought on a sickness among the slaves, of which many died, thus falling victims to the improvident avarice, as I may call it, of their purchasers. This wretched situation was again aggravated by the galling of the chains, now become insupportable, and the filth of the necessary tubs, into which the children often fell and were almost suffocated. The shrieks of the women and the groans of the dying rendered the whole a scene of horror almost inconceivable. Happily perhaps for myself I was soon reduced so low here that it was thought necessary to keep me almost always on deck, and from my extreme youth I was not put in fetters.

Questions to Consider

1. What effect did the deplorable conditions on the slave ship have on the psychology of the slaves?
2. What impact do you think Equiano's description of conditions on the slave ship might have had on the campaign in England to abolish slavery?

From Paul Edwards, ed., *Equiano's Travels: His Autobiography, The Interesting Narrative of the Life of Olaudah Equiano or Gustavus Vassa the African* (London: Heinemann Educational Books, 1967).

An African Pamphleteer Attacks Slavery

Denmark was the first European state to end the slave trade in 1803, but it was Britain's decision to abolish the trade four years later that had the most far-reaching consequences. The ideals of the Enlightenment, in addition to the lobbying efforts of abolitionist movements in England, had prepared the way for this act, but even more decisive factors were the declining profitability of Britain's Caribbean plantations, a rise in the price of slaves, and pressures from British industrialists, who found it more profitable to invest in wage labor in European factories than in the sugar plantations. Although a British squadron did patrol the Atlantic after 1807, looking for slavers, the slave trade was not dramatically affected. Around that time, however, West Africans began making adjustments to their trading relations with the outside world.

There was more to the Atlantic exchange than the trafficking in human beings. Africa's population was still expanding despite the devastation of the slave trade. New foods imported from the Americas, such as manioc (cassava), which could be grown in poor soils in forested areas, and maize (corn), soon became staples because they could contribute many more calories to people's diets than other mainstays, such as sorghum and millet. Europeans also introduced oranges, lemon, limes, pineapples, groundnuts (peanuts), and guavas to the African continent. In return, yams (sweet potatoes, which were the main provision for slaves on slave ships), sorghum, plantains, bananas, and melegueta pepper ("grains of paradise") made their way from Africa to the Americas. Groundnuts, which had come from South America, had made their way to the lower Congo region, where local people gave it the name *nguba*. After slaves from this area transplanted *nguba* to the Caribbean, peanuts were then taken to North America, where it was known as the "goober pea."

Whatever its unintended consequences, the Atlantic slave trade was a degrading experience for all the Europeans, Arabs, and Africans who participated in it. An estimated 12 million people were lost to Africa through the Atlantic slave trade over three centuries, and this number does not include the hundreds of thousands of slaves who died en route from their point of capture to the slave ports, in the cramped barracoons, and in the "floating tombs" that transported slaves to the New World.

African States and the Atlantic Slave Trade

Mungo Park, "Slavery in Africa"

Forms of domestic slavery were practiced in most African societies. Slaves were part of households and worked with the master's family in chores and agricultural labor. The slave status did not last long, and slaves were usually freed within one to two generations. In centralized states, more demands were imposed on slaves, who lived in separate quarters and were less likely to end their bondage through **manumission.** As the demand for slaves from plantations across the Atlantic escalated, African societies were confronted with the choice of whether or not to participate. Although some refused to participate, others seized advantage of the heightened demand for slaves to amass more power by investing in firearms and horses.

One example was the Yoruba kingdom of Oyo, situated inland on the savanna. Drawing on revenues derived from the slave trade, the Oyo *alafin* or king traded for horses from the north and assembled a cavalry that conquered the savanna region to the southwest all the way to the coast. Oyo's royal farms were tilled by slaves captured in warfare and the Sahelian slave trade, but as Oyo's rulers tapped into the Atlantic trade, surplus slaves were sold to European traders in exchange for firearms, cloth, and **cowrie shells,** which were a widespread form of currency in West Africa.

The *alafin* was not an absolute ruler. He governed with the advice of a seven-man council of state, the *oyo mesi*, and they in turn were overseen by a secret society of religious and political notables. If the *alafin* lost the backing of his counselors, they could force him to commit suicide. A turning point in Oyo's history came in the late eighteenth century when a senior counselor in the *oyo mesi* usurped the authority of the *alafin*. This bid for power set off a period of instability and internal revolts by tributary states and the Sokoto Caliphate (SOH-ko-to) that led to Oyo's collapse by the 1830s.

Of all the West African states, Dahomey (dah-HOH-may), located west of the Oyo kingdom, was particularly affected by the slave trade. Although a tributary state to Oyo for many years, Dahomey managed to maintain its autonomy, and in the mid-seventeenth century, it became a major power in its own right when its authoritarian rulers created a highly centralized state. Power revolved around the king, who passed his throne directly to his eldest son and appointed local chiefs who did not come from an established lineage. An influential figure in the palace was the queen mother, who was usually chosen from a recently conquered territory. Her presence helped to integrate her people with the king; she played a pivotal role in selecting a new king.

The royal elite rigidly monopolized the slave trade and every aspect of the economy. Everyone was required to perform military service, even women, who provided an elite palace guard and who, in the early nineteenth century, served as a key regiment in major wars against Dahomey's rivals, including Oyo. As a way of balancing power with male officials, the king allocated offices and responsibilities to the 5000 to 6000 women known as *ahosi* who served the royal court. Some were wives captured in warfare; some were wives provided by different lineages; and some were slaves. Although the legal status of female slaves

---

manumission—The practice of freeing slaves from bondage. Conditions in Africa for granting freedom might include a female slave who bears a child by her master or a slave buying freedom from a master for an agreed-upon price.

cowrie shells—The cowrie, a marine gastropod, is common in the Indian Ocean, particularly around the Maldive Islands. Used as a currency in West Africa, cowrie shells were but one trade item offered by Europeans in exchange for slaves.

From 1500 to 1800, Africans lived under a variety of political systems, ranging from small-scale societies to expansive monarchies. Powerful kingdoms emerged in every region.

was fixed, they were allowed to accumulate wealth and to assume many roles, including managing the king's resources, trading, owning private property, and serving as soldiers and ministers of state. Because of their unquestioned loyalty to the throne, female slaves were regularly appointed to the highest offices, including that of the queen mother, who did not have to be related to the king.

Another prominent regional state was Asante, a kingdom founded by Akan peoples in the gold-producing forests of the Gold Coast interior. Akan peoples had formed states based on the trade in gold, kola nuts, and slaves to the north and gold, slaves, and ivory to the Portuguese on the coast. But in the late seventeenth century, the Akan states were absorbed into the Asante kingdom, founded by *Asantehene* (king) Osei Tutu (OH-say too-too; d. 1717). Ruling from his capital at Kumasi, Osei Tutu transformed a loose confederation into a centralized state. He boosted his authority by using a consultative body, the Kotoko Council, and the Akan judicial system. He adopted the Golden Stool as the unifying symbol of Asante kingship and identity. When Osei Tutu died in battle, his successor, Opoku Ware (c. 1720–1750), extended Asante's boundaries to the savanna regions in the north and to the fringes of the forests in the south. As many as three million people lived within its dominion. The wars of expansion from the 1680s on were major factors in Asante's involvement in the Atlantic slave trade. Slaves captured in war or sent as tribute by conquered territories were deployed in gold mines and food-producing plantations or assimilated into families. However, once the Asante kingdom began selling slaves to European traders, its revenues from slave sales eventually eclipsed the proceeds from the gold trade.

The southwest coast, from the Congo River to the Cunene River, was the largest source of slaves for

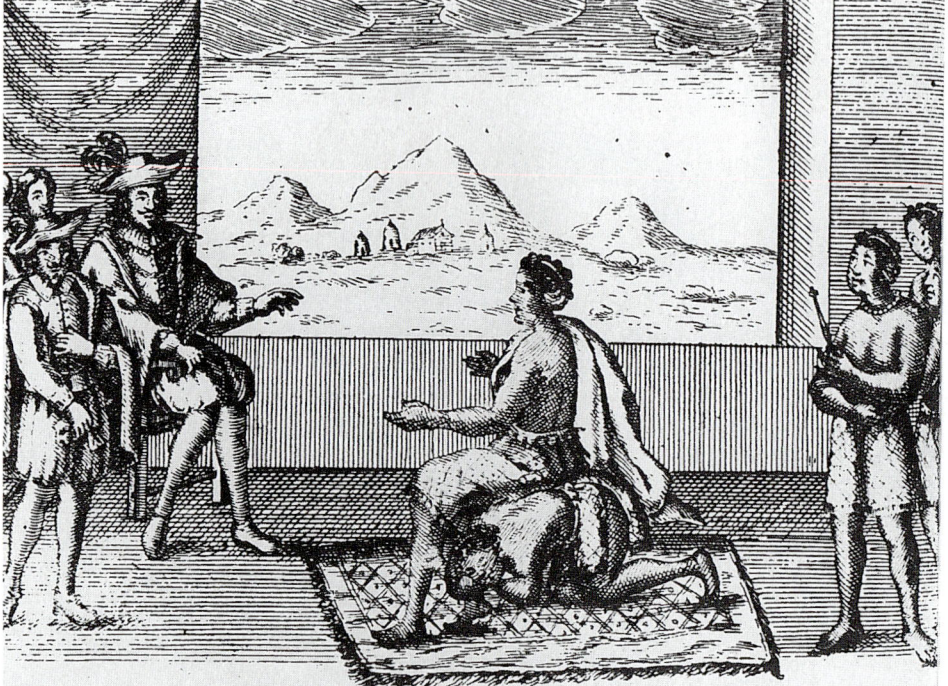

Queen Njinga of the Ndongo kingdom of Angola negotiated a treaty with the Portuguese in 1622. When an African had an audience before a Portuguese official, the African was normally expected to stand. Queen Njinga, however, ordered a female servant to kneel on all fours and sat on her back.

the transatlantic trade. Roughly 40 percent of all slaves taken during the slave trade era came from this region. Although Dutch and British slavers were active in the area, Portuguese involvement in the Kongo kingdom's affairs was particularly intrusive. The kingdom witnessed civil strife throughout much of the seventeenth century. The Portuguese took advantage of the disorder to invade Kongo in 1685, leaving the central government in shambles and fragmenting the kingdom into ministates.

A movement to restore stability and cohesion to the kingdom was inspired by Kimpa Vita (known to the Portuguese as Doña Beatrice), a woman of noble birth. As a teenager she claimed to have died and been reborn and to have been possessed by the spirit of St. Anthony in 1702. Her Antonian movement combined Kongo and Christian beliefs. She preached a personal religious experience that did not rely on Catholic priests, and her acolytes advocated the reunification of the kingdom under a king that she would choose. Although her message was very popular among peasants who longed for peace, it threatened Capuchin priests and royal factions vying for the kingship. After her opponents captured her, she was tried and convicted of treason and heresy and burned at the stake in 1706.

The Angolan hinterland suffered even more than the Kongo, and rulers had to maneuver constantly to protect their sovereignty. Queen Anna Njinga (c. 1581–1663) of the Ndongo kingdom was a survivor who was prepared to deal with most anyone. Succeeding her brother in 1618 in a kingdom that did not have a tradition of female sovereigns, she had to fend off hostile lineage groups that traditionally chose kings. To counter their opposition she signed a treaty with the Portuguese in 1622 that allowed slave traders to operate in her kingdom, and she converted to Catholicism. However, Portuguese support was short-lived, and Queen Njinga, who led her troops into battle, organized a spirited resistance. She also moved east, resuscitating the nearby Matamba kingdom and taking advantage of their recognition of queens as rulers. Proceeds from slave trading gave her the resources to build up an army. When the Dutch entered Angola in 1641, she seized an opportunity to break free from the Portuguese and allied with the Dutch. However, after the Portuguese counterattacked with troops from Brazil, she negotiated another treaty with Portuguese officials in 1656 that opened her kingdom to Catholic missionaries and to Portuguese slavers in return for Portuguese recognition of her rule.

The Portuguese eventually conquered Ndongo and other kingdoms. When Brazil's sugar plantations required massive numbers of slave laborers in the 1600s, the Portuguese, operating from their coastal ports of Luanda and Benguela, turned Angola into a vast slave-hunting preserve. Armed bands of Portuguese mercenaries regularly intervened in conflicts in African kingdoms, while the kingdoms of Kasanje, Matamba, and Ovimbundu (OH-vim-BOON-doo) assisted the Portuguese by trading or raiding for slaves in remote inland areas.

THE END OF THE SLAVE TRADE IN WEST AFRICA

■ *What changes took place in African societies as the Atlantic slave trade came to an end?*

On the West African coast, African societies were adapting to the tapering off of the Atlantic slave trade. Britain, which in the late 1700s was responsible for more than half of the slaves exported from Africa, and the United States had abolished the slave trade in 1807. Other European nations followed suit in subsequent decades. A British antislavery squadron patrolled the West and East African coasts, intercepting slave ships. Although the antislavery squadron managed to free about 160,000 slaves, it was a fraction of the overall slave trade. Between 1807 and 1888, close to 3 million more Africans were enslaved and shipped overseas, largely to sugar, coffee, and cotton plantations in Cuba and Brazil (see pp. 734, 736).

Britain and France established colonies in Sierra Leone and Gabon respectively for freed slaves. Sierra Leone's capital, Freetown, became the center for assimilating Africans from West, Central, and even East Africa and created a Krio or Creole community. A significant number of Krios were Yorubas who had been sold into slavery as a result of Oyo's wars. Some were Muslims who established mosques in Freetown. Others were among the first to take advantage of mission schools and to convert to Christianity. Some became missionaries in their own right. Samuel Crowther returned to his Yoruba homeland, and rose to become Bishop of the Anglican Church. Other Krios applied their entrepreneurial skills and knowledge to establish an extensive coastal trading network and tap into the legitimate trade.

Freed African-American slaves were settled in a territory established by the **American Colonization Society** (ACS) for former slaves that wished to return voluntarily to Africa and for blacks captured on slave ships by the American antislavery squadron. The ACS selected a strip of territory in the Cape Mesurado area and pressured local Africans into ceding them the land. However, the black settlers who landed after 1821 had a difficult time adjusting. They were susceptible to diseases and looked down their noses at agriculture. When they declared themselves independent from the ACS and founded Liberia (from the Latin word liber, "free") in 1847, their population numbered only a few thousand.

The Americo-Liberians (as the settlers came to be called) patterned themselves on the United States, adopting the English language and a constitution based on the U.S. model and naming their capital Monrovia (after President James Monroe). Although their official motto was "Love of Liberty Brought Us Here," they did not extend freedom to indigenous Africans, who were regarded as uncivilized and backward. A caste system developed in which Americo-Liberians dominated politics and exploited the labor of indigenous Africans, who were not allowed to qualify for citizenship until 1904. Although Liberia's economy sputtered in the face of intense competition with European traders and the civil service was riddled with corruption, Liberia managed to survive the European scramble for Africa and to remain an independent republic through the colonial period.

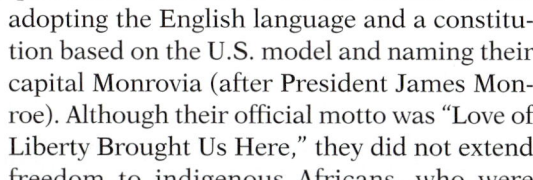
DOCUMENT
The History of Mary Prince

African societies involved in the transatlantic slave trade adjusted to its winding down in various ways. Some societies were so dependent on slave exports that they found it difficult to cope. Other societies shifted from exporting slaves to trading for more domestic slaves. The Asante kingdom in the Gold Coast acquired more domestic slaves to increase gold and kola nut production for trading with Europeans and the West African interior.

For many societies, the slave trade had been a negligible part of their overall trade, and African entrepreneurs and European merchants expanded their trading links. One African export Europeans sought was gum arabic, extracted from acacia trees and used for dyes in European textile factories. Another was palm oil, a key ingredient in candles and soap and the main lubricant for Europe's industrial machinery before the discovery of petroleum oil. Peanuts (called groundnuts) and latex were also important exports.

This shift to "legitimate" commerce did not necessarily lead to improvements or opportunities in the lives of many Africans. There was an increased demand for domestic slaves to till fields for certain products as well as porters to carry goods to the coast. Along the coast east of the Niger delta, where palm oil was a major export, palm oil production was organized on gender lines: Men cut down the nuts from trees, and women extracted the oil. Although the male heads of households were the main beneficiaries of palm oil production, they gave women the proceeds from palm kernels. The demand for palm kernel oil escalated in the 1880s when William Lever began selling Sunlight, a sweet-smelling soap made from palm kernel oil and coconut oil, to a mass market in England. Some women entrepreneurs used the profits from palm kernel sales to expand their involvement in palm oil production. However, the most important beneficiaries of the trade were not the producers but the rulers and merchants. In the Niger River delta, towns vying for control of the trade fought a series of wars.

ISLAMIC AFRICA

■ *What explains the rapid expansion of Islam in the West African Sudan in the eighteenth and nineteenth centuries?*

American Colonization Society—An organization founded in the United States in 1816 to promote the emigration of free African Americans to a settlement along the coast of West Africa that eventually was known as Liberia.

At the end of the eighteenth century, Islam remained a vibrant force in certain regions of Africa. Muslim West Africa was beginning to experience a cultural revival and was expanding its following beyond traders and rulers. Islam was carried by a wave of religious zeal, which arose on the Senegal River and spread east across the savanna regions to Guinea and the Hausa states and to the upper Nile. In East Africa, however, Islam remained a coastal religion with limited appeal beyond the Swahili city-states.

Meanwhile, across the continent in the west, Morocco was under the control of a dynasty that established itself in 1631 and remains in power today. Sultan Mulay Ismail (1672–1727) corresponded with Louis XIV of France and sent an ambassador to the court of Charles II in England. His uncontested power was based on a large standing army, including a force of black slaves who were recruited or captured in the Sudan as children and trained for specialized tasks. The sultan proved himself an exceptionally competent administrator, a wily military commander, and a patron of the arts. Morocco's economy was based on a combination of agriculture, trade, and privateering, although its piratic activity was minor compared to that of Algiers and Tunis. Under Mulay Ismail's successors, Morocco prospered. It was not integrated into the Islamic heartlands but remained connected to them by long-standing traditions of commercial and intellectual exchange. Each year Moroccan pilgrims and scholars made their ways by land and sea to the shrines of Mecca and to the great academic institutions of the Middle East.

In the West African savanna region, Muslim states had languished as the trans-Saharan gold trade declined after 1650. The Moroccan conquest in 1591 had broken the Songhay Empire into many rival small kingdoms, but as Moroccan administrators intermarried with local people, their ties with Morocco weakened. The Moroccans themselves were displaced by the Tuaregs, another group of desert invaders, in 1737.

The region around Lake Chad was the center of one of the region's most important states, Kanem-Bornu, which became an important center of Islamic learning. The high point of Bornu's power was during the reign of *Mai* (king) Idris Aloma (c. 1542–c. 1619). After being exposed to the wider Muslim world on a pilgrimage to Mecca, he imported firearms from North Africa and employed Turkish musketeers and advisers to command his army. To lessen the possibility of revolt, which had plagued his predecessors, he placed trusted allies, rather than close relatives, in key positions around his kingdom. For over a century, Kanem-Bornu exerted a stabilizing force in the region around Lake Chad, but its power steadily waned during the eighteenth century. By that time, the Hausa city-states, notably Kano, Katsina, and Gobir, were becoming prominent, as they profited from the expanding trade in slaves now moving across the central Sahara to the Mediterranean.

In West Africa the political map of the interior savanna dramatically changed in the eighteenth century as Fulani Muslim holy men launched a series of jihads and established new Muslim states across the region: Fulani-Tukolor kingdoms along the Senegal River in the west, the Sokoto Caliphate among the Hausa states and the sultanates of Tunjur, Darfur, and Funj in the region south of Egypt.

In the west, Islam rapidly spread through a series of successful holy wars led by Fulani holy men who criticized the lax moralities and heretical policies of West African Muslims, particularly the rulers. The Fulani were cattle-keepers who, by the fifteenth century, had spread across the West African savanna, often pasturing their herds in regions controlled by farming societies. In the highlands of Futa Jalon, the Fulani chafed at their Jalonke rulers' taxation and restrictions on pasture land. In 1725, they joined with Muslim traders and clerics to launch a *jihad* that by 1776 brought the area under Muslim and Fulani domination. Because of the war, slave raiding increased, and many captives were sold to work on local plantations or to European slavers at the Senegambian coast. In Futa Toro, in the middle valley of the Senegal River, other Fulani reformers joined with Tukolor Muslims to wage another *jihad*. They claimed that the Fulani elite had strayed from the Muslim faith, and they aimed to reestablish a kingdom based on Islamic law.

Their efforts inspired Fulani Muslims in the eastern Sudan—the most notable being Usman dan Fodio (1754–1817), son of a Muslim teacher and himself a scholar of some repute. When he began preaching in 1774, he stressed the fundamental principles of living a disciplined and devout Muslim life. Several decades later he began denouncing Muslim rulers in his home state of Gobir for ignoring Sharia law, for enslaving other Muslims, and for tolerating what he perceived to be immoral practices such as public dancing and the playing of drums and fiddles. Because his criticisms drew the ire of Gobir's ruling elite, he and his followers decided to leave for a safe haven to the west. When a Hausa ruler lifted the exemption of Muslims from taxes, Usman mobilized his students, Fulani pastoralists, and Hausa peasants and declared a holy war against Hausa rulers in 1804. Usman's movement succeeded in overthrowing most of the Hausa states and unifying them into the centralized Sokoto Caliphate. This new state, with a capital at Sokoto on the lower Niger, encompassed several hundred thousand square miles.

Usman was Caliph, while his brother Abdullahi and son Muhammad Bello (1781–1837) consolidated the caliphate. Usman retired in 1817 and Muhammad

Bello succeeded him. Sokoto's rulers introduced a government based on Muslim administrative structures and were patrons of Muslim scholarship and schools. Although a Hausa aristocracy was replaced by a Fulani nobility, the latter allowed Hausa political and religious elites in the emirates a measure of local autonomy as long as they paid an annual tribute and recognized the caliph's political and religious authority.

Usman dan Fodio's revolution brought mixed results for women. He encouraged education among elite women and supported women who disobeyed husbands who did not educate them. His wives and daughters were educated and became noted for their writings. However, women were expected to remain in seclusion and were excluded from meaningful roles in elite decision-making. The queen mother *(magajiya)* lost her power to veto decisions by male rulers and found her influence restricted to ritual matters.

The creation of the Sokoto Caliphate made little difference to the Hausa peasantry and slaves who served in households and tilled the fields of large plantations. Although elite women were freed up from agricultural production and expanded their production of indigo-dyed cloth, they were replaced in the fields by female slaves imported into the Caliphate. Hausa traders maintained their prosperous links with Tripoli to the north and the Atlantic coast. Their trade items included kola nuts, grain, salt, slaves, cattle, and cloth, which made their way to countries as far away as Egypt and Brazil.

AFRICANS AND EUROPEAN SETTLEMENT IN SOUTHERN AFRICA

■ *What was the impact of European settlement on African societies in southern Africa?*

While tropical diseases such as malaria prevented Europeans from permanently settling in many parts of Africa, southern Africa had a temperate climate that made it possible for first the Dutch and then the English to establish colonies of trade and settlement in the Cape. Although the Dutch settlers later created a myth that the region south of the Limpopo River was unsettled and thus open to whoever could claim it (see p. 577), the area had been populated for many centuries by indigenous African societies with varied economies and political systems. They vigorously resisted the expansion of European settlers into the interior.

The earliest inhabitants of southern Africa were San (SAHN) hunters and gatherers and Khoikhoi (koi-koi), hunters and gatherers who had taken up sheep and cattle-keeping. These were followed by Bantu-speaking groups that crossed the Limpopo River around the third century of the Common Era. These groups relied on mixed agriculture and herding cattle and sheep for their livelihoods. As they migrated into different parts of the region, the Bantu-speaking societies divided into two linguistic subfamilies. The Nguni (Swazi, Zulu, and Xhosa) largely settled to the east of the Drakensberg mountain range and spread down the Indian Ocean coast as far south as the Great Fish River, the point where the summer rainfall was insufficient for their agriculture. As this strip of land was hilly and well watered by rainfall coming off the ocean, Nguni families established scattered homesteads and formed small clan-based chiefdoms. Although splits in ruling families were common, as long as land was plentiful, factions could break away and form their own chiefdoms. The other Bantu-speaking group, the Sotho/Tswana (SOO-too/TSWAH-nah), populated the drier, rolling plains west of the Drakensberg Mountains. Because the grasslands were sparse, Sotho/Tswana cattle-keepers managed their scarce resources by clustering in villages and pasturing their cattle in outlying areas. Those nearest the Kalahari Desert created extensive villages, some containing as many as 10,000 to 20,000 people.

Small groups of Khoikhoi that inhabited the southwestern Cape were the first to make contact with European seafarers. In the late sixteenth century, Portuguese and English ships on the long voyage to India and Southeast Asia began making the harbor at Table Bay a regular stopover for rest and replenishment. Because they needed a reliable source of fresh meat, Europeans depended on the Khoikhoi, who were usually willing to part with their old and sick cattle, in exchange for iron, copper, tobacco, and beads.

The English and Portuguese were followed by the Dutch East India Company, which founded a permanent settlement at Table Bay in 1652. European settlers encountered a mix of African societies that had populated the region for many centuries. Because the company's primary goal was providing meat, fruits, and vegetables for its employees, its first governor, Jan van Riebeeck, had strict instructions to avoid friction and win the cooperation of the Khoikhoi. Only a few years later, however, the company made several fateful decisions that led to clashes with Khoikhoi bands.

Because their fruit and vegetable gardens did not yield enough, in 1657, the company allowed some of its soldiers to establish their own farms a short distance from the main company settlement. Dependent on its cattle trade with the Khoikhoi, the company decided to import slaves from elsewhere to work the farms. The first batches of slaves came from western and central Africa, but, thereafter, the company turned to the Indian Ocean for most. The majority of slaves came from Mozambique and Madagascar, while the rest were brought over from India, Malaya, and Indonesia.

Over the next 150 years the Dutch colony, populated by a mix of Dutch, German, and Scandinavian settlers and Huguenot refugees fleeing persecution in France, developed a distinctive character. Company officials and personnel made up an elite at Cape Town; a second group included slaveholders whose plantations in the Cape Town vicinity produced fruit and wine; and a third group, the Boers (*boer* is the Dutch word for "farmer"; the settlers did not begin calling themselves Afrikaners until the late nineteenth century), consisted of migratory pastoralists called **trekboers**. By 1800 there were about 21,000 Europeans in the colony, compared to a slave population of about 25,000.

The gradual expansion of company farms into the interior alarmed the Khoikhoi, who saw their grazing lands threatened by Dutch takeover. As wars broke out with Khoikhoi groups in the Cape peninsula, the trekboers steadily began conquering Khoikhoi territory farther and farther from the company settlement.

Boer families lived a pastoral lifestyle, relying largely on their own resources and preferring infrequent contact with company officials in Cape Town. Boer men believed that it was their birthright to stake out farms of around 6000 acres apiece. They expected their sons to claim other farms of the same size, usually at the expense of indigenous people. By 1800 the Boers had extended the colony's boundaries 300 miles north and 500 miles east along the Indian Ocean coast.

For most of the eighteenth century, Khoikhoi and San bands resisted Boer expansion by carrying on guerrilla skirmishing. The Khoikhoi and San groups that wanted to maintain their autonomy migrated farther into the interior; others, who lost their herds, supplemented the slave population as servants or apprentices to Boers. White settlers began to refer to Dutch-speaking Khoikhoi and San, freed slaves, and mixed-race servants as "Cape Coloureds."

The Boers' first contacts with Xhosa chiefdoms were at the Great Fish River in the early 1700s. Although they initially worked out a mutually beneficial trading relationship, as more Boers moved into Xhosa territory, conflicts erupted, largely over land and cattle. The first war between the two groups broke out in 1779. Over the next century, eight more were to take place between Xhosa chiefdoms and Europeans. Unlike the small Khoikhoi and San bands, which lacked unity, Xhosa farmers outnumbered the Boers and lived in chiefdoms prepared to defend their land vigorously. Moreover, the Boers' advantage in armaments was slight. Two wars between Xhosa and Boers ended in stalemates, broken only by the entrance of the British into the Cape in 1795.

When France invaded the Netherlands in 1795, the British responded to an appeal by the Dutch royal house and colonized the Cape. Controlling the sea route around the Cape of Good Hope also allowed the British to protect the passage to India. After handing control of the Cape back to the Dutch in 1803, the British returned several years later and established a dominant presence in the Cape and southern Africa for the next century. The British were primarily interested in increased commercial ties with the Cape by expanding wine and wool production. The British relationship with European farmers who actively participated in the market economy was more amicable than that with Boer cattle-keepers, who kept their involvement in the market economy to a minimum. Throughout the nineteenth century, British strategic and economic interests would repeatedly clash with the desires of Boer pastoralists to maintain their independent lifestyle.

African State Formation

In the first decades of the nineteenth century, African societies in southeastern Africa were swept up in a period of political transformation known as the **Mfecane** ("the scattering"). Its origins can be traced to increased competition by chiefdoms for grazing land following a series of severe droughts and for control of first the ivory and then the cattle trade with the Portuguese at Delagoa Bay. However, it was the Zulu clan, a minor actor when the Mfecane began, that became the region's most formidable military power.

The Zulu owed their rise in prominence to their king, Shaka (c. 1786–1828). When he was born about 1786, his father was chief of the Zulu clan, which was later part of the Mthethwa (im-TE-twah) Confederacy ruled by Dingiswayo (DEEN-gis-WAI-yoh; c. 1770s–1816). When Shaka's father rejected his mother, Shaka was forced to spend his childhood among his mother's people. As a young man, he enrolled in one of Dingiswayo's fighting regiments. Young men of about 16 to 18 traditionally went to circumcision schools for a number of months to prepare themselves for manhood. Because Dingiswayo needed soldiers who could be called into battle on short notice, he abolished the circumcision schools and enrolled his young men directly into regiments.

Shaka soon distinguished himself as a warrior, and he rose rapidly in Dingiswayo's army. On his father's death in 1815, Shaka assumed the chieftaincy of the Zulu. Shaka assumed the chieftaincy of the Zulu on his

---

trekboers—Migrant farmers who moved eastward from the Cape of Good Hope in the eighteenth century.

Mfecane—A term that historians use to describe a period of heightened warfare and state formation in the early nineteenth century in southern Africa.

Print of Shaka, King of the Zulus. Shaka established a major kingdom based on innovations in battle tactics and weaponry.

power was centered in his kingship and status was based not on descent but on achievement in the military regiments. He assigned his generals (indunas) to regimental villages around his kingdom. Groups of young women were also attached to regiments to produce food and carry out domestic chores. They eventually became the wives of the warriors who were not allowed to marry until Shaka gave his permission.

Shaka's repeated raids for cattle and captives throughout the area proved to be his downfall, as his regiments tired of constant campaigns. Several of his half-brothers and one of his generals conspired against him and assassinated him in 1828.

During the Mfecane, refugee groups escaped Shaka's domination by migrating to other parts of the region. Some headed much farther north, adopting Shaka's fighting methods and establishing kingdoms on the Shakan model in Mozambique, Zimbabwe, Malawi, and Tanzania. Still other peoples survived by creating new kingdoms that knit together clans and refugees. One kingdom forged in this way was Moshoeshoe's Basotho kingdom.

The son of a minor chief, Moshoeshoe (moh-SWESH-shwee; c. 1786–1870) gained a reputation as a cattle raider as a young man. He succeeded his father as refugee groups began streaming into his area in the foothills of the Drakensberg. To escape their raids, in 1824 Moshoeshoe moved his small following to an impregnable, flat-topped mountain called Thaba Bosiu. Over the next several decades, he creatively built a kingdom that became one of the most powerful in the region. Moshoeshoe accumulated vast cattle herds through raiding, and he used **mafisa**, a traditional practice of lending cattle to destitute men so they could establish their own homesteads, to win

father's death in 1815 and became leader of the entire confederacy a few years later, after Dingiswayo was killed in a trap laid by enemies. He regrouped his followers and won over others; eventually, he vanquished his opponents. He then began constructing, primarily by cattle raiding, a major kingdom between the Phongolo and Tugela rivers that dominated southeastern Africa.

Shaka was best known for adopting new weapons and battle strategies that revolutionized warfare. He armed the Zulu army with a short stabbing spear that was not thrown but used in close fighting. He employed the buffalo horn formation, which allowed his soldiers to engage an opponent while the horns or flanks surrounded them. He drilled his soldiers so that they could march long distances on short notice. He also transformed his clan into a major kingdom of about 25,000 people by assimilating large numbers of war captives. He created a new hierarchy in which

Moshoeshoe photographed in 1860, during the visit of Prince Alfred to South Africa. Although he liked to wear European dress on formal occasions with whites, he preferred traditional dress among his own subjects. Renowned for his diplomatic skills, he was able to maintain his kingdom's independence for many decades from Afrikaner and British colonizers.

their loyalty. Moshoeshoe married many times to build up political alliances with neighboring chiefs and placed his sons and brothers as governors in different part of the expanding Basotho kingdom. He

mafisa—A traditional practice among South African tribes of lending cattle to destitute men so they could establish their own homesteads.

> ## Document: "Song of the Afflicted"
>
> This song, collected in the 1830s by a French missionary residing in the Basotho kingdom, was a lament sung by women who were mourning their menfolk lost in battle.
>
> ### Song of the Afflicted
>
> Older Widows:
> *We are left outside!*
> *We are left to grief!*
> *We are left to despair,*
> *Which only makes our woes more bitter!*
> *Would that I had wings to fly up to the sky!*
> *Why does not a strong cord come down from the sky?*
> *I would tie it to me, I would mount,*
> *I would go there to live.*
>
> The new widow:
> *O fool that I am!*
> *When evening comes, I open my window a little,*
> *I listen in the silence, I look;*
> *I imagine that he is coming back!*
>
> The dead man's fighting sister:
> *If women, too, went to war,*
> *I would have gone, I would have thrown darts beside him;*
> *My brother would not be dead;*
> *Rather, my mother's son would have turned back half way,*
> *He would have pretended he had hurt his foot against a stone.*
>
> All the women:
> *Alas! Are they really gone?*
> *Are we abandoned indeed?*
> *But where have they gone*
> *That they cannot come back?*
> *That they cannot come back to see us?*
> *Are they really gone?*
> *Is the underworld insatiable?*
> *Is it never filled?*
>
> ### Question to Consider
>
> 1. Look for other songs sung by women in wartime or by men as they went off to war. How do the sentiments of this song compare with them?
>
> From M. J. Daymond et al., eds., *Women Writing Africa The Southern Region* (Feminist Press, 2003), pp. 85–86.

armed his warriors with battle-axes and formed a cavalry using ponies bred for the rugged mountain terrain.

Moshoeshoe is best remembered for his diplomatic skills. He was prepared to fight if necessary, but he preferred to negotiate wherever possible. On many occasions he managed to salvage difficult situations by engaging in diplomacy and exploiting divisions among opponents. When a band of Ndebele warriors raided his kingdom for cattle in the late 1820s, Moshoeshoe's forces easily repulsed them. However, Moshoeshoe sent cattle to the retreating Ndebele warriors so they would not go home empty-handed and provoke another raid from their ruler.

The Great Trek and British-Afrikaner Relations

As African kingdoms in southern Africa were undergoing a period of transformation, groups of Boers were preparing to escape British control by migrating into the interior of southern Africa. Prompted by the Napoleonic wars, Britain resumed control over the Cape Colony in 1806 to protect the sea-lanes around the Cape of Good Hope. The British were intent on expanding commercial opportunities through wine and wool production; the Boers resented any interference with their pastoral way of life.

Relations between the two groups deteriorated in the next decades. At first the British won Boer approval for a law that tied Khoikhoi servants to white farmers, but after a humanitarian outcry from missionaries over abuses of servants, the British instituted an ordinance giving Khoikhoi farm laborers equal rights. Britain also abolished the slave trade in 1807, driving up the price of slaves, and in 1834, it emancipated the slaves. However, this action did not improve the conditions of former slaves as most of them, unskilled and uneducated, ended up as free but servile labor on white farms. The last straw for the Boers came in 1836 when the British handed back land to Xhosa chiefdoms whose land had been conquered in a recently completed war.

Before the European conquest of Africa in the late nineteenth century, Africans in all parts of the continent were establishing new kingdoms or expanding old ones.

To many Boers, who had very little personal capital other than their herds and found it virtually impossible to purchase land in the Cape Colony, the solution was to escape further British interference by heading northeast for the high plateau, or **veld**. In the mid-1830s bands of migrants known as *voortrekkers* undertook a migration called the Great Trek in their ox-drawn wagons to lands where they could restore their way of life and maintain their domination over blacks. Each band numbered several hundred people. A total of about 15,000 *voortrekkers* eventually participated in the migration.

---

veld—The high plateau region within the interior of South Africa.

voortrekker—An Afrikaner farmer who migrated into the interior of South Africa in the 1830s as part of the Great Trek.

The primary transportation of *voortrekker* groups that migrated into the interior of southern Africa were light and strong wagons that were ideally suited to the rough terrain they were forced to cross. Despite their maneuverability, they could carry a surprising amount of household and other goods. This picture shows a wagon crossing a particularly difficult river.

Because the Boers were pastoralists, many African rulers treated them initially as another group of cattle-keepers migrating through their lands. When *voortrekker* groups reached Moshoeshoe's kingdom, he allocated land for them to pasture their cattle temporarily. Because African societies did not have a concept of private land ownership, Moshoeshoe was not ceding the land. However, the Boers regarded the land as their own and refused to part with it. One of Moshoeshoe's sons compared the situation to a person inviting a guest to sit down in his home and the guest taking ownership of the chair.

The *voortrekkers* established two republics: the Orange Free State and the Transvaal. For the rest of the century they solidified their control by engaging in wars of land conquest against African kingdoms. In the meantime, the British prevented the Boers from having direct access to the Indian Ocean by extending their own settlement along the eastern coast north of the Cape and founding the colony of Natal.

African rulers such as Moshoeshoe became adept at dealing with both the Boers and the British and taking advantage of the rivalry between them. He invited three French Protestant missionaries to reside in his kingdom so that he could draw on their knowledge of European life and politics. He used them as scribes to send diplomatic exchanges to British officials.

Moshoeshoe's overtures to the British were initially successful. When the British drew a boundary line between the Basotho and the Boers in 1843, they favored Moshoeshoe's claims. British policy shifted a few years later to absorb the Boer states, and Moshoeshoe saw the boundary redrawn to favor Orange Free State claims. He fought a British force to a draw in 1852 and, after the British changed their policy again and withdrew from the Boer Republics in 1854, he waged two wars with the Orange Free State. The first war in 1858 ended inconclusively, but in the second, the Boers were on the verge of destroying his kingdom when Moshoeshoe successfully appealed to the British government for protection in 1868.

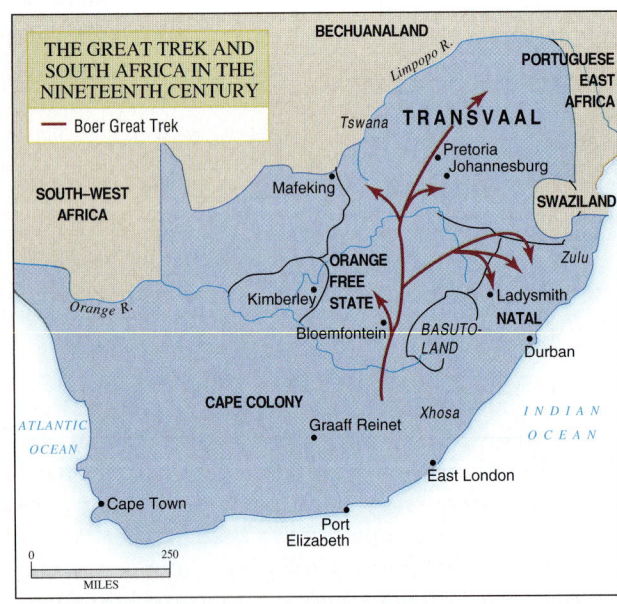

In the 1830s bands of Afrikaners migrated from the Cape into the interior of South Africa. Through the conquest of African lands, they established two republics, the Transvaal and the Orange Free State.

Discovery Through Maps

The Myth of the Empty Land

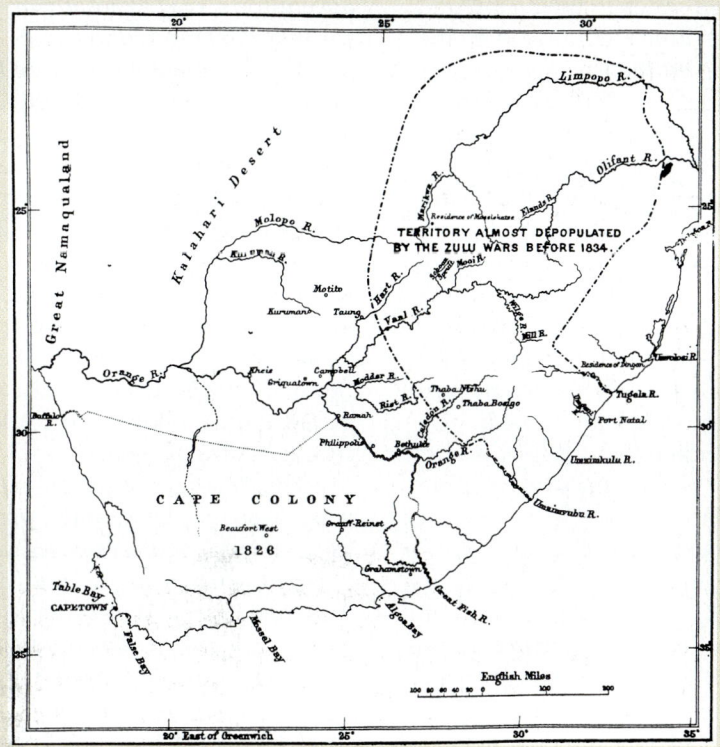

European settlement in various parts of the world was usually accompanied by the conquest of land from indigenous peoples. Because the settlers did not have a historic claim to the land, they often constructed their own versions of the past to justify their right to be there. In South Africa, one myth that white settlers created was that Dutch settlers arrived in southern Africa about the same time as Bantu-speaking peoples, the ancestors of most present-day Africans—in the mid-seventeenth century. Hence, white settlers could claim that, as they migrated from the western Cape into the interior of South Africa, they were moving into an unpopulated land that was up for grabs. Europeans could lay claim to the land, and they had just as much right to it as Africans did.

A variation of the "myth of the empty land" was based on a late-nineteenth-century map drawn by George McCall Theal, a Canadian who settled in the Cape in 1861. Theal's map shows the South African interior virtually depopulated because many Africans had been displaced by the wars of the Zulu king Shaka in the 1820s and 1830s (see p. 573). Thus, the Boers who trekked into the interior in the 1830s were settling on land no longer occupied by Africans. In a speech delivered to a Cape Town audience in 1909, Theal clearly revealed his motives for the way he drew his map. "We must ... prove," he declared, "to these people [Africans] that we were no more intruders than they were, and that they enjoyed as much as they were entitled to." He added, "In reality this country was not the Bantu's originally any more than it was the white man's, because the Bantus were also immigrants ... most of their ancestors migrated to South Africa in comparatively recent times."

Theal's "myth of the empty land" became an article of faith for many white South Africans until late in the twentieth century. His interpretation was a standard feature in South African history textbooks used in both white and black schools, and South African government propaganda relied on it to justify the apartheid system to the international community.

Questions to Consider

The ownership of disputed land has been a thorny issue in many countries.

1. Are there myths that settler groups have devised in other parts of the world to justify their conquests and domination of indigenous peoples and the land?
2. How accurate is the claim of Theal's map that "Zulu Wars" had depopulated the interior of South Africa before Afrikaners set out on the Great Trek?

From Christopher Saunders, *The Making of the South African Past: Major Historians on Race and Class* (Cape Town: David Philip, 1988), p. 39; Marianne Cornevin, *Apartheid Power and Historical Falsification* (Paris: UNESCO, 1980), p. 79.

In 1877 British policy shifted in response to diamond discoveries in the interior of the Cape Colony. Desiring to create a unified regional labor market, Lord Carnarvon, the Colonial Secretary, established a confederation of white-ruled states in the region and took over the Transvaal with little resistance from the Afrikaners (the name taken by the Boers about this time). The British attempted to win Afrikaner compliance by launching offensives against their main African rivals, the Pedi and Zulu kingdoms.

Although the Zulu had coexisted peacefully with British and Afrikaners for many decades, the British now perceived them as an obstacle to white control and manufactured a war against the Zulu kingdom. They launched a propaganda war, depicting the Zulu King Cetshwayo (c. 1832–1884) as an oppressive tyrant who had lost the support of his people and threatened the stability of the region. After the British issued an ultimatum demanding that Cetshwayo disband the age regiments, the basis of his power, within 30 days, a war was inevitable.

Contrary to British expectations, Cetshwayo had the full support of his army and most of his kingdom. The war started disastrously for the British when, in January 1879, the Zulu army caught a British column by surprise at Isandhlwana and overwhelmed them. A handful of British soldiers survived the battle. Cetshwayo hoped the British would end their aggression following their defeat, but they renewed their efforts and, six months later, put an end to the Zulu kingdom by carving it into 13 small pieces and exiling Cetshwayo.

MAP
South Africa

This victory did not improve British relations with Transvaal Afrikaners. In 1881 they rebelled against British rule and scored a series of military successes. The British agreed to pull out of the Transvaal, although they still claimed to have a voice in its foreign affairs.

AFRICAN STATE FORMATION IN EASTERN AND NORTHEASTERN AFRICA

■ *How was eastern Africa integrated into the global economy?*

During the eighteenth century, strong new kingdoms arose in the south central and eastern sections of Africa. Portuguese intervention in these regions, like that elsewhere in Africa, proved equally calamitous. In the seventeenth century Portuguese settlers in Sena and Tete in the Zambezi River valley had intervened to support the *Mwene Mutapa* or king in a civil war within the Mutapa state; they won concessions from the king to extend trading fairs and gold-mining operations in the Zimbabwean highlands. When the *Mwene Mutapa* then attempted to curb Portuguese adventurers, they deposed him and installed a successor they could influence.

The fragmentation of the Mutapa Kingdom created a power vacuum on the Zimbabwean plateau. Young men who lacked cattle to start their own homesteads joined the armies of wealthy patrons who were contesting for power. The most successful of these warlords was Dombo (d. 1695), who took the title *Changamire*. In the late seventeenth century his *Rozvi* soldiers conquered the remnants of Mutapa and other kingdoms in the region. Then, Dombo's army turned its attention to the Portuguese, expelling them from the trading fairs. Thereafter, the Portuguese were allowed to trade in the interior only through African agents.

The Portuguese presence in the Zambezi River valley was restricted to the **prazos,** huge estates run by Portuguese settlers (*prazeros*) who, over time, intermarried with Africans and assimilated into local African cultures. When they failed to eke out a living from agriculture, the prazeros became warlords whose slave armies exacted tribute from clients and hunted elephants for the ivory trade.

In East Africa, most states remained small, except in the region west of Lake Victoria, where two kingdoms, Bunyoro and Buganda, vied for power. Bunyoro dominated a confederation based on village-based chiefdoms that paid tribute to Bunyoro and contributed regiments for cattle raids against neighboring societies. Bunyoro's economy was based on hunting, herding, and agriculture. In the late eighteenth century, those clans most likely to protect themselves against Bunyoro's raids, formed Buganda, a rival kingdom to the northwest of Lake Victoria. Buganda's king (*kabaka*) allocated lands to territorial chiefs and distributed land to lesser chiefs. Buganda's staple food was the banana, which had a high caloric yield and thrived in the rich, fertile soils bordering Lake Victoria. The banana could be produced on an annual basis, unlike the shifting cultivation practiced in most savanna regions of Africa. Because cattle did not thrive within Buganda's borders, Buganda's regiments regularly carried out cattle raids in neighboring chiefdoms to the west.

In East Africa, Islam was largely restricted to the coastal area, despite the fact that two centuries of Portuguese tyranny were brought to an end in 1698

---

prazos—Leased crown estates in the Zambezi River valley under Portuguese control.

Buganda, a kingdom situated west of Lake Victoria, became a regional power in the late eighteenth century. A wide avenue led to the royal palace at its capital, Rubaga.

after a three-year siege of Fort Jesus by Omani Arabs responding to appeals of the Swahili city-states. The Portuguese retreated to their bases in southern Mozambique, but their expulsion did not bring peace and stability to the Swahili states, which fought among themselves. Pate, benefiting from immigrants from the Hadramaat that developed its trading capacity, eclipsed Kilwa as the leading Swahili state.

Oman, on the southeastern coast of the Arabian peninsula, was a major producer of dates. Oman's rulers took advantage of their new position and exported dates to East Africa in exchange for slaves for their plantations. In the late eighteenth century the Omani ruling dynasty, the Busaids, set up a headquarters on Zanzibar and established a stranglehold over commerce along the East African coast. Non-Omani traders were excluded from trading along the coast, and Zanzibar merchants had to give the Busaids a 5 percent tax on the worth of their goods.

Zanzibar became so important to the Busaids that Sultan Sayyid Said (1791–1856), who had made trips to the island for over a decade and who had built palaces for himself and his family, transferred most of his court and government there in 1840. The sultan also welcomed a British agent of the East India Company to reside in Zanzibar and to keep the lines of communication open with the British government.

The British had dispatched an anti-slavery squadron to the Indian Ocean. They first established a boundary that prohibited slave trading to India, but allowed the Omanis to sustain their slave operations on the East African coast to Oman and the western Persian Gulf region. Eventually the British began pressuring Said to give up his slave operations, and his compromise was to build up clove plantations on Zanzibar. In 1848, the British limited the slave trade to eastern Africa and its naval squadron aggressively stopped any Arab vessel thought to be transporting slaves. Zanzibar became a base for British ships and British officials dictated policy to the Omanis. Although Zanzibar did not become a British protectorate until 1890 it had long since lost its autonomy.

Throughout the nineteenth century East and Central Africa were increasingly drawn into the world economy through long-distance trade. Gold and ivory had long been exported to China and India, but now ivory was in demand by European middle classes for luxury items such as combs, billiard balls, piano keys, and cutlery handles. Elephant herds paid an enormous price; 33 elephants were slaughtered for every ton of ivory exported. The scourge of slavery also ravaged the region. During the nineteenth century, several million people were enslaved. Half of them were sent to southern Arabia, Sudan, and Ethiopia, while the rest ended up on French sugar plantations on the Indian Ocean islands of Mauritius and Réunion; on Brazilian sugar plantations, whose owners found West African slaves too highly priced; and on Arab-run clove plantations on Zanzibar and nearby islands.

The long-distance trade largely consisted of ivory and slaves brought from the interior to the coast in exchange for trade beads and cotton cloth, much of it produced by American textile mills. The trade between the coast and the interior opened up new opportunities for middlemen trading groups. The Yao, Nyamwezi (nyam-WAY-zee), Afro-Portuguese, Kamba, and Swahili Arabs controlled routes in different parts of the region and recruited thousands of porters for their caravans. As Swahili merchants established trading centers such as Tabora in the interior to facilitate and oversee their networks, the Swahili language increasingly became the lingua franca along trading routes. With imported firearms and slave armies, some of the leading warlords established conquest states based on their control over the slave trade. Mirambo (1840–1884), a Nyamwezi chief, and Tippu Tip (c. 1830–1905), who was of Arab and Nyamwezi parentage, carved out domains east and west of Lake Tanganyika, respectively.

This was the era when a distinct Swahili identity developed along the coast and the maturing Swahili language, assimilating Arabic words to a greater degree into its vocabulary, produced its earliest poetry. The primary language of traders was Swahili, which spread from the coast to far into the interior.

Many African kingdoms such as Rwanda were not dependent on the long-distance trade for their survival. Rwanda was composed of three main groups: the Twa, who were hunter-gatherers; the Hutu, Bantu-speaking farmers; and the Tutsi, a pastoral Nilotic people who were the last to settle in the area. Over the centuries Tutsi clans had established a patron-client relationship with Twa and Hutu clans, but the lines between the groups were not clearly drawn. Hutu and Tutsi intermarried and shared a common language, religious beliefs, and cultural institutions, and the distinctions between Tutsi patrons and Hutu clients were often blurred.

However, in the late nineteenth century the Nyiginya, a Tutsi clan led by King Rwabugiri, conquered other Tutsi and Hutu clans. Rwabugiri's state was highly centralized and favored the Tutsi minority, who served as administrators, tax collectors, and army commanders and controlled grazing land. Hutu chiefs were in charge of agricultural lands but tended Tutsi cattle and paid tribute to their Tutsi overlords.

While new states were rising in East Africa, the oldest African polity, the Kingdom of Ethiopia, was fragmenting. A source of trouble was the presence of Catholic missionaries. In 1607 Emperor Za-Dengel, hoping to attract more Portuguese arms and musketeers to counter his rivals from the nobility, invited Jesuit priest Pedro Pais to his court as a teacher, diplomat, and adviser. However, when Za-Dengel ignored Pais's advice and issued a proclamation banning the customary observance of the Saturday Sabbath, the nobles rose up and overthrew him. The Emperor Susneyos (soos-NAY-yohs; 1604–1632) consolidated the relationship with the Jesuits and secretly converted to Catholicism in 1612. He, too, subsequently forbade the observance of Saturday Sabbath as well as renouncing the monophysite belief that Christ had both human and divine qualities. Susneyos's public conversion to Catholicism in 1622 and the zealous policies of Bishop Alphonso Mendez, head of the Jesuit mission after 1625, incurred the wrath of the Ethiopian church. Mendez tried to Catholicize the Ethiopian orthodox faith by reordaining Ethiopian priests, reconsecrating the

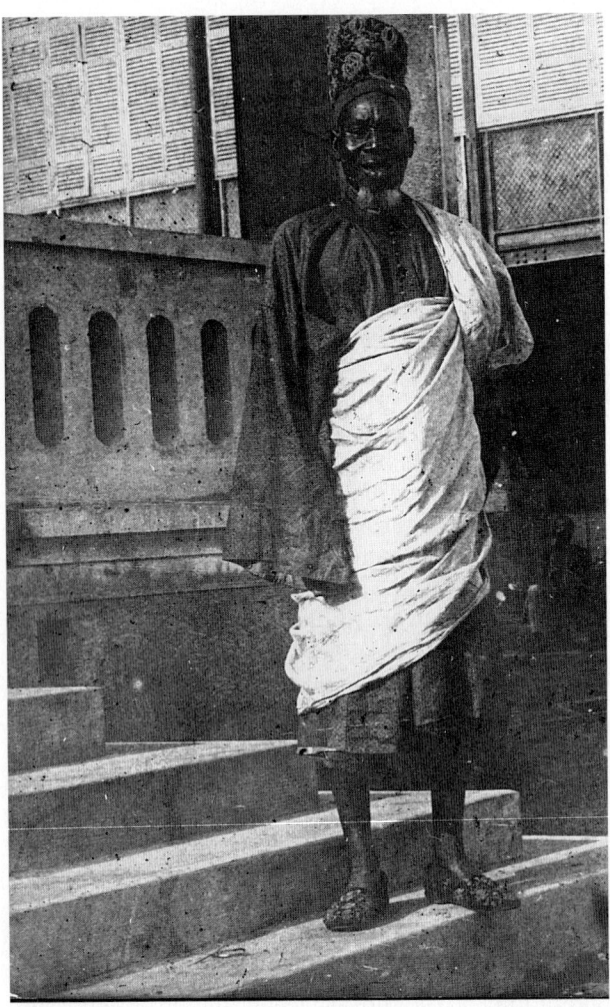

Born of Arab and Nyamwezi parents, Tippu Tip was a warlord who established a state west of Lake Tanganyika to exploit the slave trade.

churches, and banning circumcision. Land was transferred from the Ethiopian church to the Catholics. A bloody rebellion forced Susneyos to reestablish the orthodox faith in 1632. However, he had lost so much support that he abdicated. When his son, Fasilidas (fah-SIL-e-deez; 1632–1667), expelled the Jesuits several years later, a popular song captured Ethiopian sentiment:

> At length the Sheep of Ethiopia free'd
> From the Bold Lyons of the West . . .
> Rejoyce, rejoyce, Sing Hallelujahs all,
> No More the Western Wolves
> Our Ethiopia shall enthrall.[2]

During that era, Ethiopia's trading relationships with Europe and the Ottoman Empire declined, but slaves, coffee, and salt were still exported through the Nile valley and the Red Sea. Fasilidas founded his capital around 1635 at Gonder, a prosperous market town north of Lake Tana. The capital was situated close to the fertile agricultural lands of the Blue Nile and the juncture of three major caravan routes. Muslim traders, who dominated the trade between Ethiopia and Muslim states, lived in a separate part of town from the Christians.

During his reign, Fasilidas began reshaping the monarchy, continuing his father's policy of outmaneuvering his rivals by integrating the Muslim Oromo into his nobility. However, his policies eventually reduced Gonder's power, as the nobles expanded their personal fiefdoms around the kingdom and the Oromo asserted their autonomy. In effect Gonder's emperors became local potentates. One exception was Iyasu II (c. 1730–1755), who ruled with the support of his astute mother, Mentewab, who was crowned queen at his coronation and served at the same time as his queen mother. Her leadership abilities were demonstrated in 1732 when a rebel faction assaulted Gonder's castle, and she presented a plan of action to the council. "If I am a woman by the manner of my creation," she candidly told her councilors, "my gifts, which I have received from God, from below [on earth] and from above [heaven], are those of a man amongst men."[3]

An Oromo, Mentewab brought many of her ethnic group into the court and the army, and she became a master at dealing with court factions and intrigues. When her son died and was succeeded by her grandson, Iyo'as, she continued to play a pivotal role in his court. One of her strategies for extending her influence was granting *gults* (land grants) and endowments to churches, which in turn legitimized her and her ruling line through their chronicles.

However, following Iyasu's reign, civil war erupted, and provincial rulers asserted their power over Gonder. The lowest point came in 1769 when Tegray's ruler, Mika'el, conspired to strangle one emperor and poison another four months later. The years between 1769 and 1855 are known as the "era of the princes" because nobles entrenched their power at the expense of a series of powerless emperors who reigned in Gonder. A royal chronicler plaintively asked: "How is it that the kingdom has become contemptible to striplings and slaves?"[4]

This state of affairs ended in the mid-nineteenth century when Kasa Haylu, a noble from western Ethiopia, began conquering various provinces and consolidating the kingdom under one ruler. In 1855 he took the name Téwodros II (tay-WHO-drohs) and was crowned emperor. His goal was to modernize Ethiopia and build up relations with European nations. He depicted himself as a latter-day Prester John, the ruler of a Christian outpost surrounded by hostile Muslim states. He made overtures to the British government for support on that basis, but to the British, Ethiopia counted for little when compared to the Ottomans and Egypt. When Téwodros grew frustrated at the absence of a British response, he took hostage a group of Europeans, including the British consul to Ethiopia. Although he was trying to win concessions by holding the prisoners, the British grew tired of his impudence and dispatched a large Anglo-Indian expeditionary force to lay siege to Téwodros at his fortress, Maqdala, in 1868. By then, his iron-fisted rule had lost him the support of most of his nobles who refused to send soldiers. The British won a quick victory and freed the prisoners, but rather than submit to the British, Téwodros put a gun into his mouth and killed himself.

CONCLUSION

By the mid-nineteenth century many parts of Africa had been integrated into the world economy to varying degrees. In the mid-seventeenth century parts of Africa were harshly introduced to global commerce through the slave trade that wrenched millions of people from sub-Saharan Africa to service plantation economies in the Americas, North Africa, and the Middle East. Although the slave trade introduced new plants such as cassava and maize to the African continent from the Americas, the slave trade contributed little to African economic development and to the kingdoms that participated in it.

Some kingdoms such as Kongo and Oyo collapsed through their involvement in the slave trade, while many new ones were established. Islamic jihads created a series of Muslim kingdoms in the Sudanic region of West Africa. In southern Africa, new political states such as the Zulu and Basotho kingdoms were established during the Mfecane.

Once the plantation economy declined and the slave trade began to wind down in the nineteenth century and as Europe's industrial economy expanded, Europeans sought new trading relationship with Africans. A legitimate trade developed in resources such as palm oil and palm kernels that could be converted into soap, lubricants, and lamp oil for the European market. However the relationship favored Europeans as Africans sold raw resources and bought manufactured goods or finished products from non-African traders.

With the exception of southern Africa, where Dutch and British settlers seized African lands first on the coast and then in the interior, European contacts with the rest of Africa were largely limited to economic relationships in coastal areas and were controlled by Africans. However, in the last quarter of the nineteenth century, rivalries among the major powers of Europe led to a mad scramble in which European nations conquered and took direct control of almost all of Africa. The European colonizers imposed their own political boundaries and initiated economic and social changes that Africans are still coping with.

Suggestions for Web Browsing

You can obtain more information about topics included in this chapter at the websites listed below. See also the companion website that accompanies this text, **http://www.ablongman.com/brummett,** which contains an online study guide and additional resources.

Excerpts from Slave Narratives
http://www.vgskole.net/prosjekt/slavrute/primary.htm

This site contains over 40 first-person accounts of slavery in the Americas and African life written between 1682 and 1937.

Liberian Letters
http://etext.lib.virginia.edu/subjects/liberia/

This site features more than 50 original letters from freed American slaves in nineteenth century Liberia to their former masters and associates in Virginia.

Cape Slavery in South Africa
http://www.museums.org.za/iziko/slavery/slavery_world.html

A presentation of aspects of slavery (slave lives, resistance, emancipation) in the Dutch Cape Colony from 1658 to 1838.

End of the Slave Trade in Africa
http://www.fordham.edu/halsall/africa/africasbook.html

Documents regarding the termination of slave trade in Africa, from the Internet African History Sourcebook.

Literature and Film

A prominent early twentieth-century South Africa politician and journalist, Solomon Plaatje set his novel *Mhudi* (Passagiatta Press, 1986) during the wars of the Mfecane, while contemporary writer Andre Brink treated a slave uprising in the western Cape in the early nineteenth century in *A Chain of Voices* (Morrow, 1994). Beverly Mack and Jean Boyd, *The Collected Works of Nana Asma'u* (African Historical Sources, No. 9, 1998) is a collection of the poetry and other writings of the daughter of a famed West African cleric, Usman dan Fodio. Marcia Wright's *Strategies of Slaves and Women* (Lillian Barber Press, 1993) presents the life histories of nineteenth-century East and Central African women.

Suggestions for Reading

Several general studies on the transatlantic slave trade are Joseph Inikori and Stanley Engerman, eds., *The Atlantic Slave Trade* (Duke University Press, 1992), and Edward Reynolds, *Stand the Storm: A History of the Atlantic Slave Trade* (Alllison and Busby, 1989). For the effects of the slave trade on Africans, see Patrick Manning et al., eds., *Slavery and African Life* (Cambridge University Press, 1990), and John Thornton, *Africa and Africans in the Making of the Atlantic World, 1400–1680*, 2nd ed. (Cambridge University Press, 1998).

Usman dan Fodio's jihads and the creation of the Sokoto Caliphate are treated in Mervyn Hiskett, *The Sword of Truth: The Life and Times of the Shehu Usman dan Fodio* (Northwestern University Press, 1994). The decline of the Atlantic slave trade and the expansion of trade with Europe are traced in Robin Law, *From Slave Trade to "Legitimate" Commerce: The Commercial Transition in Nineteenth-Century West Africa* (Cambridge University Press, 1996).

Long-distance trade and state formation in eastern Africa are treated in Abdul Sheriff, *Spices and Ivory in Zanzibar* (Ohio University Press, 1987), and Edward Alpers, *Ivory and Slaves in East Central Africa* (Heinemann, 1975). Ethiopia's church and state are dealt with in Donald Crummey, *Land and Society in the Christian Kingdom of Ethiopia* (University of Illinois Press, 2000).

Slavery in the Cape Colony is examined in Nigel Worden, *Slavery in Dutch South Africa* (Cambridge University Press,

1985), and Robert Shell, *Children of Bondage: A Social History of the Slave Society at the Cape of Good Hope, 1652–1838* (Wesleyan University Press, 1994).

Norman Etherington's *Great Treks: The Transformation of Southern Africa, 1815–1954* (Longman, 2001) provides overviews of the Mfecane in southern Africa. John Laband has written a comprehensive treatment of nineteenth-century Zulu history, *The Rise and Fall of the Zulu Nation* (Arms & Armour, 1997).

Moshoeshoe's life is treated in biographies by Leonard Thompson, *Survival in Two Worlds: Moshoeshoe of Lesotho, 1786–1870* (Oxford University Press, 1975).

Studies on nineteenth-century South Africa include Timothy Keegan, *Colonial South Africa and the Origins of the Racial Order* (University of Virginia Press, 1996), and Jeff Peires, *The Dead Will Arise: Nongqawuse and the Great Xhosa Cattle-Killing Movement of 1856–7* (Indiana University Press, 1989).

GLOBAL ISSUES

SLAVERY

Why has slavery been so widespread?

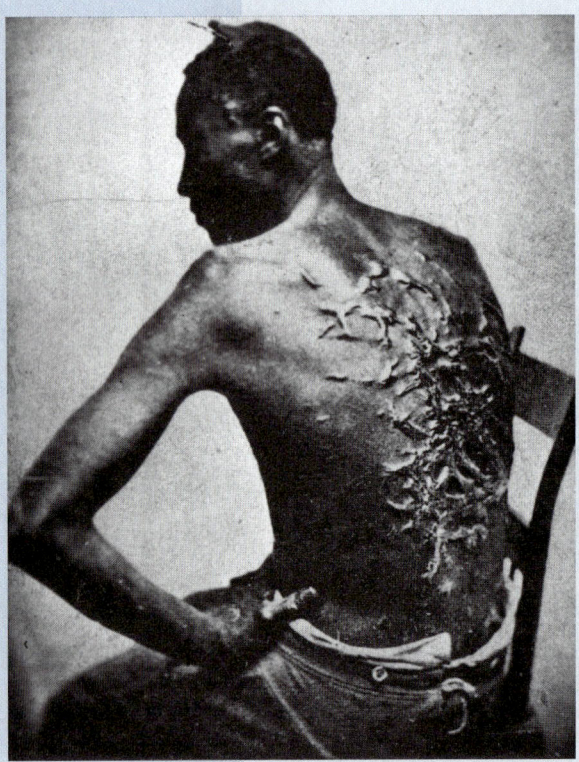

Back of plantation slave whipped by his owner, Captain John Lyon, Louisiana, 1863.

Slavery—the practice of people forcing other people into servitude and treating them as property—has existed for most of history. While the specific reasons why any one culture practiced slavery have varied, the simplest explanation for the existence of slavery is that, wherever and whenever it has occurred, certain people possessed the power to control other people absolutely, found it economically rewarding to do so, and faced little ethical or political opposition to their actions.

Traditionally, most slaves have been taken from outside the tribe, nation, or ethnic group that enslaved them, usually as war captives or kidnap victims. Most societies only extended social rights and protections to their own members, which made outsiders or "others" vulnerable to exploitation, particularly if they came from hostile communities. When slavery occurred within a group, those enslaved were generally singled out as punishment for criminal behavior, as debt repayment, or, as in the case of women and children, because of economic and physical vulnerability.

Most slaves have been used as agricultural workers. Agriculture was the primary source of wealth up until the nineteenth century, and the labor of slaves was needed to generate income for their masters. Slaves, however, have also served as artisans, soldiers, domestic servants, laborers, courtesans, prostitutes, and eunuchs. In certain cultures, notably the Ottoman and Arabic civilizations, slaves could rise to comparatively high stations when they showed great abilities as military leaders or administrators. In some cultures, slaves could buy their freedom or win it on the death of their masters. In others, slavery was a permanent condition, passed on from one generation to the next.

No one knows exactly when or where slavery originated. Some claim the institution is almost as old as the first *Homo sapiens*. The early Sumerians owned slaves who were usually captives taken in raids or wars. Early legal documents from the region between Mesopotamia and Egypt show the existence of debt slavery, a practice in which a person who could not repay his debt presented himself as payment. In fifth century B.C.E. Athens, one person in four was a slave, but their treatment varied widely, with some slaves considered members of the family while other slaves were forced to work in mines or as rowers in galleys. In ancient Rome, large numbers of slaves were taken from the various conquered peoples throughout the empire. Slave revolts were commonplace, often the result of brutal treatment in the large agricultural estates, where slaves served as both laborers and overseers. The founders of the Christian Church offered conflicting views on slavery. In the book of Colossians in the New Testament, St. Paul instructed slaves to obey their masters. Paul also urged the masters to treat their slaves as they would their brothers.

In China, war captives, criminals, and women of poor families made up the enslaved class as early as the Shang dynasty (1600–1027 B.C.E.). The archaeological record shows slaves toiling in workshops and fields, constrained by leashes and under the control of whips. Despite a long history of slavery, the Chinese showed an ethical discomfort with it. When the Emperor Wang Mang (8–23 C.E.) came to power, he forbade the buying and selling of slaves. Despite attempts to prevent slavery, the selling of indentured slaves remained a fixture of Chinese culture into the twentieth century.

Various forms of slavery have also existed in other Asian civilizations. Longstanding Hindu and Muslim legal codes justified the conditions under which bondage was lawful. Criminal activity could lead to enslavement as could being the target of a holy war. In the thirteenth and fourteenth centuries, the Mongols took so many Russian artisans as slaves that the knowledge of several crafts disappeared from Russia. Between 1400 and 1650, the Ottomans took over 200,000 mainly Orthodox Christian boys from their parents in the Balkans, converted these slaves to Islam, and trained them to be janissaries, elite infantry soldiers. Some of these slaves eventually rose to high positions within the Ottoman government.

Slavery was also practiced in the Americas. Mayan, Aztec, and Incan civilizations enslaved conquered peoples. Evidence of slavery can be found at the archaeological site at Cahokia in present-day Illinois and among the Plains Indians in the eighteenth and nineteenth centuries. When the Spanish conquistador Francisco Coronado traveled through the Pueblo towns of New Mexico in the sixteenth century, he found that people owned the slaves from present-day Kansas. Though a slave trade in the Americas predated European penetration, Europeans greatly intensified the trade after they integrated the region into their global trading networks after 1492.

Africa became the major source of slaves for both the Indian and Atlantic Ocean trades after 1300. The overseas trade grew progressively over the years as first Arabs along Africa's east coast and then later Europeans along the continent's west coast began to participate in and expand Africa's own internal slave trade. In the foreign and domestic market, slaves were paid for in cloth, tobacco, metal goods, weapons, or alcohol. Both African sellers and the European and Arab buyers found the slave trade to be profitable and continually tried to tilt the advantage of transactions in their favor.

In the Atlantic trade, Portuguese, Spanish, Dutch, French, and English merchants dealt in African slaves as part of their global commerce after the fifteenth century. Portugal started the Atlantic trade, and Spain and Holland followed suit thereafter, but by the mid-seventeenth century and throughout the eighteenth century England and France assumed leading roles in the trade. Ironically, at the same time these two nations were profiting from the slave trade, they also served as seedbeds for the Enlightenment, the intellectual and political movement that led to the principles of universal human rights. Enlightenment writers such as John Locke and Voltaire made fortunes investing in companies that participated in the slave trade, just as many of the nobles and bourgeoisie of their countries did. From the sixteenth century to the nineteenth century, some 12 million Africans were shipped across the Atlantic to the Americas and the Caribbean where most were forced to work in agriculture. Racism, specifically the belief that Africans were inherently inferior to Europeans and so deserving of enslavement, was a distinguishing characteristic of the Atlantic slave trade and slavery in the Americas.

In the Indian Ocean slave trade, Arab traders dominated from the fourteenth century through the sixteenth century. Beginning in the seventeenth century, however, the Dutch integrated the East African, South Asian, and Southeast Asian circuits of trade across the Indian Ocean, which had long been the "great highway" for eastern hemispheric migration, trade, and cultural diffusion. The Dutch transported slaves to their colonial holdings in the Netherlands East Indies (now Indonesia) and to other Indian Ocean ports. The volume of the Indian Ocean trade fluctuated between 15 and 30 percent of the Atlantic slave trade. By the end of the seventeenth century, slaves made up more than half the population of Dutch colonies and other Indian Ocean ports.

The international effort to abolish slavery is a relatively new movement that only began to take shape in Europe and its colonies in the middle of the eighteenth century. As the Enlightenment and English reform movements stressed the equality of all human beings, a growing number of people started to oppose slavery. Slaves began to resist enslavement more vigorously. Haitian independence in 1804 marked the conclusion of the world's first successful slave revolt. In the United States, many freed slaves joined the abolition movement. At the same time, the development of machines and more efficient methods of production began to reduce the demand for labor in agriculture, and other economic areas. By the middle of the nineteenth century the United States and most European nations had made slavery illegal. In other parts of the world, slavery continued into the twentieth century. Today, all governments of the world condemn slavery. Nevertheless, traditional forms of slavery still exist in remote and lawless regions of Mauritania, Sudan, Myanmar, Pakistan, and Brazil. The growing number of women and children transported across international borders and forced into prostitution or unpaid factory work also represent a new form of involuntary labor that has been likened to slavery.

Questions

1. Why have so many societies kept slaves?
2. Why did the treatment of slaves vary so much from one culture to another?
3. What conditions do you think finally led to the abolition of legal slavery? What allows various forms of illegal slavery to exist today?

CHAPTER 20
Asian and Middle Eastern Empires and Nations, 1650–1815

CHAPTER CONTENTS

- The Ottomans in the Early Modern Era
  DOCUMENT: Lady Montagu, Florence Nightingale, and the Myths of "Orient"
- Muslim Politics in Persia
- Early Modern India Under the Mughals
- The Qing Dynasty Before the Opium War
  DOCUMENT: Lan Dingyuan, County Magistrate: Depraved Religious Sects Deceive People
- Korea in the Seventeenth and Eighteenth Centuries
- Early Modern Japan: The Tokugawa Period
  DOCUMENT: Ihara Saikaku: "The Umbrella Oracle"
- Southeast Asia: Political and Cultural Interactions
- Europeans on New Pacific Frontiers

1600

1622 Ottoman Sultan Osman II deposed

1640 Tokugawa trade limited to Chinese, Koreans, Dutch

1644–1912 Qing dynasty

1650

1658–1707 Reign of Mughal emperor Aurangzeb in India

1662–1722 Reign of Emperor Kangxi in China

1680–1720s Golden age of literature and arts in Tokugawa Japan

1700

1707–1720 Maratha and Rajput rebellions curtail Mughal power

1718–1730 Tulip Period, Ottoman Empire

1720 Müteferrika Ottoman language press founded in Istanbul

1723 Afghan invasion of Iran

1724–1776 Reign of King Yŏngjo in Korea

1736–1739 Nadir Shah becomes shah in Iran, invades India

1736–1796 Reign of Qianlong in China

1750

1750s Beginning of Dutch domination in Indonesia

1752 Burmese invasion of Thailand

1757 Battle of Plassey

1759 Chinese confine European traders to Guangzhou

1768–1779 Three voyages of Captain James Cook

1771–1801 Tay Son Uprising in Vietnam

1782 Founding of Chakri dynasty in Thailand

1789–1807 Reign of Selim III, Ottoman reformer

1794 Dutch East India Company collapses

1794 Qajar dynasty emerges in Persia

1796–1804 White Lotus Uprising in China

The late seventeenth through the early nineteenth centuries were a period of sometimes gentle and sometimes violent transformation for the countries of Asia and the Middle East. The states in these regions faced a set of challenges prompted primarily by internal upheavals and but also by new external threats. The internal upheavals took the forms of regional conflict, economic turmoil, and population growth. The external threats coalesced around the ambitions of certain European states whose growing military and economic power enabled them to launch wars of expansion to the far corners of the globe.

For the three countries of East Asia—China, Japan, and Korea—these centuries were an era of great growth and continued domination of Eurasian trade and production. By the nineteenth century, however, these East Asian countries would face the kind of internal turmoil, fueled by external pressure, experienced earlier in Asian countries farther to the west.

In 1650 most of India and the Middle East was incorporated into traditional agrarian empires ruled by the Ottomans, the Safavids, and the Mughals. These dynasties capitalized on their military successes and durable state structures to project a sense of legitimacy and permanence to their populations. They cultivated and benefited from extensive trading networks reaching from East Asia to Europe. But no dynastic system exists free of internal struggles for power. As each empire experienced the effects of systemic changes in world economic systems in the seventeenth century, it simultaneously contended with challenges from within. For the Ottomans, the challenge came from the pasha households resisting the central authority of the sultan. In Persia, the shahs (kings) struggled to retain the loyalties of their tribal military forces. In India, the long rule of Aurangzeb was a high point in Mughal power. Soon after his death, though, sustained military struggles with the Hindu Maratha confederacy sapped the power of the empire, which had, before Aurangzeb's rule, sought to accommodate the faith of its Hindu subjects.

Southern Europeans, particularly the Portuguese, penetrated the Indian Ocean in the sixteenth century and, relying on advances in naval weaponry, rapidly militarized this important trading zone. Soon after the Portuguese and the Spanish altered the configuration of trade, the Dutch, French, and English moved into Asia, bringing with them their own contests and rivalries with one another. In 1600, these rivalries were mainly for a share of the Asian trade. Dutch power throughout East Asia peaked in the seventeenth century, and thereafter was confined to Indonesia. France and Britain then moved their rivalries to India (and the New World). By the middle of the eighteenth century, what had begun as the Europeans' quest for a share of Asian trade became both an effort to dominate that trade and a bold imperialist grab for territory. The Europeans' actions fundamentally changed the configuration of trade and politics in South, Southeast, and West Asia.

At the end of this period, large areas of Asia and the Middle East were still free of European political domination, but their continued independence was becoming more doubtful. The Ottoman Empire continued to rule an empire spanning three continents, and the Qajar dynasty had consolidated its rule in Iran. The major contenders for power in India were the Marathas, the Mughals, and a variety of regional warlords. Europeans, however, had begun to expand their influence in Asian economic affairs, and the British East India Company had itself become a regional force in South Asia.

East Asia continued to play the dominant role in the world economy until the early nineteenth century. Before the Industrial Revolution in England transformed the European economy, the inhabitants of China, Japan, and Korea enjoyed more access to a variety of products and lower rates of abject poverty than anywhere else in the world. China produced one-third of the world's entire economic output in 1750. Japan was the largest producer of silver until the late seventeenth century, which, together with the silver from the New World, supported the world's trade system. Many of the world's largest cities—sustained by sophisticated banking systems and complex transportation and communication networks—were located in East Asia in the eighteenth century. In the next century, the Industrial Revolution, however, gave Western imperialists operating in Asia decisive economic and military advantages, and this, together with internal wars and agricultural distress, led this dynamic region into a rapid decline.

THE OTTOMANS IN THE EARLY MODERN ERA

■ *Did attempts at modernization using European models strengthen or weaken the Ottoman Empire in the eighteenth century?*

By the seventeenth century the Muslim world stretched from the Atlantic to the Pacific. In a millennium, the spread of Islam from Arabia had indeed been phenomenal. But after 1700, Muslim rulers from Anatolia to Indonesia, like their counterparts in Africa, found it increasingly difficult to keep the European imperialists at bay. As European states expanded their military power and infringed on the routes of maritime trade from East to West, they developed new world systems of interregional trade that in part supplanted older commercial systems based in and controlled by Middle Eastern and Asian states and merchants. Control of trade in the eighteenth-century world slipped out of the hands of merchants in Istanbul, Isfahan, and Cairo. For the Ottoman sultans, who for centuries had terrorized European armies and dictated the terms of trade, that ideological and economic adjustment was not easily made. Even in the great Islamic empires, economic changes, vested interests, and prolonged warfare drained state treasuries and made it difficult for traditional rulers to restructure their empires and compete with the emergent powers of Europe.

CASE STUDY
The Ottoman Empire in the Late Sixteenth Century

Ottoman Reorganization and Reform

The early seventeenth century in the Ottoman Empire was marked by a series of rebellions, one culminating in the deposition and execution of the ill-starred Sultan Osman II in 1622. Although the empire was still vast and powerful, it had lost the glory of the Golden Age associated with the reign of Suleiman (SOO-leh-mahn) the Magnificent. Many explanations have been advanced for the weaknesses of the empire in this time period: corruption, the intrigues of harem women, retention of princes in the harem rather than their being sent out to govern and fight in the provinces. Although these were factors, the more telling reasons were changes in the global economy (linked to late-sixteenth-century inflation and population growth), competition among the various pasha households for position and prestige, and the reorganization required when the empire reached the limits of its expansion. Economic factors fuelled Ottoman rebellions when **janissaries** did not receive their pay, peasants fled the plots that could no longer sustain the burgeoning population, and demobilized auxiliary soldiers (with no hope of earning a living) became bandits preying upon the countryside.

The Ottoman Empire was surprisingly large and surprisingly long-lived. No empire of any duration can remain static, and the institutions of the Ottomans had to change over time. As the ranks of the janissaries were inflated, as the *timar* ("fiefs") of the traditional cavalry became hereditary, and as a state based on expansion and conquest exhausted its resources fighting long wars on two fronts, the empire began to take a different form from the one it had in the days of Mehmed the Conqueror. All of these changes occurred in the context of a shift in the global economy due to transatlantic discoveries and the rise of oceanic merchant empires like those of the Dutch and the English.

The Age of the Köprülü Vizirs

Mehmed IV became sultan in 1648, facing rampant inflation, a Venetian blockade of the Dardanelles, rebellion in the provinces, and a violent struggle among palace factions, including his mother, Turhan (TOOR-hahn) Sultan, and her rival, the old Valide Sultan Kösem (KOO-sem). These senior women wielded considerable influence and controlled considerable wealth in the palace system. In 1651 Turhan ended Kösem's long-term dominance of the harem by having her strangled, but Mehmed remained enmeshed in factional politics. This internal strife was compounded by a vehement struggle between groups of conservative mullahs representing the **ulama** (oo-LAH-mah) and **sufis,** both of which were contending for spiritual authority and influence in the capital. By 1656 Istan-

---

janissaries—An elite Ottoman infantry corps armed with gunpowder weapons and comprised mostly of converted Balkan slaves.

ulama—Islamic religious authorities; men versed in Islamic sciences and law.

sufis—Islamic mystics who sought contact with Allah through prayer and ritual dance; considered a heretical movement by conservative Muslims.

In the late seventeenth and early eighteenth centuries the Ottomans began to lose territory on their northern frontiers. As the eighteenth century progressed Russia emerged as a primary threat to Ottoman dominance in the region.

bul was in a panic as the Venetians vanquished the Ottoman fleet in the Dardanelles, provincial rebels seized much of eastern Anatolia, and food supplies became scarce. In the midst of this crisis, the empire required drastic measures; it found a man willing to take such measures in the person of a 79-year-old pasha named Mehmet Köprülü (MEH-met koo-PROO-loo; 1586–1661). Köprülü is a striking example of the power that elderly members of the military-administrative class could achieve if they managed to survive the challenges of multiple military campaigns and the competition within the palace system.

The sultan granted Mehmed Köprülü extraordinary powers. The pasha then suppressed the rebels in the provinces and broke the Venetian blockade of the Dardanelles. He used the sweeping powers granted him by the sultan to quell opposition and gain some control over the military. For two generations Köprülü and members of his family served as reformist **vizirs** (veh-ZEERS), attempting to bring some power back into the hands of the central government. They launched campaigns against Austria and Poland, took Crete, and reformed taxes. They also struck thousands of men from the rolls of the janissaries, which had become bloated with nonmilitary men who collected pay but did not fight. The problems of the empire, however, were not solved; conscription had depopulated the countryside, and Russia was emerging as a major threat to the north. **"Tax farms"** which the government sold to finance its wars, were becoming hereditary. The empire thus entered the next century in a precarious military and economic state.

The Tulip Period

The eighteenth century for the Ottomans is framed by a period of literary and artistic florescence at its beginning and a period of concerted military reform at its end. The century began inauspiciously, with a massive revolt in the capital that deposed the sultan and brought Ahmed III (1703–1730) to the throne. During his reign, the Ottomans were successful in battle against Russia but lost decisively to the Austrians. In 1718 Ibrahim Pasha became grand vizir and under his influence Ahmed launched a program of building, entertainments, and patronage of the arts that was later called the Tulip Period because of the fashion for extravagant gardens. Tulips were the rage, and rare varieties sold for fabulous sums. Ibrahim supervised the building of a pleasure palace for the sultan called the "Place of Happiness," a model for other palaces and their luxurious lifestyles.

In the Tulip Period, Ottoman elites became great consumers of European, particularly French, styles in fashion and decor, and European artists were imported to enhance life among the elite. Yirmisekiz Chelebi Mehmed (YEER-mee-SEH-keez she-LEH-bee), sent to Paris by Ibrahim, sent back reports on French zoos, gardens, women, publications, and shops as well as on arms and military schools. It was an era when the Ottomans became highly conscious of the need to emulate Western military tactics and technology and when the fashions of the French court were admired and imitated, in part, by elite Ottoman women. The luxuries of the Tulip Period were cele-

Images of women appeared more frequently in eighteenth-century Ottoman miniatures than in earlier Ottoman art. This late-eighteenth-century work depicting childbirth in the harem also illustrates the influence of European fashions in ladies' dress styles. While the midwife delivers the child, a cradle stands by to receive it.

---

vizir—A chief minister in the Ottoman government.

tax farms—Farms controlled by government administrators who could collect revenues from the farmers, remit most to the ruler, and use the rest to support their own interests.

brated in verse by poets, such as Nedim (d. 1730), who were experimenting with new styles: "This year, border your crimson shawl in mink, / And if the tulip cups are lacking, bring wine cups in their stead."[1] Tulips, fur-lined garments, and wine cups were all markers of elite status and wealth. Scholarship also continued to flourish under the sultan's patronage. The first Ottoman Turkish language press was founded by Ibrahim Müteferrika (EE-brah-heem MOO-teh-FEH-ree-kah) in 1720, producing maps, a dictionary, and works on science, history, and geography. The press had been opposed by some of the religious authorities but was permitted so long as it did not print books on religious subjects. The extravagance of the Tulip Period, however, did not mesh well with the conditions of economic depression and political conflict in which the empire found itself. Ahmed's reign ended as it had begun, with a violent rebellion in the capital that produced prolonged rioting and forced the sultan's abdication.

Eighteenth-Century War, Relations, and Reform

Although the empire still had its share of cultural and military successes, overall, the eighteenth century was characterized by the extension of more special commercial privileges (capitulations) to European states, loss of Ottoman territory, and a growing willingness to employ European military advisers, tactics, training methods, and technology. Travel, of Ottomans to Europe and of Europeans to the Ottoman Empire, intensified beyond the merchant activities that had for centuries connected the two regions. The Ottomans also began sending ambassadors to European courts and receiving ambassadors from more European states in return, a sign of the empire's growing weakness and need for communication. The empire had been a dominant power for centuries, and its rulers were generally persuaded of their own cultural superiority. But Ottoman military defeats prompted some Ottoman elites to consider significant military reform in order to duplicate or (they hoped) even surpass the successes of Europe. To that end, Sultan Mahmud I (r. 1730–1754) brought in the French mercenary Comte de Bonneval to help modernize the military; Mustafa III (r. 1757–1774) hired the Hungarian Baron de Tott to revamp his artillery corps and establish a military school; and Abdül-hamid I (ahb-dool-HAH-mid; r. 1774–1789) imported numerous foreign military advisers. All of these attempts were vehemently opposed by the janissaries, who saw them as a threat to their own status and position.

Throughout the century, the Ottomans fought intermittently with European foes and with a series of new military leaders in Persia. The government was entangled, in alliances and competing interests, with Britain, France, Austria, and Russia, all of which had designs on certain segments of Ottoman territory. The empire had already lost Hungary and Transylvania to Austria by the Peace of Carlowitz in 1699, and it surrendered to the Austrian emperor the right to intervene in the affairs of Catholics in Ottoman territory. A series of eighteenth-century wars with Russia culminated in the 1774 Treaty of Küchük Kaynarca (koo-CHOOK kai-NAHR-kah), under which the Ottomans paid a large indemnity, gave up the Crimea, allowed Russia to interfere in the affairs of Orthodox Christians in the empire, and granted Russia commercial access to the Black Sea. By granting foreign powers like Austria and Russia rights to intervene on behalf of Ottoman Christian subjects, the empire was allowing these states to undermine its sovereignty and autonomy. These concessions suggested that Christians in the empire could appeal to outside powers and circumvent the authority of Ottoman law.

Several factors demonstrate the weakness of Ottoman central control over the provinces. The semi-independent governors *(ayan)* and their private armies challenged the dictates of the palace in the provinces. In Iraq, Egypt, Tunis, Tripoli, and Algeria, Mamluk ("slave") or janissary garrisons created their own military regimes, often intermarrying with the local elites and refusing to cooperate with Ottoman decrees. A puritanical religious revival in Arabia, the Wahhabi (wah-HAH-bee) movement, founded by Muhammad ibn Abd al-Wahhab (1703–1792), joined forces with the Sa'ud family and seized control of Mecca in 1803, an enormous blow to Ottoman prestige. The Wahhabis were a true fundamentalist movement; they argued that Islam had to be purified and all innovations (such as Sufism) eliminated. This movement had a long-term and powerful influence on the development of Arabia.

Meanwhile, European powers also aggressively intervened in Ottoman affairs; Austria and Russia stirred up revolts in the Balkans, and in 1798 Napoleon invaded Ottoman Egypt. The Ottoman regime was powerless to stop Napoleon, requiring British assistance to defeat his forces. Although the British destroyed Napoleon's fleet and forced him to flee shortly after the invasion, the French occupation both demonstrated Ottoman weakness and left a lasting legacy of scholarship on Egypt produced by Napoleon's entourage. Their studies and images of Egypt, brought back to France, helped fuel a new European interest in travel to, and interpretation of the "Orient," its goods, and its culture.

Document: Lady Montagu, Florence Nightingale, and the Myths of "Orient"

In the eighteenth and early nineteenth centuries, the Ottoman Empire stepped up its exchange of ambassadors with the states of Europe. This same time period, particularly after Napoleon's invasion of Egypt in 1798, witnessed a dramatic increase in the number of affluent European travelers who journeyed to various parts of the empire. They came not only for diplomatic and military purposes but also to seek adventure, acquire antiquities, and see the sights. Among these travelers were women of the elite classes like Lady Mary Wortley Montagu, wife of the British Ambassador to Istanbul in 1716, and Florence Nightingale, who later served as a nurse in the Crimean War. Florence Nightingale traveled to Egypt in 1849–1850, nominally for her health, but actually to seek out and explore the remains of ancient Egypt and to avoid her parents' efforts to have her marry. Lady Montagu, well educated and a member of London's literary circles, came as the young and independent-minded wife of a foreign ambassador.

Like the accounts of all travelers, the letters of these women were colored by their own knowledge and expectations and by the limitations (affected, among other things, by gender and class) on what they saw and experienced of the cultures they visited. But attitude is also an important factor in the tales of travelers, and these two women were very different from one another. Both traveled in elite circles, were interested in buying up antiquities (including Egyptian mummies), and employed ethnic stereotypes; neither had much regard for the poorer classes. But while Ms. Nightingale was seeking a religious "mission," Lady Montagu was ecumenical and irreverent. While Nightingale found the Egyptians barbaric and less than human, Montagu learned Turkish, visited harems, and characterized the Ottomans as very human (and sometimes superior to the English). Nightingale seemed to prefer the architecture of Cairo to the Cairene people, while Montagu traveled veiled as a Turkish woman so that she could explore the city. Each woman suggested in her letters that she was communicating an image of the "real" Egypt or the "real" Turkey. But, in the end, Nightingale's letters convey a romantic reverence for lost antiquity combined with a horror of the Egyptian people (especially the peasants), while Montagu, writing more than a century earlier, presented a much more complex image of Ottoman beliefs and society.

You cannot conceive of the painfulness of the impression made upon one by the population here. . . . One goes riding out, and one really feels inclined to believe that this is the kingdom of the devil and to shudder under this glorious sun. . . . I cannot describe it. In Italy one felt they were children, and their dawn was coming; here one feels as if they were demons; and their sun was set . . . and out of these huts come crawling creatures, half-clothed, even in this country, where it is a shame for a woman to show her face. They do not strike one as half-formed beings, who will grow up and grow more complete, but as evil degraded creatures. I have never seen misery before but I felt, "Oh, how I should like to live here! What would I give to take this field!" But here, one turns away one's face . . . thanking God that one is not here to stay.

From Florence Nightingale, *Letters From Egypt: A Journey on the Nile, 1849–1850*, ed. Anthony Sattin (New York: Wiedenfeld and Nicholson, 1987), pp. 39–40.

[Letter to a Lady friend, 17 June 1717] I heartily beg your ladyships' pardon, but I really could not forbear laughing at your letter and the commissions you are pleased to honor me with. You desire me to buy you a Greek slave who is to be mistress of a thousand good qualities. The Greeks are subjects and not slaves [of the Ottoman Empire]. Those who are to be bought in that manner are either such as are taken in war or stolen by the Tartars from Russia, Circassia, or Georgia, and are such miserable, awkward, poor wretches you would not think any of them worthy to be your housemaid. The fine slaves that wait upon the great ladies or serve the pleasures of the great men are all bought at the age of eight or nine years old and educated with great care to accomplish them in singing, dancing, embroidery, etc. They are commonly Circassians and their patron never sells them except as a punishment for some great fault. If ever they grow weary of them, they either present them to a friend or give them their freedoms.

From *The Turkish Embassy Letters of Lady Mary Wortley Montagu*, ed. Malcolm Jack (London: Virago Press, 2000), pp. 103–105.

Questions to Consider

1. Lady Montagu was not an expert on slavery in the Ottoman Empire, but she did know more than her correspondents. What does her letter suggest about certain types of slavery in the empire and about English misperceptions?
2. What kinds of difference do you think it makes whether or not a traveler learns the language of the country she or he is visiting?
3. What do these letters suggest about the differences class and gender make in the ways a traveler portrays the society he or she is visiting?

The Reforms of Selim III

Selim III (seh-LEEM; 1789–1807) is often considered the first major Ottoman reformer, but his reform program was not new. Like several of his eighteenth-century predecessors, he proposed military and tax reforms as avenues to restore the empire to its past glory. Selim opened new technical schools to train officers and modernized arms production. He drastically cut the janissary rolls to get rid of noncombatants, but he mollified the traditional military corps by increasing pay and modernizing barracks. Offending the janissaries had proved disastrous for various of his predecessors. Most of Selim's efforts and resources, however, went to modernizing the navy and training a "new model" army of 23,000 men. It was a European-style infantry corps (with European-style uniforms), composed primarily of Turkish peasants and staffed in part with French officers. Selim hoped that this new army would help restore the empire to its former position of power and be more amenable to modern techniques of warfare. But the empire was not yet ready to break the entrenched power of its traditional military forces; Selim was deposed by a janissary uprising in 1807. Eliminating the janissaries was a task that would fall to his successor, Mahmud II (1807–1839). Although Selim's new army was disbanded, his reforms opened up the empire to further European influence, especially in the realm of military training.

MUSLIM POLITICS IN PERSIA

■ *How did Persian relations with the Europeans change in the early modern era?*

The Safavid (sah-FAH-vid) Empire in Persia suffered from many of the same problems that afflicted the Ottomans, although Persia was more isolated from the conflicts of the European great powers than the Ottoman Empire was. The tribal confederations in Persia remained powerful throughout the period of Safavid rule and, after the reign of Abbas (1588–1629), increasingly challenged the central government's authority. Despite weak rulers and an Ottoman invasion of Iraq, however, the Safavid Empire remained intact and relatively secure for almost a century after Abbas died. But the eighteenth century would bring in new warlords to rule the Safavid domains and place Persia in a military squeeze between the Russians to the north, the Ottomans to the west, the Mughals to the east, and the British to the south.

The end of Safavid rule was initiated by an Afghan invasion in 1723 that forced Shah Husein to surrender. Although members of the Safavid family controlled parts of Persia for some years afterward, this invasion effectively ended the dynasty's rule over the region. Both the Russians and the Ottomans capitalized on Safavid distress by invading northern and western Persia. Afghan rule was not destined to last long, however. A new Turkic military commander of the Afshar tribe from eastern Persia allied himself with a Safavid prince and defeated the Afghans. By 1736, Nadir (na-DEER) Khan had defeated the Ottomans in an engagement near Tabriz and declared himself shah ("king"). This new warlord reformed the government, reorganized the army, and favored both Sunni and Shia branches of Islam, thereby alienating the Shi'ite *ulama* and gaining some favor with the Ottomans. By 1747 Nadir had regained lost territories, conquered western Afghanistan, plundered the Mughal capital at Delhi, and extended Persian hegemony over the Uzbeks to the north. But his visions of unifying and ruling a Sunni and Shi'ite empire came to nothing when he was assassinated by his own men.

Persia was once again politically fragmented, but soon—between 1750 and 1779—another tribal warlord, Karim Khan Zand, emerged and gained control

Selim III's efforts to reform the Ottoman state were thwarted by the janissaries, who deposed the sultan, imprisoned him, and later assassinated him.

Middle East and South Asia

1622	Sultan Osman II deposed in an Ottoman rebellion
1637–1680	Shivaji Bhonsle, celebrated early leader of Marathas in India
1656–1691	Age of the Köprülü vizirs in the Ottoman Empire
1658–1707	Rule of Mughal emperor Aurangzeb in India
1690	British East India Company acquired land to develop base at Calcutta
1700	Mughal emperor grants British the right to trade and collect taxes in Bengal
1718–1730	Tulip Period
1723	Afghan invasion of Iran leads to end of Safavid Empire
1739	Invading army of Nadir Shah sacks Mughal capital at Delhi
1747	Durrani dynasty comes to power in Afghanistan
1765	Mughal emperor grants British administrative control over Bengal
1774	Treaty of Küchük Kaynarca after Russian defeat of Ottomans
1789–1807	Reign of the reformist Ottoman sultan Selim III
1794–1924	Qajar dynasty in Iran
1800	Anglo-Persian defense treaty

over most of the region. Karim Khan's reign was one of relative success and prosperity. He invaded Iraq, raided Ottoman territory, and encouraged trade relations with the British in the Persian Gulf. At his death, the country lapsed again into savage contention among tribal leaders. Zand successors ruled parts of Persia until 1794, but the Qajar (kah-JAR) dynasty, which was to rule until 1924, finally managed to replace them.

As the century drew to a close, Russia, Britain, and France were all competing for Persian trade, and Persia was drawn more directly into European power politics. An Anglo-Persian defense and commercial treaty in 1800 encouraged the Qajar shah to expect aid against the Afghans and Russia; when this was not forthcoming, he accepted a French military mission to train his troops. This entente collapsed when the French and Russians signed a temporary truce, demonstrating the precarious nature of alliances made with European states. The British then regained the advantage as advisers and commercial partners of the shah.

Thus Persia, like the Ottoman Empire, was increasingly drawn into the economic and military spheres of European powers, where once those same powers had come as petitioners seeking trade privileges in the Middle East. This shift in the balance of power in the late eighteenth and early nineteenth centuries did not radically alter life for the vast majority of citizens of these large agrarian empires. But it did begin to alter basic structures of economic and military organization and to produce a group of elite men who were more conversant with European ways.

EARLY MODERN INDIA UNDER THE MUGHALS

■ *Which domestic and international factors eroded Mughal power in the seventeenth and eighteenth centuries?*

The Mughal Empire was one of the world's wealthiest and most powerful states: Its rich traditions, art, and literature affected the whole Indian subcontinent. Mughal power culminated in the long reign of Aurangzeb (ow-RAHNG-zeb; r. 1658–1707), a period marked by military and administrative success. Aurangzeb's policies, however, began to alter the imperial order, based on tolerance, established by the great Akbar (r. 1556–1605). The new emperor, who learned the entire Qur'an by heart, was a champion of Islamic orthodoxy; he saw himself as a man of great piety and patronized Islamic leaders, reversing his predecessors' balanced respect for all religions. He destroyed a number of Hindu temples and schools, although it should be noted that he did support some other Hindu temples. His attacks on some religious institutions may have had as much to do with his punishment of those temples' Hindu patrons for their presumed disloyalty as it did with anti-Hinduism. He reimposed the *jizya,* the poll tax on non-Muslims, and dismissed Hindus from government service (he cut their numbers on his staff to just 25 percent). Until about 1679, he was occupied in securing his northern frontiers, so he did not push these pro-Muslim policies vigorously at first; this changed later when he adopted a less tolerant policy.

DOCUMENT
Aurangzeb, Mughal Ruler

These abuses did not provoke mass rebellion among the Mughal subjects, who were primarily Hindu peasants, but they did make Mughal rule intolerable to many. They provoked military challenges from Hindu warlords, which, accompanied by social and economic changes, weakened Mughal rule. Several factors may have undermined the Mughals after the reign of Aurangzeb. Though some historians blame the emperor himself for failure of administration, others contend that his era was fairly successful, leading to the rise of competing forces. For instance, the Mughals rewarded the Marathas (ma-RAH-tahs), a powerful tribal confederation in the south that had ambitions to expand their territory and power, with government posts for their successes and their support. The Marathas and others soon became political and military competitors. The growth of the Mughal economy and international trade also brought in New World silver; this, together with the development of cash crops, new technologies, and new trading opportunities—all desirable developments—led to competing economic elites. The Mughals had never controlled certain areas of India, and those areas' rulers saw an opportunity to develop increasing independence from the Mughals.

The Delhi Sultanate and Mughal India

One such group was the Marathas. To fight them, Aurangzeb virtually moved his capital to a battle camp in the Deccan, staying in a tent city in the field and heading an unwieldy host of 500,000 servants, 50,000 camels, and 30,000 elephants, in addition to fighting men. By 1690, after terrible losses, he had overcome most resistance, but the south could not be permanently pacified. Time and again, the aging ruler was forced to undertake new campaigns; when he died in 1707, it was in the Deccan.

Architecture and the arts during the reign of Aurangzeb were austere and religious. Wine, song, and dance were not allowed in courtly festivals. The emperor did encourage various projects in law and theology. As in the Ottoman Empire, when revenues declined, Aurangzeb employed tax farming to provide quick government income; tax farms were farms controlled by administrators who could collect revenues from the farmers, remit most to the emperor, and use the rest to support an army. The farms enriched corrupt officials at the expense of both Hindu and Muslim peasants. Peasants had little recourse against the government although they could take their complaints to the Islamic Sharia courts. After Aurangzeb died, Mughal authority was further decentralized, and South Asia was increasingly divided among rival kingdoms. A period of civil war ensued until Muhammad Shah (r. 1719–1748) succeeded to the imperial throne. Described by one contemporary as "never without a mistress in his arms and a glass in his hand," this indolent monarch made some effort to placate Hindus, with little practical result. Local Muslim dynasties ruled in the south and in Bengal; the Sikhs (SEEKS), a sect based on a Hindu-Muslim synthesis, became autonomous in the northwest; the Hindu Rajputs (RAHJ-poots), once Mughal allies, began to break away; and the fierce Hindu Marathas, whom Aurangzeb had tried to subdue over a period of 30 years, extended their sway over much of central India. The impotence of the empire was most effectively demonstrated in 1739 when the army of the Persian Nadir Shah burned and looted the Mughal capital at Delhi, killing some 30,000 and carrying away the imperial Peacock Throne, which would become a centerpiece of the Persian treasury.

Nadir Shah's invasion was but a prelude to the anarchic conditions that prevailed after Muhammad Shah's death in 1748. Mughal power met major military challenges from three directions: the Afghans in the north, the Marathas in the south, and later the British from their base in Bengal in the northeast. When Nadir Shah (1736–1747) was assassinated in 1747, his Afghan troops elevated one of their commanders, Ahmad Khan (1747–1773), to the position of shah. He took the title *Durr-i Durran* ("Pearl of Pearls"), after which his line was called the Durrani. Uniting the Afghans and conquering a vast territory—which comprised eastern Persia, present-day Afghanistan, the major part of Uzbek Turkestan, and much of northwestern India including Kashmir and the Punjab—he established a dynasty that would survive in Afghanistan into the twentieth century. During one campaign in India, Ahmad sacked Delhi (1756), decisively defeating the Marathas and helping to open the country to the British. At Panipat in 1761 his Afghans (employing their superior light artillery) crushed a huge Maratha army. But after Ahmad's death in 1772, the Afghans lost power in India, and his sprawling tribal state lapsed into almost continuous civil war.

The Afghans were a serious threat, but it was the Maratha Confederacy in the northwestern Deccan that had earlier emerged as the most powerful force to challenge Mughal supremacy. The first great Maratha leader was Shivaji Bhonsle (shee-VAH-jee BONS-le; 1630?–1680). At the age of 17, Shivaji began to build a small regional state by capturing forts and passes through the Western Ghat Mountains. He seized some territory from the kingdom of Bijapur, whose sultan sent an army under the general Afzal Khan to discipline him. Shivaji retreated to one of his hill forts, and in a famous episode, the two generals met to negotiate. Both bore arms, and in close combat Shivaji managed to disembowel Afzal Khan with a "tiger claw" (a steel weapon) concealed in the palm of his hand. Aurangzeb sent several armies to discipline Shivaji, but the Maratha chief proved illusive, raiding Mughal territory and the prosperous port of Surat on the west coast of India. When Shivaji was called to court to negotiate with the Mughal emperor, Aurangzeb publicly humiliated him. This episode set the stage for a new series of campaigns, during which Shivaji challenged the Mughal armies and extended his territory in the Deccan.

Shivaji's family had been agriculturalists, not members of the Hindu warrior or ruling caste (Kshatriya). But Shivaji was functionally a warrior nonetheless, and his rise to power illustrates the movement of a family over time from one caste group to another. To legitimize his rule, Shivaji sent to the holy Hindu city of Varanasi, where he persuaded a distinguished brahman to supply him with a Kshatriya genealogy and devise ceremonies of Hindu kingship. In these elaborate ceremonies, Shivaji offered sacrifices to the gods and received gifts from brahmans and nobles, thus reviving the notion of Hindu kingship in the subcontinent. In general, Hindu ceremonial was resurrected under the Marathas after long centuries of Muslim Mughal rule. After his death, Shivaji was immortalized in Maratha tales and ballads, and today he is celebrated as a hero figure by Hindu nationalists.

From the base established by Shivaji, various Marathas continued their wars of resistance against the Mughals, sometimes fragmented by civil war, sometimes losing territory or being co-opted by Mughal offers of position and wealth. Shortly after Aurangzeb's death, several Maratha leaders began to expand their territories into Malwa, Gujarat, and Rajasthan. In the second half of the eighteenth century, the Marathas gained control over central and north India, reducing the Mughal emperor to the status of puppet ruler. Elsewhere in India, Mughal power was challenged by the rise in power of tax farmers, princely rulers of territories, and provincial governors as well as ambitious lawbreakers. In the north and east, the Mughals also came up against the forces of a new power jockeying for position in the subcontinent, the British East India Company.

The Europeans in India

As was the case in Africa, the Portuguese were the first European power to establish themselves along the coasts of South Asia and exploit the rich commerce of the subcontinent. The Dutch, French, and English followed, and by the seventeenth century, all four powers had commercial bases in India. All were attracted by the rich trade in spices and jewels and especially by the wonderful variety and volume of Indian textiles. As in Africa, the Europeans did not initially penetrate inland; their commercial ventures were dependent on the elaborate and complex networks of traders, financiers, and middlemen already conducting trade into the interior and along the routes connecting India to China, Southeast Asia, Africa, and the Middle East.

Portuguese Church in Southern India

Of the European powers, the Dutch dominated in Southeast Asia, but it was the British who managed to gain ascendancy in South Asia. They established bases in India through negotiation and commercial exchange then later extended their power and territory by force. In 1601 a group of British merchants petitioned Queen Elizabeth to grant them a monopoly over trade with "the East." Although the newly chartered East India Company (EIC) claimed a monopoly over all trade between India and Europe, what it actually acquired was a monopoly over all trade between British territory and India. The peoples of "the East," of course, had no obligation to honor such charters, but this was an era of sweeping European claims to trade and territory in various areas of the globe; the charters did give such merchant companies a legal advantage over competitors among their own countrymen.

The Marathas in the Deccan rebelled against Mughal rule and won many victories against the Mughal kings. In the seventeenth and eighteenth centuries, first the Marathas and then the British posed formidable challenges to Mughal sovereignty.

The British presence in India exerted an increasing influence on the arts. This work of an Indian painter, inscribed in Persian and dated about 1760, depicts an official of the British East India Company smoking a water pipe and receiving an Indian visitor. Some British officials, like the one shown here, adopted South Asian furnishings; others adopted Indian styles of dress, food, and entertainment or married Indian women.

From an early **"factory"** in Surat, the British expanded to bases in Madras, Bombay (ceded to Britain by the Portuguese as a dowry for the English King Charles II's bride), and Bengal (the territory surrounding the mouth of the Ganges river). In 1690 a Company agent acquired a piece of land in the Ganges delta that the British swiftly developed into the commercial entrepot known as Calcutta. By 1700 the Company had a charter from the Mughal emperor to trade and collect taxes in the area, and by 1750 the population of Calcutta reached around 500,000. It was a major port for the Company and for Indian and independent European traders.

Calcutta provides an interesting case study for the ways (besides direct conquest) in which the British established their power in India. The Company used its bases to extend its commercial affairs inland and employed its own private army to forge alliances with local rulers. Both sides benefited (the local rulers receiving money and military assistance against their enemies from the British) although various local lords resisted British incursions. Because the balance of trade was much in favor of India, Britain sent thousands of pounds in silver to pay for its purchases. By 1800 the wealth (especially taxes) generated by the Company's activities provided a substantial portion of Britain's income.

Abu Taleb on the West and Western Influence

The British East India Company in the eighteenth century provides a clear illustration of the establishment of a new world order based on seaborne circuits of trade and the extension of European imperial power beyond the port cities of Asia and Africa. Where the Dutch, British, and French established agricultural estate colonies in Africa and Southeast Asia, in South Asia they directed their attentions, at least initially, primarily to commercial establishments. There were direct links, however, between these regions, as the Indian Ocean served not only as a medium for the transport of goods to the West but also as an arena for the circulation of slaves, workers, and mariners among the burgeoning colonies of imperial Europe.

The trade conducted by the EIC is also noteworthy for its role in **mercantilism** in the eighteenth century and for its political role in the latter part of the century. By 1750, the British market was saturated with Indian calicoes and other fabrics of high quality and low cost. Low cost was possible because Indian textile workers could maintain a decent standard of living at lower wages than could their counterparts in Europe. This was due to the higher productivity of India's agriculture, which led to lower food prices in India than in Europe; workers thus needed less income to feed themselves. The cost of fabric was kept down, and resources were freed up for other types of investment. Indian textile production grew rapidly. India accounted for 25 percent of all world manufacturing in 1750 due to enormous textile sales to Europe, Asia, and the Americas. Though the British government responded to the large volume of textile

---

factory—European commercial office and warehouse in India or China, headed by a factor.

mercantilism—Economic and political policy that regarded wealth as a measure of a nation's strength; mercantilist countries promoted companies that helped produce a favorable balance of trade.

imports by imposing stiff tariffs, the volume of trade remained high; the EIC carried this profitable trade.

In the second half of the century, the East India Company became increasingly involved in local politics, building its own domain in Bengal and challenging the authority of the local ruler, Siraj ud-Dawla (see-RAHJ ood-DOW-lah), who asserted his independence as Mughal power declined. In 1756, Siraj ud-Dawla retaliated by seizing Calcutta and demanding increased payments from the EIC for the privilege of trading there. The Company then sent a military force of 2000 men under Robert Clive, who crushed Siraj ud-Dawla's army in the battle of Plassey in 1757. Clive went on to defeat the French and Dutch establishments in Bengal. In 1760, the British defeated the French at Pondicherry, a decisive battle in the Seven Years' War (1756–1763). By the Treaty of Allahabad (al-LAH-ah-bahd) in 1765, the Mughal emperor granted the British administrative control of Bengal. The Company thus became one of many Indian provincial "lords." The British then extended their power inland using a combination of military force and commercial treaty. They gained hegemony over a great circuit of trade from India to China and to England, exchanging Indian opium for Chinese tea (all the rage in England) and English silver for Indian silk.

By the end of the century, the Mughal ruler Shah Alam II was collecting a British pension, and William Jones and other officials were cultivating British interest in Sanskrit classics (as the entourage of Napoleon cultivated scholarship in Egyptian and Arabic cultures). While the Ottoman and Persian empires suffered military defeats and increasing economic subordination to European powers in this era, the Mughal Empire surrendered large segments of its territory, first to the Marathas and then to the British. The Mughals could only look on as the British East India Company, employing Indian armies, extended its sway over the subcontinent.

THE QING DYNASTY BEFORE THE OPIUM WAR

■ *How did the Manchu emperors make their dynasty acceptable to ethnic Chinese?*

Between 1644, when the Qing rulers took Beijing, and the early decades of the nineteenth century, China was the most populous and prosperous country on earth. In 1700, China, Europe, and India each accounted for approximately 23 percent of the world's gross domestic product. In 1820, China's share had risen to about 33 percent and Europe's to about 27 percent, while India's declined to about 16 percent. China produced one-third of the world's manufactured goods in 1750, but that percentage began to decline rapidly after 1820. What historians call the "long eighteenth century"—from the late seventeenth century to the early nineteenth—was an era of splendor and growth for China. Its economy grew steadily while its literature, art, and philosophy evoked admiration from Asian and European intellec-

A major opponent to British incursion into India was Tipu Sultan, called the "Tiger of Mysore." This painting by an unknown Indian artist shows British soldiers unsuccessfully fighting Tipu's forces in 1780. The British defeated Tipu in 1799.

Qing China

1644	Founding of the Qing (Manchu) dynasty
1662–1722	Reign of Kangxi
1736–1796	Reign of Qianlong
1759	Guangzhou (Canton) system established
1793	Macartney Mission to China
1796–1804	White Lotus uprising

tuals alike. Although impossible to predict, however, the seeds of later decline were already being sown by 1820.

The Manchus came to power after Ming loyalists called on them to help put down the rebel Li Zicheng (LEE zuh-CHUNG) in Beijing. The Manchus had developed a state north of the Great Wall in the decades before 1644. The inhabitants of Manchuria were controlled by military units called "banners"; their previously tribal government was organized as a bureaucracy with laws modeled on the Ming code; and script was created to represent the spoken language. In the 1630s, Hong Taiji (TAI-jee), the son of the Manchu Nurhachi (noor-HAH-chee; 1559–1616) who had begun the process of Manchu state-building several decades earlier, proclaimed the founding of the Qing (CHING) dynasty, thereby challenging the Ming's right to rule China. Still, the Manchus seemed preferable to the rebel Chinese, and Ming loyalists like General Wu Sangui (WOO sahn-GWEH; 1612–1678) asked for Manchu assistance.

Manchu Imperial Rule

Upon coming over the Great Wall, the Manchus showed they meant to rule. They honored the Ming by giving a proper burial to the last Ming emperor but soon moved the Chinese inhabitants of Beijing to the southern part of the city while they occupied the northern part. Land was confiscated from Chinese farmers to support the Qing military banner forces. Men were required to adopt the Qing queue hairstyle as an indication of loyalty, and women were prohibited from binding their feet. The former, of course, could be enforced, while the latter, a more private practice, could be continued by Han Chinese as a covert indicator of their non-Manchu ethnicity, as women were more often indoors and their feet remained unseen.

The Manchus' first order of business was establishing military control of the Chinese realm. Emperor Shunzhi (SHOON-jih; r. 1644–1661) and his powerful successor Kangxi (KANG-shee; r. 1662–1722) conquered Ming loyalist factions in the south with the help of General Wu Sangui. When the Ming loyalists mounted armed resistance, they were brutally suppressed. One resister, Zheng Chenggong (ZHUNG cheng-GONG; 1624–1662), known to Westerners of his day as Coxinga, fled to Taiwan where he ousted the Dutch occupiers in 1662. His son held out until Kangxi's forces defeated him in 1683. The last uprising against the Qing was staged by Wu Sangui himself, but like the others, he and his followers were defeated in 1681.

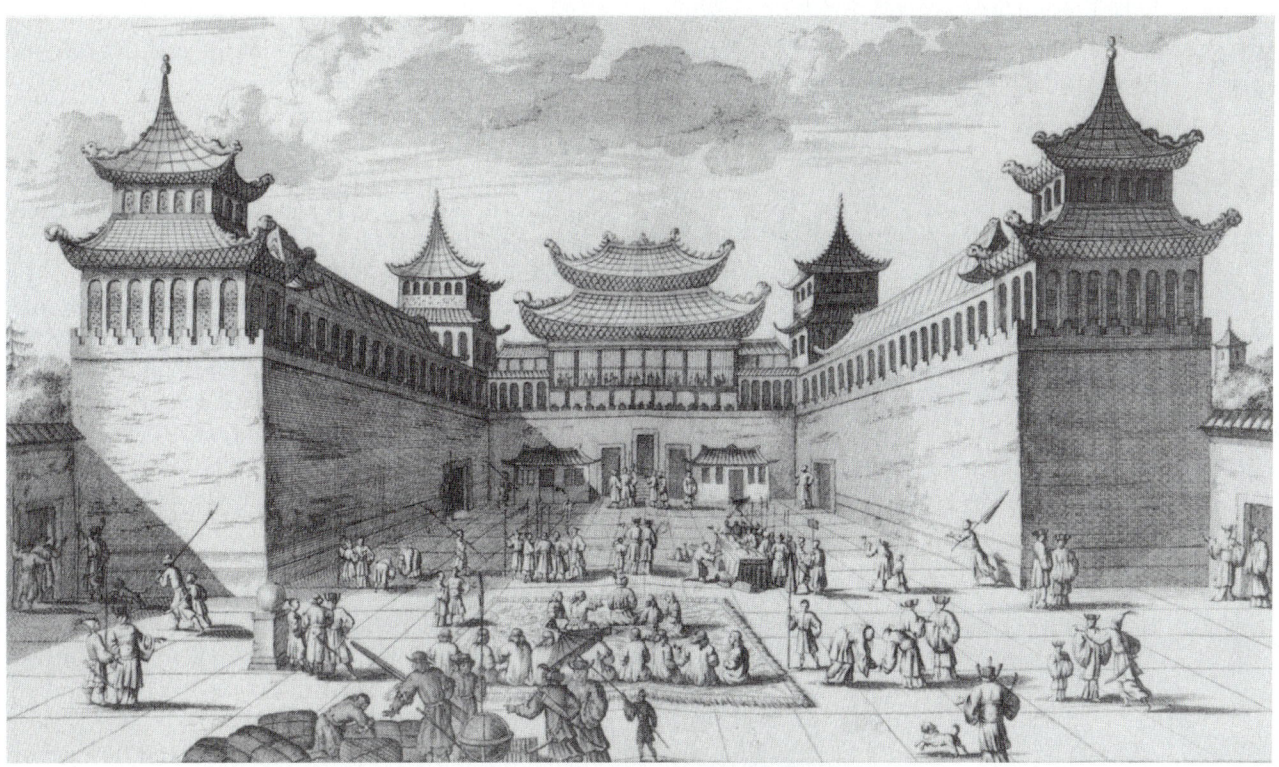

The 1689 treaty between Russia and China was the first treaty that China concluded with any Western power. In this contemporary engraving, the Russian ambassador is ceremonially greeted as he arrives for an audience with Emperor Kangxi. Note how the scale of the Chinese Imperial Palace in relationship to the Chinese figures and to the Russians suggests Chinese power over the foreign presence. Notice also how the Russians in this image have a globe of the world with them.

Kangxi extended Qing control over an enormous realm. After defeating opponents, using Chinese troops and generals, the emperor destroyed a Russian Cossack base and signed the Treaty of Nerchinsk in 1689. This treaty both eliminated the possibility of a Russian alliance with the Mongols against China and established normal relations between Russia and the Qing without imposition of a tributary relationship. In 1696 and 1697, Kangxi led troops against the Mongols and defeated them. In 1720, his armies invaded and installed a pro-Chinese Dalai Lama in Tibet. Later, during the reign of his son, the Russians recognized Chinese sovereignty over Mongolia under the Treaty of Kaikhta (1727). And, under his grandson, the Qing extended their control to Chinese Central Asia, an area with a large Muslim population permitted to retain its religion.

To underscore Qing legitimacy as a Chinese dynasty, Kangxi held a special examination in 1679 to recruit scholars to write a Ming history and other works. He patronized Zhu Xi (JOO SHEE) Confucianism. At the same time, he was fascinated by Western mathematics and sciences, and supported the Jesuits at the court. He issued an edict of religious toleration in 1692, permitting conversion to Christianity, provided Chinese converts continued to practice ancestral rites of respect. The Vatican, however, rejected Kangxi's position and sent an envoy to Beijing to assert control over Chinese Catholics. Kangxi then expelled missionaries who would not accept Chinese Christians' performance of ancestor worship.

Though the Qing tried to maintain their identity and dominance, they recognized the need to bring Chinese into the government. Paralleling the Manchu military banners, the Qing created banner forces made up of Chinese troops. In civil administration, the Qing encouraged Chinese to take exams for bureaucratic posts, most of which Chinese came to occupy. At the top levels of government, a dual administrative structure was formed in which most provinces had Chinese governors while governors-general, who were usually Manchus, ruled over two provincial governors. At the level of the top government ministers, each of the six boards had a Manchu and a Chinese minister, and half the Grand Secretaries were Chinese.

The Kangxi era was a time of creative artistic work. While many scholars took part in the compilation of the Ming history, many others refused to serve the Qing. The latter included nonconformist painters like Bada Shuren (c. 1626–1705) and philosophers like Gu Yanwu (1613–1682) whose focus on practical learning influenced later Qing philosophers.

Kangxi died an old man with 56 children. His designated heir became cruel and mentally unstable, but Kangxi, disappointed, failed to appoint an alternative before his death. The next emperor, Yongzheng (YONG-jung; r. 1723–1735), staged a coup, overthrew his incompetent brother, and ascended the throne. Like his father, Yongzheng was an effective, hard-working ruler. He established a new senior bureaucracy, the Grand Council, headed by the ministers of the six boards. He simplified the tax system and reformed the payment of local administrators so they would not be dependent on informal channels of income which opened them up to corruption. He also outlawed hereditary servitude, thus freeing members of enslaved classes.

Yongzheng's death was not followed by turmoil or a coup, as he had set up a secure system to make sure his designated heir would assume the throne. Qianlong (chen-LONG; r. 1736–1796, d. 1799) ushered in the most prosperous period in China's early

Jesuit missionaries were welcome at both the Ming and early Qing courts. This engraving shows a pioneering Jesuit in China, Matteo Ricci, and a Chinese convert in the late Ming dynasty.

The Kangxi Emperor attempted to model himself on the ideal Chinese ruler, permitting him to consolidate Manchu power over the country during his 60-year reign.

modern history. The territorial boundaries of China extended far into Central Asia, and its wealth and productivity dwarfed those of any other country in the world.

Qianlong's capital at Beijing and numerous other cities were among the world's largest in 1800, but China was primarily agricultural. Farm production grew steadily because of crop specialization, improved irrigation and fertilizers, and new plants from the Americas that could be grown where Chinese crops could not thrive. Silk production engaged many farmers, requiring the cultivation of mulberry trees (their leaves were the silkworms' food) as well as the careful tending of the worms. Farmers and urban folk alike had to buy food—especially farmers who planted tobacco, cotton, or mulberry trees—spurring the expansion of markets throughout the countryside. Chinese products were sold all over the realm and exported throughout the world. Chinese vessels shipped much of this trade until the end of the eighteenth century, when foreign shippers replaced them. The Chinese economy absorbed a great deal of silver from the mines of Japan and South America—that is, until the British discovered a product that the Chinese would consume in ever greater amounts and which would reverse the balance of trade by the early nineteenth century, opium.

Economic growth in the first half of the Qianlong reign was great, but its benefits were localized. Some regions did much better than others. The coastal region and towns along the Yangzi River and Pearl River delta were much more involved in local and international trade, and grew much faster. New industries led to new social arrangements such as "sisterhoods" for unmarried women or married women who worked away from their husbands' families. Sisterhoods offered lodging and support to women in silk and other kinds of production in the southeastern region of China.

Economic growth had some serious negative effects as well. Families decided to have more children than they could have had in more difficult economic times. While individual families did not notice any ill effects of having large families—in fact, having more children to help on the farm would lead to higher family income—after several decades of population growth, China as a whole began to experience population pressure at the end of the eighteenth century, leading to migration and conflict with indigenous people living in areas to which the Chinese migrated. Population growth also led to depletion of resources, especially trees whose wood was used as fuel, and deforestation led to serious flooding.

The Qianlong emperor's reign was the pinnacle of Qing success. Qianlong ruled wisely and expanded the realm until the last 25 years of his reign, when he allowed a corrupt underling to manipulate the strings of power. As a vigorous young man, depicted here at his inauguration in 1735 with his empress, Qianlong sponsored the collection of a great encyclopedia.

Society and Culture

Eighteenth-century society was more conservative than earlier times. Laws against behaviors considered sexually deviant became much more stringent. From time to time, officials banned plays or novels for violating Confucian morality. At the same time, the government fostered education as conducive to ethical behavior, and this led to the expansion of literacy. Public governance and popular society were seen as intertwined and most efficient and ethical when locally influential families took on the responsibility for promoting the livelihoods of their nonelite neighbors. Of course, this led to meddling by puritanical officials in their neighbors' lives.

The status of women was also affected by puritanical values. Widows continued to be discouraged from remarrying, and arches commemorating "virtuous widows" (widows who did not remarry) sprang up all over China. Young girls continued to have their feet bound. On the other hand, women writers were encouraged to express their creativity in the eighteenth century. Families prided themselves on having talented daughters, and prospective bridegrooms sought out brides with poetic sensibility. Male poet Yuan Mei (yoo-AHN MAY; 1716–1797) was a particular fan of women poets, gathering a group of lively women writers around himself and declaring that they surpassed men in many ways. His detractors believed he was encouraging too much sensuality in women.

Though Confucianists disparaged novels, some of China's finest fiction writing was produced during the Qing dynasty. Wu Jingzi (WOO JING-zuh; 1701–1754) wrote *The Scholars*, a satire on the examination system. The best-loved novel was *The Dream of the Red Chamber* (also called *The Dream of Red Mansions* and *The Story of the Stone*) by Cao Xueqin (TSOW shweh-CHIN; 1715–1764). The novel has a large number of characters and is centered around three cousins, one boy and two girls. The three lead an idyllic upper-class life of culture and literature until the boy is forced to marry one of the girls and the other cousin dies. The male protagonist passes the exams but then abandons his declining family to seek truth in religion. The novel is an exquisite study of relationships between generations, the sexes, and masters and servants. Elite family politics are played out against the tale of family decline.

The eighteenth century came to an end with the death of the emperor Qianlong. Years earlier, however, Qianlong had become attached to a handsome, bright young bodyguard named Heshen (huh-SHEN), whom he appointed to high-ranking posts. Heshen developed a network of graft and corruption; however, his fall came immediately after Qianlong's death. His plundering of China's wealth was devastating. Heshen's confiscated wealth was 800 million ounces of silver, and his cronies serving in appointive posts throughout China stole millions more. When impoverished commoners joined the White Lotus religious uprising

Document: Lan Dingyuan, County Magistrate: Depraved Religious Sects Deceive People

Lan Dingyuan (1680–1733) was a magistrate in a county near Guangzhou. Magistrates served at the lowest level of the Chinese bureaucracy but had wide-ranging responsibilities, including administration, collecting taxes, and enforcing laws, at the local level. Educated as Confucian public servants, magistrates, like all government officials, found religious deviance from Confucianism particularly unethical. White Lotus beliefs were also threatening because of the role White Lotus adherents had played in dynastic change at the end of the Yuan dynasty several hundred years earlier. Lan Dingyuan kept notes of his trials, and here we see how he dealt with this heretical sect.

The people of Chaoyang believed in spirits and often talked about gods and Buddhas.... [L]adies of the gentry families joined together to go to the temples to worship the Buddha. In this way, heretical and depraved teachings developed and the so-called Latter Heaven sect became popular.... The sect also called itself the "White Lotus" or the "White Willow."

Zhan Yucan's wife, Lin, was thought to be the "Miraculous Lady." She claimed to possess the ability to summon wind and rain and to give orders to gods and spirits. She was the leader of the Latter Heaven sect and was assisted by her paramour, Hu Aqui, who called himself the "Ben Peak Divine Gentleman." These two cast spells and used magic charms and waters to cure illness and to help pray for heirs. They also claimed to be able to help widows meet their deceased husbands at night.

The people of Chaoyang adored them madly; hundreds of men and women worshipped them as their masters.... [M]embers of the sect had ... already constructed a large building in the northern part of the county where they established a preaching hall and gathered several hundred followers ... I dispatched runners (office assistants to the magistrate) to apprehend the sect leaders, but the runners were afraid to offend the gods lest the soldiers of hell punish them. Besides the local officials and many of the influential families favored the sect. So they all escaped.

I, therefore, went to the place myself, pushed my way into the front room, and arrested the Divine Lady. Then I went further into the house to search for her accomplices.... It was indeed an ideal place to hide criminals.... Finally, the local rowdies as well as certain influential families, knowing they could no longer hide him, handed over Hu Aqiu (the Divine Gentleman).

In fact, these people had no special powers whatsoever, but used incense and costumes to bewilder people. The foolish people who trembled on just hearing the names of gods and spirits were impressed when they saw the Divine Lady had no fear of gods and goddesses. Hu Aqiu, who accompanied her, wore rouge, female clothing, and a wig. People believed Hu was the genuine Empress Lady of the Moon and never suspected he was a man.

When these pious women entered his bedroom and ascended to the upper chamber, they would be led to worship the Maitreya Buddha and to recite the charms of the Precious Flower sutra. The stupefying incense was burned and the women would faint and fall asleep so the leaders of the sect could do whatever they pleased.... Later members would cast spells and give the women cold water the drink to revive them. The so-called "praying for heirs" and the "meeting with a deceased husband" occurred while the women were dreaming and asleep.

The members of the Latter Heaven sect were extremely evil; even hanging their heads out on the streets would have been insufficient punishment for their crimes. However, this had been a year of bad harvest, so the villagers already had lots of worries.... Therefore, sympathetic to the people's troubles and wanting to end the matter, I destroyed the list of those involved which the culprits had divulged during the trial.

I had Lin, the "divine Lady," and Hu Aqui beaten and put in the collar, lacing them outside the court so the people could scorn them, beat them, and finally kill them.... I inquired further into the matter so that the other accomplices could repent and start a new life. I confiscated the sect's building, destroyed the concealed rooms, and converted it into a literary academy dedicated to the worship of the five great [neo-Confucian] teachers. Thus the filthy was swept away and the clean restored.

... I went to the academy to lecture or discuss literature with the people of the county.... As formal study developed, heretical beliefs ceased to exist...

Questions to Consider

1. Was the county magistrate more concerned about the criminals' sexual exploitation of women or about the rise of heretical sects?
2. How did the punishment of the criminals and the rehabilitation of the local inhabitants validate the ethical role of Confucianism in the Qing dynasty?

From Patricia Buckley Ebrey, ed., *Chinese Civilization and Society: A Sourcebook* (New York: The Free Press, 1993), pp. 295–296.

(1796–1804), government resources were not immediately available to meet the challenge. The **White Lotus movement** promised social equality among classes and a better status for women, all to be delivered by the Buddha of the future, Maitreya (mai-TRAY-ah). Eventually the movement was suppressed. At the same time, ethnic tensions arose as Chinese migrated to border regions in search of better farmland.

The next challenge came from overseas. Concerned about the rise of trade with the English and others, in 1759 the Qing sought to regulate foreign commerce by restricting it to Guangzhou (gwahng-JOH) and placing an official merchant guild in charge of dealing with Britain's official counterpart, the East India Company. For several decades, this system worked, but as England began to sell massive quantities of opium to offset its purchases of Chinese tea, China began to suffer (see Chapter 24). The world's greatest empire in 1700 would, by 1900, succumb to imperialism, famine, and civil war. China's way of relating to the world—the **tribute system**—was fundamentally at odds with Western practices of international relations. When King George III of England attempted to set up a permanent trade representative in Beijing in 1793, Qianlong rebuffed the British attempt because it did not accord with the practices of the tribute system. China did not need foreign products, Qianlong stated; moreover, Britain's representative, Lord George Macartney, failed to perform the kowtow, a bow of submission, to the emperor.

Asia and Oceania, 1800. Most of Asia was still free of imperialism in 1800. The Philippines were under Spanish control, and Indonesia was under Dutch control, but British inroads into India had just begun. French domination of Vietnam and Europeans' encroachment on China would occur in the nineteenth century.

KOREA IN THE SEVENTEENTH AND EIGHTEENTH CENTURIES

■ *Late Chosŏn history has long been seen as stagnant and rigidly old-fashioned. In what ways is this characterization incorrect?*

The struggles against the Japanese and the Manchus in the 1590s and from the 1620s to 1630s showed Koreans that they needed to strengthen their military. During the early seventeenth century, the Chosŏn dynasty refocused its attention on defense and strengthened its military. At the same time, serious factional struggles disrupted effective administration at Seoul. The factions were mainly concerned about power and influence, often framing their differences in terms of morality. Feuding factions disputed such issues as the proper length of the mourning period for the king's mother or the propriety of a concubine's son being designated an heir. Factionalism abated in the eighteenth century, when two strong kings ruled ably—King Yŏngjo (YONG-joh; r. 1724–1776) and his grandson King Chŏngjo (CHONG-joh; r. 1776–1800). Korea's economy, scholarship, and arts flourished during the eighteenth century.

King Yŏngjo was a patron of Confucian propriety. A scholar himself, he sponsored Confucian ceremonies

White Lotus movement—A millenarian religious movement combining elements of Confucianism and Daoism along with its predominantly Buddhist emphasis on salvation by the Buddha of the future.

tribute system—Foreign relations system placing China in a dominant position with neighboring countries who must pay tribute to China and receive protection in return.

Korea

1627, 1636	Manchu invasions
1724–1776	Reign of King Yŏngjo
1776–1800	Reign of King Chŏngjo
late 17th–early 18th centuries	*Silhak* scholarship flourished

and rituals. His behavior inspired the factions to cool their rivalries. He reduced one of the taxes paid by commoners and instituted land taxes on wealthy landowners. He ended the problem of homelessness. The economy developed rapidly, and the population increased by 50 percent. Though an effective and conscientious monarch, Yŏngjo committed a controversial and, to many, a cruel act; in 1762 he executed his son Sado, the designated heir, when the latter was clearly deranged and guilty of murder himself. This led to a renewal of factional divisions between the supporters and opponents of Yŏngjo. When Chŏngjo ascended the throne, he honored his executed father's spirit, thereby challenging his grandfather's actions and keeping the factionalism alive. Despite the disputes within the ruling class, however, the eighteenth century was a time of growth both economically and culturally.

Painters like Kim Hongdo (b. 1745) and Shin Yunbok (b. 1758) focused on Korean themes rather than simply following the previously dominant Chinese conventions. Kim, in particular, was known for his depictions of the everyday life of people at work or children in school. Other artists refined ceramic crafts. Writers, a number of them women, made **han'gul** (HAHN-gool) their medium of expression in the eighteenth century. Diaries, novels, and poetry written in han'gul were more expressive than the stiffer works written in the foreign language used for official government work, Chinese.

Yangban thinkers also were developing new approaches to learning. Observing that the farmers were not enjoying the wealth that accompanied economic growth, seventeenth-century scholar Yu Hyŏngwŏn (YOO HYONG-won) decided to undertake an extensive "investigation of things," the practice advocated by Zhu Xi, China's great Neo-Confucian scholar (see Chapter 10). Yu's massive work, which called for reform in government, the military, and the land system, inspired eighteenth-century scholars to undertake *silhak* (SHIL-hahk) or "practical learning." *Silhak* scholars, appalled by the plight of the peasants, advocated reforms that threatened the privileges of their fellow yangban. Some scholars who had international experience in China suggested that Koreans should emulate their Chinese counterparts who called for changes when circumstances demanded new policies. Some were impressed with Western studies they observed in China, including knowledge of astronomy, medicine, and Christianity. A few *silhak* scholars even formed an underground circle of Christians in 1754. In time, the number of adherents to the Western religion grew, and the government cracked down in bloody purges in 1801, 1811, 1849, and 1866.

Other social changes in the nineteenth century— new economic and power configurations—appeared following a century of growth. For example, many who had been slaves either bought their freedom or abandoned their owners, and became a new group of laborers who worked for wages. At the ruling class level, sons of concubines were entering the government as trained specialists (clerks, accountants, and other jobs), challenging the old aristocracy. These new specialists were often concerned with social reform, and many were attracted to Catholicism. Even yangban disrupted the old order, especially in areas far from Seoul. At the other end of the spectrum, farmers and miners revolted on several occasions during the nineteenth century. Thus, the stage was set for the end of the Chosŏn dynasty, as Western and, later, Japanese pressure challenged the Seoul government.

han'gul—An indigenous Korean script.

Shin Yunbok, Enjoying Lotuses While Listening to Music *(late eighteenth/early nineteenth century). Shin was one of Korea's most beloved painters. Shin's favorite themes were romantic and he often portrayed kiseang (artistic courtesans) with yangban men. The hats in this picture are the black horsehair hats that were the mark of the yangban male.*

Japan

1600–1868	Tokugawa shogunate
1640	Restriction of trade to Holland, Korea, China
1657	Death of Hayashi Razan, Neo-Confucian scholar; Great Edo fire
1688–1704	Genroku era, golden age of arts and literature
1730–1801	Motoori Norinaga, proponent of National Learning

EARLY MODERN JAPAN: THE TOKUGAWA PERIOD

- *What developments in early modern Japan helped set the stage for modernization in the late nineteenth century?*

Tokugawa Ieyasu's victory in the battle of Sekigahara in 1600, his assumption of the title of shōgun in 1603, the pacification of rowdy masterless samurai, the establishment of means of controlling the *daimyō*, and the regulation and limitation of foreign trade and contacts cemented Tokugawa rule by 1650. Japan was not yet a modern state, with its reach extending to every segment of society. But the Tokugawa shogunate did establish mechanisms to control the realm, acting as a superordinate ruler over self-regulating status groups. These statuses were the four Confucian status groups, recast for Japanese use as samurai, farmer, artisan, and merchant. In reality, the status groups were more fractured than that. Villages, cities, and towns had a variety of means of governance, depending on their relationship to their *daimyō* (for more on *daimyō*, see Chapter 13). Groups that did not fit into one of these four statuses, including those involved in the theatre or sex trades, had their own governing structure. Professional physicians and scholars could come from any status background.

The shogunate involved itself as little as possible in the day-to-day oversight of the status groups. If these groups stayed out of trouble and paid their taxes, the Tokugawa shōguns generally left them alone, sometimes issuing a warning to behave in a moral way but rarely finding reason to enforce such a decree. The one group that the Tokugawa did control was its own status group—the *daimyō*—by moving *daimyō* around for strategic placement and by the **alternate attendance system.**

The alternate attendance system required *daimyō* to spend alternate years in their domain castle and their Edo-based mansion, from which they performed attendance on the shōgun. The *daimyō's* wives and children had to remain in Edo like hostages in fancy cages. Travel was closely controlled both to prevent clashes between the huge retinues of samurai that accompanied the *daimyō* and to make sure no firearms were being smuggled into Edo or *daimyō* wives smuggled out—signs of a possible *daimyō* plot against the shōgun. Two-thirds of the *daimyō's* tax revenues were consumed in maintaining an elegant mansion in Edo to show off in front of their *daimyō* neighbors, in going back and forth across the countryside every year, in feeding and housing samurai both on the road and in Edo, and in having duplicate staffs in the domain and in Edo.

The *daimyō* were technically the top rulers within their domains, with their own legal and fiscal systems. The Tokugawa collected taxes from the rice crops of their own lands, which produced about one-quarter of the realm's rice output at the beginning of the period. The *daimyō* took in taxes from their own domains. Though the *daimyō* did not have to pay regular taxes to the shogunate, they did have to respond to demands to pay for projects the shogunate desired. For example, the domain of Satsuma was ordered to build 300 wooden ships to transport rocks for Tokugawa Ieyasu's castle. The costs were high, but the economic consequences were even greater. New jobs were created for lumberjacks, sailors, shipbuilders, and suppliers of food, clothing, and lodging. The transported rocks were cut from quarries with tools made of iron, which itself had to be mined, smelted, and crafted into tools. Resources were spread around when workers used their wages to buy other goods. This is but one example of thousands in which the Tokugawa's political attempts to control the *daimyō* led to unintended economic and social growth which, in the eighteenth century, came to define Japan as a nation rather than a collection of status groups.

The Tokugawa and the World

Although later Japanese considered Japan to have been a "closed country" during the Tokugawa period, Tokugawa Ieyasu had no interest in completely cutting off trade with the Chinese, Koreans, and selected Europeans. Gold, silver, and copper were plentiful in Tokugawa mines in the seventeenth century, affording the Japanese plenty of funds to buy silk from China, herbs and medicines from Korea, and

Closed Country Edict of 1635

---

alternate attendance system—Tokugawa system of controlling *daimyō* (nobles) by requiring them to attend shogunal court every other year and to leave their wives and children at the shogunal court when they were away.

exotic plants and woods from Southeast Asia. What the shōguns did not want was Christian missionary activity, leading them to seek alternate ways of trading without bringing in missionaries.

Although Portuguese traders hauled much of the silk and other products entering Japanese ports in the early years of the Tokugawa regime, they were soon supplanted by others, especially Korean, Chinese, and, until 1640, Japanese traders. Trade with Korea went through the island of Tsu. The volume of trade with Korea and China was huge. In one decade alone (1615–1625), a conservative estimate asserts that Japan exported 130,000–160,000 kilograms (286,000–352,000 pounds) of silver for imports from China. Japan's silver exports, entering the world monetary system through the China trade, played a significant role in global commerce until the 1680s when the Tokugawa silver mines began to be depleted.

Soon, however, diplomatic and commercial relations became increasingly controlled. By the 1640s, relations with foreign countries were limited, and Japanese ships were no longer permitted to take part in international trade. Sailors blown off course were not allowed to come home—unless they were returning from Korea or the Ryūkyū Islands—under penalty of death.

Tokugawa policy changed because they became serious about controlling the introduction of Christianity to Japan. The Dutch, who had already driven the English out of the Japan trade by their more aggressive trade practices, next persuaded the Tokugawa to kick out the Spanish and Portuguese merchants, whom they considered too interested in promoting Christianity. The Dutch convinced the shōgun that Holland would not be interested in proselytizing. For the next two centuries, only the Chinese, Koreans, and Dutch could take part in the lucrative trade with Japan.

At the dawn of the Tokugawa era, the shōgun was worried about Buddhists as well as Christians. But by the middle of the century, Buddhism had been brought under government control. Confucian attacks on Buddhism deprived it of the intellectual vitality it had demonstrated in the medieval period. In addition, the requirement that every Japanese register as a member of a Buddhist temple to indicate rejection of Christianity, which may have appeared supportive of Buddhism, actually made the religion an instrument of Tokugawa policy. This deprived it of vitality as well. Christians were controlled more aggressively, with converts forced to renounce their religion. The Shimabara uprising, put down by the Tokugawa with Dutch assistance in 1638, was the last major Christian rebellion.

Both Korea and China were countries the Tokugawa could trust, but the relations with each of these differed greatly, as the Tokugawa rejected involvement with the Chinese tribute system which would have required Japan to subordinate itself to the Ming and later the Qing. The Tokugawa unease with the Manchu emperors may have also contributed to their lack of desire to become involved in the tribute system. The Manchu occupation of Seoul in 1627 raised fears that the Manchus would continue on to invade Japan as the Mongols had 350 years earlier. The Tokugawa even debated sending troops to aid the Koreans in repelling the Manchus; in the end, they did not. With Korea, the Tokugawa conducted foreign relations on the basis of equality. Unlike the case of Korea's relations with the Chinese court, Korean envoys to Edo did not prostrate themselves in a gesture of subordination.

At the end of the seventeenth century, Qing Emperor Kangxi lifted the century-long limits on official Chinese trade with Japan. This encouraged even greater trade between the two countries. Once the maximum official trade was reached, unlicensed trade was conducted at ports throughout western Japan. The Dutch, worried about increased competition from the Chinese, told the Tokugawa that Kangxi was influenced by Jesuits. The shogunate began inspecting imported Chinese books for references to Christianity and decided in 1687 to restrict Chinese merchants to the tiny island of Deshima in Nagasaki Harbor, where the Dutch had been forced to live and operate since 1640. Nagasaki grew quickly as a center of trade in the late seventeenth century. In the next century, however, the volume of trade leveled off due to use of domestically produced goods instead of imports and to growing shortages in silver and other precious metals. In addition, concern about the detrimental environmental effects of mining to promote trade began to surface in the 1680s.

Economic Growth and Social Change

The seventeenth century was an era of rapid growth. Peace permitted farmers to look forward to predictable harvests. The Tokugawa and the *daimyō* regularized weights and measures. They established policies for village self-governance: They prohibited the sale of people and possession of luxury goods; and they required more fortunate villagers to help the poor, maintain roads and bridges, and organize village families into mutual-responsibility groups.

Self-governance, a prime example of the Tokugawa policy of rule by status, was at the heart of the system. Taxes were assessed on the whole-village level by local officials. The village leadership, which varied among villages from a single individual to a council of influential families, then determined each family's annual portion of the village tax bill. Villages often hid a large part of their productivity increases from the tax assessor. Not all farmers were equally able to stash away income. Some domains experienced exploitative or corrupt government or bad weather while others prospered.

Woodblock print of Mt. Fuji by Hokusai. Landscape prints flourished during the nineteenth century in Japan. Mt. Fuji, which could be clearly seen from Edo, was a favorite theme. Here Hokusai shows a bustling rural road.

Peace was not the only reason for rapid growth. Policies like the alternate attendance system and the requirement that samurai live in castle-towns were also instrumental in both rural and urban growth. The *daimyō* converted the rice they received as taxes into cash in two major rice markets—Edo for domains in the east and Osaka for domains in the west. By 1720, these cities, as well as the castle towns and the old capital of Kyoto, accounted for 10 percent of the population. Edo was by then the world's largest city, with over a million inhabitants, and Kyoto and Osaka together had about 800,000. All those people needed to eat and be housed and clothed.

The alternate attendance system forced most *daimyō* to live beyond their means, so merchants extended them high-interest loans in advance of their next tax receipts. Determining rice futures as well as handling the transfer of cash from the merchant house to the *daimyō's* Edo mansion or castle in his domain turned some of these merchants into bankers and created a system of Japan-wide financing that transcended the official fiscal independence of the *daimyō* domains. Roads, sea-routes, transportation companies, and communications companies sprang up in the seventeenth and eighteenth centuries to meet the needs of the alternate attendance system, leading to economic growth unintended by the Tokugawa when they set that system up.

Money flowed into the guest houses and restaurants along the *daimyō's* procession routes, and from there to the villages that supplied the workers in those establishments. That cash was used to buy commercial fertilizers and to develop new irrigation devices and farm tools like threshing machines. These new technologies opened new fields and permitted farm families to work more efficiently. New technologies were spread to remote villages through printed agricultural guidebooks as literacy expanded for both, men and women. Urban demands for fruits, vegetables, and fibers (silk, hemp, and cotton) encouraged farm families to use some of the surplus available from their increased productivity for goods sold by traveling merchants. Villagers were connected to the cities in additional ways, especially as carpenters and artisans. The demand for labor drove up the cost of labor, making the large extended family of the Warring States period less efficient than the nuclear family. The old village structure, dominated by a few large families, changed to one of numerous nuclear families.

Growth of the urban economy was even more remarkable. In the medieval period, Kyoto had been the only large city. Markets had developed near Buddhist temples, but they were relatively small. Seventeenth-century castle-towns gathered purveyors of goods and services to the *daimyō* and samurai; most had a population that was half commoner and half samurai. The alternate attendance system led to post-station towns every few miles along the highways, and material and artistic culture flowed easily as the samurai rotated between Edo and the small provincial towns. Though the population of the biggest cities stopped growing around 1720, regional towns continued to grow and become integrated across the various regions of Japan.

Officials were not the only ones who moved about the country. Traveling merchants brought goods to the rural areas, and maritime companies developed freight lines to haul goods cheaply. Pilgrims and sightseers, a large number of them women over the age of 40, added to the bustle and excitement of inter-urban travel. Few Japanese remained untouched by urban culture and goods by the end of the eighteenth century. The long arm of the city reached into the rural environment as well. During the building frenzy of the first few decades of the Tokugawa period, hundreds of castles and mansions, thousands of houses for samurai and merchants, and countless ships, temples, and shops depleted the resources of wood throughout Japan. Fires also ravaged the wooden cities, making lumber even more scarce. The 1657 Edo fire dwarfed all previous fires; much of the city was destroyed and 100,000 people were killed. In the eighteenth century, planners began reforestation and other environmental programs, but it took disasters like the great Edo fire to alert them to the need for environmental policies.

Economic growth, the development of cities whose culture and wealth were increasingly dominated by people of the lowest Confucian status (merchants), and the declining wealth of samurai were unintended and ironic consequences of policies undertaken to preserve a political order with the shōgun on top, the *daimyō* and samurai under control but supported by tax revenues and the right to rule, and agriculture at the center of the economy. Economic development eroded the conservative system the Tokugawa had tried to create.

When disasters occurred, such as famines in the 1730s and 1780s caused by crop failures due to unusually bad weather, the government tried a variety of reform measures in response. Most of these were conservative, seeking to reinforce Confucian morality and cutting government expenditures. During the famines of the 1730s, the shōgun Yoshimune (YOH-shee-MOO-neh; r. 1716–1745), widely respected as moral and conscientious, attempted to cut expenses, encourage agriculture, regularize taxes, standardize the diverse legal systems throughout Japan, and relax the ban on foreign technical books. He also ordered the dismissal of nearly half the court ladies to save money. With such policies, Yoshimune hoped to restore the efficiency of the past, but his policies were only temporary remedies rather than permanent solutions for the country's problems. More innovative solutions were sought in the 1780s by the shogunal advisor Tanuma Okitsugu (TAH-noo-mah OH-kee-TSOO-goo; 1719–1788), who tried to encourage foreign trade, develop the northern island of Hokkaido, open new mines, and charter new monopolies. But his reforms, which took a completely different path from Yoshimune's policies of retrenchment, were also unsuccessful in stemming the disasters brought on by the forces of nature. A few *daimyō* were able to implement economic policies in their domains that allowed their own areas not only to pull through the hard times but also to grow, but economic policies at the highest levels of the shogunate were generally unsuccessful in the middle and end of the Tokugawa period. By the middle of the nineteenth century, when the shogunate was facing American pressure to open its ports (see Chapter 24), it was the economically successful domains that were able to challenge the Tokugawa shogunate's claim of political legitimacy.

In other important ways, the system the Tokugawa intended to create was undermined by the actual behavior of the people. Samurai men were transformed by their occupations as bureaucrats and their education at state expense from warriors willing to lay down their lives for their feudal lords to diligent organization men striving to get ahead in life.

Women also challenged stereotyped notions of their behavior. Neo-Confucian ideology placed women below men in the status hierarchy, but women's roles and status varied greatly by class. Samurai women were dependent on their husbands, who received annual stipends. To continue to receive those stipends, samurai had to have male heirs, so their wives had to be tolerant of their husbands' taking of concubines or secondary wives to guarantee the family's continuity. Samurai marriages were usually arranged with little or no input from the future bride and groom. Samurai women were expected to be submissive to their husbands and their parents-in-law.

Merchant-class women were often well educated in math and literature, helped to run their families' shops, and frequently had a voice in the selection of their husbands. In fact, business owners often adopted a talented employee as a son-in-law, who then inherited and ran the business along with his wife, the daughter of the original owner. If the marriage did not work out, the hapless son-in-law might be divorced and a better match found. Merchant-class women often enjoyed the arts and culture of the cities.

Farm women's opportunities were very much determined by their families' wealth. The poorest had rough lives, with many of them forced to work as day laborers, domestic servants, or even as prostitutes in brothels located along the highways used by the *daimyō's* processions. Middle and upper-income farm women, however, had in some ways more opportunities than their urban counterparts. Many were educated alongside their brothers in the Buddhist temple schools that sprang up all over Japan to teach the children of the commoner classes. When they reached adolescence, village girls, like the boys in boys' associations, became members of girls' associations where they learned crafts like needlework and made important friendships. During major festivals, the boys' and girls' associations mingled, and young men and women often chose their own marriage partners based on friendships and intimate relations formed at those times. Divorce for marital incompatibility was common, and multiple marriages were not looked down upon as long as the partners were monogamous during the marriage. Farm men and women were equally important to their families' economic well-being; women planted while men reaped, and both, as well as their children, threshed the rice. Sons usually inherited, but daughters, if particularly respected by their parents or in the absence of sons, could inherit and marry a man expected to become an adopted son-in-law. Women became the skilled silk workers, bringing in cash incomes to their families. And when some farmers became entrepreneurs in the late Tokugawa period, setting up silk-reeling mills and other enterprises, teenage girls were often the wage earners for their families. Women were usually not members of the village assembly, but in some cases, they did represent their families at official events.

The official ideology concerning women was grim, but in reality most played a more important role and had greater latitude in relation to their families than that suggested in official documents. No women had "rights" in the modern sense, but neither did men.

Early Modern Scholarship and Ideology

Urbanization in the seventeenth and eighteenth centuries produced new cultural and social practices in the cities and towns. At the dawn of the seventeenth century, urban culture was samurai culture. Most scholars called Kyoto their home in the seventeenth century, but in the eighteenth, many lived in Edo as well. Many scholars were outside the four-status system; some were scholars in official posts and many of those had samurai status. But other scholars came from every type of background and earned their living as teachers, advisors, or physicians. Zhu Xi Confucianism enticed a number of scholars in the seventeenth century. Hayashi Razan (HAH-yah-shee RAH-zan; 1583–1657) and Yamazaki Ansai (YAH-mah-ZAH-kee AHN-sai; 1618–1682) both started out as Buddhist clerics but later abandoned religion for the more secular Confucian learning. Hayashi's school of thought was particularly appreciated by the shogunate. Hayashi contended that the five Confucian relationships were natural and proper. The shōgun should be elevated above all others, except for the politically powerless emperor, who was to be considered, Yamazaki added, the "heaven" from which the shōgun received the Japanese Mandate of Heaven. Thus, Zhu Xi Confucianism was blended with Shintō, the ancient Japanese indigenous religion.

Hayashi's school was considered orthodox by the shogunate, but not all scholars agreed with its point of view. Some followed the Chinese thinker Wang Yangming and called for activism in the face of social injustice. These scholars often courted banishment or other forms of punishment. Another scholar created a cult of masculinity called the "Way of the Warrior" or ***bushidō*** (BOO-shee-DOH) that elevated the samurai and shōgun as upholders of military values. Yet others, such as Ogyū Sorai (OH-gyoo so-RAI; 1666–1728) rejected Neo-Confucianism and called for a study of ancient texts themselves.

Confucianism was not the only school of thought in the Tokugawa period. Early in the period, students of history began the study of Japan's past. In the eighteenth century, an eminent literary scholar, Motoori Norinaga (MOH-toh-OH-ree NOH-ree-NAH-ga, 1730-1801) undertook a massive study of *The Tale of Genji* and other classics from the Heian and pre-Heian eras (see Chapter 10). His work, which stressed the centrality of Japan and the role of Japan's ancient Shintō gods, was not intended as political, but it inspired later scholars who advocated the restoration of the power of the emperor.

Another strand of scholarship was called "Dutch Learning." While not specifically Dutch, this scholarship started with the translation of Dutch books—the only Western books allowed in Japan and only after 1720 at that—and expanded to encompass a wide variety of studies in medicine, geography, astronomy, ship building, and other technical subjects. At the end of the eighteenth century, scholars of Dutch Learning were able to comprehend the growth of Western expansionism and, alarmed, wished to discuss military and political subjects. But these were restricted by shogunate law.

Other important schools of thought supported the way of the merchant class. Merchants were at the bottom of the Confucian hierarchy, but the Kaitokudō (KAI-TOH-koo-doh) Merchant Academy in Osaka stressed the importance of commerce and the morality of merchants. In Kyoto, Ishida Baigan (EE-shee-dah BAI-gan) attracted thousands of followers with his "Heart Learning," a religion based on a synthesis of Buddhism, Confucianism, and Shintō that honored merchants who were honest and frugal and carried out their trade as if it were a "calling." Respect for merchants facilitated the transition to modern economic development in the Meiji era (see Chapter 24).

Culture and Society

Non-samurai folk, with the help of creative samurai, developed a lively urban society whose values were exemplified through its arts. Arts and culture were increasingly accessible to less elite consumers as new materials and techniques, particularly printing, brought literature and visual arts into many hands.

The art prized during the late sixteenth century, such as paintings of the Kanō school, were still valued in the seventeenth century. In addition, a new aesthetic was developing among cultivated gentlemen—the polite accomplishments of skilled amateur poetry, painting, tea ceremony, music, and calligraphy—that resembled similar movements in China and Korea at the time. Less refined culture appealed to an enormous market of commoners and samurai. Sensuality was at the heart of this great cultural outpouring. Much of this culture was produced in sections of large cities like Edo, Kyoto, and Osaka, which set aside as zones of sexuality called "pleasure quarters," initially created to marginalize and control sexuality so that the samurai could focus on their duty to their *daimyō* lords. Brothels, teahouses, artists' and writers' studios, theatres, and restaurants were crammed into these zones. Although these zones were aimed at men, many women did take part, both as workers in the brothels and as audience members at plays and other artistic performances. To be sure, life for

---

bushidō—Literally "the way of the warrior," this philosophy called on samurai to dedicate themselves unto death to their feudal lord and to live frugally and ethically.

those in the brothels was not all pleasurable. The quarters were surrounded by moats and gates, and women sex workers were not permitted to leave. Sold to brothels as young girls, many experienced a tough life, despite their often elegant clothing, artistic accomplishments, and genteel bearing.

The culture of the "pleasure quarters" had its own rules, which countered Confucian sensibility and morality. For example, according to conventional belief, actors were to be looked down upon, but they were the heroes of this culture, along with the finely dressed "dandies" who prided themselves on their knowledge of song lyrics, literature, and the latest gossip from the world of the theatre. Its heroines were famous courtesans and gifted geisha (GAY-shah) or female entertainers, who were trained in the arts from an early age. The restrictions on the freedom of these women, however, belied the exalted status they seemed to enjoy.

It was in these crowded areas of sexuality that urban culture flourished. Perhaps because so many there seemed to be tossed about by the uncertainties of life and fortune, the world of the arts came to be known as the **"floating world,"** a concept taken from Buddhism. Poets, playwrights, novelists, and wood-block artists created art meant for mass consumption. The consumer market was increasingly sophisticated, and printing and literacy exploded in the late seventeenth century. There were over 700 publishing companies in Kyoto alone around 1800. Texts and pictures alike were produced by woodblock prints and were cheap enough to be readily accessible.

Artists like poet Matsuo Bashō (1644–1694), novelist and storyteller Ihara Saikaku (1642–1693), playwright Chikamatsu Monzaemon (1653–1724), and woodblock artists Hishikawa Moronobu (1620?–1694), Katsushika Hokusai (1760–1849), and Andō Hiroshige (1797–1858) were esteemed during their own lifetimes and continued to be highly regarded for their artistic accomplishments.

Son of a minor samurai, poet Matsuo Bashō (MAH-tsoo-oh ba-SHOH) established himself as the major practitioner of a poetic form called haikai. But he felt constrained by the conventional haikai style, so developed a new form called haiku. His own studies of Zen, Chinese literature, and medieval Japanese poetry informed his enormous poetic output. The haiku, a 17-syllable form, evokes mood and suggests linkages between seemingly dissimilar objects.

*On a withered branch
A crow has settled—
Autumn nightfall*[2]

floating world—The area in which art, literature, and prostitution flourished in early modern Japan.

Bashō's most popular work was his travel writing, *Narrow Road to the North*, a volume of poetry and prose recounting his long journey throughout the island of Honshū.

Bashō's contemporary, Ihara Saikaku (EE-hah-rah SAI-kah-koo), was one of many highly successful prose writers of his day. Until the last year of his life, his tales were racy stories laced with a bit of propriety. His characters revel in pleasure—popular book titles included *The Life of an Amorous Man* (published in 1682) and *The Life of an Amorous Woman* (1686)—but despite their hedonistic lifestyle, they suffer loneliness at the end of their lives. In his 1688 novel, *The Eternal Storehouse of Japan*, Saikaku focused on practical

Woodblock prints, like this portrait of a courtesan and her attendants, depicted the life of workers and customers in the "floating world" of urban culture in the Tokugawa period. These prints made art readily available to a mass audience. They also helped to spread new fashions and culture beyond urban areas.

Document: Ihara Saikaku: "The Umbrella Oracle"

Ihara Saikaku embodied the lively urban culture of Japan's "floating world" in the late seventeenth century. This short story is from his 1685 collection, *Tales from the Provinces*. Japanese loved to travel throughout the Japanese islands in the Tokugawa period—foreign travel was not permitted at that time—and for those who could not get away, tales of exotic places were an enjoyable substitute. Note the urbane city-based writer's humorous treatment of country folk.

To the famous "Hanging Temple of Kannon" in the Province of Kii, someone had once presented twenty oil-paper umbrellas which ... were hung beside the temple for the use of any and all who might be caught in the rain or snow....

One day in the spring of 1649, however, a certain villager borrowed one of the umbrellas and, while he was returning home, had it blown out of his hands by a violent "divine wind." ... Borne aloft by the wind, the umbrella landed finally in the little hamlet of Anazato, far in the mountains of the island of Kyushu. The people of this village had from ancient times been completely cut off from the world ... and had never even seen an umbrella! ...

Finally, one local wise man stepped forth and proclaimed, ... "Though I hesitate to utter that August Name, this is without a doubt the God of the Sun...." All present were filled with awe.... The whole population of the village went up into the mountains and, gathering wood and rushes, built a shrine that the deity's spirit might be transferred hence from [the Great Shrine of] Ise....

At the time of the summer rains the site upon which the shrine was situated became greatly agitated, and the commotion did not cease. When the umbrella was consulted, the following oracle was delivered: "All this summer the sacred hearth has been simply filthy.... [L]et there not be a single cockroach left alive! I have also one other request. I desire you to select a beautiful young maiden as a consolation offering for me. If this is not done within seven days, ... I will rain you all to death! ..."

The villagers were frightened out of their wits.... [T]he young maidens, weeping and wailing, strongly protested the umbrella god's cruel demand.... They had come to attach a peculiar significance to the odd shape the deity had assumed.

At this juncture, a young and beautiful widow from the village stepped forward, saying, "Since it is for the god, I will offer myself in place of the young maidens."

All night long the beautiful widow waited in the shrine, but she did not get a bit of affection. Enraged, she charged into the inner sanctum, grasped the divine umbrella firmly in her hands and screaming, "Worthless deceiver!" she tore it apart, and threw the pieces as far as she could!

Questions to Consider

1. What was Ihara Saikaku's attitude toward rural people?
2. Contrast the behavior of widows advocated in Qing China with that accepted in Tokugawa Japan.
3. How does this short story show that Japanese worshipped both Buddhist and Shintō religion?

Excerpt from Ihara Saikaku, "The Umbrella Oracle," in Donald Keene, ed., *Anthology of Japanese Literature* (New York: Grove Press, 1955), pp. 354–356.

---

concerns of the merchant class rather than sensual pleasures, and his last book (*Worldly Mental Calculations*, 1692) was a pessimistic tale of poverty.

Theatre was most dynamic in the seventeenth and early eighteenth centuries. Nō plays from the medieval period continued to be performed but were rapidly supplanted by plays with secular themes. Many of these new plays highlighted the dilemmas of life of the merchant class, contrasting the all-too-human struggle between fulfilling one's duty and following one's heart. Two major forms predominated: kabuki (kah-BOO-kee), which used human actors, and bunraku (BOON-rah-koo), which used almost life-sized puppets and an on-stage chorus.

Kabuki was developed by a woman dancer named Okuni who brought this new form of performance to Edo in 1603. Soon female kabuki troupes were all the rage. But when these performance troupes were linked to prostitution, women actors were outlawed in 1629. Women's roles came to be performed by men and boys, just as in English theatre in Shakespeare's day. Kabuki plays used highly sophisticated staging, with revolving stages, opulent costumes and make-up, and grandiose gestures by the actors. The actors had widely enthusiastic followers who bought prints of those they idolized.

Chikamatsu Monzaemon (CHEE-kah-MAH-tsoo mon-ZAH-eh-mon), who wrote both kabuki and puppet plays, was Japan's greatest playwright of the Tokugawa period, and arguably of all time. He preferred writing puppet plays, as kabuki actors took liberties with the lines playwrights penned. Like Shakespeare, Chikamatsu wrote both historical plays and plays with deep human emotions. The latter often focused on tragic lovers whose duty to their families or employers prevented them from marrying. The lovers had no recourse but to run away and commit double suicide, deemed a pure gesture of intense romantic love. Chikamatsu's plays, in which emotion was always balanced with duty, showed that even in the floating world hedonism had its consequences. The Tokugawa government was so appalled by the rash of love suicides that followed the performance of some of Chikamatsu's plays that it banned all plays about love suicides.

Pictorial art was intimately connected with prose and poetry in the Tokugawa period. Illuminated books combined text and images, bringing affordable art to a mass readership. Woodblock prints were the breakthrough artistic form of the late seventeenth century. Earlier in the century, erotic themes in paintings called *shunga* (SHOON-ga) or pictures of spring were popular, and these themes were continued when woodblock prints first developed. Hishikawa Moronobu (HEE-shee-KAH-wa MOH-roh-NOH-boo) elevated the humble print to a major art form, depicting travel scenes, handsome actors, beautiful courtesans, gardens, and the bustle of urban street life as well as erotica. His work set the standards for the ukiyo-e (OO-kee-yoh EH), the pictures of the floating world, that characterize the Tokugawa period for many modern viewers. The form he developed continued to reign during the rest of the period. Katsushika Hokusai (kah-TSOO-shkah HOHK-sai) and Andō Hiroshige (an-DOH hee-ROH-shee-gheh) perfected the art of landscape prints that are still immensely popular in Japan and the rest of the world.

SOUTHEAST ASIA: POLITICAL AND CULTURAL INTERACTIONS

■ *Was the fact that Southeast Asia had for centuries been an international crossroads a factor in its colonization by Europeans in the early modern era?*

The late seventeenth century was a time of turmoil on the Southeast Asian mainland. Only Laos had enjoyed sustained peace and a degree of good relations with its neighbors during the long reign of Souligna-Vongsa (soo-LIG-na-VONG-sa; r. 1633?–1694). In addition to struggles among the states of Southeast Asia, European pressure altered interstate relations. The Dutch and English chartered trading companies competed for commercial dominance. The Dutch pushed the English out of the Indonesian archipelago in 1623 and captured Malacca from the Portuguese in 1641. Though the Dutch were at first more interested in trade than administration, by the end of the eighteenth century the Dutch claimed administrative control of Indonesia, forcing the inhabitants to grow crops like coffee, sugar, indigo, and spices and destroying any products the Indonesians might wish to grow that could undercut Dutch profits.

The French also attempted to trade in Southeast Asia, but placed equal emphasis on missionary activity. Alexhandre de Rhodes, a Jesuit priest, spent four decades in Vietnam, converting some Vietnamese to Christianity. He is most noted for devising the Roman-alphabet-based script for the Vietnamese language. Because of Vietnamese antagonism toward Christian missionary activities in the late seventeenth century, the French turned toward Thailand, where the king was more hospitable toward missionaries. But the French pushed their luck too far, attempting to capitalize on their acceptance in Thailand by sending warships and demanding special privileges. While the Thai king was away from the capital, Thai nobles pushed the French out in 1688, thereby ending French hopes in Southeast Asia until they moved into Vietnam in the nineteenth century.

The Spanish came to Southeast Asia in 1521, when Ferdinand Magellan, on his round-the-world

Southeast Asia

1633–1694	Reign of King Souligna-Vongsa in Laos
1623	Dutch begin exclusive trade in East Indies/Indonesia
1624	Alexhandre de Rhodes arrives in Vietnam; later develops script
1752–1782	Burmese incursion into Thailand
1771–1802	Tay Son uprising ends Le dynasty in Vietnam
1782	Chakri ascends Thai throne; founds dynasty
1802–1820	Reign of Gia Long in Vietnam

journey, arrived (and was promptly killed) in the Philippines. Four decades later, the Spaniards established their colony there, focusing on establishing Christianity in the islands not already converted to Islam. Catholic priests dominated villages in the Philippines, acting as administrative as well as religious leaders. The Filipinos were generally allowed only religious education and were denied the learning necessary to assume self-government. Spain's presence in the Philippines allowed the triangular trade between South America, Japan, and the Philippines, which permitted silver to become the basis of the great East Asian trade machine.

Meanwhile, domestic and interstate turmoil rent the Southeast Asian mainland. In 1752, Burmese leader Alaungpaya (AH-lowng-PAH-yah; r. 1752–1760) drove the Mons from the Burmese capital and continued fighting southward. In 1760 Alaungpaya entered Thai territory and destroyed the beautiful Thai city of Ayuthaya (AH-yoo-TAI-yah). The Burmese assault on Thailand was halted when the Qing threatened Burma. Burma fended off the Qing, but later Burmese attacks on Thailand proved futile as the Thais gradually gained power on the Southeast Asian mainland. At first, the Thais were hampered by factionalism. But in 1782, General Chakri (CHAHK-ree) emerged on top, assumed the royal title, and united Thailand. He extended Thai influence over Laos, Cambodia, and Malaya. The Chakri dynasty continues to reign in Thailand. The first Chakri ruler, Rama I, restored culture and religion after the Burmese sack of Ayuthaya. He convened a major Buddhist council in 1788, wrote and supervised an extensive collection of royal writings, and established a climate for lively production of prose and poetry.

Vietnam also underwent turmoil in this era. The Le dynasty, founded in 1428, had suffered defeat at the hands of the Mac dynasty (1527–1592). But in 1592, the Trinh (TRIN) helped the Le to regain the throne in the northern part of Vietnam. The Le's power did not extend to the south, where the Nguyen (noo-EN) family ruled. The Nguyen continued moving southward; by 1720, they wiped out the old Cham (Cambodian) kingdom and controlled both Saigon and Phnom Penh (PNOM PEN). Southern Vietnamese culture became a blend of Cambodian and Vietnamese traditions. Chinese institutions, so influential in the north, were less important in the south. Indigenous deities were incorporated into culture under the Nguyen. As elsewhere in Southeast Asia, the status of women was relatively high.

By the middle of the eighteenth century, government mismanagement and excessive taxation, accompanied by natural disasters, led to great suffering among the peasants. Rebellions, the most significant of which exploded in the region of Tay Son in 1771, broke out throughout Vietnam. The Tay Son Uprising was led by three brothers and gained the support of hill people, farmers in the lowland river basins, and small-scale merchants. One of the brothers was declared emperor, and for the first time in centuries, the north and south were united. The Qing sent in 200,000 troops to support the Le, but they failed. The Trinh were driven out in the north, and the Nguyen were almost defeated in the south. But one Nguyen prince, Nguyen Anh (noo-EN AHN), fled to Thailand, and with the help of a French priest, Pigneau de Behaine (pee-NEEOH duh be-EN), Chinese merchants in Saigon, and other foreigners, Nguyen Anh reclaimed the throne. De Behaine got the French throne to agree to help the Nguyen, but the French monarchy fell in the Revolution of 1789, and when Nguyen Anh took the royal capital at Hue in 1801 only four Frenchmen were among his forces. Nevertheless, the French had gotten their feet in Vietnam's door, and later the whole country fell under French imperialism.

Nguyen Anh declared himself Emperor Gia Long (r. 1802–1820) in 1802. Gia Long and his successor Minh Mang (r. 1820–1841) restored the power of the throne, wrote a legal code modeled on that of the Qing, and set up a Chinese-style administration. They built roads and fortifications. They encouraged the arts. Poetry by both men and women flourished. The most revered writer was Nguyen Du (1765–1820), author of *The Tale of Kieu*, whose protagonist was a dutiful daughter who suffered great sexual adversity to rescue her father. Nguyen Du, a supporter of the Trinh, saw his work as paralleling his life under rulers he deemed illegitimate. Ho Xuan Huang (HO shoo-AHN hoo-AHNG), a woman poet who lived around the same time as Nguyen Du, wrote poems that called for sexual equality and mocked stuffy social norms.

Farther south, in Indonesia, the European presence was much more compelling and the native resistance much weaker, in part because thousands of migrating Chinese had diluted the Islamic values and loyalties of Muslim societies in the Malay Archipelago. By 1750 the Dutch had subordinated most native dynasties in Malaya, Java, Sumatra, and the other islands. In the process, imported plantation agriculture brought an economic revolution that conditioned much life and labor in the whole area. For more than a century, a Muslim Malay people, known in history as the Bugis (BOO-ghees), challenged Dutch supremacy. Originating on the island of Celebes, the Bugis first won fame as sea rovers and mercenary warriors, serving all sides in the competitive spice trade through the city of Macassar (mah-CAH-sar). When the Dutch took Macassar in 1667, the Bugis scattered from Borneo to the Malay Peninsula, where they concentrated at Selangor. Through conquest, intermarriage, and intrigue, they gained control of Jahore, Perak, and Kedah on the mainland while extending their influence to Borneo and Sumatra. The Bugis fought two wars against Dutch Malacca in 1756 and 1784 but were ultimately forced to accept Dutch overlordship.

While the Dutch were consolidating their control over the Indonesian islands, the British were also expanding their trade through the Malacca Straits and seeking a naval port to counter the French who still had a presence in India in the Bay of Bengal until 1760. In 1786 the British obtained Penang on the Malay coast. Later, when France made the Netherlands a satellite state during the Napoleonic era, Britain temporarily took Malacca and Java. Penang then became a rapidly expanding center of British influence in Malaya. By the nineteenth century, Dutch fortunes shifted, and they gained control of present day Indonesia.

EUROPEANS ON NEW PACIFIC FRONTIERS

■ *How did the quest for trade turn Europeans into major actors in the Pacific region?*

Except for Spanish traders and colonists in the Philippines, the North Pacific area was almost unknown to Europeans before 1550, but many came during the next two centuries. Some of this contact involved Russian ships cruising southward toward Japan from Kamchatka (kahm-CHAHT-kah); at the same time, the French and British penetrated the North Pacific from Polynesia. By the late eighteenth century, when Western ships regularly arrived at Guangzhou from Hawaii or other Polynesian islands, East Asians began to feel the Western world crowding in on them.

DOCUMENT
A European View of Asia

Russians moved out toward the Pacific in 1632, when they established Yakutsk (yah-KOOTSK) in eastern Siberia. From there, adventurers drifted down the Lena, first reaching the Arctic and later sailing east to the open Pacific. Their discoveries were ignored until 1728, when Vitus Bering (VEE-toos BE-ring; 1680–1741), a Danish navigator sailing for Peter the Great, charted what was later named the Bering Strait, which links the Arctic and Pacific Oceans. This discovery opened the North Pacific to Russia during the eighteenth century. Meanwhile, the Russians founded Okhotsk (aw-KOTSK) on the Pacific coast opposite the Kamchatka peninsula. At Okhotsk, and at other timbered forts in Siberia, Russian governors and their Cossack soldiers exacted tribute in furs from a society of nomadic hunters. Relations between the conquerors and their subjects were not particularly friendly; indeed, local populations around the forts were often wiped out by direct violence or European diseases.

Shortly after Bering's expeditions, French and English navigators began their own extensive explorations. The most significant were those of the French noble Louis de Bougainville (loo-EE duh boo-gan-VEE; 1729–1811) and the famous English captain James Cook (1729–1779). Bougainville visited much of southern Polynesia, the Sandwich (Hawaiian) Islands, Australia, New Guinea, and New Britain. Cook's three voyages between 1768 and 1779 went beyond the known waters of the South Pacific to Antarctica and north of Alaska to the Arctic coasts, where Cook made contact with the Russians. Although he was later killed in Hawaii, Cook's journals fired European imaginations and encouraged European migration across the Pacific. Botany Bay in eastern Australia, established by the English as a penal colony in 1788, soon became a colony of settlement. Meanwhile, a swarm of Western traders, whalers, missionaries, and beachcombers descended on the South Pacific islands and the North Pacific coasts.

Perhaps the most striking feature of relations between Europeans and Pacific islanders was the contrast in gender roles. Male islanders, unlike European men, were used to female leadership; men were less possessive; and sexual indulgence was considered by both men and women as pleasurable but not overly significant. Polynesian women in Tahiti or Hawaii, when they learned that sex could be exchanged easily for European goods, met European ships when they anchored. Their preference for iron nails—no iron being found on the islands—resulted in European sailors almost dismantling their own ships.

After Cook's time, original cultures in Polynesia rapidly declined as trade goods, rum, and guns stimulated avarice, status seeking, competition for power, violence, and war. With European help, local rulers—male and female—fought to dominate their islands. Such conflict was particularly true of Hawaii in the decade after 1790, where a Hawaiian chief, Kamehameha (kah-MEH-hah-MEH-hah), used European ships and cannons to unite the three main islands. Sexual commerce with Europeans also brought

Europeans in the Pacific

1728	Vitus Bering charts Bering Strait
1779	Captain Cook killed in Hawaii
1788	Botany Bay established as British penal colony in Australia
1790	Unification of Hawaiian Islands by King Kamehameha

syphilis to the islands, blame for which was long disputed by the French and the English. Other European imports included cattle, smallpox, and missionaries. Challenged by Christian condemnation, the old religion was largely abandoned, whole communities were harmed by alcohol consumption and alcoholism, and other evidences of psychological malaise, such as suicide, became prevalent.

European expansion in the Pacific brought significant changes for East Asia, particularly in maritime commerce. After the middle of the eighteenth century, the British began replacing the Dutch as the major European traders, a trend climaxed by the collapse of the Dutch East India Company in 1794. At Guangzhou the number of British and American ships increased dramatically after 1790. Seeking a product that might be exchanged profitably for Chinese silk and tea, the British first concentrated on cotton and then later opium from India. When the opium trade created friction with Chinese officials, British merchants began seeking furs, particularly sea otter skins, which were obtained in the North Pacific. Hawaiian ports soon became busy centers for fitting ships and recruiting sailors. By 1815, European expansion into the Pacific had radically altered the structure of commerce.

CONCLUSION

At the beginning of the nineteenth century, the Ottoman Empire continued to endure, as it would into the twentieth century with the bulk of its expansive territories, including some in Europe, intact. To the east, the Qajars consolidated their power and ruled Iran for a century, despite the territorial ambitions of Russia and Britain. The Mughals, however, had lost considerable ground to their Maratha and British rivals.

Like the recently formed Sikh state, that of the Marathas remained strong and challenged the military authority of the British in India in the first half of the nineteenth century. France had recently lost influence in Vietnam—which it would regain by the end of the nineteenth century—and was acutely aware of a revived Thailand. To Vietnam's north, China continued to be the world's largest power at the end of the eighteenth century, maintaining tributary relations with its neighbors, outproducing the rest of the world, managing great domestic growth while balancing the needs of the Manchu regime with the indigenous culture of the people, and dominating international trade. But domestic corruption, social tensions at China's boundaries due to population pressures, and creeping imperialism began to undermine Chinese strength and wealth in the early nineteenth century. Korea, long accustomed to its subordinate status vis-à-vis China, developed its own fine arts and crafts. Its eighteenth-century monarchs ruled efficiently, and its creative scholars developed an exciting form of "practical learning" which produced reforms. Japan's vibrant urban society, as well as its growing regional wealth, developed institutions of government and society that set the stage for its dynamic modernization in the late nineteenth century.

Suggestions for Web Browsing

You can obtain more information about topics included in this chapter at the websites listed below. See also the companion website that accompanies this text, **http://www.ablongman.com/ brummett,** which contains an online study guide and additional resources.

Islam and Islamic History in Arabia and the Middle East:
On the coming of the West, see
http://www.islamic.org/Mosque/ihame/Sec14.htm.
On the Ottomans, see
http://www.islamic.org/Mosque/ihame/Sec13.htm.

Internet East Asia History Sourcebook:
http://www.fordham.edu/halsall/eastasia/eastasiasbook.html

Extensive online source for links about the history of East Asia, including primary documents regarding exploration, European imperialism, the legal system, and literature and arts.

Literature and Film

The following works provide an overview: Walter Andrews et al., trans., *Ottoman Lyric Poetry* (University of Texas, 1997); Kemal Silay, *Anthology of Turkish Literature* (Indiana University Press, 1998); *Evliya Çelebi in Bitlis,* ed. & trans., Robert Dankoff (Brill, 1990), the section on eastern Anatolia of the famous book of travels by the Ottoman raconteur Evilya Çelebi; and Sir John Chardin, *Travels in Persia 1673–1677* (Dover, 1988 reprint of 1927 edition).

The famous novel of Qing society *Dream of the Red Chamber* is available in various translations. See, for example, Cao Xueqin, *The Story of the Stone, The Golden Days,* trans. David Hawkes, Vol. 1 (Viking Press, 1973). For a multifaceted account of woman's place as writer during the Qing that includes representative translations of poetry, see Susan Mann, *Precious Records: Women in China's Long Eighteenth Century* (Stanford University Press, 1997). For an overview of the vibrant urban culture of Tokugawa Japan along with translations of some of the most famous short fiction of the Genroku era, see Howard

Hibbett, *The Floating World in Japanese Fiction*, 2nd ed. (Charles E. Tuttle Co., 2002).

Japanese film directors of the mid-twentieth century doted on the Tokugawa period. Numerous excellent commercial films give an insight into seventeenth-, eighteenth-, and nineteenth-century life. Kurosawa's depictions of samurai and their values may be seen in *Seven Samurai* (Toho, 1954) and *Yojimbo* ("The Bodyguard"; Kurosawa Production, 1961); a moving depiction of an early nineteenth-century physician is available in his *Red Beard* (Kurosawa Production, 1965). Filmmaker Mizoguchi Kenzo's insightful examinations of the status and roles of Tokugawa women in *The Life of Oharu: The Life of A Woman by Saikaku* (Koi Productions, 1952) are an excellent accompaniment to Ihara Saikaku's novels.

Suggestions for Reading

For background on the Ottoman Empire, see Donald Quataert, *The Ottoman Empire, 1700–1922* (Cambridge University Press, 2000); Bruce McGowan, *Economic Life in the Ottoman Empire, 1600–1800* (Cambridge University Press, 1982); Suraiya Faroqhi, *Pilgrims and Sultans: The Hajj under the Ottomans 1517–1683* (I. B. Tauris, 1994); Fatma M. Göçek, *East Encounters West* (Oxford University Press, 1987); and David Morgan, *Medieval Persia, 1040–1797* (Longman, 1988).

On the Mughal Empire, see John Richards, Gordon Johnson, and C. A. Bayly, eds., *The Mughal Empire* (Cambridge University Press, 1996); K. N. Chaudhuri, *Asia Before Europe* (Cambridge University Press, 1990); Sushil Chaudhury, Michel Morineau, Maurice Aymard, Jacques Revel, and Immanuel Wallerstein, eds., *Merchants, Companies and Trade: Europe and Asia in the Early Modern Era* (Cambridge University Press, 1999); Susan Bayly, *Caste, Society and Politics in India from the Eighteenth Century to the Modern Age* (Cambridge University Press, 1999); Matthew Edney, *Mapping an Empire: The Geographical Construction of British India, 1765–1843* (Oxford University Press, 1999); and Om Prakash, *The Dutch East India Company and the Economy of Bengal, 1630–1720* (Princeton University Press, 1985).

Among the best general surveys of Southeast Asia in this period is Anthony Reid, *Southeast Asia in the Age of Commerce, 1450–1680* (Yale University Press, 1988).

Qing China studies include Willard J. Peterson, ed., *The Cambridge History of China*, Vol. 9, part 1 (Cambridge University Press, 2001); Jonathan D. Spence, *The Search for Modern China* (W. W. Norton, 1990); and Pamela Crossley, *The Manchus* (Blackwell, 1997). R. Bin Wong, *China Transformed: Historical Change and the Limits of European Experience* (Cornell University Press, 1998), and Kenneth Pomeranz, *The Great Divergence: China, Europe, and the Making of the Modern World Economy* (Princeton University Press, 2001), place China in the world context. Jonathan Lipman, *Familiar Strangers: A History of Muslims in Northwest China* (University of Washington Press, 1998) discusses an important ethnic minority. Dorothy Ko, *Every Step a Lotus: Shoes for Bound Feet* (University of California Press, 2001) examines the meaning of foot binding in Chinese history.

Andrew C. Nahm, *Tradition and Transformation: A History of the Korean People* (Hollym International, 1988), and Carter J. Eckert et al., *Korea Old and New: A History* (Harvard University Press, 1990), offer fine treatments of major Korean developments during the period. On the roles of Korean women, see Laurel Kendall and Mark Peterson, eds., *Korean Women* (East Rock Press, 1983).

The best overview of the Tokugawa period is Conrad Totman, *Early Modern Japan* (University of California Press, 1993). Gregory M. Pflugfelder, *Cartographies of Desire* (University of California Press, 1999), offers a unique perspective on culture in the urban "pleasure quarters." On rural social change, see Anne Walthall, *Social Protest and Popular Culture in Eighteenth-Century Japan* (University of Arizona Press, 1986), and Stephen Vlastos, *Peasant Protests and Uprisings in Tokugawa Japan* (University of California Press, 1986). For Japanese intellectual developments, see Herman Ooms, *Tokugawa Ideology* (Princeton University Press, 1989). On women, see Gail Lee Bernstein, *Recreating Japanese Women, 1600–1945* (University of California Press, 1991).

Credits

Chapter 9

256 ©Archivo Iconografico, S.A./CORBIS; **259** The Pierpont Morgan Library/Art Resource, NY; **259** Belt Buckle, Visigothic (Spain), Migration Period, c. 525–560. Bronze with garnets, mother-of-pearl, green glass, traces of gilding, gold foil, W 6.7 x LL 13.3 cm. ©The Cleveland Museum of Art, 2004. Purchase from the J.H. Wade Fund, 2001.119; **262** Foto Marburg /Art Resource, NY; **270** ©Archivo Iconografico, S.A./CORBIS; **271** "Des Proprietez des Choses," 1482. British Library, London, UK/Bridgeman Art Library; **273** St. Francis Receives Approval of his 'Regula Prima' from Pope Innocent III (1160–1216) in 1210, 1297–1299 (fresco), Giotto di Bondone (c.1266–1337)/San Francesco, Upper Church, Assisi, Italy, Giraudon/Bridgeman Art Library; **279** Giraudon/Art Resource, NY; **281** Carrow Psalter detail: "The Martyrdom of Thomas a Becket," English, 1250. MS W. 34 f. 15v. The Walters Art Museum, Baltimore; **282** The Metropolitan Museum of Art, Gift of George Blumenthal, 1941. (41.100.157) Photograph ©1986 The Metropolitan Museum of Art

Chapter 10

286 Werner Forman/Art Resource, NY; **291** "Krishna Battling the Horse Demon, Keshi," 5th cent. The Metropolitan Museum of Art, Purchase, Florence and Herbert Irving Gift, 1991. (1991.300) Photograph by Bruce White. Photograph ©1994 The Metropolitan Museum of Art; **292** Ric Ergenbright Photography; **296** ©Wolfgang Kaehler/CORBIS; **298** Anonymous, Chinese, Equestrienne, Tang dynasty (618–907 CE), 2nd quarter of 8th century, Earthenware with traces of polychromy, 56.2 x 48.2 cm. Mr. and Mrs. Potter Palmer Collection, 1970.1073 Photography ©The Art Institute of Chicago; **304** Fan Kuan, "Snow Mountain and Forest." ChinaStock (WL-16); **305** Bibliothèque Nationale de France, Paris; **305** Victoria & Albert Museum, London/Art Resource, NY; **307** The National Palace Museum, Taipei, Taiwan, Republic of China (detail); **309** Special Collections, New York Public Library, Astor, Lenox and Tilden Foundations; **311** Art Resource, NY; **312** TNM Image Archives Source:http://TnmArchives.jp/; **314** Kyoto News Service; **316** Tokugawa Reimeikai Foundation, Tokyo, Japan/Bridgeman Art Library; **317** ©Sakamoto Photo Research Library/CORBIS; **319** ©Royalty-Free/CORBIS

Chapter 11

322 ©Werner Forman/CORBIS; **327** Bruce Coleman; **329** Justin Kerr; **330** Museo Nacional de Antropologia, Mexico City/Werner Forman/Art Resource, NY; **334** Ewing Krainin; **338** Mark C. Burnett, Ohio Historical Society, Columbus/Photo Researchers, Inc.; **339** Cahokia Mounds State Historic Site; **340** International Color Stock, Ltd./eStock Photo; **341** ©L. Clarke/CORBIS

Global Issue Essay

344 ©Asian Art & Archaeology, Inc./CORBIS

Chapter 12

346 British Library/Art Archive; **349** By permission of the British Library (Or. 5736.f.172v); **351** Weltkarte des piri Reis, 1513. Istanbul, Topkapi. Serail-Museum/akg – images; **352** "Suleyman the Magnificent," mid-16th cent. The Metropolitan Museum of Art, Rogers Fund, 1938. (38.149.1) Photograph ©1986 The Metropolitan Museum of Art; **354** From: Title page of Baudier's "Histoire . . . empereur des Turcs," 1631. Rare Books Division, Department of Rare Books and Special Collections, Princeton University Library; **356** "Portrait of a Sufi," 16th century. The Metropolitan Museum of Art, The Cora Timken Burnett Collection of Persian Miniatures and Other Persian Art Objects, Bequest of Cora Timken Burnett, 1956 (57.51.27). Photograph ©1989 The Metropolitan Museum of Art; **359** "Adam & Eve," detail, from a Falnama (Book of Omens), Iran, c.1550. Arthur M. Sackler Gallery, Smithsonian Institution, Washington, D.C.: Smithsonian Unrestricted Trust Funds, Smithsonian Collections Acquisition Program, and Dr. Arthur M. Sackler, S1986.251; **360** Folio from the "Haft Awrang" of Jami Iran,

1556–1565. Freer Gallery of Art, Smithsonian Institution, Washington, D.C.: Purchase, F1946.12.59a; **362** By Permission of the British Library (Or.3714. f.478); **364** J. Vidler/©SuperStock, Inc.; **365** Abu'l Hasan, "Allegorical Representation of Emperor Jahangir and Shah 'Abbas of Persia," South Asian, Mughal, c.1618. From the St. Petersburg Album. Full color and gold on paper; 23.8 x 15.4 cm. Freer Gallery of Art, Smithsonian Institution, Washington, D.C.: Purchase, (F1945.9a); **367** "Birth of a Prince" from an illustrated manuscript of the Jahangir-nama, Bishndas (Attributed to), Northern India, Mughal, c. 1620. Museum of Fine Arts, Boston, Francis Bartlett Donation of 1912 and Picture Fund (14.657)

Chapter 13

370 ©Craig Lovell/CORBIS; **374** "Portrait of Hung-Wu." National Palace Museum, Taipei. Photograph by Wan-go H. C. Weng; **375** By permission of the British Library, (Maps 33.c.13); **379** National Palace Museum, Taipei, Taiwan, Republic of China; **380** Victoria & Albert Museum, London/Art Resource, NY; **380** National Palace Museum, Taipei, Taiwan, Republic of China; **383**; **383** Courtesy, The Trustees of the Victoria and Albert Museum, Photograph by Ian Thomas; **388** ©Mike Yamashita/CORBIS; **390** ©Michael Maslan Historic Photographs/CORBIS; **393** ©Richard Bickel/CORBIS

Chapter 14

397 Vatican Museums and Galleries, Vatican City, Italy/Bridgeman Art Library; **401** Scala/Art Resource, NY; **402** Scala/Art Resource, NY; **402** Erich Lessing/Art Resource, NY; **404** SCALA/Art Resource, NY; **405** Erich Lessing/Art Resource, NY; **405** Scala/Art Resource, NY; **406** Bibliothèque de l'Institute de France, Paris; **407** Erich Lessing/Art Resource, NY; **408** Scala/Art Resource, NY; **408** Kunsthistorisches Museum, Vienna, Austria/Bridgeman Art Library; **409** akg – images; **410** Giraudon/Art Resource, NY; **411** ©National Gallery, London (NG 186); **411** ©Archivo Iconografico, S.A./CORBIS; **412** SCALA/Art Resource, NY; **413** Réunion des Musées Nationaux/Art Resource, NY; **417** Lucas Cranach the Younger, "Martin Luther and the Wittenberg Reformers," c.1543. Toledo Museum of Art (1926.55). Purchased with funds from the Libbey Endowment, Gift of Edward Drummond Libbey; **420** Erich Lessing/Art Resource, NY; **423** Giraudon/Art Resource, NY; **428** Scala/Art Resource, NY

Chapter 15

432 Elizabeth I, Armada portrait, c.1588 (oil on panel), English School, (16th century)/Private Collection/Bridgeman Art Library; **434** Giraudon/Art Resource, NY; **436** Ken Walsh Private Collection/Bridgeman Art Library; **437** ©CORBIS; **439** ©Austrian Archives; Haus-, Hof- und Staatsarchiv, Vienna/CORBIS; **444** Scala/Art Resource, NY; **446** Erich Lessing/Art Resource, NY; **449** ©Archivo Iconografico, S.A./CORBIS; **451** ©Archivo Iconografico, S.A./CORBIS; **455** Wallach Collection, New York Public Library, Astor, Lenox and Tilden Foundations; **456** Les Musées de la Ville de Strasbourg

Global Issue Essay

461 ©Bettmann/Corbis

Chapter 16

462 British Museum, London, UK/Bridgeman Art Library; **465** National Maritime Museum, Greenwich (HC0705); **466** ©Bettmann/CORBIS; **468** The Art Archive/Museo de Arte Antiga Lisbon/Dagli Orti; **470** Werner Forman /Art Resource, NY; **475** ibliothèque Nationale de France, Paris; **477** ©The Trustees of the British Museum (1950AM22 1); **481** akg – images; **483** Musées Royaux des Beaux-Arts de Belgique; **487** Library of Congress (LC-USZ62-14987)

Chapter 17

490 ©Rijksmuseum, Amsterdam; **493** ©CORBIS; **495** ©CORBIS; **497** ©CORBIS; **503** Erich Lessing/Art Resource, NY; **505** Réunion des Musées Nationaux/Art Resource, NY; **506** Réunion des Musées Nationaux/Art Resource, NY; **510** Danish Royal Collections at Rosenborg Castle (#1612); **510** ©Archivo Iconografico, S.A./CORBIS; **513** Ursula Edelmann; **515** ©Bettmann/CORBIS

Chapter 18

527 Giraudon/Art Resource, NY; **529** By permission of the British Library (Maps C.6.c.3 bet 22 &

23); **531** Erich Lessing/Art Resource, NY; **533** National Portrait Gallery, London (NPG 3846); **540** Sovfoto; **542** Giraudon/Art Resource, NY; **548** Giraudon/Art Resource, NY; **549** Giraudon/Art Resource, NY; **552** Erich Lessing/Art Resource, NY

Chapter 19

560 ©Gianni Dagli Orti/CORBIS; **563** Library of Congress/Fairstreet Pictures; **564** Library of Congress/Fairstreet Pictures; **568** Jean-Loup Charmet/Bridgeman Art Library; **573** By Permission of the British Library (1047.h.16 opp.p.58 in book); **573** South African Library of Capetown/Panos Pictures; **576** Mary Evans Picture Library; **576** George McAll Theal map of South Africa; **579** Peter Newark's Pictures; **580** Roger-Viollet/Getty Images

Global Issue Essay

584 ©Bettman/CORBIS

Chapter 20

586 Museum of Fine Arts, Boston. William Sturgis Bigelow Collection, 11.19687. Photograph ©2004 Museum of Fine Arts, Boston; **590** "Birth in a Harem," late 18th century. Los Angeles County Museum of Art, The Edward Binney, 3rd Collection of Turkish Art at the Los Angeles County Museum of Art. Photograph ©2005 Museum Associates/LACMA; **593** Mary Evans Picture Library; **597** Victoria & Albert Museum, London/Art Resource, NY; **598** ©Otto Money (photography by AIC Photographic Services); **600** Photograph Courtesy Peabody Essex Museum (Neg# 19184); **601** ©Pierre Colombel/CORBIS; **602** Giuseppe Castiglione, Italian (worked in China), 1688–1766. "Inauguration Portraits of Emperor Quianlong, the Empress, and the Eleven Imperial Consorts," 1736. Handscroll, ink and color on silk, 52.9 x 688.3 cm. ©The Cleveland Museum of Art. John L. Severance Fund, 1969.31; **605** Réunion des Musées Nationaux/Art Resource, NY; **608** Erich Lessing/Art Resource, NY; **611** Isoda Koryusai, "Hinagata Wakana Hatsumoyo" series, c.1775. Collection of The Newark Museum, Louis V. Ledoux Collection. The Newark Museum/Art Resource, NY

Notes

Chapter 10

1. Stanley Wolpert, *A New History of India*, 7th ed. (New York: Oxford University Press, 2004), p. 79.
2. Hermann Kulke and Dietmar Rothermund, *History of India*, 3rd ed. (London: Routledge, 1998), p. 147.
3. *Alberuni's India*, trans. Edward Sachau (New York: Norton, 1971), p. 100.
4. Minhaju-s Siraj, quoted in John Keay, *India: A History* (New York: Grove Press, 2000), p. 245.
5. Excerpt from poem by Xu Yeueying, in Kan-I Sun Chang and Haun Saussy, eds., *Women Writers of Traditional China* (Stanford, Calif.: Stanford University Press, 1999), p. 78.
6. Quoted in H. H. Gowen and H. W. Hall, *An Outline History of China* (New York: Appleton, 1926), p. 117.
7. *The Works of Li Po*, trans. Shigeyoshi Obata (New York: Dutton, 1950), no. 71.
8. Du Fu, "A Song of War Chariots," in Cyril Birch, ed., *Anthology of Chinese Literature* (New York: Grove Press, 1965), pp. 240–241.
9. Marco Polo, *The Travels of Marco Polo* (New York: Grosset & Dunlap, 1931), pp. 30, 133–149.
10. Donald Keene, ed., *Anthology of Japanese Literature: From the Earliest Era to the Mid-Nineteenth Century* (New York: Grove Press, 1955), pp. 39–41.
11. Murasaki Shikibu, "The Diary of Murasaki Shikibu," in Donald Keene, ed., *Anthology of Japanese Literature* (New York: Grove Press, 1960), p. 152.

Chapter 11

1. Quoted by Clements Markham, in Edward Hyams and George Ordish, *The Last of the Incas* (New York: Simon & Schuster, 1963), p. 88.

Global Issues: Location and Identity

1. Emanuel Bowen, *Complete Atlas of the Known World* (London, 1752), cited in Martin W. Lewis and Kären Wigen, *The Myth of Continents: A Critique of Metageography* (Berkeley: University of California Press, 1997), p. 29.
2. Just as the European-initiated paradigm of East and West influenced people outside of Europe in the past century, China's view of itself as the "Middle Kingdom" has influenced non-Chinese views of the rest of Asia. On maps of Asia, Japan sometimes gets chopped off, and in teaching about East Asia, Korea and Vietnam have only recently joined China and Japan as deserving of treatment.
3. Cited by Lewis and Wigen, p. 69.
4. Robert B. Marks, *The Origins of the Modern World: A Global and Ecological Narrative* (Lanham, Md.: Rowman and Littlefield, 2002), pp. 52–53.
5. Lewis and Wigen, p. 23.
6. An early critic of the arbitrary binary divide between East and West is Edward W. Said, *Orientalism* (New York: Pantheon, 1978).
7. Karl Wittfogel, *Oriental Despotism: A Comparative Study of Total Power* (New Haven, Conn.: Yale University Press, 1957). Because Asian agriculture—uniquely—required irrigation, Wittfogel alleged, autocratic government came into being there. The argument may be logical, but the ecological premise is wrong.

Chapter 12

1. Vincent A. Smith, *Akbar, the Great Mogul*, 2nd ed. (Mystic, Conn.: Verry, 1966), p. 522.
2. Zahiruddin Muhammad Babur, *Baburnama*, trans. and ed. Wheeler Thackston (New York: Oxford University Press, 1996), pp. 350–351.
3. Babur, p. 351.
4. Quoted in Bamber Gascoigne, *The Great Moghuls* (New York: Harper & Row, 1971), p. 128.

Chapter 14

1. Quoted in Roland Bainton, *Here I Stand: A Life of Martin Luther* (New York: Abingdon Cokesbury, 1950), p. 54.
2. Quoted in Heiko A. Oberman, *Luther, Between God and the Devil* (New Haven, Conn.: Yale University Press, 1982) p. 190, see also pp. 187–188.
3. From Henry Bettenson, ed., *Documents of the Christian Church* (New York: Oxford University Press, 1963), pp. 280–283.
4. Quoted in Harold Grim, *The Reformation Era* (New York: Macmillan, 1968), p. 17.
5. From "Institutes of the Christian Religion," in Harry J. Carroll et al., eds., *The Development of Civilization* (Glenview, Ill.: Scott, Foresman, 1970), pp. 91–93.
6. From Lowell H. Zuck, ed., *Christianity and Revolution* (Philadelphia: Temple University Press, 1975), pp. 95–97.

Chapter 15

1. Charles Tilly, ed., *The Formation of the National States in Western Europe* (Princeton, N.J.: Princeton University Press, 1975), p. 42.
2. See Charles Tilly, *Coercion, Capital, and European States, AD 990–1992* (Oxford: Blackwell, 1992).
3. Lonnie R. Johnson, *Central Europe: Enemies, Neighbors, Friends* (New York/Oxford: Oxford University Press, 1996), p. 63.
4. See K. Bosl, A. Gieysztor, F. Graus, M. M. Postan, F. Seibt, *Eastern and Western Europe in the Middle Ages*, ed. Geoffrey Barraclough (London: Thames and Hudson, 1970).
5. Wallace T. MacCaffrey, *Elizabeth I, War and Politics 1558–1603* (Princeton, N.J.: Princeton University Press, 1992), p. 6.
6. Peter F. Sugar, *Southeastern Europe under Ottoman Rule: 1354–1804*, Vol. 5 of Peter F. Sugar and Donald W. Treadgold, eds., *A History of East Central Europe* (Seattle and London: University of Washington Press, 1977), pp. 55–59, 273–274.

Chapter 16

1. Quoted in David Killingray, *A Plague of Europeans* (New York: Penguin, 1973), p. 20.
2. Quoted in Robert Rotberg, *A Political History of Tropical Africa* (New York: Harcourt Brace, 1965), pp. 85–86.
3. Quoted in John Middleton, *The World of the Swahili: An African Mercantile Civilization* (New Haven, Conn.: Yale University Press, 1992), pp. 46–47.

Chapter 17

1. Quoted in F. Tyler, *The Modern World* (New York: Farrar & Rinehart, 1939), p. 186.
2. Quoted in Robert B. Asprey, *Frederick the Great: The Magnificent Enigma* (New York: Ticknor & Fields, 1986).
3. See the superb book by Simon Schama, *The Embarrassment of Riches: An Interpretation of Dutch Culture in the Golden Age* (New York: Vintage, 1997).
4. Quoted in Pierre Gaxotte, *Frederick the Great* (London: Bell, 1941), p. 357.

Chapter 18

1. Quoted in Stillman Drake, *Galileo at Work* (Chicago: University of Chicago Press, 1978), p. 41.
2. Quoted in Stephen F. Mason, *A History of Sciences* (New York: Collier Books, 1962), p. 206.
3. Quoted in James Harvey Robinson and Charles A. Beard, *Readings in European History*, Vol. 1 (Boston: Ginn and Co., 1908), pp. 202–205.
4. Quoted in E. Neville Williams, *The Ancient Régime in Europe* (New York: Harper & Row, 1970), p. 424.

Chapter 19

1. Hilary Beckles, *Natural Rebels: A Social History* (New Brunswick, N.J.: Rutgers University Press, 1989), p. 155.
2. Richard Pankhurst, *The Ethiopians* (London: Blackwell Publishers, 1998), p. 109.
3. Donald Crummey, *Land and Society in the Christian Kingdom of Ethiopia from the Thirteenth to the Twentieth Century* (James Currey, 2000), p. 95.
4. Crummey, p. 131.

Chapter 20

1. From Walter Andrews et al., trans., *Ottoman Lyric Poetry* (Austin: University of Texas Press, 1997), p. 137.

Index

Note: Page numbers followed by letters *i* and *m* indicate illustrations and maps, respectively. Boldface page numbers indicate key terms.

A

Aachen (Aix-la-Chapelle), Germany: Charlemagne's palace in, 262i; as "New Rome," 262
Abbasid dynasty, 305; Crusades and, 275; Delhi sultans and, 293; Mongols and, 307
Abbas the Great (Safavid), 359–361, 365i
Abbots: as vassals, 267
Abdullahi (Sokoto Caliphate), 570
Abdülhamid I (Ottoman), 591
Abolitionism, 585
Absolutism, 491, **502**; in Continental Europe, 507–512; decline of, 522–524; diplomacy and war during, 516–520; in England, 515–516; Enlightenment thinkers on, 539; in France, 505–506; Locke on, 533; of Louis XIV (France), 491, 502–505; philosophes critique of, 537; in Prussia, 508–510; in Russia, 510–512
Academies: in Florence, 403; in Korea, 383; of Science (France), 532; scientific, 532
Accolade, 268
Acre, 276
Acton, Lord: on tyranny of the majority, 553
Adam and Eve: Islamic story of, 359i
Adams, Abigail, 536
Adena culture, 337–338; Great Serpent Mound of, 338i
Administration: of Carolingian Empire, 262; of manor, 270; of Ming China, 376; of Mughal Empire, 365–367; Ottoman, 352. See also Government; specific countries
Adrianople: Ottoman conquest of, 452
Afghanistan/Afghans, 307; Ahmad Khan and, 595; Persia and, 593, 594
Afonso (Don): Nzinga Mbemba as, 470, 473

Africa: 1650–1850, 561–582; American crops in, 566; Atlantic slave trade and, 566–568; Bantu-speaking societies in, 571; before Europeans, 575m; Europeans and, 563; French in, 486; Islam in, 569–571; kingdoms in, 567m; myth of empty land and, 577, 577m; population increases in, 566; Portugal and, 465, 469–474; "the scattering" in, 572; Sebastian Munster's map of, 471, 471i; slaves in, 566, 585; slave trade and, 474, 479m; societies in, 567m; state formation in, 572–574, 578–581. See also specific countries and groups
Afrikaners, 572; migration by, 575–576, 576i, 576m; rebellion against British, 578
Afro-Portuguese, 580
Afshar tribe, 593
Afzal Khan (India), 595
Against the Thievish and Murderous…Peasants (Luther), 419
Age of Reason, 532–539. See also Enlightenment
Agnesi, Maria, 530
Agra, 364, 487
Agriculture: in Americas, 324, 478; Aztec, 330–331; capitalist, 493–494, 493i; in China, 295, 601; French Revolution and, 541–542; increased fertility and, 498; Iroquoian, 337; in Japan, 313, 608, 609; in Korea, 382; in Lake Victoria region, 578; large-market, 398; maize and, 324; medieval, 269; of Mogollon, Hohokam, and Anasazi, 340; North American Indian, 336–337; in Turkic empires, 367–368; women and, 499. See also Farms and farming; specific countries
Ahmad Gran, Ahmad al-Ghazi, 474
Ahmad Khan (Persia), 595
Ahmed I (Ottoman), 355
Ahmed III (Ottoman), 590
Air pump, 531
Ajanta, India: sculptures at, 290

I-2

Akan peoples, 567
Akan states: Portugal and, 469–470
Akbar (Mughal Empire), 347, 363, 365
Alam II (Mughal Empire), 598
Alaska, 615; Aleuts and Inuits and, 341–342; Eskimo peoples, 324
Ala ud-Din (India), 293–294
Alaungpaya (Burma), 614
Albania, 452
Albert (Austrian Habsburgs): in Netherlands, 450
Albert of Mainz (Archbishop), 417
Albuquerque, Alfonso de, 467, 469
Alcacovas, Treaty of, 466
Alcohol and alcoholism: in London, 498–499
Alembert, Jean d', 534, 535, 536
Aleut peoples, 341
Alexander I (Russia), 555
Alexis Romanov, 451
Alexius Comnenus (Byzantium), 275
Alfonso VI (Portugal), 507
Algonquin people, 337
Allahabad, Treaty of, 598
Allen, Ethan, 536
Alliances: in 1750s, 520; between Austria and Prussia, 548. *See also* specific alliances
Allies: Aztec, 331
Alphabet(s): Korean han'gul, 383; Thai, 391
Alsace, 456, 518
Alternate attendance system (Japan), 390, **606,** 607
Alva, duke of: in Netherlands, 446
Amaterasu (goddess), 313, 314
Ambassadors: Ottoman, 591, 592
American Colonization Society (ACS), **569**
American Philosophical Society for Promoting Useful Knowledge, 536
American Revolution, 516
Americas: to 1492, 322*i*, 323–342; Dutch in, 485; Europe and, 305; French in, 485–486; human settlement of, 324; Iberian regimes in, 477–482; New Spain in, 474–477; origins of cultures in, 324; Portugal and, 467; slavery in, 585; smallpox in, 475, 476, 480; smuggling in, 521; trade and, 492. *See also* West Indies; specific locations; specific regions
Americo-Liberians, 569
Amerindians, 323; Christianity and, 481; Cortés and, 475; cultures of, 324; ethnolinguistic groups of, 324; European and African diseases among, 479–480; Hohokam, 339; Iberian effects on, 479–482; Inuit and Aleut, 341–342; Mississippian culture of, 338–339; Mogollon people and, 339; Navajo, Apache, Mandan, and, 340–341; of North America, 336–342, 337*m*; resistance to Europeans by, 481; as slaves, 478*i*; Spanish mistreatment of, 476; women of, 476–477. *See also* specific groups
Amida, 319
Amsterdam, 483; intellectual thought in, 532–533. *See also* Bank of Amsterdam
Anabaptism, **421,** 425
Anasazi culture, 339–340; at Mesa Verde, 340*i*
Anatomy, 530
Ancien régime (Old Regime), 524, 534, **534**; end of, 543; political critique of, 537–539. *See also* French Revolution (1789)
Andes region: Inca Empire in, 332–336
Andō Hiroshige (Japan), 611, 613
Anglican Church, 442, 516; in England, 419–421, 421
Anglo-American colonies, 487
Anglo-Dutch naval wars, 517
Anglo-Saxons: conversion to Christianity, 258; in England, 279
Angola, 472, 562, 568, 568*i*; Dutch and, 484
Animals: in Americas, 324
Anjou, 278
An Lushan (Tang China), 299–301, 305
Anna Ivanovna (Russia), 512
Annam, 297
Anne of Austria, 444
Annulment: for Henry VIII (England), **420**
Antigua, 487
Antioch, 275
Antwerp, 445, 483*i*; Spanish sack of, 447
Apache Indians, 341; Anasazi and, 340
Apologetic History of the Indies (Las Casas), 481*i*
Apprentices, 272, 499
Arabia, 293
Arabs and Arab world: Omani, 469; slave trade and, 561, 585; zero and, 291. *See also* Arabia; Islam
Aragon: Ferdinand of, 437
Arawak Indians, 480
Archbishop: of Canterbury, 280

Architecture: Anasazi, 340, 340*i*; in China, 379; in Japan, 314*i*, 386, 388; Mughal, 364*i*, 365; Ottoman, 356; Persian, 361; of Tenochtitlán, 330
Arctic Canada: Inuit of, 324
Argentina, 476
Arguin, 469
Arian heresy, 259
Aristocracy: in China, 297; in Europe, 261, 496–497; in France, 505; opposition by, 502; women in, 499
Aristotle, 260; geocentric theory and, 529; physics and, 528; Scholastics and, 403
Arius, 259
Armada (Spain), 450
Armed forces: Carolingian, 264; in China, 380–381; European, 433, 523–524; in France, 437, 506, 549, 550, 553–554; Incan, 335; in Japan, 315; in Morocco, 570; Ottoman, 353, 357, 593; Safavid, 359; in Spanish Netherlands, 446. *See also* specific battles and wars
Art(s): in Benin, 470*i*; Carolingian, 259*i*; in China, 304, 600; in Gupta India, 290–291, 291*i*; in High Renaissance, 406–408; in Italian Renaissance, 404–408; in Japan, 316–318, 386–389, 611–613; Korean, 604–605; in Ottoman Empire, 356–357; Persian, 361; in Turkic empires, 367. *See also* specific forms
Artifacts: Clovis spear points as, 324; in Nara, Japan, 317*i*
Artisans: in India, 288; in Korea, 382
Aryabhatta (Gupta scientist), 291
Asantehene Osei Tutu, 567
Asante kingdom, 567, 569
Asell, Mary, 535
Ashikaga shōguns, 388
Ashikaga Takauji, 384
Ashley, Lord (count of Shaftesbury, England), 532
Asia: beauty standards in, 298*i*; civilization of, 287–288; classical culture in, 312; Dutch trade with, 484; as East, 345; hegemony of, 286*i*, 287–288; imperialism and (1800), 604*m*; Portugal and, 465, 467. *See also* Central Asia
Askeri class (Ottoman Empire), 356
Assemblies: in France, 279, 554; Spanish Cortes as, 438

Assemblies of Notables (France), 541, 542
Assignats (France), 544
Astrolabe, **464**
Astronomy: Mayan, 328; in scientific revolution, 530
Atahualpa (Inca), 476
Atlantic Ocean region: Italian merchants and, 483; Portuguese sugar plantations in, 479; slave trade in, 562–568, 585
Atzcapotzalco, 329, 330
Audiencias (councils), 477
Auerstadt, battle at, 555
Augsburg Confession (Luther), 419
Augustinians, **416**, 417
Aurangzeb (Mughal), 365, 587, 594–595, 596
Australia, 615; Dutch and, 484
Austria, 262, 441; East India Company in, 493; French Revolution and, 547, 548; Habsburgs in, 508; Napoleon and, 556; Ottomans and, 590, 591; Polish partition and, 519; Spain and, 517; after Thirty Years' War, 457
Austrian Empire: Habsburgs in, 453–457
Authority: Hobbes on, 502
Autocracy: in Russia, 450–452, 510–512, 540
Avars, 262
Avignon papacy, 414, 415
Avis dynasty (Portugal), 465
Ayscough, Anne, 422
Ayuthaya, Thailand, 391, 614
Azerbaijan: Ottomans, Safavids, and, 357*m*
Azores, 438, 466
Azov, 517
Aztecs, 324, 330–332; mask of, 330*i*; Mayas and, 328; monarchy of, 324; Spain and, 474
Azuchi Castle, 386

B

Babur (Mughal dynasty), 294, 362–363, 362*i*
Babylonian Captivity: of Catholic Church, 414
Bacon, Francis (scientist), 528, 531
Bada Shuren (China), 600
Baeda Maryam (Ethiopia), 474
Bahamas, 480, 487
Bailiffs, 270
Bakewell, Robert, 494
Balance-of-power diplomacy, 416

Balance of power: France and, 557; in Habsburg Empire, 445*m*; Poland and, 519; Spanish failure and, 450; after Treaty of Utrecht, 518–520; wars over, 491
Balance of trade: mercantilism and, 506
Balasore, 487
Bali: Islam and, 394
Balkan region, 452–453; governments in, 452. *See also* Eastern Europe; specific countries
Baltic region: Hanseatic League in, 398; St. Petersburg and, 510–511, 517
Banking, 483, 496; capitalism and, 492; Italy and, 400
Bank of Amsterdam, 492
Bank of England, 492, 522
Bank of France, 554
Bankruptcy: of France, 544; of Spain, 445
Bantu groups, 571, 577, 580
Baptists, 425
Barbados, 487
Barometer, 531
Barons (England), 437; John and, 280. *See also* Aristocracy
Barracoons (slave stockades), **562,** 563
Basel: Calvin in, 423
Basotho kingdom, 573–574
Bassi, Laura, 530
Bastille: demolition of, 543
Batavia, Java, 484, 485*i*
Bathing: Safavid, 360*i*
Battle of the Nations, 557
Battles: Korea-Japan, 384; naval, 484. *See also* specific battles and wars
Bavaria, 262, 455
Bayeux tapestry, 279*i*
Bayezid I (Ottoman), 349
Bayezid II (Ottoman), 352, 354, 359
Bayinnaung (Burma), 392
Bayle, Pierre, 534
Bayonet, 506
Beatrice, Doña (Kimpa Vita) (Kongo kingdom), 568
Beauty: standards of, 298*i*
Beccaria, Cesare, 536
Becket, Thomas à, 280, 281*i*, 436
"Beggar depots" (France), 501
Beijing, 307; Ming capital in, 375; Qing rulers in, 598, 601

Belgium: France and, 517
Belgrade: Ottomans in, 352
Benedictines, 272; monasticism of, 258; as nuns, 275
Benefice: fief as, 266
Benevolent despot, 538–539
Bengal region, 293, 520, 595, 597, 598
Benguela (African port), 568
Benin, 466, 469, 470; arts in, 470*i*
Bentham, Jeremy, 535
Bering, Vitus, 615
Bering Strait, 615; land bridge across, 324
Berlin: Napoleon in, 555
Bermuda: English in, 487
Bernard of Clairvaux (Saint), 273
Bernini, Giovanni: *Ecstasy of St. Teresa,* 428*i*
Beverages: from New World and Asia, 483
Bhagavad-Gita, 289
Bhakti: as path to salvation, **289**
Bible: Complutensian, 413; in Gothic language, 259; Lutheran, 418; printed Gutenberg, 409, 409*i*
Bill of Rights: in England, 516
Biology: in scientific revolution, 530
Birmingham, England, 498
Birth of Venus (Botticelli), 405*i*
Al-Biruni, 293
Bishops: as vassals, 267
Black Death. *See* Bubonic Plague
Black Plague. *See* Bubonic Plague
Black Sea: Russia and, 591
Blockade(s): Continental System as, 555
Block printing: in China, 299
Blood flow, 530
Blücher, Gebhard von, 557
Boccaccio, Giovanni, 402
Bodhisattvas, **296**
Boers, 572, 574; Great Trek by, 575–576, 576*i*, 576*m*, 577
Boethius (scholar), 260
Bohemia, 438, 441; dynasties in, 441; Habsburgs in, 508; Hus in, 414–415; peasant rebellions in, 501
Bohemian phase: of Thirty Years' War, 453–455
Bo Juyi (Tang poet): "Song of Everlasting Sorrow, The," 300
Boleyn, Anne, 420, 421
Bologna: university in, 274
Bombay, 487, 597

Boniface (English missionary), 259–260
Boniface VIII (Pope), 413–414; Philip IV (France) and, 279
Bonneval, Comte de, 591
Book(s): in China, 303; European printing and, 409; illuminated (Japan), 613; Korean, 383
Book of Kells, 260
Book of the City of Ladies, The (Christine de Pizan), 400
"Boom and bust" market, 493
Bora, Katherine von, 418–419
Border(s): Ottoman, 352; in Turkic empires, 368. *See also* Boundaries; Frontiers
Boris Godunov (Russia), 451
Borneo, 615
Bosch, Hieronymus, 411, 412; *Hell,* from *The Garden of Earthly Delights,* 411, 412
Bossuet, Jacques, 502
Boston, 486
Botticelli, Sandro, 405; *Birth of Venus,* 405*i*
Boucier, Guillaume, 308
Bougainville, Louis de, 615
Boundaries: of France, 519
Bourbon (Réunion): France and, 486
Bourbon dynasty, 456; France and, 447, 450; in Spain, 507
Bourgeoisie: Catholic Church and, 413
Boyars, 451
Boyle, Robert, 530
Boys: in Ottoman service, 452–453
Bradstreet, Anne, 487
Brahe, Sophia, 528
Brahe, Tycho, 528
Brahmans (Indian priestly class): in India, 289
Brandenburg: elector of, 507, 509*m*
Brandenburg-Prussia: Treaty of Utrecht and, 518*m*
Brazil: Dutch and, 484, 485; government of, 478; industries in, 478; plantation system in, 479; Portugal and, 467; slavery in, 568
Bread riots: in French Revolution, 550
Breitenfeld, battle of, 456*i*
Bride price: in China, 378
Bristol, England, 498
Britain. *See* England (Britain)
British East India Company, 484, 487, 495, 520, 596; Zanzibar and, 579
British Empire, 486–487. *See also* England (Britain)

Brothels: in Japan, 610–611
Brueghel, Pieter, the Elder, 411–412; *Massacre of the Innocents, The,* 446*i*
Bruno, Giordano, 532
Brunswick, duke of, 548
Bubonic Plague, **398**; east Central Europe and, 440
Bucer, Martin, 424–425
Buddha and Buddhism: in Asia, 287; Chan sect of, **298**, 301; in China, 295, 296, 308; in India, 292; Indian trade and, 289; in Japan, 313, 314, 318–319, 319*i*, 372, 607; in Korea, 312, 384; Oda Nobunaga and, 386; Pure Land sect of, 296, 298, 301; rock carvings and, 296*i*; in Song China, 304; in Southeast Asia, 391; suppression in China, 301; in Vietnam, 393
Buenos Aires, 476
Buffalo: Amerindians and, 341
Buganda, 562, 578, 579*i*
Bugis people, 614–615
Building: Incan, 336. *See also* Architecture
Bulgaria and Bulgarians: Second Bulgarian Empire and, 452
Bullionism, **506**; critique of, 537
Bull of demarcation, 466
Bunraku theater (Japan), 612
Bunyoro kingdom, 578
Bureaucracy: in China, 600, 603; economy and, 521–522; Ottoman, 452–453; in Tang China, 297
Burgundy, 264
Burial mounds: Adena and Hopewell, 338, 338*i*
Burma, 391–392, 393, 614; Portugal and, 468; Thailand and, 614
Busaid dynasty, 579
Bushidō (Way of the Warrior, Japan), **610**
Byzantium (Byzantine Empire): Balkans and, 452

C

Cabildos (advisory councils), **477**
Cabinet: in England, 516
Cabot, John, 486
Cabral, Pedro, 467
Caciques (Amerindian chiefs), **477**, 480, 482
Cahiers, 542

Cahokia, Illinois, 324, 339*i*; Mississippian culture in, 338–339; slavery at, 585
Calais: English control of, 437
Calcutta, 598
Calendar: Aztec, 332; in France, 550; Incan, 336; Mayan, 328
Calicoes, 521
Calicut, 467
Calligraphy: in Japan, 610; in Korea, 383; Ottoman, 356; in Song China, 304
Calpulli (Aztec clans), **330,** 331
Calvin, John, and Calvinism, 423–425, 443; in Central Europe, 455; in France, 447; Knox and, 425; spread of, 426*m*
Calvinist Fury (Netherlands), 446
Cambodia (Kampuchea): Portugal and, 468; Thais and, 392, 614
Cameron, Ian, 332
Campo Formio, Treaty of, 552
Canals: Hohokam, 339; Incan, 334
Canary Islands, 464, 466, 466*i*; plantations in, 478
Cannons, 464; in China, 302
Canon law, 273
Canossa: Henry IV at, 282
Canterbury, England: Cathedral in, 421, 442; pilgrim's map of, 436*i*
Canterbury Tales (Chaucer), 400
Canton, China. *See* Guangzhou (Canton), China
Canute (Denmark), 279
Cao Xueqin (China), 602
Cape Bojador, 464
Cape Colony, 574, 578
"Cape Coloureds," 572
Cape of Good Hope, 466, 467, 572
Cape region: in southern Africa, 571
Capetian dynasty (France), 278–279
Cape Town, 572
Cape Verde Islands, 466, 469, 479
Capital (financial): for agriculture, 494
Capital cities: of Mehmed II, 356. *See also* specific cities
Capitalism, **492**; aristocracy and, 496–497; European, 463, 483; expansion of, 492–493; free enterprise, 493; industry and, 562; from Northern Europe, 488; social crises and, 496–502; in woolen industry, 400
Capitalist agriculture, 493–494, 499

Caral, Peru, 324
Caravan trade, 310, 368, 580; Muslims and, 464
Cardinal directions, 344–345
Caribbean region: Dutch in, 484; France in, 486; slaves in, 479; sugar plantations in, 564
Carib Indians, 486, 487
Carlowitz, Peace of, 591
Carnarvon, Lord (England), 578
Carnot, Lazare, 549
Carolinas: England and, 486
Carolingian Empire, 261–264, 264*m*; frontiers of, 262; Lindau Gospels from, 259*i*
Carrow Psalter, 281*i*
Carrying trade, 465*i*
Cartaz (Portuguese license), **468**
Cartier, Jacques, 485
Cartography: Ottoman, 351; Portuguese, 464
Casimir the Great (Poland), 441
Cassiodorus, 260
Caste system: al-Biruni on, 293; in India, 596
Castile: Isabella of, 437
Catalonia, 262
Cateau-Cambrésis, Treaty of, 447
Cathay (China), 308
Catherine I (Russia), 512
Catherine II the Great (Russia), 512, 539–540, 540*i*
Catherine de Medici, 447
Catherine of Aragon, 420, 421, 442
Catholic Church: Babylonian Captivity of, 414; in Bohemia, 441; in Central Europe, 455–456; in China, 600*i*; Conciliar Movement in, 415–416; Copernicus and, 528; crisis in (1300–1517), 413–416; doctrine of, 427; in Early Middle Ages, 258–260; eastern frontier of, 440–442; in England, 420–421, 442–443, 515; English immigrants and, 486; in Ethiopia, 580–581; feudalism and, 267; French Revolution and, 550; global nature of, 428; Great Schism in, 415; in High Middle Ages, 272–275; in Holy Roman Empire, 508; humanists and, 413; in Japan, 469, 607; in Kongo, 470; in Korea, 605; missionaries from, 429; in Netherlands, 446; plague and, 398; political challenges to, 415; in Prussia, 539; reform in, 416, 426–428; on

Catholic Church, *continued*
salvation, 418; in Spain, 444; spiritual and intellectual developments in, 416; after Thirty Years' War, 456. *See also* Clergy; Papacy; Pope(s); specific popes
Catholic Counter-Reformation. *See* Counter-Reformation (Catholic)
Catholic league, 455
Cattle, 494
Cavendish, Henry, 530
Cayuga Indians, 337
Çelebi, Evliya, 355
Celebes, island of, 614
Cellarius, Andreas, 528, 528*i*
Cellini, Benvenuto: *Saltcellar of Francis I*, 408*i*
Cempoala people, 475
Central Africa: long-distance trade in, 579–580
Central America, 325; civilizations of, 326*m*; smallpox in, 480. *See also* Americas; Latin America
Central Asia, 349; China and, 297, 301*m*, 600; Mongols in, 305–307; Muslims and, 293
Central Europe: 1300–1521, 438–439; Habsburgs in, 453–457; religious wars in, 443
Central government: in China, 297
Centralization: in France, 503, 523
Ceramics: in Korea, 383
Cervantes, Miguel de, 410
Cetshwayo (Zulu), 578
Ceuta, Morocco, 438; Henry the Navigator and, 466
Chaghatai khanate, 349
Chakri dynasty (Thailand), 614
Champagne, France, 271, 278
Cham people, 391
Champlain, Samuel de, 485–486
Chan Buddhism, **298**, 301
Chandra Gupta I (India), 288, 289
Chandra Gupta II (India), 288, 289, 291
Changamire (title), 474, 578
Chang'an (Xi'an), China, 297–298, 301
Charity: guilds and, 272
Charlemagne, 262–264, 262*i*; coronation of, 262; Einhard on, 263; empire of, 264*m*; successors to, 264
Charles I (England), 513–514
Charles II (England), 515
Charles II (Spain), 507
Charles V (Holy Roman Empire), 416, 439, 442; Catherine of Aragon and, 420; Netherlands and, 446; Philip II (Spain) and, 444
Charles VII (France), 434*i*
Charles IX (France), 447
Charles XI (Sweden), 507
Charles XII (Sweden), 517
Charles the Bald, 264
Charles the Great (Bohemia), 441
Châtelet, Marquise du, 534
Chaucer, Geoffrey, 400
Chemistry: in scientific revolution, 530
Chengdu, China, 306
Cheops (Egypt). *See* Khufu (Cheops, Egypt)
Chiaroscuro, 405
Chichén Itzá, 329, 330
Chichimec people, 329, 481
Chikamatsu Monzaemon (Japan), 611, 613
Childbirth: in China, 601; death during, 499; in Ottoman harem, 590*i*
Children: in forced prostitution, 585; life expectancy of, 499. *See also* Families
Children's Crusade (1212), 276
Chile, 476; humans in, 324
Chimu kingdom, 332
China: 1300–1650, 371; beauty standards in, 298*i*; Buddhism in, 296; as "Central Kingdom," 371; concubinage in, 378; Confucianism in, 296; Daoism in, 296; empires in, 294–310; England and, 598; equal-field system in, 295; eunuchs in, 374, 376; Europeans and, 604*m*, 616; expansion of, 301*m*; Indian Buddhism and, 292; Japan and, 312, 606, 607; Jesuits in, 380, 600*i*; Manchu Empire in, 599–601; map of ancient heartland from, 375, 375*i*; Ming dynasty in, 305, 373–381, 373*m*; Mongols and, 287, 304–305, 305*i*; North-South divisions in, 295; plague in, 310; political division in, 301–302; Portugal and, 468; Qing (Ching) dynasty in, 381; rock carvings and, 296*i*; Russia and, 599*i*, 600; slaves in, 584–585; Song dynasty in, 301–304; Spain and, 476; Sui dynasty in, 296; Tang dynasty in, 297–299; technology in, 287–288; Thais from, 391–392; unification of, 302; Vietnam and, 393; world locations and, 345; Yuan dynasty in, 304–310, 307–310,

373. *See also* Foot binding; specific dynasties
Chinampas, **331**
Chinese language: Japanese language and, 317
Chinese people: migration of, 376; in Qing Manchu government, 600
Chinggis (Genghis) Khan, 293, 306, 307, 348–349; law code of, 307
Chivalry, 267–268
Chŏngjo (Korea), 604
Chola kingdom (India), 293
Cholian-speaking peoples, 327
Cholula, 329
Chongzheng (China), 381
Chosŏn dynasty (Korea), 372, 381–384, 604–605
Christian IV (Denmark), 455, 455–456
Christian Church, 258–260. *See also* specific churches
Christianity: in Africa, 569; among Amerindians, 479–480, 481; in Benin, 470; in Ethiopia, 580–581; Iberian expansion and, 464–465; in Japan, 389, 390, 468–469, 607; missionary spread of, 258–260; Muslim perspective on Crusades and, 277; Ottoman, 449, 452, 591; Ottoman levy of male children and, 452–453; Portuguese and, 467; after Roman Empire, 257; of slave ship captains, 564; in Southeast Asia, 613; in Spain, 281. *See also* Catholic Church
Christine de Pizan, 400
Church(es): in Austria, 540; education and, 274; feudalism and, 267; in High Middle Ages, 272–275; land ownership by, 496; plague and, 398. *See also* specific religious groups
Church and state: separation of, 536
Circumnavigation of world: by Magellan, 476
Cistercian movement, 273
Cities and towns: in Americas, 324; Antwerp and, 483*i*; Cahokia as, 339; in China, 303; in east Central Europe, 440; in Europe, 498; European women in, 499; in Japan, 385, 608; medieval, 271–272; in Middle Ages, 261; Mughal, 364; in Netherlands, 445; Teotihuacán and, 326–327, 327*i*; worker riots in, 502. *See also* specific locations

Citizens and citizenship: in France, 543, 547, 550; women's rights and, 535
City-states: in Italian Renaissance, 400
"Civil Constitution of the Clergy" (France), 544
Civilization(s): of Central and South America, 326*m*; Incan, 332–336; in Mesoamerica, 323, 324, 325–336. *See also* China; specific civilizations
Civil service: in China, 297, 376–378, 600; in Prussia, 509
Civil war(s): in England, 514, 515*i*; in Ethiopia, 581; French Fronde and, 503; in Russia, 451
Clans: Incan, 332
Clara Isabella Eugenia (Spain), 450
Classes: Aztec, 331; in China, 298; French estates as, 279; Incan, 335; medieval, 267; in Mughal Empire, 366–367; in Ottoman society, 356. *See also* Elites; specific groups
Classical Age: in India, 288–294; in Japan, 312, 314–319
Classical learning: humanism and, 400–402; medieval preservation of, 260; Renaissance and, 397, 402–404
Classical period: in Americas, 326–327
Clement VIII (Pope), 450
Clergy: as class, 267; in England, 442; as First Estate, 542; in France, 544; reform of Catholic, 427; in Third Estate, 542
Cliff Palace: of Anasazi, 340*i*
Climate: North American, 337
Clive, Robert, 598
Cloth industry, 400
Clothing: colonies and, 483
Clovis I (Merovingian), 260
Clovis spear points, 324, 341
Cluny: Benedictine monks at, 272
Cobo, Bernabé: on Pachacuti, 333
Cocoa, 483
Code Napoléon (Napoleonic Code), **554**, 555
Code of 1649 (Russia), 451
Codes of law. *See* Law codes
Codex Azacatitlán, 475*i*
Coe, Michael, 328
Coen, Jan Pieterszoon, 484
Coffee, 483; France and, 486
Coins, 522; English, 448
Colbert, Jean-Baptiste, 505, 506, 517, 537

Cold War: East and West in, 345
College of Cardinals, **415,** 427
Colombia, 476
Colonies and colonization: Anglo-French wars over, 562; Dutch and, 484; England and, 486–487, 518; for freed slaves, 568; French-British conflict over, 518; French North American, 485; French Revolution and, 550; industries in Americas, 478; Japan and, 389; New Spain and, 474–477; Portuguese, 467, 472; slaves in Spanish America, 478–479; Smith on, 537; smuggling in, 521; in southern Africa, 571–572; Spanish North American, 475–476; Spanish society in, 482; Spanish South American, 476–477. *See also* Imperialism
Columbus, Christopher, 351, 464–465, 466; Christianity and, 464; Spanish claims and, 465
Command economy: Incan, 334
Commerce, 521; Africa and, 562; Chinese, 303, 380; Dutch, 484; end of slave trade and, 569; European in India, 596–598; French, 505–506; Indian, 394; international, 261; Japanese, 388; in Korea, 382; medieval, 271–272; Renaissance wealth from, 400; Safavid, 360; after Treaty of Westphalia, 492; in Turkic empires, 367–368. *See also* Foreign trade
Commercial Revolution, 463, 482–484
Committee of Public Safety (France), **549,** 551
Common law (England), 280
Common people: Aztec, 331; capitalism and, 496–497; in Europe, 497; Incan, 334–335; as Third Estate, 542
Commons (England). *See* House of Commons (England)
Common sense, 537
Communication: in Turkic empires, 367–368
Communion: Lutheran, 418
Compass, 288, 303
Complutensian Bible, 413
Conciliar Movement, 415–416
Concordat of 1801, 554
Concubinage: in China, **378**; in Korea, 382
Condillac, Étienne de, 535
Condorcet, Marquis de, 535

Condotierri (Italy), **440**
Confederation of Swiss Cantons, 423
Confucianism, 287, 296, 372; in China, 295, 304, 308, 600; in Japan, 313, 607, 610; in Korea, 381–384, 604; scholarship of, 376; women and, 303, 378; Zhu Xi, 379
Connecticut, 486
Conquistadores, 324, **474**; Maya and, 475–476; in Peru, 476
Consent of governed, 538
Consistory (Calvinism), 423
Consolation of Philosophy, The (Boethius), 260
Constance: Council of, 415
Constantinople: Crusades and, 275, 276; Ottoman conquest of, 348
Constitution(s): in England, 514; in France (1793), 550; in Japan, 314
Constitutional convention: in France, 548
Continental Europe: absolutism and, 507–512; city and town growth in, 498; enclosure and, 494; Enlightenment in, 534
Continental System, **555,** 556
Contracts: manufacturing, 494
Convents, 275
Conversos, 437
Cook, James, 615
Copernicus, Nicolaus, 527, 528; Galileo and, 528
Corday, Charlotte, 549
Cordova, Emirate of, 282
Corn. *See* Maize
Coronado, Francisco, 476, 585
Coronation: of Charlemagne, 262
Corrigodores (Spanish colonial officials), 481
Corruption: in China, 602
Cortés, Hernando, 475, 475*i*; Malitzin and, 481; slaves and, 480
Cortes (Castile and Aragon), 438, 444
Corvinus, Matthias, 441, 441*i*
Cosmographia Universalis (Munster), 471
Cossacks, 511; in Siberia, 615
Cotton and cotton industry: calicoes and, 521
Council(s): in Americas, 477
Council of the Indies, 477
Councils (Christian): of Constance, 415; of Pisa, 415; of Trent, 416, 427, 443, 444

Counter-Reformation (Catholic), 453; militance of, 453
Counts: Carolingian, 262
Courts (papal), 273
Courtship: in Japan, 315
Cowrie shells: as currency, **566**
Craft guilds, 271–272
Craftsmanship: Visigothic, 259*i*
Cranach, Lucas: *Martin Luther and his Friends*, 417*i*
Cranmer, Thomas, 420
Creation: Incan, 336; Japanese myth of, 313
Credit, 496
Crimea: Ottoman loss of, 591
Cromwell, Oliver, 514, 515*i*
Crop rotation, **494**
Crops: from Americas, 566; in China, 601; maize as, 324; medieval, 269; from New World, 492; in North America, 338. *See also* specific crops
Crowley, Ambrose, 495
Crowther, Samuel, 569
Crusader states, 276
Crusades, 275–278, 276*m*; significance of, 278. *See also* specific Crusades
Cuba: Spanish in, 474–475
Cuernavaca, 331
Cultivation. *See* Agriculture; Farms and farming
Culture(s): Adena, 337–338; Amerindian, 324; Asian, 287; in China, 295, 295–296, 298–299, 308, 378, 602–604; diffusion of, 288; in east Central Europe, 440–441; Fremont, 340; Hindu-Buddhist, 394; Hopewell, 337–338; in India, 288–291; Indian, 363, 364–365; Italian Renaissance and, 399–408; in Japan, 313, 386–389, 610–613; in Korea, 312, 381, 382–383, 604–605; in Latin America, 488–489; Mesoamerican, 324; in Middle Ages, 258; Mississippian, 338–339; Mogollon, Hohokam, Anasazi, and Fremont, 339–340; Mongols and, 307; Mughal, 363–365; Persian, 360–361; in Southeast Asia, 613–615; in South Vietnam, 614; Spanish colonial, 482. *See also* Amerindians; Civilization(s)
Currency: assignats as, 544; in China, 301; cowrie shells as, 566. *See also* Coins
Cuzco, 332, 476

Cyprus: fall to Turks, 449
Czech lands, 438
Czech people, 440; Catholicism of, 440

D

Da Gama family: Christopher, 474; Vasco, 466*i*, 467, 473
Dahomey, 566
Daimyō, **385**, 386, 388, 605; lifestyle of, 607–608; shogunate and, 390, 391; status groups and, 606; women of, 389
Dainichi (Great Sun Buddha), 319
Dalai Lama (Tibet), 600
Danish phase: of Thirty Years' War, 455, 455–456
Dante Alighieri, 400
Danti, Ignazio, 401
Danton, Georges-Jacques, 548; followers of, 550
Danube region: Charlemagne and, 262
Daoism, 287; in China, 296, 308
Dara Shikoh (Mughal dynasty), 365
Dardanelles, 452, 590
David (Donatello), 405
David (Michelangelo), 408*i*
David, Jacques-Louis, 542*i*; *Death of Marat, The*, 549*i*
Death of Marat, The (David), 549*i*
Death rates, 497
De Behaine, Pigneau, 614
Debt: finance crisis and, 522; in France, 524
Decameron (Boccaccio), 402
Deccan region (India), 292
Declaration of Pillnitz, 547
Declaration of the Rights of Man and Citizen (France), 543, 544, 545
Declaration of the Rights of Woman (Gouges), 546
Decline and Fall of the Roman Empire (Gibbon), 535
Dede Mohammad, 358
Deductive reasoning, 530
Defender of the Faith: Henry VIII (England) and, 420
Defenestration of Prague, **455**
Deism, **536**
Deities: Incan, 335–336; in Vietnam, 614. *See also* Gods and goddesses; specific deities

Delhi, 293, 349, 593; sack of (1756), 595; Sultanate of, 293–294, 294m, 362
Demesne, **269**
Denmark: Lutheranism and, 419; royal authority in, 507; slave trade ended by, 565; Viking raids from, 266
Descartes, René, 530–531, 536
De Soto, Hernando, 476
Despots and despotism: enlightened, 539–541; of Napoleon, 555
Devshirme (levy of Christian male children) system, 353, **452**
Dhimmis (non-Muslims), **356**
Dialectic, **274**
Diamonds: in Cape Colony, 578; Portugal and, 507
Dias, Bartolomeu, 466
Diderot, Denis, 534, 536, 539
Diet (assembly): in Germany, 439; in Poland, 508
Diet (food): Inuit, 342; in North America, 338
Diet of Worms, 418
Differential calculus, 531
Dingiswayo (Mthethwa Confederacy), 572
Diplomacy: in age of absolutism, 516–520; balance-of-power, 416; Japanese, 314, 606–607; Safavid, 359; after Thirty Years' War, 457
Directions: for location, 344–345
Directory (France), 551–552
Discourse on Method (Descartes), 530–531
Disease: Bubonic Plague and, 398; in Eurasia, 287; European and African in New World, 475, 479–480; among slaves, 564
Divan, **353**
Diversity: in Amerindian societies, 336
Divine Comedy (Dante), 400
Divine right, 502; Enlightenment thinkers on, 539; Locke on, 533; vs. social contract, 538
Divorce: in Japan, 609; Luther on, 419
Djakarta. *See* Batavia, Java
Dōgen Buddhist sect, 319
Dmitri (Russia), 451
Doctrines: Catholic, 427
Dogma, **275**
Dombo (warlord), 578
Dome of the Rock (Jerusalem), 356
Domesticated animals: in Americas, 324
Domestic system, 494–495

Dominic (Saint), 273
Dominica, 520
Dominicans, 273, **417**; in New World, 481
Donatello, 405
Donation of Constantine: as forgery, 413
Donation of Pepin, 258, 261
Dong Qichang (China), 379–380
Don Quixote de la Mancha (Cervantes), 410
Dover, Treaty of, 517
Draft (military): in China, 296
Drake, Francis, 450
Drama: Chinese, 379; in Japan, 387; Shakespeare and, 410–411
Drang nach Osten, 440
Drawing of a Flying Machine (Leonardo da Vinci), 406i
Dream(s): in Middle Eastern literature, 350
Dream of the Red Chamber (Cao Xueqin), 602
Drugs: Hindu medicine and, 291
Du Barry, Madame, 523
Duchy of Milan, 400
Du Fu (China), 299
Durga (goddess), 289, 290
Durrani dynasty (Persia), 595
Dushan, Stephen (Serbia), 452
Dutch: Africa and, 561; in Angola, 568; Benin and, 470; in Caribbean region, 479; central government of, 512; decline of, 493; in East Asia, 588; expansion by, 482; exploration by, 488m; French mercantilism and, 506; independence of, 447, 450; Indonesia and, 391, 394, 615; Japan and, 390, 607; naval wars with English, 517; privateers of, 449; Southeast Asia and, 372, 394, 613; in southern Africa, 571–572; Thais and, 392; trade with Japan, 469; Treaty of Utrecht and, 517
Dutch East Indies, 484, 485, 485i; slaves for, 585. *See also* Indonesia
Dutch Empire, 484–485
Dutch Learning: in Japan, 610
Dutch Republic, 456
Dutch West India Company, 484
Dürer, Albrecht, 411
Dynasties: in Balkans, 452; Capetian, 278–279; Chakri (Thailand), 614; in China, 294–310, 381; in east Central Europe, 440; Habsburg, 416, 507–508; in Hungary and Bohemia, 441; Koryo, 372; Le (Vietnam), 614; Ming, 371, 373–381;

Mughal, 294; in Persia, 593–594; Plantagenet, 280; of Qutb ud-Din Aibak, 293; Salian, 282; Tudor, 419–421; Valois, 416. *See also* Empires; specific dynasties

E

Early Middle Ages: church in, 258–260
East, the. *See* Eastern world
East Africa, 562, 578–580; Islam in, 570; long-distance trade in, 579–580; Portugal and, 472–474; state formation in, 578–581
East Asia: 1300–1650, 370*i*, 371–372; in 1650–1815, 587–588; Dutch in, 588. *See also* Asia
East Central Europe, 440
Eastern Europe: Lutheranism in, 419; Ottomans and, 352; peasants in, 501; royal intermarriage and, 440
Eastern Roman Empire, 348
Eastern world: Asia as, 345; balance of trade in, 368; identification of, 344–345. *See also* Asia; specific countries
East India Companies: in Austria, 493; Dutch, 484; English, 484, 487, 596, 597–598; in Prussia, 493
East Indies: Dutch, 484, 485, 485*i*
East March: Austria as, 262
East Prussia, 441
Ebstorf Mappamundi (map of the world), 309
Eck, John, 418
Economy: in 16th century Europe, 398; in 18th century, 520–521; Atlantic, 483; Aztec, 330–331; capitalism and, 463, 492–493; in Central Europe, 439, 453; in China, 380, 601; in England, 448; Enlightenment critique of, 536–537; in Europe, 562; in France, 524, 544, 553, 557; free enterprise and, 493–496; in French Revolution, 550; global, 589; gold and silver in, 483; government role in, 302; Iberian in America, 478–479; in Japan, 314, 607–608; Mayan, 328; medieval manorialism and, 268–271; mercantilism and, 505–506; in Russia, 511; in Song China, 302, 303; in Spain, 445; in Tang China, 297–298
Ecstasy of St. Teresa (Bernini), 428*i*
Ecuador, 476; Incas and, 334
Edict of Nantes, 450; revocation of, 503

Edict of Restitution, 455–456
Edict on Changing Status (Japan), 386
Edo, Benin, 470
Edo, Japan, 389, 606, 607; fire in, 608
Education: in China, 301; of Chinese women, 298, 303; in France, 554; of Japanese women, 609; Mayan, 328; medieval, 274; in Middle Ages, 260; of Mughal women, 367; in Russia, 540
Edward I (England), 281, 414
Edward VI (England), 421, 425
Egypt: Napoleon and, 552–553, 591
Einhard: on Charlemagne, 263
Eisai (Japan), 319
Elba: Napoleon in, 557
Eleanor of Aquitaine, 280*m*; Henry II (England) and, 280
Elect: in Calvinism, 424
Electors: in Germany, 439; of Holy Roman Empire, 441
Eleni (Ethiopia), 474
Elephants: ivory trade and, 579
Elites: African slave trade and, 566; Aztec, 475; in Japan, 315, 316, 386–387; in Korea, 381; Ottoman, 590
Elizabeth (Valois, France), 444, 449
Elizabeth (Russia), 512
Elizabeth I (England), 420, 448, 513; Irish rebellion and, 448; Renaissance and, 410
Elmina (Africa), 562
Emigration: from China, 380. *See also* Immigrants and immigration
Emir, 349
Emperor: Incan, 335; in Japan, 315; Napoleon as, 554. *See also* Empires
Empires: Asian, 587–588; Aztec, 330–332; Carolingian, 261–264, 264*m*; Chinese, 294–310; Dutch, 484–485; English, 486–487; European, 429; of Franks, 257; French, 485–486; gunpowder, 348*m*; Gupta, 288–291; Inca, 332–336; of Khubilai Khan, 308; Middle Eastern, 587–588; Mongol, 306, 306–307; Mughal, 347, 361–367, 361*m*; Muslim vs. European, 368; Ottoman, 347, 349–357; Portuguese, 466–469; Safavid, 347, 357–361, 357*m*, 593–594; Toltec, 329; Turkic, 347; Vijayangar, 294. *See also* Byzantium (Byzantine Empire); Dynasties; specific empires

Employment: in Japan, 606; for women, 499
Enclosure Acts, **494,** 494*m*
Enclosure movement: in England, 484, 494, 494*m*
Encomendero, 480–481
Encomienda system, **480**–481
Encyclopédie (Diderot), 534
Encyclopedias: Yongle, 379
England (Britain): to 1348, 279–281; Africa and, 561, 562, 568, 571; Canterbury in, 436, 436*i*; Canute in, 279; Cape (southern Africa) and, 572, 574; in Caribbean region, 479; Catholic Church and, 442–443; China and, 604; Christianity in, 259; church lands in, 420–421; cities and towns in, 498; Continental System and, 555; diamonds in Cape Colony and, 578; Elizabeth I and, 448, 450; empire of, 486–487; Enclosure Acts in, 494; enclosure in, 484, 494*m*; Enlightenment and, 533, 535–536; Ethiopia and, 581; exploration by, 488*m*; France and, 280, 280*m*; gentry in, 494; Glorious Revolution in, 512; government of, 491, 513–516; Hanoverian kings in, 516; in Hundred Years' War, 434–437; India and, 518, 595, 596–598, 604*m*; industrialization in, 555; iron industry in, 495; Japan and, 390; Malacca Straits and, 615; Mary, Queen of Scots, and, 450; mercantilism of, 597; migration to New World from, 498; missionaries from, 258; Moshoeshoe and, 576; Napoleon and, 553, 555, 557; naval wars with Dutch, 517; Norman conquest of, 279*i*; Parliament and, 281, 437; Persia and, 594; political system in, 495; population of, 271, 498; poverty in, 498*i*; Protestant martyr in, 422; Puritans in, 448; Quebec an, 486; religious war and, 443; Renaissance in, 410–411; republic in, 514; Safavid silk trade and, 360; after Seven Years' War, 520; slave trade and, 565; smuggling in, 522; Southeast Asia and, 372, 613; Spanish American trade and, 520; Spanish Armada and, 450; after Thirty Years' War, 457; Transvaal rebellion against, 578; Treaty of Utrecht and, 518; uniting of, 266; Viking invasions of, 266; William the Conqueror in, 279–280; wool trade and, 483; Wycliffe in, 414

English East India Company. *See* British East India Company
English language: church services in, 442
Enjoying Lotuses While Listening to Music (Shin Yunbok), 605*i*
Enlightened despotism, 539–541; Catherine the Great and, 512
Enlightenment, 522; Age of Reason and, 532–539; Catherine the Great and, 539–540; contributions to, 538*m*; Deism in, 536; economic critique in, 536–537; international responses to, 535–536; radical version of, 534; on separation of powers, 538; women and, 535
Enlightenment (religious): Tendai doctrine of, 319
Enragés (France), 549
Entertainment: in cities, 498
Epic literature: *Mahabharata*, 365; *Shahnamah*, 293; *Shakuntala*, 291. *See also* Literature
Epic of Kings (Firdawsi), 361
Epidemics: in New World, 480. *See also* Disease
Equal-field system, **295**; in China, 295; in Japan, 314
Equality: in France, 550–551
Equiano, Olaudah: slave memoir of, 565
Erasmus, Desiderius, 412, 413*i*, 416
Eskimo peoples, 324
Essay, 410
Essay Concerning Human Understanding (Locke), 537
Essays (Montaigne), 410*i*
Estates (classes): in France, 279, 542
Estates (land): Aztec, 330–331; in Japan, 315
Estates-General (France), 279, **501,** 524, **542**
Este, Isabella d', 404
Esterhazy family (Hungary), 497
Eternal Storehouse of Japan, The (Ihara Saikaku), 611–612
Ethiopia, 561, 580; Eleni in, 474; Henry the Navigator and, 466
Ethnic groups: in Central Europe, 439; in Ottoman Empire, 353
Ethnolinguistic groups: Amerindian, 324
Eunuchs, **374**; in China, 374, 376, 377
Eurasia, 348–349; China trade and, 380; Mongols and, 306, 310

Europe and Europeans: 9th and 10th century invasions and, 264–266, 265*m*; 1300–1600, 398–399; Americas and, 305; aristocracy and, 496–497; Atlantic slave trade and, 585; Bubonic Plague and, 398; cardinal directions used by, 345; China and, 308; common people in, 497; decline of absolutism and, 522–524; economy of, 483; expansion by, 433, 463, 488; exploration by, 429; in India, 596–598; during Italian Renaissance, 399–408, 399*m*; medieval towns in, 271; Middle Ages in, 256*i*, 257–285; Muslims and, 368; Napoleon's impact on, 555–556; Northern European expansion and, 482–487; during Northern Renaissance, 399*m*; Ottomans and, 590, 591; in Pacific region, 615–616; politics in (1300–1500), 434–442; population and, 497–499; power politics in, 594; prostitution and, 499; smuggling and, 521; Southeast Asia and, 394; states in, 278–283; after Thirty Years' War, 457*m*; as West, 345; women in, 499. *See also* specific countries

Examination: for Chinese civil service, **297**, 302, 376–378, 600

Exarchate of Ravenna, **261**

Exchange: in Korea, 382

Excommunication, 273; of Hus, 415

Expansion and expansionism: in 15th century, 463; by Assante, 567; of China, 301*m*; of Europe, 433; of European population, 497–499; by Hohenzollerns, 509; by Ming China, 376, 380; Northern European, 482–487; Portuguese, 464–474; religion and, 464–465; Viking, 266. *See also* Imperialism; specific countries

Experimentation: scientific, 532

Exploration: European, 429, 488*m*, 615; maps of, 471; Ming Chinese, 376, 380; by Portugal, 438

Expulsion from Eden (Masaccio), 405, 405*i*

F

Factions: in Korea, 383, 604; in Song China, 302

Factories (European commercial offices and warehouses): English, in India, **597**

Fairfax, Lord (England), 514

Fairs: trade, 271

Faith: Calvin on, 424; reason and, 536; salvation by, 418

Falconry, 268

Families: in China, 303–304, 601; in Japan, 315, 385, 608; noble, 497

Famine: in Japan, 609

Fan Kuan (Song China), 304; *Snow Mountain and Forest*, 304*i*

Farms and farming: in India, 288; in Japan, 315; Japanese women and, 385, 609; in Korea, 382; medieval, 269–270; in southern Africa, 571–572; Xhosa, 572. *See also* Agriculture

Farnese, Alexander: in Spain, 447

Fasilidas (Ethiopia), 581

Fatehpur Sikri: palace at, 365

Fatih Mosque (Turkey), 356

Fatma Sultan, 355

Faxian (Buddhist monk): on Gupta society, 289, 290

Fedor (Russia), 451

Female infanticide: in China, 303

Feminism: in French Revolution, 544

Ferdinand I (Holy Roman Empire), 439, 444

Ferdinand II (Habsburg, Holy Roman Empire), 455

Ferdinand and Isabella (Spain), 437–438, 437*i*; Columbus and, 466

Fertility: European population growth and, 498

Feudal incidents (lord's rights), 267

Feudalism, 266–268; in Europe, 257–258; Japanese Kamakura system and, 384

Ficino, Marsilio, 403

Fiction: in China, 602. *See also* Literature

Fiefs, **266**; in England, 279; Ottoman, 353

Finances: crisis in, 522; in England, 448, 514, 521; in France, 521, 554. *See also* Economy

Firdawsi (Muslim scholar), 293, 361

Firearms: in Japan, 389

First Coalition: against France, 549, 550

First Consul: Napoleon as, 553

First Crusade, 275, 277; trade and, 271

First Estate (clergy), 542

First Republic: in France, 548

Fishing: in Newfoundland, 482
Fish Market at Leiden, The (Steen), 513*i*
Fitzwilliams family (Ireland), 497
Flanders, 278; Hundred Years' War and, 434
Fleury, Cardinal (France), 523, 524
Floating world (Japan), **611,** 611*i*; pictures of, 613
Florence, Italy, 416; Bubonic Plague and, 398; republic of, 400
Florentine Codex, 480
Florida: Amerindians in, 323; Spanish in, 475–476
Food(s): from Americas, 482, 566; demand for, 493; Japan and, 608; population growth and, 271
Foot binding: in China, 303, 378, 602
Foreign affairs: in Japan, 388, 390–391
Foreigners: Chinese religion and, 301
Foreign policy. *See* Diplomacy
Foreign trade: Chinese, 602; Japanese, 606–607
Formative period: in Mesoamerica, 325–326
Fort Jesus, 579
Forty-Two Articles (England), 421
Foundling children: in Russia, 540
Fourth Crusade, 275–276
France: absolutism in, 505–506; Africa and, 562, 568; after Armada, 450; boundaries of, 519; Bourbons and, 450; Calvinism in, 424; Capetians in, 278–279; in Caribbean region, 479; church land ownership in, 496; city and town growth in, 498; Code Napoléon in, **554**; continental dominance by, 517–518; Continental Europe and, 507; economic critiques in, 536–537; economic problems in, 524; England and, 598; estates (classes) in, 279; exploration by, 488*m*; First Coalition against, 549; government of, 554; Henry II (England) and, 280, 280*m*; humanism in, 409–410; in Hundred Years' War, 434–437; India and, 518; influence of, 491; Italy and, 440; Louis XIV and, 502–505, 522, 523; mercantilism in, 505–506; Muslim raids of, 265; under Napoleon, 553–557; Netherlands and, 615; Old Regime in, 524, 527; peasant living conditions in, 500; Persia and, 594; population of, 498; privileged orders in, 496–497; reforms and, 540; religious wars in, 443, 447–448; Second Coalition against, 553, 554; after Seven Years' War, 520; Southeast Asia and, 613; Spanish peace with, 450; Thailand and, 613; Third Coalition against, 555; Third Estate in, 497; after Thirty Years' War, 456; trade in, 521; Treaty of Utrecht and, 517–518, 518*m*; upper class extravagance in, 497*i*; Valois dynasty and, 416; Vietnam and, 604*m*, 614; Vikings and, 266; war with Russia, 556. *See also* French Revolution (1789)
Francis I (France), 503
Francis II (France), 447
Francis II (Holy Roman Empire), 548
Franciscans, 273, 273*i*; in China, 308; in Japan, 389, 469
Francis of Assisi (Saint), 273
Frankish state: breakup of, 261–262
Franklin, Benjamin, 536
Franks: under Charlemagne, 262–264; empire of, 257; Merovingians and, 260, 261; papal alliance with, 261
Frederick I Barbarossa (Germany), 275, 282
Frederick I (Prussia), 508, 517, 520
Frederick II (Germany), 283
Frederick II the Great (Prussia), 509–510, 510*i*; as enlightened despot, 539
Frederick III (Denmark), 507
Frederick III (Holy Roman Empire), 439, 439*i*
Frederick of Saxony (Elector), 417*i*, 418
Frederick William "the Great Elector" (Prussia), 508
Frederick William I (Prussia), 508, 509
Free blacks, 479; in French colonies, 550
Freedom(s): in England, 516; Enlightenment thinkers on, 537
Freed slaves: African colonies for, 569
Free enterprise: growth of, 493–496
Freemen, 267, 270
Freetown, 569
Fremont culture, 340
French Academy of Science, 532
French Empire, 485–486, 506
French phase: of Thirty Years' War, 456
French Republic, 548
French Revolution (1789), 541*m*; domestic phase of, 541–552; moderate phase of, 543–547; Napoleonic phase of, 552–557;

radicalism in, 547–549; West Indies treatment during, 544; women in society and, 535
Fresco, **406**; of Raphael, 406–407
Friars, 273
Friedel, David, 328
Friedland, battle of, 555
Friends of Truth, 544
Fronde (civil war), 503
Frontiers: Catholic, 440–442; Chinese, 302. *See also* Boundaries
Fugger family (Augsburg), 492; banking house of, 483
Fujiwara family (Japan), 314, 315–316
Fulani Muslims: in West Africa, 570, 571
Fundamentalists: Wahhabi, 591
Funerals: Japanese, 312
Fur trade, 483; French and, 486; in Siberia, 511
Fushimi, castle at, 386

G

Gabon, 569
Gaçon-Dufour, Madame, 535
Galilei, Galileo, 528, 530, 532
Gama, Vasco da, 466*i*
Games, 268
Ganges River region, 293
Gaozong (Tang China), 297
Gaozu (Tang China), 297
Garden of Earthly Delights (Bosch), 412, 412*i*
Gardens: in Ottoman Tulip period, 590
Gardes-françaises, 543
Gargantua and Pantagruel (Rabelais), 409–410
Gaul: peasants in, 261
Geisha (Japan), 382
Gender: in Korea, 382; in Ottoman society, 356; in Pacific islands, 615
General Directory (Prussia), **508**–509
Geneva, Switzerland: Calvin and, 423, 443; Protestantism in, 423
Gentry: economic position of, 494; in England, 494, 516
Geocentric view, 528
Geography, 344–345; as destiny, 345
George I (England), 516

George II (England), 516
George III (England), 516; China trade and, 604
Germanic tribes: movement of, 440
German people: in east Central Europe, 440
Germany, 282–283, 443; city and town growth in, 498; Danish invasion of, 455; division of, 283, 283*m*; Enlightenment in, 536; Gustavus Adolphus and, 456; Habsburgs in, 508; Holy Roman Empire and, 507, 555–556; humanism in, 410; Lutheranism in, 416–419; Magyars and, 266; monarchy in, 439; peasants in, 419, 498; Slavs in, 261; Thirty Years' War and, 453, 456; unification and, 517
Ghana (Gold Coast): Dutch and, 562; Portugal and, 469
Ghent: Pacification of, 447
Gia Long (Vietnam), 614
Gibbon, Edward, 535
Gibraltar, 518
Gin Lane (Hogarth), 498*i*
Giotto, 404; *Innocent III*, 273*i*; *St. Francis Receiving the Stigmata*, 404*i*
Girls: in Japan, 609
Girondins, **547,** 548, 549, 550
Global economy, 398
Glorious Revolution (England), **512,** 513, 516
Glyphs, **328**
Goa: Dutch and, 484; Portugal and, 467
Gobir (Hausa city-state), 570; Usman dan Fodio and, 570
Goddess cult: Incan, 335
Gods and goddesses: Aztec, 331–332; Enlightenment and, 536; Incan, 332; in India, 289. *See also* specific deities
Gog and Magog, 309
Gold: in Americas, 478; capitalism and, 492; imports of, 483; Portugal and, 471, 474, 507
Golden Age: of Chinese drama, 379; European Renaissance and Reformation as, 397; Iberian, 464–469
Golden Bull, The, **439,** 440, 441
Golden Lotus, 379
Gondar, Ethiopia, 581
"Goober pea," 566
Gouges, Olympe de, 544; *Declaration of the Rights of Woman*, 546

Government: Aztec, 330; in Balkan region, 452; in Brazil, 478; Calvinist, 443; in China, 297, 308, 376, 380; of Chinese cities, 303; church, 258; in classical Japan, 314–316; Dutch, 512; economic role of, 302; in England, 513–516, 514; of English colonies, 486; Enlightenment thinkers on, 537–538; feudal, 266; in France, 503, 523, 551, 554; guilds and, 272; of Iberian New World, 477–478; Incan, 334, 335; in Japan, 313, 314, 320, 607; in Japanese villages, 385; Korean, 381; Locke on, 533; Mayan, 328; of Mongol territories, 307; of New Spain, 477; of Ottoman Empire, 353–356; poor and, 501; of Prussia, 508–509; of Qing (Manchu) China, 600; in Russia, 511, 540; by Suleiman, 353; in Vietnam, 614. *See also* Absolutism; Administration
Granada, Spain, 437, 520; Muslims in, 282; Spain and, 438
Grand Canal (China), 296, 297, 374
Grandparents: in Japan, 315
Gravitation: Newton and, 531–532
Great Britain. *See* England (Britain)
Great Fear (France), 543
Great Khan: Chinggis as, 306
Great Northern War, 517
Great Pyramid of Khufu (Cheops): Pyramid of the Sun and, 327i
Great Schism, 415
Great Serpent Mound (Ohio), 338i
Great Trek, 573–576, 576i, 576m, 577
Great Wall (China), 374
Greece (ancient): division of world by, 345; learning from, 260. *See also* Classical learning
Greenland: Vikings in, 266
Gregory I the Great (Pope), 258
Gregory VII (Pope), 272–273
Gregory XIII (Pope), 401
Grenville, George, 516
Gros, Antoine-Jean: Napoleon by, 552i
Guadeloupe, 486
Guangzhou (Canton), China, 297; foreign commerce in, 602; Western ships at, 615
Guatemala, 325, 327; Maya resistance in, 481; Spain and, 474
Guericke, Otto von, 530
Guest houses: in Japan, 608
Guide to Geography (Ptolemy), 471

Guilds, **271**–272, 271i; domestic system and, 494; in Europe, 398, 484; in France, 521; women in, 499; worker living conditions and, 499–501
Guillotine, 548i; in French Revolution, 544
Guise family (France), 447
Gujarat, 293, 467
Gunpowder, 288; in China, 302, 303; Safavids and, 359
Gunpowder empires, 348m, 368
Gupta dynasty (India): classical age under, 288–293
Gustavus Adolphus (Sweden), 456, 456i
Gustavus Vasa (Sweden), 419
Gutenberg, Johann, 409
Gutenberg Bible, 409i
Gu Yanwu (China), 600

H

Habsburg dynasty, 416, 439, 507–508; in Austrian Empire, 453–457; Germany and, 455, 507; Ottomans and, 357; Philip II (Spain) and, 444; in Spain, 482; Spanish holdings and, 517; Switzerland and, 440; after Thirty Years' War, 456; Treaty of Utrecht and, 518m
Haciendas (plantations or estates), **482**
Haikai poetry, 611
Haiku poetry, 611
Haiti, 486
Halecki, Oscar, 440
Halifax, England, 498
Hamzanamah manuscript, 365
Han dynasty (China), 294; Korea and, 310
Han'gul (Korean script), **381**, 383, **604**
Hangzhou, China, 302
Hannibal (ship): slaves on, 564
Hanoverian kings (England), 516
Hanseatic League, 398, **439**, 445
Harem, **354**; in China, 298; Mughal, 367i; Ottoman, 354i
Harsha (India), 292
Harvey, William, 530
Haugwitz, Count, 508
Hausa, 570; Usman dan Fodio and, 571
Hawaii: Europeans and, 615–616
Hawkhurst gang, 522
Hawkins, John, 450, 486

Hayashi Razan (Japan), 610
Hébert, Jacques, 549
Head tax. *See* Jizya (head tax)
"Heart Learning" (Japan), 610
Heaven's mandate (China), 373
Hegemony: Asian, 286*i*, 287–288; Mongol, 306*m*
Heian Period (Japan), 314; architecture from, 314*i*; religion in, 319
Heliocentric theory: of Copernicus, 528, 529; Galileo and, 528
Hellenic Greece: Renaissance and, 397
Hellenistic world: Renaissance and, 397
Helvetius, Claude, 535
Henry II (England), 280, 436; France and, 280, 280*m*; successors of, 280
Henry II (France), 447
Henry III (France), 447–448
Henry IV (France), 448, 450, 503
Henry IV (Germany), 282
Henry IV (Holy Roman Empire): Gregory VII and, 273
Henry VII (England), 437
Henry VIII (England), 436; Anglican Reformation and, 419–421; break with Rome, 442–443; church after death of, 421; More and, 413
Henry of Guise (France), 447–448
Henry the Navigator (Portugal), 438, 465–466, 466*i*; slave trade and, 562
Heptameron (Margaret of Navarre), 423*i*
Heresy: Arian, 259; medieval, 273–274; Wycliffe and, 414
Heshen (China), 602
Hideyori (Japan), 388, 389
Hierarchy: in Cahokia, 339; in Confucian society, 394; in Japan, 312; in Muslim society, 293
Hieroglyphics: Egyptian, 553
High Middle Ages. *See* Later Middle Ages
High Renaissance: Italian arts in, 406–408
Hildegard of Bingen, 275
Himeji Castle (Japan), 388, 388*i*
Himiko (Pimiko, Japan), 312
Hindus and Hinduism, 287, 288, 292, 294, 372; Akbar and, 363; of Gupta dynasty, 289; in Majapahit, 394; Marathas and, 595–596; Mughal culture and, 364–365, 595; in Southeast Asia, 391; Vijayangar Empire of, 294. *See also* India
Hindustan, 362

Hishikawa Moronobu (Japan), 613
Hispaniola: smallpox on, 480
Historical writing: in China, 299
History: in Japan, 313, 610; maps and, 309, 309*i*; in Song China, 304. *See also* specific historians
Hōjō Masako (Japan), 316, 320
Hōnen (monk), 319
Hōryūji, Japan, 314
Hobbes, Thomas, 502; Locke and, 538; women and, 535
Hogans, 341*i*
Hogarth, William: Gin Lane, 498*i*
Hohenzollern family, 508; German unification and, 517
Hohokam people, 339
Hokkaido, Japan, 609
Holbach, Paul Henri d', 535
Holbein, Hans, the Younger, 411; *Portrait of Erasmus*, 413*i*
Holland: central power in, 512. *See also* Dutch
Holy Land: Crusades and, 275, 275–278, 276*m*. *See also* Jerusalem
Holy League, 449, 450
Holy Roman Empire, 283, 283*m*, 438, 439; Brandenburg and, 509*m*; destruction of, 555–556; electors of, 441; German principalities in, 507; Habsburgs and, 508. *See also* specific rulers
Homage, **267**
Honduras, 325
Hong Taiji (Manchu), 599
Hongwu (Ming China), 374, 374*i*
Honor: female chastity and, 384
Hooke, Robert, 530
Hopewell people, 337–338
Hormuz: Portuguese capture of, 467
Horses: for plowing, 269
Horseshoes: from China, 303
Hospitalers, 276
House of Burgesses (Virginia), 486
House of Commons (England), 281, 516
House of Lancaster (England), 437
House of Lords (England), 281, 516
House of Savoy, 517
House of York (England), 437
Housing: Adena and Hopewell, 338; Aztec, 331; of medieval peasant, 270–271; of Mogollon, Hohokam, and Anasazi, 340; Navajo, 341*i*

Howard, Charles, 450
Huari, 332
Huascar (Inca), 476
Huayna Capac (Inca), 334, 476
Hudson, Henry, 485
Hudson Bay, 518; England and, 486
Hugh Capet, 278
Huguenots, 424, 447, 503, **534**; Dutch, 534; Edict of Nantes and, 503; Enlightenment and, 534; massacre of, 447; migration by, 498
Huitzilopochtli (god), **332**
Humanism, 400–402; classical learning and, 402–404; in France, 409–410; in Germany, 410; in Northern Europe, 408–409, 412–413; reform and, 416; use of term, 400
Humanists: Luther and, 418
Human rights: Enlightenment and, 538–539
Humans: in Americas, 324
Human sacrifice: Aztec, 332; in Cahokia, 339
Humayun (Mughal dynasty), 363
Hume, David, 535
Huna people, 292
Hundred Years' War, 398, 434–437
Hungary and Hungarians, 438; in 15th century, 441–442; battle of Mohacs and, 442; Catholicism and, 440; dynasties in, 441; Habsburgs in, 508; Ottomans in, 352. *See also* Magyars (Hungarians)
Hunter-gatherers: Amerindians as, 324
Hunyadi, János, 441
Hus, John, 414–415, 418, 441
Husein (Safavid Shah), 593
Hussite Church, 441
Hussite wars, 415
Hutchinson, Anne, 487
Hutten, Ulrich von, 410
Hutu people, 580
Hülegü (Mongols), 307
Huygens, Christiaan, 530
Hydrostatics, 530

I

Iberian Peninsula: Amerindians and, 479–482; Golden Age of, 464–469; regimes in New World of, 477–482; Spain and, 437
Ibn Battuta, 308
Ibn Majid, 394
Ibrahim Pasha (Ottoman), 590
Ice Age: Bering Strait land bridge and, 324; in Japan, 312
Iceland: Norsemen from, 266
Identity: Chinese, 376
Ideologies: in Japan, 609, 610; of Napoleon's armies, 555
Idris Aloma (Kanem-Bornu), 570
Île-de-France, 278
Iltutmish (India), 293
Imams, 358
Immigrants and immigration: by English nonconformists, 486; to New World, 498
Imperial Diet (Holy Roman Empire), **418**, 439
Imperialism: in Asia and Oceania (1800), 604*m*; maritime, 463; Portuguese, 465–474; Spanish, 465, 474–477. *See also* Colonies and colonization
Import-export trade, 400
Inca Empire, 324, 332–336, 476
Indentured servants: for capitalist agriculture, 493*i*; women in colonies as, 487
Indentured slaves, 585
Index of Forbidden Works, 427; Copernicus and, 528
India, 287; 1650–1815, 587–588; Ahmad Khan and, 595; after Aurangzeb, 595; Babur in, 362, 362*i*; Buddhism in, 289; Classical Age in, 288–294; da Gama and, 466*i*, 467; division of, 292; England and, 487, 518, 604*m*; Europeans in, 596–598; France and, 518; geographers in, 345; Gupta art and literature in, 290–291, 291*i*; Huna people in, 292; Mughal painting in, 361; Mughals in, 361–367, 361*m*, 594–598; Muslims in, 293–294; Portuguese trade and, 467, 468; sea route to, 466, 466*i*; slaves from, 572; Thai people and, 391; Turkic invaders of, 305; universities in, 291; women in, 367. *See also* specific rulers and dynasties
Indianization: of Southeast Asia, 293
Indian Ocean region: anti-slavery squadron in, 579; Dutch in, 484; French in, 486; Ottomans and, 357; Portugal and, 467; slave trade in, 585; trade and, 288, 393*m*
Indians. *See* Amerindians; specific groups
Indies. *See* East Indies; specific countries
Indigenous people: American, 324

Individual: place in universe, 557
Individualism: in High Renaissance, 406–407
Indochina: China and, 301*m*. *See also* Cambodia (Kampuchea); Laos
Indonesia: Chinese migration to, 380; Dutch and, 394, 613, 615; England and, 613; Majapahit and, 393; Ming Chinese trade with, 380; Muslims in, 391; slaves from, 572
Inductive reasoning, 530, 531
Indulgences: Luther and, 417
Industrialization: in England, 555
Industry: in China, 303; domestic system in, 494–495; slave labor for, 562. *See also* Industrialization
Infallibility of the pope, **418**
Infanticide: female, 303
Infant mortality, 499
Inflation, 492–493, 495; in Europe, 483; in France, 494
Inheritance: in Japan, 315, 320, 385; in Korea, 382; by women, 303
Inner lights, 425
Innocent III (Giotto), 273*i*
Innocent III (Pope), 273, 413; Fourth Crusade and, 275–276; Frederick II (Germany) and, 283; John (England) and, 280
Innocent IV (Pope), 308
Inoculations: in Song China, 304
Inquiry into the Nature and Causes of the Wealth of Nations, An (Smith), 537
Inquisition, 273, **437,** 444; in Netherlands, 446
Institutes of the Christian Religion (Calvin), 423, 424
Instrument of Government (England), 514–515
Instruments (musical): in Japan, 317*i*
Insurance: companies, 496
Intellectual thought: in cities, 498; in Enlightenment, 532–539; in Gupta India, 291; monastic preservation of, 260; new approaches to, 530–531; scholasticism and, 274–275; women and, 275. *See also* Humanism
Intendants (French officials), **496**
Interdict: by church, 273
Interior Castle (Teresa of Avila), 427
Interregnum (England), **515**
Inuit peoples, 324, 341–342

Invasions: in 9th and 10th centuries, 264–266, 265*m*; from Central Asia, 305; of Europe, 261, 264–266; of India, 292; of Mughal India, 595. *See also* specific invaders
Inventions: scientific, 531
Investiture: feudal, 267
Investiture Controversy, 282
Invincible Armada (Spain), 450
Invisible hand: Smith on, 537
Iran: Qajar dynasty in, 588
Iraq: Karim Khan in, 594; Ottoman conquest of, 357; Safavids and, 357*m*
Ireland: migration from, 498; missionaries in, 259; revolts against England in, 448
Iron and iron industry: in England, 495
Iroquois (Native American) people, 324, 337
Irrigation: by Anasazi, 339–340; Incan, 334; in Korea, 382
Isabella (Castile). *See* Ferdinand and Isabella (Spain)
Isandhlwana (Transvaal region), 578
Isfahan (Persia): size of, 361; trade in, 360
Ishida Baigan (Japan), 610
Islam, 287; in Africa, 569–571; Akbar and, 362; in East Africa, 578–579; European Renaissance and, 397; Iberian expansion and, 464; in India, 294; in Indonesia, 393; in Majapahit kingdom, 394; in South Asia, 361–362; in Southeast Asia, 394. *See also* Arabia; Arabs and Arab world
Ismail (Sasfavid), 357–359
Italian Renaissance, 397, 399–404; arts in, 404–408; Europe during, 399*m*; humanists and, 400
Italy, 264; 1300–1500, 440; banking and, 400; Enlightenment in, 536; Germany and, 282–283; humanism in, 400; Muslim raids of, 265; population of, 498; Switzerland and, 440; unification of, 517
Itzcoatl (Aztec), 330
Ivan III (Russia), 450–451
Ivan IV the Terrible (Russia), 451
Ivory: Portugal and, 471; trade in, 579–580
Iyasu II (Ethiopia), 581

J

Jacobins, **547,** 548, 549; France under, 549–551

Jahan (Mughal Shah), 365; Taj Mahal of, 364*i*
Jahangir (Mughal dynasty), 363, 365, 365*i*, 366
Jalonke rulers: of Fulani, 570
Jamaica, 479
James I (England), 513
James II (England), 515–516; Newton and, 532
Jamestown, Virginia, 486
Jami (poet), 361
Janissaries, **353**, 452, **589**, 590
Japan, 312–320, 384–391; 1300–1650, 372; architecture from, 314*i*; arts in, 386–389; Buddhism in, 318–319; China and, 380, 381; Christianity in, 389, 390, 468–469; classical age in, 312, 314–319; Columbus and, 466; constitution in, 314; culture in, 386–389, 610–613; economy in, 607–608; emperor in, 315; Europeans expelled from, 469; Fujiwara family in, 315–316; government in, 314–316; ideology in, 610; Korea and, 312, 383–384; Mongols and, 306, 320; Neolithic culture in, 312; Portugal and, 467–468; regents in, 315–316; Russia and, 615; sakoku (closed-country policy) in, 390; scholarship in, 610; society in, 608–609, 613; Tang China and, 297; tea ceremony in, 388; Tokugawa period in, 605–613; tomb period in, 312, 313; trade and, 310, 390; Warring States period in, 384–386
Japanese language: written, 317
Japanese pirates, 388
Java, 485*i*; Dutch in, 394, 484; England and, 615; Mongols and, 306
Jefferson, Thomas, 536
Jena, battle at, 555
Jerusalem: Crusades and, 275, 276; Ottomans and, 352
Jesuits, 427; in China, 380, 600*i*; in Ethiopia, 580; in Japan, 389, 468, 607; in New World, 481; in Southeast Asia, 613; in Spain, 444
Jews and Judaism: in east Central Europe, 440; in France, 279, 547; in Ottoman states, 452; Sephardic, 437; in Spain, 437
Jihad (holy war, struggle): in West Africa, 570
Jin Empire (China), 295; Mongols and, 307
Jingdezhen: Ming kilns at, 380
Jito (Japan), 314

Jivaro peoples, 324
Jizya (head tax), **356,** 363, 366
Jōmon culture (Japan), 312
Joan of Arc, 434–437, 434*i*; trial of, 435
John (England), 280
John II (Portugal), 466
John V (Portugal), 507
John of Leyden, 425
John of Monte Corvino, 308
John of Plano Carpini, 308
Joint-stock companies, **492**; in 17th century, 495; northern, 483–484
Jones, William, 598
Joseph II (Austria), 540
Journal des Dames, 535
Journeymen, 272
Journey to the West (Monkey), 379
Judaism. *See* Jews and Judaism
Judges: Ottoman, 353
Judicial board: in Japan, 320
Julius II (Pope), 406
Jurchen people, 302, 311
Jury system: in England, 280
Justification by faith alone, 424
"Just price," 272, **399**

K

Kabuki theater (Japan), 387, 612–613
Kabul, 362; trade in, 368
Kaifeng, China, 302
Kaikhta, Treaty of, 600
Kailasanatha Temple (India), 292*i*
Kaitokudō Merchant Academy (Osaka), 610
Kakinomoto Hitomaro: poem by, 317
Kalahari Desert: peoples near, 571
Kalidasa (poet and dramatist), 291
Kaliningrad (Koenigsberg), 441
Kamakura Period: in Japan, 319–320
Kamakura system (Japan), 384
Kamba peoples, 580
Kamchatka, 615
Kamehameha (Hawaii), 615
Kami, 313
Kamikaze (divine winds), 320
Kaminaljuyu, 327–328
Kampuchea. *See* Cambodia (Kampuchea)
Kan'ami (Japan), 387
Kana script: in Japan, 317

Kandahar (Afghanistan), 365
Kanem-Bornu, 570
Kangxi (Qing China), 599, 600, 601*i*; Japan and, 607
Kanō (Hausa city-state), 570
Kanō school of painting (Japan), 610
Kano Eitoku (Japan), 386
Kantō plain, Japan, 389
Karanga kingdom, 471
Karim Khan Zand (Persia), 593–594
Kasa (Lady) (Japan): poem by, 317
Kasa Haylu (Ethiopia), 581
Kasanje (African kingdom), 568
Katsina (Hausa city-state), 570
Katsushika Hokusai (Japan), 611, 613
Kayaks, 342
Keating, Richard W., 332
Kepler, Johannes, 528
Khanates, **348**; Mongol, 307, 308
Khans: Mongol, 305*i*
Khmer state, 391
Khoikhoi hunters and gatherers, 571, 572
Khubilai Khan (Mongol), 304, 307, 307–308
Khufu (Cheops, Egypt): pyramid of, 327*i*
Khurasan province, 362
Kilwa (Swahili state), 473, 579
Kim Hongdo (Korean painter), 604
Kingdom of Jerusalem, 276
Kingdom of Sicily, 440
Kings and kingdoms: in Afghanistan and Persia, 293; in Buganda, 578; in China, 295; Chola (India), 293; division of India into, 292; Harsha (India) and, 292; Incan, 332; in Korea, 310–312, 381; in Later Middle Ages, 278; Merovingian, 260; in Poland, 441; Zulu, 573. *See also* Absolutism; specific kings and kingdoms
Kinship: Aztec, 331; Incan, 335
Kipling, Rudyard, 344
Kirk (church, Scotland), 514
Kisaeng (women entertainers), 382
Kūkai (Japan): Shingon Buddhism and, 318
Knights: chivalry and, 267–268; in England, 279; feudal, 266–267
Knights of St. John of Jerusalem, 276, 352
Knights of the Temple (Templars), 276
Knowledge. *See* Intellectual thought
Knox, John, 425, 448
Ko Chosŏn (Korea), 310
Koguryŏ, 310–311

Kojiki (Japanese history), 313
Kongmin (Korea), 312
Kongo, 466, 469; kingdom of, 470–472, 568; Portugal and, 470–472, 473; slaves from, 472
Koran: Ottomans and, 452
Korea, 307, 310–312; 1300–1650, 372; in 17th and 18th centuries, 604–605; China and, 296, 310, 381; Chinese tribute system and, 381, 385*m*; Confucian society in, 381–384; female chastity in, 382, 384; Japan and, 384, 606, 607; Koryo dynasty in, 372; Manchu invasions of, 384; Mongols invasion of, 306; Qing dynasty (China) and, 384; syllabary in, 381; Tang China and, 297
Koryo dynasty (Korea), 311, 372
Kosovo: Ottomans in, 452
Kotoko Council, 567
Köprülü vizirs (Ottomans), 589–590
Krakow: university in, 441
Krio (Creole) community: in Sierra Leone, 569
Krishna (god), 289, 291*i*
Kul system (Ottoman Empire), 353
Kumaradevi (India), 289
Küchük Kaynarca, Treaty of, 591
Kwanghaegun (Korea), 384
Kyūshū, Japan, 312, 320, 389
Kyme, Mrs. Thomas. *See* Ayscough, Anne
Kyoto, 607
Kyoto (Heian), Japan, 313, 314, 320

L

Labor: Amerindian, 477, 478; for capitalist agriculture, 493*i*; in Japan, 386; in New Spain, 477; peasant, 269–270
Lacombe, Claire "Rose," 544
Ladder of Perfection, The (Teresa of Avila), 427
Lafayette, Marquis de: French Revolution and, 544
La Gioconda (Mona Lisa) (Leonardo da Vinci), 406
Lagoon of Venice, 401, 401*i*
Laissez-faire economics, **537**
Laity, **419**
Lake Chad: Kanem-Bornu and, 570

Lake Texcoco, 330
Lake Victoria region, 578
Lancaster, House of, 437
Lancaster, John, 487
Land: Chinese equal-field system and, 295; church ownership of, 496; of English church, 420–421; Korean Rank Lands and, 381–382; manorial, 269; nobility and, 496; Portuguese African cessions of, 474
Land bridge: across Bering Strait, 324; in Japan, 312
Lan Dingyuan (China), 603
Landlords, 494
Landowners: inflation and, 492
Landscapes: Japanese prints of, 613; painting in Song China, 304, 304i; in Tang Chinese arts, 299
Land trade: between Europe and China, 310
Language(s): of English church, 442; in Holy Roman Empire, 508; Iroquoian, 337; in Japan, 312, 313, 317; Korean, 383; Nahuátl, 480; North American, 336; Quechua, 335; Swahili, 580; of Yucatec- and Cholian-speaking peoples, 327
Laos, 613–615; Burma and, 392; Portugal and, 468; Thailand and, 614
Laplace, Pierre, 530
Large-market agriculture, 398
Las Casas, Bartolomé de, 481, 481i
Last Supper, The (Leonardo da Vinci), 406
Lateen sail, **464**
Later Middle Ages, 258; Crusades in, 275–278; European state development in, 278–283; Roman Catholicism in, 272–275
Latin America: culture of, 488–489
Latin Americans, 477
Latin Empire of Constantinople, 276
Latin Kingdom of Jerusalem, 275
La Venta: pyramid at, 325
Lavoisier, Antoine, 530
Lavoisier, Marie-Anne, 530
Law(s): of church, 273; in England, 280; in France, 547; in Korea, 311; Mongol, 307; in Ottoman Empire, 452; in Prussia, 539; regulating women, 303; studies in, 274; in Tang China, 298; in Yuan China, 308. *See also* Law codes
Law codes: Code Napoléon as, 554; in France, 547; on slavery, 585

Laws (scientific): of conservation, 530; of falling bodies, 530; of gravitation, 532; of planetary motion, 528; of supply and demand, 537
Lay investiture: prohibition of, 272–273
League of the Five Nations, 337
Learning: Charlemagne and, 264; classical, 402–404; in Ming China, 378–379; monastic preservation of, 260. *See also* Education; Intellectual thought
Le dynasty (Vietnam), 614; Le Loi, 393; Le Thanh Tong, 393
Leeds, England, 498
Leeuwenhoek, Antonie van, 530
Legal reform, 536
Legends: of Indian gods, 289
Legislation: Parliament and, 281
Legislative Assembly (France), 547; Paris Commune and, 548
Legislatures: in France, 542; House of Burgesses as, 486; Third Estate (France) as, 543. *See also* Assemblies
Leibniz, Gottfried Wilhelm, 531
Leipzig: Battle of the Nations at, 557
Leisure: medieval, 268; of peasants, 271
Le Mire, Noel: engraving by, 519i
Leo X (Pope), 417
Leon, Pauline, 544
Leonardo da Vinci, 406; *Drawing of a Flying Machine,* 406i
Leopold I (Holy Roman Empire), 508
Lepanto, battle of, 449, 449i
Letter of a Bourgeois of New Haven (Condorcet), 535
Levée en masse, 550
Levellers (England), **514**
Lever, William, 569
Leviathan (Hobbes), 502
Li (principle): in China, 304
Liao people (China), 302, 311
Liberal education: in Italy, 400
Liberation movement: in Netherlands, 512
Liberia, 569
Liberum Veto, **441**
Li Bo (Li Bai, China), 299
Libraries: Hungarian, 442
Licchavi princess (India), 289
Licensing Act (England), 516
Life expectancy, 497; for women, 499
Life of an Amorous Man (Ihara Saikaku), 611

Life of an Amorous Woman (Ihara Saikaku), 611
Life of Charlemagne (Einhard), 263
Lifestyle: of Boer families, 572; in English colonies, 487; of European poor, 499–501; in Korea, 311; on manors, 270; Mayan, 328; of peasants, 270–271; of poor, 501; Safavid, 360*i*; in Tang China, 298
Lima, 477
Limited monarchy, 533–534; in England, 516
Lindau Gospels, 259*i*
Li Qingzhao (Chinese poet), 303, 304
Literacy: in China, 378; in Japan, 316, 611
Literature: by Chinese women, 298, 602; classical, 402; in classical Japan, 317–318; European before Renaissance, 400; in France, 409–410; in Germany, 410; in Gupta India, 290–291; Japanese, 386, 611; Japanese women in, 315; Korean, 383; Middle Eastern, 350; in Ming China, 379; Ottoman, 356–357; in Song China, 304; in Spain, 410; in Tang China, 299; *Upanishads* and, 292–293; in Yuan China, 308. *See also* Epic literature; Humanism
Lithuania: Poland united with, 441
Liu Bang. *See* Gaozu (Tang China)
Liverpool, England, 498
Living conditions. *See* Lifestyle
Li Zicheng (China), 599
Lloyds of London, 495
Location: identification by, 344–345
Locke, John, 527, 532, 537, 539; on powers of people, 539; on role of government, 537–538; slave trade and, 585; women and, 535
Lodi, Treaty of, 440
Lodi Afghan dynasty, 362
Logic, 274, 530
Lollards, 414, **448**
Lombard League, 282
Lombards: Charlemagne and, 262
London: banks in, 496; Bubonic Plague and, 398; growth of, 498; poverty in, 498*i*
London Company, 486
London Stock Exchange, 496
Longbow, 434
Long Parliament (England), 514, 515*i*
Lord, 266; contract with vassals, 267; demesne of, 269; in Japan, 385, 386

Lord Protector: Cromwell as, 514–515, 515*i*
Lorenzo de' Medici, 402*i*, 405*i*
Lorraine, 264
Lothair, 264
Lotus Sutra, 319
Louis II (Hungary), 439
Louis VIII (France), 278
Louis IX (St. Louis, France), 278
Louis XI (France), 437
Louis XIII (France), 456, 503
Louis XIV (Sun King, France), 496, 502–505; absolutism of, 491, 505–506; diplomacy and warfare by, 517; French Empire and, 485; memoir to son, 504
Louis XIV in Robes of State (Rigaud), 503*i*
Louis XV (France), 522–524, 540; peasants and, 501
Louis XVI (France), 540, 543–544, 547, 548; execution of, 548, 548*i*. *See also* French Revolution (1789)
Louis XVIII (France), 557
Louis the German, 264
Louis the Great (Hungary), 441
Louis the Pious (Frankish emperor), 264
Louvois, Marquis de (France), 506
Love suicides: in Japan, 613
Loyola, Ignatius, 427
Luanda (African port), 472, 568
Luoyang, China, 295
Luther, Martin, 410, 442; Copernicus and, 528, 529; German Reformation and, 416–419; marriage by, 418–419; Ninety-Five Theses of, 417–418; salvation and, 417–418
Lutheranism: in Denmark, 419; human obligation in, 419; salvation in, 418; spread of, 426*m*
Lützen, battle at, 456
Luxury goods: China trade and, 380; Italian trade in, 400

M

Macao, 380; Portugal and, 468
Macartney, George, 604
Macassar (Malay Archipelago), 614
Macaulay, Catherine, 535
Mac dynasty (Vietnam), 614
Macedonia: Ottomans in, 452

Machiavelli, Niccolò, 403, 428
Machinery: knitting, 495i
Machu Picchu (Peru), 334i, 336
Mactan Island (Pacific Ocean), 476
Madagascar: slaves from, 571–572
Madeira Islands, 466, 479
Madonna of the Meadow (Raphael), 407i
Madonna with the Long Neck (Parmigianino), 408
Madras (India), 597; English in, 487
Maestricht (Netherlands): Spanish siege of, 447
Mafisa (cattle lending), **573**
Magellan, Ferdinand, 476, 613–614
Maghada, India, 288
Magistrates: in China, 603
Magna Carta, 280
Magyars (Hungarians): in Germany, 266; invasions by, 265, 265m
Mahabharata (Indian epic), 365
Mahal, Mumtaz, 365
Mahayana Buddhism, 296; in Japan, 318
Mahmud I (Ottoman), 591
Mahmud II (Ottoman), 593
Mahmud of Ghazna (Turkic warrior), 362
Mahmud of Ghazni (Muslim ruler): raids in India by, 293
Ma Huan: on Siam, 392
Maine, 486
Maitreya (future Buddha), 310, 602
Maize, 324, 482; in North America, 338
Majapahit kingdom, 372, 393, 394
Malacca, 393, 613; England and, 615; Portugal and, 467
Malawi: kingdom in, 573
Malaya: slaves from, 572; Thailand and, 614; trade and, 310
Malay Peninsula, 614
Malay people: Bugis as, 614
Malaysia, 394; Portugal and, 467
Mali: Portugal and, 469
Malindi, 471
Malitzin, 475, 475i, 480
Malnutrition: among women, 499; among workers, 499
Mamluks, 310
Manchu people: in China, 600
Manchuria, 599; Tang China and, 297
Manchus, 384; Qing (Ching) dynasty and, 381
Manco (Inca), 476, 481
Mandan Indians, 341

Mandate of Heaven (Japan), 610
Manhattan Island, 485
Manila, Philippines, 476; Spain and, 394
"Manila Galleons," 380; Spain and, 394
Mannerism, 408
Manor, 269m; administration of, 270
Manorialism, 268–271; restrictions of, 494; trade, towns, and, 271–272
Mansabdars (military administrators), **364**
Manuel (Portugal), 471
Manufacturing: domestic, 494–495; in Europe, 484; in Italy, 400
Manumission, **566**
Manuscripts: Mughal, 365; Persian, 361
Man'yōshū (The Collection of Ten Thousand Leaves), 316
Map(s): of Africa, 471, 471i; of ancient Chinese heartland, 375, 375i; in China, 303; of China's ancient heartland, 375, 375i; of exploration, 471; history and, 309, 309i; of Lagoon of Venice, 401, 401i; world map of Piri Reis (Ottoman cartographer), 351, 351i
Marat, Jean-Paul, 548; death of, 549, 549i
Maratha Confederacy (India), 595
Marathas (India), 595, 596m
Margaret of Navarre, 423i
Margaret of Parma, 446
Margraves: Carolingian, 262
Maria Habsburg, 439
Maria of Burgundy, 439
Maria of Portugal, 444
Maria Theresa (Austria), 508, 520
Marie Antoinette (France), 540, 548; execution of, 549
Marie de' Medici (France), 503
Marina, Doña. *See* Malitzin
Mariner's compass. *See* Compass
Maritime countries: England and, 486; European, 589; Portugal and Spain and, 467m; in Southeast Asia, 393–394
Maritime imperialism, 463
Maritime Southeast Asia, 372
Maritime trade, 288, 310; of Ming China, 380; in Song China, 304
Market(s): Antwerp as, 483i; in China, 297–298; European, 482–483; in Japan, 607; New World and, 492; in Tenochtitlán, 331; towns and, 271
Market towns: in Ming China, 378

Maroons: in Jamaica, 479
Marriage: alliances in India, 289; by Chinese widows, 378; by Eastern European royal families, 440; by Henry VIII (England), 420; in Japan, 315, 385, 609; by Luther, 418–419; Mongol, 306; in Ottoman Empire, 355; royal, 439
Marston Moor, battle at, 514
Martel, Charles (Franks), 261
Martin V (Pope), 415
Martinique, 486, 544
Martin Luther and his Friends (Cranach), 417*i*
Martyrs and martyrdom: Becket and, 436; English Protestant, 422; Protestant, 425, 427
Mary, Queen of Scots, 448; Elizabeth I (England) and, 448; England and, 450
Mary I Tudor (England), 420, 421, 444, 449
Maryas (India), 288
Maryland, 487
Mary of Guise, 448
Masaccio, 405; *Expulsion from Eden*, 405*i*
Mason, J. Alden, 332
Masons, 533–534
Mass: Catholic, 418
Massachusetts Bay Company, 486
Massacre of St. Bartholomew's Eve, 447
Massacre of the Innocents, The (Pieter Brueghel the Elder), 446*i*
Masulipatam (English trading post in India), 487
Matamba (African kingdom), 568
Materialists: French, 535
Material reality, 557
Mathematics, 530–531, 531; in India, 291; Mayan, 328; Newton and, 531–532
Matriarchies: in Americas, 324; Incan, 335; Mayan, 328
Matrilineal societies: Amerindian, 337; Incan, 335
Matsuo Bashō (Japan), 611
Matter: Lavoisier on, 530
Maurice, James, 448
Mauryan Empire (India), 288
Maximilian I (Holy Roman Empire), 439
Mayan civilization, 325, 326; classical, 327–329; conquistadora and, 475–476; resistance to Europeans by, 481
Mayapán (Central America), 329, 330
Mayor of the palace: Martel as, 261

Mazarin, Cardinal (France), 503
Mbundu kingdom, 472
Measles, 480
Mecca: Portugal and, 352; seizure from Ottomans, 591
Medici family, 400, 440; Catherine de, 447; Greek scholars and, 402–403; Lorenzo de', 402*i*, 405*i*; Marie de', 503
Medicine: Hindu, 291; in Song China, 304; studies in, 274
Mediterranean region: Crusades and, 276, 276*m*; England and, 518; Hellenic and Hellenistic societies in, 397; Muslim control of, 266; Ottomans and, 352
Mehmed II (Ottoman), 350–352, 356, 378
Meiji era (Japan), 610
Melanchton: Copernicus and, 528
Men: enslavement of African, 563; on medieval farms, 270*i*
Mencius (China), 304
Mendelssohn, Moses, 536
Mendez, Alphonso, 580
Mene Mutapa (king): in Mutapa state, 578
Mennonites, 425
Mentewab (Ethiopia), 581
Mercantilism, **505**–506, **597**; critiques of, 536–537; England and, 597; in Russia, 511
Mercenaries, 498; in African kingdoms, 568; condotierri as, 440; in Ottoman Empire, 591
Merchant(s): in China, 297, 298; Italian, 483; in Japan, 608; in Korea, 382; in Mughal Empire, 367; wives of, 609
Merchant-capitalists: in Italy, 400
Merchant guilds, 271–272
Merovingians, 260
Mesa Verde National Park, Colorado, 340*i*
Mesoamerica, 323, **325**; Aztecs in, 330–332; civilizations in, 325–336, 327*m*; classical civilization in, 327–329; formative period in, 325–326; postclassical civilization in, 329–336; sacrifices in, 329*i*
Mestizos (Spanish-Indian people), **477**
Metalwork: in Benin, 470
Mettrie, Julien de la, 535
Mexican-Guatemalan region, 325
Mexico: agriculture in, 324; Aztecs in, 330–332; civilizations of, 325; Olmec and, 325; silver from, 478; smallpox in, 480; Spanish in, 474; viceroyalty of, 476

Mexico City, 330, 475, 476
Mfecane (the scattering, Africa), **572,** 573
Miao people (China), 376
Michael Romanov, 451
Michelangelo Buonarroti, 407–408; *David,* 408*i*
Middle Ages, 256*i*, 257–258; chivalry in, 267–268; Christian missionary activities in, 258–260; church in, 258–260, 272–275; feudalism in, 266–268; manorialism in, 268–271; nobility in, 268; state development in, 278–283
Middle classes: discontent in, 502; social change and, 522
Middle East: 1650–1815, 587–588; literature of, 350; Ottoman Empire in, 350*m*; Turkic invaders of, 305. *See also* Arabs and Arab world
Middle Passage, **563**–564; slave ship in, 564*i*
Migration: into Americas, 324; China and, 376, 380, 601, 602; in Europe, 498; in New England, 486; in Portugal and Spain, 465; by voortrekkers, 575–576, 576*i*. *See also* specific groups
Milan, 517; duchy of, 400
Militarism: Toltec, 330
Military: in England, 434; Europe and, 433; in France, 506; Frederick the Great and, 509–510; in India, 288; in Korea, 311–312; Martel and, 261; Mexican-Mayan, 330; in Ming China, 380–381; Mongol, 307, 308; Mughal, 364, 365; under Napoleon, 554–555; Ottomans and, 593; in Silla, 311; in Song China, 302; in Tang China, 297, 299; Zulu, 572, 573. *See also* Armed forces; Janissaries; specific battles and wars
Military orders: in Crusades, 276
Millet system, 452
Minamoto shōguns, 389
Minamoto Yoritomo (Japan), 316, 319–320
Ming dynasty (China), 305, 347, 371, 373–381, 373*m*, 599; 16th-century world and, 380–381; administration of, 376; Great Wall of China and, 374; Japan and, 388; Korea and, 312, 384; location of, 375; opposition to Manchus by, 599; society of, 374–380; Taizu in, 310
Minh Mang (Vietnam), 614
Miniatures: Mughal, 365*i*
Mining, 484

Minorca, 518
Mir Ali, Sayyid, 361, 364
Miramo (Nyamwezi chief), 580
Mirza, Ibrahim, 361
Missi dominici (king's envoys), 262
Missions and missionaries: Amerindians and, 481; Catholic, 429; in China, 308, 600*i*; European, 394; in Japan, 389; Jesuits as, 380; in Middle Ages, 258–260; in Southeast Asia, 613; sufi, 360–361, 393
Mississippian culture, 338–339
Mississippi Company, 496
Mississippi River region, 324
Mistresses: of Louis XIV (France), 503–505
Mnemonic devices: Incan, 336
Mobility: social, 502
Mobilization: in France, 553
Moctezuma II (Aztec), 475
Model Parliament (England), 281
Mogollon people, 339
Mohacs, battle of, 352, 442
Mohawk Indians, 337, 487*i*
Moldavia, 452
Molucca Islands, 394; Dutch in, 484
Mombasa: Portugal and, 471
Mona Lisa (Leonardo da Vinci), 406
Monarchs and monarchies: in Americas, 324; aristocratic opposition to, 502; in Central Europe, 441; in England, 280, 281, 515–516; in Ethiopia, 580–581; failures of reform of, 539–541; in France, 279; German, 439; Hobbes on, 502; in Japan, 384; nobility and, 496; Thai, 391. *See also* specific monarchs and monarchies
Money: in Korea, 382. *See also* Coins; Currency
Moneylenders: Italian, 483
Mongol Empire: China under, 308–310; khanates within, 308
Mongolia: Chinese sovereignty over, 600
Mongols, 287, 288; in China, 295, 304–305, 374; before conquest of Song China, 306–307; in east Central Europe, 440; expansion of, 305–306; hegemony of, 306*m*; in Japan, 320; in Korea, 312; Russia and, 600; Southeast Asia and, 391; views of, 305*i*
Monks and monasteries, **261**; Buddhist, 289, 293; Dominican, 417; French Revolution

and, 544; in Ireland, 259; learning and, 260; medieval reforms of, 272–273; in Middle Ages, 259
Monogamy: in Japan, 315
Monopolies: joint-stock companies as, 495–496
Monotheism: of Pachacuti, 336
Monroe, James, 569
Monrovia, Liberia, 569
Mons (Burma), 614
Montague, Mary Wortley, 535, 592
Montaigne, Michel de, 410, 410*i*
Monte Alban, 327
Montespan, Athénaï de, 505*i*
Montesquieu, Baron de, 534, 539; *Spirit of the Laws,* 538
Montezuma I (Aztec), 330
Montezuma II (Aztec), 330
Montreal, 486
Montserrat, 487
Moors: Spain and, 261, 444
Moravia, 438
More, Thomas, 412 413, 416, 421, 436
Moriscos (Spanish Muslims), 445
Morocco: Islamic dynasty in, 570; Portugal and, 438, 466; Songhai and, 570
Mortality: in Europe, 497; of slaves in Middle Passage, 564; of workers, 499. *See also* Life expectancy
Mortgaten, battle of, 440
Moscow: French occupation of, 556
Moshoeshoe (Basotho), 573*i*; Basotho kingdom of, 573–574; voortrekkers and, 576
Mosques: in Isfahan, 361
Motoori Norinaga (Japan), 610
Möngke (Mongol), 307
Mound Builders, 324
Mounds: Adena, 338; at Cahokia, 338; Great Serpent Mound, 338*i*; Hopewell, 338
Mt. Fuji: print of, 608*i*
Mt. Hiel, 386
Movable type: in China, 298, 303; in Europe, 409; in Korea, 312
Mozambique: kingdom in, 573; Portugal and, 467, 471, 579; slaves from, 571
Mthethwa Confederacy, 572
Mufti, **355**–356
Mughal Empire (India), 294, 347, 348, 361–367, 361*m*, 587, 594–598; administration of, 365–367; Marathas and, 595–596, 596*m*; religion in, 365–366; society in, 366–367; state and culture of, 363–365
Muhammad Bello (Sokoto Caliphate), 570–571
Muhammad-Hadi (historian), 366
Muhammad Shah (Mughal India), 595
Mulattoes (European-African people), **479**; in French colonies, 550; West Indian, 544–547
Mulay Ismail (Moroccan Sultan), 570
Multiculturalism: in Malacca, 394; in Ottoman Empire, 353
Munster, Sebastian: map of Africa, 471, 471*i*
Muomachi period (Japan), 384
Murad I (Ottomans), 452
Murad IV (Ottoman), 357
Murals: Mayan, 329
Murasaki (Lady) (Japan), 316, 317, 318
Murhachi (Manchu), 599
Muromachi period (Japan), 386–387, 388
Music: in Japan, 316, 317*i*
Muslims: in Africa, 562; African trade and, 469; caravan routes and, 464; Charlemagne and, 262; in Chinese Central Asia, 600; Christian perspective on Crusades and, 277; European raids by, 265–266; fall of Jerusalem to, 275; Hindu-Buddhist culture and, 394; in India, 293–294, 294*m*; in Ottoman states, 452; in Persia, 593–594; Portugal and, 467–468; in Southeast Asia, 391; in Spain, 281, 437; Sufi, 294; in West Africa, 570. *See also* Arabia; Islam
Mustafa III (Ottoman), 591
Mutapa state, 471–474, 578
Mutinies: by slaves, 564
Mutiny Act (England), 516
Münster: siege of, 425
Müteferrika, Ibrahim, 590

N

Nadir Shah (Persia), 593; in Mughal Empire, 595
Nagasaki, Japan: growth of, 607
Nahuátl language, 480
Nakatomi family. *See* Fujiwara family (Japan)

Nalanda: university at, 291
Nanjing (Nanking), China, 302, 374
Nantes, Edict of. *See* Edict of Nantes
Naples, 517; kingdom of, 400
Napoleon I Bonaparte (France), 550, 552–557, 552*i*, 556*m*; Continental System of, 550; downfall of, 556–557; in Egypt, 552–553, 591; as emperor, 554; military under, 554–555
Napoleonic Code. *See* Code Napoléon (Napoleonic Code)
Napoleonic Empire, 555–557, 556*m*
Nara Period (Japan), 313, 314; artifacts in, 317*i*; pagodas of Yakushi-ji in, 319*i*
Narrow Road to the North (Matsuo Bashō), 611
Naseby, battle at, 514
Natal, 576
Nation(s): in Asia, 587–588; in Middle East, 587–588. *See also* State (nation); specific nations
National Constituent Assembly (France), 543, 544; West Indies and, 547
National Convention (France), 548, 549, 550, 551
National Guard: in France, 544
Nationalism: in Europe, 557; German, 410, 556; Lutheranism and, 419
Nationalities: in Holy Roman Empire, 508
Nationalized land: in China, 297
Nations, Battle of the, 557
Native Americans. *See* Amerindians
Natural rights: Locke on, 538
Nature: Deism and, 536; in Enlightenment, 533
Navajo Indians, 340, 341*i*
Naval wars: Anglo-Dutch, 517
Navarre, 437; Spain and, 438
Navies: Dutch, 484; in France, 506, 555; Korean, 384; Ottoman, 357, 590, 593; Portuguese, 464; Spanish, 450, 484; Turkish, 449
Navigation, 463; European Pacific exploration and, 615
Ndebele warriors: Moshoeshoe and, 573
Ndongo kingdom, 568, 568*i*
Near East: trade in, 271
Nedim (poet), 591
Nelson, Horatio, 553, 555
Neo-Confucians: Japanese women and, 609; in Korea, 312, 382, 383, 384, 605; in Song China, **304**

Neolithic (New Stone Age): in Japan, 312
Nerchinsk, Treaty of, 600
Netherland East India Company, 484, 495, 616; in southern Africa, 571
Netherlands: France and, 615; government of, 491; Habsburgs in, 450; Spain and, 445–447, 447, 449, 517; after Thirty Years' War, 457. *See also* Dutch
Netherlands East Indies. *See* Indonesia
Nevis, 487
New Amsterdam, 485
New Britain, 615
Newcastle family (England), 497
New England: population of, 486
Newfoundland, 482, 518; England and, 486; France and, 485
New Guinea, 615; Dutch and, 484
New Spain, 474–477
New Testament: of Tyndale, 421
Newton, Isaac, 530, 531, 531–532; Enlightenment and, 533; religion and, 536
Newton, John, 564
New World: "discovery" of, 351; Enlightenment in, 536; Iberian regimes in, 477–482; Korean trade and, 382; migration to, 498; New Spain in, 474–477; products from, 380; rebellions against France in, 555
Ngola (Mbundu king), 472
Nguni peoples, 571
Nguyen Du (Vietnam), 614
Nguyen family (Vietnam), 614; Anh, 614
Nichiren Buddhism, 319
Nigeria, 470. *See also* Hausa
Nightingale, Florence, 592
Nihongi (Japanese history), 313
Ninety-Five Theses (Luther), 417–418
Nizhni Novgorod, 310
Njinga (Ndongo kingdom), 568*i*
Njinga, Anna (Angola), 568
Nō plays (Japan), **387,** 612
Nobility, 496; Aztec, 331; in Central and Eastern Europe, 441; as class, 267; in England, 516; feudal, 266–267; in France, 437, 447, 503; Incan, 334–335; as lords and vassals, 266; medieval, 268; Merovingian, 261; in Poland, 441, 508; in Portugal, 507; Prussian, 508, 509–510; in Russia, 451, 540; as Second Estate, 542;

in Spain, 445, 465, 507. *See also* Aristocracy
Nobunaga (Japanese daimyō), 389, 468–469
Nomads: from Central Asia, 288; in China, 295
Nonconformists: migration of English, 486
Normandy, 266, 278
Normans: conquest of England by, 279*i*
North Africa, 561
North America: Amerindians in, 336–342, 337*m*; England and, 486–487; French in, 485–486; Hohokam in, 339; Mississippian culture in, 338–339; Mogollon people in, 339; Paleolithic migration into, 324; Vikings in, 266
North China, 295; Wei in, 295
Northeastern Africa: state formation in, 578–581
Northeast Woodlands: Iroquois of, 337
North-South: use of terms, 345
Northern Europe: expansion of, 482–487; humanism in, 412–413
Northern Renaissance, 397, 408–413; Europe during, 399*m*; painting in, 411–412; printing in, 409
Northern Song period (China), 302
Northern Wei (China), 295; rock carvings and, 296*i*
North Sea region: Hanseatic League in, 398
Northumberland, duke of (England), 421
Norway: Lutheranism and, 419; Viking raids from, 266
Norwich, England, 498
Notation system: Mayan, 328
Nova Scotia, 518; French in, 485
Novels: in China, 308
Novum Organum (Bacon), 531
Nuclear families: in Japan, 608
Nuns: Buddhist, 289
Nurjahan (wife of Jahangir): seclusion and, 366
Nyamwezi peoples, 580
Nyiginya people, 580
Nzinga Mbemba (Kongo), 472, 473
Nzinga Nkuwu (Kongo), 470–472

O

Oaxaca, 325, 328, 329; Monte Alban and, 327
Obas (Benin), 470
Oceania: imperialism and (1800), 604*m*
Oda Nobunaga (Japan), 385–386, 388
Ogyū Sorai (Japan), 610
Ohio River region: Adena and Hopewell cultures of, 337–338
Okhotsk, 615
Old believers (Russia), 512
Oldenbarnveldt, John, 512
Old regimes (Europe): nobility and, 496; women's protests and, 502. *See also* Ancien régime (Old Regime)
Olmec society, 325–326
Oman, 579
Omani Arabs, 469; in East Africa, 579; Portugal and, 471
Oneida Indians, 337
Onondaga Indians, 337
On the Fabric of the Human Body (Vesalius), 530
On the Revolutions of the Heavenly Spheres (Copernicus), 528
Opium trade, 598, 616; China and, 601, 602
Opoku Ware (Asante), 567
Oprichniki, 451
Optics, 530
Orange Free State (South Africa), 576
Orbit: planetary, 528
"Orient," 591; myths of, 592
Orléans, France: in Hundred Years' War, 437
Oromo people: Mentewab as, 581
Orthodox Christianity, 450–453; in Russia, 511, 512
Osaka, 607
Osei Tutu (Asante), 567
Osman (Ottoman), 349
Osman II (Ottoman), 588
Otto I the Great (Germany), 282*i*, 283*m*
Ottoman Empire, 347, 348, 349–357, 350*m*, 587, 588; in 17th century, 588; in 18th century, 518, 591; ambassadors from, 591, 592; arts in, 356–357; bureaucracy in, 452–453; challenges to, 357; in early modern era, 588–593; European influence on, 590; European intervention in, 591; harem in, 354*i*; Köprülü vizirs in, 589–590; at Lepanto, 449; maps in, 351; Safavids and, 359; under Selim III, 593; after Seven Years' War, 520; under Suleiman, 353–356; Tulip Period in, 590–591

"Ottoman Official's Wedding Night, An" (Çelebi), 355
Ottoman (Osmanli) Turks: in Balkans, 452; Hungary and, 442; Safavids and, 359
Ögödei (Mongol), 307
Outline of Herb Medicine, The (China), 378
Overseers: African slaves as, 482
Ovimbundu (African kingdom), 568
Oxford: university in, 274
Oyo (Yoruba kingdom): slave trade and, 566
Ozuola (Benin oba), 470

P

Pachacuti (Inca), 332, 333, 335–336
"Pachacuti, the Greatest Inca" (Cobo), 333
Pacification of Ghent, 447
Pacific Ocean region: Europeans in, 615–616
Padded horse collar: from China, 303
Padua, University of, 403
Paekche (Korean state), 311, 313
Pagodas: in Korea, **311**; in Nara, 319*i*; stupas and, 311
Paine, Thomas, 536
Painting: in Italian Renaissance, 404–405, 406–408; in Japan, 317–318, 386, 610; in Korea, 383, 604; Mayan, 329; in Ming China, 379–380; Mughal, 364–365; in Northern Renaissance, 411–412; Ottoman, 356–357; Persian, 361; in Qing China, 600; in Song China, 304; in Tang China, 299; in Yuan China, 308
Pais, Pedro, 580
Palaces: in Benin, 470; in Ming China, 379; Topkapi, 356; at Versailles, 505. *See also* specific palaces
Palenque, 328
Paleolithic (Old Stone Age): migration into Americas during, 324
Pallavar dynasty (India), 293
Palmer, Elihu, 536
Panchatantra, 291
Pantheism, **534**
Papacy: after 1300, 416; alliance with Franks, 261; in Avignon, 414; criticisms of, 413; in Early Middle Ages, 258; England and, 421; Ferdinand and Isabella and, 437; Germany and, 282; under Innocent III, 273; missionaries and, 259; Philip II (Spain) and, 444; political power of, 442
Papal bull: *Unam Sanctam* as, 414
Papal court: Inquisition as, 273
Papal States, 258, 400, 416, 440; Pius VII and, 554; pope as ruler of, 261
Paper, 299
Paper money: in China, 303
Paraguay: mestizos in, 477
Paris: count of, 278; French Revolution and, 543; Huguenot synod in, 447; Napoleon's return to, 557; parlement of, 540; university in, 274; women's protests in, 502
Paris Bourse, 496
Paris Commune, **548,** 549
Parishes, **260**
Parlement of Paris, 540
Parlements (French courts), 541
Parliament (England), 281, 437; Charles I and, 513–514
Parmigianino, 408
Partition: of Poland (1772, 1793), 519. *See also* Germany; Korea
Pasha, **353**
Pasha, Melek Ahmed, 355
Pate (Swahili state), 579
Patriarch: of Russian Orthodox Church, 511
Patriarchies: in Americas, 324; in China, 303–304; Mayan, 328; in Mughal Empire, 367
Patriotism: in Italy, 400
Patrons: popes as, 400
Patroons, **485**
Paul III (Pope), 427; Copernicus and, 529
Peace of Aix-la-Chapelle, 520
Peace of Augsburg, 419, 442, 443, 453
Peace of Carlowitz (1699), 591
"Peace of God," 267
Peace of Paris: of 1763, 520
Peace of Prague, 456
Peace of Utrecht, 508; slave trade and, 562
Peace of Vervins (1598), 450
Peace of Westphalia, 456–457; France after, 517
Peasants: in Austria, 540; in China, 373–374, 380; as class, 267; enclosure and, 494; in Europe, 497; in France, 505; in French Revolution, 543; in India, 288; inflation and, 492; in Japan, 315, 390; in Korea,

382; large-market agriculture and, 398; living conditions in 18th century, 500; medieval, 270–271, 270*i*; in Middle Ages, 261; in Mughal Empire, 364, 367; in Ottoman Empire, 589; in Vietnam, 614
Peasants' revolts, 501; of 1524–1525, 419, 442; in Russia (1770s), 501, 540
Pecs (city): university in, 441
Pedro II (Portugal), 507
Pegu, Burma, 392; Shwemawdaw Pagoda and, 393*i*
Penal reform, 536
Penang: British in, 615
Pendulum, 530
Pendulum clock, 531
Peninsular War, 555
People's Republic of China (PRC). *See* China
Pepin II the Short (Franks), 261; donation of territory to pope, 258
Persecution: of Protestant sects, 425
Persia and Persian Empire, 348, 349; fragmentation of, 593–594; Mongols and, 305*i*, 307; Muslims and, 593–594; Ottomans and, 357; Safavid Empire in, 357–361, 357*m*. *See also* Iran
Persian Gulf region: Ottomans and, 352; slave trade in, 579
Persian Letters (Montesquieu), 534
Peru: agriculture in, 324; city in, 324; Inca in, 476, 481; silver from, 478
Peter I the Great (Russia), 496, 510–512, 510*i*, 511*m*, 517
Peter III (Russia), 520
Petition of Right (England, 1628), 513
Petrarch (Francesco Petrarca), 402
Philip I (Spain), 439
Philip II Augustus (France), 275, 278; John (England) and, 280
Philip II (Spain), 444*i*; Elizabeth I (England) and, 448, 448–449; failure of, 450; Lepanto and, 449; Mary I Tudor and, 421; Netherlands and, 449; Portugal and, 438, 478; religion and, 443, 444–445; wives of, 444
Philip III (Spain), 450
Philip IV the Fair (France), 279, 414
Philip V (Spain), 507, 517
Philippines, 394; Chinese migration to, 380; Magellan in, 614; Ming Chinese trade with, 380; Spain and, 394, 476

Philosopher king, 539
Philosophes, **534**; radical Enlightenment and, 534–535
Philosophy: in Song China, 304. *See also* Intellectual thought
Phoenix Hall (Japan), 314*i*
Physicians: Hindu, 291
Physics: in scientific revolution, 530
Physiocrats, **536**; French Revolutionary policies and, 544
Physiology: in scientific revolution, 530
Piast dynasty (Poland), 440, 441
Pico della Mirandola, 403
Pictographs, **328**
Pictorial art: in Japan, 613
Pilgrimages: to Canterbury, 436, 442; Crusades and, 275
Pillow Book, The (Sei Shōnagon), 317, 318
Pirates: in East Asia, 372; Ming China and, 381
Piri Reis (Ottoman cartographer): world map of, 351, 351*i*
Pisa: Council of, 415
Pius VII (Pope): Concordat of 1801 with, 554
Pizarro, Francisco, 476, 477
Plague: Bubonic, 398; in China, 310
Planetary motion: Copernicus and, 528; Kepler on, 528
Plantagenet (Angevin) dynasty, 280
Plantation(s): in Americas, 478; Dutch, 484; slavery on, 562
Plantation agriculture, 492; Dutch, 394
Plassey, battle of, 598
Plato, 260; humanist study of, 403
Playwrights: Chinese, 379; in Japan, 613
Pleasure quarters: in Japan, 610
Pocahontas, 486
Poets and poetry: in China, 296; in Japan, 312, 316–317; Japanese haiku and, 611; Korean, 383; by Petrarch, 402; in Song China, 304; in Tang China, 298, 299, 300
Poland, 438; in 18th century, 518; absolutism in, 508; Catholicism in, 440; destruction of, 519; Lithuania united with, 441; partitions of (1772, 1793), 519; peasant rebellions in, 501; Russia and, 451; after Seven Years' War, 520
Police: in Russia, 511
Politics: British industry and, 495; Calvin and, 443; Catholic Church and, 415;

Politics, *continued*
English East India Company in, 598; in Europe (1300–1500), 434–442; in Gupta India, 292; Lutheranism and, 419; medieval church and, 267; Muslim, in Persia, 593–594; Ottoman, 354–356; religion and, 442–443; in Song China, 301–304; in Southeast Asia, 613–614; under Tang dynasty, 297. *See also* specific countries
Polo, Marco: Columbus and, 466; on Yuan China, 308
Poltava, battle at, 517
Polygamy: among Anabaptists, **425**; Mongol, 306
Polynesia, 615; Europeans in, 615
Pomerania, 508
Pompadour, Madame de, 520, 522
Pondicherry, battle at, 598
Poniatowski, Stanislaus (Poland), 519
Poor: conditions for women and, 499; misery of, 499–501
Pope(s): Council of Constance and, 415; Henry IV (Germany) and, 282; infallibility of, 418; Papal States and, 400; Pepin the Short and, 261; Philip IV (France) and, 279; as Renaissance patrons, 400; temporal authority of, 258; Treaty of Tordesillas and, 466
Popular sovereignty: in England, 516
Population: of Agra, 364; American losses after European arrival, 481; Amerindian, 336; Bubonic Plague and, 398; in China, 303, 380, 601; explosion in Europe, 497–499; Incan, 334; of Isfahan, 361; in Japan, 607; living conditions and, 499–501; in Portugal and Spain, 465; town growth and, 271
Porcelain: in Ming China, 380, 380*i*; trade in, 297
Portrait of a Sufi (Shaykh-Zadeh), 356*i*
Portrait of Erasmus (Holbein the Younger), 413*i*
Port Royal, Nova Scotia: French in, 485
Portugal, 438; Africa and, 469–474, 473, 568; Americas and, 467; Angola and, 568*i*; Brazil and, 467; carrying trade and, 465*i*; China trade with, 380; decline of empire, 469; Dombo and, 578; Dutch trade and, 484; East Africa and, 472–474; empire of, 466–469; expansion by, 464–474, 467*m*; exploration by, 488*m*; expulsion from Zimbabwean plateau, 474; Indian Ocean and, 587–588; Indonesia and, 391; Japan and, 389, 467–468, 607; Kongo and, 470–472; Mozambique and, 579; New World claims of, 465; Ottomans and, 357; population growth in, 465; rebellion against Napoleon, 555; royal authority in, 507; Safavids and, 359, 360; in Sena and Tete, Africa, 578; ships and, 465*i*; slave trade and, 469–470; Southeast Asia and, 372, 394, 613; and southern Africa, 571; Spain and, 437, 449, 482; sugar plantations of, 479; West Africa and, 466*i*, 469–470. *See also* Iberian Peninsula; Latin America
Postclassical civilization: Mesoamerican, 329–336
Potatoes, 482
Pottery: in Korea, 383; in Ming China, 380, 380*i*
Poverty: in London, 498*i*; rural, 501; urban, 499–501
Power (authority): of Europe, 433; Habsburg, 439; Ottoman Empire and, 357; of Philip II (Spain), 444–445; religion and, 442–443
Power politics: Persia in European, 594
Prabhavati Gupta (India), 289
Prague, 441; defenestration of, 455; Peace of, 456; university in, 441
Praise of Folly, The (Erasmus), 412
Prazos (land grants), **474, 578**
PRC (People's Republic of China). *See* China
Predestination: Calvin on, 424
Presbyterians: in Parliament, 514; in Scotland, 448
Prester John, 474; myth of, 465
Preston, battle at, 514
Price, just, 272, 399
Price, Richard, 535
Priest-king: Mayan, 328
Priestley, Joseph, 530, 535
Priestly culture: in Teotihuacán, 327
Principe, 472
Principia (Newton), 532
Printing: in Central and Eastern Europe, 441; in China, 299, 303; in Hungary,

442; in Korea, 312; in Northern Renaissance, 409; in Ottoman Turkish language, 591
Privateers: Dutch, 446, 449; English, 450
Profession(s): education for, 274
Property: of aristocrats, 497; in France, 543; as voting qualification, 547
Prostitution: in Europe, 499; in Iberian American colonies, 479; women and children forced into, 585
Protest(s): by poor in Europe, 501–502
Protestantism, 429; Anabaptism and, 421; in Bohemia, 455; Calvinism and, 443; of Christian IV (Denmark), 455; Council of Trent and, 427; Edict of Nantes and, 450; Elizabeth I (England) and, 448; in England, 419–421, 442; in English civil war, 514; in Holy Roman Empire, 508; martyrs of, 422; in Netherlands, 446; politics and, 442; radical, 421; in Spain, 444; splinter groups in, 425; in Switzerland, 423; after Thirty Years' War, 456; use of term, 419; Zwingli and, 423. *See also* Huguenots; specific groups
Protestant Reformation: geographical spread of, 426*m*
Provinces: Ottoman, 591
Prus people, 441
Prussia, 441; absolutism in, 508–510; Austria and, 520; craftsmen for, 498; East India Company in, 493; France and, 548; French Revolution and, 547, 548; Polish partition and, 519; after Seven Years' War, 520; War of Jenkins's Ear and, 520
Ptolemy, Claudius (scientist), 471, 528, 529
Public assistance: for poor, 501
Public finance: crisis in, 522
Publishing: in Japan, 611
Pueblo people, 324
Pugachev revolt (Russia), 501
Puisseux, Madame de, 535
Punjab region: Mongols in, 294
Puranas (books), 289
Purchase brides: in colonies, 487
Pure Land Buddhism, **296,** 297, 301; in Japan, 319, 385; in Korea, 311
Puritans, **448**; in colonies, 487; in England, 514; in Massachusetts Bay, 486
Pyramids: in Americas, 325; Aztec, 332; at Cahokia, 338; Mayan, 328–329; in Peru, 324; of the Sun (Teotihuacán), 327, 327*i*, 328

Q

Qajar dynasty (Persia/Iran), 588, 594
Qianlong (Qing China), 600–601, 602*i*
Qing (Ching, Manchu) dynasty (China), 381, 599–601; Burma and, 614; Korea and, 384; before Opium War, 598–604; Vietnam and, 614
Qin Liangyu (China), 381
Quakers, 425
Quattrocento painters, 405
Quebec, 485–486
Quechua, **335**
Queens: in Africa, 568
Quesnay, François, 536–537
Quetzalcoatl (god), **329**
Quipus (knotted strings), **336**
Qutb ud-Din Aibak, 293

R

Rabban Sauma, 310
Rabelais, François, 409–410
Racial mixture: in New World, 477
Radicals and radicalism: in England, 514; in French Revolution, 547–549; Protestant, 446
Radziwill family (Poland), 497
Ragusa-Dubrovnik, 452
Rajput Confederacy, 362
Rajputs (India), 292, 293, 595
Rama I (Chakri, Thailand), 614
Rama Khamheng (Thai), 391
Rank Lands (Korea), **381**–382
Raphael, 406–407; *Madonna of the Meadow*, 407*i*
Rationalism: British, 535
Ravenna: Exarchate of, 261
Raziyya (India), 293
Reaction: against French Revolution, 551–552
Reason, 530–531; faith and, 536; politics and, 519. *See also* Enlightenment
Reconquista (Spain), 281–282, 437–438
Red Turbans (China), **374**

Reform and reformers: in Austria, 540; in Catholic Church, 426–428; in China, 302; in England, 280; in France, 540; in Holy Roman Empire, 508; humanist, 416; in Japan, 314, 609; in Korea, 312, 605; legal, 536; of monarchies, 539–541; monastic, 272–273; in Ottoman Empire, 593; prison, 536; in Prussia, 539; in Russia, 540

Reformation: Anglican, 419–421; Catholic, 426–428; in Europe, 397; in Germany, 416–419; Lutheran, 416–419; Protestant, 416–425; in Switzerland, 423

Refugees: from Shaka, 573

Regency Council (England), 421

Register of Licentious Women, The (Korea), 382

Regulation: of Japanese trade, 390

Reid, Thomas, 537

Reign of Terror (France), **550**; end of, 551–552

Religion(s): Aztec, 331–332; Buddhism and, 287; in Central Europe, 439, 453; Edict of Nantes and, 450; English migrants and, 486; Enlightenment and, 536; in French Revolution, 550; Hohokam, 339; in Holy Roman Empire, 508; Iberian expansion and, 464–465; Incan, 335; in India, 289, 294; in Japan, 312, 318–319; in Korea, 311, 312; in Mayan life, 328; in Middle Ages, 272–273; Mississippian, 338–339; in Netherlands, 446; in Ottoman Empire, 355–356; politics and, 442–443; Puritans and, 448; Shintō as, 313; in Song China, 304; in Southeast Asia, 391; state and, 418–419; in Switzerland, 423; in Tang China, 298; in Yuan China, 308

Religious orders, 427; in French Revolution, 544

Religious toleration: by Akbar, 363; in Austria, 540; by Mongols, 308; in Mughal Empire, 363, 365; in Qing China, 600; after Thirty Years' War, 456–457

Remedies Against Fortune, 402i

Renaissance: arts in, 404–408; in England, 410–411; in Europe, 397; Hungary and, 441–442; Italian, 399–408; northern, 408–413; Northern humanism in, 412–413; Scholasticism during, 403

Rents: from Japanese farmers, 315

Representative legislature: House of Burgesses as, 486

Republic(s): Boer, 576; in England, 514; in France, 548. *See also* specific republics

Resistance: by Amerindians, 481

Resources: in China, 601

Restoration (England), 515

Restoration (France), 551

Revolts and rebellions: in Africa, 474; by Irish, 448; in Japan, 390; in Ming China, 381; in Mughal India, 595; against Napoleon, 555; in Ottoman Empire, 588; by peasants, 419; by poor in Europe, 501–502; in Spanish Netherlands, 445–447; in Vietnam, 614

Revolution(s): American, 516; scientific, 528–532

Revolutionary War in America. *See* American Revolution

Rhineland: France and, 517

Rhode Island, 486

Rhodes: Ottomans in, 352

Rhodes, Alexhandre de, 613

Ricci, Matteo, 380

Rice industry: in China, 303

Richard I the Lion-Hearted (England), 275, 280

Richard II (England), 414

Richelieu, Cardinal (France), 456, 503

Rigaud, Hyacinthe: *Louis XIV in Robes of State*, 503i

Rights: Enlightenment thinkers on, 537; feudal, 266; in France, 543; Locke on, 538

Rinzai Buddhism, 319

Riot(s): in China, 380; among European workers, 502; by poor in Europe, 501–502

Ritual: Incan, 335

Rivers. *See* specific rivers and river regions

Rōnin (masterless samurai), 389

Robespierre, Maximilien, 548, 549, 550, 551

Rocroi, battle at, 450, 456

Roman Catholicism. *See* Catholic Church

Romance of the Three Kingdoms (China), 308

Romanians, 452

Romanov dynasty (Russia), 451–452

Rome (ancient): Charlemagne and, 262; Frankish state and, 261. *See also* Byzantium (Byzantine Empire)

Rome (city): Indian trade with, 289; papacy and, 258, 415; sack of (1527), 416, 442
Rosetta Stone, 553
Rousseau, Jean-Jacques, 535, 538
Royal courts: in England, 280; in Japan, 316; Japanese women in, 315; in Ming China, 380; of Suleiman, 352–353; of Yuan China, 308
Royalists: in France, 551; Parliament (England) and, 514
Royal Society of London, 532
Royalty: Aztec, 331. *See also* Absolutism
Rozvi soldiers: in Mutapa kingdom, 578
Rubaga, Buganda, 579*i*
Rudolf I (Holy Roman Empire, Germany), 439
Rudolf II (Holy Roman Empire, Bohemia), 455
Rulers. *See* Dynasties; Kings and kingdoms; specific rulers
Rump Parliament (England), 514
Rural areas: in Korea, 382; poor women in, 499; poverty in, 501
Rurik rulers (Russia), 451
Russia, 441, 519; autocracy in, 450–452, 510–512; Bering Strait and, 615; China and, 599*i*, 600; craftsmen for, 498; expansion by, 517; in Great Northern War, 517; Japan and, 615; Napoleon and, 556; Ottomans and, 357, 590, 591; peasant rebellions in, 501; Persia and, 594; Polish partition and, 519; population of, 498; after Seven Years' War, 520; Slavic migration from, 261; Vikings in, 266; war with France, 556
Rwaburgiri (Tutsi), 580
Rwanda, 562, 580

S

Sacks: of Rome (1527), 416, 442
Sacrifices: Aztec, 332; in Cahokia, 339; Mesoamerican, 329*i*
Sado (Korea), 604
Safavid Empire (Persia), 347, 348, 357–361, 593–594; Ottomans and, 352
Safavi mystical order, 357–359
Safety: in Safavid Empire, 360
Safi al-Din (Safavid), 357
Sagres, 466
Saichō (Japan), 318, 386
Said, Sayyid (Omani Sultan), 579
Saikaku, Ihara (Japan), 611–612
Sailing: by Vikings, 266
Sails: lateen, 464
St. Augustine, 475–476; Scholastics and, 416
St. Bartholomew's Eve Massacre, 447
St. Francis Receiving the Stigmata (Giotto), 404*i*
St. Helena: Napoleon on, 552, 557
St. Kitts, 486, 487
St. Lawrence River region, 520; French in, 485
St. Lucia, 520
St. Peter's Basilica (Rome), 408, 417
St. Petersburg, 510–511, 517
Sakoku (closed-country policy), **390**
Saladin (Salah al-Din): Crusades and, 275
Salian dynasty (Germany), 282
Salonières, **534,** 535
Salonika: Ottomans in, 452
Saltcellar of Francis I (Cellini), 408*i*
Salvation: in Calvinism, 424; by faith alone, 418; by faith and good works, 418; Hindu, 289; Hus on, 414; Luther and, 417–418; Tendai doctrine of, 319
Samad, Abdus, 364
Samad, Khwaja Abdus, 361
Samudra Gupta (India), 288
Samurai (warriors, Japan), 315, 316, 319–320, 385–386, 389, 607; Kamakura and, 320; wives of, 609
Samurai board: in Japan, 320
Sandwich Islands. *See* Hawaii
San hunters (Africa), 571; Boers and, 572
San Lorenzo: Olmec site at, 325
San Salvador, 466
Sanskrit language: England and classics in, 598; literature in, 291; *Mahabharata* epic in, 365
Santa Fe, 476
Santiago, Chile, 477
Santo Domingo, 486, 544; slaves freed in, 550. *See also* Haiti
Saracens: Muslims as, 275
Sardinia and Sardinians, 517
Sasfavid Empire, 587
Sassanids (Persia), 293
Sati (burning of widows, India), **363**
São Tomé, 472, 479

São Vicente, 467
Sa'ud family: Mecca seized by, 591
Savonarola, 426–427
Savoy, 517
Saxons, 262
Scandinavia: invasions of Europe from, 264–265, 266; Lutheranism and, 419; royal authority in, 507
Schele, Linda, 328
Schism: in Catholic Church, **415**
Schmalkaldic League, **442**
Scholars: Greek, 402–403
Scholars, The (Wu Jingzi), 602
Scholarship: in 12th and 13th centuries, 274–275; Confucian in Japan, 313; Gupta, 291; in Japan, 610; in Korea, 382–383; at Mahmud's court, 293; Ottoman, 356–357; silhak, 605; in Song China, 304; in Tang China, 299. *See also* Intellectual thought; Learning
Scholasticism, 274–275, 403, 416
Schonbrün family (Bohemia), 497
Schools: in France, 554; in Korea, 383; in Prussia, 539
Science(s), 527; Aztec, 332; contributions to, 538*m*; Gupta, 291; in India, 287; in Japan, 610; Mayan, 328; popularity of, 532; scope of, 530; in Song China, 304. *See also* Intellectual thought
Scientific instruments, 531
Scientific method: Newton and, 532
Scientific Revolution, 528–532
Scotland, 281; Christianity in, 259; England and, 514; Knox in, 448
Script: in Japan, 317
Scriptures, 418
Sculpture: in Gupta India, 290, 291*i*; Indian, 290–291, 291*i*; in Italian Renaissance, 405; Mayan, 328–329; of Michelangelo, 408, 408*i*
Scurvy, **476**
Second Bulgarian Empire, 452
Second Coalition: France and, 553, 554
Second Estate (nobility), 542
Second Peace of Kappel, 423
Second Rome. *See* Constantinople
Second Treatise on Civil Government (Locke), 533, 538
Secret society: Masons as, 533–534
Secular rulers: church and, 415

Secular state: in Russia, 540; after Thirty Years' War, 458
Sei Shōnagon (Japan), 317, 318
Sejong (Korea), 381, 382, 383*i*
Sekigahara, battle of, 389
Selective breeding, 494
Selim I the Grim (Ottoman), 350–352
Selim II (Ottoman), 357
Selim III (Ottoman), 593
Seljuk Turks: Crusades and, 275; Ottomans and, 350
Sena, Africa, 578
Seneca Indians, 337
Senegal, 438
Senegambia, 469
Sen no Rikyō (Japan), 388
Sensation: Enlightenment thinkers on, 535
Seoul, 384
Separation of church and state, 536
Separation of powers, 538
Sephardim, 437
September Massacres (France), 548
Serbia: Stephan Dushan in, 452
Serfs and serfdom, 267, 270; in Prussia, 539
Serious Proposal to the Ladies (Astell), 535
Servants. *See* Indentured servants
Servetus, Michael, 424
Settlement(s): Dutch, 484, 485; in Siberia, 511–512. *See also* Colonies and colonization
Seven Sages of the Bamboo Grove (China), 296
"Seventeen-Article Constitution" (Japan), 314
Seventh Crusade, 276
Seventh Ecumenical Council (Nicaea II), 429
Seven Thrones (Jami), 361
Seven Years' War, 520, 598
Seville, 282
Sex and sexuality: in Japan, 315, 610; in Korea, 382; in Polynesia, 615–616
Seymour, Jane, 421
Sforza, Battista, 404
Shahnamah (Persian epic), 293
Shaibani Khan (Uzbek ruler), 359
Shaka (Zulu), 572–573, 573*i*, 577
Shakespeare, William, 410–411
Shakuntala, 291
Shankara (Hindu philosopher), 292

Sharia (Islamic law): in Ottoman Empire, 452; in West Africa, 570
Shaykh-Zadeh: *Portrait of a Sufi*, 356i
Shaykhs, **349**; Safavid, 357
Shelter. *See* Housing
Shen Zhou, 379
Shenzong (Song China), 302
Sher Khan, 363
Shia (Shi'ite) Muslims, 357–358; Nadir Khan and, 593; Safavid, 360
Shimabara revolt (Japan), 390
Shingon Buddhism, 318–319
Shinran (Japan), 319
Shintō (Japan), 313, 318; Zhu Xi Confucianism and, 610
Shin Yunbok: *Enjoying Lotuses While Listening to Music*, 605i
Ships and shipping, 484; Chinese trade and, 376; navigation, technology, and, 464; slave ships and, 563–564; Spanish, 449; Viking, 266
Shire reeve, 270
Shiva (god), 289, 292i
Shivaji Bhonsle (India), 595–596
Shōen (Japanese estates), **315**
Shōgun (great general), **384**; in Japan, 319; Tokugawa Ieyasu as, 389
Shōtoku (Yamato ruler), 314
Shogunate, 386; Muromachi, 386
Shona kingdoms, 471
Short Parliament (England), 514
Shrines: of Becket, 436
Shunga (erotic paintings), 613
Shunzhi (Qing China), 599
Shwemawdaw Pagoda, Pegu, 393i
Siberia: Russia and, 511, 615
Sichuan, 381
Sicily: Kingdom of, 440
Sierra Leone, 569
Sieyès, Abbé, 553
Sikhism, **294**
Sikhs (India), 595
Silesia, 520
Silhak (practical learning), 605
Silk and silk industry: in China, 601; Safavid, 360; trade and, 305, 310
Silk Roads: Buddhism spread along, 287
Silla (Korean state), 311, 311i
Silver: in Americas, 478; China trade and, 381; imports of, 483; from Japan and South America, 601; from New World in India, 595; Peruvian, 477; Spanish trade in, 476
Sima Guang (Song China), 304
Simplicissimus: on Thirty Years' War, 453, 454
Sind, 293
Sinification (sinicization), 295
Siraj ud-Dawla (India), 598
Sisterhoods: in China, 601
Six Articles of Confederation (England), 421
Six Licensed Stores (Korea), 382
Six Nations, 337
Sixteen Kingdoms (China), 295
Skanderbeg (Albania), 452
Skavronska, Marfa: Peter the Great and, 511
Slaves and slavery: abolition and, 585; African colonies for freed slaves, 569; for Americas, 478–479; Amerindian, 478i; for capitalist agriculture, 493i; in Central Africa, 579–580; current existence of, 585; in East Africa, 579–580; in English islands, 487; Equiano's memoir and, 565; from Kongo, 472; in Korea, 382; major source of, 567–568; Mayan, 328; in New Spain, 477; Ottomans and, 353–354; Portugal and, 469–470; reasons for, 584–585; in southern Africa, 571–572; treatment of slaves, 564
Slave trade, 474, 479m, 493, 585; abolition of, 565; Arabs and, 561; Assante and, 567; Atlantic, 562–568; domestic African, 569; Dutch and, 484; end in Denmark, 565; end in West Africa, 568–569; England and, 486, 487, 518, 574, 579; France and, 486; Portugal and, 469–470, 472; in Sahara region, 570; West African center for, 563i
Slavs, 262, 452; migration from Russia, 261. *See also* Balkan region
Sōtō Buddhism, 319
Smallpox: in Americas, 475, 476, 480
Smith, Adam, 535, 537
Smith, John, 486
Smuggling, 521–522
Snow Mountain and Forest (Fan Kuan), 304i
Sobloff, Jeremy, 328
Social contract: theory of, 538
Social Contract, The (Rousseau), 535
Social orders: French Third Estate as, 497. *See also* Classes

Society: African, 567m; Amerindian, 336–342; of Anglo-American colonies, 487; Aztec, 331; Bantu, 571; Bubonic Plague and, 398–399; Calvin on, 424; capitalist revolution and, 496–502; in Europe (1300–1600), 398–399; feudal, 266–267; in France, 505; impact of slave trade on, 569; in India, 289, 290; in Japan, 608–609, 613; Korean, 310, 381–384, 604–605; Mayan, 328; in Ming China, 374–380; Mughal, 366–367; Ottoman, 356; in Qing China, 602–604; in Song China, 303–304; Spanish colonial, 482; in Tang China, 298; women in, 535. *See also* Classes; Culture(s); specific countries and cultures

Society of Jesus. *See* Jesuits

Society of Republican Revolutionary Women (France), 544

Sofala, 471

Sofia: Ottomans in, 452

Soga family (Japan), 313–314

Sokoto Caliphate (Nigeria), 570–571; Oyo and, 566

Solar system. *See* Astronomy

Soldiers: in China, 374; Martel and, 261. *See also* Armed forces; specific battles and wars

Somerset, duke of (England), 421

Song dynasty (China), 294, 297, 301–304; economy in, 302, 303; paper money in, 301; philosophy, literature, and art in, 304; society in, 303–304

Songhai (Songhay Empire), 570

"Song of Everlasting Sorrow, The" (Bo Juyi), 300

"Song of the Afflicted" (Basotho kingdom), 574

Song Taizu (China), 302

Sophia (Russia), 510

Sotho/Tswana peoples, 571

Sotoba Komachi (play), 387

Souligna-Vongsa (Laos), 613

South (worldwide), 345

South Africa: Dutch and, 484; "myth of the empty land" and, 577, 577m

South America: civilizations of, 326m; cultures in, 324; Inca Empire in, 332–336; Spain in, 476–477

South Asia: division of, 595; Mughal Empire in, 361–367, 361m

South China, 295

Southeast Asia, 288, 391–394, 613–615; Europeans in, 394; India and, 289, 293, 372; Islam in, 394; maritime, 372, 393–394; Portugal and, 467; Tang China and, 297. *See also* specific countries

Southern Africa: Africans and European settlement in, 571–572; British in, 572; Dutch in, 571–572; myth of empty land and, 577, 577m

Southern Song period (China), 302

South Korea. *See* Korea

South Pacific: Dutch and, 484; Europeans in, 615

South Sea Company, 496; stock failure of, 522

Southwest (U.S.): native cultures of, 339–340; Navajo housing in, 341i; Spanish colonies is, 476

Spain: to 1348, 281–282; American silver in, 478; Armada of, 450; Charlemagne and, 262; Columbus and, 466; Dutch independence from, 447; Dutch struggle against, 512; expansion by, 467m; exploration by, 488m; Ferdinand and Isabella in, 437–438; Habsburgs in, 444–445; Japan and, 469, 607; Jews in, 437; Mary I Tudor and, 421; Moors and, 261; Muslims in, 437; nation-building in, 437–438, 438m; New Spain and, 474–477; Philippines and, 614; population growth in, 465; population of, 498; rebellion against Napoleon, 555; *Reconquista* in, 281–282, 437–438; religious wars and, 444–445; Renaissance literature in, 410; royal authority in, 507; shipping of, 449; South American colonies of, 476–477; Southeast Asia and, 372, 394, 613–614; after Thirty Years' War, 457; Treaty of Utrecht and, 518; Turkey and, 449; unification with Portugal, 482; wars of religion and, 443–444. *See also* Iberian Peninsula; Latin America; specific colonies

Spanish America: England and, 518, 520; society and culture in, 482. *See also* Latin America; specific colonies

Spanish Empire: decline of, 482

Spanish March, 262

Spanish Netherlands, 443, 449; regents of, 446; revolt in, 445–447. *See also* Belgium

Speculation, 496

Spice Islands: Dutch in, 484
Spices and spice trade, 310, 482–483; Portugal and, 467, 471
Spies and spying: in Russia, 511
Spinoza, Baruch, 534, 535; on abuse of power, 538; religion and, 536
Spirit of the Laws, The (Montesquieu), 534, 538
Spirits. *See* Gods and goddesses
Sri Lanka (Ceylon), 293; Buddhism in, 289; Dutch in, 484
Srivijaya kingdom (Southeast Asia), 293
Stadtholders (Dutch), 512
Standard of living. *See* Lifestyle
Standing armies: in Europe, 523–524; in France, 550
State (nation): absolutist, 491; in Africa, 572–574; banks of, 496; in Central Europe, 438–439; characteristics of, 433; in eastern and northeastern Africa, 578–581; economic control by, 521–522; end of absolutism in, 522–524; European, 278–283, 432–458; Holy Roman Empire and, 439; in Italy, 400; Mughal, 363–365; religion and, 418–419; separation from church, 536; in Spain, 437–438, 438*m*; in Switzerland, 440; after Thirty Years' War, 457
State of nature: Locke on, 539
Status, 496; of Japanese women, 389; in Korea, 382; in Tokugawa Japan, 605–606. *See also* Classes
Steel and steel industry: in Gupta India, 291
Steen, Jan: *Fish Market at Leiden, The*, 513*i*
Steppes, 348–349; nomads from, 288
Stereotypes: of East and West, 345
Stock exchanges, **495**–496
Storytellers: in Japan, 386
Strait of Magellan: Dutch and, 484
Stuart dynasty (England), 450, 513; Parliament and, 515
Stupas (Buddhist funeral mounds), 289
Suarez, Ines, 477
Subinfeudation, 266–267
Succession: to Charlemagne, 264; in England, 280; to Japanese throne, 316. *See also* Dynasties
Sufis and sufism, 294, 350, 358, **589**, 591; Akbar and, 363; as missionaries, 360–361, 393; Safavid, 359

Sugar and sugar industry, 483; Amerindian slaves for, 478*i*; China, India, and, 292; Dutch and, 485; France and, 486; Portuguese, 479; slaves for, 565, 568
Sui dynasty (China), 294, 295, 296; Japan and, 314; Korea and, 311
Sukhothai, Thailand, 391
Suleiman (Ottoman), 352–353, 588; Ottoman Empire under, 353–356; *tughra* (signature) of, 352*i*
Sully, duke of (France), 503
Sultana: Raziyya as, 293
Sultanates: in Africa south of Egypt, 570; of Delhi, 293–294, 294*m*; in India, 362
Sultans: Ottoman, 349, 354; Qutb ud–Dina, 293
Sumatra, 394, 615; Dutch in, 484
Summa Theologica (Thomas Aquinas), 275
Sun-god (Aztec), 331
Sunlight (soap), 569
Sunni Muslims, 357, 593; in Mughal Empire, 365–366
Superpowers. *See* Cold War
Supply and demand: Smith on, 537
Surat (Indian port), 487, 596
Su Shi (China), 304
Susneyos (Ethiopia), 580
Suzerain (lord), **267**
Swahili Arabs, 580
Swahili city-states, 472, 579; Islam and, 570; Portugal and, 467
Swahili culture and language, 580
Swazi peoples, 571
Sweden, 441; bank of, 496; in Great Northern War, 517; Lutheranism in, 419; royal authority in, 507; Viking raids from, 266
Swedish phase: of Thirty Years' War, 456
Switzerland, 440; Protestantism in, 423; Zwingli in, 423
Sword Hunt edict (Japan), 386
Syllabary: in Korea, 381
Syphilis: in Hawaii, 616
Szlachta (nobility), 441

T

Table Bay, 571
Tabriz, battle at, 593
Tabula rasa: Locke on, 537

T'aejo (Korea), 311, 381, 382
Tahiti: gender roles in, 615
Tahmasp (Safavid), 359; Humayun and, 363
Taika (Great Change) Reforms (Japan), 314, 315
Taille (land tax), 497
Taira warrior band, 319
Taizong (Tang China), 297
Taizu (Ming China), 310
Taizu (Song China), 302
Taj Mahal, 364*i*
Tale of Genji, The (Japan), 316, 316*i*, 317, 318, 610
Tale of Kieu, The (Nguyen Du), 614
Tales from the Provinces (Ihara Saikaku), 612
Tamerlane (Timur the Magnificent), 294*m* 347, 349*i*, 350
Tang dynasty (China), 294, 296; Buddhism and, 292; decline of, 299–301; economy and society under, 297–298; Japan and, 313, 314; Korea and, 311; political developments under, 297
Tangut state (Central Asia), 305, 307
Tang Yin: *Whispering Pines on a Mountain Path*, 379*i*
Tannenberg, battle of, 441
Tanuma Okitsugu (Japan), 609
Tanzania: kingdom in, 573
Tasmania: Dutch and, 484
Taxation: Aztec, 331; in China, 301; of church, 414; in France, 279, 524, 543; in India, 288; in Japan, 315, 606, 607; in Mughal Empire, 363; of New World colonies, 477; in Ottoman Empire, 356; of peasants, 497; protests against, 502; in Russia, 540; along trade routes, 368; in Vietnam, 614; in Yuan China, 308
Tax farms, **590**; in Mughal India, 595; Ottoman, 590; power of, 596
Tay Son Uprising (Vietnam), 614
Tea, 483; Chinese, 602
Tea ceremony: in Japan, 388
Technology: Anasazi, 339; Chinese, 287–288, 302, 303; Europe and, 433; Inca, 334; in Japan, 608; navigational, 463, 464
Tehuacán, 324
Telescope: of Galileo, 528
Temmu (Japan), 314
Templars, 276
Temple mounds: in Mexico, 325

Temple of the Golden Pavilion, 388
Temple of the Silver Pavilion, 388
Temples: in India, 290, 292*i*; Kamakura, 320; in Korea, 384; in Ming China, 379
Temporal authority: of pope, **258**
Temujin. *See* Chinggis (Genghis) Khan
Tenant farmers: Aztec, 331
Tenants-in-chief, 279
Tencin, Madame de, 534
Tendai Buddhism, 318
Tennis Court Oath (France), 542*i*, 543
Tennō (emperor, Japan), 384
Tenochtitlán, 330; Cortés and, 475
Teotihuacán, 326–327, 327*i*, 328
Teresa of Avila (Saint), 427, 428*i*
Tete, Africa, 578
Tetzel, Johan, 417
Teutonic Knights, 276, 441
Tewodros II (Ethiopia), 581
Textiles and textile industry: domestic system in, 495; in India, 597–598
Tezcatlipoca (god), **329**
Thailand, 392, 613; Burma and, 392, 614
Thai people, 391–392, 393
Theal, George McCall, 577
Theater: in Japan, 612. *See also* Drama
Theocracy: Anabaptist, 425; Ottoman, 452
Theology: in England, 421; studies in, 274
The Prince (Machiavelli), 403
Theravada Buddhism: in Burma, 391
Thermometer, 531
Third Coalition: against France, 555
Third Crusade, 275
Third Estate (common people), 542; in France, 279, **497**
Third World, 345
Thirty Years' War, 441; Bohemian phase of, 453–455; Danish phase of, 455–456; Europe after, 457*m*; French phase of, 456; Simplicissimus on, 453, 454; Swedish phase of, 456
Thomas (ship): slave rebellion on, 564
Thomas Aquinas (Saint), 274–275
Tiahuanaco, 332
Tibet, 307
Tierra del Fuego: peoples of, 324
Tikal, 328, 329; pyramid at, 328–329
Tilly, Charles, 433
Tilsit Treaty, 555, 556
"Time of troubles" (Russia), 451

Timurid Empire, 348–349
Tintoretto, 449*i*
Tippu Tip (Africa), 580, 580*i*
Tithes, **413**; in France, 544
Tiyanoga (Mohawk), 487*i*
Tlatelolco (god), 331, 332
Tlaxcalan people, 475
Tobacco and tobacco industry, 483; labor for, 493*i*
Tokugawa shogunate (Japan), 389–391, 605–613; Hidetada (Japan), 390; Iemitsu (Japan), 390; Ieyasu (Japan), 385, 386, 389; international relations of, 606–607
Tokyo. *See* Edo, Japan
Toland, John, 534, 536
Tollan, 329
Toltecs, 327, 329–330; Aztecs and, 330
Tomb period: in Japan, 312, 312*i*, 313
Tombs: Taj Mahal as, 364*i*, 365
Tools: agricultural, 269; in Americas, 324; in Japan, 312
Topa Yupanqui (Incan), 332–334
Topiltzin (Toltec), 329
Topkapi Palace, 356
Tordesillas, Treaty of, 466
Tories (England), 516
Torture: abolition in Prussia, 539
Tott, Baron de, 591
Tours, battle at, 261
Townshend, Charles ("Turnip Townshend"), 493–494
Toyotomi Hideyoshi (Japan), 384, 385, 386, 388, 389
Trabriz, Persia, 310
Trade: African long-distance, 579–580; Amerindian, 338; Aztec, 331; in Central Asia, 305; in Central Europe, 439; Chinese, 297, 376, 602; Dutch, 484–485, 512; in East Asia, 372; in England, 448; English control over India and China, 598; Ethiopian, 581; Eurasian, 310; European with India, 596–598; expansion of, 463; French, 505–506, 521; in Iberian colonies, 478; illegal, 521; India-China, 393; Indian, 289; in Indian Ocean region, 587–588; in Italy, 400; Japanese, 388, 606, 609; maritime, 288; medieval, 271–272; mercantilism and, 505–506; in Middle Ages, 266; by Ming China, 376, 380; Muslim, 293; by Netherlands, 445–446; New World and, 492; Omani, 579; Portuguese West African, 470; Safavid, 360; Smith on, 537; by Sokoto Caliphate, 571; in Song China, 304; Tokugawa and, 390; in Turkic empires, 367–368; Turks and, 305. *See also* Commerce; Foreign trade; Joint-stock companies
Trade goods, 487*i*
Trade routes: across Indian Ocean, 393*m*; fairs along, 271; Portugal and, 467
Trade winds, 464
Trading communities, 368
Trading companies, 484; French, 505–506. *See also* British East India Company
Trading networks: Portugal and, 468
Trading posts: Portuguese, 466–467
Trafalgar, battle of, 555
Trailok (Thai), 393
Transatlantic trade: Ottoman Empire and, 589
Translations: of classical works, 274
Transoxiana, 349
Transvaal, 576; rebellion against British, 578
Transylvania, 452
Travel: in Japan, 606; Ottomans and, 591
Treaties: China-Russia, 599*i*. *See also* specific treaties
Trekboers, **572**
Trent, Council of, 415, 427, 443, 444
Trials: of Joan of Arc, 435
Tribute system (China), 345, **602**; Korea and, 381, 385*m*; in Ming China, 376; in Qing China, 602–604; Sumatra and, 394; Vietnam and, 372, 393
Trinh people (Vietnam), 614
Tripoli: Hausa trade with, 571
"Truce of God," 267
True Pure Land sect: in Japan, 319
Tsars (caesar): use of title, 451
Tsu, island of, 606
Tuareg people, 570
Tudor dynasty (England), 419; Elizabeth I and, 448; Henry VII and, 437; Henry VIII and, 420–421
Tughluks (Delhi), 294
Tukolor Muslims: jihad and, 570
Tulip Period: in Ottoman Empire, 590–591
Tull, Jethro, 493
Tumbrels, 549–550
Turco-Mongols, 349; Timur as, 294

Turgot, Robert, 537
Turkestan, 307, 595
Turkey: Philip II and, 449
Turkic empires, 305, 347; Mughal, 361–367; Ottoman, 349–357; Safavid, 357–361; trade in, 367–368
Turks, 288; China and, 305; Ethiopia and, 474; Muslims and, 293; Russia and, 517
Tuscarora Indians, 337
Tutsi peoples, 580
Twa people (Africa), 580
"Two kingdoms": Luther on, 419
Two tax system (China), **301**
Tyndale, William, 421

U

Uighur Turks (Central Asia), 288, 305, 307
Uji leaders: in Japan, 312*i*, 313, 314–315
Ukiyo-e (Japanese pictures), 613
Ulama (Islamic religious authorities), **353, 589**; in Mughal Empire, 363; in Ottoman Empire, 356
Ulfilas (missionary), 259
"Umbrella Oracle, The" (Ihara Saikaku), 612
Umiak (boat), 342
Unam Sanctam, 414
Understanding of History, The, 299
Unemployment: in European cities, 498–499, 498*i*
Unification: of Germany, 517; of Italy, 517; of Spain, 437, 438; of Spain and Portugal, 482, 507
United East India Company, 394
Universal laws of nature: Newton on, 532
Universe: Descartes on, 531; Newtonian, 531–532. *See also* Astronomy
Universities: Buddhist in India, 294; in east Central Europe, 441; origins of, 274; in Spanish America, 482
University of France, 554
Upanishads, 292–293
Upper classes: Enlightenment and, 536; extravagance of, 497*i*; wives in, 499
Urban areas: Japan and, 608, 611; poor in, 499–501
Urbanization: in China, 303; in Japan, 610
Ursins, Princesse des, 507
Usman dan Fodio, 570; women and, 571

Utilitarianism, **535**
Utopia (More), 412–413
Utrecht: Peace of, 508, 562; Treaty of, 518*m*
Uxmal, 328
Uzbeks, 349, 359, 593

V

Vakataka dynasty (India), 289
Valide sultan, **354**
Valla, Lorenzo da, 413, 428
Valley of Mexico, 325
Valmy, battle at, 548
Valois dynasty, 416, 450
Van Eyck, Jan, 411; *Wedding Portrait*, 411*i*
Vasa family (Sweden). *See* Gustavus Vasa (Sweden)
Vassals, 266; Balkan states as, 452; contract with lords, 267; tenants-in-chief as, 279, 280
Veld, **575**
Venereal disease, 499
Venice, 416; Fourth Crusade and, 275–276; Lagoon of, 401, 401*i*; Ottomans and, 590; republic of, 400; Turkey and, 449
Veracruz, 325
Verdun: Treaty of, 264
Verrazzano, Giovanni da, 485
Versailles palace, 505; French Revolution and, 543; women's march to, 544
Vervins, Peace of, 450
Vesalius, Andreas, 530
Viceroyalties: Mexico as, 476, 477; Peru as, 477
Vienna: Habsburgs of, 453; Hungarian capture of, 442
Vietnam, 393, 604*m*, 614; China and, 297, 372, 393; France and, 614; Ming dynasty and, 376; Portugal and, 468
Vietnamese language: Roman-alphabet-based script for, 613
Vijayangar Empire, 294, 362
Vikings, 266
Vilacamba: Inca in, 476
Villages: Inuit, 342; in Japan, 385, 607, 608; in southwestern United States, 339
Violence: in cities, 498–499; in France, 549; in French Revolution, 543; by poor, 501
Viracocha (Inca), 332, 336
Virginia: England and, 486

Vishnu (god), 289, 290
Visigoths: belt buckle of, 259*i*; missionary to, 259
Vizirs, **353, 590**; Köprülü, 589–590
Voltaire, 534, 536, 539; slave trade and, 585
Voortrekkers, **575**–576, 576*i*
Voting and voting rights: in France, 547, 550–551
Voyages of exploration: expansion of trade and, 463; maps of, 471; Ming Chinese, 376, 380. *See also* Trade; specific voyages

W

Wage labor, 398
Wages: inflation and, 492, 495
Al-Wahhab, Muhammad ibn Abd, 591
Wahhabis (puritanical movement), 591
Wales, 281; England and, 281
Wallachia, 452
Wallenstein, Albert von, 456
Walpole, Robert (England), 516
Wang Anshi (Song China), 302, 304
Wang Mang (China): slavery and, 585
Wang Yang-ming (China), 379
Wanli (Ming China), 380
War criminals: as slaves, 584–585
Wardship, 267
Warlords: in China, 374
War of Jenkins's Ear, 520
War of Liberation: against Napoleon, 557
War of the Spanish Succession, 517, 562
"War of the three Henries" (France), 447–448
Warren, Mercy, 536
Warri (Benin vassal state), 470
Warring States period: in Japan, 384–386, 388
Warrior-monks: in Japan, 319
Warriors: in Japan, 385–386; Japanese samurai as, 315; nobility as, 267
Wars and warfare: 18th–century Ottoman, 591; in age of absolutism, 516–520; between Boers and Xhosa, 572; Europe and, 433; feudal, 267; foreign, during French Revolution, 548, 550; Hussite, 415; Korea-Japan, 384; Mayan, 328; Napoleonic, 552–557; in Southeast Asia, 391. *See also* Civil War(s); Weapons; specific battles and wars

Wars of religion, 443–450; in Bohemia and German principalities, 453; in France, 447–448; Spain and, 444–445, 449–450
Wars of the Roses (England), 419, 437
Wartburg Castle: Luther at, 418
Waterloo, battle of, 557
Water Margin, The (All Men Are Brothers), 379
Watson Brake (Louisiana): Native Americans of, 338
Wealth: in China, 308; from commerce, 400; of Heshen (China), 602; Iberian desire for, 465; of Mughal Empire, 364; in Teotihuacán, 327; Vietnamese, 393; women of, 499
Wealth of Nations (Smith). *See Inquiry into the Nature and Causes of the Wealth of Nations, An* (Smith)
Weapons: in France, 506; in Hundred Years' War, 434; in Japan, 389; Mayan, 328; on ships, 464; Zulu, 573. *See also* specific weapons
Wei dynasty (North China), 295, 296*i*
Wei Zhongxian (China): eunuchs and, 377
Well-field system (China), 295
Wellington, duke of, 557
Wendi (China), 296
Wen Zhengming, 379
West Africa, 466; Dutch and, 484; France and, 486; Muslims in, 570; Portugal and, 466*i*, 469–470; slave trade and, 487, 563*i*, 566–567, 568–569; trade relations of, 566
Western Europe: feudalism in, 266–268
Western Hemisphere: Spanish claims to, 465
Western world: Europe as, 345; identification of, 344–345
West Indies, 520; Columbus in, 466; Dutch in, 485; English migrants in, 487; French in, 486, 544; mulattoes from, 544–547; plantations in, 478; smuggling and, 521. *See also* Barbados; Jamaica
Westphalia, 508; Peace of, 456–457, 517; Treaty of, 456, 457*m*, 491
West Prussia, 441
"What Is the Third Estate?" (Sieyès), 553
Wheelbarrow: from China, 303
Whigs (England), 515, 516, 533
Whispering Pines on a Mountain Path (Tang Yin), 379*i*
White Deer Grotto Academy (China), 304
White Lotus Society (China), **310, 602,** 603

White Mountain, battle of the, 455
Widows: in China, 378, 602; in Korea, 382; in Mughal Empire, 367; in Spanish American society, 482
William I of Orange (the Silent), 446, 447
William and Mary (England): Locke and, 532
William of Rubruck (Franciscan), 308
William the Conqueror (duke of Normandy), 279–280
Window on the West: St. Petersburg as, 510–511, 511*m*
Winds: trade winds, 464
Wittenberg: Luther in, 417, 418, 419
Wives: conditions of, 499; in Lutheranism, 419
Wollstonecraft, Mary, 535
Women: in Adena and Hopewell cultures, 337–338; in Anglo-American colonies, 487; Aztec, 331; Calvin on, 424; in China, 378, 601, 602; Christine de Pizan and, 400; under Code Napoléon, 554; as concubines, 378; conditions after 1648, 499; conquistadora and Amerindians, 476–477; on encomiendas, 481; in English colonies, 487; Enlightenment thought and, 535; in forced prostitution, 585; in France, 551; in French Revolution, 542, 544, 550; in guilds, 272; Incan, 335; Iroquois, 337; in Japan, 312, 315, 316, 385, 389, 609, 610–611; in Korea, 382, 383; in Lutheranism, 418–419; march to Versailles by, 544; on medieval farms, 269–270, 270*i*; medieval learning and, 275; in Middle Ages, 260; in Mughal Empire, 367; mulatto, 479; noble, 268; in Ottoman Empire, 354, 590*i*; in Paris, 548; in Protestant sects, 425; protests by, 502; in Renaissance, 403–404; as Russian monarchs, 512; as salonières, 534; as slaves, 563; slave trade and, 566–567; in Sokoto Caliphate, 571; in Song China, 303; Spanish, 477; Spanish American, 482; in Tang China, 298; in Vietnam, 614; as workers, 398; in Yuan China, 308
Woodblock prints, 611*i*; in Japan, 611, 613; of Mt. Fuji, 608*i*
Woodlands Indians: Iroquois as, 337
Wool industry, 400, 483; Hundred Years' War and, 434; Italy and, 440

Woolston, Thomas, 536
Word (Scripture): in Calvinism, 424
Workers: in Korea, 382; living conditions in Europe, 499; peasants as, 267; protests by European, 501–502; wage system and, 495; women as, 398. See also specific countries
Workhouses: in England, 501
Worldly Mental Calculations (Ihara Saikaku), 612
Worms: Diet at, 418
Writing: Incan, 336; in Japan, 317; Korean, 383; Korean han'gul as, 604; Mayan, 328; Vietnamese, 393, 613. See also Literature
Wu (Chinese Empress), 297, 298
Wu Daozi (Tang painter), 299
Wudi (China): Korea and, 310
Wu Jingzi (China), 602
Wu Sangui (China), 599
Wycliffe, John, 414, 421; Hus and, 414–415

X

Xhosa chiefdoms, 571, 574; Boers and, 572, 574
Xia people (China), 302
Ximenes (Cardinal), 413, 427
Xiongnu people: China and, 295. See also Huna people
Xochicalco, 329
Xuanzong (Tang China), 297, 299
Xu Yueying (Tang poet), 298

Y

Yakutsk: Russia and, 615
Yamato family (Japan), 313, 314
Yamazaki Ansai (Japan), 610
Yangban reformers (Korea), 381, 382, 605
Yangdi (China), 296
Yang Guifei (Tang China), 299, 299–301
Yao people (China), 376, 580
Yaxchilán, 328
Yayoi period (Japan), 312
Yi (Chosŏn) dynasty (Korea), 312
Yirmisekiz Chelebi Mehmed (Ottoman), 590
Yi Sunsin (Korea), 384
Yi T'oegye (Korea), 383

Yongjo (Korea), 604
Yongle (Ming China), 374, 376
Yongle Encyclopedia, **379**
Yongzheng (Qing China), 600
York, House of, 437
Yoruba people (Africa): Krios as, 569
Yoruba states: Oyo as, 566
Yoshimasa (Ashikaga Japan), 388
Yoshimitsu (Ashikaga Japan), 388
Yoshimune (Japan), 609
Young, Arthur, 494, 499, 500, 501
Yuan dynasty (China), 295, 304–310, 307–310, 373; culture of, 308
Yuan Mei (China), 602
Yucatán peninsula, 325, 327, 475; Amerindian resistance in, 481; Maya of, 326
Yucatec-speaking peoples, 327
Yuezhi people, 295

Z

Za-Dengel (Ethiopia), 580
Zambezi River region, 471, 472, 578
Zambos (Indian-Africa people), **482**
Zand, Karim Khan (Persian warlord), 593–594
Zanzibar, 579; Portugal and, 467
Zapotecs, 329
Zara (Adriatic town): Venice and, 276
Zar'a Ya'kob (Ethiopia), 465
Žižka, John, 441
Zeami Motokiyo (Japan), 387
Zeeland, 446–447
Zell, Matthew and Katherine, 424
Zemski Sobor (Russian representative assembly), **451**
Zen Buddhism, **319**; in Korea, 311
Zero: in India, 291
Zheng Chenggong (Coxinga, China), 599
Zheng He (China), 376; Siam and, 392
Zhongguo (Central Kingdom, China), 375
Zhongyuan region (China), 375
Zhu Xi (Song China), 304, 383, 604
Zhu Xi Confucianism, 379, 600; in Japan, 610
Zhu Yuanzhang (China). *See* Hongwu (Ming China)
Zimbabwe, 578; kingdom in, 573; Portugal and, 471, 474
Zoroastrians and Zoroastrianism, **363**
Zulu peoples, 571, 572–573, 573*i*, 577, 578; end of kingdom, 578
Zurich, Switzerland, 423
Zwingli, Ulrich, 423